MAR - 9 2021

Praise for *The Making of Asian America*

Winner of the ALA Asian/Pacific American Award for Literature
A *Kirkus Reviews* Best Book of 2015
****New York Times Book Review* Editors' Choice***

"Lee's comprehensive history traces the experiences of myriad Asian-American communities, from Chinese laborers in 1850s California to Hmong refugees in 1980s Minnesota. . . . Fascinating. . . . I suspect Erika Lee will soon join [the canon of key Asian-American histories]."

—Oliver Wang, *The New York Times Book Review*

"*The Making of Asian America* is a path-breaking approach to Asian American history. Professor Lee will challenge and surprise most of her readers. . . . She is clearly now a distinct and important voice in a debate of growing complexity."

—Roger Daniels, author of *Coming to America* and Charles Phelps Taft Professor Emeritus of History, University of Cincinnati

"Monumental. . . . Lee handles her scholarly materials with grace, never overwhelming the reader with too many facts or incidents. . . . Powerful Asian American stories . . . are inspiring, and Lee herself does them justice in a book that is long overdue."

—Viet Thanh Nguyen, Pulitzer Prize–winning author of *The Sympathizer*, in *The Los Angeles Times*

"A stunning achievement, *The Making of Asian America* establishes the centrality of Asians to American history, and poses alternatives to US national and immigration histories. Asians, this remarkable text reveals, transformed the face of America, and they locate the US firmly within a hemispheric and global order."

—Gary Y. Okihiro, Professor of International and Public Affairs, Columbia University

"In this fascinating retelling of the American creation story, Lee uses incisive scholarship, a wide historic lens and rich detail to fill in the long missing Asian-American pieces. Starting with ancient Greece and the Age of Exploration, from enslavement to modern day challenges, Lee tracks the epic Asian-American journey to North and South Americas, East Indies to West Indies, and in doing so, she breaks new ground and inverts the master narrative."

—Helen Zia, author of *Asian American Dreams: The Emergence of an American People*

"A sweeping study of the fastest growing group in the United States that underscores the shameful racist regard white Americans have long held for Asian immigrants. . . . A powerful, timely story told with method and dignity."

—*Kirkus Reviews* (starred review)

"Building on the best and newest scholarship, Erika Lee has written a sweeping yet personal and critical history of Asian Americans across centuries, continents, and diverse cultures without losing sight of the global, racial, and historical contexts of Asian migration, exclusion, and resettlement. A definitive and ideal text for college classes and the general public, *The Making of Asian America* is truly an enjoyable, informative, and insightful read."

—Judy Yung, Professor Emerita of American Studies, UC Santa Cruz, and author of *Unbound Feet*

"Epic and eye-opening."

—*Minneapolis Star-Tribune*

"A fascinating narrative. . . . Deftly weaving together a masterful synthesis of the existing literature with new information culled from hitherto untapped archival sources and with analytical insights on the global currents that have shaped the last five centuries, Erika Lee has created a richly textured tapestry enlivened by vivid stories of hundreds of individuals and groups who played significant, though often unsung, roles in the making of Asian America."

—Sucheng Chan, Professor Emerita of Asian America Studies, University of California, Santa Barbara

The MAKING of ASIAN AMERICA

A History

Erika Lee

SIMON & SCHUSTER PAPERBACKS

New York London Toronto Sydney New Delhi

For my students

Simon & Schuster Paperbacks
An Imprint of Simon & Schuster, Inc.
1230 Avenue of the Americas
New York, NY 10020

Copyright © 2015 by Erika Lee.

All rights reserved, including the right to reproduce this book or portions thereof in any form whatsoever. For information, address Simon & Schuster Paperbacks Subsidiary Rights Department, 1230 Avenue of the Americas, New York, NY 10020.

First Simon & Schuster trade paperback edition September 2016

SIMON & SCHUSTER PAPERBACKS and colophon are registered trademarks of Simon & Schuster, Inc.

For information about special discounts for bulk purchases, please contact Simon & Schuster Special Sales at 1-866-506-1949 or business@simonandschuster.com.

The Simon & Schuster Speakers Bureau can bring authors to your live event. For more information or to book an event, contact the Simon & Schuster Speakers Bureau at 1-866-248-3049 or visit our website at www.simonspeakers.com.

Interior design by Ruth Lee-Mui

Manufactured in the United States of America

13 15 17 19 20 18 16 14 12

The Library of Congress has cataloged the hardcover edition as follows:

Lee, Erika.
The making of Asian America : a history / Erika Lee.
pages cm
1. Asian Americans—History. 2. Asians—United States—History. 3. United States—Emigration and immigration—History. 4. South Asia—Emigration and immigration—History. 5. United States—Ethnic relations—History. 6. Racism—United States—History. 7. United States—Race relations—History. I. Title.
E184.A75L43 2015
973'.0495—dc23 2015010372

ISBN 978-1-4767-3940-3
ISBN 978-1-4767-3941-0 (pbk)
ISBN 978-1-4767-3942-7 (ebook)

"An impressive work that details how this diverse population has both swayed and been affected by the United States. Highly recommended."

—*Library Journal* (starred review)

"A well-written, panoramic view of Asian America from the colonial era to the present that sheds light on how Asian immigrants have sought to make their place in American society and, at the same time, continually changed it."

—Nancy Foner, coauthor of *Strangers No More* and Distinguished Professor of Sociology, Hunter College and Graduate Center, CUNY

"Accessibly written for a wide readership, *The Making of Asian America* opens important, new perspectives on the relationship of the U.S. and the world."

—Donna Gabaccia, Professor of History, University of Toronto Scarborough

"Ambitious, sweeping, and insightful."

—*Publishers Weekly*

"Erika Lee's new narrative of Asian American history deserves consideration to complement, if not supplant, celebrated earlier syntheses. Incorporating compelling revisionist approaches, Lee peels back several centuries of time to locate the origins of Chinese in America to the founding of the Spanish empire in America in the sixteenth century. . . . She further insists on the mainstreaming of Asian American history in the United States."

—Evelyn Hu-DeHart, Professor of History and American Studies, Brown University

"Informative and engaging. . . . *The Making of Asian America* is full of fascinating stories about immigrants who left a mark on their adopted country."

—*The Oregonian*

Contents

PART THREE

Asian America in a World at War

PART FOUR

Remaking Asian America in a Globalized World

PART FIVE

Twenty-first-Century Asian Americans

Introduction

The 19.5 million Asian Americans in the United States today make up almost 6 percent of the total U.S. population. They increased in number by 46 percent from 2000 to 2010 and are now the fastest-growing group in the country. They are settling in places that have traditionally welcomed immigrants like New York City, San Francisco, and Los Angeles, as well as in other cities where such large-scale immigration is new: Atlanta, Las Vegas, Houston, Phoenix, and Minneapolis-St. Paul.[1] Asian Americans are changing the face of America. But most people know little about their history and the impact that they have had on American life.

The Making of Asian America tells this story.

Over the centuries, millions of people from Asia have left their homes to start new lives in the United States. They have come in search of work, economic opportunity, freedom from persecution, and new beginnings that have symbolized the "American Dream" for so many newcomers. During the nineteenth and twentieth centuries, Asian immigrants joined millions of others from around the world to turn the United States into a "nation of immigrants." In the past fifty years, more have come as a result of new immigration policies, as refugees following the wars in Southeast Asia, and as part of increasing globalization.

The making and remaking of Asian America is the story of these global journeys and histories. This book digs deep into the historical record with sources like the first world atlas (printed in 1570), newspaper accounts, and long-forgotten immigrant autobiographies. It also explores contemporary American life through the latest census statistics, policy reports, and social media campaigns. There is an extraordinary range of Asian American lives and experiences.

Consider, for example, Afong Moy, a nineteen-year-old "beautiful Chinese lady" who arrived in New York in 1834 aboard a ship full of snuffboxes, walking canes, and fans imported to satisfy Americans' taste for imported Chinese goods. She was the first-recorded Chinese woman to arrive in the United States. A decade or so later, Jacinto Quintin de la Cruz and other Filipinos founded a fishing village in Barataria Bay south of New Orleans. They named it Manila Village to remind them of the home they left behind. While South Asian and Chinese indentured laborers were being brought to the Caribbean, Peru, and Cuba, my great-great-great-grandfather joined another stream of Chinese heading across the Pacific to seek their fortunes in the California Gold Rush. In 1919, Shizu Hayakawa left her home in Japan as a "picture bride" to marry a man she had never met. Around the same time, Whang Sa Sun and his wife, Chang Tai Sun, fled from Japanese rule in their native Korea and arrived as refugees. Vaishno Bagai, an Indian nationalist, also sought freedom in the United States and entered the country through Angel Island with his wife, Kala, and their three children. By the 1920s, Francisco Carino had learned from his teachers in the Philippines that America was full of riches and glory, so he too boarded a ship bound for the United States.

Small numbers of family members, students, and professionals began to come after World War II and during the Cold War. They have been joined by even more immigrants and refugees since 1965. Chiyoko Toguchi Swartz married an American soldier and left her home in Okinawa in 1966. That same year, Kang Ok Jim was adopted from Korea and brought to Palo Alto where she grew up as Deann Borshay. Fear of persecution forced Le Tan Si and his family to flee from Vietnam in 1979 while Yeng Xiong joined an exodus of Hmong from Laos after the communists took control of the country. Korean engineer Han Chol Hong arrived in 1983 and after failing to find work, he opened a store in South Central Los Angeles. Vicki Diaz, originally from the Philippines, works as a housekeeper in LA to support her family back home. Rashni Bhatnagar, from India, recently joined her husband, who is an IT worker here on a temporary visa, and Chinese students are now the largest group of international students in the United States.

These Asian American journeys may not be well known, but they have been central to the making of Asian America and of America itself.

Broadly speaking, Asian Americans are people who can trace their roots to countries throughout East Asia, South Asia, and Southeast Asia.[2] Obscured by the broad definition of "Asian" and "Asian American" is a staggering diversity of peoples that represent twenty-four distinct groups. Chinese and Japanese were the largest Asian American communities in the United States before World War II, but South Asians, Koreans, and Filipinos also came in significant numbers. New immigration since 1965 has brought an even greater diversity of Asians to the United States, including new immigrants from China, Korea, the Philippines, India, Pakistan, Bangladesh, Hong Kong, and Taiwan, as well as refugees from Vietnam, Cambodia, and Laos.[3]

Asian Americans have differed not only in their country of origin, but also in their immigration and generational status, class position, religion, and gender. These differences have resulted in distinct experiences and histories. It is fair to ask whether there is even one "Asian America," or one "Asian American history." Asian Americans with long roots in this country may wonder what they have in common with today's recent arrivals. Similarly, new Asian immigrants and their descendants may not think that the histories of earlier Asian Americans are relevant to their own experiences. But they should. There is great diversity within Asian America and across Asian American history, but there are also significant similarities and connections. The experiences of previous generations shaped the world that Asian Americans live in today. Likewise, new immigration has helped us see the past in fresh ways. Both the diversity and the shared experiences of Asian Americans reveal the complex story of the making and remaking of Asian America. There is not one single story, but many.

Asian American history begins long before the United States was even a country and has its roots in world history. Asia and the Americas first became connected through European colonization and global trade after Christopher

Columbus embarked on his search for Asia and "discovered" America. Even though Columbus missed his mark, the idea of Asia remained central to the invention of America, and European colonization on both sides of the Pacific Ocean led to the first migrations of Asians to the Americas.[4]

Beginning in the sixteenth century, Spanish trading ships known as "Manila galleons" brought Asian sailors, slaves, and servants to present-day Mexico as part of the creation of Spain's Pacific Empire. Thereafter, Asian immigration followed the ebbs and flows of global history. The rise of the British Empire led to the movement of South Asian indentured laborers from British-controlled India to British colonies in the Caribbean while Chinese coolies were sent to Cuba after the end of the African slave trade. And as the United States became a world power and expanded its reach into Asia beginning in the late eighteenth century, Asians have steadily come to our shores. Seen through the lens of world history, Asian American journeys are part of longer and larger patterns that help us understand the making of America in a global context.

The history of Asian Americans is also immigration history. The most common view of immigration to America is still framed around the "push and pull" idea: conditions in one country—like war, natural disaster, civil unrest, and economic instability—push desperate peoples out while the United States pulls them in with better-paying jobs, land, and freedom from persecution. Once uprooted, these immigrants successfully transplant themselves into the United States where they achieve American dreams of success.[5]

But this is just part of the story. We know that people and families move for complex reasons. Asian immigration has been particularly tied to the U.S. presence in Asia. Americans first crossed the Pacific Ocean in search of trade, investment, and empire. Nineteenth-century trading vessels gave way to massive transpacific steamships that soon brought both Asian goods and laborers to the United States. American labor recruiters and transportation companies encouraged and facilitated Asian immigration into the early twentieth century. Immigration to the United States became an economic lifeline for many families on both sides of the Pacific Ocean even after immigration laws greatly restricted and even excluded Asian immigrants from the country.

U.S. colonial and military occupations and engagements in the Philippines, Japan, Korea, and Southeast Asia also brought Asians to the United States as colonial subjects, military brides, adoptees, and refugees. And U.S.-Asian international relations, including U.S. relationships with its allies, neighbors, and enemies, continue to affect both Asian immigration patterns and the treatment of Asian Americans in the United States.[6]

Asian immigration is about moving from Asia to the United States and making new homes in America. But it is also about moving temporarily or moving multiple times across the Pacific Ocean and throughout the Americas in search of education, employment, family, and freedom from persecution. The multifaceted journeys that have brought Asians to the United States reveal new ways of understanding both Asian American life and American immigration history in general.[7]

Once here, Asian immigrants have "become American" by becoming U.S. citizens when they could and by participating in American life.[8] There are some stunning individual success stories that show how Asian Americans have contributed to American society and the American economy. Most recently, the "rise of Asian Americans" as the "highest-income, best-educated and fastest-growing racial group" in the United States has been widely covered in mainstream media.[9] Pro basketball player Jeremy Lin, Yale law professor Amy Chua, aka the "Tiger Mom," and Bobby Jindal, Republican governor of Louisiana, are all cited as examples of the proven success of Asian Americans. But Asian Americans have often encountered an America that has excluded them from full participation in American life based on their race. The history of Asian Americans is thus also a history of how race works in the United States.

Broadly speaking, the concept of race has been used to divide humanity into distinct groups. Racism exists when race is used to treat people unequally and to confer different rights and freedoms upon some groups while denying them to others. In the United States, the concept of race was used to justify the enslavement of Africans and the dispossession of indigenous peoples because these groups were believed to be naturally inferior to whites. After the United States became an independent nation, the definition of American became tied to white settlers, and the privileges of American citizenship were extended to whites only as early as 1790. As successive groups of European immigrants came to the United States, they were mostly deemed "white on arrival" and were granted the benefits of citizenship and belonging that were denied to Asian immigrants, who were classified as "aliens ineligible for citizenship" on racial grounds.[10]

Throughout the nineteenth and early twentieth centuries, these racial beliefs were accepted and supported by pseudoscientific research that allegedly proved the biological basis of human difference and ability. Only after Nazi Germany's genocidal regime was condemned at the end of World War II did scientific racism lose its credibility. In the United States, new attitudes about race paved the way for new laws, and discrimination based on race was outlawed by the Civil Rights Act of 1964. More than fifty years later, however, discrimination and inequality still exist, and we have recently seen the rise of new kinds of racism that use racial difference in complicated ways. There's color-blind racism, which claims that since race no longer matters, racial discrimination and race-based inequality are now things of the past. There's also cultural racism, in which the term "culture" has come to stand in for "race" to describe how certain cultures possess inherent beliefs, mores, and traditions that determine a group's abilities.[11] Moreover, racial micro-aggressions, or everyday indignities and racial slights that differentiate and denigrate peoples of color, have become increasingly common.[12] Simply put, race still matters in the United States.

There are two main ways in which this history of race has played out for Asian Americans. The first is the simultaneous lumping together of diverse Asians into one homogenous group and the persistent treatment of Asian Americans as foreigners tied to Asia rather than as Americans loyal to the United States. Long before there were sizable communities of Asians in the Americas, Western ideas about Asia, or the "Orient," circulated widely and laid the foundation for how Asia and Asians would be viewed and treated in the West. Asia was consistently viewed as the West's Other, an array of exotic lands and peoples that both fascinated and terrified Europeans. Opinions about the vast differences between East and West, what theorist Edward Said called "Orientalism," justified European conquest and domination of Asia and treated the diverse peoples and empires of Asia as one, homogenous land and culture.[13]

Americans formed their own type of Orientalism. By the time that large-scale Asian immigration to the United States began in the mid-nineteenth century, diverse Asian peoples were considered one monolithic group, regardless of national origin, ethnicity, class, and religion and were fixed in the American mind as backward, submissive, and inferior. They were seen as the opposite of the forward-thinking expansionist American: always Asian and never American.[14] Thus, when Chinese immigrants—the first group to come in large numbers to the United States from Asia—were labeled as foreigners who were racially inferior to whites and incapable of assimilation, all succeeding Asian immigrants were similarly classified with only slight variations. From the mid-nineteenth to the mid-twentieth centuries, Asian immigrants were considered a single "despised minority." They faced discrimination in every part of their lives. Asian Americans fought for equal rights in the workplace, in the courts, and on the streets, but they remained largely excluded, segregated, and disfranchised until during and after World War II.

Class and education sometimes made a difference. In the early twentieth century, immigration laws granted privileges to merchants, students, and professionals that were denied to working-class immigrants. International relations and U.S. imperialism also differentiated some Asians from others. But more often than not, laws and practices that treated Asians the same were obstacles to all.

Gender discrimination added another layer of complexity for Asian immigrant women, for both their right to enter the United States and to stay in the country were linked to their husband's or father's immigrant status. U.S. citizenship had a gendered dimension as well. Barred from becoming naturalized citizens, Asian Americans could only gain U.S. citizenship through birth in the country. But for some years, native-born Asian American women lost their U.S. citizenship if they married Asian immigrant men, a consequence that did not apply to Asian American men.

How Asian Americans have been defined in relation to the enduring racial divide between African Americans and whites in the United States is the second way in which race has affected Asian American life. Until after World War II, Asians were treated as peoples unfit for U.S. citizenship and as outsiders in American society. They were, as historian Ellen Wu has explained, "definitely not white" and were denied equal rights alongside

African Americans and Native Americans.[15] For Asian Americans, this took multiple forms. They were barred from becoming naturalized citizens, prohibited from owning or leasing land and marrying whites in some states, and harassed, driven out, and segregated from the rest of America.

Most importantly though, Asian immigrants were simply denied entry to the country. In response to fears that Asians were threats to the economic, social, and political well-being of the country, new laws like the Chinese Exclusion Act of 1882 were passed to prevent most Chinese immigrants from entering the United States. America became a "gatekeeping nation," and new policies to inspect, interrogate, detain, identify, and deport immigrants followed. So did undocumented immigration. By the 1930s, all other Asian immigrants were largely excluded from the country as well. These policies almost destroyed Asian America before World War II.[16]

Moreover, the U.S.'s Asian exclusion laws had a global impact. Anti-Asian racism moved across national boundaries and contributed to an emerging worldwide system of immigration regulation. By the early twentieth century, the United States had set the terms and logic of the Asian "immigration problem" that nearly every country in the Western Hemisphere—from Canada to Argentina—adopted or adapted to. During World War II, these policies merged with new concerns about national and hemispheric security. Japanese Americans were uprooted from their homes and incarcerated in the name of "military necessity." Similarly, Japanese Canadians were sent into exile. Japanese Latin Americans faced restrictions in their daily lives and some were even expelled.

Even as discriminatory laws were struck down and as social attitudes have mellowed, Asian Americans have still not achieved full equality in American life. In contemporary America, Asian Americans occupy unique and constantly shifting positions between black and white, foreign and American, privilege and poverty. Depending on what is happening inside and outside the United States, certain Asian American groups have been labeled as "good Asians" ("model minorities," "honorary whites," cultural brokers, and loyal citizens), while others have been labeled as "bad Asians" (perpetual foreigners, religious others, unassimilated refugees, spies, terrorists, and the enemy within). These labels and stereotypes serve myriad purposes. During the Cold War, the Asian American model minority who achieved the

American Dream was held up as proof of American democracy at a time when the United States was being criticized by communist rivals abroad and civil rights activists at home. Today, the privileged model minority continues to be a useful reminder that American success is still achievable even as income inequality grows, the achievement gap between whites and African Americans and Latinos persists, and the United States' power in the world diminishes.

But this portrait of Asian American success is uneven and incomplete. While some Asian Americans have achieved economic success and cite hard work and perseverance as the keys to their positions of privilege, others—especially working-class immigrants, undocumented immigrants, and refugees fleeing the ravages of war—remain mired in generational poverty and struggle at the margins of American society. Even some of those who have been touted as models continue to occupy an unstable status that can change overnight. Korean storeowners in South Central Los Angeles were targeted in the aftermath of the verdict in the Rodney King case in 1992. South Asian Americans, along with Muslim and Arab Americans, became the victims of hate crimes and labeled as terrorists after 9/11.

On a more daily basis, Asian Americans continue to be seen as outsiders in the United States despite the fact that many are U.S. citizens and are from families who have been in the country for generations. "Where are you from?" they are continually asked. And when the answers "Oakland," "New York," or "Chicago" do not satisfy the questioner, they are asked, "No, where are you *really* from?" The underlying assumption behind these questions is that Asians cannot possibly be real Americans and do not belong in the United States. Instead, they are perpetual foreigners at worst, or probationary Americans at best.[17] The persistence in treating Asian Americans as outsiders in their own country has resulted in everyday racial slights as well as targeted violence, murder, and hate crimes.

Race has never been just a matter of black and white in the United States. Asian Americans have been both included and excluded from the country, sometimes simultaneously. In exemplifying this complicated and contingent history of American race relations, Asian Americans remain absolutely central to understanding the ongoing ways in which race works today.

• • •

The history of Asian Americans is lastly a history of America in a global age. Like many Americans today, Asian Americans live transnational lives and form their identities across national borders. Over the decades, Asian American families, businesses, as well as social, political, and religious organizations have all existed and flourished both within the United States and across nations. During the late nineteenth century, the majority of Chinese immigrant families, including my own, lived in so-called split households. Fathers and husbands worked in American Chinatowns while mothers and children remained in China.[18] The same was true for many South Asians and Filipinos. Today, H-1B visa holders from India toil in Silicon Valley separated from their families back home. Taiwanese high schoolers leave their parents behind to attend American schools and universities. Lao refugee grandparents living in the upper Midwest leave their American-raised children and American-born grandchildren during the bitter winter months and become long-distance snowbirds in sunny Laos.

Asians' pursuit of equality in the United States has also been connected to homeland politics, whether it was the Chinese Revolution or Korean and Indian nationalism during the early twentieth century, the anti–martial law campaign in the Philippines during the 1980s, or human rights issues in Southeast Asia today. Asian Americans continue to confront both American racism and global inequalities through their transnational lives, activities, and identities that are simultaneously effecting change in the United States and across the Pacific Ocean.[19]

Furthermore, contemporary Asian Americans are creating new, multilayered identities. They are simultaneously racial minorities within nations, transnational immigrants who engage in two or more homelands, and diasporic citizens making connections across borders. Like many contemporary immigrants around the world, they "don't trade in their home country membership card for an American one," as anthropologist Peggy Levitt explains. Rather, they "belong to several communities at once."[20] They might raise their children in the United States, yet send money to elderly parents or extended family in India. They might shop at Walmart as well as the local Korean grocery store, contribute to their children's local parent-teacher association and to their alma mater in the Philippines, or vote in both the United States and Taiwanese national elections.

Today's immigrants challenge the either/or dichotomy of becoming American or not. They are transnational not because they don't want to or cannot become fully American. They are transnational because it allows them to achieve something that is quintessentially American: to improve their lives and socioeconomic status for themselves and their families whether that may be solely within the United States, or often, in the United States and somewhere else at the same time.[21] These transnational immigrants are helping us all become global Americans.

Exploring how Asian Americans have made and remade American life over the centuries, this book offers a new and timely history of this important and diverse community. But more than that, it offers a new way of understanding America itself, its histories of race and immigration, and its place in the world today.

PART ONE

Beginnings: Asians in the Americas

1

Los Chinos in New Spain and Asians in Early America

Long before Asians came to the United States, they went to Latin America. The earliest came as part of Spain's Pacific empire stretching from Manila in the Philippines to Acapulco in New Spain (present-day Mexico)—an empire that had been built on Christopher Columbus' accidental "discovery" of America while searching for Asia.

Europeans, dating as far back as ancient Greece, had long been fascinated with Asia—including the Middle East and Far East—its people, its civilizations, and its fabled riches.[1] In the European imagination, Asia was Europe's polar opposite, its Other. Asia and Asians differed in "every respect" from Europe and Europeans, as the Greek physician and recognized father of medicine Hippocrates explained in the fourth or fifth century BCE.[2] For centuries this difference between East and West was the subject of endless speculation, informing a Western-held understanding of a masculine, conquering Europe and a feminized Asia ripe for conquest.[3] This worldview helped direct the West's search for Asia and influenced its presence there. It was also a significant factor in propelling Asian peoples to the Americas.

During the Roman Empire, trading networks were established that eventually stretched from the British Isles to the Indian subcontinent. European pilgrims, merchants, and others shared their first impressions of Asia through sporadic travel writings. Crusaders rediscovered Asia when they set off for the Middle East on their quest to reclaim Jerusalem from the Muslims in 1095. Lasting almost 200 years, the Crusades gave generations of western Europeans firsthand knowledge of the Middle East and some idea of the vastness and richness of the rest of Asia. European travelers described the bizarre creatures, alien plants, and strange customs of the "East" and helped to define Asia as an "other world" that stood in opposition to Europe.[4]

Sustained long-distance travel and trade between Europe and Asia followed the establishment of the Mongol Empire that stretched across Asia to the eastern fringes of Europe in the early thirteenth century. The so-called Pax Mongolica of the thirteenth and fourteenth centuries brought Asia and Europe closer together as both Asians and Europeans ventured far from their homelands. Asian goods and Asia itself came within reach of more and more Europeans. During this period travelers could journey eastward and back in relative safety and those who returned found ready audiences for their tales of exotic lands and abundant riches.[5]

Among the most well known in western Europe was the story of Marco Polo, a young Italian merchant who journeyed 15,000 miles throughout the Middle East and Asia over a twenty-four-year period at the end of the thirteenth century. *The Travels of Marco Polo* contained accounts of fantastical unicorns, exotic sexual customs, and mountain streams flowing with diamonds. Marco described the court of the Mongol leader Kublai Khan as having "so many vessels of gold and silver that none without seeing could possibly believe it."[6]

Published in 1356, *The Travels of Sir John Mandeville* also told incredible tales of the East, becoming a highly popular and influential book among a large audience of Europeans interested in understanding the larger world and the place of both Asia and Europe in it. Written under a pseudonym and allegedly the autobiography of an English knight, it described the Holy Land, Egypt, Arabia, and China as a region filled with cannibals and headless beasts as well as tantalizing spices, gems, and abundant quantities of gold and silver.[7]

By the dawn of the European age of exploration and conquest in the fifteenth century, wealthy Europeans had developed a growing taste for Asian imports such as spices, silks, and sugar, and they demanded more. Portuguese explorer Vasco da Gama relied upon an Indian navigator to become the first European to sail directly to Asia from Europe in 1497. His route took him around the Cape of Good Hope along the Atlantic coast of present-day South Africa to the legendary spice routes of India. When he returned to Portugal two years later, his spice-laden cargo yielded a 600 percent profit, paved the way for Portugal's colonial empire in Asia, and spurred further European exploration of Asia that would last through the twentieth century. Profit was far from the only motivation. As England's Sir Walter Raleigh predicted in 1615, "whosoever commands the sea commands the trade; whosoever commands the trade of the world commands the riches of the world, and consequently the world itself."[8]

Technological advances in shipbuilding and navigation as well as breakthroughs in astronomy and geography made Europe's oceangoing exploration possible. Spanish seafarers used the latest oceanic sailing ships to explore the Pacific and followed the Polynesian voyagers who preceded them. By the late fifteenth century, the ocean sea was no longer a barrier and soon became a passageway to the other side of the world.[9]

Inspired by Marco Polo, Christopher Columbus dreamed of Asia. His well-worn copy of Marco's *Travels* contained numerous comments in the margins; it was through these adventures that Columbus formed his impressions of the Christian converts and fabulous riches that Asia promised. When he and his crew first spotted land in the Caribbean on October 12, 1492, Columbus imagined that he would soon be viewing Asia's rich spice markets and gold-roofed houses. When he and his landing party rowed to the beach the next morning in the *Santa María*'s launch, however, nothing matched the men's expectations.

Nevertheless, Columbus explored the surrounding islands over the next few months and returned to Spain in February of 1493 believing that he had accomplished his dream of reaching Asia. His accounts echoed the fantastical descriptions of exotic peoples and fabulous riches that numerous travelers to Asia had told before him. The new lands, he claimed, were full of boundless wealth and populations ripe for conversion to Christianity. Columbus would make three more voyages across the Atlantic to the New World before his death in 1506, forever convinced it was Asia.[10]

Columbus's voyages and subsequent discoveries by other explorers such as Amerigo Vespucci helped Spain dispossess the indigenous peoples of

Mesoamerica and establish its huge land-based American empire, *Nueva España*.[11] Between 1520 and 1540, the Spanish added over three quarters of a million square miles to their empire in the Americas. In 1519, Spanish conquistador Hernán Cortés founded the town of Veracruz on the Mexican Atlantic Coast. The Aztec Empire was defeated by 1521, and Francisco Pizarro conquered the Incas of Peru a decade later. The wars of conquest and dispossession were violent affairs that cost many human lives among the indigenous peoples. But this death toll paled in comparison to the untold millions who perished as a result of the introduction of European diseases like smallpox.

1. "Americae Sive Novi Orbis, Nova Descriptio." This map of the Americas, prominently featuring Manila galleons sailing across the Pacific from Manila to Acapulco, was included in what is considered to be the first world atlas, by Abraham Ortelius, initially printed in 1570.

Long after they realized that the lands Columbus had discovered were not in fact Asia, the Spanish continued to seek routes to Asia's fabled empires. Asia and the Americas were linked in Spain's imagination and became two parts of the New World, *ambas Indias*, both Indies, that could be conquered and converted to Christianity.[12] Spain's new American empire allowed explorers to continue the search for a transpacific trading route with Asia, but the vast size of the Pacific and the general lack of knowledge of winds and currents made this difficult. By 1522, Portuguese explorer Ferdinand Magellan's crew had successfully circumnavigated the world, traveling from the Atlantic to the Pacific and back again. In doing so, they proved that Europeans could indeed sail westward to reach the riches of Asia. Of far greater consequence for Spain was navigator and friar Andrés de Urdaneta's 1565 discovery of a route from Asia to New Spain by way of the Philippines, the new Spanish colony and seat of its Pacific empire. Urdaneta's route set in motion a wave of Pacific exploration and conquest that was motivated by "God, gold, and glory." *Presidios* (military bases), missions, and *pueblos* (settlements) rose up from Mexico to northern California.[13] It also inaugurated a new era of transpacific migration and global trade.

Asia's own history of maritime exploration and trade played an equally important role in connecting Asia and the Americas. Long before Europeans began their oceangoing missions, the Chinese navigator Zheng He commanded seven expeditions to explore the waters of Southeast Asia and the Indian Ocean in 1405. Zheng's fleets ventured as far as the Persian Gulf, Aden, East Africa, and the south coast of Arabia.[14] Following these successful expeditions, however, the Chinese emperor officially isolated China from the rest of the world and ended China's maritime expansion. An imperial decree prohibiting private overseas trade was in place until 1567. Throughout the years of the ban, however, private Chinese traders from Fujian and Guangdong sailed their Chinese junks to ports throughout the Indian Ocean and South China Sea. As a result, Chinese junks came yearly to Manila, bringing a wealth of goods from throughout the Asian maritime world.[15] At the crossroads of a flourishing trade established by both Chinese traders and the Portuguese in India, Manila became a vibrant global marketplace through which flowed the "riches of the Orient and the Occident," as a Jesuit historian explained in 1663.[16]

With Urdaneta's new route connecting Asia and the Americas in place by 1565, transpacific trade began. The first Spanish ship, known as a Manila galleon (*nao de China* or *nao de Acapulco*), left Manila and arrived in

Acapulco in late 1565. The Manila galleon trade took off eight years later, when the *Santiago* and the *San Juan* carried 712 pieces of Chinese silk and 22,300 pieces of Chinese porcelainware to Acapulco. By 1576, the galleon trade was firmly established and controlled by a monopoly of merchants from Seville, Spain.[17]

From 1565 to 1815, 110 Manila galleons traveled across the Pacific between Manila and Acapulco. By imperial decree, all trade between Spain and Asia went through the Philippines, then by sea to Acapulco, overland to Veracruz via *el camino de China* (the China highway), and then across the Atlantic to Spain. Two ships were allowed to sail from each port annually, accompanied by several other vessels that protected the trading ships from British and Dutch pirates. These enormous teakwood "castles in the sea" ranged in size from 78 to 174 feet long and displaced from 300 to 2,000 tons.[18] On the lengthy and arduous voyage to Acapulco, ships were at sea around six difficult months and had to sail northward to avoid westerly trade winds. A 1620 order required that the galleons leave Manila by the last day of June in order to guarantee their arrival in Acapulco by the end of the year. The return trip to Manila typically took seventy-five to ninety days and was mandated to begin by the end of March.[19]

The galleons brought to New Spain an enormous array of goods: porcelain, spices, furniture, and silk, cotton, satin, velvet, and linen fabric from China; emeralds, rubies, and diamonds from India; ivory from Cambodia; ebony from Siam; cinnamon from Ceylon; pepper from Sumatra; Persian carpets from the Middle East; and fans, umbrellas, and lacquered wood and silverware from Japan. Over the centuries, the Manila galleons also sent 2 million Mexican silver pesos to China, turning it into the world's first currency. This unprecedented era of world trade would last for 250 years.[20]

Representing the first migrations of Asians to the Americas, some 40,000 to 100,000 Asians from China, Japan, the Philippines, and South and Southeast Asia crossed the Pacific from Manila and landed in Acapulco during the 250-year history of the galleon trade.[21] Among the very first may have been Filipino crewmembers on Friar Urdaneta's trailblazing voyage to New Spain in 1565. Also, a small number of Filipino crewmembers were likely on the Manila galleon that made a brief stop in Morro Bay, California, in

1587, where they battled with locals before heading back out to sea. According to some reports, Filipinos were also among the first settlers of Alta California after it became a province and territory in the Viceroyalty of New Spain in 1769.[22] Others—mostly sailors, servants, and slaves—also came during the two and a half centuries of the Manila galleon era. Native Filipinos and mestizos (mixed race peoples) of Filipino/Chinese/Spanish descent were in the majority, but there was a sizable number of Chinese, Japanese, and South Asians as well.[23]

Filipino and Chinese sailors were among the most numerous, arriving as members of crews that ranged in size from 60 to 200. By the 1600s, they made up the majority of crewmembers sailing out of Manila to New Spain.[24] Filipino sailors, called "Indians," were highly valued. In a memorial to the Spanish king in 1765, Francisco Leandro de Viana, a Spanish official in Manila, praised the sailors, saying, "There is not an Indian in those [Philippine] islands who has not a remarkable inclination for the sea; nor is there at present in all the world a people more agile in manoeuvers on ship board, or who learn so quickly nautical terms and whatever a good mariner ought to know."[25]

The ships they sailed, however, were filthy and often unseaworthy. Disease ran rampant and killed many crewmembers and passengers. During one voyage in the late seventeenth century, Pedro Cubero Sebastián's ship barely survived a massive storm that lasted for eighty hours. Of 400 passengers and crew, 208 died before reaching Acapulco.[26] In his book about his voyage around the world, Italian adventurer and traveler Giovanni Francesco Gemelli Careri titled the chapter describing his 1697 passage on a Manila galleon "the Author's tedious and dreadful Voyage, to the port of Acapulco," claiming that the transpacific voyage was "enough to Destroy a Man, or make him unfit for any thing as long as he Lives." As he described it, the provisions brought on board the ship were full of maggots and the galleons swarmed with "little vermine"—bugs that "ran all over the cabin, in the food, and onto human passengers and crew." With all available space devoted to cargo, he also noted, the ships often lacked proper crew quarters, and the sailors were required to sleep on deck.[27]

Despite their skill, Asian crewmembers received half the rations provided to Spanish crewmembers or were never paid the wages they were promised.

And when provisions grew scarce near the end of the transpacific voyages, they were given even less.[28] They were treated "like dogs," according to Hernando de los Ríos Coronel, a Spaniard living in the Philippines who served as the Procurator General, the sole representative of the Philippines at the Spanish court. In his appeal for reform, Ríos Coronel explained that the crew arrived on board ship without adequate clothing for the cold weather, and because they slept in the open air many froze to death. "When each new dawn comes there are three or four dead men," Ríos Coronel recounted. The Asian sailors suffered so much, Ríos continued, that to "tell in detail the evil that is done to them, would fill many pages."[29]

The perilous and long journey, unfair wages, and harsh working conditions convinced many sailors that their fortunes lay in the New World. To prevent desertion, ship captains paid sailors only a portion of their wages when they sailed out of the Philippines toward America. Only on their return to the Philippines was the rest of their promised pay to be given. The outbound journey was so horrendous, however, that many sailors opted to forfeit their pay rather than suffer through another ship voyage. Many even came prepared with a few bundles of Asian fabrics to sell. On one ship alone in 1618, only five out of an original crew of seventy-five Asian sailors returned to their ship for the journey back to Manila. The remaining seventy easily blended into local society with their ability to speak Spanish. Some married and settled down.[30]

Some Asian servants also accompanied their Spanish masters across the Pacific to New Spain. The galleons carried a good number of Spanish passengers traveling across the Pacific as returning residents, new settlers, colonial and church officials, soldiers, and travelers. Their Asian servants catered to their needs on the sea voyage and in the new homes.[31]

After sailors, slaves made up the next largest group of Asians coming to the Americas. The importation of Asian slaves began in Manila with Portuguese slave traders traversing Portugal's extensive Southeast Asian empire. European travelers in Asia and Spanish officials in Manila regularly recorded Portuguese ships arriving in Manila with both spices and slaves in their holds. These ships brought African slaves as well as slaves from Macao, the Malabar Coast of India, Pegu (Burma), Malacca, Java, and other areas where they conducted trade in the Indian Ocean. In 1625, for example, one

Portuguese ship left the port of Bengal with rice, oil, textiles, and slaves in its hold on its way to Malacca and Manila. Japanese sources chronicle how Portuguese slavers bought "several hundred men and women" in the Goto islands, Hirado, and Nagasaki, and took them aboard their "black ships," where they were chained hand and foot. Portuguese slavers were known to use deception and outright kidnapping in acquiring slaves. As a result, several hundred Asian slaves are estimated to have arrived in the Philippines each year from the Indian Ocean world.[32]

Licenses to transport slaves to the New World through the ports of southern Spain date back to the early sixteenth century, and African slaves had been brought to the Americas by the first conquistadors. When epidemics ravaged the indigenous populations during the first half of the seventeenth century in New Spain, slaves became a much sought-after commodity. By 1607, the Indian population of central Mexico had fallen to between 1.5 and 2 million, down from an estimated 20 million in 1520. Approximately 300,000 African slaves arrived in Spanish America and another 335,000 in Brazil from 1492 to 1650.[33]

In the sixteenth and early seventeenth centuries Manila became a center of transpacific slave trading. Facilitated by the Manila galleon trade, Asians constituted another pool of slave labor in New Spain, albeit much smaller than the African population. Colonial merchants, priests, and military and civil officials involved in the trade all profited handsomely. In 1604, Father Pedro Chirino observed that slaves from India, Malacca, and Maluco fetched the highest prices, because "the men are industrious and obliging, and many are good musicians; the women excellent seamstresses, cooks, and preparers of conserves, and are neat and clean in service."[34] An estimated 6,000 entered the colony each decade during the seventeenth century.[35]

Some of the Asian male slaves were skilled workers; others were not. A man named Francisco Corubi testified in 1616 that he had been captured by fishermen when he was a young boy and then sold to Portuguese masters, who took him from Goa to Malacca and then to Manila. He eventually ended up in Mexico.[36] In 1642, a twenty-five-year-old slave named Gaspar sailed from Manila to Acapulco. Gaspar's owner, who was a "citizen of the city of Manila" named Francisco de Araujo, put Gaspar into the custody of Manuel Joan de Alcántara, a sailor on the *Nuestra Señora del Rosario*, anchored in Manila Bay. Their contract stipulated that Alcántara would "give him [Gaspar] food and drink on the entire voyage" and "keep him comfortably in his quarters." When the ship reached New Spain, Alcántara was instructed to "sell the said slave at the highest price offered." Upon returning to Manila, Alcántara was to deliver the proceeds to Araujo. In return, the sailor could keep one third of the profits.[37]

Some women were captured for sale on the concubine market or as sex slaves. They faced particularly harrowing ordeals. Spanish officials and nobles were known to bring Filipina women on board as concubines and then abandon them once they reached Acapulco. One prominent official reportedly embarked with fifteen women. "Several were delivered of children by him, while others left the ship at Acapulco in a pregnant condition," an observer noted with disgust. This abuse of women caused a "great scandal," and a 1608 decree sought without much success to abolish the practice.[38] Spain tried to restrict transpacific slavery, but the trade continued for many decades. In 1626, a tax of 4,000 reales was levied on every slave brought from the Philippines. In 1672, Asian slaves were emancipated in New Spain, and in 1700 a royal order prohibited the Asian slave trade. Only then did the number of Asians transported as part of the transpacific slave trade drop dramatically.[39]

Historians estimate that the first Asians—collectively known as *los chinos*—landed in Acapulco in the 1580s.[40] Small but stable populations of *chinos*, the indigenous women they married, and their descendants formed communities along the Pacific coast in cities and *pueblas* like Acapulco, Coyuca, and San Miguel. The towns of Guerrero, Jalisco, and Michoacán were also popular settlements, as were the large settlements along *el camino de China* that connected Acapulco on the west coast to Mexico City, Puebla, and Veracruz on the east coast. According to historian Edward Slack Jr., Asians could be found in almost every corner of colonial Mexico during the late sixteenth to the early nineteenth centuries, from Loreto in Baja California to Mérida in Yucatán.[41]

A small Japanese community traces its origins to the arrival of an official Japanese delegation in 1611, when Ieyasu, the powerful shogun of Japan, sent twenty-three tradesmen and an official to New Spain in the hopes of negotiating a trade agreement with Spanish American officials. They stayed for five months and returned to Japan with wine, cloth, and velvet, but no agreement. Three years later, Masamune Date, a lord of Sendai, sent a delegation via New Spain on the first leg of his journey to pay homage to the Spanish court in Madrid and then to the pope in Rome. One hundred eighty samurai and merchants led by Tsunenaga Hasekura arrived in Acapulco in January of 1614. While the majority traveled on to Spain and eventually returned to Japan, a small number settled in New Spain and started families.[42]

Other Asians ventured to different locales in the Americas. A 1613 census of the inhabitants of Lima, Peru, found "Indians of China and Manila."[43] Chinese shipbuilders worked in Spanish-controlled lower California, present-day Baja California in northwestern Mexico, during the late sixteenth and early seventeenth centuries. Chinese from the Philippines were employed in the textile mills of Peru in the seventeenth century, and reports of Chinese miners in the gold mines of Minas Gerais in Portuguese Brazil were recorded in the early 1700s.[44]

Along the Pacific coast of New Spain, Asians worked as fishermen or as farmers or farm laborers tending rice, corn, cotton, and tobacco fields. They transported goods and people along the coast and labored in the silver mines, textile workshops, or sugar mills. In Acapulco, Mexico City, and Puebla they took up a variety of occupations, including as laborers and craftsmen in the Acapulco royal shipyards, and as dancers, tailors, shoemakers, and butchers. Large numbers were peddlers, barbers, or merchants, selling Asian cotton and silk textiles or food in Mexico City's Plaza Mayor. On a visit to Mexico City in the 1620s or 1630s, Dominican monk Thomas Gage marveled at the number of "people of China" who had converted to Christianity and excelled in goldsmithing. They had "perfected the Spaniards in that trade," he observed.[45] And Asians so dominated the field of barbering in the city that Spanish barbers filed a petition in 1635 complaining of unfair practices and competition.[46]

Filipinos were notably successful in making palm wine, or *tuba*, a liquor made from palm trees that was popular in the Philippines. In 1619, Philippine official Hernando de los Ríos Coronel reported that "Indian natives of the Filipinas Islands" who had arrived in Mexico as seamen had deserted their ships and were now turning a profit making the wine along the coast.

Palm wine was so popular, Ríos observed, that the indigenous peoples in the colony were now drinking "none except what the Filipinos make," which was as "strong as brandy." This entrepreneurial success worried Ríos. Not only did the new palm wine threaten the import (and tax revenue) of Castilian wine, but Ríos predicted that its ready availability would cause harm to the natives of Nueva España, "a race inclined to drink and intoxication."[47]

Some Asians in New Spain became well integrated into their local societies. They formed Catholic confraternities that provided charitable services and served in militias on the west coast of New Spain.[48] They also rose to prominent and respected positions in their communities. Take, for example, the life histories of two Japanese merchants in seventeenth-century Guadalajara. Born in 1595 in northern Japan, a man who adopted the Spanish name of Luis de Encío had settled in the town of Ahuacatlán by 1620 and worked as a peddler. Fourteen years later, he and some business partners opened a shop in Guadalajara's city center, and he married a local woman named Catalina de Silva. By the 1640s, Encío managed the monopoly of all coconut and mescal wine sales and became the major supplier of delicacies popular with local elites. He was also a leader in the Asian community in Guadalajara that developed as small numbers of new immigrants trickled into the city over the years. One of these newcomers was a Japanese-born man known as Juan de Páez.[49]

Born in 1608 in Osaka, Juan de Páez was just ten years old when he arrived in New Spain on a Manila galleon. He may have been an orphan in the care of Jesuits expelled from Japan during an anti-Christian purge. Despite his humble beginnings, Páez had become well established by the 1630s through his financial and legal services business and gained the approval of Luis de Encío to marry his daughter Margarita. One of the richest businessmen in town, Páez became part of the city's elite, the mayor of Zapopan, as well as the steward of the Guadalajara cathedral. He drew his friends from among other social elites, clergy, and Spanish colonial authorities and was listed as the executor of a remarkable number of estates. When he died at the age of sixty-nine in 1675, Páez's final resting place was at the foot of the Altar of the Santo Cristo in the Guadalajara cathedral.[50]

Perhaps the most well known and revered *chino* in New Spain was Mirrha-Catarina de San Juan, who in 1610 arrived in Puebla a sexually abused slave and died a holy woman respected by rich and poor alike. Mirrha's exact birthplace and family origin are unknown. Seventeenth-century church biographies tell us that Mirrha was born in the "distant provinces" of China, Mogor, or India.[51] She was just twelve years old when she was abducted from her home by Portuguese slave traders in 1618 or 1619 and confined and raped. She sailed with her captors to several port cities in the Indian Ocean. In Cochin, on the west coast of India, she was baptized before being sold in Manila to Spanish captain Miguel de Sosa.[52]

Mirrha crossed the Pacific Ocean on a Manila galleon with her new owner and then lived and worked in Captain de Sosa's household in Puebla. When the captain died in 1624, Mirrha was granted her freedom. She continued to work as a domestic servant in the home of Padre Pedro Suarez, who ordered her to marry an Asian slave named Domingo Suarez. The two were married in 1627, but by that time, Mirrha had decided to dedicate her life to Christ. After both husband and master died by the 1640s, Mirrha began her life as a lay holy woman. In her later years, she became known as a healer and a Catholic visionary who worked among the poor and sick. When she died in 1688, devotees unofficially turned her former homes into shrines and Mirrha's funeral was attended by crowds that included some of the most prominent members of colonial Mexican society. The Jesuit order also nominated her for sainthood.

The Church rejected the nomination in the 1690s during the Mexican Inquisition, an extension of the Spanish Inquisition that sought to reaffirm the practice of traditional Catholic tenets in the New World. Biographies of Mirrha were condemned as witchcraft and the Church ordered that all copies be destroyed along with any portraits of her. Despite this official condemnation, Mirrha-Catarina de San Juan remained a highly respected figure in Mexico, especially in her hometown of Puebla. Located on *el camino de China* that ran from Acapulco to Veracruz, Puebla had a large criollo population of American-born Spaniards who sought to promote the city's importance in Spanish imperial and Christian history. Mirrha became a heroine to the emerging criollo class in Puebla, who revered her as a local saint even if she had arrived as a foreigner. Mirrha's own holy visions connected Asia and the Americas together in complementary ways. She reportedly made numerous spiritual journeys in which she traveled to various nations in the

Americas and Asia and witnessed the Christian conversions of the kings of Japan, India, and China. A *chino* from Asia who had become Christian and local, she represented two important historical linkages and aspirations at work in New Spain at the time: Europe's search for Asia and Christian converts, and the successful spiritual conquest of the New World.[53]

2. "Poblanas," a nineteenth-century painting of *La China Poblana* (the Chinese girl from Puebla), by Carl Nebel (1829).

In the nineteenth century, Mirrha-Catarina de San Juan became the inspiration for *la china poblana*, "the Chinese girl from Puebla," an iconic symbol of Mexican womanhood that ironically glorified Mexico's *mestizaje* (mixed race) and indigenous peoples rather than Mirrha's own Asian origins. Representing the beauty and strength of local culture over imported European tastes, *la china poblana* is known for her indigenous country origins, distinctive behavior, hairstyle, and dress, typically a white blouse with silk and beaded embroidery, similarly decorated full skirt, and shawl resembling textiles from India, perhaps in honor of Mirrha. The red, green, and white colors of her clothes mirror the colors of the Mexican flag, and her skirt often has Mexico's eagle and serpent on it.[54] *La China Poblana* was captured in paintings, figurines, and other forms of popular culture throughout the nineteenth century. To this day, she remains one of Mexico's most iconic symbols. Mirrha's tomb lies inside the sacristy of Puebla's eighteenth-century Jesuit church in the city's historic center. And an enormous statue and fountain dedicated to her is a local landmark.

Spain's Pacific empire had first connected Asia and the Americas together through colonization and trade. But as other European powers extended their reach into Asia and its markets, the Spanish monopoly on trade with Asia came to an end. By the 1760s, Britain was the world's leading colonizer and its East India Company exported goods from the Indian subcontinent and China to the rest of the world. As a result, the American colonies, and later the new United States, became increasingly connected to Asia and Asian goods. Eventually, Asian immigrants followed.

Just as the peoples of New Spain had become enamored with Asian porcelain and fabrics through the Manila galleon trade, North American settlers also experienced a "China-mania" for Asian goods beginning in the eighteenth century. Everything from Chinese tea, teapots, and porcelain figurines to Japanese lacquerware and East Indies furniture, textiles, trinkets, and pictures made their way into the colonies and were viewed as symbols of civilization and refinement. George Washington, for example, was known for his love of exotic goods like Chinese tea sets and kept these items close at hand even as he battled the British. With tea drinking a popular pastime in the British colonies, millions of pieces of Chinese porcelain were imported for display and use in early American homes.[55]

Tea from China, of course, also helped fuel the opening acts of the American Revolution. It was both a coveted staple of American life and culture and a potent symbol of the "treachery of Britain's mercantile establishment." Americans were consuming more than a million pounds of tea each year (much of it smuggled in from non-British sources), and some suspected that American dependency on the "evil weed" was a British plot to make them weak and slavelike. When the British Parliament passed the Tea Act of 1773, which made it easier for the British-owned East India Company to import tea directly into the colonies and maintain taxes on tea, popular discontent turned into a protest movement. Americans believed that purchasing East

Indies tea meant accepting the right of the British Parliament to levy direct taxes on them; one more example of "taxation without representation." Boston patriots decided to act. On December 16, 1773, they famously boarded three East India Company ships and dumped 342 chests of Darjeeling tea into the Boston Harbor. The Boston Tea Party became one of the major turning points leading to the War of Independence.[56]

Asia remained important to Americans in the new United States. It continued to be imagined as a place of fabulous luxuries and advanced civilizations that America's founding generation sought to emulate. But it was the lucrative trade with China (from which Europe's great powers were already profiting) that Americans most immediately wanted to engage in. It symbolized, as historian Kariann Yokota explains, "both America's independence and future promise."[57] Americans set sail for China only days after the British departed New York harbor in November 1783. The first vessel to embark on this journey was the *Harriet* from Boston. She sailed in December 1783 with a cargoful of North American ginseng, a native root the Chinese used as a health supplement. This was one month before the Continental Congress of the new United States of America ratified the Treaty of Paris on January 14, 1784, establishing its independent statehood.[58]

Then on February 22, 1784, the *Empress of China* set sail from New York as excited crowds gathered to witness the first U.S. vessel to travel to Canton under the United States flag. From the same harbor on the same day, another ship departed for London to deliver the congressional ratification of the Articles of Peace between the United States and Great Britain. The timing of the two launches had great significance. Finally free from King George III's grasp, Americans were eager to voyage to the "golden regions" of the East Indies, where they had long been forbidden to go. Through China, Americans believed that the economic prosperity and the promise of the new nation itself would be secured.[59]

The *Harriet* and the *Empress of China* did not disappoint. The *Harriet*'s captain traded the ginseng for tea. When the *Empress* returned in 1785 after a fifteen-month voyage, it brought a cargo hold full of Chinese teas, silks, porcelains, and fans and made a handsome profit. China was now open to the United States. Within six years of American independence, fifty-two ships sailed from the United States into the Indian Ocean and beyond. By 1814, some 618 U.S. vessels had sailed to Macao or Canton. The China trade, which involved trading ginseng (from the mountainous backcountry regions of the northeastern United States) and pelts and furs from otters, seals, beavers, bears, and cattle (from the Pacific Northwest and California) to China in exchange for tea, porcelain, silk, furniture, and other goods, became a central part of the new U.S. economy. It helped build the fortunes of many East Coast families, turned New York into the U.S.'s commercial center, and connected European, Asian, American, and native communities on both sides of the Pacific Ocean together in a new era of global trade.[60]

The growing U.S. presence in Asia also led to new migration from Asia to the United States and Canada. Many U.S. ships recruited Filipinos to serve as deckhands, cooks, servants, and other members of the crew, and as a result Filipinos ended up in many of the Pacific islands and all the way to Alaska. Small numbers of Asian sailors and merchants also made their way to the East Coast of the United States by the late eighteenth century. In 1784 the *Pallas* arrived in Baltimore with "Chinese, Malays, Japanese and Moors" along with some European crewmembers. John Huston, a seaman and naturalized U.S. citizen, arrived as a young child in 1829 from China. When New York State census takers knocked on his door in lower Manhattan in 1855, he was married to an Irish woman. There were others as well, such as Lesing Newman and John Islee, Chinese-born naturalized U.S. citizens living in New York and serving on board transatlantic ships in the 1830s and 1840s.[61]

The first recorded Chinese woman to arrive in the United States was brought into New York harbor in November 1834 aboard the *Washington*, a trading vessel owned by two U.S.-China traders, brothers Nathaniel and Frederick Carne. The ship's hold was full of new Chinese goods aimed at the American middle class (shawls, lacquered backgammon boards, snuffboxes, walking canes, fans, and baskets), as well as nineteen-year-old Afong Moy, advertised as a "beautiful Chinese Lady" with bound feet whom the Carnes hoped would attract buyers for their wares. Within three weeks of her arrival in New York, the brothers had secured an exhibit space and placed Moy in a re-created "Chinese Saloon" with paper lanterns, gold and red satin drapes, Chinese furniture, and paintings. Newspapers reported widely on Afong Moy's arrival and upcoming appearances. Soon tickets were on sale to viewers eager to see the exotic traveler from the Far East.[62]

3. Afong Moy, the first recorded Chinese woman in the United States, 1834.

Wearing her "national costume," or richly embroidered robes that fit a "lady of her rank," Moy was on display for eight hours a day, from 10:00 a.m. to 2:00 p.m., and then again from 5:00 p.m. to 9:00 p.m. Viewers watched her use chopsticks and listened to her speak in Chinese. An interpreter helped viewers communicate with her, and Afong Moy was instructed to walk around the room to display her bound feet, which were the source of great fascination among men and women alike. The cost for viewing her was 50 cents. Afong Moy's exhibit sent a clear message: China and the Chinese were exotic, different, and as Moy's bound feet further illustrated, degraded and inferior. By relegating her to an exotic curiosity, the Carne brothers and all who came to gawk at her reaffirmed the West's superiority as well as the great differences between the United States and China. Moy eventually departed New York and embarked on an East Coast tour that took her to New Haven, Philadelphia, Washington, Baltimore, Richmond, Norfolk, Charleston, New Orleans, and Boston. During her visit to the nation's capital, she even met with members of Congress and paid a visit to President Andrew Jackson in the White House. By 1848, Afong Moy was sharing an exhibition space with Tom Thumb and working in a P. T. Barnum show. But two years later, she was cast aside when Barnum promoted a show featuring another "Chinese Belle" in New York. Afong Moy's fate remains unknown.[63]

By the early nineteenth century, small pockets of Asians had settled in the southern United States as well. Some may have arrived through Mexico as early as the late eighteenth century.[64] The earliest documented settlement dates back to the 1840s, when the Filipino fishing village of St. Malo, near the mouth of Lake Borgne in Louisiana, was founded. In 1883, Padre Carpio, one of the original inhabitants, told two journalists from the New Orleans–based *Times-Democrat* and *Harper's Weekly* that he had been a sailor, but had deserted his ship to settle in St. Malo for its good harbor and excellent fishing and shrimping. Living in houses on stilts on the banks of the lake, the 100 male residents of St. Malo endured long, hot summers and cold winters with only mosquitoes, fleas, sand flies, alligators, and poisonous snakes for company. They worked long, hard hours to send alligators, fish, and shrimp to New Orleans for export to Asia, Canada, and South and Central America. Isolated enough to be ignored by the U.S. Postal Service and tax collectors, St. Malo residents still regularly sent money and letters to the Philippines and maintained relationships with the larger Filipino community based in New Orleans. Another Filipino named Jacinto Quintin de la Cruz founded a larger fishing village called Manila Village in Barataria Bay, and a number of Filipinos settled in New Orleans between 1850 and 1870. Long before the Philippines had become a U.S. colony in 1898 and U.S. imperialism launched a larger wave of mass migration from the Philippines during the early twentieth century, these Filipinos, or "Manila men," had carved out a strong community for themselves.[65] They represented both the continuation of a long line of Asians who had come as part of European colonization of the Americas as well as the forerunners in a new era of mass migration that would follow during the next centuries.

2

Coolies

While small numbers of Asian immigrants were beginning to form communities in the United States in the early nineteenth century, a much larger migration of peoples was taking place between South Asia and China to Latin America. Between 1838 and 1917, more than 419,000 South Asians went to British West Indian plantations in British Guiana, Trinidad, and Jamaica as "coolies," or indentured laborers bound under contract.[1] An estimated 140,000 Chinese men also went to Cuba as coolies from 1847 to 1874, and 90,000 more went to Peru from 1849 to 1874. In all of these locations, they entered worlds of hard, bitter labor.[2]

By the end of the nineteenth century, Asian indentured laborers had gone to Cuba, Peru, British Guiana, Trinidad, Jamaica, Panama, Mexico, Brazil, and Costa Rica in addition to other places around the Americas. Conditions and experiences varied across location and from plantation to plantation, territory to territory, and over the decades. South Asian men and women who left their homelands as indentured laborers from 1838 to 1917, for example, migrated within a larger British imperial web that connected people, capital, and goods within and across the British Empire. Every aspect of the system was under British regulation, and both Britain's strong antislavery stance and imperial oversight affected the conditions and contracts under which they labored.[3]

On the other hand, the migration of Chinese, mostly men, to Cuba and Peru from 1847 to 1874 was part of an unregulated multinational business involving the transport of both indentured and nonindentured Chinese overseas while African slavery was still in effect in these two countries. The Chinese coolie trade was not as long-lived, and it was smaller than the British system. Nevertheless, it was characterized by a high level of abuse and exploitation. Many of the laborers were recruited through kidnapping, coercion, or deception. Disease led to shockingly high mortality rates on crowded and unsanitary ships, including some that had previously been used in the African slave trade. Chinese coolies in Cuba especially stand out for their status as "slaves all but in name" struggling to survive within a system that was grafted onto African slavery.[4]

The stereotype of Asian workers as coolies, cheap workers who drive down wages, take away jobs, and are servile pawns of factory owners and greedy capitalists, has a long history. Although the nineteenth-century migration of indentured Asian labor to the Americas was a Latin American phenomenon, the coolie label was effectively used to fuel violent anti-Asian movements in the United States that resulted in widespread discrimination. Consequently, both Asian immigrants in the United States and the historians who have studied them have been careful to distinguish the free Asian immigration to the United States from the unfree migration of Asian indentured laborers to Latin America that constituted what historian Hugh Tinker called a "new form of slavery."[5]

Nevertheless, just as the roots of Asian immigration to the United States extend back to Europe's search for Asia and the arrival of Asian sailors, slaves, and servants in New Spain, the mass movement of Asian laborers to the United States beginning in the nineteenth century overlaps with and connects to the arrival of Asian coolies in Latin America. Both movements were made possible by the growing European and American presence in Asia and the West's search for labor following the end of African slavery in the Americas. Western slave traders, labor recruiters, steamship companies, missionaries, and officials helped to build the infrastructure that made both unfree Asian migration to parts of Latin America and free Asian immigration to North and South America possible. And the idea of the Asian coolie—an unfree laborer who represented a new kind of slavery—would shape Americans' perceptions of Asian immigrants for years to come.

• • •

Enslaved Africans had been brought to the Americas as early as 1501, but it was the expansion of the sugar industry in the mid- to late 1500s that set in motion the tremendous growth in slavery in the region. At first a luxury product, sugar became a staple in European households after 1700. Demand skyrocketed and sugar plantations in the Americas and elsewhere multiplied and expanded. Masses of African slaves were used to grow, cultivate, and process this notoriously labor-intensive crop.

From the beginning of the 1500s, when the first African slaves were transported across the Atlantic Ocean, to 1888, when the last slaves were emancipated in Brazil, some 10 to 12 million African slaves made European expansion and settlement of the Americas possible. Slavery became integral to many economies and shaped everyday life in the Americas. But slavery always represented a profound contradiction: how could nations that professed to value liberty and equality rely upon slave labor? By the early nineteenth century, abolitionists around the world had successfully lobbied for the end of the transatlantic slave trade. In 1807, Great Britain abolished the trade throughout the British Empire. The United States followed the year after, and by 1817 the slave trade had been banned in Spanish America north of the equator as well.[6]

As a consequence, the cost of African slaves increased, and their dwindling numbers created a labor shortage in the West Indies, Cuba, Brazil, and Peru at a time of economic expansion. Sugar continued to drive many economies, especially in Cuba, which by 1870 produced over 40 percent of the world's sugarcane. Throughout the Caribbean, the southern United States, and Latin America, the demand for minerals, raw materials, coffee, cotton, rum, tobacco, and guano fertilizer also kept the demand for labor high.[7] In the West Indies, Cuba, and Peru, planters, labor recruiters, and politicians all looked to India and China to provide the labor needed to maintain the plantations that sustained both local and imperial economies.

It began in the British West Indies. There, the African slave population experienced a steep decline in the two decades after the end of the slave trade, from 800,000 in 1808 to 650,000 in 1830. Planters watched in dismay as estates closed and the entire economy suffered. In Jamaica, one planter described streets overgrown with weeds and abandoned houses that "look as though something much less than a hurricane would level them with the ground."[8] In 1802, planters began an experiment to bring Chinese contract laborers to their overseas colonies. One hundred ninety-two Chinese men landed in Trinidad that year. In 1810, several hundred Chinese tea growers were taken to Brazil by the Portuguese. About 2,947 Chinese were brought to Brazil from 1810 to 1874.[9]

The formal end of British slavery in 1834 placed the West Indies' sugar economies in a precarious situation. Freed Blacks left the plantations in droves to find other occupations, purchase small plots of land, and even organize to bargain for higher wages and better working conditions. Jamaica, Trinidad, and British Guiana experienced the greatest losses. Large numbers of freed men and women continued to work as wage laborers on sugar plantations, but planters complained that they insisted on working shorter hours and fewer days. Sugar production fell drastically, and a number of plantations shut down.

To solve their problems, planters turned to foreign immigration. The goal was, in the words of John Gladstone, one of the largest slaveholders in British Guiana, to make the planters "independent of our negro population . . . as far as possible."[10] European immigrants were preferred, and many governments, including that of British Guiana, subsidized the cost of European immigration to encourage the "whitening" of their populations. But the Europeans who came fell far shy of satisfying the demand for labor, so planters turned to Asia instead. The first group of 396 Asian indentured laborers arrived in May of 1838 and were subsequently known as the "Gladstone coolies." After reports of abuse of workers surfaced, the experiment ended the next year, but the system resumed in 1844, and from 1838 to 1917, 429,623 South Asians and 17,904 Chinese went to the British West Indies as indentured laborers.[11]

The search for labor in Asia resulted from Europe's growing presence and power in the region. Europe's quest to trade with Asia in the 1500s led to European colonization. Portugal had established its colonial empire of Portuguese India by 1503, but its dominance of the Asian spice trade was challenged by the Dutch East Indies Company, which set up its headquarters in Indonesia a century later. The English were the next challengers. In 1600,

Queen Elizabeth granted the East India Company full trading rights on all English trade east of the Cape of Good Hope. The East India Company set up a permanent trading post in Bengal in 1608. A fort at Madras followed in 1639. During the seventeenth and eighteenth centuries, the company built settlements and trading posts with the protection of a private army. By the mid-nineteenth century, the British—through the East India Company—had become the dominant European power in the Indian subcontinent. The India Act of 1784 and the 1813 Charter Act formally transferred governing power to the United Kingdom. The British expanded its rule by force and by annexation, sometimes with the cooperation of local rulers. They met heavy resistance, especially in the Punjab province of what is now present-day India and Pakistan. Annexation was finally completed in 1849. A small legion of colonial administrators fanned out throughout the region as part of the British Raj (present-day India, Pakistan, Bangladesh, and Myanmar) and British India became the "jewel in the Crown," representing Britain's immense imperial, military, and commercial power in the world.[12]

British imperial rule transformed South Asia. Economic policies contributed to a century of economic dislocation. The colonial government built railroads, roads, and irrigation canals to aid colonial projects, but it was the local population who funded them by paying new and increased taxes. The British also instituted major economic changes that were geared toward the development of products, crops, and raw materials for British consumption or for British markets and manufacturers. These changes mostly benefited Great Britain while exploiting local farming families and subjecting them to diminishing economic returns. The self-sufficiency of traditional village communities eroded while exploitation by landlords and moneylenders increased. Conditions worsened even more as the region's population exploded to 100 million over the nineteenth century.[13]

These social and economic pressures were felt most acutely in the northern provinces of Bengal, Bihar, Assam, and the United Provinces, and Madras in the south, and it is from these regions that the earliest migrants came. In later years, migrants came from the Punjab. Known as the region's breadbasket, the Punjab had once been one of the most fertile regions in South Asia. But by the mid-nineteenth century, it mostly supplied raw materials and cash crops to the British Empire, while local farmers suffered the effects of overcrowded and overused farmland, high rents, and famines.[14]

People left their homes in droves. Representing a broad cross section of the rural population, they sought out new fortunes close to their families and villages and then began to venture farther and farther away. By the mid-nineteenth century, British colonial officials and labor recruiters were sending South Asian men and women around the world as part of the British-controlled indentured labor system that was created to serve its colonies abroad and its markets and industries at home.

It all began with the *arkatia*, or local labor recruiter, who was deeply connected to the communities. Spending his days in the markets, bazaars, and railway stations, he learned who had lost their lands, was in debt, or had been cast out by their families. Then he made his pitch for work and easy money abroad. Through the efforts of these *arkatias*, over one million people migrated from throughout the region to British colonies and other locations around the world as indentured workers.[15]

South Asians went to Ceylon, Burma (present-day Myanmar), and the Malay peninsula in South and Southeast Asia; Mauritius, Réunion, and Madagascar in the Indian Ocean; Fiji in the Pacific Ocean; and South and East Africa. In the Americas, the largest number went to the British West Indies. The importance of their contribution to the global economy cannot be overstated. As historian Hugh Tinker has explained, it was their labor that "created the overseas wealth of Britain."[16]

In 1838, the first indentured laborers from South Asia arrived in British Guiana. More than half a million South Asians were brought to the Caribbean over the next seventy-nine years. Most went to British Guiana (238,900) or to Trinidad (143,939), but some 42,326 went to Guadeloupe, 36,420 went to Jamaica, 34,304 went to Dutch Guiana, and 25,509 went to Martinique.[17]

They had diverse social, religious, linguistic, regional, and caste backgrounds. The first recruits came from both Madras and Calcutta, but over the years they hailed from all parts of British-controlled India as the system stabilized and expanded under the management of British colonial officials and labor recruiters. Some were Muslim; others were Hindu. They were largely men. Planters wanted male farmhands, and recruiters found very few women who were willing to indenture themselves or families who wished to go abroad together. As long as the journey was considered temporary, most married men decided to venture abroad alone.[18]

Some of the male recruits had been domestic servants, entertainers, artisans, and shopkeepers. Even a few priests made the voyage. But the majority were agricultural laborers swept up in the labor recruiter's net. Their reasons for leaving home varied. Some had already traveled far in a vain search for employment. Some had been involved in the failed 1857 mutiny against the British and were fleeing arrest. Others were ex-soldiers or farmers in search of livelihoods. Most had been lured by promises made by labor recruiters who fanned throughout the countryside in search of willing (and sometimes unwilling) bodies to fill their quotas. One British Guiana planter observed in 1909 that the recruiters "tell the coolies lots of nonsense, I am sure, because a coolie has often told me that he was told . . . [that] all he had to do was to lie on his back and the cocoanuts would drop into his mouth, and the gold, and everything else."[19]

As the South Asian indentured labor system became established and planters sought to stabilize the overwhelmingly male labor force, new efforts to recruit women began. In 1855, a new ordinance required a ratio of 33 women to every 100 men on board the ships sailing abroad. From 1868 onward, women made up a little over 40 percent of those heading overseas as indentured laborers.[20]

But not all women were acceptable. Planters and colonial officials only wanted "virtuous" women (i.e., docile and "moral" women who were widowed or who came with their husbands or parents) who could tame the mostly male population. Single women were purported to be "shamelessly immoral" and likely to encourage prostitution, competition for sexual partners, worker unrest, and loss of worker productivity.[21] The women who were able to pass the morality test set by colonial officials came with diverse working backgrounds. On the SS *Zanzibar*, which arrived in Dutch Guiana in 1878, for example, there were fifty-six maids, thirty-six unemployed women, and fifteen midwives. Others listed their occupations as milkmaids, water carriers, vegetable women, peasants, fieldhands, and weavers.[22]

Not all South Asian indentured laborers came willingly. Cases of kidnapping and coercion were not uncommon. An 1873 British government study found that "very grave abuses" accompanied the recruitment of both male and female indentured laborers. In many cases, emigrants had been "entrapped by force and fraud." Many had been "systematically plundered" of their signing bonuses and advance wages as well.[23] Rev. Thomas Evans, a missionary in Allahabad in northern India, complained to British officials in 1871 that an "Indian slave trade" was at work.[24]

South Asian indentured laborers began their journeys in Calcutta, where they were inspected, registered, and housed in special British government-regulated emigration depots. Some were even "seasoned" for their new lives on the plantations by being kept outdoors for long periods of time doing light work.[25] From there, they boarded crowded sailing ships that carried as many as 510 people. The trips to the Caribbean lasted anywhere from three to four months and were plagued by the killing diseases of cholera, typhoid, and dysentery, as well as severe seasickness. While conditions and mortality rates varied, and did improve over the years, many observers recorded grim anecdotes. Mrs. Swinton, a captain's wife who accompanied her husband on the coolie ship *Salsette* as it sailed from Calcutta to Trinidad in 1858, likened the journey to the African slave trade and called it "the other middle passage." Swinton recorded almost nothing but deaths—which occurred on a daily basis among the old and young, male and female—in her journal:

> May 3: A woman died of dysentery. This makes seventy dead. It is dreadful mortality.
>
> June 3: One child died of dropsy . . . Woman died.
>
> June 7: Infant died, and many sick found who are afraid to take our medicine. Doctor gave me his list . . . and makes 110 [dead] all told . . . Fearful!
>
> June 30: Mustered the coolies, and find only 108 men, 61 women, 30 children, two infants, and two interpreters left of the 323 or 324 we sailed with from Calcutta.

Over one third of the 324 coolies on the *Salsette* died on the voyage from disease and poor diet. The death toll on this ship may have been extreme, but between 1857 and 1862 the mortality rate on ships heading to British

Guiana was 10.9 percent. By the 1870s, it had decreased to between 2 and 3 percent.[26]

Transported halfway across the world to a foreign and hostile land, under contract to perform backbreaking work, and thrust among strangers who spoke different languages, ate strange food, worshipped different gods, and practiced different social customs, South Asian indentured laborers struggled every day to survive. Their contracts generally bound them to five years of indenture working nine to ten hours a day, six days a week. They were supposed to receive a daily wage of 16 to 24 cents, return passage, free housing, medical attention, and some food rations. Reality did not often match the terms of the contracts. In some colonies, like Trinidad and British Guiana, for example, return passage was granted only after workers had worked an additional five years in the colony after their contracts had expired.[27] And the entire system was inhumane. Some of the first workers to arrive in British Guiana were treated with severe brutality just like the African slaves they had recently replaced. The first reports out of British Guiana described conditions of "unalleviated wretchedness" and "hopeless misery." The workers had a mortality rate of almost 25 percent.[28]

4. Coolies. Demerara, British Guiana, c. 1890.

Over the decades, South Asian indentured laborers became central to the production of sugar in the West Indies. By 1891, they were over 80 percent of the workforce on British Guianan sugar plantations, and the terms "sugar worker" and "Indian" became almost synonymous in British Guiana and Trinidad.[29]

Work on the sugar plantations was divided according to sex, age, ability, and experience. Gangs of men, for example, took on the heaviest and hardest work of forking and cutting sugarcane. They sometimes worked alongside freed blacks who also performed the heaviest manual labor. Monotony and brutal labor were the norm. "Sahib, we are not donkeys to work so hard, give us time," Jhangir Khan protested to his overseer on the Rose Hall estate in British Guiana.[30]

Women were supposed to be in the fields as many hours as the men, and they kept up their work even when they were in the advanced stages of pregnancy. They earned less than their male counterparts and were prohibited from working in the higher-paying and higher-status positions on the plantations. And when their work in the fields ended, their work at home began: cooking, cleaning, and taking care of the men and children in their own homes. Their double duty often meant waking before dawn and toiling until the late hours of night.[31]

Female indentured workers were additionally vulnerable to sexual exploitation. Overseers commonly kept "Hindu and Muslim females as paramours or concubines," according to a government commission. In the 1840s, a medical doctor even reported to the governor of Trinidad the scandalous case of seven indentured women on one plantation simultaneously pregnant with the estate manager's children. On another estate, South Asian women were regularly brought in by the South Asian overseer to serve as prostitutes for the male workers.[32]

Like black slaves, South Asian indentured workers were severely punished and convicted under the law for neglect or refusal to work, absenteeism, desertion, vagrancy, and insufficient or incomplete work. Some estate drivers prided themselves that the laborers were "always either at work, or in hospital, or in gaol" (prison).[33] Labor ordinances imposed penalties for damaging, breaking, or losing estate tools and equipment. Laborers were also bound to certain plantations and could not switch employers at will.

Punishment involved physical violence, imprisonment, and withholding of the pass that allowed indentured laborers to travel outside the plantation boundary.[34]

If this system of criminal penalties and social and disciplinary control was a legacy of African slavery, so, too, were the racist attitudes that planters used to justify mistreatment and unequal status. Indentured laborers were, in the eyes of the planters who brought them, "more akin to the monkey than the man."[35] Indentured laborers inherited old slave quarters that were often sparse, lacked latrines, and suffered from leaky roofs, bad ventilation, and poor drainage. Colonial authorities and plantation managers justified the poor conditions by claiming the quarters were "much more sanitary than that of the houses in an ordinary Indian village."[36]

South Asian workers who had been recruited for their supposed subservience turned out to be quite militant. Strikes, mass marches, violent demonstrations, mass desertions, and organized work stoppages—even though they were illegal—were common throughout the years of the indentured labor system in the West Indies. Usually, these protests were sporadic, small-scale, and quickly repressed. But occasionally, worker-led riots and work stoppages took place on a larger scale and spread across plantations. For example, one hundred strikes occurred between 1886 and 1889 alone, and another 141 erupted between 1900 and 1913.[37]

Even though the indentured labor system had been designed to bring South Asian laborers to the West Indies on a temporary basis and then return them to their homeland to be replaced with a fresh crop of laborers, the majority chose to remain. Some had failed to acquire the wealth and riches they had hoped for and did not wish to return home in disgrace. Others had married partners of different castes and believed that these unions would not be accepted in their home villages. Still more tried to find economic opportunities in the islands after their contracts ended. They reindentured themselves, sometimes for two, three, or four one-year terms. Others hired themselves out as wage laborers or became landowners themselves.[38]

By 1920, South Asians represented 33 and 42 percent of the populations in Trinidad and British Guiana, respectively. Replacing Africans as the largest part of the population in the islands, they transformed the fabric of everyday life in the Caribbean, becoming part of the callaloo (mixed) societies there.[39] A small middle class also formed, and community activism around the general welfare and rights of South Asians became more noticeable.

Some of this activism centered around abolishing the entire indenture system. Critics had consistently railed against it from its earliest days. But between 1900 and the beginning of World War I, opposition to the indentured labor system grew in South Asia, Britain, and elsewhere as the suffering of indentured laborers and the discrimination that South Asians faced worldwide was tied to the plight of India under British colonialism. Nationalists like Mahatma Gandhi attacked the system with new fervor. In 1912, G. K. Gokhale, leader of the Indian National Congress, declared indenture "degrading to the people of India . . . [and] a grave blot on the civilization of any country that tolerates it."[40]

The British government defended the system, but the colonial government of India, headed by Viceroy Charles Hardinge, came to a different conclusion. Describing the system as "differing but little from a form of slavery," he argued that "it is not the duty of the Government of India to provide coolies for the colonies." Connecting the indenture system to growing nationalist sentiment in India, Hardinge strongly urged the total abolition of the system in order to "remove a racial stigma that India deeply resents."[41] In 1917, the Indian government suspended emigration altogether. By 1920, the entire indenture system was abolished and outstanding indentures were terminated.[42]

Just as British imperialism influenced modern migration from South Asia, the growing presence of European powers in China similarly resulted in Chinese migration abroad. Ruled by the Qing Empire since 1644, China was already suffering from weak political leadership and corruption, a population explosion, regional factionalism, and economic instability before Britain, France, Germany, and Portugal sought to carve the nation up in the nineteenth century. When unequal economic relationships between China and European powers caused even greater instability in the mid-nineteenth century, Chinese began to move around the world in ever greater numbers.

The European interest in China in the late eighteenth century began with tea. An expensive luxury afforded by only the European elite in the 1600s, tea became by the 1800s Britain's favorite drink and a national pastime. The tea and the Chinese porcelain that British and European consumers desired most could only be bought in China. But European traders were strictly controlled by the Chinese government, which allowed business to be conducted only through specific treaty ports. Additionally, Chinese officials insisted that there was nothing that it desired from Europe. In a letter to Britain's King George III in 1793, Chinese emperor Qianlong famously declared that "our Celestial Empire possesses all things in prolific abundance and lacks no product within its own borders."[43] As European consumers clamored for more tea and porcelain, European traders became concerned about the growing trade imbalance with China.

British traders found a solution in opium, which they began to illegally import from British India to make a profit on their tea export businesses. As the Chinese demand for the drug increased, so did British power in the region. Chinese attempts to end the opium trade led to war. Britain's victories in the Opium Wars (1839–1842 and 1856–1860) forced the opening of several southern Chinese ports to international trade: Canton, Fuzhou, Amoy (Xiamen), Ningbo, and Shanghai.

As a result of this dramatic economic restructuring, a dynamic market economy sprang up around Canton, and the Pearl River Delta became one of China's busiest centers for domestic and international trade. Hong Kong, which became a British colony after the first Opium War, grew into a center of the expanding Pacific economy, and, under British control, both Chinese trade and labor markets were opened to the rest of the world. As foreign labor recruiters and agents descended upon South China, transpacific trade networks expanded to include a growing market in both indentured and nonindentured laborers.[44]

In the southern Chinese provinces of Guangdong and Fujian, economic, political, and social conditions set the stage for mass migration. By 1850, the country's population had grown exponentially to 450 million from 150 million in 1700.[45] And a seemingly endless stream of natural disasters struck southern China beginning in the early nineteenth century. Droughts, storms, typhoons, earthquakes, plagues, floods, and famines all took their toll on the Chinese people. High taxes and dissatisfaction with the Qing led to a number of rebellions and civil unrest in the form of the Taiping

Rebellion (1850–1864), the Red Turban uprisings (1854–1864), and feuds between the Punti and Hakka ethnic groups. At the same time, unequal treaties between China and Western imperial powers resulted in higher taxes on local peasants.

Chinese who could no longer make a living as farmers or laborers increasingly began to leave their home villages and head to larger cities in Guangdong province. This migration from the rural areas to the cities became the first stepping-stone to migration abroad, and 96 percent of Chinese came to the Americas from Guangdong. From 1801 to 1900, an estimated two and a half million Chinese migrated to Southeast Asia as well as to the United States, the Pacific islands of Hawai'i, Tahiti, and Western Samoa, and to Canada, Australia, New Zealand, the West Indies, South America, and Africa. The most widely dispersed group of Asian migrants, Chinese worked and lived abroad on almost every continent on earth by the 1940s.[46]

Chinese migration was more varied than migration from South Asia. In general, there were three ways to go abroad. The first was to pay one's own way across the Pacific, a choice reserved for only the most prosperous. The second was to borrow the necessary funds from family members or from a moneylender with the promise to pay back the loan with interest after arrival. This was known as the credit-ticket system and was the primary way that Chinese made it to the United States, Canada, Southeast Asia, and Australia. The Chinese who were able to pay their own way or use the credit-ticket system were not the poorest of the poor; as a rule, they had resources and saw migration as a way to remain upwardly mobile. The third way, which 11 or 12 percent of emigrants leaving Hong Kong chose, was to migrate as indentured laborers. These individuals were more likely to be "very poor and needy . . . and destitute," according to one British investigator. Some ultimately ended up as coolies in Latin America.[47]

Eighteen forty-seven was the first year that Chinese were sent to Cuba as part of the coolie trade. By 1874, 142,000 Chinese had been brought to Cuba. From 1849 to 1874, another 90,000 Chinese went to Peru.[48] *La trata amarilla* (the yellow trade) of Chinese indentured laborers to Cuba was horrific in its barbarous recruitment and transportation practices as well as its exploitation of laborers on the plantations. Unlike in South Asia, where the indenture system was regulated (if somewhat negligently) by British colonial officials, the Chinese coolie trade was largely unregulated. That Chinese coolies were introduced into Cuba while African slavery was still in full swing (it would not be abolished until 1886) meant the latter also greatly influenced the experiences of the former.[49]

Cuban planters initially relied upon the Real Junta de Fomento y Colonización, a company led by the Zuluetas, the most powerful slave-trading family in Cuba, to secure Chinese labor. The Chinese coolie trade became a profitable multinational business involving shipping companies, labor recruiters, government agencies, and banks based in Great Britain, Spain, Portugal, the U.S., the Netherlands, and France—the same countries that had been the top traffickers in African slaves.[50] Because of the demand for labor, profits from *la trata amarilla* were huge. A *New York Herald* correspondent noted in 1872 that one ship had brought 900 laborers into Cuba at a cost of $50,000 and netted over $400,000. "Never in the palmiest days of the African trade were such tremendous profits realized," he observed.[51]

These profits motivated foreign and Chinese labor recruiters to use deception and force to fill coolie ships. Chinese commissioners investigating the abuses of the coolie system in Cuba concluded that 80 or 90 percent of all Chinese laborers had been brought there against their will.[52] Indentured laborer Ren Shinzen wrote a lengthy petition for the commissioners that described how Cuban recruiters were "crafty in their hearts and greedy and cruel in their nature. . . . Their ships go into China and collude with wicked civilians [who] pointed falsely at a gold mountain and promised to show the way."[53] Cheng A-mou and other workers explained that they had been "induced" to go to Macao "by offers of employment abroad at high wages." They were even told that "the eight foreign years specified in the contracts were equivalent to only four Chinese [years]" and that then they would be free.[54]

Recruiters were also deliberately vague about the types of work and the exact locations that Chinese were headed to. The 400 Chinese on board the *Robert Browne* heading out of Amoy on March 21, 1852, for example, believed they were heading to San Francisco and the promise of the gold fields. Instead, they were destined for Peru, where they were to work as coolies on the guano islands. When this news was revealed on board the ship, they organized a mutiny. The captain, two officers, and four crewmembers were killed. The Chinese mutineers were eventually captured and brought to trial.[55]

Portuguese-controlled Macao was the main center of the Chinese coolie trade in Asia. New recruits were sent there and were restrained in "pigpens" while awaiting sale to European and U.S. ship captains in a process that the Chinese called "the buying and selling of pigs." One such pigpen was a wooden shed "like a slave baracoon," 120 feet by 24 feet, holding 500 nearly naked and suffocating men. White letters were stamped or painted on their chests to indicate their intended destination. A "C" meant California, a "P" meant Peru, an "S" referred to the Sandwich (or Hawaiian) Islands.[56] The kidnapped, deceived, and voluntary migrants were all mixed up together, and it was sometimes impossible to distinguish among them. Over the next four to eight months, they slowly made their way across the Pacific to the Americas on American, British, Spanish, Dutch, Italian, and French ships that were often nothing more than overcrowded prisons.[57]

Ships heading to Cuba took a westward route from China sailing through the Indian Ocean, around Africa's Cape of Good Hope, and then across the Atlantic. Ships heading to Peru sailed across the Pacific on journeys lasting 80 to 140 days.[58] To control the passengers—especially those who were victims of kidnapping or deceit—ships were commonly outfitted with "iron gratings over hatchways, walls between crew and coolie quarters, armed guards, [and] cannons trained on hatchways."[59] There was insufficient food and water, and coolies were often crowded together and chained in the suffocating hold. They were frequently beaten and killed. One hundred seventy-three men were chained with foot irons and 160 men were stripped and flogged with rattan rods during the journey that brought Huan A-fang to Cuba. Three hundred died of thirst on Chen A-sheng's ship. Twenty men cast themselves overboard to escape the misery on Liu A-san's ship.[60] During a twenty-six-year period, approximately 16,400 Chinese, or one third of all Chinese coolies destined for the Americas, reportedly died from physical violence, suicide, and thirst on European and American ships to Cuba. The Chinese began calling them "devil ships" and others referred to them as "floating coffins." The mortality rate on the coolie ships rivaled those on African slave ships, when an average of 20 percent of all Africans died during the Middle Passage from 1590 to 1699.[61]

5. Chinese immigrants were often beaten and chained on board the coolie ships that brought them from China to Cuba. "Preserving the Peace," *Harper's New Monthly Magazine* 29 (June 1864).

Facing such horrific conditions, mutiny was not uncommon. In 1871, the crew on the *Dolores Ugarte* responded to a threat of mutiny by its several hundred Chinese coolies by firing shots through the iron grates down into the hold. A fire began below deck and the flames spread. The captain and his crew abandoned the ship by lifeboat, but left the Chinese passengers remained locked in the hold, where they either suffocated or burned to death. Some survivors managed to struggle on deck. As the ship burned, they jumped into the sea, where some were saved by fishermen. Of the 650 Chinese coolies who boarded the ship in Macao, only 50 survived the journey.[62] An estimated 3,000 to 4,000 Chinese died during mutinies on their way to Cuba, Peru, and the British West Indies during the coolie era.[63]

Upon arrival in Havana, Chinese coolies were taken from the ship and readied for sale. "Once we got to the Havana Selling People House, our plaits were cut off, our clothes were changed, and people were allowed to choose and buy," coolie Xian Zuobang later recalled. "No matter what status one had in China, one will become a slave."[64]

By 1860, the Chinese had become the main solution to the labor problems in both Cuba and Peru. Planters and labor agents wanted laborers, not settlers, and therefore recruited men almost exclusively. Chinese cultural constraints also frowned upon women traveling or immigrating abroad. This gender imbalance was apparent in government population statistics. Women were less than one percent of Chinese arriving in Cuba from 1847 to 1874. The 1861 Cuban census recorded only fifty-seven Chinese females out of a population of 34,807. In Peru, women were less than one percent of the country's total Chinese population from 1847 to 1874.[65]

Because the bondage system ensnared a vast array of peoples in its nets, the Chinese coolies who arrived in Cuba and Peru were occupationally very diverse. The largest group (around 20 percent) of Chinese coolies worked in agriculture, but an amazing array of craftsmen, traders, business owners, and even doctors and government employees were brought on the coolie ships bound for Cuba. They were mostly young, and mostly from Guangdong province. But there were also children and some who came from central, northern, and eastern provinces like Tianjin, Henan, and Anhui.[66]

Ninety percent of Cuba's Chinese coolies worked in the sugar plantations on the western half of the island. On some plantations, they made up as much as 50 percent of the labor force. A small percentage worked as carpenters, cigar makers, or machinists in the cities or in mines or the railroads. In Peru, Chinese picked cotton and sugarcane on coastal plantations and toiled in the noxious guano pits on the Chincha Islands, but they also built railroads in the mountains and worked as domestic servants in the cities.[67]

Coolies in Cuba and Peru were legally free men who signed labor contracts. Unlike slaves, who were considered property, coolies were legally bound to eight years' servitude (three years longer than South Asians in the British West Indies) and could become free upon the completion of their contracts. They could enter into marriages, assume parental control over their children, and could not be separated from spouses. They could also buy and sell property and bring charges against their *patrones*, the owners of their contracts. They were supposed to receive a monthly wage, adequate food and health care, lodging, and one day of rest on Sundays, plus holidays. These elements made coolie labor unique from both slavery and the free labor system. Freedom was theoretically an option, and coolies had certain rights during their terms of indenture that were denied to slaves.[68]

In reality, however, the daily experiences of Chinese coolies in Cuba did not follow the terms of their contracts or reflect their status as free laborers. Whatever freedoms they had were temporary and arbitrary. Coolie life on the plantations revolved around backbreaking work, routine beatings and intimidations, little or poor-quality food, and exploitation by cruel overseers. They worked daily for twenty to twenty-two hours, from 2:00 and 4:00 a.m. until midnight. "I had to labour night and day, suffered much from cold and hunger, was flogged when seriously ill, and was chained and imprisoned even for resting a few moments," Yang Wan-sheng testified. The mortality rate among Chinese coolies was shockingly high.[69]

The status of Chinese coolies and African slaves—Cuba would not abolish slavery until 1886—often overlapped. They worked alongside each other and often lived in close proximity. They lacked the same basic freedoms and were subjected to the same systems of control. Coolies were required, for example, to "renounce the exercise of all civil rights which are not compatible with the compliance of contract obligations." Thus, marriage and any buying and selling of property had to be approved of by the *patrón*, and coolies had little freedom of movement. They could not leave the plantation without written permission, and if they were caught without it, they could be arrested as runaways, beaten, and even killed.[70] As one Chinese laborer told visiting Chinese commissioners in 1874, "The police are bent solely on profit and oppress the Chinese . . . you could die easily like an ant."[71]

Even their punishments were the same. The 1849 regulations issued by the Spanish government to guide the coolie system lifted—almost verbatim—language from existing Cuban slave codes. Chinese indentured laborers who did not follow orders or who ran away could be flogged, shackled, and confined. The consequences were horrific. "There are shackles on my feet and chains around my neck," one coolie testified in 1874.[72] Due to mistreatment and malnourishment, over 50 percent of Chinese coolies in Cuba perished before their contracts ended.[73]

Moreover, the terms of the contracts, which were subject to interpretation by masters, were routinely ignored or manipulated to further exploit the laborer. For example, regulations allowed Chinese coolies to purchase their contracts at any time, but they had to pay their masters back for their purchase price, any value added to their contract since the time of purchase, including clothing and sick days, and the cost of finding a replacement laborer. Owners set the terms and price of these costs.[74]

In short, Chinese coolies were slaves in all but name. At best, they inhabited a unique status as unfree laborers, somewhere between slave and free, that allowed them to demand better treatment and eventual freedom. In practice they were, according to historian Philip S. Foner, "bought, sold, and transferred like slaves, and treated like slaves."[75]

Like South Asian laborers in the British West Indies, the Chinese in Cuba and Peru found ways to challenge exploitative work conditions. They routinely slowed the pace of their work, refused to work, committed acts of sabotage, and stole from their plantations. Chinese coolies also took their rights to sue employers very seriously. They filed protests and complaints against *patrones* who mistreated them and local authorities who failed to enforce the laws. Chinese often tried to escape their indentures by running away, and in extreme cases Chinese attacked their overseers and *patrones*.[76]

Suicides were also common. Ch'en Ming-yuan told commissioners that "no count can be made of the number of those who have thrown themselves into wells, cut their throats, hanged themselves, and swallowed opium."[77] Wen Changtai gave specific details: "I witnessed nine workers who hanged themselves, one who jumped into a hot sugar cauldron . . . and some who ran into the mountains and starved to death."[78]

Others joined the fight to overturn the entire Spanish political system in Cuba and joined insurgents to overthrow Spanish colonialism. They fought in *la Guerra de los Diez Años* (the Ten Years' War of 1868–1878), *la Guerra Chiquita* (the Little War of 1878–1879), and *la Guerra de Independencia* (the War of Independence, 1895–1898). Many histories of Cuban independence tell the inspiring tale of Chinese indentured laborer Bu Tak (José Bu), who joined insurgents in 1860 and eventually rose up the ranks to become a celebrated Cuban freedom fighter. In 1869, Bu guided Cuban forces through treacherous terrain in order to deliver orders to a Cuban general. He was known for charging into battle ferociously waving a machete and shouting in Spanish, "For Cuba! Spanish go to hell!" Bu fought in all three wars for Cuban independence from Spain over a thirty-year period and eventually became a lieutenant colonel.[79]

By the 1860s, the Chinese coolie system prompted a global debate over race and labor that would shape Chinese immigration to the United States. On the one hand, Chinese indentured laborers were seen as a necessary cure for the labor shortages that plagued industrializing settler societies after the end of slavery. Chinese laborers were cheap, easily available and exploitable, and their labor made it possible for plantation economies to prosper. However, at a time when most countries were debating abolishing slavery or had already abolished it, the advantages of Chinese coolie labor came under fresh scrutiny.[80]

This was especially true in the United States, where the impending Civil War over slavery shaped every news report and traveler's account of the coolie labor system in the Caribbean. Both abolitionists and pro-slavery activists in the United States closely studied the "coolie problem" in Latin America and the Caribbean and used the specter of Asian coolies to further their political agendas. Coolies were either portrayed as an industrious labor force that would make slavery unnecessary or as another inferior race that was vulnerable to cruel exploitation. After African slaves were emancipated in 1863, southern planters championed coolie labor in order to revitalize the southern economy and to counter the effects of black enfranchisement. Political battles between federal officials and Louisiana planters and merchants over the status of coolies erupted in the late 1860s. In the end, the United States outlawed coolie labor and U.S. involvement in the coolie trade in 1862. The Coolie Trade Act of that year became the first step in the eventual exclusion of all Chinese laborers that occurred in 1882.[81]

By the 1870s, condemnation of the coolie trade had spread internationally. On December 27, 1873, the Portuguese governor of Macao closed the colony to the coolie trade. The last coolie ships set sail to Latin America three months later.[82] In 1874, an international commission traveled to Cuba to investigate coolie conditions. Representatives from China, Britain, and France heard 1,176 oral testimonies and read 1,665 written petitions. One after another, Chinese coolies described their experiences, begged for help, and called attention to the abuses and exploitation of the coolie system, or what one called "a hell on earth."[83] As a result of the commission's findings, the Chinese emperor issued a decree calling for the immediate end of the coolie trade in 1875. In 1877, Spain and China signed a treaty terminating all contracts of Chinese laborers still under indenture in Cuba and established a Chinese consulate general in Cuba to protect the interests of Chinese still there. Peru and China reached a similar treaty in 1876.[84]

Freedom, however, remained elusive for Chinese coolies in Cuba. Even after the coolie trade was abolished, slavery remained in place until 1886 and affected the mobility of all slave, indentured, and free laborers. Laws, such as one that required coolies to reindenture themselves or leave Cuba within two months at their own expense, also forced some to continue their terms of indenture. And many *patrones* refused to give the papers documenting a coolie's freedom at the end of his contract period.[85]

Those who were able to secure their freedom found limited opportunities available to them. Some organized themselves into *cuadrillas*, or contract work gangs under Chinese management, and were slowly able to transition into agricultural wage work. A small number of Chinese became engaged in retail and truck farming. A larger number concentrated in the laundry business or as domestic servants, like their compatriots in the United States and Canada.[86]

By the 1860s and 1870s, a large community of free Chinese had settled in Havana. Two former coolies, Chung Leng and Lan Si Ye, are credited with establishing Havana's Chinatown near Zanja Street by opening up a café and grocery store in 1858. Other businesses followed. By the early 1870s, a recognizable *barrio chino* had been formed around the market plaza.[87]

Other former Chinese coolies remigrated within the Americas to countries like Panama, Mexico, and the United States. The first Chinese cigar makers in New York City, for example, were transplants from Cuba. The largest number went to Louisiana, where planters and labor recruiters hoped that the Chinese could help replace emancipated African Americans, and by 1867 at least 2,000 Chinese had left Cuba for New Orleans.[88]

By then, thousands of other Chinese immigrants were crossing the Pacific

Ocean and working throughout the Western United States in search of what they called "Gold Mountain." Building on the first transpacific Asian migrations to the Americas during the Manila galleon era and overlapping with the migrations of coolies to Latin America, they helped to create early Asian America.

PART TWO

The Making of Asian America During the Age of Mass Migration and Asian Exclusion

3

Chinese Immigrants in Search of Gold Mountain

On January 24, 1848, James W. Marshall discovered gold along the American River in northern California. Gold seekers from around the world swept into California, and the Gold Rush was on. The news took some time to reach China, but once it did, it spread like fire. "Good many Americans speak of California," wrote one man in Canton to his brother. "They find gold very quickly. . . . I think I shall go to California next summer."[1]

Three hundred twenty-five Chinese forty-niners made their way to California in 1849. In 1850, 450 more came. Within a year, the numbers grew exponentially: 2,716 Chinese came to California in 1851 and 20,026 in 1852. Only a few struck it rich in the goldfields, but there were enough economic opportunities in the United States as well as problems back home in China to set in motion a new era of Chinese immigration. Labor recruiters in China bombarded prospective immigrants with the message that, as one advertisement proclaimed, "Americans are very rich people. They want the Chinaman to come. . . . Money is in great plenty and to spare in America." By 1870, there were 63,000 Chinese in the United States, most of them (77 percent) in California.[2]

Among the thousands of gold seekers who flocked to California was Moy Dong Kee, my maternal great-great-great-grandfather. He arrived in San

Francisco in 1854 as a twenty-year-old married father from Sun Jock Me Lun village in the Pearl River Delta of southern China. He left his wife and two sons behind while chasing dreams of *Gum Saan*, or Gold Mountain, as the Chinese called the United States. By the time he made it to California, there was little gold left in the foothills. He stayed anyway. We don't know much about what he did in these early years. When he shows up in official U.S. records, some forty-five years later, it is in an affidavit filed with the U.S. Bureau of Immigration stating his intention to travel to China and return to the United States.[3]

This type of paperwork was required only of Chinese immigrants. Beginning in 1882, the United States passed a series of Chinese exclusion laws that barred Chinese laborers from entering the country and allowed only certain "exempt" classes of merchants, students, teachers, diplomats, and travelers to enter or reenter the country. After protests by the Chinese American community, U.S. citizens of Chinese descent and the wives and children of citizens and merchants were also allowed to apply for admission or readmission. But all Chinese in the United States were under strict surveillance, and my great-great-great-grandfather found that he needed to fill out a number of government forms, subject himself to interrogations and investigations, and provide affidavits from two white witnesses who vouched for him and his status as a merchant whenever he left or reentered the country.

6. Moy Dong Kee's business card, 1899.

His 1899 application was filed in New York City, where he had been a resident and merchant for twenty years. He had followed the growing number of Chinese who left the West Coast in search of better opportunities and friendlier neighborhoods. He opened the Yuet Sing & Company store at No. 10 Chatham

Square in New York's Chinatown in 1882 and then moved it to No. 6 Mott Street a few years later. By the 1890s, he had another store in Philadelphia's Chinatown, and had opened the Kwong Wah Tai & Co. at No. 14 Mott Street. His bilingual business card identified the company as "importers and dealers in Chinese Groceries, also General Merchandise."

But like many Chinese immigrants during this time, Moy Dong Kee's life stretched across the Pacific. His family remained in Sun Jock Me Lun village, and he traveled back and forth to China at least three times over his forty-five-year sojourn in the United States before he retired in the village where he was born. He passed on his business to his oldest son, Moy Quong Shee, who continued the transpacific shuttle between China and the United States, leaving his wife and children in China while running the family business in New York and Philadelphia and adopting the name of John Moy.

By 1907, my great-grandfather Moy Wah Chung entered the United States. With him, the transnational family pattern that the Moy family had practiced for three generations eventually broke. In 1911, he married Yuen Si, and a daughter named Sau Bik, my grandmother, was born in 1912. A son named Chong Mon followed in 1918. The next year, my great-grandfather decided to settle in the United States permanently and became Raymond Moy. As a Chinese merchant, he was eligible to bring his wife and his children to the United States. But when he filed the necessary forms with the U.S. government to sponsor them into the country, Raymond listed his wife and two sons. One was Chong Mon. The other was his nephew, Chong Don. Sau Bik was never mentioned, and according to the records of the U.S. Bureau of Immigration, she did not exist. Chong Don, given her immigration slot, came to the United States in her place. My grandmother remained in Canton with her grandparents and attended school.[4]

There are many reasons why my great-grandfather might have made the decision to leave his daughter behind in China. Perhaps he believed that boys were more likely to find steady work and contribute to the family economy. Maybe there was no other way for Chong Don to immigrate, and giving him the immigration slot was great-grandfather's way of performing some act of filial duty. Perhaps he thought it was safer for my grandmother to remain in China. Whatever the reason, his actions effectively excluded my grandmother from the United States. She would never see her mother alive again, and she would not immigrate herself until 1933, when she married my grandfather Huie Bing Gee (Ben Huie), a merchant and restaurant owner in New York City.

7. Huie Bing Gee (Ben Huie) and Moy Sau Bik (Gladys Huie) wedding portrait, 1931.

My grandmother deeply resented being left behind in China, but once in New York, she and my grandfather started new lives and had three daughters. My grandfather ran two successful restaurants in Brooklyn. One was named the New Deal Chow Mein Inn after President Franklin D. Roosevelt's federal program, and it catered to a mostly Jewish clientele in the

Brighton Beach neighborhood nicknamed Little Odessa. The restaurant was a family affair. My grandfather ran the business side of things and many of the cooks came from my grandfather's home village in China. My grandmother wore elegant cheongsams, Chinese-style dresses, and served as the restaurant's hostess. My mother and her sisters made eggrolls after school, earning a penny a piece. Dishes at the New Deal included Lobster Cantonese, Chicken Chop Suey, and New Deal Lo-Mein. The New Deal wontons became locally famous and were remembered years later in a cookbook featuring New York City's great culinary traditions.[5] By the 1930s, my mother and aunts attended public school in Brooklyn, went off to college, and grew up identifying as "Americans first, Chinese second."[6]

After four generations of immigrating back and forth between China and the United States, my family was finally becoming Chinese American.

The Moy family offers a window into the worlds of Chinese immigrants during the late nineteenth and early twentieth centuries. Families were split across the Pacific Ocean but remained connected to each other through visits home—infrequent as they were—letters, and remittances. Moy Dong Kee spent almost fifty years in the United States, but when it was time to retire, he returned to the village where he was born having fulfilled the dream of returning home a rich, successful "Gold Mountain Man."

The Moys "became American" in ways that were common for many immigrants. Moy Dong Kee did not become a U.S. citizen, because naturalization laws barred Chinese and other Asians from naturalized citizenship. But he lived most of his life in the United States, first in San Francisco, then New York and Philadelphia. His businesses in the Chinatowns of New York City and Philadelphia were likely among these cities' first. He conducted business with non-Chinese suppliers and customers and learned enough English to read and write. (His signature on all of his U.S. government documents is in English.) And even though he retired in China, the family's future was tied to the United States.

Moy Dong Kee's immigration file also reveals how U.S. immigration law—and specifically the Chinese exclusion laws—intruded on the lives and movements of Chinese immigrants in the United States and their families in China. When he first arrived in 1854, Moy Dong Kee needed no documentation to enter the country, and there were no interrogations, medical examinations, or testimony required from white witnesses. As another early immigrant remembered, "In those days . . . people came and went freely. We rolled up our bedding, packed our baskets, straightened our clothes . . . and pile[d] into one of the waiting wagons."[7] But by the time that Moy Dong Kee filed his affidavit in 1899, everything had changed as race- and class-based inequality became part of immigration law and everyday experiences. As a merchant family, the two successive generations of Moy sons were able to enter the country with little difficulty. But my grandmother's exclusion from the United States reveals how gender inequality also became part of immigration law and Chinese immigration strategies.

The Moys were just one part of the massive global migrations of Chinese around the world. The Chinese who came to the United States paralleled the movement of those who went to Southeast Asia, Australia, New Zealand, and other parts of North and South America. An estimated 550,000 Chinese immigrated to Southeast Asia from 1801 to 1875, while 65,000 went to Australia, 178,000 to the United States, and 30,000 to Canada.[8] The immigration of men like my Moy ancestors especially overlapped with the immigration of other Chinese immigrant men to Canada, Mexico, and Latin America in the late nineteenth and early twentieth centuries. Together, all of these migrations helped to form the modern Chinese diaspora that has lasted for generations.

Dreams of gold first propelled Chinese, most from just eight districts in the Pearl River Delta in Guangdong province, to the United States. But it was a mixture of domestic crises and foreign intervention in China that sustained and expanded the immigration of Chinese from this region to the United States over the next several decades. As the center for American and European trade in China, the Pearl River Delta was home to American labor recruiters, businessmen, and missionaries, and the growing American presence in the region helped to establish a lucrative transpacific business in Chinese immigration. By the 1860s, Hong Kong had become a "city built on migration."[9]

While public opinion often mischaracterized Chinese laborers in the United States as unfree coolies, the system that brought Chinese to the United States was different from the one sending migrants to Latin America.

Those heading to the United States did not come under contract and either paid for their own passage or borrowed money for the steamship ticket. The most common way to do this was through the credit-ticket system. Family or district associations lent money for the ticket and borrowers promised to pay it back with interest. Sometimes exorbitant rates were charged and it took years, even decades, to pay back these loans, but unlike coolies in Cuba and Peru, they were not legally bound to others.

The Chinese coming to the United States, however, did share common experiences with those going to Latin America as indentured laborers. Both were heavily recruited by foreign labor agents, for example. It started with the search for workers to build the Central Pacific Railroad in the 1860s. The recruitment of Chinese laborers grew even more after regular transpacific steamship service between Hong Kong, Shanghai, and San Francisco was established in 1867 by the Pacific Mail Steamship Company. Over the next several years, U.S. and Japanese steamship companies launched new routes to Seattle, Vancouver, and a number of other ports along the West Coast of the United States and Canada.[10] A new era of immigration began.

Foreign and domestic crises also continued to propel Chinese abroad during the late nineteenth and early twentieth centuries. Political, economic, and social unrest in China deepened as the Qing Empire faltered, Japan defeated China in the Sino-Japanese War (1894–1895), and European imperialist powers strengthened their economic positions in the country. The 1911 Chinese Revolution led by Sun Yat-sen brought an end to China's history of imperial rule, but it could not bring long-lasting political stability. Instead, powerful warlords emerged as the dominant power brokers in many parts of the country and internal rivalries between the Kuomintang (Nationalist Party) and the communists increased in the 1920s. By the 1930s, China was at war again with Japan, and by the end of the decade, Japan controlled parts of the country. World War II and the Communist Chinese Revolution in 1949 brought new upheavals.

Meanwhile, the United States continued its imperialist expansion westward through a war with Mexico and further dispossession of Native Americans. Industrialization and the growth of American capitalism created an insatiable desire for labor in the United States. Large numbers of workers were especially needed in western states to tap natural resources and build a transportation infrastructure. The Chinese filled a need. They were hired again and again for jobs that were believed to be too dirty, dangerous, or degrading for white men. But they were also paid on a separate and lower wage scale from whites.

Soon, a culture of Chinese immigration was established through letters, returning migrants, and even folksongs. "Try to leave the village," Wong Sing Look's brother (already in the U.S.) advised him in a letter. "You can never make a living there."[11] Early-twentieth-century Cantonese folksongs praised the "sojourner [from] Gold Mountain" who had at least "eight hundred," if not "one thousand in gold."[12] Young men like Lee Chew saw firsthand how fellow villagers left home poor and returned home rich. One Gold Mountain man in Lee's village made enough money to build a massive four-block-long family compound complete with a palace, summer house, streams, bridges, walks, and roads.[13] By the 1930s, Chinese heard time and time again that "anyone who comes to *Gam Saan* will make money fast and go home a rich man."[14]

For some, immigration was simply about survival. Lee Chi Yet, orphaned at a young age in Poon Lung Cheng village, was "kill[ing] himself for nothing" as a farmer in the early 1900s. People were starving to death around him, and the situation in his village was desperate. He immigrated to the United States in 1917. More than eighty years later, he explained his decision: "What the hell kind of life I have? I suffer! I got to look for a way to go. I want to live, so I come to the United States."[15] Conditions were equally bad in other villages. "The reason we Chinese come to the United States," one Chinese American organization explained in 1910, "is because . . . we have no other method by which we can keep our bodies and souls together. Should we be blocked in this . . . will our calamity not be inexpressible?[16]

Once the initial stream of people had gone abroad, an immigration chain fell easily into place helped by a number of international businesses. Transpacific steamship agents sold tickets for passage aboard a growing number of modern vessels to San Francisco, Victoria, and Callao, Peru. Letter offices, banks, and *gam saan jong*, or Gold Mountain firms, moved people, information, money, and goods from China to locations around the world. Prospective immigrants could buy tickets, have health exams, arrange documentation, and fill out consular forms all at their local *gam saan jong*. The firms also provided emigrants with a place to stay in Hong Kong while they waited for their paperwork to be processed and sold them the essential items needed for the long journey, such as comforters, food, trunks, and toiletries. Immigrants traveled to where they already had relatives or fellow villagers, and they in turn encouraged more people from home to follow in their footsteps. Through these chain migrations, or immigrant "grooves," Chinese spread throughout the United States and to other places around the world.[17]

Chinese American communities were predominately made up of men—more than half of them married—during the late nineteenth and early twentieth centuries. Like many European immigrant groups, Chinese men often came to the United States as sojourners, or immigrants who intended to return home after working and living abroad temporarily. They were known as *gam saan haak*, or Gold Mountain men. Chinese women did immigrate to the United States, but their numbers were small. During the nineteenth century, the traditional Chinese patriarchal family system discouraged and even forbade "decent" women from traveling abroad. Chinese folk sayings said as much: "A woman's duty is to care for the household, and she should have no desire to go abroad."[18] Married women were expected to remain in China, take care of their husband's parents, and perform the filial duties of their absent husbands. The harsh living conditions in California, high levels of anti-Chinese violence, expensive transpacific transportation, and the lack of available jobs for women were also factors that discouraged Chinese women from immigrating.

But U.S. immigration laws presented some of the most formidable barriers to female Chinese immigration. The 1875 Page Act barred Asian women suspected of prostitution as well as Asian laborers transported to the country as contract laborers. The Exclusion Act of 1882 further discouraged the entry of Chinese women. Although they were not explicitly barred from the United States, the exempt categories listed in the exclusion law—merchants, students, teachers, diplomats, and travelers—were professions that were held almost exclusively by men in nineteenth-century China.

Court cases initiated by Chinese in the United States eventually allowed the wives and children of Chinese merchants and U.S. citizens of Chinese descent to come. But Chinese women could not initiate immigration on their own. Because their admission into the country was based on their relationship to a male relative, they were dependent upon their husbands or fathers to sponsor them. Moreover, their own right to enter and remain in the United States was based on their sponsor's legal immigration status. If their husband or father lost his right to remain in the country, so did they. Still, these families were among the lucky ones. For the vast majority of working-class Chinese, like laundrymen and restaurant workers, bringing their wives to the United States was virtually impossible.

As a result, women accounted for only 0.3 percent of the total number of Chinese admitted into the United States in 1880. In 1900, they made up only 0.7 percent of the total number of Chinese entering the country. The situation was slightly different in Hawai'i, where plantation owners encouraged Chinese immigrant women to come as a way of tying down the Chinese immigrant labor force in the islands. In 1900, women made up 13 percent of the Chinese population in Hawai'i compared to just 5 percent of the Chinese population in the continental United States.[19]

Most Chinese immigrant families during the late nineteenth and early twentieth centuries were thus split across the Pacific Ocean. Visits were infrequent if they happened at all, and many women were essentially "Gold Mountain widows" or "grass widows."[20] If they were fortunate, they could at least rely on letters and remittances to support them. But surviving letters discovered in the Kam Wah Chung Company Building in John Day, Oregon, record some of the broken relationships, disappointment, and sadness that characterized many transnational Chinese immigrant families. A small town that supported the area's mining, ranching, farming, and logging industries, John Day had a population of 500 to 600 Chinese in its heyday in the 1870s and 1880s. The Kam Wah Chung store served as an employment agency, social gathering place, and post office for letters coming in and going to China. These letters—discovered almost a century after they were written—were either never sent or were not picked up.

From an unknown husband, undated:

My Beloved Wife:

It has been several autumns now since your dull husband left you for a far remote alien land . . .

Because I can get no gold, I am detained in this secluded corner of a strange land.

From a mother in China, February 2, 1898:

Chin-Hsin My Son, Take Notice:

You have been away from home for years. During that time, your second elder brother died, then your father died, and then your eldest brother died, too. . . . I am old and weak now and I may die at any moment. . . .

You should save some money and should come back at least next year. . . . Come back, don't forget your mother, please.

Your Mother.[21]

Small numbers of women did begin to immigrate by the end of the nineteenth century, though the number of Chinese men always outnumbered Chinese women in the United States until after World War II. Some of the first to make the journey came as prostitutes who had been kidnapped, lured, or purchased and imported as indentured or enslaved laborers. One woman testified in 1892 that she had left China after being promised marriage to a rich and good husband in the United States. But when she arrived in San Francisco, she was sold for $400 to a slave dealer. The dealer then sold her to another man for $1,700. "I have been a brothel slave ever since," she told investigators.[22]

A small number of Chinese prostitutes became concubines or mistresses to wealthy Chinese men. Most were sold to parlor houses in Chinatown that catered to well-to-do Chinese and white men. Those who ended up in alley cribs—small, sparsely furnished shacks—were forced to entice customers until they were sold again or died from venereal disease. Called *lougeui* ("always holding her legs up") and *baak haak chai* ("hundred men's wife"), Chinese prostitutes were virtual slaves.[23]

The rare Chinese prostitute escaped. Polly Bemis (Lalu Nathoy) had been sold into prostitution as a young girl in China for one thousand pieces of gold and brought to San Francisco and then to Idaho. Through perseverance and luck, she eventually gained her freedom, married, and owned and operated a well-known business and ranch. Over the years, she became respected as a businesswoman and community member. Her house is now a museum registered on the National Register of Historic Places.[24]

Some Chinese prostitutes were able to turn to Christian missionary women who managed two "rescue" homes in San Francisco to provide an escape from prostitution, arranged marriages, and abusive relationships. The largest was the Presbyterian Mission Home run by Margaret Culbertson and then Donaldina Cameron, which claimed to have rescued 1,500 women. Many Chinese mission home women gained valuable skills that served them in later years. Tye Leung, for example, escaped an arranged marriage at the age of twelve by fleeing to the Presbyterian Mission Home. She stayed to work as an interpreter and helped missionaries rescue Chinese prostitutes. Her work earned her praise by Cameron, who personally recommended her for a position with the U.S. Bureau of Immigration as an interpreter and assistant matron for Chinese women detainees at the Angel Island Immigration Station. Christian missionary women were among the prostitutes' only allies, but with their missionary zeal and self-righteousness, these women and their rescue efforts also perpetuated negative stereotypes about Chinese immigrant men as immoral slave dealers and Chinese immigrant women as degraded sex slaves that contributed to growing anti-Chinese sentiment.[25]

As Chinese men decided to stay in the United States, an increasing number of women came as wives or daughters. Changing attitudes about gender roles and an easing of cultural restrictions on Chinese female emigration made it easier for some women to leave China. By 1910, women were 9.7 percent of the total number of Chinese immigrants entering the country. Ten years later, they were 20 percent, and by 1930 the percentage of women immigrants had risen to 30 percent.[26]

Many of these women viewed both marriage and immigration in terms of economic opportunity. Wong Lan Fong's experience was not uncommon. A lack of steady work plagued her family following the 1911 revolution in China, and they were forced to move around Canton in search of work. "I remember moving every couple of years," she reflected. "The house would become smaller and not so nice." The Wongs sold off their possessions with mounting sadness. After Wong Lan Fong's mother fell ill and died, her father and new stepmother urged her to look for a *gam saan haak*, a Gold Mountain man, to marry so that she could go to the United States. It was the only way to secure her economic future, they explained. In 1926, she married Lee Chi Yet and came to the United States a year later.[27] Law Shee Low's family was in even worse shape. Bandits had robbed them of all of their possessions and destroyed their farmland. "We became so poor that we had no food to go with rice," she remembered. Some of the neighboring families started begging for food or even sold their daughters. "That was when my parents decided to marry me off to a *gam saan haak* from the next village. They thought I would have a better future in Gold Mountain."[28]

The men they joined, however, were often barely scraping by working in difficult jobs for low pay. The Chinese first found work in the mines, and by 1860, 70 percent of all employed Chinese in California were miners.[29] Most worked independently, but some organized themselves into small companies. Only a few found gold. Others supported themselves by opening up restaurants and laundries in mining country. The Chinese also spread out to mine in other states throughout the U.S. West. In every location, they endured a great deal of hostility. Whites resented their large numbers and competition in the goldfields. Harassment, robberies, and mob violence were so common that Chinese tried to work in isolated and inaccessible places to avoid conflict.

Over the decades, the demand for Chinese labor increased. Chinese immigrant men quickly became indispensable as they worked on railroads and in factories, canneries, fisheries, and fields. In 1869, the *Daily Alta California* praised the role that Chinese immigrants were playing in developing the state's economy. "The Chinamen are ploughmen, laundrymen, placer miners, woolen spinners and weavers, domestic servants, cigar makers, shoemakers, and railroad builders to the great benefit of the State," the reporter pointed out.[30]

8. Chinese workers building the Loma Prieta Lumber Company Railroad in Santa Cruz County, California, c. 1885.

Western railroad companies were the largest employers of Chinese laborers. In 1865, the first Chinese were hired by the Central Pacific Railroad as track layers on the great transcontinental railroad heading east from Sacramento. Company president Leland Stanford praised the Chinese as "quiet, peaceable, industrious, economical," and rightly acknowledged that "without them it would be impossible to complete the western portion of this great National highway."[31] As the railroad was being built eastward, the Union Pacific Railroad was being built westward, beginning with construction from Omaha, Nebraska, to Promontory Point, Utah, where the two railroads would meet and finally link the country by rail for the first time from east to west. Chinese laborers proved to be such a capable and reliable workforce that Central Pacific agents sent for more laborers from China and paid their passage over to the United States. By 1867, 12,000 Chinese, representing 90 percent of the workforce, were building the railroad.[32]

The Chinese cleared trees, blasted rocks with explosives, picks, and shovels, carried away debris, and laid tracks. The rugged mountains of the Sierra Nevada "swarmed with Celestials, shoveling, shoveling, carting, drilling and blasting rocks and earth," described one observer. The work was difficult and dangerous. Many Chinese died during the winter of 1866, when snowstorms covered construction workers and trapped them under snowdrifts. Others lost their lives in explosions while trying to dynamite tunnels through the mountains. One newspaper estimated at least 1,200 Chinese immigrants died in the building of the railroad.[33]

In 1867, 5,000 Chinese went on strike. They were working long hours for little pay. "Eight hours a day good for white men, all the same good for Chinamen," they declared. Railroad baron Charles Crocker responded by cutting off the miners' food supply. Isolated and starving in their work camps in the mountains, the strikers surrendered.[34] A final indignity occurred when the Central Pacific and Union Pacific railroads met at Promontory Point on May 10, 1869, to lay the last spike to link the transcontinental railroad: the Chinese workers who had made it all possible were nowhere to be found in official photographs commemorating the occasion.

9. On May 10, 1869, the western and eastern halves of the transcontinental railroad were linked together at Promontory Point. Chinese railroad workers, who made up 90 percent of the workforce building the western half of the railroad, are noticeably absent from the official photographs celebrating this historic event. "East and West Shaking Hands at Laying Last Rail, 1869," Andrew J. Russell (1829–1902).

Chinese and other Asians were also heavily recruited to harvest sugarcane on the Hawaiian Islands (just as they were in the Caribbean), where sugar was king during the nineteenth century. More than 300,000 Asians arrived in Hawai'i between 1850 and 1920. The Chinese came first, recruited by planters in the Royal Hawaiian Agricultural Society. Seven hundred came during the 1850s. Another 25,497 Chinese arrived between 1875 and 1887. By 1890, Chinese were almost 19 percent of the total population in the islands.[35] Unlike Chinese laborers on Cuban sugar plantations, the Chinese in Hawai'i worked under contracts, but were unindentured. They called Hawai'i *Tan Heung Shan*, or fragrant sandalwood mountains. Sugar planters praised the Chinese for being "prompt at the call of the bell, steady in their work, and quick to learn." They encouraged even more Chinese to come and to stay. But the Chinese had other ideas. The vast majority left the plantations after their contracts expired to grow rice, coffee, bananas, and taro and to raise livestock. Many found opportunities in towns and in the city of Honolulu. Others left the islands altogether and went to other parts of the United States.[36]

When railroad construction jobs dried up in the western U.S. after 1869, thousands of Chinese laborers drifted into San Francisco, where they helped to expand the city's emerging industries in shoes, textiles, and cigars. By 1872, nearly half the workingmen employed in factories were Chinese.[37] They were paid low wages, and in shops where they worked alongside whites performing the same work, Chinese were paid less than their white counterparts. The charge that Chinese competed unfairly with white workers would become one of the central arguments in the anti-Chinese movement by the 1870s.

The demand for Chinese immigrant labor was not just in the West. Chinese were also recruited to work in shoe factories in North Adams, Massachusetts, and on plantations in the South. By 1880, there were small communities based in New Orleans and in Mississippi. In the racially segregated South, Chinese occupied an in-between, "partly colored" place among blacks and whites. They had more freedom of movement and other privileges that were denied to African Americans. But they were never accepted as equal to whites.[38]

In California, Chinese also turned to agriculture. In the Sacramento–San

Joaquin River deltas, they were hired to construct irrigation channels, levees, dikes, and ditches. Working with shovels in waist-deep water, they drained the swamplands and turned them into some of the most productive and fertile farmland in the country. Chinese immigrants also constructed roads, cleared land, planted, pruned, and harvested grapes for the Napa and Sonoma valleys' wine industry. They grew citrus fruits, beans, peas, and sugar beets. On their own small farms, they grew potatoes, vegetables, and fruit and trucked their produce into cities and small towns. By the turn of the century, 95 percent of the Chinese population in the Sacramento and San Joaquin delta region worked as farmers, farmworkers, fruit packers, and in other agriculture-related occupations.[39] "They were *the* vital factor" in making California's agricultural transition possible, noted historian Carey McWilliams.[40] But wage inequality followed the Chinese into the fields. They were paid around $10 to $20 less per month than whites doing the same work.[41]

Among the Chinese in agriculture were two horticulturalists who helped transform the industry. One was Ah Bing, who bred the famous Bing cherry in Oregon. The other was Lue Gim Gong of Florida, who succeeded in growing a hearty, juicy orange that could be shipped around the country in large quantities. In 1911, the Lue Gim Gong orange won the American Pomological Society's distinguished Wilder Medal. He went on to develop a new grapefruit strain and several other unusual plant combinations. When he died in 1925, Lue Gim Gong, known as the "citrus wizard," was memorialized for the significant role he played in the Florida citrus industry.[42]

By the early 1900s, Chinese immigrants had spread out to big cities and small towns throughout the West and into the Midwest, Northeast, Mid-Atlantic, and South. More often than not, they supported themselves by running small businesses, especially laundries, restaurants, or stores. In 1920, 48 percent of the Chinese in California worked in small business.[43] In spite of the stereotypes, these enterprises were in no way traditional Chinese occupations. "The Chinese laundryman does not learn his trade in China," laundryman Lee Chew explained in 1906. "There are no laundries in China. The women there do the washing in tubs and have no washboards or flat irons."[44] Nor did the Chinese particularly like this kind of work. Rather, the Chinese became laundrymen, writer and activist Wong Chin Foo explained in 1888, "simply because there is no other occupation by which they can make money as surely and quickly."[45]

It all seemed to start with a man named Wah Lee, who hung up a "Wash'ng and Iron'ng" sign over a storefront at the corner of Dupont and Washington Streets in San Francisco in 1851. With so few women, including washerwomen of any ethnic background, in Gold Rush California, the city faced an acute shortage of launderers. It cost $8 to wash and iron a dozen shirts. At one point, the cost of cleaning clothes was so high that some resorted to shipping their laundry to Honolulu, which was actually less expensive than having it done in San Francisco. The one downside was that it could take several months to get the clean clothes back. Lee and others capitalized on an opportunity. By 1860, there were 890 Chinese laundrymen in the state. Ten years later, almost 3,000 Chinese were recorded as washing and ironing clothes for a living.[46]

Chinese restaurants had similar origins. Gold Rush era California was filled with few women and even fewer men who were willing to cook and feed others. Like the entrepreneurial Wah Lee, Chinese immigrants seized on the opportunity to support themselves and worked as camp cooks and as operators of small eating establishments. By the early twentieth century, restaurants were a mainstay for many immigrant families, who opened up chop suey houses catering to non-Chinese clientele across the country.

As Chinese moved across the United States, so did Chinese laundries and restaurants. Shut out from other jobs because of racial discrimination, Chinese were forced into self-employment, ethnic economies, and work that no one else wanted. But these two businesses also fit the needs of Chinese immigrants as well. Neither required professional skills, proficiency in English, or education, and the businesses could be operated by single owners, small families, or larger group partnerships. Moreover, they filled an economic niche in many cities and towns. Lee Chew, who got his start washing clothes in a California railroad camp, left the state in the 1880s after he and his partner were robbed and driven out of town. When he arrived in Chicago, he supported himself by operating another laundry before moving to Detroit, Buffalo, and New York City, where he also opened up laundries.[47]

The work was difficult and physically punishing. Boston laundry worker Tung Pok Chin remembered that his workday lasted from seven in the morning until two the next morning, "day in and day out, six days a week." He and the five other workers in his laundry ate supper at two in the morning and slept at two-thirty, leaving them only four and a half hours of sleep.[48] Still, the wages earned in the United States were better than what most could earn in China. During a good week in the 1920s, a laundryman could earn up to $50. He could generally support his family in China on that income if he was frugal. An enterprising laundryman might eventually own his own business. Sociologist Paul Siu found that in the 1920s and 1930s, a laundry could be set up for the relatively low investment of $2,800 to $3,000.[49]

Working long hours in laundries and restaurants, often in small towns far away from other Chinese communities, immigrants retreated to the Chinatowns that began to spring up around the country. Home to the oldest and largest Chinese community in the United States, San Francisco and its Chinatown—known as *Dai Fou*, or "Big City"—was the economic, cultural, and political center of Chinese America for most of the nineteenth and twentieth centuries. A bustling Chinese section of the city had sprung up during the Gold Rush with general merchandise stores, restaurants, boardinghouses, and butcher, herb, and tailor shops. By the 1870s, the Chinese quarter was six blocks long starting at California Street and running all the way to Broadway. By 1900, 45 percent of all Chinese in California lived in the San Francisco Bay Area.[50] Most Chinese immigrants and Chinese goods entered the United States through the port of San Francisco, and from there, people and things were dispersed around the country and to other places within North and South America.

San Francisco Chinatown was also home to a number of organizations that provided support and mutual aid to make life easier in America. There were fraternal organizations, political parties, chambers of commerce, secret societies, regional associations, and labor unions. *Fongs* were formed by family associations to assist clan members in the United States. Meaning "house" or "room," *fongs* were clubhouses that served as boardinghouses and community centers where members could meet, exchange news, mail and receive letters, and arrange for the remains of deceased relatives to be shipped back home. *Tongs* (fraternal lodges or organizations) were organized around sworn brotherhood loyalty and patterned after the secret societies, or triads, that were formed in opposition to the Qing Empire in China. They also helped immigrants find jobs, pool economic resources, and provided other forms of mutual assistance. As they grew and expanded, *tong* activities also extended into the opium, gambling, and prostitution trades, all common vices in bachelor societies.

Above the *tongs* and *fongs* were *huigan*, or regional associations based on immigrants' native districts. In San Francisco, the first Chinese immigrants formed six district associations linked to areas in the Pearl River Delta. They later joined together as the Chinese Six Companies, which acted as a representative for Chinese in the United States, settled inter-district conflicts, and provided legal, educational, and health services. Eventually, it managed overseas branches in Canada and Latin America from San Francisco as well.

These organizations may have provided the social and economic backbone of the Chinese community in the United States and other parts of North and South America, but for most Chinese immigrants San Francisco's Chinatown was simply home. This is where they could speak their native language, eat favorite foods, stock up on supplies and Chinese foodstuffs, visit with family and fellow villagers, and hear news from home. On their days off, Chinese immigrant men would stroll through the streets of Chinatown or maybe gather in Portsmouth Square. There would be tea to drink and wall notices to read about the latest political news from China, changes in U.S. immigration laws, and community announcements. In the evening, they might gamble or visit the theaters, temples, and brothels. As one Chinatown resident told an interviewer in the 1920s, "most of us can live a warmer, freer, and more human life among our relatives and friends than among strangers. . . . It is only in Chinatown that a Chinese immigrant has society, friends and relatives who share his dreams and hopes, his hardships, and adventures."[51] As Chinese moved throughout the state and across the country, other Chinatowns sprung up in cities like Sacramento and Minneapolis and towns like Butte, Montana. And there were growing Chinatowns as well in the big cities of Chicago, Boston, St. Louis, Philadelphia, and New York.

Between 1880 and 1890, the number of Chinese in New York tripled to over 2,000, for example, with most settling in the Five Points neighborhood on the Lower East Side of Manhattan.[52] The first Chinese in New York had arrived as sailors. By the 1850s, there was a small community of Chinese who worked as street peddlers, cigar makers, laundrymen, cooks and restaurant owners, and Chinese grocery store operators. And while social reformer Jacob Riis described the Chinese as "a homeless stranger among us," the Chinese in New York City were busy building a vibrant world that included strong community institutions, families, and organizations.[53]

Some Chinese immigrants married Irish immigrant women, like the well-known "exemplary Chinaman" Quimbo Appo, an English-speaking tea seller who was born on Zhusan, an island off the Chinese coast southeast of Shanghai. The island was frequently visited by Western opium traders, and it was probably through them that Appo secured passage on a ship heading to California (then Mexican territory), in 1847. From there, he sailed to Boston as a cook and steward. In New Haven, he met and married Catherine Fitzpatrick, an Irishwoman. They moved to New York, where Appo worked at a tea store in lower Manhattan. When their son was born on the Fourth of July, 1856, they named him George Washington Appo.[54] By the 1860s, such Chinese-Irish marriages were so common that the *New York Tribune* remarked that "these Chinamen have a peculiar fancy for wives of Celtic origin."[55]

Mott Street was the center of the city's Chinatown and was crowded with boardinghouses, family association lodges, grocery stores, herbalists, and restaurants. While other immigrant groups, including the Irish, Italians, and Jews, eventually left the neighborhood where Chinatown now stands, the Chinese stayed, and New York's Chinatown remains one of the largest and most dynamic in the world.

While the streets of Chinatown bustled with activity, Chinese homes were often places where Chinese immigrant women were "doubly bound by patriarchal control in Chinatown and racism outside" as historian Judy Yung has explained.[56] Early immigrant women—including both the prostitute at one end of the social and economic ladder and the merchant's wife at the other—lived circumscribed lives. They often spoke no English and were confined to the enclosed world of their families and communities by their husbands and fathers and by the patriarchal values in both Chinese and American societies. "Poor me!" one Chinese immigrant woman complained. "In China I was shut up in the house since I was ten years old, and only left my father's house to be shut up in my husband's house in this great country. For seventeen years I have been in this house without leaving it save on two evenings."[57]

By the early twentieth century, the women who were coming to the United States found their lives shaped by changing attitudes about women's roles and status in both China and the United States. They began to educate themselves, work outside the home, and participate in community activities. And they began to take an active role in the nationalist movement in China and in the struggle for equality in the United States. As Chinese women in China became "new women," so did Chinese women in the United States.[58]

In 1902, Chinese student and social reformer Sieh King King stood before a packed San Francisco crowd and introduced the idea that the emancipation of Chinese women was central to the emancipation of China. An ardent believer in the reform movement in China, which viewed modernization as a way to free China from foreign domination, Sieh made history by being the first Chinese woman to introduce feminist ideas to San Francisco's Chinatown. As the *San Francisco Chronicle* reported, Sieh "boldly condemned the slave girl system, raged at the horrors of foot-binding, and . . . declared that men and women were equal and should enjoy the privileges of equals."[59]

Other Chinese immigrant women took advantage of changing attitudes and new educational and professional opportunities for women. Chinese immigrant Jane Kwong Lee earned a master's degree in sociology at a time when few women pursued advanced degrees. She went on to direct the Chinese Young Women's Christian Association's programs that provided women with English classes and assistance with immigration issues, employment, education, and domestic problems. In her role as a community worker, Lee served as a crucial link between different groups and generations of Chinese women in San Francisco, between the Chinese and non-Chinese communities, and between the Chinese and the United States governments.[60]

Chinese immigrant women also worked alongside their husbands in Chinese-owned restaurants, shops, and laundries. Or they worked for wages in factories, canneries, and other businesses. By World War I, Chinese women dominated the garment industry in San Francisco. Some immigrant families also took in boarders as a way of adding to their income, and in these homes it was the wife's job to prepare food and clean for the additional household members. Juggling their dual responsibilities as homemakers and wage earners, Chinese women were indispensable partners in their families' struggles for economic survival in the United States.[61]

10. A Chinese American family in Golden Gate Park, San Francisco, California, 1890s.

The same immigration laws that barred or discouraged Chinese women from immigrating to the United States slowed the growth of Chinese American families. With so many families split between the United States and China, the presence of women and children in many communities was rare until after the 1920s. But as increasing numbers of Chinese women immigrated as wives (and less commonly as daughters) of merchants and U.S. citizens, women and children became more common on the streets of Chinese communities across the country. Between 1900 and 1940, the U.S.-born Chinese population quadrupled.[62]

Chinese American families learned to adapt Chinese cultural practices to their new American environments. Children's births were often celebrated with a traditional Chinese "full moon" celebration 100 days after birth. But newborns were also baptized in Catholic and Protestant churches. Families celebrated Chinese New Year and the Fourth of July. Children were given both Chinese and American names, which signaled the family's growing attachment to the United States. Pardee Lowe's father named him after the governor of California. His siblings were given names of U.S. presidents, vice presidents, and their wives: Woodrow Wilson, Thomas Riley Marshal, Helen Taft, Alice Roosevelt, and Mabel.[63]

Family life often revolved around the family business and school. Children headed off to public school in the morning, like San Francisco's Oriental Public School, and then attended Chinese school in the afternoon, where they studied the Chinese language, and for the older kids, Chinese history and classics. Faith-based social service organizations like the Chinese Young Men's Christian Association (YMCA) and the Chinese Young Women's Christian Association (YWCA) in San Francisco also offered opportunities to learn music, play basketball, take classes in English, Mandarin, and mechanical drawing for boys, and classes in English, sewing, piano, and cooking, as well as recreational sports like table tennis and badminton for the girls.[64] In the evening, children were put to work in the family restaurants and laundries washing dishes, preparing food, or ironing clothes.

Like other immigrant groups, the coming of the American-born second generation brought new ways of becoming American. Learning English was one way in which Chinese learned to navigate through American life, and many Chinese immigrants relied on English-Chinese phrase books. A common edition was an 1888 version that focused on "dialogues on ordinary and familiar subjects for the use of the Chinese resident in America." With sections on meeting friends, conducting business at the post office, serving customers in the laundry, getting a job as a cook or waiter, and handling immigration matters with government officials, the phrase book offered basic English communication skills that readers might expect to use in daily life, such as: "Is this the right way to the post office?" "Can you tell me where No. 10 Fifth Avenue is?" "I heard, sir, that you wanted a waiter."[65] Phrase books also revealed some of the hardships and other experiences Chinese faced with entries like: "He took it from me by violence." "He was choked to death with a lasso, by a robber." "She is a good-for-nothing huzzy."[66]

Chinese immigrants additionally adapted to life in the United States by changing their clothing, eating habits, and social customs. Some married white, Native American, Mexican, Native Hawaiian, and African American women and blended into non-Chinese local communities when and where permitted. They became Christian, changed their names, and a small number of Chinese immigrants even managed to become naturalized citizens in spite of federal law. But Chinese immigrants also became American by drawing on American values of equality in their protests against discrimination and in using the U.S. justice system to try to overturn discriminatory laws.

A few Chinese made American legal history with their attempts to guarantee equality for the Chinese in America. In 1884, Mary and Joseph Tape went to enroll their daughter Mamie in San Francisco's Spring Valley School. Citing state education codes that allowed schools to exclude children who had "filthy or vicious habits, or children with contagious or infectious diseases," school officials and the San Francisco School Board refused their application. Characterizing all Chinese children as dangerous or diseased, the School Board trustees used these codes to maintain a strict policy of racial segregation in the public schools. The Tapes launched a legal battle for equal access to education. In a letter of protest to the board, Mary Tape wrote: "I see that you are going to make all sorts of excuses to keep my child out of the Public Schools. . . . Is it a disgrace to be born a Chinese? Didn't God make us all!!! What right! Have you to bar my children out of the school because she is of chinese Descend." The Tapes eventually sued the San Francisco School Board and argued that as a native-born citizen of the United States, Mamie was entitled to the free education that was every American's birthright. A San Francisco superior court judge agreed, but the San Francisco School Board refused to allow Mamie to attend school with whites and established a separate Chinese primary school in the Chinatown district. Although it was not the outcome that the Tapes would have liked, Mamie and her younger brother, Frank, were the first two students to show up for class when the school opened in April 1885. The Tapes' legal challenge had affirmed that Chinese children in the United States had the right to a public education.[67]

Wong Kim Ark was a native-born American citizen of Chinese descent whose 1898 Supreme Court challenge affirmed the constitutional status of birthright citizenship for all persons born in the United States. A restaurant cook and native of San Francisco, Wong was twenty-four in 1894 when he returned to California after a visit to China. To his surprise, he was denied reentry into the United States. John H. Wise, U.S. collector of customs in charge of immigrant processing in San Francisco, claimed that Wong, though born in the United States, was not a citizen because his parents were Chinese nationals who were ineligible for citizenship under the Chinese exclusion laws. A self-described "zealous opponent of Chinese immigration," Wise attempted to apply the exclusion laws as broadly as possible, including to second-generation Chinese Americans. Wise ordered that Wong be "returned" to China.

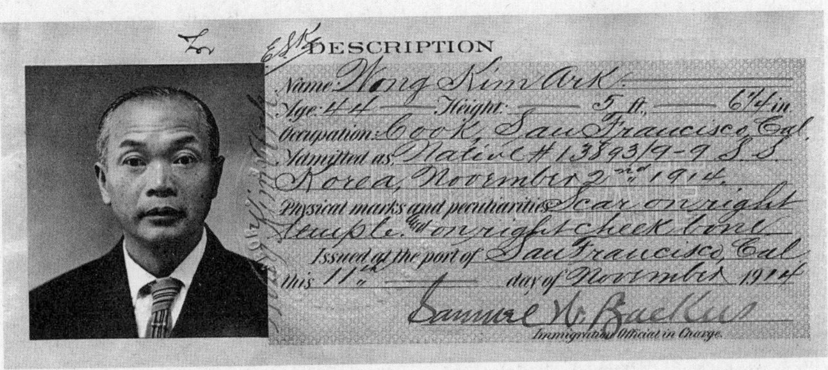

DESCRIPTION

Name Wong Kim Ark.
Age 44 Height 5 ft. 6¼ in.
Occupation Cook, San Francisco, Cal.
Admitted as Native #13893/9-9 S.S. Korea, November 2nd 1914.
Physical marks and peculiarities Scar on right temple. Mole on right cheek bone.
Issued at the port of San Francisco, Cal this 11th day of November 1914
Samuel W. Backus
Immigration Official in Charge.

11. Despite the fact that his 1898 Supreme Court case affirmed the right of birthright citizenship to all persons born in the United States regardless of race, Wong Kim Ark was still treated as an unequal citizen in the United States. Like all Chinese immigrants and Chinese Americans in the country, he was forced to carry this certificate of identity (c. 1914) with him at all times to demonstrate his legal residence in the United States.

Wong and his lawyers challenged the decision with a writ of habeas corpus. He claimed that he had a right to be readmitted into the United States based on his status as a United States citizen under the Fourteenth Amendment. The question for the court was: how does the United States determine citizenship—by *jus soli* (by soil) or by *jus sanguinis* (by blood)?

The District Court for the Northern District of California ruled for Wong, but the U.S. attorney appealed the decision and the case was argued before the United States Supreme Court in March 1897. With a majority opinion by Justice Horace Gray, the court ruled in Wong's favor. *United States v. Wong Kim Ark* affirmed that all persons born in the United States were, regardless of race, native-born citizens and entitled to all the rights of citizenship.[68]

Other Chinese in America, like writer and activist Wong Chin Foo, used the public sphere to challenge discrimination in the U.S. Born in 1847, Wong was twenty years old when he came to the United States with an American missionary woman who, with her late husband, had taken care of him in China after his family fell on hard times. He studied in schools in Washington, D.C., and Pennsylvania before returning to China to marry and start a family. But when he began to criticize the Qing Empire, he was expelled from China and returned to the United States in 1873. The next year, he became a naturalized U.S. citizen in Grand Rapids, Michigan. (Federal laws prohibited the naturalization of Asian immigrants, but they were not enforced rigidly around the country until after the Chinese Exclusion Act of 1882 was passed and explicitly spelled out the prohibition against naturalized U.S. citizenship for Chinese.) Wong lectured throughout the country on topics related to China and the Chinese in the United States. As the anti-Chinese movement grew during the 1870s and 1880s, he defended the Chinese community, attacked anti-Chinese leader Denis Kearney, and established the *Chinese American*, the first Chinese newspaper in New York City. During the next decade, he formed the Chinese Equal Rights League in 1892 and continuously spoke out against the Chinese exclusion laws, including when he testified before the U.S. Congress in 1893 (likely the first Chinese person to do so).[69] His was an unequivocal voice for justice. "We claim a common manhood with all other nationalities," Wong's Equal Rights League stated in an 1892 appeal, "and believe we should have that manhood recognized according to the principles of common humanity and American freedom."[70] Wong continued to push for Chinese American citizenship rights until his death in 1898.

While Chinese were fighting for equality in the United States, they were also fighting for "a modern strong Chinese nation." Because China's weak status in the world translated into the weak status of Chinese abroad, the two movements were inextricably connected, explained the Chinese language newspaper *Chung Sai Yat Po* (Chinese Western Daily) in 1900.[71] European and American powers continued to dominate China through unequal treaties and territorial expansion in the late nineteenth century. The Qing imperial court was largely powerless to resist. A growing number of Chinese began to advocate for reforms that ranged from modifying the traditional imperial system to a complete revolution to replace the empire with a republic. Banned from China because of their subversive views, reformers and revolutionaries went abroad to gain financial and political support for their causes. They found eager audiences.

Sun Yat-sen, a Chinese Christian who had attended school in Hawai'i, was the recognized leader of two major political organizations active in the Chinese nationalist movement abroad. The Xingzhonghui, founded in Hawai'i in 1894 with the assistance of the Chinese Hawaiian middle class, introduced the Chinese revolutionary movement to the Chinese in the Western Hemisphere. In 1905, he formed the Tongmenghui in Japan, which brought several groups together in one coalition and offered a more sophisticated and detailed revolutionary ideology based on nationalism, democracy, and people's livelihood.

Another major Chinese nationalist organization had its roots in North America. In 1899, Kang Youwei, a scholar and former advisor to the Chinese emperor, arrived in North America preaching reform of the imperial system. Along with his student Liang Qichao, Kang and his followers formed the Baohuanghui, Chinese Empire Reform Association, in Victoria, British Columbia. With its focus on reform rather than on revolution, the Baohuanghui proved to be popular. At its peak, it published its own Chinese-language newspaper, the *Chinese World*, and boasted 5 million members. These reform efforts—supported in part by the Chinese in North and South America—helped lead to the overthrow of the Qing Dynasty in 1911. A Provisional Government of the Republic of China was established in 1912 with Sun Yat-sen as president. The Tongmenghui formed a coalition with other political groups to become the Kuomintang, or Chinese Nationalist Party. The Chinese in the United States would continue to support the new Republic of China, especially during the war of resistance against Japan

(Sino-Japanese War) beginning in 1937 and during World War II. "To save China, to save ourselves" became the rallying cry for Chinese throughout the Americas during the long war years.[72]

But "saving" China and challenging discrimination in the United States was not easy. Inequality continued to shape Chinese Americans' daily lives. In the 1930s, sociologists studying the Chinese community in the U.S. found that Chinese immigrants and Chinese American citizens suffered from a deep-rooted sense of insecurity and a "psychology of fear" brought on by the fact that the Chinese "did not feel at home under the conditions of exclusion and race prejudice."[73] Unwelcome in the United States and prevented from becoming full-fledged citizens, many Chinese immigrants continued to view the country as a sojourner would: a place where they could make money and then leave. As one Chicago laundryman explained: "I have no other hope but to get my money and get back to China. What is the use of staying here; you can't be an American here."[74]

Discrimination was keenly felt among the second generation of Chinese Americans who grew up acculturated into American society and yearned to realize their full potential as U.S. citizens in their pursuit of education, professions, and American social and political life. But racism in the larger society dashed many of these dreams. Discrimination, limited work opportunities, and social segregation followed them wherever they went. For many Chinese American women, becoming American additionally meant going against traditional gender role expectations of their parents.

Many also found that their citizenship status offered little protection from discrimination. In 1913 and 1923, politicians introduced bills in Congress designed to disfranchise citizens of Chinese ancestry. The Immigration Act of 1924 explicitly excluded "aliens ineligible to citizenship," a reference to all Asians, and the 1922 Cable Act revoked the citizenship of women who married "aliens ineligible for citizenship." The main victims of this law were Asian American women who married Asian male immigrants. Once a woman lost her citizenship, her rights to own property, vote, and travel freely were also revoked. This law would not be changed until 1931.[75]

Chinese Americans expressed a marked loss of admiration for the United States as well as a frustrated sense of alienation. One explained to an interviewer that "I feel that I am more American than Chinese. I am an

American citizen by birth, having the title for all rights, but they treat me as if I were a foreigner." Another observed that "I thought I was American, but America would not have me. In many respects she would not recognize me as American. Moreover, I find racial prejudice against us everywhere. We are American citizens in name but not in fact."[76] It would not be until World War II that Chinese Americans started feeling like they were part of American society.

4

"The Chinese Must Go!": The Anti-Chinese Movement

On February 28, 1882, Senator John F. Miller of California introduced into the United States Congress a bill to exclude Chinese immigrant laborers from the country. Over the next two hours, the California Republican presented his case. He first spelled out the imminent danger that Chinese immigration posed to the United States, including the fact that, according to Miller, Chinese immigrants came from a "degraded and inferior race." Other senators jumped in to compare the Chinese to "rats," "beasts," and "swine." "Oriental civilization," they claimed, was incompatible with the United States and threatened to corrupt the nation. Chinese immigrants were also an economic danger according to Miller. They competed with white workers with their "machine-like" ways and their "muscles of iron," he claimed. As a result, the U.S. laborer, whether on the farm, the shoe bench, or the factory, simply could not compete with the low-paid Chinese worker. Miller proclaimed that a vote for Chinese exclusion was thus a vote for both American labor and the "public good" of the country.[1]

There was minimal opposition to the law. Former Radical Republicans, like Massachusetts senator George Frisbie Hoar, called the discriminatory Chinese Exclusion Act "old race prejudice," a crime committed against the Declaration of Independence.[2] But overall, politicians in both the Senate and House agreed that the menace of Chinese immigration needed to be stopped. "The gate . . . must be closed," Representative Edward Valentine of Nebraska succinctly declared.[3] Just over two months later, the United States passed the Chinese Exclusion Act of 1882, the country's first immigration law that singled out an immigrant group for large-scale exclusion based on race.[4]

The Chinese who entered the United States in the late nineteenth century were only a small fraction of the total immigrant population in the United States. From 1870 to 1880, 138,941 Chinese immigrants entered the country, representing only 4.3 percent of the total number of immigrants (3,199,394) who were admitted during the same decade.[5] Nevertheless, their presence in the United States sparked some of the most violent and destructive racist campaigns in U.S. history that would transform the United States and shape the regulation of international migration around the world.

Americans were first introduced to the Chinese through reports from U.S. traders, diplomats, and missionaries in China. Their portrayals of Chinese as heathen, crafty, and dishonest "marginal members of the human race" quickly set Chinese apart. At first seen as exotic curiosities from a distant land, Chinese immigrants came to be viewed as threats, especially as their numbers increased throughout the Gold Rush period and other changes in the United States shaped ideas about race and what it meant to be American.[6] Belief in U.S. Manifest Destiny and white superiority had driven the U.S. expansion westward. Indian wars, struggles over African slavery, and the conquest of the West were all tied to race-based ideas of who belonged in the United States and where they fit into the country's racial hierarchy. Chinese were the largest group of nonwhite immigrants to come to the United States. And as soon as they arrived, questions were raised about whether they should be welcomed or expelled.

On the one hand, the Chinese were praised by industrialists as an ample source of cheap, available labor to build the transcontinental railroad and help develop the lumber, fishing, mining, and agricultural industries of the West. Others believed that Chinese immigrants represented unfair economic competition. They were also concerned about the vices that the mostly male population of Chinese immigrants was accused of bringing to the United States, such as drug use, prostitution, and gang activity.

Demagogues, such as Workingmen's Party of California leader Denis Kearney, capitalized on the deep sense of economic insecurity among the working classes in San Francisco during the depression of the 1870s. Blaming Chinese workers for unfavorable wages and the scarcity of jobs, anti-Chinese leaders such as Kearney drew upon earlier debates over Asian indentured labor in the Caribbean and Latin America and charged that Chinese were imported coolies engaged in a new system of slavery that degraded U.S. labor. Samuel Gompers, president of the American Federation of Labor, framed this issue explicitly by asking the question: "Meat vs. Rice—American Manhood vs. Asiatic Coolieism. Which Shall Survive?"[7]

Many of the arguments in favor of restricting Chinese immigrants also framed the problem explicitly around the sexual danger that both Chinese women and men allegedly posed to the country and its citizens. Chinese female prostitutes caused "moral and racial pollution" through their interracial liaisons, while Chinese men lured pure and innocent white women into their dens of vice and depravity. Moreover, Chinese men were depicted as undermining acceptable gender roles in American society, because they engaged in "women's work" of cleaning and cooking.[8]

Nineteenth-century popular culture in the form of theater and illustrated magazines capitalized on these images of Chinese immigrants and helped to spread them far and wide. One cartoon titled "A Statue for Our Harbor," published in 1881 in the San Francisco–based magazine *The Wasp*, seemingly captured all of white California's fears about Chinese immigration. A statue of a grotesque Chinese male coolie in San Francisco Bay mocks New York's Statue of Liberty, then under construction. His ragged robes, rat-tail-like queue, stereotypical facial features, and opium pipe symbolize the unassimilability and immorality of the Chinese. The message that Chinese immigration would bring destruction to California and the entire nation is made clear with the skull upon which the statue rests his foot, the rats scurrying around the pedestal, the capsized ships and crumbling statue foundation, the slant-eyed moon, and the rays of light emanating from the coolie's head informing readers that Chinese bring "filth," "immorality," "diseases," and "ruin to white labor." With the wide dissemination of such racist images in mainstream popular culture, the anti-Chinese movement spread.

By the time that this cartoon was published, Californians had tried to regulate Chinese immigration for decades. As early as 1850, anti-Chinese sentiment in California became part of state law in the form of a foreign miner's tax. Although the law was aimed at all foreigners, it was primarily enforced against the Chinese. In 1870, the state had collected $5 million in taxes from the Chinese alone, an amount that equaled a quarter to half of California's entire revenue.[9] In 1854, Chinese were officially granted unequal status along with other racial minorities when the California Supreme Court ruled that Chinese immigrants, African Americans, and Native Americans, were prohibited from giving testimony in cases involving a white person. In support of its decision, the court argued that Chinese immigrants were a "distinct people . . . whom nature has marked as inferior."[10] In 1855, California governor John Bigler set in motion the first attempt by Californians to prohibit Asian immigration by signing a bill that taxed any master or owner of a ship found to have brought Asian immigrants to the state. Although the law was invalidated by the state Supreme Court on the grounds that only the federal government had the power to legislate immigration, it foreshadowed later laws that would be successful at the national level.[11]

12. "A Statue for Our Harbor." By George Frederick Keller, *The Wasp*, November 11, 1881.

13. The massacre of the Chinese at Rock Springs, Wyoming, drawn by T. de Thulstrup, *Harper's Weekly*, September 26, 1885.

Anti-Chinese sentiment also turned violent. Beginning in the 1850s and continuing to the end of the nineteenth century, Chinese were systematically harassed, rounded up, and driven out of cities and towns across the West. During the winter of 1858–1859, a veritable race war began in the goldfields as armed mobs forced Chinese out of various campsites and towns. In 1853, 3,000 Chinese had been working and mining in California's Shasta County. At the end of the decade, only 160 remained.[12]

By the 1870s, vigilante anti-Chinese violence was common throughout the West in cities big and small. On October 24, 1871, seventeen Chinese were lynched in Los Angeles after a policeman was shot by a Chinese suspect. A mob of nearly 500, which represented nearly a tenth of the population of Los Angeles at the time, went on the attack and dragged Chinese out of their homes while others hastily built gallows downtown to hang the victims. Police did little as a broad cross section of Angelenos, including women and children, assisted the mob in what would become the largest mass lynching in U.S. history.[13]

During the 1880s, the violence increased. In February 1885, the entire Chinese population of Eureka, California—300 in total—was rounded up within forty-eight hours after a city councilman was accidentally killed in the crossfire between two Chinese rivals. On September 2, 1885, twenty-eight Chinese miners were killed and another fifteen were wounded in Rock Springs, Wyoming, before the rest of the Chinese population in the town—numbering in the hundreds—were driven out into the desert. On November 3, 1885, a mob of 500 armed men descended upon the two Chinese neighborhoods in Tacoma, Washington, and forced all 800 to 900 Chinese residents out of the city. Some were dragged from their homes and were forced to watch as their businesses were pillaged and their belongings thrown into the street. By the afternoon, Chinese residents were marched out of town in the heavy rain to the Lake View Junction railroad stop, part of the Northern Pacific Railroad that Chinese laborers—possibly some who had just been forced out of Tacoma—had built. Others walked, some as far as 100 miles, to Portland, Oregon, or British Columbia—anywhere but Tacoma. Three days later, Seattle also demanded that all Chinese leave town.[14]

Opposition to Chinese immigration also began to show up in federal laws. Beginning in the 1860s, the U.S. government passed a series of laws restricting Chinese immigration. The 1862 Coolie Trade Act outlawed coolie labor and U.S. involvement in the coolie trade. The 1875 Page Act banned Asian women suspected of prostitution as well as Asian laborers brought to the United States involuntarily. Finally, the Chinese Exclusion Act became law on May 6, 1882. The new law barred the entry of Chinese laborers for a period of ten years, allowed entry only to certain exempt classes of Chinese (students, teachers, travelers, merchants, and diplomats), and prohibited all Chinese from obtaining naturalized citizenship. The message was clear: Chinese could come for business, travel, or study, but not to settle. In 1888, a second law, known as the Scott Act, imposed further restrictions. Laborers who had returned to China were forbidden to reenter the United States unless they had wives, children, parents, or property or debts in excess of $1,000 there. The act also nullified 20,000 return certificates that had already been granted to Chinese laborers in the country. In 1892, the exclusion laws were extended for another ten years under the Geary Act. Beginning the next year, all Chinese in the United States were required to register with the federal government to obtain certificates of residence (precursors to today's Green Cards) that proved their legal right to be in the

United States. The Chinese Exclusion Act was renewed again in 1902 and made permanent in 1904.[15]

The Chinese in the United States referred to the Chinese exclusion laws as a "hundred kinds of oppressive laws."[16] They affected every aspect of Chinese immigration to the United States. They determined who would be able to immigrate and cast a shadow on Chinese immigrant lives in the United States. They also inspired the Chinese in America to protest. The fact that Chinese immigrants had been singled out for discriminatory treatment was clear. "Why do they not legislate against Swedes, Germans, Italians, Turks and others?" Yung Hen, a Chinese poultry dealer in San Francisco asked a newspaper in 1892. "There are no strings on those people. . . . For some reason, you people persist in pestering the Chinamen."[17] They engaged in fierce battles to challenge the legality of the laws and the ways they were enforced. When the constitutionality of Chinese exclusion was upheld, Chinese immigrants and their organizations turned their attention to opening up additional immigration categories within the confines of the exclusion laws. They hired lawyers and used the courts to affirm the rights of merchant families, returning laborers, and U.S. citizens of Chinese descent and their families to enter and reenter the country.[18]

From 1882 to 1943, some 300,000 Chinese were admitted into the United States as returning residents and citizens, exempt-class merchants, family members, and others. Many Chinese hired immigration lawyers or brokers to assist with their cases and prepare paperwork. Others learned to evade or circumvent the exclusion laws. As immigrant Ted Chan explained, "We didn't want to come in illegally, but we were forced to because of the immigration laws. They particularly picked on the Chinese. If we told the truth, it didn't work. So we had to take the crooked path."[19]

The most common strategy that immigrants used was to falsely claim membership in one of the classes exempt from the exclusion laws, such as merchants or native-born citizens of the United States. A multinational business in false papers and relationships, or "paper sons," aided their efforts, and an estimated 90 to 95 percent of Chinese immigrants entered the United States with false papers during this time. The first to be restricted, Chinese became the first "illegal immigrants."[20]

Nearly 100,000 Chinese entered the United States through San Francisco from 1910 to 1940. About half were admitted directly from their ships and another half were detained at the Angel Island Immigration Station.[21] While popularly called the "Ellis Island of the West," the immigration station on Angel Island was in fact very different from its counterpart in New York. Ellis Island enforced U.S. immigration laws that restricted, but did not exclude, European immigrants. Angel Island, on the other hand, was the chief port of entry for Chinese and other immigrants from Asia, and as such, enforced immigration policies that singled out Asians for exclusion.

14. The Angel Island Immigration Station, San Francisco, California, c. 1910.

Chinese were first subjected to a primary inspection on board the steamship. After receiving identification numbers, new arrivals were sent to the hospital for a medical examination. The medical staff examined Chinese bodies for physical defects and even measured body parts to determine age. They looked for evidence of the parasitic "Oriental diseases" such as uncinariasis (hookworm), filiariasis (round worm), and clonorchiasis (liver fluke), which were all grounds for exclusion if untreated after arrival. Chinese immigrants found these examinations extremely humiliating. They were unaccustomed to being naked in front of strangers, let alone forced to provide stool samples on demand so that the hospital staff could test for disease. "When the doctor came, I had to take off all my clothes. It was so embarrassing and shameful," Lee Puey You explained about her medical examination in 1939. She was detained for twenty months before being sent back to China. She later told interviewers that she cried a "bowlful of tears" on Angel Island.[22]

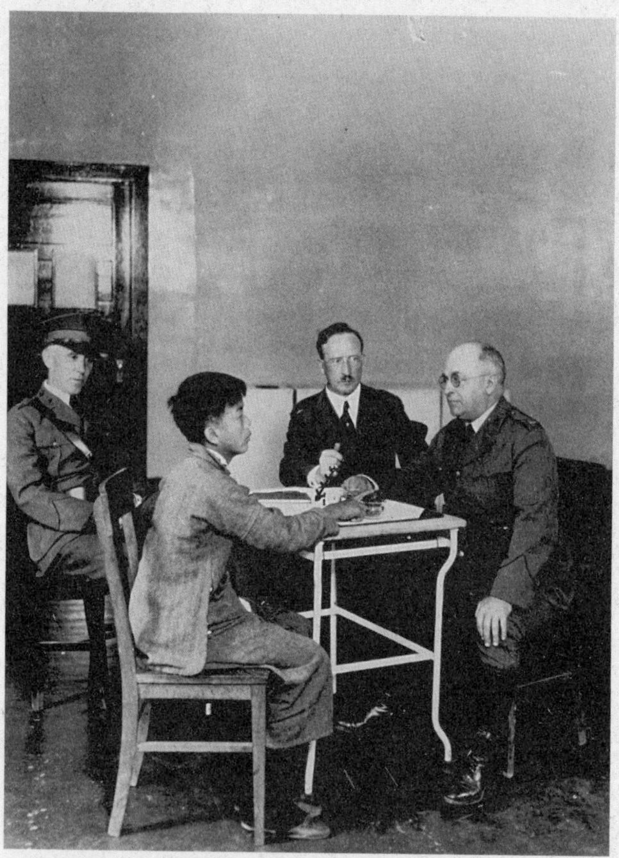

15. Interrogation at the Angel Island Immigration Station, 1923.

Chinese immigrants next had to make their case for admission into the country before immigration officials. Chinese merchants, for example, were required to provide detailed documentation of their business activities, the volume of merchandise, and lists of all business partners. Returning merchants also had to have "two credible witnesses, other than Chinese" to testify on behalf of the applicant's status and state of business. Wives and children of merchants and citizens had to confirm that their husband or father still qualified as a person exempt from the exclusion laws. They also had to prove that their relationship was genuine.

Because of the popularity of the paper son system, Angel Island officials particularly scrutinized cases involving families. As a routine part of the interrogations, family members were questioned about a wealth of minute details concerning their family history, relationships, and everyday life in the home villages—what immigration officials believed should be common knowledge to all parties: What are the marriage and birth dates of your family members? When did you last see your father? How many steps lead up to your house? How many windows are in your house? How many clocks are in your house? How many rows of houses in your village? Who lives in the third house, fourth row? In some cases, applicants were required to draw extensive maps of their villages, complete with the locations of major buildings and all houses. Sometimes wives were required to recall minute facts about their husband's extended family and native village or share intimate details about their marital relationship with the immigration officials. If any major discrepancies were discovered in the testimonies, immigration inspectors concluded that the claimed relationship did not in fact exist, and the entire case was discredited.

These interrogations were terrifying. They typically lasted two or three days, but it could take much longer if witnesses had to travel to the island to testify or if applicants had to be recalled and interrogated again. Applicants were often asked two hundred questions.[23] Some were asked up to a thousand questions. Immigrants worried about forgetting minor details or having to answer difficult or impossible questions. Law Shee Low, who was detained on Angel Island in 1922, recalled the anxiety and despair in the women's barracks over the interrogation: "One woman was questioned all day and then deported. She told me they asked her about life in China: the chickens and the neighbors, and the direction the house faced. How would I know all that? I was scared."[24]

Because of these harsh interrogation methods, Chinese immigrants had one of the highest rejection rates at the Angel Island Immigration Station. Of the 95, 687 Chinese who applied for admission into the United States through Angel Island from 1910 to 1940, 9 percent were rejected. The vast majority appealed their decision through attorneys, and in the end, 5 percent of Chinese applicants were ultimately returned to China.[25] Chinese also made up the overwhelming majority (70 percent) of the detainee population at the immigration station. Between two hundred and three hundred men and thirty to fifty women were detained in the Angel Island barracks at any given time. Their average stay was for two weeks, the longest of all the immigrant groups. Kong Din Quong, who arrived in San Francisco in 1938, spent the longest recorded time in detention: 756 days. His grandfather was a native of the United States. His father, though born in China, also held U.S. native status, but Kong was born before his father had resided in the country. His admission into the United States was denied on the grounds that a father cannot transfer citizenship rights to his children until he becomes a U.S. resident. Kong appealed his case, but he was eventually deported after spending twenty-five months detained on Angel Island.[26]

Chinese immigrants bitterly resented their long detentions on Angel Island. They watched other immigrants from Japan, Russia, and South Asia come and go while they remained imprisoned. The barracks were crowded and sparsely furnished. They were guarded at all times and were not allowed visitors. Some wallowed in feelings of helplessness and despair. Others petitioned the Chinese Six Companies in San Francisco or the Chinese consul general for help. Chinese men formed a Self-governing Association to provide assistance to the detainees. Many Chinese men expressed their frustration, anger, resentment, loneliness, and despair by writing poems on the walls. More than 200 poems from the Angel Island barracks have been recorded.[27] Written anonymously, they are found in almost every corner of the men's detention barracks of the immigration station (now preserved as a National Historic Landmark) and serve as powerful reminders of the costs and hardships of immigration under such a discriminatory regime. One reads:

There are tens of thousands of poems composed on these walls.
They are all cries of complaint and sadness

The day I am rid of this prison and attain success,
I must remember that this chapter once existed.[28]

While Ellis Island has come to represent the United States' welcome to (European) immigrants and a celebration of America's immigrant heritage, Angel Island symbolized America's clear rejection of Asian and other immigrants. Through Angel Island, the United States became a gatekeeping nation designed to restrict immigration, monitor immigrants already in the country, and deport those considered dangerous or undesirable. For their part, Chinese immigrants never forgot their time on Angel Island or the shadow of exclusion they lived under for decades. For them, Angel Island became a place that symbolized broken dreams, or hard-won dreams at best.[29]

The Angel Island Immigration Station was not the only site of Chinese exclusion in the country. The Chinese exclusion era coincided with the birth of the U.S. as an empire. As the United States advanced across the Pacific, colonizing Hawai'i and the Philippines in 1898, the restriction of Chinese immigrants became a central aspect of U.S. imperialism in these new territories, a reflection of both local conditions and new American power in the Pacific.

The U.S. presence in Hawai'i began soon after British explorer James Cook discovered the islands in 1778. European and American settlers, missionaries, and traders flocked to the islands, and foreign advisors and weapons helped Kamehameha I unite the separate island governments into the Kingdom of Hawai'i in 1810. By 1875, the United States was the dominant foreign power in the kingdom. American plantation owners were soon acquiring large tracts of land, wresting political power from the Hawaiian monarchy, and expanding the sugar plantation economy with the help of Chinese and other Asian immigrant laborers.

Many planters viewed Chinese immigration as an economic necessity that made possible the huge and profitable production of sugar and the future economic success of the islands. At the same time, they recognized that Chinese immigration posed great challenges. American missionaries, journalists, and others were quick to identify Chinese immigration as an immense social threat. The almost exclusively male character of the immigrant population and the resulting interracial mixing between Chinese and Native Hawaiians was a primary source of concern. The alleged threat Chinese immigrants posed to public health was also an issue.[30] Others complained of the "grasping tendencies of the Mongolian," referring to the movement of Chinese from the plantation economy into small business and economic competition with whites.[31] Commentators agreed that the Chinese were simply "not good citizens from principle."[32]

Meanwhile, many Native Hawaiians viewed the Chinese as another group of settlers who contributed to their displacement and dispossession. Native Hawaiians first suffered terribly from the diseases brought by the foreigners. The Hawaiian censuses recorded an alarming decline in the native population. In 1853, there were 71,109 Native Hawaiians recorded in the islands. In 1890, that number had dropped to 40,622.[33] During this period, Native Hawaiian land ownership and political power was also diminishing as foreign settlers gained influence and control in the islands.

By the end of the nineteenth century, Chinese immigration had become a central issue affecting the internal affairs of the kingdom. And as the Hawaiian Islands grew more closely involved with the United States economically, politically, and socially, the debate over Chinese immigration in Hawai'i became entangled with a larger transpacific discussion as well. Portrayals of Chinese as unassimilable, disease-ridden, cheap workers in Hawai'i traveled over from the continental U.S. with the arrival of new white settlers and visitors, Hawaiians returning from the states, and newspaper reports from both sides of the Pacific.

Transplanted missionaries from the United States were an especially dominant force in shaping public opinion about Chinese immigration in Hawai'i. Henry Whitney, son of missionaries and the editor of *The Pacific Commercial Advertiser* newspaper, organized the first meetings against Chinese immigration in 1869. Mormon missionary Walter Murray Gibson succeeded Whitney in both the editorship of the *Advertiser* and the leadership of the anti-Chinese campaign in the 1880s. Under Whitney and Gibson, the *Advertiser*, an influential English-language newspaper with a primarily white readership, explicitly connected the growing population of Chinese in the Hawaiian Islands to the "Chinese problem" in the continental U.S.

and elsewhere. "The Chinese generally are not desirable acquisitions to any country to which they emigrate," the *Advertiser* declared.[34]

By 1882, when the U.S. Congress passed the Chinese Exclusion Act, the anti-Chinese movement in Hawai'i had also fully matured. The establishment of the anti-Chinese Workingman's Union in Hawai'i in 1883 was likely modeled after the anti-Chinese Workingmen's Party organized in California in 1877. In 1881, King David Kalakaua and his cabinet (including the anti-Chinese leader Walter Gibson) sought to model the kingdom's immigration agreement with China after a recently negotiated treaty between China and the United States. By 1892, Chinese immigration was virtually prohibited, and Chinese were barred from engaging in any nonagricultural work to prevent them from competing with Hawaiians and whites in business enterprises. At the same time, Chinese and other Asians were explicitly disenfranchised. The 1887 Bayonet Constitution forced upon King Kalakaua by the planter elite granted the privilege of voting only to male residents of Hawaiian, American, or European birth.[35]

On January 14, 1893, white business leaders forced the abdication of Queen Lili'uokalani, formed the provisional Republic of Hawai'i, and asked that Hawai'i be annexed to the United States. Annexation was fiercely debated, but both the pro- and anti-annexation forces also fixed their arguments on Asian immigrants, who in 1890 constituted 32 percent of the total Hawaiian population.[36] Former U.S. minister to Hawai'i John Stevens argued that the "American and Christian Caucasian people" needed to acquire the Hawaiian lands as soon as possible to prevent the islands "from being submerged and overrun by Asiatics."[37] When Hawai'i was formally annexed to the United States on July 7, 1898, Chinese exclusion was automatically extended to the islands. The final treaty also prohibited the emigration of Chinese residents in Hawai'i to any part of the continental U.S., a concession to labor organizations in the United States.[38]

Hawai'i was not the only new U.S. possession in 1898. Military campaigns in Cuba, Puerto Rico, and the Philippines brought all of these territories under U.S. control. And the newly colonized peoples, including Chinese immigrants in these lands, became subject to U.S. policies. In the Philippines, U.S. military and diplomatic officials promoted Chinese exclusion as an integral part of U.S. colonization of the islands, one that focused on the "benevolent assimilation" of the Philippines. U.S. politicians argued, for example, that Filipinos lacked the capacity to compete with Chinese. The latter's exclusion from the Philippines was therefore a policy that would benefit the Filipinos and assist them in their development under American protection. With the support of organized labor in the United States, Chinese exclusion became established policy in the Philippines in 1902.[39]

In Cuba, restrictive anti-Chinese immigration legislation, similar to the U.S. Chinese exclusion laws, was imposed during the U.S. occupation from 1899 to 1902 and again from 1906 to 1909. On May 15, 1902, Military Governor Leonard Wood issued Order No. 155 banning Chinese laborers from entering Cuba. Diplomats, merchants, students, and Chinese workers who had resided in Cuba since 1899 were exempt. After independence in 1902, Order No. 155 was confirmed by Presidential Decree No. 237.[40] The ban on Chinese laborers remained in force until the need for laborers made necessary the liberalization of some of the old restrictions. The exclusion laws were suspended for five years from 1917 to 1921 to respond to wartime labor shortages, but after 1921, the law was enforced again, and in 1926 new prohibitions were enacted that refused admission to all Chinese except for consular officials.[41]

In all three cases, the United States also took the unusual step of prohibiting the free movement of certain peoples *within* the empire, as Chinese immigrants already in Hawai'i, Cuba, and the Philippines were prohibited from entering the continental United States. In this way, the Chinese exclusion laws became a central aspect of U.S. imperialism.

Outside the United States and its territories, debates over Chinese immigration also resulted in similar actions and policies, often influenced by what was happening in the United States. In Canada, for example, Chinese were just a fraction of the more than 3.5 million immigrants who entered the country from 1885 to 1914 (in 1901, there were 17,312 Chinese in Canada), but as in the United States, they were greeted with racial animosity disproportionate to their numbers. Calls to keep British Columbia a "white man's province" and to rally around a "white Canada forever" fueled the movement to restrict Chinese, and later, Japanese and South Asian immigration.[42] U.S. actions and perspectives were instrumental in shaping the anti-Chinese movement in British Columbia. Anti-Asian organizations, modeled after ones in the United States, adopted slogans like "The Chinese Must Go!" and called for the exclusion of all Asian immigrants.[43]

Beginning in the 1870s and 1880s, the Canadian government considered solutions to the Chinese "problem" and strategically studied U.S. methods and tactics. Due to British relations with China, an all-out exclusion of Chinese immigrants was not feasible for Canada. Thus, instead of the United States' explicit policy of exclusion, Canadian commissioners suggested a head tax policy that would permit entry to every Chinese, provided that he or she paid the landing fee. The federal government waited until construction of the Canadian Pacific Railway was mostly completed (with Chinese labor) and then yielded to the demands of British Columbians to restrict Chinese immigration in 1885 by imposing a $50 head tax on laborers. In 1900, Canada raised its head tax to $100. Three years later, the tax was raised again to $500.[44]

For some years, the Chinese head taxes were effective. But one unintended consequence was that the lower immigration rates turned Chinese laborers into a scarce and increasingly valuable commodity in British Columbia. Chinese immigrant wages doubled and, in some cases, tripled. By 1908–1909, the $500 head tax was no longer useful as a deterrent to Chinese immigration, although it proved to be an effective source of revenue for the Canadian government. From 1885 to 1923, Chinese immigrants paid $22.5 million to the Canadian government for the privilege of entering and leaving the country.[45] No other group was required to pay these taxes.

In 1923, Canada transformed its regulation of Chinese immigration altogether. Closely modeled on U.S. Chinese exclusion laws, the 1923 Exclusion Act abolished the head tax system and instead prohibited all people of Chinese origin or descent from entering the country. Consular officials, children born in Canada, merchants, and students were the only exemptions. The act also required every person of Chinese origin in Canada, regardless of citizenship, to register with the Canadian government and obtain a certification of registration as in the United States. For the Chinese in Canada, the act was a major setback. July 1, 1923, the day that the law was passed, became known by Chinese Canadians as "Humiliation Day."[46]

NUMBER 88103

NEW C.I. 5 SERIES

DOMINION OF CANADA

IMMIGRATION BRANCH — DEPARTMENT OF THE INTERIOR

RECEIVED FROM

Jung Bak Hun whose photograph is attached hereto, on the date and at the place hereunder mentioned, the sum of Five Hundred Dollars being the head tax due under the provisions of the Chinese Immigration Act. The above mentioned party who claims to be a native of in the District of of the age of 11 years arrived or landed at Vancouver on the 3rd day of January

Dated at Vancouver on 3rd January 1919

CONTROLLER OF CHINESE IMMIGRATION.

16. Canadian Chinese Immigration Certificate #88103: Jung Bak Hun, January 3, 1919.

As the U.S. and Canada cracked down on Chinese immigration, Chinese immigrants headed to Mexico. By 1910 Chinese lived and worked in almost every state and territory in the country. They made up the second largest number of foreigners (around 24,000) residing in Mexico in 1926.[47] The rise of the *antichinistas* (anti-Chinese activists) followed.

By the early twentieth century, Mexican newspapers were describing the Chinese as "savages," "uncivilized," and "lazy." Chinese immigration itself was described in catastrophic terms: "*onda amarilla*," "*peste amarilla*," "*invasión mongólica*" ("yellow wave," the "yellow plague," the "Mongol invasion").[48] An organized anti-Chinese movement developed in the northern state of Sonora, where *antichinistas* focused on the unfair economic competition that Chinese immigrants allegedly posed to Mexicans. Although the Chinese population was never large, they dominated local commerce in groceries, dry goods, and general merchandise in border towns such as Nogales and Agua Prieta, where American companies were busy establishing mines and building railroads. Sonorans, who already felt disadvantaged by the large presence of U.S. capital in the region, greatly resented the Chinese-owned businesses.[49] The *chino* was "impossible to compete with," charged anti-Chinese leader José Angel Espinoza.[50]

Antichinista attacks on interracial marriages between Chinese men and Mexican women added another layer to the anti-Chinese rhetoric. Chinese men were described as lecherous, Mexican women who married Chinese men were labeled traitors to their race, and Chinese Mexican children were denigrated as "freaks of nature." Race, economics, masculinity, and sexual power were all bound together in these attacks.[51]

Anti-Chinese sentiment especially flourished after the Mexican Revolution of 1911 tried to destroy all aspects of President Porfirio Díaz's reign, including its support of U.S. trade and its policies that encouraged Chinese immigration. Intense xenophobia based on a revolutionary *indigenista* nationalism resulted.[52] Anti-Chinese leader José María Arana's fiery speeches, for example, pitted the "evils and vices of the Chinese" against the progress and national regeneration of the Mexican nation.[53] José Angel Espinoza similarly identified the campaign against the Chinese as a movement "*por la patria y por la raza*" (for the fatherland and for the race). To drive the Chinese out of Mexico was "the moral duty of all true Mexican nationalists," he proclaimed.[54] The cover of Espinoza's 1932 book, *El Ejemplo de Sonora* (*The Example of Sonora*), boldly illustrated this message: a Mexican politician kicks a Chinese immigrant—greedily holding on to a bag of gold and a brick of opium—out of Sonora while holding a newly passed anti-Chinese law in his hand. A worker stands behind him to make sure that the will of the people is carried out while the sun looks on approvingly and heralds the victory.

Although leaders called for immigration restriction laws to limit or stop Chinese immigration to Mexico, violence was the most common response. There was an anti-Chinese riot in Mazatlán in 1886, and several unprovoked attacks on Chinese occurred in Mexico City that same year. Then came the massacre of Chinese in Torreón on May 5, 1911. The "two-day orgy of unbelievable brutality" resulted in the deaths of 303 Chinese (out of an estimated 600 to 700) and $850,000 worth of property damage to Chinese businesses and homes.[55]

17. The cover of *El Ejemplo de Sonora* by José Angel Espinoza, 1932.

In the heart of the anti-Chinese movement in the state of Sonora, citizens turned to local laws and regulations that restricted where Chinese could live, how they conducted their businesses, and who they could love. In 1922, for example, the Sonoran legislature passed a law (similar to the U.S.'s Geary Act) requiring the registration and identification of all Chinese in the state. The next year, another law mandated the segregation of Chinese through the creation of residential ethnic barrios and prohibited interracial marriages between Mexican females and all Chinese males, including those who were naturalized Mexican citizens. In 1931, the legislature went after

Chinese businesses by requiring that 80 percent of all employees in foreign-owned businesses be Mexican.[56]

The federal government soon acted. In 1908, a new immigration law, inspired by U.S. policies, was passed to regulate immigration and to create the Mexican Immigration Service.[57] In 1927, the treaty between Mexico and China was canceled, and in July of that year, another race-based immigration law was passed, restricting the immigration of blacks, British Indians, Syrians, Lebanese, Armenians, Palestinians, Arabs, Turks, and Chinese.[58]

By the 1930s, the so-called Chinese problem throughout North and South America had largely been resolved. In addition to the restrictions put in place in the United States, Canada, and Mexico, most countries in Latin America had restricted Chinese immigration in one way or another, varying from total exclusion to various regulations that limited the number of Chinese immigrants allowed in each year.[59] The campaign to restrict Chinese immigration begun in the United States ended up having far-reaching consequences for the regulation of immigration around the world. By the early twentieth century, a "restrictive international migration regime" was in place. Comprehensive immigration reform would not occur in the United States until 1965.[60] The Chinese in America would live with the consequences of the exclusion laws for generations. And as other Asian immigrants followed in their footsteps, so did new anti-Asian laws that separated them from the rest of America as well.

5

Japanese Immigrants and the "Yellow Peril"

In 1893, Inota Tawa pleaded with his parents to let him leave their village and seek his fortune in the United States. He had heard fantastic stories of how a simple day laborer like him could earn up to $2 a day, or almost a thousand yen in one year. This was as much as what a governor in Japan earned. "By all means," he begged his parents, "let me go to America."[1] Tawa's parents reluctantly gave in. Tawa sailed for the United States and landed in Portland, Oregon. He was one of 380,000 Japanese to immigrate to Hawai'i and the continental U.S. between 1885 and 1924.[2]

Japanese immigrants, or issei, were the second largest group of Asian immigrants to come to the United States during the late nineteenth and early twentieth centuries. They left Japan as part of a mass movement of Japanese around the world, and overlapped with the Chinese who remained in the United States as well as the new Chinese immigrants who continued to come during the exclusion era.

Like other Asian immigrants in the United States, most of the early Japanese immigrants were young, male *dekasegi* (sojourners) who intended to return to their homeland. Over time, however, they settled down, called for their families to join them, and built strong ethnic communities. They tried to become American while also maintaining strong connections to Japan.

But as anti-Japanese movements gained momentum and Japanese were subjected to violent riots and discriminatory laws that kept them outsiders in America, issei and their children struggled to survive.

As early as the early sixteenth century, small numbers of Japanese began emigrating to other countries. But in 1639, the shogunate instituted a policy of isolation in an attempt to protect Japan from European colonialism spreading throughout Asia. It traded only with China and the Netherlands and issued a ban on Japanese emigration that would remain in place until 1858. By the mid-nineteenth century, the United States, seeking to expand its influence in the Pacific, had grown impatient with Japan's refusal to trade. In 1853, it sent four navy ships armed with guns to Edo (Tokyo) Bay under the command of Commodore Matthew C. Perry. Under orders from President Millard Fillmore, the commodore threatened to use force unless the Japanese government opened its ports. Japan acquiesced. Thereafter, it allowed foreign traders into the country and lifted its ban on emigration.

American traders and labor recruiters quickly established themselves in Japan and flooded the countryside with agents charged with recruiting laborers to Hawai'i's sugar plantations. They described the islands in glowing terms, and "Hawai'i Netsu," or emigration fever, swept through villages.[3] By the 1880s, the Japanese government also took an active role in emigration abroad. In fact, immigration became a central feature of its larger project of imperial expansionism in Asia. Influenced by the West, Japan sought to compete with European empires in the scramble for new territories and export markets. Sending Japanese to newly acquired territories like Hokkaido, Okinawa, and Korea served state interests and made it easier to bring the new lands and peoples under Japanese control.[4]

There were other benefits to Japanese emigration as well. By sending its people abroad, the Japanese government hoped to alleviate a population explosion at home. It was also believed that poor farmers and "low-class citizens" threatened Japan's national progress by being a drain on the economy. Once they were sent abroad, they might prosper and send money home to their families, thereby contributing to the country. Japanese emigrants could also serve as national emissaries to lay the foundation for international trade.[5]

The first private Japanese emigration company was established in 1891, and soon other companies were competing to send Japanese laborers to the Hawaiian Islands, the United States, Australia, Fiji, the Philippines, Mexico, Peru, and Canada. Both emigration companies and labor recruiters targeted young men who could withstand hard labor. Most were from farming families who struggled to make ends meet as the Meiji government imposed higher and higher taxes to fund its modernization and industrialization programs (known as the Meiji Restoration) from 1868 to 1912. These programs were designed to protect Japan from encroaching European and American dominance in Asia, but the high taxes hit Japanese farmers, especially those in the southwestern agricultural prefectures of Hiroshima, Yamaguchi, Kumamoto, and Fukuoka, particularly hard. Farmers were required to pay fixed taxes every year regardless of the success of their crops or the market prices for their products. And during the 1880s, government economic policies depressed the price of rice and increased the financial burden on small farm owners even more. Three hundred thousand farmers were forced to sell their land when they could no longer pay the taxes. They joined a growing population of landless peasants. Even those who successfully held on to their farms struggled with plots that were often too small to support their families. A growing number of Japanese men chose emigration abroad instead of compulsory military service, and inflation, sharp increases in the price of rice, and a devastating earthquake in 1923 contributed to the ongoing interest in immigrating abroad. Okinawans, a minority group whose islands had been annexed by Japan in 1897, and whose homeland was and still is Japan's poorest prefecture, made up another large group going to the United States. Between 1926 and 1941, 15 percent of all people leaving the country were from Okinawa, and at least one third of the Japanese population in Latin America came from the prefecture.[6]

On January 20, 1885, the first group of Japanese immigrants boarded the *City of Tokyo* at Yokohama and headed to Honolulu. They included 666 men, 158 women, 69 boys, and 48 girls. Between 1885 and 1924, 200,000 Japanese went to Hawai'i and 180,000 more went to the continental U.S.[7] Emigration was not cheap. Initial expenses for the journey could total $100. But word spread back across the Pacific Ocean that a common plantation laborer in Hawai'i could earn four to six times more there than in Hiroshima.[8] Japanese used a saying, *kokyo ni nishiki o kazaru* ("return home in golden brocades"), to express their wishes. In the states, the wages were even higher. In 1902, Japanese plantation laborers at the top of the pay scale in Hawai'i earned $16 a month while their counterparts working as railroad section hands in the continental United States might earn close to double that.[9] Labor contractors and emigration companies kept feeding the emigration fever, and Japanese could talk only of going to *Amerika*, which collectively referred to Hawai'i, the United States, and Canada.[10] One poet captured the feelings of many issei dreams:

Huge dreams of fortune
Go with me to foreign lands
Across the ocean.[11]

Families mortgaged their properties and borrowed money from moneylenders to buy passage on a transpacific ship. The first Japanese immigrants, predominantly young men, intended to return home. Many of them were second and later sons who had no prospects of inheriting the family farm due to Japanese traditions that granted land only to first sons. Expecting their fathers and husbands and sons to return, few women immigrated to the United States until the early twentieth century. But a small number of female prostitutes, often tricked by Japanese men, were part of early Japanese immigrant society.

By the early twentieth century, Japanese immigrants had established a measure of economic security in the United States and Hawai'i. At the same time, future immigration of Japanese laborers was prohibited by the 1908 Gentlemen's Agreement between the United States and Japan. Many Japanese men already in the United States focused on settling down. They engaged in *yobiyose*, or the "called immigrant" system, and asked relatives and matchmakers back home to introduce them to suitable wives. They went to photography studios, put on their best clothes, and sent home photographs. Sometimes, reality did not match the images of youth, wealth, and good looks that they wanted to convey. So they did what many singles looking for love have done: they sent photographs of themselves in their younger days or paid extra to have receding hairlines and blemishes touched up. These photographs were sometimes accompanied by exaggerated reports about their status and wealth in the United States.[12]

Many Japanese women answered the call to come to the United States. Some were eager to embark on an adventure abroad. Others reluctantly followed their parents' wishes to agree to a match. When Ai Miyasaki decided that she was willing to go abroad, the news spread throughout her town. "From here and there requests for marriage came pouring in like rain!"[13] From 1908 to 1920, 20,000 Japanese "picture brides" traveled to Hawai'i and to the continental U.S. to join the men to whom they were promised.[14]

Shizu Hayakawa was one of these women. She left her home in Fukuoka in March of 1919 to marry Shuneki Hayakawa in the United States. They had never met. Her family ran a dairy, but was poor. Hayakawa, a window washer, was believed to be a good prospect. Obeying her parents, Shizu sailed on the *Korea Maru* bound for San Francisco. During the month-long journey, she met many other young brides, and the women spent hours talking to each other about their future husbands and lives in America. They were strikingly similar: daughters of farmers between the ages of eighteen and twenty-three destined to husbands who were ten to fifteen years older and who worked as farmers, wage laborers, or ran small businesses in the U.S. West.

Many picture brides entered the United States through the Angel Island Immigration Station in San Francisco. With the backing of their powerful homeland and government-issued passports, most Japanese immigrants were generally admitted into the country within a day or two. Unlike Chinese immigrants, less than one percent were excluded or deported. Thus, when Japanese picture brides arrived in San Francisco, they were more likely to be worried about what their husbands were going to be like rather than whether they would be admitted into the country or not. As their ship slowly made its way into San Francisco Bay, the women crowded onto the steamship decks. Clutching photographs in their hands, they scanned the large numbers of Japanese men waiting on the docks. Their husbands, too, grasped photographs of their wives and anxiously sought out a matching face on deck. Some women collapsed in shock when they realized that the photograph of the handsome, young, and well-dressed man did not at all resemble the older, wrinkled, and pockmarked farmer who appeared before them. Their dashed expectations and the reality of their harsh lives in the United States often led to lifelong disappointment and difficult, if not failed, marriages. A few disillusioned brides even asked to return to Japan on the next ship. Others left their husbands, and notices of these desertions often appeared in the Japanese language press.[15] Shizu Hayakawa, however, was not disappointed. Shuneki had brought some sushi to the dock, and she was pleased with his thoughtfulness.[16]

18. Picture brides arriving on Angel Island, c. 1910.

Once in Hawai'i and the United States, Japanese laborers faced lives of hard, endless work. In Hawai'i, the Japanese joined a pool of 300,000 Chinese, Japanese, Korean, and Filipino laborers on the islands, and together they helped to transform the sugar industry in the U.S. colony.[17] The loud scream of the 5:00 a.m. siren roused the tired workers out of bed. "Awake! Stir your bones! Rouse up! Shrieks the Five O'Clock Whistle," one plantation work song described the harsh morning routines. "Don't dream you can nestle for one more sweet nap. . . . Wake up! Wake up! Wake up! W-a-k-e-u-u-u-up!"[18]

19. Harvesting pineapples on a Hawaiian plantation, c. 1910–1925.

Grouped in work gangs of twenty to thirty, the plantation laborers were marched into the fields or brought there by wagons and trains. The cane fields stood twelve feet high. It was their job to cut and collect the cane stalks and hoe weeds. They also stripped the dry, withered leaves from the stalks. It was hot, dusty, and backbreaking work. "We worked like machines," one Japanese laborer complained.[19] Eight *lunas* (foremen) and a field boss supervised their work constantly. The *luna* carried a whip and rode a horse, another Japanese plantation worker explained. "If we talked too much the [*luna*] swung the whip."[20] Plantation work continued like this until the whistle blasted again at 4:30 p.m. To pass the time, many of them sang plantation songs that captured their frustrations and sustained their spirits during the hard workday. "*Kane wa Kachiken. Washa horehore yo. Ase to namida no. Tomokasegi*," some women sang. (My husband cuts the cane stalks and I trim their leaves. With sweat and tears we both work for our means.)[21]

The work of Japanese women on the plantation never seemed to end. Those who were not in the fields washed laundry, cooked, and sewed clothes. Women who operated boardinghouses prepared three meals a day for twenty to thirty laborers, rising well before the 5:00 a.m. whistle and retiring long after their tenants had come in from the fields.[22]

Chafing under the rigid system of control, hard labor, and physical punishment, Japanese plantation workers used repeated work stoppages in the 1880s and 1890s to protest mistreatment by plantation bosses or to complain about the lack of proper living conditions on the plantations. In the early 1900s, Japanese labor activism sparked a full-fledged revolt, culminating in the Japanese strike of 1909, one of the most massive and sustained strikes in the history of Hawai'i. Strikers demanded higher wages, equal pay for equal work, and an end to the racially discriminatory wage system that paid Japanese laborers less than laborers of other nationalities. On the evening of May 9, 1909, several hundred Japanese laborers gathered at the Aiea Plantation on Oahu to organize. By morning time, they were on strike. Over the next few weeks, the strike spread from plantation to plantation. At its height, 7,000 Japanese participated in the "Great Strike of 1909." Planters responded by evicting the strikebreakers and their families from the plantation. By the end of June, more than 5,000 strikers and their families were homeless and straggled into Honolulu. The evictions forced many strikebreakers back to the plantations, but the organized resistance of Japanese plantation laborers also forced the Hawaiian Sugar Planters' Association to raise the wages of Japanese laborers and end the discriminatory wage scale. In 1920, Japanese plantation laborers in Hawai'i joined with Filipinos to continue to push for better working conditions and higher pay. The 1920 strike was the first significant interethnic strike in the islands. But by then, most Japanese were leaving the plantations and the islands altogether to pursue other economic opportunities.[23]

From 1891 to 1900, 27,440 Japanese, mostly male laborers, were admitted into the United States. Over the next seven years, 52,457 more were admitted, and another 38,000 came from Hawai'i until President Theodore Roosevelt signed an executive order in 1907 banning aliens from entering the continental United States via its territories, like Hawai'i. In the United States, Japanese filled the jobs that Chinese immigrants once had. Labor contractors sent them to railroads, mines, lumber mills, fish canneries, farms, and orchards throughout the Pacific Coast states. In the cities, Japanese worked as domestic servants. In 1909, 40,000 Japanese worked in agriculture, 10,000 on the railroads, and 4,000 in canneries.[24]

Workdays started early and ended late. In the fields of central and southern California, the temperature could soar to 120 degrees. Railroad workers, on the other hand, suffered bitter cold in the mountain states where the temperature could get as low as 20 degrees below zero. In Alaska, Japanese cannery workers processed huge catches of salmon as conveyer belts sped as many as 200 fish per minute their way. The "Alaskan smell" of "rotten fish, salt, sweat, and filth" stayed with them for days.[25]

Japanese women's labor was essential to the survival of their families. They worked alongside their husbands in the fields and shops, or as domestic servants in private homes, and in laundries or other small businesses. Many women cooked for large gangs of male laborers managed by their husbands in addition for their own families. They fit their work around their family responsibilities and continued to perform all of the tasks of homemaking and raising children. Tsuruyo Takami, for example, who helped her husband run the Rainier Laundry in Spokane, Washington, performed laundry tasks and cooked for all of the laundry workers on staff during the day and then ironed and pressed clothes at night, often working until past midnight.[26]

But Japanese did not remain laborers forever. As they began to consider permanent residency in the United States, many turned to agriculture. Issei leader and newspaper publisher Abiko Kyutaro played a key role in urging his fellow Japanese to abandon the *dekasegi* mind-set and commit to staying in the United States. Farming, he suggested, was perfectly suited to the Japanese. Their timing could not have been better. Chinese immigrant laborers had helped to reclaim much of California's Central Valley with their labor on irrigation projects. With a steady water supply, California's fertile land could now be processed for intensive agriculture and fruit and vegetable production. An increased demand for fresh produce in the cities and the development of a distribution system that carried produce across the nation in refrigerator cars helped fuel an agricultural revolution in the state. Japanese contracted, shared, and leased farmland throughout the West. In 1900, there were thirty-seven Japanese farms in the United States with a combined acreage of 4,674 acres. By 1910, Japanese had 1,816 farms with a total acreage of 99,254. On the eve of World War II, they grew 95 percent of California's fresh snap beans and peas, 67 percent of the state's fresh tomatoes, and 44 percent of its onions.[27]

20. Packaging berries, Sumner, Washington, c. 1908.

One of the most successful Japanese farmers was Kinji Ushijima, known as George Shima, the "Potato King." Shima arrived in the United States in 1887 and began working as a potato picker in the San Joaquin Valley. He eventually saved up enough money to lease a small plot of land that soon expanded into a large operation near Stockton. By 1912, Shima had 10,000 acres of potatoes under his control and was transporting half a million dollars' worth of potatoes to San Francisco and the surrounding area on a fleet of a dozen steamboats, barges, tugboats, and launches all emblazoned with the "Shima" name. When the Potato King passed away in 1926, his estate was worth $15 million.[28]

As they began to establish themselves economically, Japanese Americans also formed tight-knit communities. Organizations, businesses, and associations connected Japanese immigrants together across wide distances, fostered support and community, and helped sustain Japanese culture and traditions far away from home. *Kenjinkai* were established to support Japanese who shared roots in the same prefecture (*ken*) in Japan. Japanese language newspapers reported on news from Japan and from other Japanese communities in North and South America. Japanese immigrants formed economic associations to pool resources through a rotating credit system that could be used to purchase or expand businesses. Japanese also formed farming cooperatives to buy supplies and market crops.

When they could, Japanese retreated to *Nihonmachi*, the Japanese sections of big cities like Los Angeles, San Francisco, and Seattle. By 1910, a vibrant ethnic economy of Japanese-owned boardinghouses, restaurants, barbershops, poolrooms, grocery stores, and laundries served Japanese communities in these cities and beyond. San Francisco alone had over 3,000 Japanese-owned businesses.[29] Masajiro Furuya, who arrived in Seattle via Vancouver in 1890, eventually built a business empire that catered to growing Japanese immigrant communities up and down the Pacific Coast and in the West. His Seattle-based department store specialized in Japanese foods and products and had branches in Portland and Tacoma. He also ran a labor supply agency, a post office, and the Japanese Commercial Bank. Furuya became known as one of the most important and prominent Japanese businessmen in Seattle. His salesmen, known as "Furuya men," traveled in their trademark dark blue suits into rural Japanese immigrant communities to take orders. Until it went bankrupt during the Great Depression, the Furuya company filled an important economic and cultural niche in the Japanese immigrant community.[30]

As they opened businesses, started families, and gradually became settled into their new lives in the United States, the issei forged a transnational immigrant identity that was shaped by their experiences of discrimination in the United States as well as by their homeland ties to imperial Japan. They continued to identify and take pride in their homeland, but immigrant leaders also urged their countrymen to assimilate into mainstream American society by wearing only Western-style clothing, following American customs, and celebrating American holidays. Nisei, the American-born children, were sent to American public schools, spoke English, and played baseball.[31]

By 1930, nisei made up 52 percent of the Japanese population in the continental U.S. Ten years later, they were 63 percent of the community. Many felt stuck between two worlds. At American public school, they saluted the American flag and learned to become American citizens. In the afternoons, they went to Japanese-language school, where they learned Japanese language and culture. The switch between the two schools sometimes mirrored niseis' split personalities. "At Bailey Gatzert School I was a jumping, screaming, roustabout Yankee," wrote Monica Sone about her childhood in Seattle. "But Nihon Gakko [Japanese school] was so different. . . . I found myself switching my personality back and forth daily like a chameleon. . . . I suddenly became a modest, faltering earnest little Japanese girl with a small, timid voice."[32]

Yoshiko Uchida and her sister never considered themselves anything other than American while growing up in Berkeley, California. But as she entered adolescence, Yoshiko and her other Japanese American friends began to be singled out and excluded. In order to avoid embarrassment and humiliation at clothing stores, theaters, beauty salons, swimming pools, and other public venues, Yoshiko would call ahead to ask if Japanese were welcomed: "Can we come swim in the pool? We're Japanese . . . Will you rent us a house? Will the neighbors object?"[33]

In response to the racial discrimination that shadowed their daily lives, nisei formed their own organizations and social clubs, often sponsored by the YWCA, Buddhist temples, and Christian churches. These organizations allowed them to compete in sports, take part in community service, enjoy social outings, dances, and parties with other Japanese Americans, and develop a strong Japanese American identity before World War II. In 1940, there were 400 nisei youth organizations in southern California alone.[34]

Nevertheless, Japanese American efforts to be fully accepted as Americans were largely unsuccessful. Labeled another "Oriental" problem, Japanese became the targets of discriminatory laws at both the federal and state levels that restricted Japanese immigration and prohibited Japanese immigrants from becoming naturalized citizens. Japanese were denied membership in mainstream labor unions. And in many western states, Alien Land Laws prevented them from owning or leasing land.

Like Chinese Americans, Japanese Americans fought these laws in order to gain equal rights in the United States. In 1922, Japanese immigrant Takao Ozawa challenged the United States' ban on naturalized citizenship for Japanese immigrants with a test case before the U.S. Supreme Court. Born in Japan in 1875, Ozawa emigrated to the United States as a student in 1894. He graduated from high school in Berkeley, California, and attended the University of California for three years before moving to Hawai'i to raise a family. He was fluent in English, a practicing Christian, worked for an American company, and was, as historian Yuji Ichioka described, "a paragon of an assimilated Japanese immigrant, a living refutation of the allegation of Japanese unassimilability."[35] On October 14, 1914, Ozawa filed an application for citizenship but was denied. He challenged the ruling in the U.S. District Court for the Territory of Hawai'i two years later. He was denied again. The court found that Ozawa was "in every way eminently qualified under the statutes to become an American citizen," except for his race. He was not white as the country's naturalization laws required.

21. Takao Ozawa, 1916.

Ozawa appealed the decision and the case went to the U.S. Supreme Court on May 31, 1917. With the assistance of the Pacific Coast Japanese Association Deliberative Council, an immigrant civic association, and his attorney, former U.S. Attorney General George Wickersham, he made a passionate plea for the right of naturalization. He argued that although he was of Japanese descent, his skin was "white in color." Some Japanese, he contended, were even "whiter than the average Italian, Spaniard, or Japanese." Ozawa argued that as a resident of the United States for twenty-eight years, he had been educated in American schools, taught his children English, and forswore any connections to Japanese churches, schools, or organizations. Lastly, and most emphatically, he explained that "in name, I am not an American, but at heart I am a true American." He sought to "return the kindness which our Uncle Sam has extended me" by becoming a naturalized citizen. To no avail. Ruling that the U.S.'s 1790 Naturalization Act expressly allowed the naturalization of only white persons, the court argued that since Ozawa was not white or Caucasian, he was ineligible.[36]

As their lives became more and more circumscribed by anti-Japanese laws and policies like the Ozawa decision, Japanese Americans became disillusioned. "America . . . once a dream of hope and longing, now a life of tears," one issei explained.[37] Some returned to Japan. Others, including community leaders, tried to counter the growing anti-Japanese racism in the country by molding the mass of Japanese immigrants into upstanding, respectable subjects. Japanese associations were established to control the behavior of immigrants, maintain connections to Japanese consulates in the United States, conduct educational campaigns to promote understanding among non-Japanese, and challenge discriminatory laws.[38]

At the same time, Japan and its expanding empire encouraged Japanese immigrants in the United States to participate in Japanese nationalist goals. Issei community leaders responded by creating their own type of immigrant nationalism that claimed both Japaneseness and Americanness. By helping Japan and being patriotic Japanese, historian Eiichiro Azuma has explained, they were also helping themselves survive as a community in the United States. Some sent their American-born children to Japan for schooling and maintained strong transnational ties at the same time that they struggled to survive and be accepted in the United States.[39]

Japanese immigrants largely lost their struggle for equality in the United States, because no matter how hard they tried to demonstrate how American they were, they were still seen as Japanese. And with Japan growing as a world power that might threaten U.S. interests in the Pacific, Americans' views of Japan were increasingly negative. In this context, the threat of Japan and the threat of Japanese immigrants were linked together as part of a global discourse that would reshape immigration patterns, policies, and international relations. What would become known as the "yellow peril" began in Germany.

One morning in 1895, German Kaiser Wilhelm II awoke from a terrible nightmare. He had dreamt that the great nations of Europe were threatened by ruthless foreign invaders from the East. Convinced that he had witnessed some terrible future event, Wilhelm commissioned a painting of his vision and sent reproductions to several European leaders and to President William McKinley. The painting shows the great nations of Europe—Austria, England, France, Germany, Italy, and Russia—represented as women warriors preparing for battle. The winged archangel Michael wields a sword and points to the foreign "calamity which menaces them" in the distance, as the painting's caption explains. The "heathen idol" Buddha rides a Chinese dragon that represents "the demon of Destruction" heading toward Europe. A burned and ruined city lies in their wake, and ominous storm clouds accompany the "invaders in their onward career."

Kaiser Wilhelm's commissioned painting, *Die Gelbe Gefahr* (The Yellow Peril), helped to coin the term "yellow peril" and popularized long-standing European fears of an Oriental invasion of the West. Published in the London *Review of Reviews* in 1895, it became the most influential political illustration of the late nineteenth century. It is no coincidence that Wilhelm dreamt of an Asian menace in 1895. That year, Japan surprised the world with its stunning defeat of China in the Sino-Japanese War. The Kaiser was convinced that Japan would attempt to conquer Europe next. With his personal inscription of the original painting, "Nations of Europe, defend your holiest possession," Wilhelm hoped to encourage Europe and the United States to form an alliance against the shared threat from the East.[40]

22. "Die Gelbe Gefahr," (the "Yellow Peril") reproduced in *The Review of Reviews* (London), December 12, 1895.

Kaiser Wilhelm's message found a ready audience in the United States. Apprehension about Japan's expanding empire heightened existing fears that Japanese immigrants were growing in number, taking away jobs, and preparing for an eventual invasion of the Western Hemisphere. These "yellow peril" anxieties became part of larger transnational conversations about hemispheric security and the future of the "white race" circulating throughout North and South America.

Organized anti-Japanese sentiment in the United States followed the successful campaign to restrict Chinese immigration. With the Chinese exclusion laws in place, Americans turned their attention to the growing numbers of Japanese immigrants arriving on their shores. Japanese were often viewed along the same lines as the Chinese: both groups were inassimilable cheap laborers who were threats to white workers and to existing race relations. But restrictionists also made important distinctions. Whereas China was believed to be a backward civilization burdened by massive civil unrest, Japan had modern industries and a powerful military. It had proven its might and standing among world powers in its decisive defeat over Russia in the Russo-Japanese War of 1904–1905 and was thus considered to be a greater danger to the West. By extension, Japanese immigrants were viewed as both superior to and more threatening than other Asians. And unlike Chinese immigrant communities, the Japanese population included a substantial number of women and an increasing number of children, meaning that the Japanese were likely in the U.S. to stay. In 1900, there were only 2,039 Japanese in the continental United States. By 1920, there were 72,257.[41] Adding to the anxiety, many whites suspected that Japanese immigrants were actually a colonizing force sent from Japan to take over the West Coast of North America. San Francisco newspapers expressed as much with alarmist headlines like: "YELLOW PERIL—HOW JAPANESE CROWD OUT THE WHITE RACE."[42]

Anti-Japanese sentiment grew without check. Racial epithets like "Yellow Jap!" and "Dirty Jap" were hurled at Japanese Americans on the streets of big cities and small towns. Signs reading "Japs Go Away" and "No More Japs Wanted Here" were scrawled on sidewalks, on the walls of railroad stations, and in the case of a small town in the San Joaquin Valley, even on a highway sign. "People even spit on Japanese in the streets," one Japanese immigrant told an interviewer.[43]

Opponents to Japanese immigration in the United States demanded that the national government take action. Total exclusion along the lines of the Chinese Exclusion Act was the goal. But officials in Washington, D.C., proceeded cautiously. Japan was a proud and powerful country and would not submit to a humiliating exclusion law. Tensions between exclusionists on the West Coast and officials in Washington increased, coming to a head in the early 1900s. By the fall of 1907, three cities in the United States and Canada were engulfed in racial hatred and violence.

San Francisco was first. Tensions over Japanese immigration had been brewing for years, and on May 14, 1905, delegates from sixty-seven local and regional labor, political, and fraternal organizations met to form the Japanese-Korean Exclusion League. Their goal was the total exclusion of Japanese immigrants from the United States, including the then territory of Hawai'i. At stake, they believed, was the survival of the white race. With their slogan, "Absolute Exclusion of the Asiatics," the league concentrated their efforts on spreading their message through legislation, boycotts, and propaganda.[44] It also lobbied the San Francisco School Board to segregate Japanese students from whites in the city's public schools. On October 11, 1906, the board responded to public pressure and ordered all Japanese and Korean students to the city's Oriental School, which Chinese students already attended.

The segregation order set off a flurry of diplomatic activity. President Theodore Roosevelt privately sympathized with exclusionists, but he also believed that exclusion could only be accomplished through delicate diplomacy. Intense negotiations between San Francisco officials, the California congressional delegation, and members of Roosevelt's administration took place in Washington in February 1907. Roosevelt demanded that the school segregation order be revoked. Californians demanded restrictions on new Japanese immigration and on the Japanese from Canada, Mexico, and Hawai'i. Japanese immigrants remigrating from Hawai'i were especially worrisome to California exclusionists. Since the 1898 annexation of Hawai'i, more than 40,000 Japanese had left the islands for the states.[45] Because

Hawai'i was a U.S. territory, immigrants could not be barred from passing from one part of the United States to another. On this issue, the federal government was reluctant to take action, but the anti-Asian lobby stood firm. Finally, an agreement was reached. On March 13, 1907, the school board rescinded the segregation order. The very next day, Roosevelt issued an executive order that excluded from the continental United States any aliens involved in secondary migration from Hawai'i, Canada, or Mexico.[46] Roosevelt also began diplomatic negotiations with Japan to restrict Japanese laborers altogether.

In San Francisco, however, the anti-Japanese movement continued to grow, and violent attacks on Japanese residents increased. In the summer and fall of 1906, local police recorded nearly 300 attacks on San Francisco Japanese. In the spring of 1907, tensions erupted again. On the night of May 20, a mob of about twenty whites entered the Japanese-owned Horseshoe Restaurant at 1213 Folsom Street, drove out its customers, broke all the windows, and wrecked the interior. The mob then crossed the street and attacked a Japanese bathhouse. The next night, a white mob congregated in front of the Japanese-owned Lion Restaurant at 124 Eighth Street and began attacking Japanese homes, businesses, and restaurants throughout the city. The violence lasted for several nights. Japanese repeatedly called the police for help, but none came. Local and national officials dismissed the violence, but Japanese leaders continued to protest against the systemic harassment of Japanese in San Francisco. "Hardly a day goes by . . . that some threatening demonstration is not made by roughs and hoodlums against the Japanese," complained the Japanese Association of San Francisco.[47] As a result of Japanese immigrant and diplomatic protests, Secretary of State Elihu Root urged California officials to protect Japanese residents. President Roosevelt also stationed troops near San Francisco and gave them orders to quell the next riot should it occur.[48] The violence in San Francisco would prove to be the least destructive of all of the 1907 riots, but it laid the groundwork for more violent outbreaks in Bellingham and Vancouver.

The events in San Francisco inspired supporters of Asian exclusion in the Pacific Northwest. Arthur E. Fowler, a former cook, soldier, and cartoonist, became the driving force in organizing the anti-Asian movement in Seattle, for example. In 1906, he launched a new magazine called *The*

Yellow Peril and began lecturing on the evils of Asian immigration. He soon organized a Seattle branch of the San Francisco–based Japanese-Korean Exclusion League and gathered 10,000 signatures on an "anti–Japanese coolie" petition.[49]

While Fowler orchestrated the anti-Japanese campaign in Seattle, new immigrants from South Asia began to arrive in Washington, and tensions flared up over job competition and race relations. The Japanese-Korean Exclusion League formally changed its name to the Asiatic Exclusion League to better confront the new threat. On September 4, 1907, a mob of thirty to forty white men forced 200 South Asians out of the city to shouts of "Drive out the Hindus." All South Asians were forced to leave the city over the next few days. Bellingham's Asian immigration "problem" was apparently solved. But the issue of Asian exclusion was just coming to a head up north in Vancouver.

In the summer and fall of 1907, British Columbia experienced a sudden increase in Asian immigration. Government reports listed 11,440 Asians, including 8,125 Japanese, disembarking at Pacific Coast ports in Canada.[50] Some of this immigration was a direct result of President Roosevelt's 1907 executive order, which made it impossible for Japanese to go from Hawai'i to the continental U.S. without a passport issued by the Japanese government. As a result, Japanese in Hawai'i began to travel north to Canada. Newspapers reported that Japanese were "swarming in by shiploads from Japan and Honolulu" and that "feeling[s] of panic" were strong in the coastal cities.[51] "White Canada Forever" became the favorite song of exclusionists, who often sang it on the streets of Vancouver:

For white man's land we fight.
To Oriental grasp and greed
We'll surrender, no never.
Our watchword be "God save the King."
White Canada for ever.[52]

Much of the anti-Asian sentiment in Canada was local and national in nature. But British Columbian exclusionists increasingly drew inspiration from their fellow activists south of the border. The Vancouver Trades and

Labour Council formed British Columbian branches of the San Francisco–based Asiatic Exclusion League in July 1907. In early August, Olaf Tveitmoe, president of the Exclusion League in San Francisco, was invited to Vancouver to offer advice, and Vancouver newspapers excerpted a speech by Washington exclusionist Fowler on that state's efforts to "shut out the Japanese."[53]

The league's first meeting on August 12 drew 400 men from "many shades of public opinion" and "many classifications of citizens" to discuss the economic threat that Japanese immigrants posed to white workers, merchants, and industrialists. Participants passed a resolution calling for the prohibition of Asian immigration.[54] The idea of an anti-Asian parade was soon suggested as a way to "bring the white people to a state of enthusiasm."[55] They set a date for Saturday, September 7. Just a few days before the parade, organizers cheered the news of the successful expulsion of South Asians from Bellingham. And American leaders of the Asiatic Exclusion League rushed to Vancouver to lend their support.[56]

The crowd that gathered at seven o'clock on the night of September 7 made their way to Vancouver's City Hall with the assistance of three marching bands and a parade marshal. Carriages carrying officials of the Asiatic Exclusion League, the evening's speakers, and "lady sympathizers" led the way. Five thousand men marched behind them shouting slogans until they were hoarse. An estimated crowd of 10,000 eventually gathered, "giving evidence of their dislike for the Mongolian race."[57] Union men and members of fraternal organizations unfurled banners proclaiming: "Stand for a white Canada" and "A white Canada and no cheap Asiatic labor."[58]

City Hall was packed to the doors with a mass of people. The president of the Asiatic Exclusion League of Vancouver chaired the meeting and welcomed the international gathering of anti-Asian leaders. W. A. Young, an American Federation of Labor leader from Seattle, deplored the "yellow blight." J. E. Wilson, a visiting New Zealand labor leader, described to the crowds what the other colonies in the British Empire had done to exclude Chinese. But it was Arthur E. Fowler from Seattle who delivered the most rousing speech. He reportedly addressed the mob outside from a telegraph pole in the middle of the business district. "What will you do?" he asked, according to a reporter at the scene. "What did they do to the Hindus in Bellingham?" he called out. Then around nine o'clock, he proposed a march through Chinatown. "The mob was off like a pack of hounds," the reporter described.[59]

Soon the mob turned violent. Many Chinese and Japanese kept indoors. But when objects were hurled through the windows of their shops and homes, Japanese residents armed themselves with clubs and bottles, guns, or knives and paraded in front of their houses and places of business on Powell Street. Another group guarded the entrance to the Japanese quarter, while others hurled bottles, bricks, stones, and chunks of wood from the rooftops of their buildings.[60] Japanese immigrant Akisaburo Sato was in his room in a boardinghouse on Powell Street when the mob descended. He described how "hundreds of white rioters poured down from the direction of Main Street, violently screaming, throwing stones and flaying about with clubs." A stone broke a nearby window, and a piece of glass cut Sato's face. "When I saw the damage incurred by all the other shops and businesses, I was really scared to death," he recalled.[61]

By three the next morning, virtually every building occupied by Chinese was damaged. In the Japanese quarter, fifty-nine properties were wrecked and the Japanese-language school was on fire. Two thousand Chinese were driven from their homes. Many immigrants and rioters were wounded. The official Canadian investigations did not record any deaths, but Asian-language newspapers claimed that four rioters and one Chinese man were killed.[62]

Pushed to act by the violent outbreaks, both the United States and Canada began to negotiate with Japan to restrict Japanese immigration. Because Japan agreed to these regulations voluntarily (rather than be subject to a humiliating Japanese exclusion bill), these policies were known as the Gentlemen's Agreement. The negotiations were finalized within three days of each other. The U.S. agreement was signed on January 25, 1908; Canada's on January 28, 1908. They were nearly identical. In the U.S. agreement, the Japanese government agreed not to issue passports to any laborers, skilled or unskilled, bound for the continental U.S., but passports would be issued to "laborers who have already been in America and to the parents, wives, and children of laborers already resident there."[63] What this meant was that Japanese immigrants already in the U.S. could re-enter the country if they left. They could also bring their families over if they wished. But any new Japanese immigrants seeking entry into the United States would find the door firmly closed against them.

The 1907 riots revealed just how much "yellow peril" fears were part of larger Western anxieties about demographic and political changes occurring around the world. Many believed that the white race, and by extension "white" nations like the United States, Canada, Britain, France, and Australia, would become vulnerable as "colored races" and "colored nations" grew in power and in number. In books like Charles H. Pearson's *National Life and Character: A Forecast* (1893), Madison Grant's *The Passing of the Great Race; or, The Racial Basis of European History* (1916), and Homer Lea's *The Valor of Ignorance: The Inevitable Japanese-American War* (1909), authors reached wide audiences with their predictions of an impending race war.[64]

Historian and eugenicist Lothrop Stoddard sounded an even louder alarm in his 1920 book, *The Rising Tide of Color Against White World-Supremacy*, which reached a broad audience and went through fourteen editions in just three years. One of Stoddard's goals was to demonstrate the naturalness of geographic and racial divisions like the "Yellow Man's Land" of Asia, the "Black Man's Land" of Africa, and the "White Man's Land" of Europe, Australia, New Zealand, the United States, and Canada. The problem facing the world, Stoddard warned, however, was that a "colored peril" was rising. Population increases, mass immigration, and the rise of anticolonial movements threatened both the sanctity of these racial borders and the hegemony of the white race.[65] *The Rising Tide of Color* depicted as much on its cover: the newly powerful and vengeful peoples of Africa (represented by a spear-carrying naked man with a headdress, earrings, and full lips) and Asia (depicted by an armed man wearing a coolie hat and Fu Manchu–style mustache and a gun-toting man wearing a turban) were angry and ready to dominate the world.

The threat emanating from Japan in the "Yellow Man's Land" caused Stoddard the most concern. While Asians had previously been dismissed as inferior or strangely exotic, the Japanese were proving to be very skilled at "adapting white ideas and methods" to their own needs. In fact, it was because Japanese were *not* inferior to whites that made them so dangerous, he argued.[66] Stoddard identified three dangers coming from Asia in general and from Japan in particular: the peril of arms (military expansion), the peril of markets (economic competition), and the peril of immigration. Japan's economic and military rise to world power status represented the first peril to the white world, because Japan's' thirst for expansionism could not be contained within the "Yellow Man's Land" of Asia. Asia's ongoing industrial transformation would not only monopolize markets within Asia, but would also propel the "invasion" of white markets and severely thwart Europe's and America's economic dominance in the world, he argued.[67] As frightening as the perils of arms and markets were, however, it was the peril of immigration that was the most dangerous according to Stoddard. The permanent settlement of Japanese in the white world, and especially North and South America, threatened "our very race-existence, the well-springs of being, the sacred heritage of our children," he warned.[68]

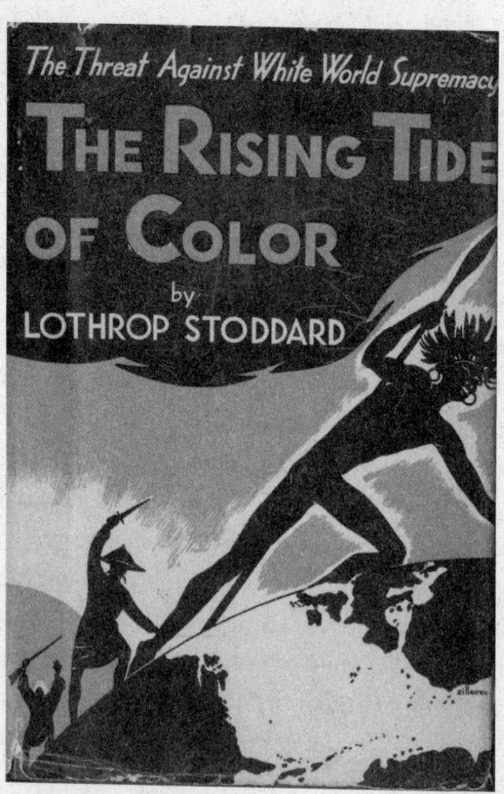

23. The cover of Lothrop Stoddard's *The Rising Tide of Color Against White World Supremacy* (New York: Scribner's Sons, 1921).

• • •

Stoddard's identification of Japanese immigration as the ultimate peril facing the West built upon and further strengthened the decades-old campaigns to exclude Japanese immigrants from the United States and Canada. It did not take long for the two countries to realize that the 1908 Gentlemen's Agreements were ineffective. The two policies barred the immigration of Japanese laborers, but family members of Japanese already in the United States and Canada could still apply for admission. From 1909 to 1920, almost 93,000 Japanese entered or reentered the United States. The largest number of new immigrants, 20,000, were picture brides. During that same period, 17,382 Japanese entered Canada, the majority being women as well.[69] Supporters of Asian exclusion viewed the new increase and permanency of Japanese immigration with alarm.

First was the problem of sheer numbers. In 1924, California anti-Japanese leader V. S. McClatchy warned an audience at the Lions Club of San Francisco that the Japanese population of California had "quadrupled within the past fifteen years" and that the growth of this "unassimilable population" presented nothing less than "a deadly menace to the nation."[70] Second was the problem of economic competition between Japanese and whites. In the U.S. West, Japanese immigrants were proving to be highly successful farmers. By 1920, Japanese leased, contracted, or owned over 458,000 acres of farmland in California alone.[71]

Japanese success in agriculture sparked a great deal of resentment. The *San Francisco Examiner* bemoaned the spectacle of "thousands of acres of our richest and most productive farmlands" being under the control of "an unassimilable race."[72] Laws aimed at checking Japanese economic competition followed. In California, the 1913 Alien Land Law permitted "aliens ineligible to citizenship," a legal category applicable only to Asian immigrants, to lease land for only three years and barred them from further land purchases. Japanese immigrants deftly worked around this law by securing leases and land in their U.S.-born children's names or in jointly owned corporations. Amendments to this law in 1919 and 1920 closed these loopholes. By 1923, Washington, Colorado, Arizona, Texas, Oregon, and Idaho had all adopted similarly restrictive alien land laws as well.[73]

Japanese immigrant demographic growth and economic competition were major sources of anxiety in the United States, but they were largely overshadowed by the pure racial threat that Japanese immigrants allegedly posed. Japanese immigrants were believed to be inassimilable aliens. Moreover, as American sociologist Jesse F. Steiner explained in 1917, an "immigrant invasion" from Japan would only add to the existing racial conflict in the United States relating to African Americans.[74]

Even more troubling was the conviction that Japanese immigrants were merely an advance guard of an invading imperial Japanese army coming to conquer the West. An extensive amount of yellow peril literature expounded on this specific point. Homer Lea's *The Valor of Ignorance* laid out just how the Japanese invasion of the Pacific Coast would occur, complete with maps and strategic plans. He argued that with 149,000 Japanese immigrants in Hawai'i, Japan had already completed the occupation of the islands. Lea also pointed out that the similar "invasion" of Japanese soldiers well under way in California and Washington would allow Japan to conquer the entire Pacific Coast with ease.[75] Senator James Phelan of California picked up on Lea's assertions and warned that the Pacific Coast "would be an easy prey in case of attack" because Japanese immigrants in California were not peaceful settlers, but rather the "enemy within our gates."[76]

The yellow peril theme also became a central topic in North American and European popular culture. American writers like Jack London, Peter Kyne, Montaville Flowers, and Wallace Irwin focused on either the Japanese conquest of the Western world or on the heroic struggles waged by whites in the United States and Canada against evil Japanese barons who acquired American land and white women as part of Japan's scheme of world domination.[77] Sax Rohmer's Fu Manchu novels illustrated the mass appeal of the yellow peril in popular culture. As a servant to "Eastern dynasts," Fu Manchu secretly plotted the destruction of the entire white race in books, comics, radio dramas, films, and TV shows for much of the twentieth century. By the 1920s, Hollywood had brought the yellow peril of Asian-white miscegenation to a number of popular films, including Cecil B. DeMille's *The Cheat* in 1915 and D. W. Griffith's *Broken Blossoms* in 1919.[78]

With such wide circulation of yellow peril fears, support for restricting Japanese immigration expanded. As James Francis Abbott, a Washington

University professor, argued in 1916, the "yellow peril in the white man's country . . . is not a Californian, nor a Canadian, nor an Australian problem, but a *world problem*."[79] In the United States, Madison Grant and Lothrop Stoddard spelled out the situation with rhetorical flourish. "Colored migration is a *universal* peril, menacing every part of the white world," Grant wrote in his introduction to Stoddard's book. "There is immediate danger that the white stocks may be swamped by Asiatic blood," he warned. "Unless [the white] man erects and maintains artificial barriers [he will] *finally perish*."[80]

Stoddard himself mapped out the battle lines of the coming race war and called for the white world to take action. But the question remained: what could the white world do? Stoddard bemoaned the fact that in the aftermath of World War I, "the white world [was] ill-prepared to confront—the rising tide of color." But he noted approvingly that the "lusty young Anglo-Saxon communities [that] border the Pacific," including Australia, New Zealand, British Columbia, and the West Coast of the United States, "have one and all set their faces like flint against the Oriental and have emblazoned across their portals the legend: 'All White.' " White solidarity, however, was insufficient. Stoddard argued that only the "rigorous exclusion of colored immigrants" could really save the white race. "The gates must be strictly guarded," Stoddard exhorted his readers.[81] The United States was the first to act.

The U.S.'s 1924 Immigration Act was a result of decades of activism on the part of nativists who lobbied for immigration restriction as a way to "stem the tide" of undesirable foreigners. Since the Chinese Exclusion Act of 1882, the number of excludable classes had increased dramatically. During and after World War I, wartime xenophobic nationalism, economic depression, and new international systems of regulating immigration helped establish a "regime of restriction."[82] The 1917 Immigration Act had established the "Asiatic Barred Zone." The Quota Act of 1921 limited annual admissions to 355,000 and restricted the number of aliens admitted annually through a national origins quota system designed to limit the immigration of southern and eastern European immigrants. (The number of aliens admitted annually was restricted to 3 percent of the foreign-born population of each nationality already residing in the United States in 1910, when immigration from southern and eastern Europe had been much smaller.) After 1921, nativists pushed for even greater restrictions. The 1924 Immigration

Act, also known as the Johnson-Reed Act, thus reduced the total number of admissions to 165,000 and redesigned the quotas to further reduce the slots available to southern and eastern European immigrants (2 percent of the foreign-born population of each nationality already residing in the United States in 1890). No restrictions were based on immigration from the Western Hemisphere, but the act closed the door on any further Asian immigration by denying admission to all aliens who were "ineligible for citizenship" (i.e., those to whom naturalization was denied). This clause was specifically aimed at the Japanese. And it was effective. After decades of activism by anti-Japanese activists, the gates to the United States were finally barred to Japanese immigrants.[83]

Other countries followed. In 1928, Canada's Prime Minister Mackenzie King informed the Japanese government that Canada would admit only 150 agricultural laborers, domestic servants, clergy, and women and children into the country per year. After some negotiation, Tokyo agreed to the limit and an end to the picture bride system. Japanese immigration to Canada soon slowed to a trickle.[84]

The gates to North America were now closed to Japanese immigrants. But the struggle for Japanese exclusion in the Americas did not end; it merely shifted southward. From 1908 to the beginning of World War II, 190,000 Japanese immigrants entered Brazil, constituting 75 percent of all Japanese arrivals in Latin America before World War II. In 1934, there were 20,385 Japanese in Peru.[85] As the Japanese population grew in Latin American countries, so did anti-Japanese sentiment and hostility. In 1934, Brazil put into effect an immigration quota system modeled after the U.S.'s Immigration Act of 1924 that allowed in only 2 percent of the total number of nationals settled in Brazil during the past fifty years.[86] Like the U.S. act, Brazil's law clearly targeted Japanese immigrants. The quota set for 1935 allowed only 2,711 Japanese into the country, almost a tenth of the number of Japanese arrivals during the previous year.[87]

By the 1930s, anti-Japanese sentiment in Peru was also on the rise and was greatly influenced by similar movements in Brazil and the United States. The Peruvian media paid close attention to the passage of the 1924 Immigration Act in the United States.[88] The newspaper *La Prensa* held up the "United States of North America" as an example of how to "impede successive yellow immigration."[89] The Peruvian government soon passed a series of anti-Japanese laws. The first established an immigration quota of 16,000 per nation, which was approximately two tenths of one percent of Peru's total population. It also specifically barred the immigration of "racial groups," like the Japanese.[90] Other laws curbed the rights of Japanese immigrants already in the country, dictating that only 20 percent of employees in all businesses and professions could be foreigners, limiting the number of Japanese-owned businesses in certain industries, and making it difficult for foreign residents of Peru to return to Peru after a visit to their native land.[91] A new constitution went further by requiring foreigners to renounce their dual citizenship and denying aliens the right to be naturalized altogether. Second-generation Peruvians were also stripped of their citizenship if they left Peru for their immigrant parents' homelands to live, study, or undergo military training before they reached adulthood. One last law required all foreign newspapers in Lima that printed in type other than roman type to publish a parallel translation of the text in Spanish. In all of these cases, Japanese Peruvians were the clear targets.[92]

On May 13, 1940, an anti-Japanese demonstration organized for that day developed into a full-scale riot during which almost all Japanese-owned shops in Lima were destroyed. By the time that Peruvian troops finally had the situation under control the next day, 620 households had lost $1.64 million in property damage. Scores of individuals were injured and ten Japanese had been killed.[93]

The widespread success in banning Japanese immigration to North and South America was all too clear to Japan, as was the important role of the United States in shaping these transnational discussions and encouraging parallel policies of exclusion. As Iichiro Tokutomi, a member of the Japanese House of Peers, explained in 1922, "there can be no doubt that the anti-Japanese sentiment of today is . . . an epidemic." The United States seems inclined, he continued, "to set up on both continents of America the sign board with this inscription: 'The Japanese Shall Not Enter.' "[94] Such sentiments from both sides of the Pacific foreshadowed the impending tragedies to come for Japanese communities in the Americas during World War II.

6

"We Must Struggle in Exile": Korean Immigrants

In 1905, Mary Paik Lee's family was driven out of their home by Japanese soldiers who had taken control of Korea. They walked for several days and nights until they reached the port city of Inchon. There, they saw two ships ready to recruit Korean laborers to work on the Hawaiian plantations. Mary's father signed a contract, and they sailed for Hawai'i on the SS *Siberia* in May 1905. They joined 7,400 other Koreans who left their homeland for Hawai'i between December of 1902 and May of 1905. Another 1,000 immigrated to Mexico in 1905, and 600 political refugees and over 1,000 picture brides also made it to the United States from 1905 to 1924.[1]

Korean immigrants shared many of the same experiences and challenges that Chinese and Japanese faced while working and living in Hawai'i, the continental U.S., and Mexico. Recruited as part of the U.S.'s ongoing search for Asian labor, they often sailed on the same transpacific ships and worked in many of the same jobs, often side by side. As Asians, they were also subjected to anti-Asian laws and attitudes that treated them unfairly, subjected them to racial violence, and made them outsiders in the United States. But as peoples fleeing colonialism at home, Koreans also faced unique challenges that shaped their lives in the United States in different ways.

Japanese colonialism in Korea affected every aspect of Korean immigration.

The Japanese-controlled government allowed Koreans to leave beginning in 1902 but then banned emigration in order to prevent Koreans from competing with Japanese laborers already in Hawai'i and to keep an ample supply of Koreans at home to support Japanese expansionist projects. Koreans chafed under Japanese control, and the cause of Korean independence became central to almost everything that they did and how they thought of themselves. This extended to Korean immigrants in the United States as well. "We Have No Country to Return To. We are a conquered people," an editorial in the San Francisco Korean language newspaper *Sinhan Minbo* (New Korea Newspaper) declared. "We must struggle in exile."[2] Both a stateless people and another despised "Oriental" menace, Koreans felt keenly the colonized status of their homeland and their unequal status in the United States.

"A shrimp among whales," Korea had long been the site of international rivalry among European powers, the United States, China, and Japan. Already weakened and impoverished, in the nineteenth century Korea became a tributary state of China until 1876, when Japan tried to exert more control over the country. Korea soon became a battleground between the two powers, and this rivalry eventually led to the Sino-Japanese War in 1894 in which Japan emerged victorious. Ten years later, after Japan defeated Russia in the Russo-Japanese War, it declared Korea a protectorate, and then formally annexed the country in 1910.[3]

Annexation brought harsh policies designed to control the Korean population. The colonial government made it easy for Japanese to purchase land, and Japanese settlers began to arrive in Korea in large numbers. The Korean army was disbanded, Korean teachers were replaced with Japanese ones, the Korean language was no longer taught in schools, newspapers were closed down, and the Japanese controlled Buddhist temples and Christian churches. Koreans lived in daily fear of the Japanese secret police and deeply resented the colonization of their country. "The Japanese are buying property right and left," reported an American missionary during the early years of Japanese occupation. "The people are highly enraged and see no hope of redress. They . . . are driven out of house and land."[4] "The Japanese were cruel oppressors," Korean immigrant Duke Moon explained even more bluntly.[5]

Chafing under a corrupt and debt-ridden Korean monarchy followed by Japanese colonial policies, Koreans suffered from heavy taxes and unemployment. Farmers were forced off their lands, and when two disastrous years brought a cholera epidemic, drought, flood, and locust plague in 1901 and 1902, many Koreans looked to leave their homeland. "We left Korea because we were too poor," one Korean immigrant explained.[6]

U.S. diplomats and businessmen saw an opportunity. Hawaiian sugar plantation owners wanted an additional source of labor to address a labor shortage and to counter the growing militancy among Japanese plantation workers. Korea seemed to present a ready solution. An 1882 treaty between the United States and Korea already allowed Koreans to immigrate to the United States, and small numbers of students and ginseng merchants had made their way to the country. U.S. foreign minister Horace Allen convinced King Kojong to sign an edict establishing a Korean Department of Emigration. The king also gave American businessman David Deshler permission to recruit and assist "free laborers" interested in immigrating to Hawai'i. Many prospective immigrants were too poor to pay their own way, however. The resourceful Deshler solved this problem by funneling funds provided by the sugar plantation companies through his company and then on to prospective immigrants as loans. Sugar plantation official C. M. Cooke noted with satisfaction that it was a win-win situation. "As the people there are in a starving condition we hope that we shall be able to get a number of them as they seem to be just what our plantations need."[7]

The promises of good wages, free housing, and medical care on the Hawaiian sugar plantations appealed to Koreans. Newspapers, posters, government announcements, American missionaries, and labor recruiters all portrayed Hawai'i as a "paradise" where "gold dollars were blossoming on every bush."[8] Koreans could expect to make up to $15 a month, five times what laborers were making in Korea at the time. "We heard of a man who was talking a lot about the opportunities in Hawai'i," one Korean immigrant explained. "He promised to give us work, free houses, and adequate pay." Thirteen in his family signed on and sailed for the islands.[9]

The Koreans who went to the United States and Hawai'i were predominately young and male, just like other Asian immigrants. But they came from more diverse occupational backgrounds. Some were clergymen, scholars, former soldiers, and students. Others were farmers and laborers. About 70 percent were literate and 40 percent were Christian, having been converted by American missionaries. Ten percent were women. The imbalanced gender ratio would continue to shape Korean immigrant communities in Hawai'i and in the continental U.S., but it would gradually grow more even. In 1920, 75 percent of the Korean population in the U.S. was male. In 1930, it was 66 percent.[10]

In Hawai'i, they found no promised life of riches. Plantation life involved overcrowded camps with run-down shacks and the long, hard labor of cutting cane in the oppressive heat. Hands became blistered, and faces and arms were torn and scratched by the sharp cane leaves. The barracks were segregated by race, with the Japanese in one area, the Chinese in another, and the Koreans in yet one more. The living quarters were provided by the plantation company, but workers had to pay for everything else, including meals and laundry. Moreover, plantation owners mistreated the Korean laborers. "We [were treated] like draft animals . . . rather than as human beings," said one Korean laborer. "Every worker was called by number, never by name."[11] And the work never seemed to end. "The sugar cane fields were endless and the stalks were twice the height of myself," a Korean woman recalled. "Now that I look back, I thank goodness for the height, for if I had seen how far the fields stretched, I probably would have fainted from knowing how much work was ahead."[12]

Many Koreans left the Hawaiian plantations within a year or two to work in canneries, grow rice and coffee, or move to the cities where they worked in restaurants, as gardeners, janitors, and domestic servants. Some opened businesses like laundries, retail stores, and boardinghouses. Over 1,000 Koreans also moved from Hawai'i to the continental U.S. until 1907, when a U.S. executive order aimed at curbing Japanese migration from Hawai'i was applied to Koreans as well.

While many left Korea to improve their economic condition, others crossed the Pacific to be free from the "Japanese enemy." Between 1910 and 1918, 541 refugee students were able to escape Japan and get to the United States via Manchuria, Shanghai, or Europe. Eighty percent arrived at the port of San Francisco and were processed at the Angel Island Immigration Station, where David Lee, president of the Korean National Association and U.S. immigration interpreter at Angel Island, helped hundreds of Korean immigrants get landed.[13] One of these was Whang Sa Sun, who with his wife, Chang Tai Sun, had become involved in the national independence movement; both were members of the anti-Japanese Sinminhoe (New People's Society). Facing likely capture and torture, the couple fled across the northern Korean border into Manchuria by disguising themselves as Russian refugees and crossing the half-frozen Yalu River. They made their way to Shanghai and then disguised themselves as Chinese citizens to book passage on a U.S.-owned steamer going to San Francisco. Like many other Korean refugee students, they arrived in the country without passports, but managed to be admitted into the United States with the help of the Korean National Association and sympathetic U.S. government officials. Their sense of relief was palpable. "I wanted to come to America, a free country," Whang told his granddaughter sixty years later. "When I left Korea, I felt like a free man." Whang Sa Sun settled in San Francisco, where he opened a dry cleaning shop, and became the minister of the Korean Methodist Church and a leader in the Korean independence movement.[14]

Other Koreans who were able to immigrate to the United States after the formal end of Korean immigration in 1905 were picture brides. The expansion of Japanese colonial rule in Korea, with its unfair economic policies and oppression, made many Korean immigrants reconsider their initial plans to return to Korea. Letters published in the *New Korea* newspaper from those who had returned warned them to stay in the United States. Korea under the Japanese was "like hell now," one letter writer explained.[15] Many immigrants heeded this advice. They began to send for wives through the picture bride system and prepared to make the United States their home. The Japanese government allowed small numbers of women to leave the country as a way of calming some of the passionate nationalist politics brewing in Korean communities abroad. From 1910 to 1924, 1,066 women went to Hawai'i and the continental U.S. They came from throughout Korea, but the majority were from poor rural families in the south. They were young, between the ages of eighteen and twenty-four.[16]

As in the Japanese picture bride system, Korean men and women relied upon go-betweens and pictures for introductions. Matchmakers, usually older women, recruited young women into going to the United States. Photographs of the young men in the United States and Hawai'i fed these women's imaginations of new lives and new freedoms. "If you marry here, you become a slave to your husband and his parents until you die," one matchmaker told a prospective bride. "In Hawai'i, no one bothers you."[17] The photographs of the prospective grooms usually featured handsome young men in Western suits. Some posed in front of large plantation houses or fancy automobiles. What the women did not know was that these photographs had been carefully staged and even doctored. More often than not, the houses and automobiles were owned by the plantation manager, the suits were borrowed, and the photographs were years old.[18]

Thus, when the women arrived in San Francisco or Honolulu, they were in for a shock. "[My aunt] came to Hawai'i as a 'picture-bride' at the age of sixteen to be married to a man who, to her horror, she later found out, was 72," one woman recounted.[19] Another woman's husband had sent a photograph of him when he was twenty-five years old and handsome. But when she arrived in Honolulu, the resemblance to his photograph was negligible. "He came to the pier, but I see he's really old, old looking. He was forty-five years old, 25 years more old than I am. My heart stuck. I was so disappointed, I don't look at him again."[20] Many felt betrayed, but few had any recourse. Some cried out "*Aigo omani*," or "O dear me, what shall I do?"[21]

In addition to the shock of deception by their husbands, many Korean picture brides were unprepared for the harsh lives that awaited them in the United States. Their husbands were barely scraping by as plantation laborers or migratory farmworkers. They expected and needed their wives to work for wages, too, on top of performing the work to maintain the house and raise children. "Look at me now," one woman in Hawai'i lamented. "My husband doesn't earn enough so I have to scrimp and save. I have to take in washing and ironing for unmarried men. And a baby keeps coming every year!"[22] The bitterness and disappointment were deep and enduring.

Picture brides also faced another harsh reality. Because their husbands were often so much older than they were, there was a very real possibility that they would need to work even harder to support their families when their husbands became infirm. Or worse yet, they could become widows at a very young age. One woman was in Hawai'i for only seven years when her husband passed away after being ill for two years. She was left with five young children. She worked so hard without sufficient rest or nourishment that she fainted and fell into a coma for twenty days, though she eventually recovered.[23]

But not all picture brides faced such difficult lives. Shinn Kang-ae was lucky. Her husband-to-be, Shinn Han, had a dry cleaning business in San Francisco, was a local community leader and well-known Korean nationalist, and was caring and thoughtful. When they were courting, he sent Kang-ae a Korean-English book to prepare for her new life in the United States. And he was waiting for her at the San Francisco dock when her ship arrived. "He wasn't too bad looking, much like the photograph," she told her daughter many years later. With a Japanese passport, Kang-ae was readily admitted into the country, and the couple went to the Korean Methodist Church to get officially married. She dressed in a white gown and veil, and he rented a black tuxedo. They eventually made a home for themselves and their four children in San Francisco's Chinatown.[24]

24. Korean weddings, Korean Methodist Church in San Francisco, 1914. Shinn Han and Shinn Kang-ae, the couple in the middle, pose with two other newly married Korean immigrant couples.

The arrival of so many Korean women and the establishment of an American-born generation of Korean Americans marked an important turning point in Korean immigrant communities. The skewed gender ratio became more equitable, and the children born in the United States were U.S. citizens who would live to see increased opportunities for themselves and their communities.

In California, Korean immigrants found work as farm laborers who, like other Asian immigrants, helped to turn California agriculture into a multimillion-dollar business in the twentieth century. They often worked together in cooperative Korean "gangs," following the crops or working in light industry. The agricultural towns of Dinuba, Reedley, Sacramento, and Delano attracted nearly 83 percent of the Korean population in the United States. Many of them became tenant farmers and truck farmers and worked alongside California's multiracial farm-laboring populations of Mexicans, Chinese, Japanese, South Asians, Filipinos, whites, and African Americans.[25]

Mary Paik Lee's family was one of these early settlers who struggled to make ends meet in several California towns. They were constantly on the move in search of better economic opportunities and followed the crops and other jobs. Their migratory lives of hardship reflected the reality for most Koreans. Mary's mother cooked and cleaned for thirty men who boarded with the family for four years in Riverside. "Father did not like her to work," Mary explained. "But it seemed to be the only way we could make a living for ourselves." Her mother would rise before dawn and make their breakfast at five, pack their lunches, work all day, and cook supper at seven. This was on top of doing laundry and keeping house for her own family. Mary herself began to help out with chores when she was six and became a domestic servant for a white family in town when she was eleven.[26]

As Korean immigrants settled into their new lives in the United States, their family life also revolved around community. They formed many organizations to offer community support and assistance. *Dong-hoe*, or village councils, were organized on each plantation. Social, community, and political organizations were established in San Francisco and Los Angeles, and separate women's organizations were formed as well.[27]

Korean churches on the plantations became among the first centers of Korean immigrant society and Korean nationalist politics. Christianity—first introduced by American missionaries—acted as a bulwark against Japanese colonialism at home. In the United States, it became a continuing source of strength and a center of nationalist activity. Koreans in Hawai'i lost no time establishing Korean-language church services, and by 1918 there were thirty-three Korean Protestant churches on the islands. In California, Koreans began worshipping together in Los Angeles in 1904, and the Korean Methodist Church was established in San Francisco in 1905.[28] Churches not only served as places to meet, worship, and retain the Korean language; they also served as centers for political activities. Church organizations raised funds and helped organize activities for independence movement leaders like Seo Jae-pil (more commonly known as Philip Jaisohn), Syngman Rhee, An Ch'ang-ho, and Park Yong-man.[29]

Like many Asian immigrants, Koreans retained strong ties to their homeland. But because of the colonized status of Korea, their homeland ties took on a fierce nationalism that focused on Korean independence. The welfare of their country and of the Koreans living under Japanese colonial rule weighed heavily on their minds. "My parents were constantly fearful of what might happen to their loved ones back home," Mary Paik Lee recalled.[30]

Japanese colonization of Korea between 1910 and 1945 turned Koreans abroad into stateless exiles. They were united in the shared goal to rid Korea of Japanese control and formed a cohesive community around Korean nationalism. "We are not sojourners . . . and we are not laborers," the *Sinhan Minbo* newspaper declared in 1910, "but political wanderers . . . and righteous army soldiers."[31] Korean immigrant nationalist activities took place at the international level, on the streets, and in the back rooms of stores and church basements. Although there were sizable Korean communities in Manchuria, Siberia, China, Europe, Mexico, and Cuba, Koreans in the United States played especially important roles in the global Korean independence movement. Their presence and connections in the United States—a growing international power, especially in the Pacific—provided key opportunities to publicize the cause of Korean independence to an international audience.[32] They faced significant obstacles, including internal dissension, but one of the biggest challenges was to get the United States—which refused to interfere with Japanese colonization of Korea in exchange for Japan's noninterference in the U.S.'s colonization of the Philippines—to recognize Korean nationalist organizations (and not the Japanese embassy) in the affairs of Korean immigrants in the United States.

As early as 1903, Koreans in Hawai'i formed a political organization, *Sinmin-hoe* (New People's Association), to unite Koreans around the cause of Korean independence. As Japan exerted more control in Korea between 1905 and 1908, nationalist activities in the United States and abroad grew. During these years, Japanese troops entered Korea as part of its war against Russia, the Korean king was forced to abdicate, the army was disbanded, and a new Japanese-led regime was installed. Koreans resisted and 14,556 were killed and another 32,993 wounded during the period of armed resistance between 1907 and 1909. After Japan formally annexed Korea in 1910, the nationalist movement entered another highly active phase, and Korean independence would become, according to historian Richard S. Kim, the "single most important issue for Korean immigrants."[33]

In 1909, the Korean National Association was formed in San Francisco to unify Koreans around independence, to provide religious, educational, and cultural activities, and to raise funds. It eventually had 130 chapters in San Francisco, Hawai'i, Siberia, Mexico, and Manchuria. In 1914, there were over 2,300 members in the Hawaiian chapter alone.[34] Korean language newspapers were established to spread the independence message, and Koreans in the United States tried—mostly unsuccessfully—to engage the wider international community around the freedom cause. In 1907, the Korean king sent a secret mission to the Second Hague Peace Conference arguing that Japanese rule had been wrongfully forced upon the Korean people, but the conference refused to receive the delegation or hear the petition. Korean nationalists became incensed when Durham White Stevens, an American in Korea who served as an advisor to the Japanese-led colonial government, visited San Francisco in 1908 and defended Japanese rule. The Korean people, he remarked, were too backward to govern themselves and were much better off under the Japanese. Nationalist Chang Chae-Kwan shot Stevens dead outside the San Francisco Ferry Building. That same year, another nationalist who had worked in Hawai'i and California before returning to Korea attacked a pro-Japanese Korean prime minister, and the next year another nationalist assassinated a Japanese official in Manchuria.[35]

The Korean National Association took a leading role in building the cause of Korean independence among Korean communities in Hawai'i, the continental U.S., and Mexico. After 1910, the association held mass protests and a huge rally to declare Japan's annexation of Korea null and void. At its rallies, protesters sang the Korean national anthem and displayed the Korean flag. Its founding resolution declared, "All Koreans in America regard Japan as an enemy nation." In an effort to exert some control and authority over Korean affairs in the United States, the Korean National Association also identified itself as "the only legitimate official agent of all Korean residents."[36]

A violent racial incident in Hemet, California, in 1913 gave the association an opportunity to push its case. When in June of 1913 an angry crowd of whites mobbed a small group of Korean laborers and expelled them from Hemet, the Japanese consulate in San Francisco offered assistance and began negotiating with Secretary of State Williams Jennings Bryan. Koreans protested the involvement of the Japanese. "We don't want to see the Japanese Consul, or for that matter have any Japanese interfere with our affairs," one Korean immigrant told the *Los Angeles Times*. "We are Koreans, not Japanese, and Japan has no reason to protest at Washington because of our troubles."[37]

Bryan soon released an announcement asserting that the Koreans in the United States were not Japanese subjects and that the government should deal directly with the Korean National Association. The organization went on to establish a military training program in Hawai'i, the continental U.S., and Mexico. Over the years, it continued to advocate on behalf of Korean immigrants seeking entry into the United States while also advancing the cause of Korean independence throughout the Americas.[38]

Korean women played especially important roles in the nationalist movement in Hawai'i and the United States. They knew from firsthand experience the terror of Japanese colonial rule, sometimes even more than their husbands who had left Korea before the Japanese annexation. They infused their family lives with the Korean language, customs, and culture while also helping to form Korean American ethnic identities as well. They spearheaded important nationalist activities through Korean churches and other groups. And they also organized their own separate women's organizations to support Korean independence by raising funds and spreading the nationalist message.[39]

Korean nationalism in the United States reached another important turning point in 1919 after the cause of Korean independence was rejected at the Paris Peace Conference that concluded World War I and former Korean King Kojong died. On March 1, 1919, Korean political and religious leaders gathered in Seoul to proclaim Korea's independence. The "March First Movement" would become a massive anticolonial uprising involving an estimated one million people. The Japanese tried to repress the nationwide demonstrations with brutal violence. Thousands of Koreans were killed and almost 20,000 were arrested. However, Koreans abroad in the continental United States, Hawai'i, Manchuria, Siberia, and China carried on the movement.[40]

On March 15, the Korean National Association held the first Korean Liberty Congress in Philadelphia. Korean nationalists in the United States had long identified with American political ideologies and institutions in the cause of Korean independence. At this crucial moment, Korean American nationalists chose the United States' "cradle of liberty" to launch their own declaration. Two hundred representatives from twenty-seven organizations in the United States and Mexico as well as a few from Europe were there to witness the public Proclamation of Independence of Korea and to recognize the newly established Korean Provisional Government. Prominent American supporters joined leading Korean nationalists at the rally. The conference ended with a massive march through Philadelphia to Independence Hall, where the Proclamation of Independence of Korea was read and the representatives formally asked the U.S. government to recognize the new government. The American revolutionaries and Korean nationalists were one and the same, Philip Jaisohn (Seo Jae-pil) argued, and he strategically called upon the United States to live up to its reputation as a defender of liberty. "We believe that America will champion the cause of Korea as she has that of other oppressed peoples," Jaisohn declared.[41] On April 9, 1919, nationalist leaders gathered in Shanghai and formed the Korean Provisional Government led by Syngman Rhee. It would eventually lay the foundation for the formation of the Republic of Korea (South Korea) in 1948.[42]

Korean immigrant communities helped sustain the Korean independence movement, but in the United States, Koreans confronted the same racial discrimination faced by Japanese and other Asians in the country. Koreans were routinely lumped together as inassimilable "Orientals" who stole jobs from deserving whites and contributed to the country's race problems. The Japanese-Korean Exclusion League was founded in San Francisco in 1905 and soon became a major political force that advocated for the exclusion of all Asian immigrants from the United States. In 1912, the Democratic Party in California opposed all immigration from Asia and included Koreans on its list of immigrants to be immediately excluded from the country.[43]

Koreans also faced harassment and violence in their everyday lives. When Mary Paik Lee's family arrived in San Francisco from Honolulu in 1906, a group of young white men harassed them. "They laughed at us and spit in our faces; one man kicked up Mother's skirt and called us names we couldn't understand." Throughout her childhood, Mary would feel the sting of discrimination. She was barred from attending a white church and from playing with white classmates in Willows, California. She had to endure the derogatory remarks her history teacher made about "stinking Chinks and dirty Japs" in class.[44] Koreans were also often barred from certain occupations and neighborhoods. Do-Yun Yoon remembered that a Korean could never rent in the "white town" in Delano, California, but only in the "Mexican town" or "black town." Even the local movie theater was segregated. "The Americans would not let us sit anywhere in the public movie theater," Yun explained. "They permitted us to sit in one corner with the Mexicans but not with the Americans."[45] They were routinely refused service in restaurants, public recreation facilities, and barbershops. As Asians, Koreans were also barred from becoming naturalized U.S. citizens.

Like other groups, Koreans contested this policy with a court case. In 1921, Easurk Emsen Charr, a U.S. Army veteran, petitioned for citizenship in a federal district court, arguing that his military service entitled him to it. The court disagreed and ruled that since Koreans were "of the Mongol family," they were excluded from citizenship.[46] And after many western U.S. states passed Alien Land Laws and made it illegal for "aliens ineligible to citizenship" to own or lease land, Koreans were pushed out of agriculture. "We left California because the state had passed the alien land act," one Korean immigrant recalled. "Then we went to Washington. But after we lived there for a few years, Washington passed an anti-alien exclusion law."[47]

"I felt the discrimination and realized that America was not a free country," Whang Sa Sun concluded. With no home government advocating on their behalf like the Japanese, Koreans were left to fend for themselves.[48]

Mary Paik Lee never grew accustomed to the rampant discrimination that she and other Koreans faced in the United States. Her father taught her from a young age that Koreans needed to "show Americans that we are just as good as they are" through both words and actions. She bristled at the ignorance, bigotry, and racism that she felt every day when she and her family were forced to live in the worst parts of town, called names, and forced to sit in the worst sections of the movie theater. But more often than not, she called attention to these actions and demanded equal treatment. When Mary was not allowed to enter the doors of the local Presbyterian church in Willows, California, by the minister, who told her "I don't want dirty Japs in my church," she told her friend's father, who happened to be a local judge and a member of the church. The next weekend, the minister himself came out to welcome Mary. When her English teacher consistently gave the nonwhite students lower grades than the whites, Mary protested. She recognized that Koreans were "in the same hopeless state" as African Americans and Mexicans, and in the multiracial neighborhoods in which she lived, the three groups bonded and patronized each other's stores to help out. "The first generation laid the foundation for the future by teaching their children," she explained.[49] Like many others in this first generation of Korean Americans, Mary and her family struggled through their first years in the United States, keeping their dreams of a better future in both Korea and the United States alive.

7

South Asian Immigrants and the "Hindu Invasion"

On April 6, 1899, San Francisco newspapers reported on four Sikh men who had just arrived on the steamship *Nippon Maru*. The quartet—described as a "picturesque group"—included some of the first South Asians to ever arrive in the city. Former British Army soldiers, they had been away from their native district of Punjab for twenty years. For much of that time, they had been in Hong Kong, where at least one of them was a sergeant with the British police. Bakkshield Singh, who spoke English fluently, told reporters that the men intended to "make their fortunes" in the United States and then return home. The *San Francisco Chronicle* gushed with praise for the dashing soldiers in the service of the British crown.[1]

Less than ten years later, however, the same newspapers had nothing but condemnation for a different group of South Asians arriving to work in the lumber mills and on the farms and railroad lines up and down the Pacific Coast. Like other Asian immigrants, South Asians made up a fraction of the total number of foreigners coming to the United States at the time. Compared to groups like the Chinese, Japanese, and Filipinos, South Asians were even smaller. A mere 8,055 were admitted into the United States from 1910 to 1932. Nevertheless, a virulent pattern of anti-Asian racism had been set. They arrived at a time when anxieties over Chinese and Japanese immigration were at a peak, and as headlines of a "Hindu Invasion" splashed across newspapers, all the public saw was another Asian immigrant threat.[2] By 1917, South Asians were excluded from the United States.

But as British subjects whose homeland was an integral part of the British Empire, South Asians occupied a unique place in the United States, and their experiences and status in America were shaped by the U.S.'s relationship with Great Britain. South Asian demands for fair treatment in the United States were also tied to British imperialism in India, for many immigrants were convinced that their unequal status in the country was directly tied to India's subjugation under the British. Like Korean immigrants, they became increasingly involved in anticolonial and nationalist struggles to free their homeland from foreign rule. Thus, as they struggled to make a living, create families, and sustain communities in America, they also worked hard to keep the dream of a free India alive.

British colonial rule in South Asia, the end of the African slave trade in the British Empire, and the campaign to bring Asian labor to British colonies like the British West Indies helped propel 419,000 South Asians to British Guiana, Trinidad, and Jamaica as indentured laborers from 1838 to 1918. The immigration of South Asians to Canada and the United States overlapped with this mass migration. By the early twentieth century, decades of economic dislocation, high taxes, and farming losses caused by British colonial policies in South Asia had further destroyed farming families. Making matters worse, the emigrant-sending region of the Punjab (in present-day India and Pakistan), also suffered from a population explosion, droughts, famines, and severe epidemics.[3]

At the same time, modern transportation routes made immigration more accessible than ever before. By the end of the nineteenth century, 2,000 miles of new roads combined with 2,000 miles of railway connected the Punjabi heartland to all major cities and ports in the country. Immigrants commonly took the Grand Trunk Road and the British-built railway from Punjab to New Delhi. They could then travel by train to Calcutta, where they could board steamers to the British colony of Hong Kong. From there, international steamships could take them anywhere in the world.[4]

Passage to North America was much more expensive and longer for

South Asians than it was for Chinese, Japanese, and Koreans, but steamship companies were eager to facilitate immigration between South Asia and North America.[5] After exclusionary laws in the United States and head taxes in Canada halted their lucrative business in Chinese immigration, company agents advertised cheap fares and flooded the Punjabi countryside with flyers describing "opportunities of fortune-making" in Canada and the United States. As one immigrant from Julundra explained, the circulars typically stated that "if men were strong, they could get two dollars a day." Forty men went abroad from his village alone in just two years.[6]

Relatives and friends already in North America also promoted immigration. One Punjabi immigrant recalled how reports "on the ease with which [immigrants] could make money in America" came from numerous sources and convinced him that his future lay on the other side of the Pacific. "So I decided to go," he explained.[7] Dr. D. R. Davichand, a Punjabi immigrant in Vancouver, wrote such convincing letters to friends and relatives back home that he is credited with bringing several hundred Punjabis to Canada to work in British Columbian sawmills in the early 1900s.[8]

They were a diverse group of Sikhs, Muslims, and Hindus. The vast majority came from the Punjabi districts of Jullundur, Hoshiarpur, Gurdaspur, Ludhiana, Ferozepur, and Amritsar. Like other Asian immigrants at the time, most were young single men in their early twenties who had been independent farmers in their native villages and were seeking work as laborers in North America. But there was also a small number of students, merchants, and peddlers. Given the cost of emigration, U.S. and Canadian policies, and their intention to return home, many who were married generally left their wives and children at home. They often ended up being away for years, migrating throughout the British Empire before landing in Canada and the United States. For them, North America was often just another stop in their circuitous life of migration.

Tuly Singh Johl's journey to Canada and the United States mirrors the experiences of many early-twentieth-century South Asian immigrants. The youngest of four brothers, Tuly grew up in the Punjabi village of Jundialla in the 1880s. With two older brothers working in the sugarcane fields of Australia, his family was just one of many that survived by sending some members abroad. By the time that Tuly himself was old enough to immigrate, the news of good money to be made in Canada lured him away from his wife and young son. He traveled first to Hong Kong and then to Vancouver. The morning after his ship arrived in Vancouver, Tuly went to work in a lumber mill. Four months later, a visit from friends who were working in the Washington lumber mill town of Bellingham convinced him and three other men to cross the U.S. border, where South Asians could quickly find jobs at the Bellingham Bay Lumber Mill, the Morrison Mill, and Larson's Mill. Tuly earned up to $2 a day. It was 22 cents less than what white workers received, but it was still a fortune compared to the 5 and 15 cents a day he could have expected at home.[9]

South Asians like Tuly Singh Johl did not have any trouble finding work. They arrived on the West Coast of the United States at a time of extraordinary economic expansion in the lumber, railroad, fishing, and agricultural industries. With Chinese, Japanese, and Korean labor immigration prohibited, the resulting labor shortage caused recruiters to turn to South Asian, Filipino, and Mexican laborers. By the 1910s, South Asians were hired in droves to keep California's agricultural industry booming. They worked in the fruit orchards of the Vaca Valley, the beet fields of Hamilton, Oxnard, and Visalia, the celery, potato, and bean fields near Stockton, and the orange groves in southern California. The work was backbreaking, and white and Japanese growers routinely discriminated against the newly arrived South Asians by paying them lower wages than other groups. In 1911, a U.S. government commission found that South Asians did the "roughest, most unskilled work" that whites shunned, and they often did it for less pay than any other group.[10]

Day laborers often formed work groups ranging from two to fifty members and elected a boss who negotiated the terms of their contract and managed their interests. Men often lived together, worked as a unit, and divided earnings equally. Discriminated against in the housing market, they often lived in dilapidated houses, woodsheds, or barns, sleeping in a group in one room. Under these conditions, some were able to send as much as two thirds of their wages home. Muslim workers also found ways to manage their eleven-hour workday around their faith by bringing prayer into the fields with them. Through these and other tactics, South Asians survived and carved an economic foothold in California agriculture. By 1919, South

Asians occupied over 88,000 acres of land in the state, mostly in the Sacramento and Imperial Valleys.[11]

Most South Asian immigrants arrived at West Coast ports and remained in California, Oregon, and Washington. But there were other, smaller groups of South Asian peddlers and seamen throughout the Northeast, Midwest, and South as well. Historian Vivek Bald has traced their origins to a group of Bengali Muslim peddlers who sold embroidered silks and other "exotic" trinkets and goods to tourists in New Jersey beach towns, cities in the South, and tourist destinations in the Caribbean and Central America. In New Orleans, where a number of Bengalis married and started families with African Americans, they occupied a racial status that traversed the segregated world of white and black. As "dark-skinned men from the East," they were members of neither group. But as Bald describes, their daily lives were embedded in working-class neighborhoods, and their families played important roles in the history of black New Orleans.[12]

Hundreds of South Asian seamen, including Bengali Muslims and others from the Punjab, Kashmir, and the Northwest Frontier regions of present-day Pakistan, also made new lives for themselves in northeastern port cities and in Midwest industrial belt cities. When World War I ushered in an increase in transatlantic shipping, the number of British steamships arriving in New York, Philadelphia, and Baltimore rose, carrying dozens of South Asian workers who labored under indenture-like conditions in the ships' engine rooms and kitchens. Many deserted their ships and found work in the expanding shipbuilding, steelworks, and munitions factories. These ex-seamen became part of working-class neighborhoods in New York, Baltimore, and Detroit, marrying local women and forming blended families.[13]

Connected as they were to British imperial networks, South Asians primarily migrated to Canada and then to the United States in the early twentieth century. But small numbers came to the United States through Latin America as well. Vasaka Singh was twenty-five years old when he left his village in Lahore on a journey that took him to Europe, Central America, Mexico, and California. He first traveled to Genoa, Italy, where he boarded a steamer that took him to the Canal Zone in Panama. He worked there for a year before trying his fortune in Guatemala and then Mexico. By the time Singh arrived in Salina Cruz, revolutionary violence had made Mexico unsafe. He fled for his life and boarded a U.S. transport ship carrying refugees out of Mexico with the hope of joining his cousin in Stockton.[14]

Suchiat Singh was another whose global journey took him from his home in Punjab to the Panama Canal Zone, on to Lima, Havana, and then Veracruz. "I was a farmer in my country," he explained to U.S. immigration officials in 1914. But in Panama, he was a laborer, and in Havana he peddled cloth. His circuitous journey throughout the Americas ended at the U.S. Immigration Station on Angel Island, where he was denied admission and returned to India.[15]

Like other Asian immigrants in the United States, few women and families made the journey across the ocean. Traditional gender roles that discouraged women from leaving home, the expense of immigration, discrimination in the United States and Canada, and immigration policies that made it almost impossible for women and children to come kept the South Asian immigrant population mostly male.

Kala and Vaishno Das Bagai and their three sons were among the few families who did make the journey to the United States. Kala was just eleven years old and Vaishno twelve when they were married in the Punjabi city of Peshawar. The couple eventually welcomed three sons, Brij, Madan, and Ram, into their lives. In 1915, they decided to move to the United States. "Why did we come to America?" Kala pondered decades later. "The Ghadar [Indian nationalist] movement wanted to take the British out of India. Mr. Bagai was in that movement. He said, 'I don't want to stay in this slave country; I want to go to America where there is no slavery.'" Family and friends advised Vaishno to leave Kala and the children behind. That was the custom of most men going abroad. But Vaishno insisted, and the whole family boarded a steamship heading across the Pacific Ocean.

Unlike the majority of South Asian immigrants who came as laborers and were subjected to the U.S. government laws that barred persons "likely to become a public charge," the Bagais had no trouble entering the country. U.S. immigration officials at the Angel Island Immigration Station were at first suspicious of the family since so few women and children were coming to the United States at the time. Indeed, the sight of South Asian women in San Francisco was such a rare occurrence that Kala Bagai's arrival at the port was covered by the *San Francisco Call-Post* with a photograph of Kala and her son, Ram. The article claimed that Kala Bagai was the "first Hindu woman to enter the city in ten years" and focused on the diamond nose ring that she wore. But immigration officials' suspicion quickly evaporated when Vaishno showed them the $25,000 in cash that he had brought with him to begin his new life. The Bagais left Angel Island and started their lives in the United States.

25. Brij, Kala, Ram, Vaishno, and Madan Bagai, c. 1920–1921.

After being admitted into the country, Vaishno relished his new life in the United States. He wore American suits, spoke English fluently, and adopted Western manners. He bought a home, ran an import business and general store in San Francisco called Bagai's Bazaar, and became involved in the

San Francisco–based Ghadar Party, organized by South Asian immigrants to revolt against British rule on the Indian subcontinent. In 1921, Vaishno applied to federal court in San Francisco and became a naturalized U.S. citizen.

Kala, however, struggled with learning English and everyday tasks like shopping and caring for her three young boys. "In India we had servants to take care of our children, and mother-in-law, and so on. But here, when I came, we didn't have anybody, so I couldn't take care of my children," she explained. She also chafed at the harsh discrimination the family faced every day. The family achieved a dream when they bought their first home in the city of Berkeley. But when they pulled up to their new neighborhood on moving day, they found that the neighbors had locked up the house to prevent them from moving in. "All of our luggage and everything was loaded on the trucks," recounted Kala Bagai. "I told Mr. Bagai 'I don't want to live in this neighborhood. I don't want to live in this house, because they might hurt my children, and I don't want it.' He agreed. We paid for the house and they locked the doors? No." The family moved back to San Francisco and lived above their store at 3159 Fillmore Street.[16]

With so few South Asian women and children in the United States in the early twentieth century, the Bagais were a rare South Asian immigrant family in the country. Far more common were the multiethnic families of South Asians and Puerto Ricans, African Americans, and West Indians in the Northeast and South or Punjabi-Mexican families in southern California. In the Imperial Valley, along the Mexican border east of San Diego, Punjabis were among the newcomers who arrived after the massive Imperial Irrigation District project created hundreds of thousands of acres of fertile land. Barred from marrying white women by California's antimiscegenation laws, many South Asian men began to seek out Mexican partners around World War I. Inder Singh, an Imperial Valley farmer, told an interviewer in 1924 that his Mexican wife not only provided companionship but also economic security in spite of the Alien Land Laws that prevented him and other Asian immigrants from owning land in the state. "Through her I am able to secure land for farming. Your land law can't get rid of me now; I am going to stay." By the 1930s, a vibrant Punjabi-Mexican community had been established in the county.[17]

Worlds were also built among immigrants outside the formal boundaries of nuclear families, ethnic neighborhoods, and community organizations. Immigrant workers on the move could still form attachments and associations among one another and across racial and ethnic lines, what historian Nayan Shah describes as "stranger intimacy." Sometimes this took the form of the work gang that acted as a cooperative unit. Sometimes this took the form of interracial sex and same sex relations. Stranger intimacy helped foster community and survival in a hostile land.[18]

26. Vaishno Das Bagai.

Compared to other Asian immigrants like the Chinese, Japanese, and Filipinos, South Asians found that their smaller numbers constrained their choices. There were not as many formal organizations providing assistance, and the group lacked a central ethnic neighborhood like San Francisco's Chinatown, Seattle's Japantown, or Stockton's Little Manila. Like Koreans, South Asians were also colonial subjects and could not rely on their home government for assistance or protection.

27. Exterior photograph of the Stockton *gurdwara* printed in the January 1916 issue of *The Hindusthanee Student*.

Despite their relative numbers, South Asians did build important community, religious, and political organizations that provided communal support, a way to practice their faith, and a means to express their growing support for Indian nationalism. The Pacific Coast Khalsa Diwan Society was formed in the early 1900s in Stockton to help Sikhs practice their faith, and by 1912 it had established the first Sikh *gurdwara* (temple) in the United States. By 1915, one U.S. government official reported that there were numerous *gurdwaras* "scattered all over the Coast."[19] They were primarily places of worship and faith for practicing Sikhs. But they also served as community centers and meeting places where some of the first organizations were formed to discuss Indian nationalist politics and community affairs. The Sikh temple in Stockton also helped immigrants detained at Angel Island by summoning U.S. resident witnesses to testify in cases and paying for medical treatment at the station hospital. For many newly admitted immigrants, the Stockton *gurdwara* was often the first place they would go to in order to connect with family and friends and to find employment and housing.[20] Muslims and Hindus also relied on their own organizations. The Moslem Association of America was formed in 1919 in Sacramento. The Hindustani Welfare and Reform Society of America was founded in 1919 in El Centro, and the Hindu American Conference was formed in Sacramento in 1920.[21]

Along with their work, families, associations, and communities, another central aspect of South Asian American life in the early twentieth century was the Indian nationalist movement. British subjects in name, South Asians in the United States expected to have the same rights, privileges, and responsibilities as other British subjects. When the British government failed to protest the rampant discrimination that South Asians faced in North America, they realized that their equal status was merely a fiction. Increasingly, South Asians found the revolutionary message of Indian nationalists more and more appealing. They believed that if they could control their own country, they could also control their own destinies in North America.

Indian nationalist activities in North America were first organized in Canada by Taraknath Das in 1907. An educated Bengali who had arrived in Vancouver from Seattle via Japan, Das served as a translator for the U.S. government in Vancouver and helped found the Hindustan Association in Canada. He also began publishing the *Free Hindustan*, a nationalist newspaper that became the first South Asian publication in Canada. Because the paper openly advocated the cause of Indian independence, the British government closely monitored it and even went so far as to urge the U.S. government to repress publication. The United States declined to do so, but government officials did order Das to cease his involvement in the Hindustan Association or resign from his government post. Das chose resignation. The *Free Hindustan* was banned from the Canadian mails shortly thereafter, and Das moved to Seattle, where he attended the University of Washington. He continued his political work by organizing the growing number of South Asian students arriving in the United States and Canada. He was soon joined by fellow Indian nationalist Teja Singh. They and other Indian nationalists spread news and encouraged others to join them in revolution. The movement grew from a fledgling group into a growing political force that was connected to a global anticolonial movement.[22]

By the 1910s, the Hindustan Association of America had chapters on a number of major university campuses. Das developed strong relationships with U.S.-based anarchists and Industrial Workers of the World leaders. In 1913, Har Dayal, a recently arrived nationalist and lecturer, helped Das organize the Pacific Coast Hindustani Association. After it had established branches up and down the coast of the United States and Canada, it renamed itself as the Ghadar Party to organize against British rule in India. The word *ghadar*, meaning "mutiny" or "revolution," became the title for the association's newspaper, *Hindustan Ghadar*, printed in both Urdu and Punjabi. Ghadar activities and publications aimed to engage local South Asian communities in the cause of Indian independence and to foster a collective identity for the immigrants as nationalists. Unlike earlier nationalist movements that were either reformist or religiously based, the Ghadar movement explicitly advocated revolution, by violent means if necessary. Ghadarites hoped to invade India from outside and inspire a massive revolt against British rule. Dayal and other Ghadar leaders such as Kartar Singh Sarabha, Gobind Behari Lal, Sohon Lal Pathak, and Muhammad Manlavie Baraktullah published the newspaper and traveled to farms, lumber mills, and railroad camps in both Canada and the United States to lecture about the injustices of British colonialism.[23]

For many South Asians, the Ghadar movement promised a way to achieve both independence in India and equal treatment in the United States and Canada. As Ghadar leader Gobind Behari Lal explained, "it was no use to talk about the Asiatic Exclusion Act, immigration, and citizenship." Nationalists had to strike at the British because "they were responsible for the way Indians were being treated in America."[24] This appeal made sense to many South Asian farmers and laborers in the United States and Canada. They made donations, joined the Ghadar Party, and the movement spread.[25]

• • •

While South Asians viewed their struggles in North America as part of a global struggle for freedom in India, white Americans and Canadians viewed them as just another Asian immigration problem. South Asians were simply added to the list of despised "Asiatics" like Chinese and Japanese, and the arguments for their exclusion grew louder. The Bellingham *Reveille* editorialized that the "Hindus" were "repulsive in appearance and disgusting in their manners."[26] Religious Sikh men, who wore the dastar, a turban head covering that is a symbol of the Sikh faith, were especially targeted, with one Washington newspaper describing them as "dirty and gaunt and with a roll of pagan dry-goods wrapped around [their] head[s]."[27] South Asians were labeled the least assimilable of all the Asian immigrants, and were, according to the 1911 U.S. Immigration Commission, a government committee charged with investigating U.S. immigration policy, "universally regarded as the least desirable race of immigrants thus far admitted to the United States." Given the fact that the commission had just studied thirty-nine immigrant groups in the United States, placing South Asians at the bottom of the heap was significant. The commission recommended that the United States should reach an understanding with the British government to prevent "East Indian laborers" from coming to the United States.[28]

Racial tension and violence targeting South Asians escalated in the summer of 1907 in Bellingham, Washington, and built on the region's established pattern of organized legal and extralegal violence directed toward Asians. Chinese miners had been driven out of Bellingham, Tacoma, and Seattle as early as 1885, and Japanese mill hands had been threatened with expulsion by whites in the early 1900s. By the summer of 1907, when South Asian workers came to Bellingham, white workers were ready. They demanded a "whites only" policy at the Whatcom Falls Mill Company.[29]

When a mass firing of Asian workers in the mills did not materialize, a thousand union supporters marched down the main streets of Bellingham on Wednesday, September 4, shouting "Drive out the Hindus." At eight in the evening, a mob of white men began pulling South Asians out of their residences and bunkhouses, dragging them off streetcars, and driving them out of town or to the city jail. By the end of the night, 200 South Asians were in jail. The next day, the rest of the South Asian community gathered up what they could find of their belongings and left Bellingham by boat or train for Vancouver, Seattle, or Oakland with the taunts of the gathered crowd ringing in their ears.[30]

The "Hindu problem" in Bellingham was apparently solved. Three days later, Vancouver was ripped apart by a related anti-Asian riot that swept through the Chinese and Japanese quarters and left destruction in its wake. The Gentlemen's Agreements with Japan followed, and Japanese laborers were thereafter barred from both countries.[31] Although South Asians were not the primary targets of the Vancouver riots, exclusionists in both countries remained focused on finding a way to stop South Asian immigration as well. Canada acted first.

Exclusionists in British Columbia called for all-out immigration restriction. But as a member of the British commonwealth, Canada had to be mindful of international relationships and imperial responsibilities. The colonial India office warned against discriminating against South Asians in Canada to avoid negative repercussions within British India. And British officials gently reminded their hotheaded counterparts in British Columbia that as British subjects, South Asians could not easily be excluded from Canada anyway. In Ottawa, officials came up with an ingenious solution. Government investigations had revealed that most South Asians had to board two ships on their journey from Calcutta to Canada; one from Calcutta to another Asian port, usually Hong Kong or Shanghai, and another to cross the Pacific Ocean to British Columbia. Canadian ministers used this information to issue an order-in-council to temporarily prohibit immigrants who had not come on a "continuous voyage" from the country of their birth or citizenship when entering Canada. Since there was no direct steamship service between India and any Canadian port, the January 1908 Continuous Journey order effectively barred South Asians without exception. This law achieved exclusion of South Asians without explicitly discriminating against British Indian subjects.[32]

With Canada closed, the United States became the primary North American destination for South Asian immigrants after 1908, and the numbers of South Asians entering the country grew dramatically. San Francisco quickly became the most important port of entry, and by April 1910, Hart Hyatt North, the commissioner of immigration at San Francisco, reported that "the Hindus are coming here at the rate of 80 to 100 a week."[33] A new phase of the "Hindu invasion" began.

28. In this 1910 cartoon, an American railroad baron welcomes two South Asians into the United States as cheap laborers. Their vermin-infested clothes and impoverished and ape-like appearance clearly mark them as "undesirable citizens," but without any restriction laws in place, throngs of other South Asians line up to enter the country. "Undesirable Citizens," *San Francisco Daily News*, June 28, 1910.

San Francisco newspapers claimed that the "Hindus" were being used as cheap laborers by "moneyed capitalists" to further degrade white workingmen. National publications referred to the "Hindu Invasion" and the "Tide of Turbans" descending on the West Coast. All of these claims had been made before to exclude Chinese and Japanese immigrants. The one original argument was that South Asians were "the most undesirable," because they were dangerous "revolutionaries" pledged to overthrow British domination.[34]

That South Asian immigration needed to be stopped was clear to Asian exclusionists. But like their counterparts in Canada, officials in Washington, D.C., proceeded cautiously. South Asians were technically British subjects, and it was unclear how U.S. exclusion policies might affect British imperialism and Anglo-American relations. U.S. politicians, immigration officials, and anti-immigrant activists first looked to Canada. They praised the actions of the Canadian government in stopping the "threatened invasion of undesirable Asiatic immigrants," as California congressman Julius Kahn explained.[35] U.S. commissioner-general of immigration Daniel Keefe specifically approved of Canada's Continuous Journey law, and he exhorted his fellow immigration officials to find similar solutions.[36]

The fact that there was no legal way to exclude South Asians was of little concern to Keefe. "It is true, of course, that there is no law directed at the exclusion of Hindus as a race," Keefe conceded to a fellow immigration officer. However, the commissioner continued, there were still ways to exclude them.[37] If the immigrants were "not found to belong to some of the definitely excluded classes such as paupers, criminals, or contagiously diseased," for example, they should be excluded by other means, including being "persons of poor physique" or persons "likely to become public charges," Keefe instructed in 1913. Government surgeons would then "render certificates to that effect," thereby supporting the made-up grounds for exclusion.[38] For example, immigration officials might use immigrants' "poor physical condition" to question whether they would be able to perform hard labor or become an unemployed public burden.[39] Americans' staunch opposition to South Asians could also provide "practically the sole ground upon which the Department could exclude Hindus."[40]

Under Commissioner-General of Immigration Keefe, U.S. immigration officials began to enforce U.S. immigration policies to achieve an informal system of exclusion. The most common tactic was to try to establish that the applicant under investigation was "likely to become a public charge" and then exclude him under that provision of the general exclusion laws.[41] Because the definition and context of the "likely to become a public charge" clause was so vague and subjective, excluding South Asians under this category was effective. In 1910, for example, immigration officials on Angel Island denied entry to one immigrant because he had "a very poor physical appearance," and was "weak and emaciated looking."[42] Such practices inspired Rajani Das, a U.S. government investigator, to contend that South Asians were "illegally or on small pretext detained . . . by immigration officials."[43] Statistics from the U.S. Bureau of Immigration best illustrate the stark reality of South Asian exclusion. From 1911 to 1915, 55 percent of all South Asian applicants were denied admission. In comparison, immigrant inspectors on Angel Island rejected 9 percent of Chinese applicants during the same years.[44]

Despite this high rejection rate, opponents to South Asian immigration remained convinced that a federal immigration law was the only permanent solution to the "Hindu problem." Several bills were introduced into Congress in 1913 and 1914 proposing to exclude South Asians along the same lines as the Chinese Exclusion Act, but no bill resulted. Total exclusion would have to wait. In the meantime, South Asians began to organize a protest against their exclusion from North America that would have long-standing repercussions around the world.

It began in Canada. Canadian lawmakers were mistaken in believing that they had completely solved the "Hindu" immigration problem with the 1908 Continuous Journey decree. South Asians, already chafing under British colonial rule in India, saw the law as blatantly discriminatory, and some launched a campaign to challenge it. The most spectacular of these involved Gurdit Singh, a Sikh contractor, and a ship called the *Komagata Maru*.

In 1914, Singh chartered a boat to bring South Asians directly from India to Canada. He advertised passage on the *Komagata Maru* and pledged "not [to] return back until the real result will be out."[45] The *Komagata Maru* sailed on April 6, 1914, from Hong Kong with a Japanese crew of 40 and 165 Sikhs. In Shanghai, it picked up 111 additional passengers, and by the time it left Kobe and Yokohama, there were 376 people (340 Sikhs, 24 Muslims, and 12 Hindus, all from Punjab) on their self-designed "continuous journey" to Vancouver.[46] Rumors in the press began to fly around the world about the shipload of "Hindoos" destined to "force" their way into British Columbia in spite of the Continuous Journey law.[47] The stage was set for a showdown.

On May 21, 1914, the *Komagata Maru* arrived at Victoria harbor. Gurdit Singh announced that as British citizens, he and the passengers of the *Komagata Maru* had "a right to visit any part of the Empire. We are determined to make this a test case."[48] The *Komagata Maru* was allowed to proceed on to Vancouver, but it was not allowed to dock. Instead, she had to put down her anchor about a half mile offshore. No passengers were allowed to leave the ship, and immigration agents in Vancouver established a special patrol around the ship to prevent any passengers from escaping.

The arrival of the *Komagata Maru* set off protests by whites, who gathered at the harbor to proclaim that "yellow races are not wanted in Canada."[49] But support for the *Komagata Maru* passengers also came from far and wide. Local Sikhs in Vancouver shouted words of encouragement from the docks, provided supplies, and organized fund drives to support the legal efforts. On May 31, a mass meeting of about 500 South Asians gathered in Vancouver to pledge donations and to pass resolutions to the government of India detailing the plight of the ship and its passengers.[50] The San Francisco–based *Ghadar* newspaper lambasted the Canadian government in its pages. U.S.-based activist Taraknath Das rushed to the border town of Sumas, Washington, to lend his support.[51]

29. Sikhs aboard the *Komagata Maru* in Vancouver Harbor, 1914. Gurdit Singh is at left wearing a light colored suit.

By the end of June, Singh had been negotiating with city, provincial, and dominion officials for an entire month, and time was running out for the *Komagata Maru*. On July 6, the passengers were ordered deported by the Supreme Court. Immigration officials boarded the *Komagata Maru* three days later to negotiate the ship's departure, but tensions escalated. Passengers threatened to hold immigration official Malcolm Reid hostage unless they received food and other provisions. When the ship was again ordered to leave the harbor on July 18, passengers mutinied and refused to let the crew control the ship. Vancouver immigration officials and the local city police made plans to forcibly remove all passengers and place them on another steamship to Hong Kong. They prepared the *Sea Lion*, the largest tugboat available in the city, to effect the transfer. Immigration agent Reid brought together 175 police and special officers, including the chief of police, for the mission, which was to begin at 1:00 a.m. on Sunday, July 19.

The government's plan went awry almost immediately. A "strenuous fight" ensued as the officers on the *Sea Lion* tried to board the ship. Passengers cut the grappling ropes and defended their ship. During the fifteen-minute battle, the tug's windows were smashed, its captain suffered two broken ribs, and the chief of police was wounded. The police turned a water hose on the mutineers. Three gunshots came from the *Komagata Maru*. The *Sea Lion* limped back to shore with twenty injured men.[52]

The federal government finally intervened and sent a senior minister from Ottawa to negotiate with Gurdit Singh and the passengers. It also sent one of its two navy cruisers to assist with the task of securing the ship. By July 23, the crisis was over. The *Komagata Maru* had received provisions, the passengers gave control back to the crew, and the ship voluntarily left Vancouver harbor accompanied by the Canadian navy vessel.

The *Komagata Maru* incident had primarily been a challenge to Canada's Continuous Journey law. But it was also part of a larger anticolonial movement in which South Asians challenged British rule throughout the empire in 1913 and 1914. The extent to which British officials felt threatened by the *Komagata Maru* challenge was made clear when the ship finally arrived in the city of Bajbaj, about ten miles from Calcutta, in September 1914. The passengers wanted to disembark and make a religious procession to Calcutta, but British police refused, fearing that they would spread revolutionary unrest among the local population. Instead, the *Komagata Maru* passengers were ordered to board a special train that would take them directly to Punjab. The passengers resisted, and shots were exchanged. Twenty-six people died. Gurdit Singh and twenty-nine former passengers fled. Almost all of the rest were arrested and imprisoned as subversives.[53]

The *Komagata Maru* incident transformed the United States' own efforts to exclude South Asians. Commissioner-General of Immigration Anthony Caminetti quickly employed the specter of the *Komagata Maru* to argue that the United States was on the brink of a similar tragedy, and he urged the passage of federal legislation. In a special letter to Congressman John Burnett, chair of the Committee on Immigration and Naturalization, he concluded that the country faced nothing less than an "emergency" situation regarding "Hindu migration."[54]

The movement to exclude South Asians gained additional support as the U.S., Canadian, and British governments became increasingly alarmed that South Asians in North America were engaging in the Indian independence movement, promoting sedition against the British government, and even raising money to buy arms. By 1910, the United States had replaced Canada as the main site for organizing and promoting Indian nationalism in North America, and South Asian immigration became identified as a threat to national security. The Ghadar Party and its leaders, especially Har Dayal, were put under U.S. surveillance efforts that complemented the Canadian and British surveillance of South Asian communities throughout North America.

Beginning in 1911, William C. Hopkinson, the Canadian agent hired in 1908 to conduct surveillance within the Vancouver South Asian community, was also hired by the U.S. government as an immigrant interpreter in 1911. He was recognized by the United States as Canada's "best posted man on Hindu matters."[55] For several years, he passed information between the two governments and regularly traveled across the border to meet with informants, conduct undercover work, and gather information on Indian nationalist activities in North America. Copies of his reports routinely went to both the Canadian and U.S. governments as well as to the Colonial Office in London.

The belief that Indian nationalists posed a security threat was magnified when Hopkinson was murdered in a Vancouver courtroom in October 1914 by Indian nationalist Mewa Singh. And when 2,000 Indians left North America in late 1914 to lead a rebellion against the British in India, the British government responded with executions, arrests, trials, and more surveillance.[56] Such high-profile cases lent momentum to the cause of South Asian exclusion in the United States. Linked to revolutionaries in British India and assassinations in Canada, South Asian immigration began to be viewed with increasing alarm.

By 1916, congressional debate on South Asian exclusion resumed. This time, the discussion centered on the issue of geographic exclusion or a "barred zone." The so-called Barred Zone Act was a compromise piece of legislation. On one side were the die-hard exclusionists who had fought for a bill "openly excluding all Asians." On the other side was the administration of President Woodrow Wilson, which believed that such a blatantly discriminatory clause would infuriate the Japanese government.[57] The compromise "barred zone" law officially excluded "inhabitants of most of China, all of India, Burma (Myanmar), Siam (Thailand), and the Malay states, part of Russia, all of Arabia and Afghanistan, most of the Polynesian Islands, and all of the East Indian Islands," with an estimated population of 500 million people. Since Chinese and Japanese had already been excluded by separate laws and diplomatic agreements, South Asian immigrants were the clear targets. On February 5, the Immigration Act of 1917 was passed with the Asiatic Barred Zone in place, and another gate was closed to Asian immigration.[58] At the same time, South Asians fell victim to western states' Alien Land Laws that prevented them from owning and leasing land. And in 1923, the U.S. Supreme Court ruled in *Bhagat Singh Thind* v. *The United States* that South Asians were not eligible for naturalized U.S. citizenship.

The impact of these laws and policies on South Asian immigrants in the United States was immediate. Discrimination against South Asians became rampant. They were barred from many professions. When they did find employment, they were offered lower wages than white and other Asian workers. They were only given the hardest and "lowest kind" of work, and their complaints about unsafe working conditions or unfair wages were ignored. They faced discrimination in theaters, movies, restaurants, and

30. Photograph of Bhagat Singh Thind in his U.S. Army uniform, from 1918. Thind enlisted in the U.S. Army and trained at Camp Lewis, Washington.

hotels. They were forced to live in "the most undesirable sections of the town." They were socially ostracized and ridiculed for observing their national or religious customs.[59] One interviewee put it more poignantly. We "see discrimination in the eyes of all. We . . . feel the discrimination in every glance and action."[60]

South Asians coped as best they could and continued to challenge the discrimination they faced. One high-profile case involved Bhagat Singh Thind, a naturalized American citizen who had first entered the United States in 1913 and served in the U.S. armed forces during World War I. When officials began an effort to denaturalize the small numbers of South Asian immigrants who had been able to become naturalized citizens on the grounds that they were not white, as the law required, Thind took his case to the U.S. Supreme Court. He claimed that he was a descendant of the Aryans of India and belonged to the Caucasian race, and was thus "white" within the meaning of U.S. naturalization law. The Supreme Court disagreed. The "great body of our people," the court stated, recognize the racial differences between whites and South Asians and "instinctively . . . reject the thought of assimilation" of South Asians into [white] Americans.[61] Thind was denaturalized.

Other South Asians who had become naturalized citizens were also unceremoniously denaturalized. By 1924, Vaishno Das Bagai was stripped of his U.S. citizenship. Without citizenship status, Bagai was subject to California's Alien Land Laws. He was forced to sell his home, his San Francisco store, and other property. The final insult came when the U.S. government refused to grant him a U.S. passport to visit friends and relatives in India in 1928. They suggested that he reapply for a British passport, but having once renounced his British citizenship in the name of Indian nationalism, Bagai refused to reclassify himself as a British subject. Feeling trapped and betrayed, he committed suicide by gas poisoning in 1928. He left one letter to his family and another to the *San Francisco Examiner* explaining that he had taken his own life in protest. "I came to America thinking, dreaming and hoping to make this land my home . . . and tried to give my children the best American education. . . . But now they come and say to me I am no longer an American citizen," he wrote. "Now what am I? What have I made of myself and my children? We cannot exercise our rights. Humility and insults, who is responsible for all this? Me and the American government. Obstacles this way, blockades that way, and bridges burnt behind." Vaishno left behind his young widow, Kala, and three young sons.[62]

The Bagai family was slow to recover after Vaishno's tragic death. But he had left behind detailed instructions on how to manage the family finances, and Kala was extremely resourceful. She focused on raising her children and saw them off to college. She also remarried. Her second husband was Mahesh Chandra, a family friend in San Francisco and a fellow Indian nationalist.[63] When the 1946 Luce-Celler Act amended the Immigration Act of 1917 and allowed "natives of India" to apply for admission to the United States, Kala and her sons became naturalized U.S. citizens. India gained its independence from Great Britain the next year.

8

"We Have Heard Much of America": Filipinos in the U.S. Empire

U.S. colonial rule in the Philippines began two years before Francisco Carino was born in 1900 in a small town in the province of Ilocos Sur. By the early twentieth century, there were American missionaries, teachers, doctors, and colonial officials all over the new colony, and American-style schools taught U.S. geography, history, government, and civics. Growing up learning about "the best of America," Carino was convinced that the United States was full of "riches, beauty, and grandeur." "We have heard much of America as a land of the brave and the free, land of opportunity," he told an interviewer.[1] Spurred on by these images and facilitated by U.S. policies that classified Filipinos as "U.S. nationals" rather than as foreign immigrants, 150,000 Filipinos crossed the Pacific to Hawai'i and the continental U.S. during the early twentieth century.

The rampant prejudice and discrimination Carino experienced in the United States, however, broke his heart. Landlords would not rent apartments to him. Employment agencies did not hire him. Restaurants and barber shops refused to serve him. Signs that read "Positively No Filipinos Allowed" or "No Filipinos or Dogs Allowed" were common in many California towns. "The color of the skin makes all the difference" in the United States, Carino observed.[2] Writer Carlos Bulosan put it more bluntly: "It is a crime to be Filipino in California."[3]

U.S. imperialism and the status of Filipinos as U.S. nationals shaped every aspect of Filipino migration to the United States as well as their experiences within the U.S. empire. The U.S. colonization of the Philippines set in motion the second wave of Filipino migration to the Americas (following the thousands who came during the Manila galleon era). And the American presence in the islands had taught Filipinos that they were part of America. But when they arrived in the United States, their status as Asians and as a colonized people translated into unequal treatment. They were included in the United States, but not as citizens. They could be in the United States, but were relegated to the lowliest and most exploitable positions. They suffered racism, but in ways different from other Asians. They were "little brown brothers" in the United States, and that status came with its own set of problems.[4]

The Philippines became a U.S. colony, along with Puerto Rico and Guam, following the end of the Spanish-American War in 1898. The United States had annexed Hawai'i earlier that year, and with its new possessions became a formidable imperial power. Just as the Philippines had been central to Spain's Pacific empire beginning in the 1500s, it now became a valuable gateway for U.S.-Asian trade after 1898. But it was a hard-won victory. Filipino revolutionaries led by Emilio Aguinaldo refused to recognize the United States' sovereignty. They battled American soldiers during the brutal Philippine-American War that lasted over three years until 1902. In the end, 4,500 American soldiers lost their lives. As many as one million Filipino civilians died from battle, violence, starvation, and disease.[5]

With the colonization of the Philippines came the need to incorporate Filipinos into the United States in some way. Citizenship was out of the question. Filipinos were described in racial terms as uncivilized savages, brutal rapists, and even dogs and monkeys. At best, they were characterized as children in need of (U.S.) guidance. As the young lawyer William Howard Taft, chairman of the U.S. commission that established the colonial government and future U.S. president, explained, Filipinos were "little brown brothers" who would need "fifty or one hundred years" of close supervision "to develop anything resembling Anglo-Saxon political principles and skills."[6]

U.S. rule transformed the Philippine economy in ways that benefited American investors but not Filipinos. For example, the United States continued to expand the Philippines' export-oriented economy first established by the Spanish. American companies and owners bought farmland to use for export crops, including sugar, and by the twentieth century the Philippines was exporting so many of its agricultural products and natural resources that it could no longer feed itself. Even basic necessities like rice and textiles had to be imported, and economic policies that kept the Philippines an unindustrialized export economy led to dislocation and inequalities. Small family farms, especially in the provinces of Ilocos Norte and Sur, Pangasinan, Tarlac, La Union, and Abra on the island of Luzon, became divided into unsustainable plots by the late nineteenth and early twentieth centuries. Tenancy, landlessness, poverty, and migration followed.[7]

The United States' role in the Philippines was characterized by President William McKinley as one of "benevolent assimilation." The United States would educate, civilize, and uplift Filipinos so that they could one day rule themselves.[8] And Filipinos were considered "U.S. Nationals," an unequal legal classification that granted Filipinos "ward" status (like Native Americans) without citizenship rights. Colonized U.S. national status did, however, allow Filipinos to migrate from one part of the United States to another with few obstacles. Unlike immigrants, Filipinos were not subjected to immigration laws or immigrant inspections, and 150,000 migrated to the Hawaiian islands and the United States while other Asians faced increasing restrictions. Filipinos were also the only foreign nationals allowed to enlist in the U.S. armed forces. They were restricted to joining only the U.S. Navy and were mostly relegated to demeaning "women's work" as Navy stewards who prepared and served the officers' meals and cared for their living spaces. Still, the incentive to join was high. With military service came good salaries, exemptions from immigration laws after 1935, and expedited naturalization after 1940. Thousands of Filipinos enlisted in the U.S. Navy and joined the navy's "brown skinned servant force" as a career.[9]

The proliferation of American culture in the Philippines also spurred migration. With missionaries, teachers, doctors, and many other Americans active throughout the Philippines as part of the U.S.'s efforts to "uplift" the country, Filipinos were schooled from a very young age to admire the United States and to think of themselves as American. With its commitment to freedom and democracy and its huge cities, "beautiful streets and parks, big factories, [and] great men," as Francisco Carino described, the United States was believed to be a "land of Paradise."[10] A culture of migration took root.

The first Filipino men and women to come to the United States came at the invitation of the U.S. government under the Pensionado Act of 1903. This law brought a few thousand elite Filipino students, known as *pensionados*, to attend American universities around the country, but they were expected to return to the Philippines to become "successful and powerful [pro-U.S.] leaders" of the Philippines.[11]

By the early twentieth century, the Philippines was identified as the next site in the United States' ongoing search for Asian labor. Filipinos were attractive for a number of reasons. First, they could enter the United States easily because of their status as U.S. nationals. Second, like Koreans, they could be used to compete with the Japanese plantation workers in Hawai'i who were leading successful labor movements for higher wages and better working conditions.

Soon, labor agents known as "drummers" were flocking to the Philippines. Traveling from town to town, they showed movies in the town plaza that promoted the great adventures and economic opportunities that awaited Filipino workers in Hawai'i. One movie scene even showed bosses handing out check after check to waiting Filipinos. Migration fever quickly spread. "*Kasla glorya ti Hawaii*," "Hawai'i is like a land of glory," Filipinos would repeat to one another.[12] In 1906, the first fifteen Filipino laborers arrived in Hawai'i on the SS *Doric*. Between 1907 and 1919, recruiters from the Hawaiian Sugar Plantation Association brought over 24,000 Filipinos. From 1920 and 1929, 48,000 followed. *Hawaiianos*, or those returning from Hawai'i, were the best type of advertisement for going abroad. Some had saved up enough to purchase land. Others strutted around in shiny white shoes, expensive-looking suits, and Stetson hats. "Of course I lost no time in making up my mind to go," Dolores Quinto recalled after seeing *Hawaiianos* return to his village. Soon, he, his wife, and their children joined the throngs of others on their way to Hawai'i.[13]

• • •

Thousands of Filipinos signed contracts that took them to Hawai'i as *sakadas,* or laborers, who were part of the global sugar plantation economy that stretched from the Caribbean to Hawai'i. They were bound to work for three years at wages of $18 a month and gained transportation back home if they worked for a total of 720 days. The transition to life as a plantation laborer occurred as soon as the steamships reached Hawai'i. "As we came down the gangplank," one new arrival remembered, "we shouted the plantation of our destiny. 'Waialua Sugar Company!' 'Puunene Maui!' people shouted. I shouted 'Naalehu, Hawai'i.' " As they assembled with other laborers, plantation officials placed a *bango*, a metal tag with a number stamped on it, around their necks that identified them as lowly plantation workers. Their new lives in Hawai'i had begun.[14]

Like Chinese, Japanese, and Korean plantation laborers, Filipinos worked in a new world of labor from "siren to siren." The work was dusty, hot, physically difficult, and monotonous. Workers complained of aching backs, the sharp, spiney needles of the cane leaves, reddish clouds of dust, and the searing sun. They left camp at five in the morning and did not return until after the end-of-day whistle at eight.

Filipinos shared in these difficult tasks with other plantation laborers from Asia. But as the last group to arrive in Hawai'i, they occupied the lowest position in the plantation hierarchy. As writer Milton Murayama explained, the plantation was like a pyramid with the white plantation manager living at the top in the big house; the Portuguese, Spanish, and Japanese foremen, living in decent homes just below. Chinese, Japanese, and Korean workers lived in wooden frame houses below them, and finally there was the run-down Filipino camp. The sewer system ran downhill too, with the result that the Filipino camp was the smelliest and most unsanitary.[15] Over time, the tales of returning *Hawaiianos* were less about glory and more about hardship. "*Narigat ti Hawai'i*, hardship is Hawai'i." "Go back, brother . . . go on home," the returning Filipinos would tell those who would listen.[16]

The migration was slower to the continental United States. The first Filipinos to arrive in San Francisco were likely Filipino servants or stewards to U.S. Navy officers. There were also students or former plantation workers coming from Hawai'i. The 1920 census counted 5,603 Filipinos in the states. By the 1920s, transpacific U.S. and Japanese steamship companies were making regular trips from Manila to San Francisco, Los Angeles, and Seattle. The conditions were crowded and unsanitary, but the third-class tickets that most Filipinos bought were cheap and steamship company agents did a good job of drumming up business with "stories of 'streets strewn with gold.' "[17] The first Filipinos to arrive directly in California came in 1923 and numbered around 2,000.[18] After 1924, when new U.S. laws closed the door even further to other Asian immigrants, more than 4,000 Filipinos arrived in California each year. By 1930, there were 56,000 in the country.[19]

As U.S. nationals, Filipinos primarily migrated to the United States. But small numbers often landed first in Canada and Mexico before traveling on to the United States. A common transpacific route from Manila brought Filipinos to Hong Kong, Tokyo, or Kobe, and then to Vancouver or Victoria. If they were bound for the United States, the passengers would then take a smaller boat to San Francisco. Some were quarantined in Vancouver before they were allowed to land in the United States. There were a small number of Filipinos who landed in Mexico as well.[20]

Most of the Filipinos migrating to the United States were young men joining their fathers, uncles, cousins, brothers, and friends already laboring in farms in California's Central Valley or in canneries in the Pacific Northwest and Alaska. The few women who did migrate to the United States came as students, accompanied their husbands, or were sent to join family already there. Throughout the decades, the gender ratio remained highly unequal. In 1930, there were only 2,500 Filipino women in California out of a total of 42,500 Filipinos. Despite their small numbers, Filipinas played important roles building families, contributing to family economies, and keeping bonds of extended family strong. They formed their own women's organizations and helped promote Filipino culture.[21] Large extended families made up of relatives and nonrelatives also became central to Filipino lives in America. The small numbers of Filipino children were cherished and families often modified the traditional *compadre* (or godfather) system to include nonrelatives. It was not uncommon to have 200 men be invited to be godparents at the time of a birth, for example.[22]

In California, Filipinos worked in a variety of jobs. Twenty-five percent worked as janitors, dishwashers, and "all kinds of service boys," according to writer Manuel Buaken, chamber boys, houseboys, elevator boys, door boys, and busboys.[23] However, most Filipinos, around 60 percent, worked in what writer Carey McWilliams called "factories in the fields."[24] By the 1920s, California agriculture was a multimillion-dollar business with a long history of exploiting immigrant labor. The delta region between the Sacramento and San Joaquin rivers produced most of the world's supply of asparagus as well as large amounts of strawberries, potatoes, and lettuce. These crops required small armies of laborers who had to withstand brutal working conditions ranging from heavy winter rains to summer temperatures of over 100 degrees. Chinese, Japanese, Koreans, and South Asians had been among the state's first migrant farmworkers. Filipinos and Mexicans became the dominant workforce in the fields by the 1920s and 1930s. While growers routinely claimed that Asians and Mexicans were physically more suited to the harsh agricultural work than whites, it was likely the low wages and terrible work conditions that kept whites away. "Under these adverse conditions," Buaken explained, "white workers don't even try."[25]

By 1930, approximately 18,000 Filipino immigrants were engaged in agricultural work in the United States. Traveling between the major agricultural centers like Delano, Stockton, and other cities and towns in California, they followed the crops and kept California's farms profitable.[26] Eliseo Felipe, who began working in Stockton soon after his arrival in 1933, traveled even further to Wyoming, Montana, and Utah with the harvest. "I stayed in different camps because crops followed the different seasons," he told an interviewer. "So when asparagus is over here, we are already done, getting ready for grapes. Then when the grapes is over, the tomatoes are ready to ripen up. We had to go where the job was. Name it, baby, I was there. I was not particular. I just wanted to work."[27]

Farmworkers fought a never-ending battle against the dust from the fields that choked their lungs and covered their skin and had to make repeated visits to the doctor to swab their throats clean.[28] In Salinas, Filipinos worked eight to ten hours a day, with only brief breaks for meals. For their labor, they earned 15 cents an hour up until 1933, when the wages were raised 5 cents. They were, according to McWilliams, among the "most viciously exploited" laborers recruited by California growers to "make up their vast army of 'cheap labor.'"[29]

31. Filipino asparagus cutters in California during the 1920s.

Even if they laboriously followed the harvests throughout the U.S. West, most Filipinos could only find farmwork for ten months of the year. The growing Alaska cannery business offered other employment opportunities for some of the remaining months. The regular season began in June, and a steady stream of Filipinos made their way up north from California after the asparagus harvest to work as "Alaskeros."

By the 1930s, 15 percent of Alaska cannery workers were Filipinos. Their job was to clean, pack, cook, label, and box all the fish delivered to the cannery doors. It was difficult work that all had to be done by hand. Pablo Mabalon remembered, "ours was the work of a mule. The work schedule was indefinite and the hours were long. You needed will and strength to keep up with the work."[30] Promises of high wages kept Filipinos going up north. Workers were recruited with guaranteed seasonal earnings. In the late 1920s, this was between $250 and $300 for six months' work. This promising amount, however, was soon whittled down by debts that workers incurred to the labor contractors, who were often other Asian immigrants. Workers could purchase goods—often at grossly inflated prices—at the company store, for example. And there were also gambling debts and fees paid to prostitutes brought into the cannery districts. As a result, it was not uncommon for a worker to be left with only $30 or $40 at season's end.[31]

• • •

Stuck in what Manuel Buaken called "a pit of economic slavery," Filipinos began to organize collectively. In 1928, the Stockton-area Anak ng Bukid, or Children of the Farm, became the first formal Filipino American labor organization. The first Filipino strike occurred in Watsonville in 1930. Over the next six years, there were more than twenty Filipino labor disputes throughout the San Joaquin and Imperial Valleys, and by the mid-1930s there were seven different unions. One of them was the Filipino Labor Union, the FLU, formed by D. L. Marcuelo, a Stockton businessman, in 1933. It soon had 4,000 members.[32]

The Filipino Labor Union took its first stand for higher wages, union recognition, and improved working conditions in August 1933 in the Salinas Valley. Seven hundred Filipino lettuce workers walked off the job to protest their 20 cents an hour wage. The strike failed when growers quickly brought in Mexican, South Asian, and other Asian laborers as strike breakers. Growers continued to pit one group against the other, and it also organized Filipino labor contractors to oppose the labor union.

The FLU tried again the next summer. The Salinas lettuce strike began on August 27, 1934, with a combined group of 6,000 Filipino lettuce pickers and white laborers who packed and stored the lettuce. Soon, the lettuce industry in Monterey County had been brought to a standstill. When the white strikers agreed to negotiate, the Filipinos held their ground and faced an onslaught of violence. The growers rallied local police and armed vigilantes to threaten and beat up the strikers. The camp of FLU president Rufo Canete was burned to the ground and more than 100 rounds were fired into it. The union's headquarters were raided and the leaders arrested for unlawful assembly. By the time the FLU called an end to the strike nearly a month after it had begun, its ranks had been severely depleted, and it negotiated from a compromised position. Still, the labor union was able to win some important concessions. Wages were raised to 40 cents an hour, and the FLU was recognized as a legitimate union. More importantly, the Salinas lettuce strike helped introduce Filipinos to the larger U.S. labor movement. After the FLU organized another strike in Salinas two years later, the American Federation of Labor chartered the formation of a combined Filipino-Mexican agricultural union.[33]

Over the years, Filipino labor activism continued and matured. On April 6, 1939, an independent, all-Filipino union called the Filipino Agricultural Laborers Association (FALA) was formed. Made up of diverse groups of Filipinos (Ilocanos, Visayans, and Tagalogs), FALA represented an effort to unite Filipinos around shared goals of economic security and the campaign to fight discrimination. The union did not waste any time testing its power. It called for a general strike of all asparagus workers the next day if demands for a wage increase were not met. It was the height of the profitable asparagus season, and growers were faced with the potential loss of that season's multimillion-dollar crop. Most growers accepted the union's demands, and the nonviolent strike was considered a rousing success. By 1940, FALA had organized branches throughout California's agricultural belt.[34]

Since Filipinos were barred from living in most neighborhoods, "Little Manilas" made up of Filpino residents, families, and businesses sprang up in Los Angeles, San Francisco, Seattle, Chicago, New York, and Washington, D.C.[35] Stockton's Little Manila was the largest in the country and was well known for its many Filipino businesses and vibrant community. By the 1920s, migrant farmworkers could return from weeks or months away following the crops to recuperate and reconnect in Stockton. They might first pick up their mail and grab a plate of adobo at the popular Lafayette Lunch Counter, run by Pablo Mabalon. They might then buy food at the Manila Grocery Company, read Filipino newspapers like the *Philippine Examiner* published in the city, play pool at Philip's Philippine Billiard Parlor, get their hair cut at the Manila Barber Shop, buy a suit at Los Filipinos Tailoring Shop, have a photograph taken at J. Y. Billones' photo studio, hear the latest labor news at the Sons of the Farm offices, search for jobs at the Filipino Employment Agency, and worship at Catholic St. Mary's. And if they were looking for female companionship, they might stop in at the Lu-Vi-Min Club, named after the major Philippine regions of Luzon, Visayas, and Mindanao. Dressed in their best suits with their hair slicked back, thousands of Filipinos would meet up in Little Manila's taxi dance halls to hear live bands play the popular jazz tunes of the era and pay to dance with hired female dancers. Many blew through a whole day's wages of $1 to $2 in ten or twenty minutes.[36]

Stockton's Little Manila helped sustain and nourish the Filipino American community in the United States for generations. As historian Dawn Mabalon explains, in Little Manila, Filipinos could become something other than the "debased, exploited, faceless laborer hunched over endless miles of asparagus, celery, or beets." Instead, they gathered in their best clothes to meet with friends and "asserted their right to flourish on the streets of Stockton." The city's Little Manila remained the largest Filipino community outside the Philippines from the 1920s to 1970s.[37]

32. Filipinos in front of Manila Pool Hall in California, 1929–1934.

As their migration to the United States grew steadily in the 1920s, Filipinos were increasingly seen as a problem. No longer contained in a far-off U.S. colony, they symbolized the inherent contradiction between the U.S.'s benevolent assimilation policies of Filipinos in the Philippines and the virulent and violent anti-Asian racism that affected all Asians in the United States. By the 1930s, Filipinos were increasingly characterized not as "little brown brothers" but as another "Asiatic invasion" that was worse than the Chinese, Japanese, and South Asian "invasions" that had preceded them.[38]

The anti-Filipino movement first drew on Filipinos' colonized status and perceptions of the Philippines as a backward colony. Filipinos were often portrayed as uncivilized peoples who were criminally minded. San Francisco law enforcement officials reported in 1931 that "there is not one of them [Filipinos] who is not a potential criminal."[39] They were compared to Native Americans and called "untamed headhunters." The president of California's Immigration Study Commission went so far as to label Filipinos "jungle folk" with a "primitive moral code."[40] Judge D. W. Rohrback in Monterey County described Filipinos as "little brown men about ten years removed from a bolo and breechcloth."[41] V. S. McClatchy, editor of the *Sacramento Bee*, argued that the growing number of Filipinos "swarming into the United States . . . would lower citizenship standard[s], and if left unchecked . . . would lead to the destruction of the republic."[42] Congressman Richard J. Welch agreed and told the public in 1930 that Filipino immigration was "one of the gravest problems that has ever faced the people of the Pacific Coast." Both supported an all-out ban on the new invasion.[43]

But the primary complaint against Filipinos seemed to be that they upset the existing racial hierarchy between whites and nonwhites in the United States. Compared to other Asian immigrant communities, more Filipino men paired up with white women. As a consequence of crossing the taboo of interracial sex, Filipino men were constantly charged with having unbridled sexual passions that were dangerous to white women and to decent society. A witness from Salinas testified before the U.S. House Committee on Immigration and Naturalization that Filipinos were a "social menace as they will not leave our white girls alone."[44] In 1933, California's attorney general extended the state's antimiscegenation civil code to include Filipinos, and thereafter Filipino-white marriages were illegal.[45]

With such deep-rooted and passionate racism circulating in towns and cities in the U.S. West, it was common for Filipinos to be victims of violence. California was the most dangerous place. In January 1930, the Northern Monterey County Chamber of Commerce passed a number of anti-Filipino resolutions. In Stockton, hotels and landlords refused to rent to Filipinos. Police routinely arrested Filipinos at random or raided gambling halls. "The streets were not free to my people," Carlos Bulosan wrote. "We were suspect each time these vigilant patrolmen saw us driving a car."[46] Connie Tirona remembered the vivid shock she felt when, as a young girl, she witnessed two Filipino men being dragged by white riders on horseback for the purported crime of talking to white women.[47] Manuel Buaken chronicled arrest after arrest of his fellow Filipinos by police officers and others. His cousin Remigio Santiago was accosted by Hollywood officers while waiting for a car on Hollywood Boulevard. Wenceslao Tambolero, a journalist for the *Philippine Star Press*, was arrested and put in a Los Angeles county jail after leaving a theater in the early hours of the morning. Buaken himself was reading a magazine in Los Angeles when two policemen came up to him and tried to arrest him for no reason.[48]

Anti-Filipino violence in California escalated in the late 1920s and early 1930s. Filipino immigration was at an all-time high, the Filipino labor movement was growing in strength and number, and new white migrants entering the state as part of the great Dust Bowl migration from Texas, Oklahoma, and Arkansas brought with them a regional culture where Jim Crow segregation, lynchings, participation in the Ku Klux Klan, and racial terror were common. On New Year's Eve in 1926, white men went in search of Filipinos in Stockton's hotels and pool halls, and by the end of the night, eight men had been stabbed and beaten. Over the next few years, Filipinos were expelled from the Yakima Valley in Washington, Filipino laborers socializing with white women were attacked in Dinuba, California, and mobs attacked Filipinos in Exeter, Modesto, Turlock, and Reedley. In December 1929, a mob of 400 white men attacked a Filipino dance hall in Watsonville after a local newspaper published a photograph of a Filipino man and white teenage girl embracing. Even though the couple was engaged and had the blessings of the girl's family, the incident touched off many political pronouncements against the economic and moral threat that Filipino immigrants posed. Four days of rioting ensued after the attack on the dance hall, leaving many Filipinos beaten and one dead. In 1930, a group of white youths bombed the Stockton Filipino Federation of America building.[49]

In the wake of the Watsonville race riots, labor and patriotic organizations, including the California Joint Immigration Committee, the American Federation of Labor, and the American Legion, all made Filipino exclusion a central issue at their national meetings. They warned that current U.S. immigration policies were allowing throngs of dangerous and unassimilable Filipinos to enter the country and wreak havoc on American communities.

These supporters of Filipino exclusion, however, also recognized that they had to overcome a major legal and political obstacle. Similar to the problem that Canada faced with its attempts to bar South Asians from one part of the British Empire to another, Filipinos were U.S. nationals and colonial subjects and could not be excluded from coming to the United States.

33. Members of the Filipino Federation of America in Stockton, California, pose in front of their building after it was bombed in 1930.

An odd coalition of Philippine nationalists in the Philippines and Filipino exclusionists in the United States worked together to craft a compromise. As Congress debated proposals to exclude Filipinos in 1930, representatives from the Philippines strategically used the congressional hearings to advance the cause of Philippine independence. If Filipino exclusion bills were successful in becoming law, the Philippine delegation pointed out, the United States would be the only imperial power to ban its own subjects from entering the mother country. Such blatant discrimination targeting Filipinos might jeopardize U.S. economic and political interests in the Pacific and would tarnish the U.S.'s reputation in the world more generally, they warned. At a time when the United States was on its way to becoming a major global power, such reasoning had an impact. Filipino exclusion without independence for the Philippines, the nationalist leaders continued, would be "unjust" and "un-American." Pedro Gil, a leader in the Philippine House of Representatives, testified that if the U.S. Congress wanted to restrict Filipino immigration, it would first need to grant independence to the Philippines.[50] By the end of the 1930 hearings, support for Filipino exclusion without independence was faltering. Exclusionists began to entertain proposals for a compromise.

The result was the Tydings-McDuffie Act (officially known as the Philippine Independence Act), which was signed into law by President Franklin D. Roosevelt on March 24, 1934. It granted the Philippines commonwealth status and a promise of independence after ten years. It also changed the status of Filipinos from U.S. "nationals" to "aliens." The Philippines were henceforth to be considered a "separate country" with an annual immigration quota of fifty. The bill then went to the Philippine Senate for approval. The exclusionists had won. But so had Filipino nationalists. On the other hand, prospective Filipino migrants had lost, including a group caught in legal limbo.[51]

While the bill was traveling west across the Pacific, several steamships were bringing Filipinos east. Marcelo Domingo and a cousin traveled to San Francisco on the *President Hoover* along with dozens of other Filipinos. Domingo and his cousin were bound for Watsonville, where another cousin promised them work in the fields. But when they arrived in San Francisco, immigration officials did not know what to do with them. The Filipino passengers had sailed from Manila to the United States after the Tydings-McDuffie Act had been signed into law in the United States, but before the law had been accepted by the Philippine government in May. Filipino passengers on five other ships arrived in San Francisco under similar conditions. In total, 261 Filipinos would face questions about their legal status. Would they be considered under the old rules since they had been at sea when the law had gone into effect? Or would they automatically be excluded once they arrived in the United States?

Domingo and the rest of the Tydings-McDuffie Filipinos, as they were called, were allowed to enter the country on parole after being photographed and fingerprinted. The International Institute of San Francisco, a settlement house that had formerly been part of the Young Women's Christian Association, was tasked with taking responsibility for the parole of the Filipino "boys." But when the Filipinos' appeals were dismissed and they were given deportation orders in February 1935, institute officials could not locate their charges. Many had either moved away as part of their lives as migratory laborers or deliberately went into hiding to avoid deportation. The U.S. Bureau of Immigration and Naturalization took over, and the manhunts conducted by Angel Island officials took place up and down California, across the United States, and even into the Philippines. Immigration officials interviewed family members, neighbors, employers, Selective Service Board officers, and postmasters in their quest to find, arrest, and deport the Tydings-McDuffie Filipinos. The manhunts lasted years, and in most cases, individuals like Marcelo Domingo were never found.[52]

The new policy of treating Filipinos as aliens rather than nationals worked in concert with the U.S. government's new use of repatriation, or removal, of undesirable immigrants in the country, as another method of international immigration control. The Filipino Repatriation Act of July 10, 1935, stated that any Filipino born in the Philippines and living in the United States could apply for the "benefits" of repatriation to the Philippines. The U.S. would pay for all expenses, but there was one catch: any repatriate would be barred from entering the United States ever again.

Just as Americans had justified colonizing the Philippines through "benevolent assimilation," U.S. officials used the language of benevolence to encourage Filipinos to volunteer for repatriation. San Francisco Commission of Immigration's Edward Cahill called repatriation a "Big Brotherly gesture of help and assistance." He and other officials hoped that 30,000 Filipinos, or about half of the total Filipino population in the United States, would leave of their own accord. But others, like journalist Carey McWilliams, called repatriation "a trick, and not a very clever trick, to get [Filipinos] out of this country."[53]

Filipinos were suspicious of the law, with some linking it directly to Filipinos' unequal status as U.S. nationals and the damaging effects of U.S. imperialism in the Philippines. Pedro Buncan submitted his application to return home to the Philippines in June 1935, but he did so with great bitterness. As he wrote to the U.S. secretary of labor:

> In the Philippine Public Schools we learn your Constitution and also the American Texts books which contained the two rotten Phrases Equality and Freedom. These phrases lure the mind of the poor Filipino youths. We have come to the land of the Free and where the people are treated equal only to find ourselves without constitutional rights. . . . We . . . did not realize that our oriental origin barred us as human being in the eyes of the law.[54]

The Filipino repatriation program lasted for three years, but it did not bring the results the U.S. government hoped for. The first boat of Filipino repatriates sailed for Manila in 1936. The last one sailed in 1939. In total, only 2,190 Filipinos returned to the Philippines out of 108,260 Filipinos residing in the entire United States.[55]

Targeted for exclusion and repatriation, Filipinos grew increasingly disillusioned in the years leading up to World War II. For Filipinos who had been raised to learn, recite, and cherish American political beliefs and values, the discrimination they faced in the United States was devastating. "I was born under the American flag, I had American teachers since I was six," Manuel Buaken explained to employers who refused to hire Filipinos. "I am a loyal American," Buaken protested. "But no sale."[56] It would not be until World War II that Filipinos began to feel like they belonged in the United States.

9

Border Crossings and Border Enforcement: Undocumented Asian Immigration

In 1918, a joint sting operation between the U.S. Postal Service and the Bureau of Immigration uncovered a complicated plan to bring undocumented Japanese immigrants into the country across the the U.S.-Mexican border. The Postal Service had intercepted a letter written by a man named Nakagawa who described "a new way to come into America" via Mexico to an unknown friend. As the Gentlemen's Agreement between the United States and Japan barred Japanese laborers, Nakagawa first instructed his friend to get a passport to Mexico directly, or to Argentina or Peru, and then make his way to Mexico. "After [that], you can proceed into the United States," he wrote. Included with the letter was a hand-drawn map that showed a route heading from Salina Cruz up the coast to Acapulco, Calexico, and then on to Yuma, Arizona.

Painstakingly handwritten next to specific geographic landmarks on the map were helpful notations and bits of cautionary advice:

- On landing you go eastward to the Black Hill. Then go northward along the auto road. If you were captured by the soldiers let them take you, but when you come about a day journey from Mexicali you give them about $5.00 and you will be free.

- If you fortunately come to this lake you might stay and work for a little while for there are many Japanese cotton plantations north from this place.
- Food: take 4 cans of milk and some bread. You must be careful about water, for there is no water in the desert.
- Some people go to Nogales. But sometimes they are killed by the natives. So you had better not go that way.[1]

The Asian exclusion laws were effective in restricting immigration, but by the early twentieth century, immigration to the United States had become a thriving aspect of international business and a way of life for many families around the world. Enduring dreams of America continued to encourage immigration, including undocumented immigration across the U.S.-Canadian and U.S.-Mexican borders. Attempts by the U.S. government to secure its northern and southern borders established the country's first border security policies and practices. But these efforts did not end Asian undocumented immigration. Instead, Asian immigrants redirected their efforts to other locations and employed increasingly complex and dangerous methods to achieve their goals. The first immigrants to be excluded from the United States, Asians became the first undocumented immigrants.

Undocumented immigration was the logical if highly unintentional outcome of the exclusion laws. The efforts to exclude Asian immigrants from the United States contrasted too sharply with the demand for immigrant labor and immigrants' intense need and desire to seek entry. Government laws restricted immigration, but gaps in enforcement provided the very openings (and high profitability) of undocumented immigration. Because government statistics recorded only the numbers of immigrants caught while crossing the border, we will never know how many Asian immigrants entered the United States without documentation. Official government estimates identify 17,300 Chinese immigrants who entered the United States through the back doors of Canada and Mexico from 1882 to 1920.[2] Other sources report that as many as 27,000 Chinese and Japanese immigrants entered without documentation between 1910 and 1920.[3] Additional records reveal that the scope of Asian undocumented immigration spanned all possible entry points into the country, including the northern and southern borders on both the Pacific and Atlantic Coasts, as well as the Gulf Coast and all points in between.

As the United States attempted to control undocumented immigration, border stations and border guards appeared in previously unguarded areas. And immigrants who were on the wrong side of the line found themselves in a quandary. The first undocumented Asian immigrants were likely Chinese railroad workers who had been legally admitted into the United States but had traveled north to work on the Canadian Pacific Railway. When the Chinese Exclusion Act was passed in the United States in 1882, they found themselves stuck north of the border. Because they were not residing in the United States at the time of the passage of the act, they were ineligible for the laborers' identification certificates that allowed laborers already residing in the United States to return to the country. They did what many others would do later: they simply crossed the largely unguarded 4,000-mile border between the United States and Canada and became undocumented immigrants.[4]

The huge expanse of unguarded borders made surreptitious entry into the United States a relatively easy affair in the late nineteenth century. Because steamships routinely traveled between Hong Kong and British Columbian ports, such as Victoria and Vancouver, the U.S.-Canadian border provided the first convenient back door into the United States. Canada's Chinese head taxes (first established in 1885) did not prove to be a sufficient deterrent for immigrants motivated to enter the United States, and in the wake of the U.S. exclusion laws Chinese immigration to Canada actually increased.

Chinese first used well-established smuggling routes in the Vancouver–Puget Sound area, paying anywhere from $23 to $60 in the 1890s and up to $300 one decade later to enter the United States.[5] Other popular entry points were along the northeastern border. After the Canadian Pacific Railway was completed, immigrants could land in Vancouver, travel by train across the country to the east, and then enter the U.S.[6] In 1909, a reporter in Buffalo found that two to four Chinese were brought into the city each week, at a price of $200 to $600 apiece.[7] Chinese were then frequently taken on to Boston and New York City.[8]

Border crossings were by their very nature risky endeavors. In 1906, the

Bureau of Immigration reported on one entry that ended in tragedy. A Chinese immigrant was hidden inside a Canadian rail car full of ice traveling south from Windsor, Ontario to Detroit. The trip was normally a short one and the immigrant was supposed to be removed from the car as soon as the train crossed the border. Unfortunately a snowstorm delayed the train, and he froze to death.[9] In Buffalo, another tragedy occurred: ten Chinese attempting to cross Lake Erie were caught in a severe storm that dashed their open boat against the sea wall. Six drowned.[10]

Until 1923, when Canada passed a more complete Chinese exclusion bill, the Canadian-U.S. border remained the easiest way to enter the United States for any Chinese immigrant willing and able to pay the Canadian head taxes. This migration across the border prompted one Oregon magazine editor to complain about the growing "Chinese leak" coming in from Canada. "Canada gets the money and we get the Chinamen," he wrote.[11]

Beginning in the 1890s, Chinese began to enter the United States from the U.S.-Mexican border as well. The start of regular steamship travel between China and Mexico in 1902 led to increased Chinese immigration to that country, and while many Chinese stayed and settled in Mexico, many others, perhaps a majority, eventually tried to enter the United States. The U.S. government estimated that 80 percent of Chinese arriving in Mexican seaports eventually reached the border with the help of Mexican guides or on their own. Chinese border crossings were an "open secret," and the city of El Paso was especially known as a "hot-bed for the smuggling of Chinese."[12] According to Chinese inspector Clifford Perkins, Chinese "hid in every conceivable place on trains: in box cars loaded with freight, under staterooms rented for them by accomplices, and even in the four-foot-wide ice vents across each end of the insulated Pacific Fruit Express refrigerated cars, iced or not."[13] In 1907, U.S. immigrant inspector Marcus Braun was forced to admit that a "deplorable condition of affairs" existed along the Mexican border that, despite the "vigilance" of officers, could not prevent the steady stream of Chinese coming in.[14] Two years later, the commissioner-general of immigration added a slightly different take: "a Chinaman apparently will undergo any hardship or torture, take any risk or pay any sum of money . . . to enjoy the forbidden, but much coveted privilege of living and working in the United States."[15]

34. This cartoon illustrates the threat of Chinese undocumented immigrants coming into the United States through Canada and Mexico. Uncle Sam guards the seaport while floods of Chinese enter undetected and thumb their noses at the U.S. government. "And Still They Come!" *The Wasp*, December 4, 1880.

Just as the Chinese exclusion laws in the United States set in motion Chinese undocumented immigration across the U.S.-Canadian and U.S.-Mexican borders, Japanese, Canadian, and U.S. policies had a similar effect on Japanese immigrants. In 1900, the Japanese government began to issue U.S.-bound passports only to students and merchants. The 1908 Gentlemen's Agreements additionally made direct immigration to the United States and Canada impossible for working-class Japanese. Moreover, President Roosevelt's executive order prohibiting secondary migration from Mexico, Canada, and Hawai'i also effectively closed legal immigration from these locations. If Japanese laborers wanted to enter the country, they had to do so without documentation.

Booking passage to Canada and then crossing the border into the United States was one option. U.S. immigrant inspector Charles Babcock reported from Blaine, Washington, that the area was "most advantageous to those who desire to cross the border unnoticed." The so-called Border Road heading east of Blaine had well-trod trails leading both north and south and its heavily wooded areas provided "excellent cover" during the day when the travelers usually slept. Some of the roads heading south toward Bellingham were so well marked that "Japanese who desire to go this way find the matter easy . . . and no pilot is needed to guide them."[16]

Increased Japanese migration to Canada was a source of major concern on both sides of the border. U.S. immigration officials charged that U.S. steamship companies were using Victoria as a "dumping ground" for Japanese immigrants destined for the United States.[17] Moreover, residents of British Columbia were entering a state of panic in response to the "Japanese hordes" entering the country. Newspaper articles described the never-ending numbers of Japanese arriving in the province and officials' inability to stop it.[18]

Just as U.S. government officials were beginning to understand the cross-border Japanese migration from Canada, it was becoming clear that the Mexican border presented even larger problems. Immigrant inspector Marcus Braun was dispatched to investigate the situation in 1907 and sent back reports of an uncontrolled border. Over 10,000 Japanese had been "imported" to the United States from Mexico since 1905, but Braun observed that "at the present moment, you cannot find a thousand in all the Republic of Mexico."[19] Statistics partially bear out his point. From 1901 to 1907, 10,956 Japanese entered Mexico. But in 1909, only 2,465 still resided in the country.[20] Japanese government documents from the same period also confirmed that "hundreds of Japanese were scattered over [the U.S.-Mexico border] area just waiting for a chance to cross the border," and others observed that Japanese immigrants "went to every length to get to America, crossing over the Pacific Ocean and the deserts and mountains of Mexico."[21]

Japanese used the same routes and strategies first developed by the Chinese. Some carried passports to enter Mexico and held labor contracts to work in Mexican mines and plantations, but then quickly deserted these workplaces to immigrate to the United States. Dengo Kusakabe arrived in Mexico in 1906 destined to work at a coal mine, for example, but as his train traveled toward his destination, he jumped. He ran as far and as fast as he could but was arrested and brought to the mine. After that, opportunities to escape were few and far between. "The coal mine company personnel shot without hesitation at us Japanese trying to escape," Kusakabe explained. The mine bosses continually told Kusakabe and his fellow Japanese, "even if you escape, you can't make it because in the mountains there are huge snakes and wild animals and you will be eaten alive." Despite these dangers, Kusakabe and a small band of other Japanese workers snuck out of the mine one night and followed the railroad tracks. Local Mexicans helped them with directions and offered them food. Along the way, they met other Japanese who were also fleeing Mexico for the United States. They finally entered the country at Eagle Pass, Texas.[22]

Some Japanese entered Mexico with valid passports and then immediately crossed the border on their own or in small groups. Fukuhei Saito described how he and a group of fellow laborers landed at Salina Cruz in 1906 and set out northward. They traveled through an area dense with cactus plants and were stung by "millions of thorns." They stole vegetables from farms at night and struggled to catch rain in empty cans or bottles to satisfy their thirst. When there was no rainwater to be found, they sucked water left standing in hoofprints. "We just wanted to get into America without being caught on the way," he explained. They traveled this way for two weeks until they, too, entered the country at Eagle Pass.[23]

Undocumented Asian immigration was a big business. The disconnect between national immigration policies that restricted immigrants on the one hand and national and global economies that still depended upon immigrant labor on the other created a lucrative underground business dealing in the dreams of desperate immigrants. Steamship companies and labor agencies were either complicit or actively involved in shepherding undocumented immigrants into the country. Asian immigrants were also aided by a highly sophisticated, transnational, and interracial network of undocumented immigration agents, guides, and accomplices. Chinese and Japanese immigrants arriving in Mexico, for example, were routinely in touch with relatives and friends already in the United States who provided money, directions, Chinese-English or Japanese-English dictionaries, and maps to speed their journeys.[24]

Asian undocumented immigration also relied upon a great diversity of accomplices—men of different races, classes, ethnicities, and nationalities—who worked together and sometimes formed common bonds. In 1914, an extensive list of persons arrested for aiding and abetting the undocumented immigration of Chinese into Texas, New Mexico, Arizona, and southern California, for example, included Anglo, Chinese, and Hispanic names.[25]

Many involved in the business were longtime smugglers of opium, liquor, or other contraband goods. Others took advantage of their occupations or locations along the borders to profit from the undocumented immigration business. In Mississippi, a "certain ring of Greeks" in Bay St. Louis brought Chinese through Mexico, housing them temporarily in their store and factory. In the Pacific Northwest, an Italian named Quinto Mariano charged Chinese immigrants $50 each for safe passage into Washington. One former U.S. Army map surveyor was caught selling customized maps of the U.S.-Mexico border to Chinese immigrants and their guides. And in 1908, a government investigation found evidence that former El Paso chief of police Edward M. Fink was "the leader of one of the gangs of smugglers" in El Paso who charged $100 to Chinese seeking entry.[26]

Immigrants also relied upon experienced guides to pilot them across dangerous and unfamiliar terrain. Members of Canada's First Nations were known to guide Chinese from Canada into the United States along the northern border. Mexicans were the primary guides along the southern border, working in conjunction with Chinese and/or Americans. In 1910, Mar Been, a Chinese merchant in El Paso, spearheaded a business that employed two Mexican women to help Chinese immigrants coming in from Juárez. He also had an agreement with a "negro" brakeman on the Santa Fe railroad, who, in exchange for money, stopped the train at Montoya, Mexico, and "put the Chinese boys in the Pullman car."[27]

Asian undocumented immigration in the U.S. borderlands also inspired frequent racial crossings: attempts by Asians to "pass" as members of other races in order to cross undetected. In 1904, the *Buffalo Times* reported that white "smugglers" routinely disguised Chinese as Native Americans. Dressed in "Indian garb" and carrying baskets of sassafras, they crossed the border from Canada to the United States without raising suspicions. Along the southern border, Chinese disguised themselves as Mexicans, cutting their queues, adopting Mexican clothes, and even learning to say a few words of Spanish, especially *Yo soy mexicano*. Along the Gulf Coast in the southern United States, Chinese were even known to disguise themselves as African Americans.[28]

Frequent interethnic interactions among Chinese, Japanese, and South Asian immigrants in the U.S.-Mexico borderlands sometimes forged common understanding and cooperation. A Mexican farm manager took in Miyoji Fujita and his five companions when they were extremely ill and stranded in the desert. He found a doctor and provided food and housing for the group until they were able to continue their trek northward. "Gracias to the kind Mexican . . . who saved my life!" Fujita recalled years later.[29] In 1915, a group of twenty-three Japanese, three Chinese, and thirty-five South Asians pooled their resources together to charter a small merchant vessel at Mazatlán, Sinaloa, before heading to San Felipe and Mexicali in the northern Baja Peninsula. When the boat reached San Felipe, the group split up. The South Asians and Chinese began the trek northward into the desert. The Japanese stayed behind to care for sick compatriots. One week later, they followed their shipmates into the desert. Three days into their journey, they stumbled upon the bodies of several of their South Asian friends. They had perished from dehydration in the desert. The Japanese returned to San Felipe, losing seven members of their party along the way. While deliberating what to do next, the Japanese were reunited with the remaining fourteen South Asians, and the group shared food and medicine. Together, they then hired Mexican guides and went back into the desert for the second time. After walking for ten days, the group arrived in Mexicali.[30]

But interracial alliances forged in the underground business of undocumented immigration could be fragile. Mexicans were not always willing to assist Asian immigrants, and some were well-known informants, employees of the U.S. Bureau of Immigration, and even witnesses in U.S. courts.[31] And despite their common predicaments, not all Asians wanted to be treated similarly. Japanese, in particular, tried to distinguish themselves from other Asians. They wished to be treated like European immigrants who enjoyed better treatment and privileges from U.S. immigration officials.[32]

• • •

Beginning in the early 1900s, the U.S. government turned its attention to its border security problem and launched major investigations of Asian undocumented immigration. The first was conducted by Immigrant Inspector Marcus Braun, who was instructed by his superiors to "leave no stone unturned."[33] Braun's 1907 multivolume report, complete with photographic and other exhibits, became the blueprint for U.S. border policy for years to come. He included descriptions of undocumented immigrant smugglers at work, the safe houses they used, and the strategies they employed. His investigations included details on many undocumented European and Middle Eastern immigrants trying to evade U.S. immigration laws that barred individuals likely to become public charges, but the focus of his report was on Chinese and Japanese undocumented immigration. He issued a passionate call for "eternal vigilance" along the border.[34]

This first meant putting some boots on the ground. In 1902, there were only sixty-six U.S. border inspectors (the U.S. Border Patrol would not be formally established until 1924), mostly along the northern border. The next year, the number had increased to 116, again mostly along the Canadian border. By 1907, there were nine examining stations along the Mexican border, and inspectors were stationed at every point where the railroads crossed the line. Two years later, 300 officers and other employees of the U.S. Bureau of Immigration were working along both the northern and southern borders.[35] Even with these improvements, the border remained porous and easily passable. Rowboats could be taken over the Rio Grande, and carriage roads, paths, highways, and mountain trails remained unguarded. Immigrant inspector Marcus Braun described the Mexican border as "a joke, a hollow mockery."[36] Border enforcement also became more centralized. In 1907, the U.S. Bureau of Immigration created a new administrative unit called the Mexican Border District that included Arizona, New Mexico, and most of Texas. Demonstrating the importance of Chinese immigration in constructing southern border enforcement, the first commissioner hired to manage the new Mexican district was Frank W. Berkshire, who had overseen the Chinese service along the New York–Canadian border and in New York City.[37]

The United States also adopted other measures to induce Canada and Mexico to cooperate in its attempts to secure its national borders. With

Canada, the United States was able to use border diplomacy to achieve its means; with Mexico, it institutionalized a unilateral form of border policing. Both reflected the imperialist nature of U.S. border regulation in the early twentieth century. Along the northern border, the U.S. pressured Canada to assist in the enforcement of U.S. immigration laws, while strongly encouraging its northern neighbor to adopt Chinese immigration laws that were more compatible with U.S. goals. The "Canadian Agreements" brokered between Canadian steamship and rail companies and the U.S. commissioner-general of immigration allowed U.S. immigration inspectors to enforce U.S. immigration laws on arriving steamships and on Canadian soil at specifically designated border points. By 1923, Canada transformed its regulation of Chinese immigration altogether to more closely mirror U.S. law.[38]

The U.S. government attempted to export U.S. immigration policy south to Mexico as well. But tense relations and a long history of border conflicts between the two countries translated into different border policies. Because Mexico had few federal immigration regulations, the United States could not simply piggyback or extend its own immigration policies onto an already existing framework as it had in Canada. While the country was ruled by Porfirio Díaz, Mexico also encouraged foreign immigration and had few restrictions. Moreover, Mexican officials—already wary of growing U.S. influence in the country—were less amenable to assisting U.S. immigration officials than their Canadian counterparts. They consistently argued that Chinese undocumented immigration was an American, not a Mexican, problem. They also refused to grant official permission to U.S. agents to conduct sting operations on Mexican soil targeting Chinese immigrants attempting to cross the border, and they did not allow Mexican inspectors or police to cooperate in the enforcement of U.S. immigration policies.

Instead of border diplomacy and cooperation, the southern border became closed to Chinese immigration through policing and deterrence. Immigration officials at the border were charged with the mission of preventing undocumented entries in the first place and apprehending those caught in the act of crossing the border. To accomplish this, they imposed a three-pronged system of surveillance within Mexico and the United States, patrols at the border, and immigration raids, arrests, and deportations of Chinese already in the United States.[39]

Relying upon a large network of immigration officers, train conductors, consular officials, and Mexican, indigenous, and U.S. informants, the U.S. government tracked the movement of Chinese immigrants in Mexico and watched for any attempts to cross the border. Immigration inspectors began to inspect trains and question all Chinese passengers. The United States also greatly increased the number and duties of immigrant inspectors along the southern border and established its first border patrols to prevent Chinese immigrants, and in later years, other immigrants, from crossing into the United States.[40]

Lastly, the Bureau of Immigration instituted a "vigorous policy" of immigration raids, arrests, and deportations of immigrants suspected of being in the United States without documentation. "Let it be known," Commissioner-General of Immigration Frank Sargent declared in 1906, "that even thickly settled city districts will not afford, as in the past, a safe harbor for those who clandestinely enter."[41] Special agents, commonly known as "Chinese catchers," were assigned to find and arrest Chinese unlawfully in the country. Over the next few years, the numbers of Chinese arrested for entering the United States without documentation rose dramatically. In 1899, the ratio of Chinese admitted to Chinese deported was 100:4. Five years later, it was 100:61.[42]

At the same time, the U.S. government began to use more sophisticated equipment in their pursuit of undocumented immigrants and their accomplices. Beginning in 1914, the U.S. Bureau of Immigration launched an aggressive campaign to identify and arrest suspected agents. In 1914, the commissioner-general proudly reported that seventy-five "smugglers of contraband Chinese" and over 400 Chinese immigrants had been arrested.[43] Changes in U.S. immigration laws facilitated this work. The Immigration Act of 1917 subjected smugglers to a $2,000 fine and five years' imprisonment. Anyone who transported immigrants without documentation was fined $1,000 under the 1924 Immigration Act, and under the same act, captains were fined $1,000 if any of their crew jumped ship.[44] The U.S. Bureau of Immigration also began to use two patrol boats along the California-Mexico coasts and increased their speed and cruising radius in order to apprehend greater numbers of undocumented immigrants. In 1917, the U.S. Navy joined in the border security efforts and took over operation of the patrol boats.[45]

• • •

U.S. border enforcement measures were partially successful. Japanese immigrants noticed it right away. Japanese native Shinji Kawamoto, arrested in 1907 for attempting to bring in Japanese without documentation from Mexico, remarked that business had been much easier in the past, but that now "the laws seemed to be enforced more rigidly."[46] Nevertheless, national border enforcement measures merely redirected undocumented immigration. As some border crossing sites became more heavily patrolled, immigrants and their agents and guides began to use even more circuitous and complex routes into the United States. Many strategies involved false documents, forged identities, and long routes.

After an increase in the number of patrolmen along the border near California and Arizona, for example, Chinese turned away from the heavily trafficked areas toward more remote, interior entry points through Texas and New Mexico. The Caribbean and Gulf of Mexico also became new back doors into the United States, with Chinese being hidden on fruit vessels from Cuba and then disappearing somewhere in Florida once the boats landed. By the 1910s, U.S. diplomats based in Jamaica were observing that the island had also become a "convenient stepping-stone to gain access to other countries which do not want them."[47]

In addition to finding more complicated and long-distance routes to enter the country, Asian immigrants increasingly turned to deception as well, aided by an illicit market in forged and fraudulent documents. In 1903, the Bureau of Immigration reported that growing numbers of Chinese were crossing the border and then fraudulently claiming U.S. citizenship in order to enter the United States.[48] Forged documents and false claims were common among Japanese immigrants as well. Some Japanese who had entered the United States before 1907 possessed government-issued U.S. head tax receipts showing their legal entry into the country. After the U.S. executive order barred Japanese in Hawai'i, Mexico, and Canada from entering the continental U.S., these head tax receipts became lucrative commodities that were bought and sold on the black market. The receipts were, one immigrant inspector ruefully admitted in 1907, "the most convenient safeguard for those who enter surreptitiously."[49]

One particularly elaborate scheme involved surreptitious border crossings, Mexican guides, forged head tax receipts, and U.S. government employee accomplices. In early 1908, four Japanese immigrants were arrested in Denver on suspicion of entering the country without documentation. The resulting investigation led officers to El Paso and across the border into Juárez. Over a dozen witnesses, including Japanese immigrants, agents, immigration officials, railroad officials, El Paso police officers, restaurant owners, and waiters, were eventually interviewed in connection with the case. When the investigation was concluded, one Japanese agent was in the El Paso county jail, twelve Japanese immigrants had been arrested and deported, the white Japanese interpreter at the U.S. Bureau of Immigration office in El Paso had disappeared, and a U.S. immigrant inspector had been dismissed.[50]

The increase in long routes and elaborate undocumented immigration schemes revealed how immigrants quickly learned to adapt to the U.S. government's border policies with new strategies of their own, a pattern that would characterize undocumented immigration into the U.S. in later years. Special Immigrant Inspector Roger O'Donnell testified before Congress in 1914 that the inspectors along the Mexican line were "as vigilant as men can be," working both day and night. Still, there remained "hundreds of miles where there is no inspection whatever because we have not the men to put there."[51] The same was true for the northern border. Moreover, after new immigration restrictions were placed on other immigrant groups, including the literacy provision (1917) and the 1921 Quota Act, which restricted immigrants from southern and eastern Europe, the number of European and Middle Eastern immigrants using the border route into the United States increased sharply. Immigrant agents who had previously assisted Chinese into the country surreptitiously now turned their sights to the other immigrants.[52]

By the 1920s, historian Patrick Ettinger explains that U.S. officials had "resigned themselves to creating a border that might serve as a deterrent, rather than a barrier, to undocumented immigrants" from Asia, Mexico, and Europe.[53] Secretary of Labor James Davis conceded in 1927 that even if the U.S. government placed the army on the Canadian and Mexican borders, "we couldn't stop them; if we had the Navy on the water-front we couldn't stop them. Not even a Chinese wall, nine thousand miles in length and built over rivers and deserts and mountains and along the seashores, would seem to permit a permanent solution."[54]

In 1924, the U.S. government took one step closer to putting an army and a wall along the U.S.-Mexican border by establishing the U.S. Border Patrol. Today, immigrants seeking to enter the U.S. from Mexico are the primary targets of U.S. border security efforts. But the origins of undocumented immigration into the United States and U.S. border policies date back to the age of Asian immigration and exclusion.

As the United States increased its border security efforts, other countries, especially Mexico, were left with the unresolved problem of Asian immigrants stuck on their side of the border. Local and federal laws were passed in Mexico to address unwanted Chinese immigration, but by the 1930s anti-Chinese sentiment had reached a crisis point with the worldwide economic depression and massive unemployment. In 1930, a Mexican government report likened Asian immigration to Mexico to "una invasión como en país conquistado," an invasion of a conquered country.[55]

U.S. policies toward Mexican immigrants also helped to shape new responses to Chinese immigration in Mexico. When one million Mexicans were forcibly repatriated from the United States during the 1930s, Mexican calls to do the same to the Chinese intensified.[56] Mexican anti-Chinese leaders argued that "if the United States is permitted to practice acts of expulsion against foreigners of friendly nations . . . we would be a thousand times more justified . . . to free ourselves of such prejudicial exploiters as the Chinese. We should throw out of the country, *as is done to our countrymen in the United States*, all those foreigners who cannot prove their legal residence within our country."[57]

As calls of "out with the Chinese" came from Sonora, Governor Francisco Elías responded. He called for the strict enforcement of existing anti-Chinese laws, including a new federal law that required at least 90 percent of employees in commercial businesses be native Mexicans.[58] Chinese faced fines and forced closings if they did not comply. When their protests failed to change the laws, Chinese in Sonora began to leave in 1931.[59]

Some relocated to other parts of Mexico. Others tried to return to China. Vigilante groups in Sonora rounded up remaining Chinese and took them by the truckload to the U.S. border.[60] Mexican officials also forced Chinese without documentation to cross the international line into the custody of U.S. Border Patrol officers. In October, newly elected Sonoran governor

Rodolfo Calles (son of the president) issued two more orders against the Chinese community. The first ordered local officers to arrest any Chinese merchants who tried to reopen their businesses. The second penalized Chinese-Mexican interracial unions in violation of existing antimiscegenation laws.[61]

Then the expulsions began. Over a year and a half, an estimated 20,000 Chinese were forcibly expelled from Sonora and other neighboring states, such as Sinaloa and Nayarit.[62] Forced from their homes, suffering from heavy economic and property losses, and harassed at every point along their journey, the Chinese arrived at the U.S.-Mexico border in a miserable state. Mexican officials reportedly inflicted one last indignity on departing Chinese by demanding a 50 peso exit fee. In September of 1931, the expulsion of all Chinese residents from Sonora had been accomplished, and Governor Calles announced with satisfaction that the "bitter twenty-year campaign" to terminate the "Chinese problem" had finally been won.[63]

Mexico's attempts to solve its Chinese problem shifted the burden to the United States, where the expulsion of Chinese from Mexico became a "most vexatious and expensive" situation, as the commissioner-general of immigration described it.[64] At first, U.S. border officials speculated that the expelled Chinese could be granted political refugee status and be temporarily detained in the United States before quickly returning to China. However, only a small number of Chinese immigrants had the funds to follow this course. As the U.S. government realized, most of the Sonoran Chinese were unable to pay for either their travel from the border to a seaport like San Francisco or for a steamship ticket back to China. They remained stuck just on the other side of the border, and jails in Nogales, Douglas, Bisbee, and Tucson became overcrowded.[65] In San Francisco at the Angel Island Immigration Station, the detention barracks were also overcrowded with Chinese refugees from Mexico.[66]

Months after the expulsion had started, the United States was still grappling with the problem as anti-Chinese campaigns moved to other Mexican states, and the number of Chinese expelled to the United States continued to grow. In March 1932, U.S. newspapers reported that 1,000 additional Chinese could be expected to cross the border before the end of the month. Five months later, U.S. immigration officials reported that Chinese refugees were being rounded up almost every night along the border and placed in a detention camp until they could be deported back to China.[67] The cost of housing and transporting the Chinese became the burden of the U.S. government. From September 1931 to June 1933, the number of Chinese refugees deported from the El Paso district alone was 3,523, at a cost of about $466,000.[68]

The U.S. government attempted to return the Chinese to Mexico, but found that this was "impossible."[69] The commissioner-general of immigration and the secretary of labor vented their frustration in the pages of their annual reports. In 1933, the commissioner-general complained of the "formidable charge" that the expulsions had forced on the bureau, a financial burden it could ill afford. The most frustrating aspect of the situation, he continued, was that in his opinion this was not even a U.S. problem. "It is a serious enough expense to deport these aliens who smuggle themselves into this country, but it is much more exasperating to have to bear the burden of removing those who are virtually forced upon us."[70]

Expelled Chinese Mexicans had a very different perspective on their plight. One Cantonese folksong described the helplessness and despair Chinese Mexicans felt at being caught between two hostile nations.

Stay at home and lose opportunities;
A hundred considerations lead me to sojourn in Mexico.
Hatred and prejudice against foreigners take away our property and many lives.
Unable to stay on—
I sneak across the border to the American side,
But bump into an immigration officer who sternly throws the book at me
And orders my expulsion back to China.[71]

PART THREE

Asian America in a World at War

10

"Military Necessity": The Uprooting of Japanese Americans During World War II

Yoshiko Uchida was in her last year of college at the University of California at Berkeley when the bombs fell on Pearl Harbor. She and her family listened to the shocking news on the radio around lunchtime on December 7, 1941. By that evening, her issei father, a manager for a Japanese company, had been arrested by the FBI and classified as an "enemy alien." He was eventually sent to a camp in Missoula, Montana. In the spring of 1942, the rest of the Uchida family was given ten days' notice to leave their home in Berkeley. Labeled Family No. 13453 by the U.S. government, the Uchidas hurriedly put their affairs in order, sold or stored their possessions, gave away their beloved dog, and prepared to be "relocated" to a former horse racetrack that had been turned into the Tanforan "Assembly Center" in San Bruno, California. From there, they were sent to the Topaz camp in Utah, and Uchida spent the war behind barbed wire.[1]

On the eve of the Japanese attack on Pearl Harbor, there were 125,000 Japanese residing in the continental United States. More than 80 percent lived in the Pacific Coast states of California, Oregon, and Washington. There were 23,000 Japanese residents in Canada, 95 percent of whom lived in the Pacific Coast province of British Columbia. In both countries, Japanese represented less than one tenth of one percent of the total population.

In 1940, there were some 17,500 Japanese in Peru. Many lived in the cities, especially in the capital city of Lima, and were likewise a fraction of the total population in the country.[2]

When Japanese bombs fell in Hawai'i and the United States declared war against Japan on December 8, 1941, Japanese Americans came under intense scrutiny and their lives were turned upside down. One hundred twenty thousand Japanese Americans—two thirds of them U.S. citizens like Yoshiko Uchida—were uprooted from their homes on the West Coast because of what the government called "military necessity." Twenty-two thousand Japanese Canadians were similarly ordered to leave British Columbia for reasons of national security and were sent to what the Canadian government called "Interior Housing Centres" set up in ghost towns and on farms in the country's interior. And over 2,100 Japanese Peruvians and other Japanese Latin Americans were arrested, detained, and taken to the United States to be incarcerated in camps as "enemy aliens." Japanese Americans, Canadians, and Latin Americans were not individually charged with acts of treachery or subversion, but were instead sentenced as a group for incarceration during the war in the name of national and hemispheric security. Their only crime was their Japanese ancestry.[3]

In the years leading up to the U.S.'s entry into the war, Japanese Americans came under increased government surveillance. The 1940 Alien Registration Act required all resident aliens over fourteen years of age to register annually with the federal government and provide their fingerprints. Both the Office of Naval Intelligence and the Federal Bureau of Investigation collected information on Japanese communities and created lists of individuals suspected of potential subversive activities. The definition of "subversive activity" was broad and encompassed most Japanese community organizations and any contact—no matter how minimal—with the Japanese government. Immigrants who had led cultural or assistance organizations, Japanese language teachers, and members of the Buddhist clergy, for example, were all identified in three FBI master lists of enemy alien "suspects" to be removed and confined in case of war. By 1941, these lists were ready, and designs for camps for aliens were prepared.[4]

There was, to be sure, evidence that the Japanese government had successfully placed spies through its consulates in the United States. There were also nineteen Americans who were arrested during World War II for serving as agents of Japan. All were white.[5] The Japanese government was successful in spreading pro-Japan messages through a few well-placed journalists and scholars, and some Japanese immigrants publicly defended and celebrated the Japanese Empire's victories in Asia, including the occupation of China beginning in 1937. But this sentiment, historian Greg Robinson argues, "certainly did not mean that they would assist the Japanese military against their own countries."[6]

The vast majority of Japanese Americans, two U.S. government reports found, were overwhelmingly loyal to the United States. Navy intelligence officer Kenneth Ringle investigated the Japanese community in southern California and officially stated in 1941 that "better than 90 percent of the nisei and 75 percent of the original immigrants were completely loyal to the United States."[7] Curtis B. Munson, sent by the Roosevelt administration to secretly investigate the loyalty of Japanese communities on the West Coast and in Hawai'i, succinctly reported to the president that there was "no Japanese problem." The first-generation immigrants would eagerly become naturalized U.S. citizens if they were allowed to do so. He found that the second-generation nisei (not including those who had been educated in Japan) were 90 to 98 percent loyal and "pathetically eager to show this loyalty."[8] Despite these reports, a contingent within the U.S. military proceeded with plans—some that had been introduced decades before the attack on Pearl Harbor—for the mass removal of Japanese Americans in the event of war.[9]

Similarly, in Canada, skepticism that Japanese Canadians were truly loyal set in motion government actions that set them apart and increased surveillance of them. As early as 1921, the commissioner of the Royal Canadian Mounted Police called for an investigation of espionage among Japanese Canadians. Once Canada entered the war in September of 1939, fear of Axis collaborators increased.[10] In 1940, Prime Minister Mackenzie King appointed the Special Committee on Orientals in British Columbia to uncover evidence of subversive acts by Japanese Canadians. In January 1941, the government in Ottawa officially exempted Japanese Canadians from conscription as a matter of national security. Two months later, the government also imposed a registration requirement for all Japanese Canadians irrespective of citizenship.[11]

These actions were part of larger North American security efforts that preceded Pearl Harbor. Beginning in 1937, Canada and the United States began to strengthen the strategic alliance between the two countries in order to shore up defense along the Pacific Coast. Airbases were built along the border, and the military road known as the Alaska Highway from British Columbia to Alaska was completed. In 1940, the Canada–United States Permanent Joint Board of Defense was established to prepare for the defense of the North American continent and the northern half of the Western Hemisphere. The board was made up of Canadian and U.S. military officials and civilians (New York City mayor Fiorello LaGuardia was the civilian chairman). The U.S. influence on the board was strong, and its recommendations generally reflected American priorities. It was here that the joint "problem" of Japanese residents in Canada and the United States was discussed. At the first meetings of the chiefs of staff of the U.S. and Canadian armies, participants raised the necessity of imprisoning Japanese Americans in case of war with Japan.[12] These prewar conversations laid the groundwork for parallel wartime actions. U.S. policy especially seemed to be used to justify Canadian policies during the war.[13]

While the United States was engaging in discussions about North American defense with Canada, it was also organizing Latin American countries around similar issues of collective defense on a hemispheric level. Economic aid, diplomatic pressure, and a "Western Hemisphere idea" that defined the Americas as a "culturally unified, ideologically unique, and politically superior" realm of the globe best protected by the United States both facilitated and justified the U.S.'s growing role in Latin America.[14] At the 1938 International Conference of American States in Lima, organized by the United States, foreign ministers of all Latin American countries approved a resolution that called for joint action in the case of an outside attack. This resolution, known as the "Declaration of Lima," also included a provision that denied rights to certain foreign ethnic groups and another that opposed political activity by foreigners. Although the Declaration was aimed at Germany, it also laid the groundwork for Latin American cooperation in the deportation and incarceration of Japanese Peruvians during the war.[15] These prewar discussions took place in anticipation of a possible war with Japan. But the events of December 7, 1941, put them in motion in ways that few had anticipated.

• • •

Shortly before 8:00 a.m. on December 7, 1941, Japanese aircrews launched a surprise attack on the U.S. military base at Pearl Harbor as well as on military airfields on the Hawaiian island of Oahu. The assault was over within two hours. Twenty-one ships sank or were damaged, including eight battleships. One hundred eighty-eight aircraft were destroyed. Two thousand four hundred three people were dead, including 1,177 crewmen on the USS *Arizona* alone, and 1,178 military and civilians were wounded. The Japanese military went on to achieve striking victories in the Malay Peninsula, Hong Kong, Wake and Midway Islands, and the Philippines on the same day as the Pearl Harbor attack. The United States found itself facing a formidable enemy.

As Americans struggled to process the attack on Pearl Harbor and the U.S. declaration of war against Japan, Japanese Americans feared that their lives would change forever. Daniel Inouye's family was getting ready for church in Hawai'i on that Sunday morning. He had completed his chores and was combing his hair while listening to the radio. "And all of a sudden the announcer came on the air, cut off the music," Inouye recalled. "And he literally started to shout, yell, 'Pearl Harbor has been bombed!' He's screaming . . . 'for real—the Japanese are bombing Pearl Harbor!' " The Inouyes walked out into the street and turned to look toward Pearl Harbor. "Sure enough we can see in the sky the black puffs," Inouye remembered. "And then suddenly, three planes, they were the fighter bombers, flew overhead after they had made their run across Pearl Harbor. . . . The planes were pearl gray with the red dot." The attack on Pearl Harbor changed Inouye's life. At the time, he felt that his life "had come to an end at that point," he explained, "because obviously the pilot in that plane looked like me." He knew that life after Pearl Harbor would be different, but what it would be like, he did not yet know.[16]

Within hours of the attack, the U.S. government launched new national security measures. In Hawai'i, the U.S. Constitution was suspended and martial law was established. Japanese, German, and Italian nationals became "enemy aliens." Just hours after the attack, FBI agents began arresting those who were presumed to be dangerous. Within forty-eight hours, 1,291 Japanese (367 in Hawai'i and 924 in the continental United States) were arrested. Using the lists that the government had prepared before the war, individuals were rounded up based on their status as community leaders and their history of contact with the Japanese embassy and consulates. By February 16, 1942, there were 2,192 Japanese being held in U.S. Department of Justice camps.[17]

In addition, the U.S. Treasury Department froze the bank accounts of all enemy aliens. Approximately $27.5 million in business enterprises and real estate owned by Japanese aliens was handed over to the government. Japanese and other enemy aliens were ordered to turn in their shortwave radios and cameras. Families scrambled to hide or destroy any possessions that would link them to Japan, including treasured family heirlooms and books, letters, private papers, and business records.[18]

These arrests and other official actions caused much hardship. The majority of those arrested were male heads of households and community leaders who would be detained for the rest of the war. The families left behind struggled to survive. Communities were left leaderless. Most of the Japanese arrested were guilty by association rather than by any hard evidence. Nevertheless, the treatment of the estimated 30,000 enemy aliens (of which 20,000 were Japanese) did follow due process of law and rules and regulations set down in international law.[19] The subsequent government actions targeting all West Coast Japanese were different. These Japanese Americans were "prisoners without trial" who were, because of their ethnicity, forcibly exiled and incarcerated in one of the war's greatest human rights atrocities.[20]

In this climate of fear, it did not take long for U.S. officials to accuse Japanese Americans in Hawai'i of aiding and abetting the enemy. Within days of the attack, Secretary of the Navy Frank Knox toured the wreckage of Pearl Harbor on special assignment from President Roosevelt. When he returned from his trip, Knox told reporters that the successful attack was "the most effective Fifth Column work of the entire war." Despite the fact that he lacked any evidence, Knox repeated his accusation to the president.[21] These false claims from such a high-ranking official had far-reaching consequences. A product of decades of racism, they confirmed what many already suspected: Japanese Americans could not be trusted.[22]

Lieutenant General John L. DeWitt became head of the newly created Western Defense Command and was charged with defending the entire West Coast. A career army man who assumed his position on December 11, DeWitt was committed to his responsibilities and knew only too well the costs of failing. General Walter C. Short and Admiral Husband E. Kimmel had been removed of their commands in Hawai'i for failing to mount an effective defense of Pearl Harbor. DeWitt told a *Los Angeles Times* reporter that he was "not going to be a second General Short."[23]

DeWitt was also convinced that the Japanese in the United States constituted a major national security threat. "I have no confidence in their loyalty whatsoever," he wrote to James Rowe, assistant U.S. attorney general, in January 1942.[24] Five weeks later, he explained to Secretary of War Henry L. Stimson that it was simply a matter of race. "Racial affinities are not severed by migration," he wrote. "The Japanese race is an enemy race," and it thus followed that American-born Japanese remained "potential enemies . . . at large." A year later, he gave the same message to a congressional committee. "It makes no difference whether he is an American citizen, he is still a Japanese." And as he more bluntly told reporters the next day: "a Jap is a Jap."[25]

Unsurprisingly, DeWitt saw danger everywhere and was prone to believe every sensationalist rumor that crossed his desk. DeWitt claimed, for example, that there were "hundreds of reports" that Japanese Americans were sending signal light messages and unlawful radio transmissions to enemy surface vessels and submarines off the West Coast. However, the Federal Communications Commission reported the rumors were "without exception . . . to be baseless."[26] Major General Joseph W. Stilwell, a DeWitt colleague, could not hide his disgust. He recorded in his diary that under DeWitt, "common sense is thrown to the winds and any absurdity is believed."[27]

As early as mid-December 1941, DeWitt proposed mass removal and incarceration of peoples of Japanese ancestry. When asked to explain his rationale in light of the fact that there was no evidence of actual incidents of sabotage by Japanese Americans, DeWitt later told a congressional committee that "the very fact that no sabotage has taken place to date is a disturbing and confirming indication that such action *will* be taken."[28] Abetted by systemic prejudice, most Americans were inclined to agree with him.

For Japanese Americans, the weeks following Pearl Harbor were filled with anxiety and fear. Some nisei in the United States remained steadfast in their belief that their U.S. citizenship would serve as protection. Others became acutely aware of their vulnerability and unequal status. For fifteen-year-old Akiko Kurose, both feelings came to the surface simultaneously. She had just come home from church on December 7 when she heard the news of the attack. "My father said, 'Uh-oh, there's going to be trouble.' And

I said, 'Well, how come?' He said, 'Well, Japan just bombed Pearl Harbor.' And, he says, 'We're at war with Japan.' But, I thought, 'Why should it bother me?' You know, I'm an American." However, when Akiko went to school the next day and was confronted by a teacher who said "You people bombed Pearl Harbor," she was astounded. "All of a sudden my Japaneseness became very aware to me . . . I no longer felt I'm an equal American."[29]

Japanese Americans struggled to defend their community from attacks. Japanese American newspapers proclaimed their loyalty to the United States and groups mobilized to demonstrate their support of the U.S. war effort. Some even turned to political action and organized against removal. They found a few allies, including writer Carey McWilliams and singer/activist Paul Robeson, who were willing to speak out on behalf of Japanese Americans. But all of these efforts were largely ineffective against the tide of popular anti-Japanese sentiment.[30]

The racial hysteria grew as news from the Pacific trickled back into the country. U.S. forces under General Douglas MacArthur were forced to evacuate Manila and withdrew to the Bataan Peninsula. Over the next two months, the U.S.'s military position in the Pacific seemed increasingly precarious. Supreme Court Associate Justice Owen J. Roberts added to the public clamor with a new investigative report on the Pearl Harbor attack. The disaster had occurred because Hawai'i's military commanders had been unprepared, Roberts concluded. But he also repeated the false charge that a Japanese American fifth column had aided the attackers. Following the Roberts report, coordinated campaigns to remove Japanese began. On January 27, General DeWitt told California governor Culbert Olson that "as a result of the report, Californians no longer felt safe around any Japanese Americans." He requested military action to displace the entire ethnic population from the West Coast and secured the approval from California attorney general Earl Warren. Recommendations on removal began circulating at the national level.[31]

In the weeks and months that followed, the press, the public, politicians, and military officials all added to the chorus of voices calling for action to deal with the presumed threat represented by Japanese Americans. West Coast newspapers like the *Los Angeles Times* fanned anti-Japanese sentiment with inflammatory and irrational headlines: "Jap Boat Flashes Message Shore." "Caps on Japanese Tomato Plants Point to Air Base." "Jap and Camera Held in Bay City."[32] Individuals sent in a steady stream of dire warnings to elected officials. On January 16, 1942, farmer (and later actor) Leo Carrillo of Santa Monica asked Congressman Leland Ford "why wait until they pull something before we act? . . . Every farm house is located on some strategic elevated point," he asserted. "I urge you on behalf of the safety of the people of California to start action at once."[33]

Theodor Seuss Geisel, aka Dr. Seuss, picked up on the fifth-column characterization of Japanese Americans in a cartoon titled "Waiting for the Signal from Home," published in the New York City newspaper *PM Magazine*. In it, a long, endless line of identical Japanese men stream across the Pacific Northwest to a building on the California coast labeled "Honorable 5th Column." There, they receive packages marked "TNT." On top of the building, another Japanese man looks out across the Pacific through a telescope waiting for the order from Japan to attack the United States. Posters created during the war also used racial stereotypes to communicate the danger from Japan and Germany.

35. Waiting for the signal from home . . . published by *PM Magazine* on February 13, 1942.

36. "Warning! Our homes are in danger now! Our job: keep 'em firing." World War II poster with a Japanese soldier and Hitler creeping over the globe with weapons in hand.

By the end of the month, support for removal and mass incarceration of the Japanese reverberated up and down the Pacific Coast. In an editorial published in the *Seattle Times*, nationally syndicated correspondent Henry McLemore argued "This Is War! Stop Worrying About Hurting Jap Feelings." Reflecting the public anger and hatred growing along the West Coast at the time, McLemore continued: "Herd 'em up, pack 'em off and give 'em the inside room in the badlands. Let 'em be pinched, hurt, hungry and dead up against it." McLemore conceded that this might result in "an unjustified hardship on 80 per cent or 90 per cent of the California Japanese." But the remaining 10 or 20 percent, he was convinced, "have it in their power to do damage—great damage—to the American people." When it came to balancing individual rights with public safety, McLemore argued that the latter needed to be considered above all else. "If making one million innocent Japanese uncomfortable would prevent one scheming Japanese from costing the life of one American boy, then let the million innocents suffer." His racism was explicit: "Personally, I hate the Japanese. And that goes for all of them."[34]

By the end of January, U.S. attorney general Francis Biddle announced the creation of eighty-eight military zones from which all enemy aliens were ordered to leave within twenty-six days. Public pressure continued to demand further government action: the mass removal and incarceration of all peoples of Japanese ancestry, including U.S. citizens. Reflecting the beliefs of many, one *Los Angeles Times* journalist claimed that "a viper is nonetheless a viper wherever the egg is hatched. So a Japanese-American . . . grows up to be a Japanese, not an American."[35]

American public support for the mass removal and incarceration of Japanese Americans became national by the middle of the next month. Influential nationally syndicated journalist Walter Lippmann wrote a column in the *Washington Post* titled "The Fifth Column on the Coast" that repeated Secretary Knox's charges that both Japanese immigrants and U.S.-born Japanese Americans were loyal to Japan. "The Pacific Coast is in imminent danger of a combined attack from within and from without," Lippmann wrote.[36] Playing to the president's fears of losing control of Congress in the off-year election, the congressional delegation from the Pacific Coast states sent Roosevelt a strongly worded resolution demanding federal action.[37]

Inside the White House, a war was simmering between War Department officials who advocated for the mass removal and incarceration of Japanese Americans and Justice Department officials who sought to preserve the rights of American citizens of Japanese ancestry. Attorney General Biddle, for example, along with his Justice Department aides Edward Ennis and James Rowe, adamantly opposed the mass removal of Japanese Americans from the West Coast. Secretary of War Henry Stimson was also initially against mass removal due to his belief that it would make a "tremendous hole in our constitutional system." But continued pressure from West Coast politicians, the press, and military advisors who argued for removal on the grounds of "military necessity" eventually changed his mind. Stimson approved of mass removal, Biddle ended his opposition, and an executive order followed.[38]

On February 19, 1942, President Roosevelt signed Executive Order 9066. While irresponsible journalism, West Coast pressure groups, and U.S. military officials all played key roles leading up to the United States' decision to forcibly remove and incarcerate West Coast Japanese, the ultimate responsibility for violating the civil rights of Japanese Americans rests with President Roosevelt. In doing so, he ignored reports from the FBI, the Office of Naval Intelligence, and his own handpicked investigators who reported that mass removal or incarceration was unnecessary.[39]

The executive order, which was not put before Congress, directed the secretary of war and other military commanders to prescribe certain "military areas with respect to which the right of any person to enter, remain in, or leave shall be subject to whatever restrictions the Secretary deems necessary." Placing the responsibility with the military, it established the premise of "military necessity" and allowed for the government to round up and expel entire communities without compensation and without due process or proof of wrongdoing. Tellingly, in Hawai'i, which was still under martial law, Acting Military Governor General Delos Emmons saw no military necessity to forcibly remove Japanese from the islands. Japanese residents also represented a large percentage of the workers in vital industries like transportation, agriculture, and carpentry, and their removal would have crippled the economy. Still, 1,504 Japanese (979 aliens and 525 U.S. citizens) living in Hawai'i were taken into custody and incarcerated in camps in the continental U.S. The Japanese who remained in the islands lived under severe restrictions for the next four years.[40]

Events moved quickly in Canada in January and February of 1942 as well. West Coast groups, who had for decades advocated for a policy of "No Japs from the Rockies to the Sea," pushed the dominion government to finally act under the guise of "military necessity" like the United States.[41] By February 19, the day that the United States' Executive Order 9066 was issued, Mackenzie King's cabinet had concluded that similar action was necessary. Indeed, King's diary entry for that day indicates that he had already made up his mind about moving Japanese Canadians. Doing so presented a "very great problem," but he was resigned to the decision and congratulated himself on having the policy "definitely settled" already.[42]

On February 24, the prime minister's cabinet amended the Defence of Canada Regulations. PC 1486 gave the government sweeping emergency powers by allowing the minister of justice to "take any required security measures with regard to any person in the protected area." The order itself was unclear, but the intent was not. All peoples of Japanese ancestry, including the young and old, citizens and noncitizens, men and women, would be removed from the protected area. Mass removal and confinement had become legal.[43]

Just as the U.S. and Canada were putting their wartime policies into action, Peruvian and U.S. authorities started to initiate a massive deportation and incarceration program that would bring approximately 1,800 Japanese Peruvians as enemy aliens to the United States from April of 1942 to April of 1945. Japanese Latin Americans from twelve other countries were also deported from their homes and incarcerated in the United States, but those from Peru made up 80 percent of all Japanese from Latin America. They were among the war's unfortunate victims, "hapless pawns in a triangle of hate that involved the United States, Peru, and Japan during and after World War II," in the words of historian C. Harvey Gardiner.[44] Peruvian authorities cooperated eagerly, but it was the United States that masterminded, organized, and paid for the forcible deportation of Japanese Peruvians from their homes, their transportation to the United States on American vessels, and their incarceration on U.S. soil.

A number of factors made the wartime deportation and incarceration program possible. The first was that both the U.S. and Peruvian governments believed Japanese immigrants and their descendants in their countries and elsewhere were threats to national and hemispheric security. Peruvian officials like Jorge Larrañaga, for example, were convinced that the Japanese Imperial Army had already infiltrated Peru under the guise of immigrant laborers, domestic servants, and business owners and were spying for the Japanese empire on Peruvian soil.[45]

On the U.S. side, one individual in particular—a U.S. embassy official named John K. Emmerson—was responsible for shaping the U.S.

government's perspective that there was "no doubt" that the Japanese in Peru were "dangerous," "thoroughly organized," and would "follow implicitly the directions of their leaders." Based in Lima, Emmerson convinced his superiors that the Japanese colony in Peru represented a clear "problem of hemisphere defense." The roughly 30,000 Japanese Peruvians were unassimilated and "emotionally tied to their homeland," he reported. Even the nisei had "little sympathy for Peru" and "little pride in Peruvian citizenship." Future acts of sabotage were likely, he concluded.[46] Emmerson's views steadily became the foundation for U.S. opinion and policy on the Japanese in Peru, and the State Department soon reported its desire to "remove these persons from Peru at the earliest opportunity."[47]

As the United States embarked on its own program of forced mass removal, relocation, and incarceration of Japanese Americans, it urged Latin American governments to follow its lead. In January of 1942, the foreign ministers of all American republics met in Rio de Janeiro to make hemispheric security a reality through the newly established joint Emergency Advisory Committee for Political Defense. The committee was charged with making defense recommendations and to coordinate inter-American policy on Axis subversion. In reality it functioned as a rubber stamp for U.S. prerogatives.[48]

The problem was that U.S. officials did not trust their southern counterparts to do the job effectively. The FBI reported in 1942, for example, that the Peruvian government "has not exercised enough control over the large Japanese colonies." U.S. officials questioned whether the Peruvian government—made up of a "heterogeneous collection of races" who failed to cooperate with each other—was equipped to take on necessary action in the face of sudden danger.[49] For these reasons, the United States maintained throughout the war a desire to "have as free a hand as possible" in the matter of deportation and incarceration in what U.S. State Department officials claimed was "in the interest of hemisphere defense."[50] If they failed, they believed that the security of the entire region—especially the United States—would be in jeopardy.[51]

Another factor leading to the incarceration of Japanese Peruvians in the United States was the American desire to obtain enough Japanese nationals to use as potential hostage exchanges for U.S. citizens captured in Japan.

An Emergency Advisory Committee resolution allowed for the detention and expulsion of "dangerous Axis agents and nationals" during the war and their repatriation after the war as a necessary safeguard for "the security of the Hemisphere."[52]

Peruvian cooperation with U.S.-led efforts was the last element that facilitated the deportation and incarceration of Japanese Peruvians. During the war, President Manuel Prado worked hard to gain U.S. support and dollars. During his May 1942 visit to the United States, he secured $30 million in loans through the U.S. lend-lease agreements, the largest pledge to any Latin American country. In return, Peru granted the United States the rights to operate an airbase and contribute its part to hemispheric security by targeting its Japanese population.[53] It froze Japanese assets, curbed Japanese commerce, and restricted Japanese freedom of movement. Japanese language schools were closed, and Japanese organizations were disbanded. With the aid of the U.S. government, including the Federal Bureau of Investigation, the Office of Strategic Services, and the State Department, the Peruvian government initiated its deportation campaign. Using U.S. intelligence, Peruvian officials established a blacklist of commercial enterprises owned or operated by persons of German, Japanese, or Italian ancestry or nationality. These businesses were subject to boycott and/or expropriation without compensation. As the U.S. State Department acknowledged in 1945, the primary targets of the blacklist were Japanese business owners in Lima.[54]

On December 24, a blacklist of "dangerous Axis nationals" provided by the U.S. State Department was published in major newspapers in Peru. Eventually many such lists were published, and like the initial roundups of issei in the United States and Canada, the individuals targeted included community leaders, such as teachers, journalists, and officers in Japanese immigrant organizations.[55] Some of the most successful Japanese Peruvians were among the first to be deported. Nikumatsu Okada, known as the "Japanese cotton king," had been among the first Japanese to arrive in Peru in 1899. He rose from common laborer to manager of six cotton haciendas in the Chancay Valley. Nevertheless, his wealth and position offered little protection. He was expelled from Peru on the SS *Shawnee* on June 15, 1942.[56]

Beginning in late 1942 and into 1943, Japanese began to be randomly arrested; there was no apparent list anymore. Most Japanese businesses were ordered to close, and many of these were sold. The Peruvian government prohibited Japanese from freely traveling outside their city or town of residence. Telephones and shortwave radios were prohibited, and Japanese were barred from obtaining a license to hunt, fish, or possess firearms.[57]

Japanese Peruvians lived in a constant state of fear and anxiety following the publication of the blacklists. Whose names would appear on the lists? What would happen to them and to their families who were left behind? Japanese immigrant and schoolteacher Seiichi Higashide was grappling with these questions when his name appeared on one of the earliest lists posted in his hometown of Ica, in the southern part of the country. "I had not committed any crimes. I had not participated in any propaganda activities for the Japanese government and, of course, I had not engaged in espionage or underground activities," Higashide explained. Nevertheless, as the leader of the local Japanese association, he was still targeted as someone who had suspicious ties to Japan.[58]

Some Japanese Peruvians went into hiding to avoid arrest. They ran away into the jungle, the mountains, or laid low in town. Art Shibayama, whose family lived in Callao, remembers that "every time a U.S. transport ship came into the port of Callao, words got around and . . . [the] father or head of the family went into hiding." Shibayama's father managed to escape detection for some time, but after numerous failed searches, the Peruvian police resorted to arresting his wife and put her in jail to force him out of hiding. "As soon as my father found out about it he gave himself up and came out of hiding," Shibayama explained. The family was given a week to get ready and then they were deported on board the U.S. Army transport *Cuba*.[59]

Seiichi Higashide was issued a deportation order for March of 1942. Refusing to leave his wife and four young children, Higashide went into hiding by digging a large hole under the house to hold a little cot, tiny table, and a lamp. "Whenever someone suspicious came into the store, then he would hide in there," his daughter Elsa Kudo remembered. He remained successfully hidden for a year until January 1944, when five detectives showed up at the family home to take him to jail "under the order of the U.S.A."[60] Higashide was first sent to a squalid and disgusting prison cell in Lima. Two weeks later, he was ordered to depart on a U.S. freighter. The Japanese prisoners were marched over the gangway surrounded by U.S. soldiers carrying rifles with fixed bayonets.[61]

From April of 1942 to October of 1944, four ships operated by the U.S. government transported Japanese Peruvians and other Japanese Latin Americans to the United States. Just as in the case of Japanese Americans, Latin American deportees were not charged with any crimes of espionage, sabotage, or subversive activity, nor had they been given hearings of any kind. The first ships carried men who had been named on the proclaimed lists. On the *Etolin*, which sailed out of Callao on April 5, 1942, around 90 percent of the passengers were from the Lima-Callao area. They ranged in age from nineteen to sixty-four and had been in the country for more than fourteen years on average. They were merchants, teachers, farmers, students, restaurant owners, waiters, and barbers.[62] Over the years, more women and children traveled as "voluntary internees" to join their husbands and fathers who had already been taken to the United States. The last ship bringing Japanese deportees to the United States from Latin America was the *Frederick C. Johnson*, which departed Peru in October of 1944.[63]

Altogether, twelve Latin American countries—Bolivia, Colombia, Costa Rica, the Dominican Republic, Ecuador, El Salvador, Guatemala, Haiti, Honduras, Nicaragua, Panama, and Peru—deported Axis nationals to the United States. These included 2,118 Japanese from Chile, Bolivia, Paraguay, Uruguay, Venezuela, and Peru. The vast majority, 84 percent, were from Peru, including Peruvian citizens by naturalization or birth. One thousand twenty-four Japanese Latin Americans had been arrested and deported by their governments. One thousand ninety-four were family members who joined them. Over 900 Japanese Latin Americans were included in two prisoner of war exchanges between the United States and Japan. The remaining Japanese Latin Americans were imprisoned without due process in special camps managed by the U.S. Immigration and Naturalization Service for the duration of the war.[64]

An estimated 400,000 people of Japanese descent lived in the United States, Canada, and Latin America on the eve of World War II. The experiences of Japanese peoples in the Americas during the war varied widely. Cuba imprisoned its entire Japanese population on the Isle of Pines prison island, but neither Chile nor Argentina took actions to incarcerate its Japanese populations.[65] Panama and Mexico were among the first countries in the hemisphere to forcibly exile their Japanese communities to certain prescribed areas, and of all of the Latin American nations, Mexico alone engaged in a large-scale forced relocation of Japanese Mexicans during the war, mostly to cities like Mexico City.

With the largest Japanese population in the Americas, Brazil placed restrictions on the approximately 250,000 Japanese Brazilians (around 6 percent of the Brazilian population). President Getúlio Vargas's government arrested and detained Japanese community leaders and froze bank accounts. Around 4,000 Japanese, including around 1,000 families, were forcibly moved from the Santos and São Paulo areas down the coast to Paranaguá in July of 1943. This forced relocation happened much later and was proportionally much smaller than any of the other forced relocations in North America or Latin America.[66]

The actions by countries like Mexico and Brazil affected sizable numbers of Japanese, but communities mostly stayed intact. In contrast, Canada and the United States forcibly removed and confined almost their entire Japanese populations, and the mass incarceration of 120,000 Japanese Americans—two thirds of them U.S. citizens and comprising less than one percent of the total U.S. population—in camps located across the country was the largest in the Americas.

11

"Grave Injustices": The Incarceration of Japanese Americans During World War II

Uprooted from her home and incarcerated in the name of national security, Yoshiko Uchida spent the war years in "desert exile" at the Topaz relocation center in Utah. Her memoir describes monotonous days behind barbed wire in "crude, incomplete, and ill-prepared camps" in a "city of dust." Frustration and discontent spread among a once proud and self-reliant people as a total of 120,000 Japanese Americans, including over 1,100 transferred from Hawai'i and almost 6,000 born in the camps, were incarcerated in ten War Relocation Authority camps located throughout the United States.[1]

Within weeks of Executive Order 9066 being signed, the U.S. government began what it euphemistically called Japanese American "evacuation." On March 1, 1942, General DeWitt issued the first public proclamation officially notifying all "persons of Japanese ancestry" that they were to be removed and excluded from the western parts of Washington State, California, Oregon, and parts of Arizona. A curfew was also put into place in these areas requiring all persons of Japanese ancestry to remain at home from 8 p.m. to 6 a.m. Other exclusion orders followed. Posted on buildings, telephone poles, billboards, and other high-traffic areas, the orders identified additional geographic regions where Japanese Americans were banned. Once an exclusion order was issued, residents were generally given just one week to prepare themselves for removal. They were allowed to bring with them only what they could carry. Over the next several months, 108 exclusion orders were issued with the same instructions. Families rushed to sell stores, farms, houses, equipment, furniture, clothes, and valuables, often at huge losses. Vegetable and fruit farmers faced a particularly bitter situation. Many had struggled through the Depression years and were just starting to expand their businesses with new equipment and more acreage. The year 1942 promised to be a bumper crop. But with the removal order, they were forced to leave just before harvest time, when they would have been able to reap the rewards of the year's labor. "We gave away practically everything," Shigeko Sese Uno explained. Before the war, her family had run a profitable dairy farm in Washington. Business was booming as Seattle's population swelled with wartime workers and industries. After EO 9066 was issued, they struggled unsuccessfully to find a responsible tenant to tend the farm while they were incarcerated. They were forced to shut down their business and sell their equipment and property. "Closed everything at a loss . . . which we never recovered from, really," she told an interviewer years later.[2] Altogether, Japanese Americans filed over 26,000 claims under the 1948 Japanese-American Evacuation Claims Act totaling $148 million. Only $37 million was ever distributed.[3]

One hundred twelve thousand Japanese Americans were thus forced from their homes. They were anxious, shocked, and deeply disappointed. The second-generation nisei perhaps felt the sting of injustice the most. Tom Akashi, who was thirteen years old in Atwater, California, wondered why it was the Japanese Americans were forced to leave their homes when German and Italian Americans could stay. He kept on thinking, " 'Gee, where's my rights? What's happening to me?' As young as I was, I was impressed that all of this was wrong. I couldn't understand why, why we had to go."[4]

On the designated "evacuation" days, all persons of Japanese ancestry within the specific zones were ordered to assemble at central locations where they were met by armed U.S. soldiers. Each individual wore a U.S. government–issued identification tag. Monica Sone described how her brother returned from the mandatory registry with twenty tags numbered 10710 to hang on their coats and on their luggage. The tags represented a first act of indignity the Sone family would suffer. "From then on," Sone writes, "we were known as Family #10710."[5]

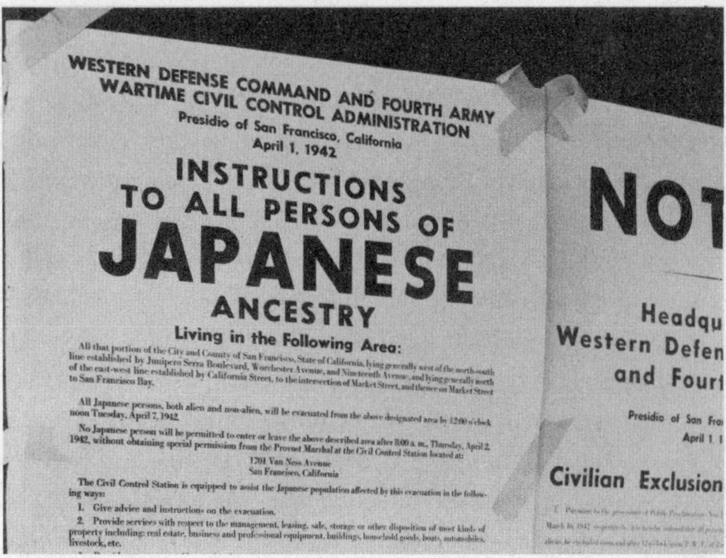

37. Exclusion Order posted at First and Front Streets in San Francisco, California, ordering the removal of persons of Japanese ancestry, April 11, 1942.

38. Following evacuation orders, this store, at 13th and Franklin Streets in San Francisco, was closed. The owner, a University of California graduate of Japanese descent, placed the I AM AN AMERICAN sign on the storefront on December 8, the day after Pearl Harbor.

Once assembled, Japanese American "evacuees" were transported to sixteen hastily erected "assembly centers" established by the Wartime Civil Control Administration (WCCA) in California, Oregon, Washington, and Arizona to implement the mass forced removal of Japanese Americans from the West Coast by the War Relocation Authority. These new "homes" were often hastily refurbished fairgrounds or racetracks where the inmates were kept in former animal stalls and barracks. Barbed wire fences and guard towers surrounded the centers. The conditions inside were appalling. Entire families were kept in rooms no bigger than twenty by twenty feet with flimsy partitions that separated one area from another but offered no privacy. Inmates were forced to make their own mattresses out of bags and straw. Dining facilities and bathrooms were all communal. The medical facilities and care were inadequate. Food was of poor quality and lacked variety. Shizuko Tokushige's first meal at the Tanforan center in San Bruno, for example, consisted of two slices of discolored meat, overcooked Swiss chard, and a slice of moldy bread.[6]

39. Grandfather and grandchildren awaiting an evacuation bus in Hayward, California, May 8, 1942. The original WRA caption notes that the "family unit is preserved during the evacuation."

The poor conditions at places like Tanforan were stark reminders of how much Japanese Americans had lost. Bob Utsumi was a thirteen-year-old Boy

Scout living in Oakland, California, when his family was forced to move out of their home and to Tanforan. "What I vividly recall is . . . getting to Tanforan and walking into the horse stable, and Mom . . . putting down her suitcase and just crying. And it [still] tears me up [today.]"[7] May K. Sasaki was just six years old when she and her family arrived at the Puyallup Assembly Center near Tacoma, Washington. A former fairgrounds, the assembly center reeked of its former animal tenants. "The one thing I remembered was the animal smells, you know," Sasaki recalled nearly thirty-five years later.[8]

40. The Konda family barrack apartment in the Tanforan Assembly Center in San Bruno, California, June 16, 1942. Mr. Konda shared this barrack with his daughter (behind him), two sons, a married daughter and her husband.

Most Japanese Americans felt powerless. They were told that cooperating with the government's plan to forcibly relocate and incarcerate them was an opportunity for American-born Japanese to demonstrate their loyalty. California congressman Leland M. Ford echoed many when he stated that if Japanese Americans were "really patriotic . . . and [are] working for us," then voluntarily removing themselves into the camps would be seen as their "contribution to the safety and welfare of this country." "Any loyal Japanese should not hesitate to do that," Ford explained to Secretary of State Cordell Hull.[9]

But a few Japanese Americans challenged the constitutionality of their wartime treatment. In late March of 1942, Minoru Yasui deliberately defied the government's curfew orders by walking the streets of downtown Portland after 8:00 p.m. When police officers failed to take notice, he went to a police station and demanded to be arrested. The federal district court agreed with Yasui's contention that the curfew was illegally applied to citizens. But it also ruled that Yasui should no longer be considered a U.S. citizen because he had briefly worked for the Japanese consulate prior to the war, a position Yasui had promptly resigned from right after Pearl Harbor. Yasui was convicted and spent nine months in solitary confinement before being sent to Minidoka camp.[10]

In Washington, Gordon Hirabayashi also disobeyed the curfew orders and challenged the constitutionality of Executive Order 9066. By refusing to comply with the forced removal from the West Coast, Hirabayashi was the "last Japanese American in Seattle." With his legal counsel, Hirabayashi argued that the U.S. government did not have the right to incarcerate Japanese Americans without due process of law. He believed that removal conferred "second-class status" on Japanese Americans. "I just couldn't accept it, and this was the only response I could make," he explained. A federal district court unanimously found him guilty of disobeying the curfew order, and the Supreme Court later upheld the conviction.[11]

Fred Korematsu also refused to comply with EO 9066 in San Leandro, California, and remained behind while his family went to the assembly center. When he was discovered in May of 1942, he was arrested and sent to prison. Ernest Besig of the American Civil Liberties Union approached Korematsu to test the constitutionality of EO 9066, and the case went to court. As Korematsu later explained, "I didn't feel guilty because I didn't do anything wrong. . . . Every day in school, we said the pledge of the flag, 'with liberty and justice for all,' and I believed all that. I was an American citizen, and I had as many rights as anyone else."[12] A federal district court convicted

Korematsu of defying military orders in September 1942 and he was forced to move to the Topaz camp.

41. Fred Korematsu, 1940s.

From within the camp, Korematsu appealed the decision and the case went to the U.S. Supreme Court. In December 1944, the court issued its ruling. Three justices found that incarceration had clearly violated Fred Korematsu's constitutional rights and that racial discrimination was a central motivating factor in Korematsu's case and in the overall treatment of Japanese Americans. But they were in the dissent. A majority of justices upheld the constitutionality of the incarceration of Japanese Americans. Justice Hugo Black, a former member of the Ku Klux Klan in Alabama, delivered the court's opinion. The high court accepted the army's position that removal and incarceration of Japanese Americans was a "military necessity" and in essence justified bowing to military demands during a time of war.[13]

• • •

While the Yasui, Hirabayashi, and Korematsu cases were weaving their way through the courts, forced removal and incarceration was U.S. policy. Beginning in June 1942, Japanese Americans were transferred to the ten newly constructed War Relocation Authority camps at Amache in Granada, Colorado; Gila River and Poston, Arizona; Heart Mountain, Wyoming; Jerome and Rohwer, Arkansas; Manzanar and Tule Lake, California; Minidoka, Idaho; and Topaz, Utah. All of the camps were located in extremely inhospitable areas. The Rohwer and Jerome camps were built on Arkansas swampland. Manzanar, Poston, and six other sites were in the desert where temperatures could climb as high as 115 degrees. In contrast, inmates at the northernmost camps at Minidoka and Heart Mountain suffered from temperatures as low as 35 degrees below zero as well as severe dust storms. Monica Sone describes how on her first day at Minidoka, she and her family "felt as if we were standing in a gigantic sand-mixing machine. Sand filled our mouths and nostrils and stung our faces and hands like a thousand darting needles."[14]

42. The War Relocation Authority Center at Manzanar, California, July 2, 1942. The original WRA caption notes that "evacuees at this . . . center are encountering the terrific desert heat."

The War Relocation Authority aimed to create communities of inmates who were as self-sufficient as possible and who could be engaged in constructive work that would rehabilitate them as loyal Americans doing their part for the war effort. The WRA provided housing, shelter, medical care, and education at no cost. Inmates could work in the camps, but their set wages of $12, $16, or $19 a month were far lower than what noninmates were receiving. Such wages were also not enough to meet even minimal needs, like shoes and clothing, or to pay for such things as mortgage payments on property owned outside the camp.[15]

Nevertheless, employment in food operations, health and sanitation, education, and camp operations like the post office and camp store provided routine and some meaning to inmates during the long months and years of confinement. Japanese Americans even started thriving enterprises within the camps, such as a huge vegetable garden at Tule Lake, a dairy at Gila River, and a silk screen poster shop at Heart Mountain. Susumu Togasaki even started a successful tofu factory and an artificial flower making manufacturing outfit within his camp in Arizona.[16]

The camps offered nursery school, elementary school, high school, and adult education, but teachers were often few in number, overworked, or untrained. School facilities needed to be built and textbooks and other supplies were in short supply. At Minidoka, high school students resorted to using the washroom as their biology and chemistry laboratories. Social science and humanities courses emphasized "Americanization" as part of their curriculum, an irony that was fully understood by many students. John Tateishi was a student at the school at the Manzanar camp where he played marbles and baseball with his friends and saluted the U.S. flag. "I was learning, as best one could learn in Manzanar," he explained, "what it meant to live in America. But I was also learning the sometimes bitter price one has to pay for it."[17]

Daily life behind barbed wire was one of monotony, anxiety, and growing discontent. Inmates were enormously creative and tried to make homes out of the barren, desolate barracks. Chairs and Japanese chests were lovingly made out of scrap lumber and turned into pieces of art. Intricate brooches were made from shells. Gardens sprang up in the desert. And there was artistic creativity, including many paintings by famed artist Chiura Obata, and in Bill Manbo's case, photographs taken in stunning Kodachrome film.[18] Nevertheless, families suffered. Proud, self-supporting issei men who had been farmers and shop owners were now dependent upon the government and worked as low-wage workers in menial jobs. Their positions as breadwinners—so important to the patriarchal Japanese and American cultures in which they lived—were threatened. And in the communal living environment of the camp, families became scattered.

Over time, discontent over camp living conditions grew. Inmates became increasingly bitter and disillusioned. They resented being prisoners when no charge had been made against them. They were also frustrated that there seemed to be no recourse available to them. There were conflicts between those who believed they should cooperate with the U.S. government and the camp administration and those who wanted to voice their dissent. Leaders of the Japanese American Citizens League, who often cooperated with and were rewarded by camp administrators, were especially criticized and suspected of being informers for the U.S. government. Violence erupted at a number of different camps, including at the Poston and Manzanar camps in late 1942. At Manzanar, the arrest of a man convicted of beating a suspected informer led to riots, martial law, and soldiers firing into an unarmed crowd, killing two and injuring nine.[19]

One of the most divisive times in the camps resulted from the government-issued loyalty review program that was initiated in early 1943. By that time, an attack by Japan was considered increasingly remote, while discontent among the inmates was growing. The War Relocation Authority began to explore options for the release of what it considered loyal detainees from the camps for either the military draft or a work release program. But first, it had to determine which ones were loyal. The government designed a questionnaire that was required of all Japanese Americans seventeen years of age and older. It asked a range of questions designed to determine Americanness versus Japaneseness.[20] Two in particular caused a great deal of concern and unrest. Question 27 asked all draft-age males: "Are you willing to serve in the armed forces of the United States on combat duty, wherever ordered?" Question 28 asked all others if they would be willing to "swear unqualified allegiance to the United States of America . . . and forswear any form of allegiance or obedience to the Japanese emperor, or any other foreign government, power or organization?" For some inmates, especially the U.S.-born nisei, answering "yes" to both questions was not difficult even if they were uneasy with the questions themselves. As Frank Miyamoto explained, "It's not a fair question directed to us, but what can we do? We want to get out of these centers. And we'll say 'yes-yes.' "[21]

Others were suspicious of the government's motives and resented the entire premise of the loyalty program. As Taneyuki Dan Harada explained, the loyalty questionnaire was just one more insult to the many injustices he and his family had already been subjected to. He objected in the only way he knew how. "My personal feeling is that I can accept a lot of things." His family's business had been lost. They had been relocated to a horse stall. They were then sent to Topaz. Now the government was asking him about his loyalty and whether he would volunteer for combat duty. "It didn't just sound right." He answered "no" to both questions.[22] Ben Takeshita recounted another common feeling of resentment and the belief that the U.S. government was trying to trick them. "Not only had our government disregarded our citizenship but put us behind barbed wire, but now was asking these same citizens to foreswear [sic] allegiance to the Emperor of Japan and to swear allegiance to the United States as if at one time all of us had sworn allegiance to the Japanese Emperor."[23]

For issei, the choice was even more heart-wrenching. Question 28 asked them to renounce their Japanese nationality even though they were barred by law from becoming U.S. citizens. Many believed that if they answered "yes" to this question, they would become stateless. However, if they answered "no," they might be forcibly separated from their families or targeted for further government reprisal. After much discussion, anxiety, and soul searching in the camps, most inmates answered "yes" to the loyalty question, and over 1,200 men volunteered for the U.S. Army. The government began to issue draft notices to Japanese Americans in the camps in January 1944.[24]

The 10 to 15 percent who had answered "no" to the two questions were considered disloyal and transferred to a segregated camp at Tule Lake. Collectively, they were nicknamed "no-no boys." Altogether, almost 12,200 inmates were brought to the segregated camp, where they joined 6,000 already there. Tule Lake Segregation Center became the largest WRA camp in the country.[25]

Various atrocities occurred at Tule Lake during the years of its operation from July of 1943 to March of 1946. The government first turned the site into a maximum security center with additional barbed wire, increased guards and tanks, and an eight-foot-high double "man-proof" fence. In the fall of 1943, discontent led to unrest, violence, and martial law. When 800 farmworkers went on strike to demand better working conditions following a work-related death, internal security forces savagely beat up the "disloyal" strikers. When massive demonstrations broke out to protest working and living conditions, authorities brought in "loyal" workers, and clashes at the camp followed. The army established martial law during which inmates were subjected to a curfew, searches, surveillance, repression, and hardship. As many as 350 men were put into a stockade, some for as long as eight months, without any charges made against them. Many of these already disaffected Japanese Americans lost even more faith in the United States.[26]

In the meantime, reports of the "Jap riots" at Tule Lake were used by anti-Asian groups as proof of Japanese American disloyalty.[27] A bill that allowed the Justice Department to denationalize Japanese Americans followed on July 1, 1944. Intended to determine (again) the loyalty or disloyalty of Japanese Americans in order to reintegrate loyal Japanese Americans back into American society, the renunciation program had another effect: it caused untold confusion and increased the distrust that many already had toward the U.S. government.

The timing also could not have been worse. Two months after renunciation program guidelines were publicized in October of 1944, the government announced that the camps would close within a year. By December of 1944, the Supreme Court had unanimously ruled in a case brought by Mitsuye Endo that "citizens who are concededly loyal" could not be held in War Relocation Authority camps. Decided during the same month that the court upheld Fred Korematsu's decision finding the mass race-based evacuation to be constitutional during wartime, *Ex parte Mitsuye Endo* did not represent the court's repudiation of the government's policy. The opinion evaded all constitutional questions regarding race-based imprisonment of American citizens. Instead, it merely found that the government did not have the right to detain a loyal citizen such as Endo. Warned that the court would rule in this way, the Roosevelt administration issued Public Proclamation 21 the day before the *Endo* ruling that rescinded the exclusion orders. The camps would be closed, and Japanese Americans would be allowed to return to the West Coast beginning in January 1944.[28]

The one exception was Tule Lake. The decision to free "loyal" Japanese Americans sent Tule Lake inmates, already branded by the government as "disloyal," into a panic. Would issei Japanese be forcibly deported and separated from their U.S. citizen children? Would Japanese Americans be sent back to hostile communities on the West Coast while the war with Japan was still raging? Widely reported incidents of violent assaults and harassment of returning Japanese Americans, including veterans, by angry whites on the coast made resettlement a frightening prospect.

With so many unanswered questions and growing anxiety, citizenship renunciation seemed like a solution. For some, renunciation was one way to keep families together. Others renounced their U.S. citizenship to avoid the draft or as a form of dissent. A few were goaded into renunciation by pro-Japanese militants. But most seemed to choose renunciation because they were terrified at the prospect of being sent back to the virulently anti-Japanese West Coast. Army officials made things even more confusing by leading many to believe that they could remain at Tule Lake for the remainder of the war if they renounced their citizenship.[29]

During these trying times, some 5,500 Japanese Americans renounced their U.S. citizenship, almost all of them residents of Tule Lake. They became "Native American Aliens," and U.S. officials proceeded to deport them from the United States. Over 1,300 were sent to Japan, including renunciants, aliens, and their U.S. citizen children. Most renunciants—over 5,400—realized that they had made a tragic mistake and took steps to reverse their renunciations right away. The Justice Department rebuffed their cases. But civil liberties attorney Wayne M. Collins appealed on their behalf on the grounds that the renunciations had taken place under duress and coercion. His efforts took fourteen years, but by 1959 the Department of Justice had restored citizenship to all renunciants who had applied.[30]

If the no-no boys, their treatment at Tule Lake Segregation Camp, and the renunciation cases point to one aspect of how Japanese American "disloyalty" was identified, controlled, and punished, then the service of the 33,000 Japanese American men who fought in the U.S. armed forces point to the ways in which Japanese American "loyalty" was proven.

The history of nisei soldiers during World War II represents one of the deepest ironies in U.S. history. Many had been forcibly removed from their homes because they and their immigrant parents were considered security risks. Despite this mistreatment, they volunteered or were willingly drafted to fight for democracy and freedom abroad and to redeem their place in the United States. In the meantime, their parents and families remained incarcerated behind barbed wire by the same government.

Japanese Americans fought in segregated units: the 442nd Regimental Combat Team and the 100th Infantry Battalion. The 100th Battalion was initially made up almost entirely of Japanese Americans from Hawai'i. Fighting under the slogan "Go for Broke," they landed on the beaches of Salerno, Italy, in the fall of 1943 to fight German forces. They suffered heavy casualties and lost seventy-eight men in the first month alone. For their bravery, many losses, and 900 Purple Hearts, the 100th came to be called the "Purple Heart Battalion."

About 18,000 men served in the 442nd Regimental Combat Team, which fought in campaigns in Italy, France, and Germany. One of their bloodiest campaigns was to rescue over 200 U.S. soldiers of a battalion from Texas surrounded by German troops in the Vosges Mountains of France during the winter of 1944. Two previous rescue attempts by other units had failed before the 442nd was called in. Fred Shiosaki remembers that his unit marched for four days up the muddy hills under constant fire. "We'd move a hundred yards, losing men, artillery coming in," he told an interviewer.[31] "The fighting was really fierce," remembered Fred Matsumura. "We were fighting, in the forest, you know. And they're throwing shells at us; every time the shell hit the tree, it burst like geysers. . . . We had a hell of a time getting through." The soldiers progressed slowly, crawling from position to position, sticking their heads out just a little bit, firing, and then moving a little more up the hill.[32] They finally reached the Lost Battalion and brought them to safety. The loss to their own troops, however, was staggering. The unit suffered 800 casualties in a single week. After the battle, Shiosaki remembers the "absolute dead" silence. "I don't know how many guys we lost right there on that hill, but we, there weren't many of us left." Dozens of trucks had carried nisei soldiers to the battlefield. After it was over, the whole company got into the back of one big truck. "That was all that was left," Shiosaki explains.[33]

The 442nd continued to play an instrumental role in the Allied effort in Europe until Germany surrendered on May 7, 1945. They were among the U.S. soldiers who discovered and liberated Jewish survivors at the Dachau camp. Over the course of the war, the 442nd became one of the most decorated combat units, with 3,600 Purple Hearts, 350 Silver Stars, 810 Bronze Stars, 47 Distinguished Service Crosses, and one Congressional Medal of Honor.[34]

While the nisei soldiers received praise and recognition during and after the war, those Japanese American men who resisted the draft faced different realities. One center of draft resistance was at the Heart Mountain camp in Wyoming, where the Fair Play Committee was established by draft-age nisei men. They demanded that civil rights be restored to all nisei before they would comply with the military draft, and they also tried to test the legality of conscripting incarcerated Americans of Japanese descent. Mits Koshiyama, a member of the Fair Play Committee, spoke for many when he recalled, "I thought that Selective Service out of the camps was not right." A Japanese American citizen, he had been put into camp, denied his constitutional rights, and was now being asked to join a segregated army unit to fight for the very democratic principles that were being denied to him.[35] Altogether, 315 men from the War Relocation Authority camps resisted the draft. Their actions were vigorously criticized by many Japanese Americans, and members of the group were often vilified and ostracized.[36]

In 1944, sixty-three members of the Fair Play Committee were convicted of willfully defying draft orders and ordered to serve three years of jail time. The committee leaders were arrested and convicted of counseling others to evade the draft and were ordered to serve up to four years in prison. In 1947, President Harry Truman pardoned them, but the mainstream Japanese American community, including U.S. Army veterans and members of the Japanese American Citizens League, largely shunned the draft resisters. Only with the passage of decades have the draft resisters been recognized for their loyalty and courage in demanding civil rights.[37]

In forcibly removing and incarcerating Japanese Americans, the U.S. government committed atrocious violations against its own people. Involving international cooperation and collusion, the deportation and incarceration of Japanese Peruvians and other Japanese Latin Americans in the United

States as enemy aliens, however, raised the level of injustice to an even greater degree.

When Japanese Latin Americans arrived in the United States, many were first taken to Immigration and Naturalization Service (INS) facilities in New Orleans, where they were forced to remove all their clothing and stand naked in groups while they were sprayed with insecticide.[38] They were also officially processed by U.S. immigration authorities in what one Immigration and Naturalization Service camp commander later acknowledged as legal "skullduggery" made possible only during wartime.[39] The INS classified the detainees as "undocumented immigrants" or "illegal aliens" who were entering the country without valid visas and passports. To many Japanese Latin Americans, this was patently preposterous. "How can you be illegal when they brought you?" Elsa Kudo asked years later.[40]

Japanese Latin Americans were then sent by train to one of six enemy alien camps run by the INS. The largest were in Texas at Kenedy, Seagoville, and Crystal City. The others were at Kooskia, Idaho; Missoula, Montana; and Santa Fe, New Mexico. The camps varied in population and size. The majority of Latin American inmates at Camp Kenedy were Germans, with some Japanese and a few Italians. The camp at Missoula was made up of mostly Italian and Japanese men, with some Germans. A large stockade housed the inmates with enclosures for Italians, another for Japanese, and a third for all others. Separate mess halls with separate cooks allowed Japanese to have rice while the Italians were offered spaghetti.[41]

Art Shibayama's family was sent to Crystal City, the largest detention camp, located about 120 miles southwest of San Antonio. Known as the family camp, it eventually held 962 families, most of whom were Japanese, who lived in shared temporary housing units with one, two, or three other families. In total, the camp held 3,000 to 4,000 people.[42]

As "interned foreign nationals," Japanese Peruvians could claim some protections and minimal standards in treatment and conditions in the camps under the Geneva Convention. Each housing unit had separate cooking facilities, cold running water, basic furniture and furnishings. There were stores, schools, a hospital, and churches in the camp. Inmates could volunteer for a paid-work program in the camp growing vegetables, caring for chickens, producing honey, slaughtering and curing meat, making and repairing clothes and furniture, and instructing classes. A number of organizations, including the International Red Cross, the YMCA, the YWCA, and the American Friends Service Committee, also tried to ameliorate conditions for the detainees.[43]

Despite these amenities, there was no mistaking the camp's purpose. It was surrounded by a ten-foot fence, floodlights, and guard towers. And lurking behind the baseball games and vegetable gardens was the constant frustration, fear, and anxiety about what the future held beyond and outside of the camps. Would the detainees be forced to "return" to Japan, a country that many had never been to or had not seen for years? Would they be allowed to return to Peru? Was staying in the United States an option? When U.S. embassy officials visited Camp Kenedy in May of 1942, they noted that inmates had been told that they would be held in the United States only for a "very brief period" and that they were "most anxious" to learn when they might expect to be repatriated to the country of their birth or returned to Latin America. The Japanese detainees also complained of discrimination, with Europeans being given preferential housing.[44]

Former inmates describe Crystal City—a "city behind barbed wire"—in mixed ways. On the one hand, all of their needs were taken care of at a time when others were experiencing wartime deprivation and rationing. There were outstanding doctors in the camp hospital, schools, clothing, work, community-led gardens, and baseball games. The Japanese could get miso, tofu, and other Japanese food products, sometimes trading their government-issued rations of butter to the Germans in exchange for fish. "We could not complain about our lives in the camp," Seiichi Higashide acknowledged. Nevertheless, the inmates had no real freedom either in their daily lives or in determining their future, and they were like "bird[s] in a cage" living in a "barbed wire 'utopia,' " according to Higashide.[45]

While the world celebrated the end of World War II in 1945, the future for Japanese American and Japanese Peruvian inmates remained unclear. After the U.S. Supreme Court ruled in the *Endo* case that the government had no authority to incarcerate loyal citizens, the blanket exclusion orders barring Japanese Americans from the West Coast were lifted in January 1945. The vast majority left the camps by the time the war ended in September, and the last camp closed in March of 1946. In the United States, the War Relocation Authority encouraged inmates to move out of the camps as soon as possible and to go to the eastern and northern areas of the United States rather than back to the West Coast. President Roosevelt had emphasized the importance and desirability of spreading the Japanese American population throughout the nation, and the War Relocation Authority used dispersal as its primary postwar policy objective. The idea was that while a few Japanese Americans spread out around the country was acceptable, the reestablishment of large, concentrated communities was unwise and detrimental to the group's ongoing rehabilitation and reentry into mainstream society.

43. Photograph of George Isoda used by the War Relocation Authority to encourage the resettlement of Japanese Americans after the war.

The government tried to encourage Japanese American resettlement by highlighting positive examples of families who had successfully integrated into new communities outside of the West Coast. One series of WRA photographs, for example, cheerfully followed the lives of the Isoda and Kaneko families, who were newly resettled in Milwaukee. Photographs showed the young families walking the shores of Lake Michigan and relaxing in their spacious and cozy homes full of domestic bliss. The original WRA caption to the photo above read: "Every man likes to put on his slippers, light up his favorite pipe, and read the evening paper before the fireplace. Mr. George

Isoda is no exception. After a hard day's work as a Milwaukee auto mechanic, Mr. Isoda likes to relax in the large living room of the home which he shares with his brother-in-law, Mr. Masumi Kaneko, who is a printing compositor. The Kanekos and the Isodas have lived in Milwaukee almost one year. The Isodas came from Los Angeles via the Granada Relocation Center while the Kanekos are Seattle, Washington, people from the Hunt Relocation Center. Beginning in summer 1942, the War Relocation Authority (WRA) began to release incarcerees and encouraged them to resettle in areas of the United States other than the West Coast."[46]

Some Japanese Americans believed that dispersal would help protect them from the racism that had led to their forced relocation and incarceration during the war. Across the country, small communities of Japanese Americans became established in new areas, including Chicago, Denver, New York, Cleveland, and Detroit.[47] They tried to follow the instructions they had been given to "assimilate," "blend in," and "don't make waves."[48] Nevertheless, institutionalized racism seethed below the surface in many of these communities, especially in housing. Some white suburbs, like the Minneapolis suburb of Edina, Minnesota, were known to be off-limits to all nonwhites, and both real estate agents and residents tried to enforce informal practices of housing discrimination. Just days after Sally Sudo's family bought a home in South Minneapolis after the war, for example, they started receiving hate mail saying "We don't want any japs in the neighborhood. Get out or else."[49]

In spite of the government's dispersal plans, many Japanese Americans wished to return to the homes and lands on the West Coast. Small numbers of Japanese had been permitted to return to the Pacific Coast to "test public reception" as early as the spring of 1944.[50] The government allowed Japanese who passed the loyalty test to return to the coast in January 1945. Those who did so found harassment, vandalized property, stolen goods, and discrimination.[51]

Housing, unemployment, underemployment, and poverty were serious problems. Many had lost their homes during the expulsion, and traditional Japanese American neighborhoods in Los Angeles, Seattle, and San Francisco had been transformed by new residents. Japanese Americans had largely been self-employed before the war. Now they were reduced to finding menial, low-paying jobs. Frank Yamasaki recalled how his parents and the other issei around him "were all having to start from scratch" again. His own father had been a factory foreman in Seattle before the war. After his return, the only work he could find was as a dishwasher at a friend's restaurant.[52]

Over time, Japanese Americans reentered society and rebuilt their lives, families, and communities. In addition to returning to school and careers, starting families, and trying to recuperate and heal from wartime injustices, they tried to demonstrate their loyalty and their Americanness to the larger American public. As Yoshiko Uchida explains, "I felt a tremendous sense of responsibility to make good, not just for myself but for all Japanese Americans . . . Sometimes it was an awesome burden to bear."[53]

Japanese Americans also continued to fight remaining vestiges of institutionalized discrimination. In 1948, the U.S. Supreme Court decision in *Oyama* v. *California* struck down provisions in California's Alien Land Law that prohibited Japanese immigrants from owning land. With the help of attorney Wayne Collins, almost all Japanese Americans who had renounced their citizenship under duress also had their citizenship restored. Moreover, the Japanese American Citizens League formed an alliance with African American civil rights groups like the National Association for the Advancement of Colored People—the NAACP—in other Fourteenth Amendment cases involving land ownership and housing.[54]

While Japanese Americans were slowly rebuilding their lives, Japanese Peruvians in the United States remained unsure about their future long after the war ended. Days and months passed as they wondered whether they would be allowed to return to Peru or be forced to go to war-ravaged Japan. As the Germans, Italians, and Japanese Americans left camps, "only we Peruvians stayed," explained Kami Kamisato, who was placed in Crystal City with her husband, daughter, and two young grandchildren. "And how lonesome it was."[55]

Most wanted to simply return to Peru. But the government of Peru was reluctant to allow any to return. As one U.S. embassy official explained, the Peruvians "look[ed] forward to the expulsion of [Japanese Peruvians] as the comforting end to a long worry."[56] But remaining in the United States was not an option either. At the end of the war, the United States classified them as "illegal entrants" who had entered the country without valid visas.

Three weeks before sending warplanes to bomb Hiroshima and Nagasaki, President Truman issued an executive order that authorized the removal of enemy aliens "who are within the territory of the United States without admission under the immigration laws" from the entire Western Hemisphere. In 1945, delegates gathered at a Mexico City Conference on the Problems of War and Peace and agreed that "any person whose deportation was necessary for reasons of security of the continent" should be prevented from "further residing in this hemisphere if such residence should be prejudicial to the future security or welfare of the Americas." In effect, both proclamations set the stage for the repatriation and expatriation of Japanese Latin Americans to Japan.[57]

Between November 1945 and June 1946, more than 900 Japanese Peruvians were repatriated to Japan. Immersed in pro-Japanese propaganda and news sources during the war, a few of the repatriates were convinced that Japan had been victorious in the war and were crushed to later learn that Japan had indeed been devastated. With their property confiscated or lost and with both the Peruvian and U.S. governments refusing to allow Japanese Peruvians to either return to Peru or remain in the United States, most believed that they had no choice but to go to Japan.[58]

The Peruvian government at first refused to acknowledge its role in the deportation and incarceration program, but ultimately did allow a total of seventy-nine Japanese Peruvian citizens and their families to return to Peru. The remainder were caught in a bind, and 364 Latin American detainees had no country to go back to. As a result, some Japanese Peruvians began to organize an effort to remain in the United States. "You brought us here with force. Now you are responsible for your own action," Mrs. Kami Kamisato protested.[59] The U.S. government's insistence that Japanese Latin Americans had entered the country "illegally" seemed incredible. After all, U.S. intelligence had provided the data for their arrest, and U.S. soldiers had guarded the U.S. transport ships that had brought them to the United States. When they arrived in New Orleans, they had been met by U.S. Immigration and Naturalization Service officers before they were put in U.S. Justice Department camps. "It [was] absurd to label us 'illegal aliens,' " Seiichi Higashide believed.[60]

44. Repatriated family preparing to board the SS *Gripsholm*, which would take them from the United States to Japan as part of a prisoner exchange program, 1943–1944.

45. Repatriated men lined up to board the SS *Gripsholm* on their way to Japan, 1943–1944.

Civil liberties attorney Wayne Collins came to the rescue again, along with his colleague A. L. Wirin. They went to herculean efforts to advocate for the Japanese Peruvians, whom Collins labeled "hapless victims of international intrigue, connivance and malice" in a 1947 letter to Secretary of State George C. Marshall. They were "guiltless of any wrongdoing," had been "kidnapped" and "abducted," and now faced "pointless and patently absurd" classifications of being unlawfully in the United States, he argued.[61] Over several years, Collins wrote to U.S. and Peruvian officials and to the public and the press in both countries, counseled and assured his clients, and in 1946, filed writs of habeas corpus on behalf of Japanese Latin Americans in the federal district court of San Francisco. As a result, they were allowed to stay in the United States on a "parole" basis and were sent to work as undocumented immigrants sponsored by Seabrook Farms in New Jersey.[62]

Some families, like the Shibayamas and the Higashides, moved to Chicago after a few years on the farm to try to rebuild their lives. They had heard the U.S. government's message to avoid the West Coast and move to places like the Midwest, where they might find a friendlier economic and social climate. An estimated 25,000 Japanese Americans lived in Chicago between 1945 and 1946, and a small but close-knit Japanese American community formed there.[63] In 1954, the "illegal entrants" from Latin America were formally given entry visas through an amendment in the Refugee Relief Act of 1953, the first step toward permanent residency in the United States. In 1958, the Higashide family became U.S. citizens.[64]

In a cruel twist of fate, Art Shibayama was drafted into the U.S. Army during the Korean War in spite of his status as an undocumented immigrant. "I couldn't believe it because here I am [an] illegal alien. But since I was fighting deportation, I thought maybe I better go in the army," he explained. He was stationed in Germany during the war and served honorably, all the while fighting for the right to remain in the United States legally. In 1970, Art Shibayama finally became a U.S. citizen.[65]

12

Good War, Cold War

World War II brought enormous changes for Asian Americans. While Japanese Americans were removed from their homes and incarcerated, other Asian Americans, including Chinese, South Asians, Filipinos, and Koreans, came to be viewed as "good Asians" whose homelands were wartime allies of the United States or were engaged in the struggle against Japan. At the same time, racism in the United States was increasingly seen as damaging the United States' war effort and its fight against the Axis powers. Decades-old Asian exclusion laws were abolished, and for these Asian Americans, World War II was a "good war" that opened up new opportunities to participate in the American economy, military, and society. Asian Americans took full advantage.

The Cold War also transformed Asian American communities and life. As the United States consolidated its position as a global superpower, Asia became a special focus of U.S. military, economic, and political power. Japan, South Korea, Taiwan, the Philippines, and South Vietnam all became crucial U.S. allies in the global war against communism and shining examples of U.S.-style democracies and capitalism. American public attitudes toward Asia and Asians softened. U.S. Cold War engagements in Asia ushered in new immigrants like military brides, adoptees, and students. Their arrival in the United States came to symbolize a new acceptance of internationalism, interracial relationships, and the benevolence and humanitarianism of the United States.

At the same time, Asian Americans in the United States actively became key figures in the ongoing debate about race in the country. With Soviet propaganda highlighting the discrimination of racial minorities in the U.S. to tarnish America's image abroad, Americans focused more seriously on ending racial inequality. Successful Asian Americans were celebrated as living proof of American democracy and actively helped to spread this message at home and abroad. By the 1960s, some Asian Americans were being characterized as "model minorities" who overcame past obstacles to achieve the American Dream. This new image would help set the stage for celebratory coverage of the "rise of Asian Americans" during the late twentieth and early twenty-first centuries. But even as the Cold War helped to open up Asian immigration again and transform Asian Americans from one of the America's most despised minorities into its model minority, it also masked persistent inequalities and the fragility of Asian Americans' new acceptance into American society.

China and Chinese Americans' involvement in what would become World War II began when Japan invaded China in 1937. Chinese American communities responded to the unfolding humanitarian crisis in their homeland with an unprecedented demonstration of support. "To Save China, to Save Ourselves" became a slogan heard throughout Chinese American communities.[1] Organizations like the Chinese Six Companies and the Chinese War Relief Association in San Francisco organized 300 Chinese communities throughout the United States, Canada, Mexico, and Central and South America to raise funds for the war relief effort. Over the next eight years, the War Relief Association collected over $20 million through door-to-door solicitations, parades, war bond sales, and what were known as rice bowl parties.[2] In San Francisco alone, more than 200,000 people packed Chinatown at its first rice bowl party in 1938.[3]

As sympathy for China grew, the international profile for both China and Chinese peoples abroad rose dramatically. Then, with the Japanese attack on Pearl Harbor, China became an American ally fighting the common

Japanese enemy. Chinese Americans volunteered for service, bought war bonds, worked in shipyards and factories, and turned their wartime efforts to supporting China *and* the United States. Public opinion turned ever more favorably toward them. As one U.S. congressman explained in 1943, "All at once we discovered the saintly qualities of the Chinese people. If it had not been for December 7th, I do not know if we would have ever found out how good they were."[4]

With both domestic and international prerogatives in mind, a nationwide media campaign began to influence Americans' ideas about the Chinese in the United States. The intent was to dismantle decades-old stereotypes of Chinese as inassimilable, cheap laborers, gamblers, and prostitutes and instead recast them as "Chinese friends" who were "law-abiding, peace-loving, courteous people living quietly among us." "That they make good citizens, there is no doubt," a group lobbying for the repeal of the Chinese exclusion laws claimed.[5] Equally important, Americans needed to unlearn their long-standing habit of viewing and treating all "Orientals" the same and instead distinguish the "good" ones from the "bad" ones.

On December 22, 1941, both *Time* and *Life* magazines ran stories helpfully guiding readers on how to distinguish their new Chinese "friends" from the enemy "Japs." *Life*'s story included photographs. The first featured a Chinese government official smiling humbly at the camera. The other featured a stern-looking General Hideki Tojo, the Japanese prime minister responsible for the attack on Pearl Harbor. Both portraits were covered with handwritten notes identifying defining features and racial rules. The Chinese, for example, had a "parchment yellow complexion," a "higher bridge," a "longer, narrower face," a "scant beard," and "never has rosy cheeks." In contrast, the Japanese had an "earthy yellow complexion," "flatter nose," "sometimes rosy cheeks," "heavy beard," and "broader, shorter face."[6]

Time's description of "how to tell your friends from the Japs" was even more specific. "Virtually all Japanese are short . . . seldom fat, [and] often dry up and grow lean as they age" whereas the Chinese "often put on weight." Chinese had more "placid, kindly, open" facial expressions, while the Japanese were "more positive, dogmatic, arrogant."[7] Perhaps unsurprisingly, some Chinese Americans sought ways to help white Americans distinguish them from Japanese Americans and wore "I am Chinese" buttons during the war.[8]

The remaking of the Chinese people and Chinese Americans into "friends" mirrored both changing U.S.-Chinese relations during the war and new racial attitudes—what historians have called "racial liberalism"—that sought to dismantle state-sanctioned discrimination and promote assimilation, integration, civil rights, and equality of citizenship for minority groups. The goals of racial liberalism were not only to improve life for America's racial minorities, but also to spread a positive message about American democracy abroad. Both of these international and national developments opened up a number of new opportunities for Chinese Americans.[9]

The war first dramatically altered Chinese Americans' domestic prospects. Twelve to fifteen thousand Chinese Americans (nearly 20 percent of the adult Chinese male population of the United States) served in all branches of the U.S. military during the war. The majority were in the army, but some Chinese Americans served in the Flying Tigers, the covert U.S.-China air force formed to defend China.[10] Two Chinese American women were even members of the Women Airforce Service Pilots (WASP) and flew military aircraft around the United States.[11]

The war economy also opened up new, well-paying jobs in shipyards and factories where Chinese Americans could earn stable wages and mix with other ethnic groups. There were six major shipyards in the San Francisco Bay Area alone, and beginning in 1942 recruitment ads appeared in Chinatown newspapers. Nearly 10 percent of the Chinese American population in the Bay Area found employment in the defense industries during the war.[12] Chinese American women made up an especially noticeable group in wartime shipyards and factories and in hospital wards and Red Cross camps. These "Chinese Daughters of Uncle Sam" caught the attention of the media and helped highlight the patriotism of the entire Chinese American community.[13] "It was the patriotic thing to do, to work in some kind of war industry," remembered May Lew Gee.[14]

Military service, wartime employment, and their new social acceptance made World War II a significant turning point for Chinese Americans. They emerged from the war with a new confidence and sense of belonging. Chinese American veterans felt the change acutely. "All of a sudden, we [Chinese Americans] became part of an American Dream," veteran Harold Lui of New York recalled.[15]

The most significant symbol of Chinese Americans' changing status in the United States and the strength of U.S.-China relations during the war was the 1943 goodwill tour by China's first lady, Mayling Soong, or Madame Chiang Kai-shek, wife of wartime China's nationalist leader, General Chiang Kai-shek. Madame Chiang started at the White House, where she was the honored guest of President Roosevelt and his wife, Eleanor. The next day, she became the first private citizen and only the second woman to address both houses of Congress. She eloquently linked the United States and China together in a common cause of freedom. Chiang charmed the assembled congressmen and senators, and when her speech ended in the Senate, the collective audience "rose and thundered" their applause.[16] Over the next two months, she traveled around the country and spoke to thousands of people. Celebrated for her intellect, beauty, grace, and message of wartime cooperation, Chiang symbolized a new China, one that was a modern, capable, and valuable ally of the United States in the war against Japan. Her popularity in the U.S. also mirrored a new acceptance of Chinese Americans. A graduate of Wellesley College and featured with her husband as *Time*'s "Man and Wife of the Year" in 1938, Chiang fit the ideal of a modern woman at home in both China and the United States.

Madame Chiang's successful goodwill tour energized an effort to repeal the Chinese exclusion laws.[17] By October 1943, President Roosevelt was urging Congress to repeal the Chinese Exclusion Laws. "China is our ally," the president proclaimed. "Today, we fight at her side." Calling the exclusion laws "a historic mistake," President Roosevelt argued that "we owe it to the Chinese to . . . wipe from the statute books those anachronisms in our law."[18] On December 17, 1943, six decades of Chinese exclusion came to an end when the president signed the Magnuson Act, also known as the Chinese Exclusion Repeal Act.[19]

The repeal of the exclusion laws marked an important symbolic gesture of the U.S.'s new wartime friendship with China. But repeal had mixed results. Chinese immigration was placed under the immigration quotas regulating other immigrants, and only 105 Chinese were allowed to enter the country per year, a fraction of the quota granted to other Allied countries. (U.S. citizens and returning residents, as well as their wives and children and members of certain professional classes and students, could continue to enter as "non-quota immigrants.")[20] The repeal of the exclusion laws did, however, allow Chinese immigrants to become eligible for naturalization. Several war-related measures also expedited naturalization for Chinese American members of the armed forces, and the War Brides Acts of 1945 and 1947 permitted citizen members of the military to bring their foreign-born spouses and minor children into the United States outside of the 105 quota.[21]

These new naturalization and immigration opportunities were enormously significant. In the immediate postwar period, more Chinese women entered the United States than ever before; almost 7,500 from 1947 to 1950.[22] Canada's Chinese Exclusion Act was also repealed in 1947, and spouses and children of Chinese Canadians entered the country at a steady pace.[23] In both the United States and Canada, Chinese sojourners and transnational families gave way to family reunification, settlement, and naturalization.

46. Madame Chiang Kai-shek, First Lady of China, and Mrs. Eleanor Roosevelt, First Lady of the United States, on the lawn of the White House, Washington, D.C., 1943, during Madame Chiang's goodwill tour.

• • •

The Japanese bombing of Pearl Harbor and the U.S. entry into World War II had a similarly dramatic effect on Filipino Americans. Seven hours after Japan bombed Pearl Harbor, Japanese forces invaded the Philippines. On the Bataan Peninsula, U.S. and Filipino troops tried in vain to repel them over four long months. On April 9, Bataan fell to Japan, but the image of the "Fighting Filipinos" allied with U.S. forces had long-lasting repercussions.

Bataan came to symbolize interracial brotherhood and sacrifice in the name of freedom and democracy, and stories of the brave Filipino soldiers who fought side by side with U.S. forces helped transform images of Filipino Americans from backward "little brown brothers" to loyal and brave allies who shared a common cause with the United States. As First Lady Eleanor Roosevelt explained, the fighting in Bataan "has been an excellent example of what happens when two races respect each other. Men of different races and backgrounds have fought side by side and praised each other's heroism and courage."[24]

Just as Chinese Americans received a boost from Madame Chiang Kai-shek's tour of the United States, Filipinos similarly benefited from the celebrated visit of Carlos P. Romulo, General Douglas MacArthur's aide-de-camp. In April 1944, Romulo marked the second anniversary of the brutal Bataan Death March with an official visit to the Stockton Filipino community. His speech repeated the themes of interracial brotherhood now familiar to American and Filipino audiences. Connecting what happened in Bataan to what could happen in Stockton, Romulo urged white Americans to adopt the same acceptance of Filipino Americans in the United States. "Take them into your hearts as the 17 million Filipinos took into their hearts the 7,000 American soldiers who fought for you, for us, for freedom in Bataan," he told the audience. "Don't discriminate against them, please. Smile at them when you meet them in your street."[25]

The change in public attitude toward Filipinos was dramatic. Whereas before the United States entered the war there was a "flood" of race hatred directed at them, afterward, writer Manuel Buaken remarked that "no longer on the streetcar do I feel myself in the presence of my enemies." But he also noted, "we Filipinos are the same—it is Americans that have changed in their recognition of us."[26]

Filipino Americans showed their patriotism to both the Philippines and the United States through military service. Worried about their families and friends in the Japanese-controlled Philippines and eager to defend their homeland, thousands of Filipinos rushed to U.S. recruiting offices. However, they found that even as U.S. nationals they were ineligible for service in the U.S. armed forces and were turned away.[27] Filipinos protested, and Roosevelt responded by changing the draft law. On February 19, 1942—coincidentally the same day the president signed Executive Order 9066 allowing for the mass removal and incarceration of Japanese Americans—the 1st Filipino Infantry Regiment and the 2nd Filipino Infantry Regiment were formed. In California, 16,000, or 40 percent of the state's Filipino population, registered for the first draft. More than 7,000 Filipinos eventually served in the two Filipino regiments and contributed to the war effort in numerous ways, including operating behind enemy lines to destroy Japanese communications and providing military intelligence.[28]

Like Chinese Americans, Filipino Americans took advantage of new opportunities like employment, citizenship, immigration, and property and home ownership. Stockton—already home to the largest Filipino community in the United States—became one of the largest centers for shipbuilding and munitions work on the West Coast. Filipino Americans left the agricultural fields for new and well-paying factory jobs. Shipyards in southern California and defense contractors like Lockheed, Douglas, and Vultee also opened up their doors. Filipino farmworkers, houseboys, and restaurant workers became welders, technicians, and assembly workers. Other economic opportunities opened up as well. The California attorney general reinterpreted the state's land laws to allow Filipinos to lease land, and they were encouraged to take over property formerly held by incarcerated Japanese Americans.[29]

On July 2, 1946, President Truman signed the Luce-Celler Act, which granted Filipinos the right to become naturalized citizens and increased the annual quota of Filipino immigration to 100 per year. Two days later, the United States officially granted independence to the Philippines. The annual immigration quota was nominal. But other laws, such as the War Brides Acts, allowed foreign-born wives of U.S. veterans to enter the country outside the quota. Filipino enlistees in the U.S. Navy and Army were also granted U.S. citizenship, assistance through the GI Bill, and the right to bring in their immediate relatives such as spouses, parents, and children outside the quota. Between 1946 and 1965, over 39,000 Filipinos immigrated to the United States, including a significant number of women.[30] Finally, after years of separation, Filipino families could be together in the United States, and Filipino Americans became more firmly rooted in the country. "For the first time in Pacific Coast history," sociologist R. T. Feria declared in 1946, "it is no longer a liability to be a Filipino."[31]

Change did not come as easily for Korean Americans. On the day of the Pearl Harbor attack, Mary Paik Lee stopped at her local grocery store in Whittier, California, to make a purchase. When she entered the store, a roomful of people stared at her with hateful expressions. One man said, "There's one of them damned Japs now," Lee recalled. The owner of the store, Mrs. Hannah Nixon, mother of future president Richard Nixon, came to her defense. "Shame on you, all of you," she told them. "You have known Mrs. Lee for years. You know she's not Japanese, and even if she were, she is not to blame for what happened at Pearl Harbor."[32] Lee's experience of mistaken identity mirrored those of other Korean Americans during the war.

For decades, Korean Americans had been waging their struggle against Japanese colonialism in Korea. While U.S. officials were aware of and sometimes sympathetic to these struggles, the U.S. government officially regarded Koreans as subjects of Japan. When the U.S. Congress enacted the 1940 Alien Registration Act, the status of Koreans became even more vulnerable. A national security measure designed to better control aliens from Axis countries, the act strengthened existing laws relating to the admission and deportation of aliens. It also required the fingerprinting of all aliens in the United States. A February 1942 editorial in the *Korean National Herald-Pacific Weekly* summed up the vexing position of Korean Americans: "The Korean here is between the devil and the deep sea for the reason that the United States considers him a subject of Japan, which the Korean resents as an injustice to his true status."[33]

Concerned about the uncertain status of Koreans in the United States, Korean nationalist leaders like Kilsoo Haan pressed the government to allow Koreans to register as Koreans and not as Japanese subjects. "Koreans are truly an unwilling subjected people under the Jap-militarist government," Haan explained to government officials. "We are loyal to America and will be always ready to serve the best interest of the United States in this time of grave National Emergency." As a result of these efforts, the director of alien registration allowed Koreans to register as Koreans, and the Immigration and Naturalization Service issued identification cards to Korean aliens in the United States that identified them as Koreans.[34]

But after the Japanese attack on Pearl Harbor, the situation changed. All Japanese aliens in the United States became enemy aliens, and the Treasury Department froze the financial assets of all Japanese nationals. In enacting these measures, the government failed to distinguish Koreans from Japanese. As a result, Koreans found themselves classified as enemy aliens and subject to many of the same restrictions imposed on alien Japanese. This classification rightly enraged Koreans. "Is there in this world a worse Jap hater than a Korean?" the editor of the *Korean National Herald-Pacific Weekly* newspaper asked.[35] Violence and hate crimes also increased. Mary Paik Lee recalled that Koreans were afraid to go out at night. "Many were beaten even during the day. Their cars were wrecked, their tires were slashed. . . . Many [perpetrators] just assumed that all Orientals were Japanese. . . . It was a bad time for all of us."[36]

The consequences of these policies and crimes were devastating. Koreans in Hawai'i and in the continental U.S. could not access their bank accounts. Businesses and livelihoods were in danger. Korean nationalist organizations and leaders pushed their case again. Nine days after the Japanese attack on Pearl Harbor, Won Soon Lee, chairman of the United Korean Committee in America, wrote Secretary of State Cordell Hull to emphatically declare their distinct status as Koreans, rather than Japanese. "Local authorities include us as Japa[nese]," Lee explained. But "we have been loyal residents of long standing having arrived in Hawai'i before Japan invaded Korea. We have never submitted to Japanese authority." Did the U.S. Department of Justice's classification of Koreans as Koreans on the alien registration census still stand? Lee asked. "We are anxious to serve America at your command. We firmly believe in the common victory of the Democratic peoples of which we claim a place."[37] Part of this show of American patriotism had—like Filipino and Chinese Americans—an anti-Japanese streak. Leaders like

Kilsoo Haan claimed that the Japanese in Hawai'i were a fifth-column danger, and he lent his voice to the chorus calling for the forced evacuation of Japanese from the West Coast.[38]

As a result of these lobbying efforts, the government unfroze financial holdings of all Koreans in the United States. But Korean Americans still faced much uncertainty in the weeks and months following Pearl Harbor. While most Korean Americans were permitted to register as Koreans under the Alien Registration Act beginning in January 1942, those in Hawai'i remained classified as enemy aliens until the end of martial law in the islands in late 1944.[39]

Koreans redoubled their efforts to prove their loyalty to the United States and to contribute to the war effort. Many believed that the U.S. war against Japan would result in Korea's independence at long last. They enthusiastically organized war bond drives, and a small, select group of Korean Americans served in the U.S. armed forces. Forced to learn Japanese in Korean schools under Japanese colonialism, Koreans in the United States now used their valuable language skills to serve as Japanese-language teachers and translators and as secret agents and propaganda broadcasters in Japanese-occupied Asia. In Los Angeles, one fifth of the city's Korean population joined the California National Guard and was organized into a Korean unit called the Tiger Brigade, known as *Manghokun*.[40]

Like Chinese and Filipino Americans, World War II presented Korean Americans an opportunity to fight for both their homeland and to advance the status and rights of Koreans in the United States. In 1944, Hawai'i territorial delegate Joseph R. Farrington introduced a bill in Congress to allow immigration and naturalization rights to Koreans. Although the bill did not pass, Koreans felt elated that the effort recognized their "forty years of fight for freedom" as well as the changing status of Koreans in the country.[41]

By war's end, Korea's fate would be determined, but it was not what Korean nationalists had been fighting for. Instead of Korean independence, the United States advocated a policy by which Korea would become independent "in due course." Plans for a multilateral trusteeship were in place by the end of the war, but by then Korea had become victim to the emerging Cold War struggle between the United States and the Soviet Union. The 1948 division of the Korean Peninsula at the 38th parallel resulted in the establishment of two separate states in the north and south and lay the foundations for the Korean War.[42]

U.S. attitudes toward South Asian immigration changed during the war as well. South Asians in the United States lobbied politicians to revise immigration laws and to build support for Indian independence. In addition, India became an important ally in the war effort. The Indian Army successfully halted the progress of the Japanese in both Central Asia and the Pacific. The Luce-Celler Act of 1946 allowed South Asians to apply for admission into the United States under existing quotas. They could also become naturalized U.S. citizens.[43] The quota for India, which won its independence from Great Britain in 1947, however, was only 100 a year, and South Asian immigration remained limited. It would not increase substantially until the 1965 Immigration and Nationality Act enacted comprehensive immigration reform.[44]

The end of World War II transformed the United States' relationship with Asia in profound ways. In 1945, Japan lay in ruins, and the United States began an occupation of its former enemy that would last for seven years. European colonial powers like France and Great Britain began to leave the region at the same time that Asian nationalist movements spread. The United States and the Soviet Union soon became engaged in their Cold War struggle for global influence in the region. The United States hoped that the decolonizing Asian countries would look to it for guidance and adopt capitalism and democracy over Soviet-style communism. But nothing was assured, and the stakes were high. The surprising 1949 victory by the communists in China put the United States on high alert.

The United States turned its attention to containing the spread of communism through direct military intervention and increased economic aid throughout Asia from Korea in the north to Taiwan, the Philippines, and into Southeast Asia and South Asia. During these tense times, the United States rejected any hint of imperial intentions, but rather insisted that the United States and the nations of non-communist Asia were allies and that the benign guidance and free world leadership of the United States benefited all. The Cold War and what scholar Christina Klein calls America's "Cold War Orientalism" shaped more than U.S.-Asian relations. It also led to new types of Asian immigration and new ways of including Asian Americans in the United States.[45]

Postwar U.S. engagement in Asia began in Japan. Between 1945 and 1952, the occupying forces, led by Supreme Commander of the Allied Powers General Douglas MacArthur, enacted widespread military, political, economic, and social reforms that transformed the country. By the end of the occupation, Japan was demilitarized, democratized, and rehabilitated. Politicians, journalists, and filmmakers helped spread glowing images of the new Japan: the evil enemy had been replaced by America's "Geisha Ally," what historian Naoko Shibusawa explains as a feminized, young nation in need of the U.S.'s benevolent guidance. By the end of the U.S. occupation, Japan was a free market democracy that served as an effective bulwark against the communist threat growing in the region.[46]

The U.S.-led Allied occupation also brought 400,000–600,000 American soldiers to the country. Some of these men married Japanese women, and from 1947 to 1975, almost 67,000 Japanese women entered the United States as wives of U.S. servicemen. Nearly half—30,000—came at the peak of the occupation of Japan from 1947 through the 1950s. These war brides made up the majority of postwar Japanese immigrants.[47]

They were a diverse group. Some were from middle-class families; others were working-class. They came from all parts of Japan, including rural areas and big cities. All had suffered from the war's massive loss of life, enormous destruction, and large-scale dislocation. With so many men in the army and then lost in battle, Japanese women went to work to support their families during and after the war. The U.S. occupation created new jobs that these women eagerly filled. They found work on military bases as clerks, sales, or service workers, or in the many restaurants and bars that sprang up to cater to the U.S. military. Miyoshi Farrow's experiences during and after the war were common. "I went to school in Osaka. I was fifteen years old when [our house] was bombed [during the war]. So we had to move to Kobe. I stayed in Kobe awhile and finished school, and then [our house] was burned again. We had to move." She was eighteen when the war ended and the United States occupied Japan. She got her first job at a dance hall that catered to American servicemen. A U.S. colonel noticed her young age and offered her a job in the military government office to take her away from the dance hall. There, she eventually met the American serviceman who would become her husband.[48]

Japanese women married white, African American, and Japanese American men. For some women, marriage to an American offered economic security. Others were swept up in the positive images of the United States that were spread by the U.S. military and other American personnel in the country. The American GI represented the power and wealth of the United States and stood in contrast to the defeated Japanese. American popular culture also fed a desire for *Ameshon* [American] fashion and culture that symbolized freedom and modernity.[49]

These interracial and international marriages, however, faced opposition on both sides of the Pacific. In occupied Japan, relationships between Japanese women and members of the U.S. occupation force were seen as symbols of Japan's defeat and humiliation. Japanese families often objected to the marriages, even to the point of disowning their daughters.[50] In the United States, the immigration of Japanese women and their entry into white America also raised anxieties. The army discouraged interracial marriage, and many states still banned marriages between whites and nonwhites. Moreover, while war brides from Europe, Australia, and New Zealand were able to immigrate to the United States at the end of the war, Japanese wives were prohibited under the racial restrictions of the 1924 Immigration Act that barred all Japanese immigrants. A Japanese American Citizens League–led campaign prompted the U.S. government to lift the racial ban on international marriages, and the United States allowed Japanese war brides to enter the country after 1947. But they were not able to become naturalized citizens until 1952.[51]

Once the issue of their immigration was solved, figuring out how to assimilate these women from a former enemy nation became "an important mission for Americans in the U.S. and Japan," according to historian Masako Nakamura.[52] Under the tutelage from American Red Cross brides' schools in Japan and social service agencies in the United States, war brides were advised on how to become good wives and mothers and good U.S. citizens. Classes were provided in U.S. history, citizenship, religion, makeup and grooming, housekeeping, and home nursing and child care. Textbooks instructed women what to read, how to perform their housework, and how to interact with their husbands. The "ideal wife," they were told, "looks her best at all times . . . is a good housewife and mother [and] a companion to her husband." She should take a great interest in his work, but she should never "make the mistake of telling him how it should be done."[53] The message was clear: creating and maintaining a proper American home and family that conformed to mainstream gender roles was akin to practicing good American citizenship. In these ways, Japanese war brides were held up as model minority brides who represented benevolent U.S.-Japan relations that the United States wanted to promote as well as racial harmony and domestic bliss at home.[54]

The lives of many Japanese war brides in the United States did not always match these positive media portrayals. Cut off from their families and support systems, they often felt like strangers in their new homes. In 1966, Chiyoko Toguchi Swartz left her home in Okinawa with Charles Swartz, her American soldier husband, and their daughter. Fear and anxiety overwhelmed her as she prepared to leave her home forever. In the few suitcases she could bring with her, Chiyoko packed a couple of kimonos, a small number of photographs, and a Japanese-language parenting book. When they arrived in the United States, the Swartzes stood out as oddities and even encountered lingering anti-Japanese sentiment. As Chiyoko raised her children among strangers in a new land, she came to rely on the Japanese parenting book that she had brought from home. Providing detailed advice and home remedies in Japanese, the book became a source of comfort, as well as a source of information. The Swartzes eventually settled in the Los Angeles area, where Chiyoko made

47. Chiyoko Toguchi and Charles Swartz wedding portrait.

new friendships in her English-language classes and became involved in the Japanese American church and the local Okinawan club. Her keepsakes from home, including the Japanese parenting book, remained an important resource and treasured family memento throughout her life.[55]

Korea was another site of expanding U.S. power after the war. Following Japan's defeat in 1945, Korea was liberated as an independent nation following thirty-five years of Japanese colonial rule. But when a civil war broke out and the new government appeared to be leaning toward communism, the United States exercised its Cold War policy of containment and intervened to militarily occupy what is now known as South Korea. With the Soviet Union and the People's Republic of China supporting the communist North Korea, the Korean War dragged on until 1953 and ended with a divided Korea. South Korea emerged from the war almost entirely reliant on the United States for its economic survival and military protection. The war also turned countless Koreans into refugees, leading many to seek safety abroad.[56]

Some came to the United States, especially two new groups of immigrants: adoptees and military brides. (The latter were so named to identify their immigration as a result of the ongoing U.S. military presence in the country that lasted long after the end of the Korean War.)[57] Since 1945, troops have regularly been deployed to South Korea to protect U.S. interests in the region. Some relationships between Korean women and U.S. military personnel—sometimes begun in the "camptowns" established near U.S. military bases where prostitution and other illicit businesses were supported and regulated by the U.S. military—ended in marriage. Cho Soonyi was a young woman at the end of World War II when American soldiers and goods became ubiquitous in the country. The soldiers began to "control everything," she remembered. Soon there were American goods in the country and even more soldiers who brought with them a distinctive American culture. The United States seemed modern, powerful, and wealthy and contrasted sharply with the ongoing struggles that postcolonial Korea faced. Cho was convinced that life in the United States was better than life in Korea. "My dream is . . . move out of Korea . . . that was my wish," she remembers. But the only way to come to America was through marriage. She eventually met a white American man, became Mrs. Mullen, and was twenty-one years old when she arrived in Seattle, Washington, in 1951.[58]

Like Cho, nearly 100,000 Korean women immigrated to the United States between 1950 and 1989. They were the largest group of Korean immigrants between 1945 and 1965, and once in the United States they often sponsored their own family members into the country in later years, directly or indirectly bringing an estimated 40 to 50 percent of all Korean immigrants to the United States since 1965.[59] Korean military bride immigration was its highest during the 1970s and 1980s, when around 4,000 women entered the country each year. It is not coincidental that these same decades were when "American fever" swept through Korea. As historian Ji-Yeon Yuh explains, the massive U.S. presence in the country combined with the powerful belief that "things American [were] vastly superior to things Korean" led to "a desire to emigrate to the United States."[60]

Transracial, transnational adoption also has its roots in the U.S.'s Cold War relationship with South Korea. Since 1953, the United States has received over 110,000 adopted children from South Korea. The first Korean adoptees were biracial children of U.S. servicemen. There were also Korean "waifs of war" and military "mascots" who were adopted by U.S. soldiers or their extended families. Other children arrived via orphanages. Surrounded by positive American media coverage, the adoption of Korean children by mostly white American parents beginning in the 1950s grew over the decades. Transnational and transracial Korean adoption became a national custom in Korea and a celebrated humanitarian project in the United States, setting in motion what historian Catherine Ceniza Choy calls "global family making," the creation of families that cross both racial and national borders.[61]

Documentary filmmaker Deann Borshay Liem was in the first generation of Korean adoptees to come to the United States. Born in 1957, she came to California in 1966 as the adopted daughter of Arnold and Alveen Borshay. Alveen explained that the couple had been moved by the television reports of the "thousands of needy children" in Korea and wanted to help out in some way. They began to send money to sponsor a little girl named Cha Jung Hee, who was described by a relief agency as a parentless eight-year-old girl. As their attachment grew, the Borshays decided to adopt her. However, like most other children adopted in the 1960s under the Cold War humanitarian movement of "orphan adoption," Cha Jung Hee was not without living parents, and her father found her at the agency before she could be sent to the United States for adoption.

The agency decided to go through with the adoption anyway and substituted Deann—whose Korean birth name is Kang Ok Jin—in Cha Jung Hee's place. Like Cha Jung Hee, Kang Ok Jin was also not an orphan. Her birth family had placed her in the orphanage temporarily while they struggled to survive. Their intention was to bring her back home when their situation stabilized, but she was sent to the United States before this could happen. Eight-year-old Kang Ok Jin was thus taken from the orphanage, boarded a plane, landed in California, and became Deann Borshay. "I was given a history and identity that didn't belong to me," she explains. The Borshays told Deann what the orphanage had told them: that her mother had died during childbirth and that her father died during the Korean War. This information did not match Deann's hazy memories of her parents and siblings still living in Korea. But she learned to dismiss them as mere dreams. Over time, even these dreams faded as her new identity as an all-American girl grew stronger in her new home under the care of her adopted family. As an adult, Borshay Liem confronted these memories and embarked on a journey to discover the truth of her identity. After a long search, she was able to reunite with her Korean mother, siblings, and large extended family and introduce her adopted parents to her birth family. She also came to understand that her birth mother's decision to place her in the orphanage was "part of a lifetime struggling to survive."[62] Since the 1950s, an estimated 200,000 Korean children have been transnationally adopted worldwide.[63]

Building on the repeal of the Asian exclusion laws during and after World War II, the 1950s and 1960s inaugurated another major transformation in Asian immigration patterns to North America. The Cold War struggle with the Soviet Union placed a premium on foreign students and professionals who had useful technical and scientific skills. Government-sponsored programs to recruit scientific workers and engineers in the field of military technology and piecemeal immigration and refugee laws brought several thousand elite intellectuals from Taiwan and Hong Kong in the 1950s. They joined a small group of 5,000 Chinese students who were stranded in the United States after the 1949 communist revolution in China.[64]

One of these new immigrants was Chang-Lin Tien. Born in Wuhan in 1935, Chang-Lin Tien was from a prosperous and politically active family. But when the communists took over in 1949, he and his family joined the exodus of anticommunist Chinese and sought refuge in Taiwan. Life was hard. Squeezed into one tiny room, Chang's parents and their ten children slept in shifts. When Tien graduated college, he applied to 240 schools in the United States in the hope of winning a scholarship. His timing was good. The United States was searching for highly skilled professionals and students in the sciences. Tien received degrees from the University of Louisville and Princeton before becoming a professor of mechanical engineering at the University of California, Berkeley, and later the first Asian American to head a major research university in the United States.[65]

The Cold War–inspired Exchange Visitor Program also brought small numbers of elite Filipina nurses to the United States to gain skills as well as firsthand knowledge about the United States and its values. They laid the foundation for the later mass immigration of Filipino nurses in the post-1965 period. These Cold War era intellectuals and professionals, the U.S.'s humanitarian acceptance of them, and their successful integration into the United States helped contribute to the new, positive images of Asian Americans circulating in the country at this time.[66]

The admission of Japanese and Korean military brides, Korean adoptees, and Chinese and Filipino professionals and students between World War II and 1965 marked an important transition period in the history of Asian immigration to the United States. The age of Asian exclusion was closing, but the gates were not wide open just yet. In 1952, the United States passed a major piece of immigration legislation that reflected this transition period. The 1952 Immigration and Nationality Act—known as the McCarran-Walter Act—kept in place the national origins quota system first established in the 1920s. It slightly revised the quotas from the 1924 Immigration Act, but the original preference toward immigrants from northern and western

Europe remained. The law did repeal the final measures excluding Asian immigrants, including eliminating the Asiatic Barred Zone. It also placed all Asians on the quota system like other immigrants. While symbolic in its seemingly equal treatment of Asian immigrants, in reality the law continued a pattern of discrimination. Each Asian nation was allotted a minimum quota of 100 visas a year. But the quotas were based on race, instead of nationality. What this meant was that persons born anywhere in the world and possessing the citizenship of any nation could immigrate only under the national quota of the Asian nation of their ethnicity. For example, Chinese coming from Jamaica and Chinese coming from Taiwan were both counted against the overall quota for all Chinese persons worldwide. The result was that Asian immigration remained very low.[67] Reflecting its Cold War origins, the act also established strict security provisions designed to target suspected subversives.

In contrast to these conservative changes, the law also set in motion some liberalizing changes. As a precursor to the 1965 Immigration and Nationality Act, it set up a system of "preferences" for certain skilled laborers and for relatives of U.S. citizens and permanent resident aliens.[68] At the same time, the McCarran-Walter Act finally abolished race as a criterion for naturalized citizenship dating back to the Naturalization Act of 1790. While Chinese, Filipinos, and South Asians had been able to become naturalized citizens through piecemeal wartime legislation, Japanese immigrants remained the one group who were barred from naturalization. Finally able to become U.S. citizens, many issei flocked to citizenship classes and then to naturalization ceremonies. The year that the law was passed also coincided with the end of the U.S. occupation of Japan. Both events symbolized the concurrent transformation of Japanese immigrants into acceptable Americans and the rebuilding of Japan into a strong U.S. ally, a hub of capitalism in Asia, and the home to some of the largest U.S. military bases in Asia.[69]

While the U.S.'s increased presence in Asia and new immigration policies brought new Asian immigrants to the United States, the ideological battle being waged between the United States and the Soviet Union also had a profound impact on the status of Asian Americans in the United States. The United States was working hard to build trust and cooperation with non-Western countries and to promote the benefits of American-style democracy and capitalism. But its efforts were hampered by the Soviet Union, which spread stories about racism and discrimination in the United States. American democracy was an "empty fraud," the Soviet Union claimed. More and more Americans began to believe that racism at home threatened the United States' power and credibility abroad. A renewed commitment to racial integration and civil rights helped usher in changes like the end of segregation and the passing of major civil rights legislation.[70]

48. After 1952, Japanese immigrants were finally allowed to become naturalized U.S. citizens. Issei naturalization ceremony, April 14, 1953, Seattle, Washington.

Asian Americans played an important role in effecting these changes. Chinese, South Asians, and Filipinos had already been recast as good Asians during the Second World War. In the 1940s and 1950s, Chinese and Japanese Americans were celebrated for both their assimilation into mainstream American society and their retention of specific Asian traits and connections that helped serve U.S. foreign policy interests. They were, according to historian Ellen Wu, "assimilating Others," people becoming, or capable of becoming, full American citizens in spite of their racial differences. Just a few decades before, their race had been viewed as a liability; now they were accepted and even celebrated as assets in the U.S.'s new role in Asia. As the United States sought to spread its anticommunist message in a positive, nonthreatening, and nonimperialist light, successful Asian Americans who bridged both the U.S. and Asia provided powerful examples of the United States' successful racial democracy.[71] Thus, Korean American Olympic gold medalist Sammy Lee, Chinese American author Jade Snow Wong, and Chinese American artist Dong Kingman were sent on cultural diplomacy tours of the Asia-Pacific region to spread positive messages of goodwill during the 1950s.[72]

Another Asian American Cold War ambassador was Congressman Dalip Singh Saund, the first Asian American to serve in the U.S. Congress. A son of an illiterate but prosperous family in India, Saund had first arrived in the United States to attend graduate school at the University of California at Berkeley in 1920. He earned his PhD in mathematics four years later. While at Berkeley, Saund—already an ardent Indian nationalist—became involved in the Hindustani Association of America and was elected its national president. His fiery anti-British speeches caught the attention of British colonial officials, and his family warned him that it would not be safe for him to return to India.

Unable to become a U.S. citizen and barred from most professions because of his race, Saund became a foreman at a fruit cannery and then at a cotton farm in southern California. He eventually turned to farming, but like other Asian immigrants, he faced obstacles like the California Alien Land Law, which prohibited "aliens ineligible from citizenship" from owning land. These experiences led him to help form the India Association of America in 1942, which lobbied to end discrimination in U.S. immigration and naturalization laws.

After he became a naturalized U.S. citizen in 1949, Saund entered politics and was elected judge of the Westmorland judicial district court in 1953. In 1956, he decided to run for the U.S. Congress out of California's 29th district, which then included Riverside and Imperial counties. Although an unknown political figure, Saund and his wife, Marian, a Czech American, and their children rang doorbells, registered voters, and visited precinct after precinct. He campaigned hardest to reach the many Mexican, African

American, Japanese, and South Asian farmers in the Imperial Valley and even had serviceable "border Spanish." His campaign message was one that celebrated the promise of the United States. "If elected to Congress," he told voters, "the first thing I would do would be to fly to India and say, 'Here I am, a living example of democracy in practice.' " On election night, he repeated the same message to his crowd of supporters: "Look at me," he said with heartfelt emotion. "I am a living proof of America's democracy."[73]

49. Representative Dalip S. Saund, the first Asian American elected to the U.S. Congress, standing in front of the Capitol Building, April 1, 1958.

After his election, Saund became an active Cold Warrior at home and abroad. He served on the House Foreign Affairs Committee and made good on his campaign promise to spread his pro-American message overseas when he went on a high-profile diplomatic mission to Japan, Hong Kong, the Philippines, Burma (Myanmar), and India. The timing was sensitive. U.S.-Indian relations were strained due to India's strong support to admit the People's Republic of China into the United Nations General Assembly. The United States also involved itself in the ongoing struggle between India and Pakistan by sending military equipment and supplies to Pakistan in its efforts to take over Kashmir. U.S. officials worried about anti-American sentiment in India and growing support for communism.[74]

During his tour, Saund tried to ease U.S.-Indian tensions and bolster support for U.S.-style democracy. He effectively used his own example of overcoming racial prejudice and achieving the American Dream to praise the power of change in democracies like the United States. "If Americans were prejudiced against Indians, how did I get elected by free vote of American people in most conservative California?" he pointedly asked his audiences.[75] Saund did not deny the vicious racism that existed in the United States, especially toward Asian immigrants. "Prejudice thrives in all countries and climates," he told his audiences. "But in a democracy things can change; people do change."[76]

The U.S. media enthusiastically reported on his tour of Asia and hailed Saund as the "Salesman" and the "Good Will Ambassador" who made his way "city by city, village by village, through his swarming native India." Bilingual and freely integrating Indian stories and parables into his speeches, he "turned in a performance that undoubtedly got closer to thousands of India's doubters than any official U.S. envoy before him," *Time* magazine reported.[77] Popular magazines like *The Saturday Evening Post* also described the mixed-race Saund family in glowing terms as the embodiment of racial tolerance, domestic happiness, upward mobility, and all-American patriotism. In 1960, Saund published his autobiography, *Congressman from India*. He was reelected two times before he resigned in 1962 during his third term due to poor health. He died in 1973.[78]

At the same time that Cold War politics at home and abroad celebrated some Asian Americans as "living examples" of American democracy and strong U.S.-Asian relations, other Asian Americans were put under surveillance as potential alien subversives loyal to communist regimes. These two stereotypes of Asian Americans coexisted during the Cold War because of persistent beliefs that Asian Americans remained directly connected to Asia, regardless of their citizenship status, place of birth, or length of stay in the United States. Whether Asian Americans were the good kind or the bad kind of Asian depended on their assimilation into American society and with which Asian country they were affiliated. Good Asian Americans were assimilated Americans whose cultural heritage and ties to noncommunist Asia were assets to the United States. Bad Asian Americans were unassimilated aliens whose ties to communist Asian countries were threats to U.S. national security. The lines between good and bad, however, were not always clear and could shift without warning.[79]

Thus, when China became communist in 1949 and then entered the Korean War in 1950, Chinese Americans' newfound status as patriotic Americans became vulnerable. An anticommunist campaign led by U.S. government officials sought to expose Chinese who were allegedly communist spies in the United States. FBI director J. Edgar Hoover, for example, connected communist China, the U.S.'s "No. 1 enemy," with Chinese Americans in the United States, "some of whom could be susceptible to recruitment either through ethnic ties or hostage situations because of relatives in Communist China," he claimed.[80] U.S. authorities began investigating Chinese American communities for communist ties and scrutinized those who had entered the country with fraudulent documentation during the exclusion era. The government's "Confession Program" was created to encourage Chinese Americans to come forward and confess their misuse of immigration documents and expose any relative or friend who had also committed an immigration-related crime. The confessions created a domino effect that wreaked havoc within families and communities. With a confession, immigrants could be in a position to legalize their status but they could also jeopardize the legal status of friends and relatives. Chinese described the Confession Program as a no-win situation. Altogether, some 30,500 Chinese immigrants confessed. In return, they were granted legal status to remain in the United States as long as they were not involved in any communist or subversive activities.[81]

And yet another new stereotype emerged out of the Cold War: Asian Americans as model minorities. Economically and academically successful, model minorities supposedly respected authority, had high moral values, adhered to strict gender roles, and enjoyed strong, stable nuclear families. Confucian traditions, social scientists said, led to upstanding youth and model families and communities. At a time when the nation was experiencing a juvenile delinquency crisis and growing numbers of rebellious and wayward white American youth, Asian American families were held up as examples of proper behavior. "Chinatown Offers Us a Lesson," a *New York Times Magazine* article claimed in 1958.[82]

The Asian American model minority stereotype was so successful during the 1950s, historian Ellen Wu tells us, because it upheld two dominant American values during the Cold War: the valorization of the nuclear family and anticommunism. Chinese American families with their alleged adherence to Confucian and patriarchal values resonated with conservatives' emphasis on traditional family values and gender roles. Chinese American success in the United States also proved the superiority of American freedom and democracy compared to communism in the People's Republic of China.[83]

After the mid-1960s, the Asian American model minority stereotype evolved in response to the ongoing civil rights movement. The significant gains of the civil rights movement—most notably the Civil Rights Act of 1964, which outlawed segregation in businesses, banned discriminatory practices in employment, and ended segregation in public places, and the Voting Rights Act of 1965, which prohibited discrimination in voting—encouraged Americans to believe that racism had safely been taken care of and was now a relic of the past. Public support wavered for the systemic change and government programs that civil rights leaders and others insisted were necessary to counter enduring discrimination and to foster lasting equality. The Asian American model minority was held up as a counterexample and to delegitimize these claims.

Explicitly compared to African Americans, Asian Americans were said to have achieved American success the old-fashioned way through hard work and perseverance. They did not protest in the streets calling for Black Power like some newly militant African Americans. The quiet success of Asian Americans, the news media claimed, provided evidence that the American Dream was still available to all those who worked to achieve it.[84]

Sociologist William Petersen, for example, praised the "superior" performance of Japanese Americans and suggested that other groups should follow their example in a 1966 *New York Times Magazine* article.[85] Sociologist and policymaker Daniel Patrick Moynihan publicly mused about the "rather astonishing" progress of Japanese and Chinese Americans as compared to African Americans.[86] Another article, in *U.S. News & World Report*, followed that same year with more explicit comparisons with African Americans. "At a time when it is being proposed that hundreds of billions be spent to uplift Negroes and other minorities, the nation's 300,000 Chinese-Americans are getting ahead on their own, with no help from anyone else," the article claimed. The "promised land" of America was still attainable for this minority who depended on "their own efforts—not a welfare check."[87]

There was some truth to these media claims. Both Chinese and Japanese Americans were able to enjoy newfound freedoms such as naturalization, intermarriage, and property ownership. They were more fully integrated into mainstream society than ever before. There were more Chinese and Japanese American college graduates and professionals in 1960 than there were in 1940. Nevertheless, their success was uneven. Generally speaking, even though they were better educated than white Americans, their income levels were lower. Take the case of California. In 1960, 29 percent of Japanese American men had completed at least one year of college compared to 24 percent of white men. Yet Japanese American men had a lower median income ($4,388) compared to white males ($5,109). Despite some upward mobility, Asian Americans were far from equal to whites, and racial discrimination in housing, employment, and social life endured.[88] Beginning a trend that would continue into the twenty-first century, the model minority trope also relied on the success of a very select group of Asian Americans—in this case mostly U.S.-born and -educated Chinese and Japanese Americans—to represent the success of all Asian Americans.

The U.S. media continued to celebrate Chinese and Japanese Americans as an American success story throughout the 1960s. Both groups, according to a front-page *New York Times* article in December of 1970, had experienced debilitating discrimination just twenty years before but had now successfully assimilated into mainstream America. The *Times* highlighted the uplifting story of J. Chuan Chu as proof of Chinese Americans' remarkable ascent. As a recent immigrant, Chu had experienced discrimination at every turn because of his "Oriental face." Just two decades after his arrival, however, Chu was now a vice president at Honeywell Information Systems and a shining example of American success. "It doesn't matter anymore if you are Chinese," Chu explained.[89]

But Chu was only partly right, because Chineseness—and other Asian cultural backgrounds—mattered very much in creating and sustaining the model minority Asian American stereotype. Just as Asianness helped frame the Asian American success story during the 1940s and 1950s, it continued to buttress the model minority stereotype in the 1960s. Social scientists and journalists argued that Asian Americans were able to succeed both in spite of their racial difference and because the allegedly Asian traits that they possessed—family values, traditional virtues of hard work, thrift, morality, respect for authority, and persistence—were perfectly suited to the U.S.'s meritocracy.[90]

PART FOUR

Remaking Asian America in a Globalized World

13

Making a New Asian America Through Immigration and Activism

Out of the 1960s a new Asian America was formed. First came the passage of the 1965 Immigration and Nationality Act, which liberalized the nation's immigration policy and ushered in new generations of immigrants from throughout Asia, many of whom had no connection to pre–World War II communities. Over the past fifty years, Asian American communities have grown exponentially, and, with the additional arrival of refugees from Southeast Asia, have become increasingly diverse and transnational.

The second major change was the widespread involvement of Asian Americans in a number of campaigns for civil rights, women's liberation, lesbian, gay, bisexual, and transgender (LGBT) rights, and an end to the war in Vietnam. Out of this political participation came the emergence of a distinctive Asian American movement that helped to define diverse peoples as Asian Americans and call them to action. After decades of being lumped together by the media and lawmakers as undifferentiated "Orientals" who were threats to American society, a new generation willingly and consciously joined together as self-identified Asian Americans to promote multiethnic alliances and action. They identified common historical and contemporary experiences, demanded fuller inclusion and recognition in American society, and formed significant and enduring institutions and organizations that addressed specific Asian American issues and inequalities.

• • •

Contemporary Asian immigration to the United States can be directly tied to the 1965 Immigration and Nationality Act. Support for immigration reform grew out of Cold War politics and civil rights activism during the 1960s. At a time when the United States emphasized its virtues of freedom and democracy over the totalitarianism of communism, the unequal treatment of immigrants based on race exposed the hypocrisy in American immigration regulation. Strong leadership came from the White House under President John F. Kennedy, whose 1958 book, *A Nation of Immigrants*, was an unabashed celebration of America's immigrant heritage and a call for immigration reform.[1]

Following Kennedy's assassination, President Lyndon B. Johnson embraced the cause and declared that the national origins quotas in the 1924 Immigration Act was "incompatible with our basic American tradition." This new support of America's immigrant heritage was cautious and partial. As congressional debates made clear, immigration from Europe was still preferred, and the president stressed the bill's primary intent to redress the wrong done to southern and eastern Europeans affected by the quotas.[2] More importantly, he connected U.S. immigration reform to America's global image and agenda. In his State of the Union address in 1964, Johnson declared that with immigration reform the "nation that was built by the immigrants of all lands can ask those who now seek admission: 'What can you do for our country?' [not] 'In what country were you born?' " A new immigration law, the president continued, would help the United States achieve its "ultimate goal" of creating "a world without war [and] a world made safe for diversity, in which all men, goods, and ideas can freely move across every border and every boundary."[3]

Supporters of immigration reform picked up on the message of caution and disputed charges that the bill would allow entry to "hordes" of Africans and Asians or that the bill would allow the United States to become the "dumping ground" for Latin America.[4] The final bill imposed the first annual global cap, or numerical limit, on immigration to the United States. And when President Johnson signed the Immigration Act into law on Liberty Island with the Statue of Liberty in the background, he assured Americans that "this is not a revolutionary bill." "It does not affect the lives of millions," he declared.[5]

50. President Lyndon B. Johnson signs the Immigration Act as Vice President Hubert Humphrey, Lady Bird Johnson, Muriel Humphrey, Senator Edward (Ted) Kennedy, Senator Robert F. Kennedy, and others look on. Liberty Island, New York City, October 3, 1965.

The president would be proven wrong. The 1965 Immigration and Nationality Act, also known as the Hart-Cellar Act, was meant to be the first incremental step in changing the nation's immigration policies, but in the absence of comprehensive immigration reform in the past fifty years, it remains the foundation of immigration policy today. The law did affect the lives of millions. And it changed the course of Asian American and U.S. history. In fact, it can be argued that no group benefited more from the act than Asian Americans. The 1965 act resulted in three major changes. First, the law abolished the national origins quotas and ushered in a new era of mass immigration that has been qualitatively different from earlier periods both in terms of volume and in terms of ethnic makeup. Prior to 1965, the peak decade for immigration was 1911–1920, when 5,736,000 immigrants entered the country, mostly from Europe. During the 1980s, a record 7,338,000 immigrants came to the United States, followed by 6,943,000 from 1991 to 1997. The 2000 census figures revealed that the United States was accepting immigrants at a faster rate than at any other time since the

1850s.[6] In 2010, there were 40 million foreign-born residents in the United States, making up 13 percent of the total population. Over half had entered the United States since 1990; one third had entered since 2000.[7]

Post-1965 immigration is also significantly different from earlier arrivals. While immigrants coming to the United States during the late nineteenth and early twentieth centuries had predominantly been from Europe, most new immigrants have come from Asia and Latin America. In the 1980s, more than 80 percent of all immigrants came from either of these two regions. This pattern has continued into the twenty-first century. In 2010, 53 percent of all foreign-born peoples in the United States were born in Latin America; 28 percent were born in Asia. The 50.5 million Hispanics (both foreign-born and native-born) make up 16 percent of the total population. In 2011, the total Asian American population, including foreign-born (59 percent) and U.S. born (41 percent), was 18.2 million, or around 5.8 percent. And the number of newly arriving immigrants from Asia is an increasing proportion of all immigrants, making up 40 percent of all foreign-born peoples who have arrived in the United States since 2008.[8]

Second, the law created immigration preference categories based on family reunification and professional skills. This policy worked to the advantage of prospective Asian immigrants, who have come to fill needed professional positions and to reunite with family already in the United States. Recent immigration laws have continued that trend. The 1990 Immigration and Nationality Act, for example, increased the flow of highly skilled "guest workers" from abroad with temporary visas known as H-1B visas, and U.S. companies, especially in the high-tech sector, have actively recruited high-skilled workers from Asia. Asian immigrants receive about three quarters of these visas; Indians alone received 56 percent of the 129,000 H-1B visas granted in 2011.[9]

The last major change resulting from the 1965 Immigration Act was the establishment of a global cap on immigration and new restrictions on immigration from the Western Hemisphere for the first time. As a result, the law ushered in a new era of undocumented immigration that has dominated immigration debates since the 1970s.

Post-1965 immigration from Asia and Latin America has resulted in the racial restructuring of U.S. society, and every sector, from politics and education, to health care and intermarriage, has been affected. Asians' growing numbers, economic investments, and contributions to the United States have transformed everyday life throughout the country. They are concentrated in the West and the Northeast, but in recent decades Asian Americans have increased in every region, and between 2000 and 2010 the Asian population also grew in every state. North Carolina, for example, now has a sizable Indian population, while Minnesota is home to the second largest population of Hmong Americans in the country after California.[10]

There are both similarities and differences with Asian immigrants from previous decades. As in the past, Asian immigrants are highly regulated by immigration laws, but the emphasis of U.S. laws in admitting family-sponsored immigrants and professional, highly skilled individuals has meant that the majority of new arrivals come to join family already here and bring a different set of educational and professional skills than earlier immigrants. In contrast to the single male laborers of the early twentieth century, women now make up a much larger number of all immigrant arrivals, and many immigrants arrive as families. Among the foreign-born Asian population in the United States, women are actually the majority (54 percent). Sixty-two percent of the most recent immigrants from China, India, the Philippines, Korea, Vietnam, and Japan received their Green Cards based on family members already in the United States.[11] And with no bans on becoming naturalized citizens as existed in the past, 59 percent of foreign-born Asian adults in the United States are naturalized citizens.[12]

There is also a much greater diversity of Asian immigration. In 1960, Japanese Americans were the largest Asian American group, making up 50 percent of the total, but immigration from Japan has been very low since 1924, and in 2010, Japanese Americans were 7 percent of all Asian Americans.[13] Chinese immigrants still come in large numbers, and the magnitude of immigration from the Philippines, India, and Korea is much higher than in the early twentieth century. In addition, there has been sustained and growing immigration from countries that had sent few immigrants to the United States before 1965, such as Vietnam, Cambodia, Laos, Pakistan, and Bangladesh.

Recent arrivals from Asia also represent great diversity in educational background and professional skills. Since the 1980s, engineers and medical professionals from India, the Philippines, China, and Taiwan have made up one third of these professions in the entire U.S. labor market. At the same time, a growing number have entered the United States with minimal education and job skills, leading to Asians being represented at both extremes of the educational and class spectrums. Unauthorized Asian immigrants also make up a significant proportion (10–11 percent) of the total number of the 11 million undocumented immigrant population in the United States from 2000 to 2010.[14]

Some of this diversity can be seen in the Chinese American community. Between 1961 and 1998, almost 1.5 million immigrants, made up almost equally of men and women, were admitted to the United States from Hong Kong, Taiwan, and the People's Republic of China (after U.S.-China relations became normalized in 1972 and China began to allow emigration in 1977). From 1960 to 1990, the Chinese population in the United States nearly doubled every decade. In 1960, there were just under 100,000 Chinese-born immigrants in the United States. In 2010, the U.S. Census reported over 3.3 million adult Chinese Americans in the country. Making up the largest group of Asian Americans and the largest ethnic Chinese population (including Taiwanese) outside of Asia, they represent 24 percent of the U.S.'s adult Asian population. Three quarters (76 percent) are foreign-born, and 69 percent are U.S. citizens. Chinese immigration has been so great in recent decades that foreign-born Chinese in the United States now outnumber native-born Chinese Americans.[15]

They come for a variety of reasons. Many Chinese first arrived in the 1960s as students or professionals under the provisions of the 1965 act. Others have come to reunite with family. Immigrants and naturalized Americans have actively sponsored their spouses, children, parents, brothers, and sisters into the country, who have arranged in turn for the entry of their family members as well. Family-based chain migration has been so extensive under the 1965 act that it is no wonder that it has been nicknamed the "Brothers and Sisters Act."[16] Some fled communism, political repression, and economic hardship in the People's Republic. Kenny Lai, for example, was only fourteen when he was sent to an agricultural commune near Canton in southern China and a life of hard labor. "The government chose for you [and] there was no way out," he explained. Convinced that if he did not escape he would condemn his children and his children's children to a life of forced labor, he planned his escape to Hong Kong when he was twenty. He and his wife eventually made it to the United States in 1978.[17]

Chinese immigration increased dramatically from Taiwan and Hong Kong after the 1989 Tiananmen Square massacre in Beijing, when the Chinese army cracked down on pro-democracy activists. Hundreds were killed and more were wounded. Pro-democracy leaders were rounded up. Hong Kong residents who were already wary of the return of the colony to mainland China in 1997 viewed having foreign passports as a safeguard against communist rule. In the 1980s, surveys of Hong Kong residents found that 60 percent of its lawyers, 70 percent of its government doctors, and 40 percent of its civil engineers planned to leave the colony before 1997. Many paid tens of thousands of dollars to establish themselves in Canada, Australia, and the United States.[18]

With its emphasis on employment-based immigration and capital investment, the U.S.'s 1990 Immigration and Nationality Act has brought in highly skilled and educated Chinese immigrants as temporary foreign workers employed in "specialty occupations" and as investors willing to apply their capital to U.S.-based enterprises in exchange for permanent residency status. Among Chinese Americans age twenty-five and older, more than half (51 percent) have a bachelor's degree, compared to the national population (28 percent). Their median annual personal earnings are higher ($50,000) than other Asian Americans ($47,000) and for U.S. adults ($40,000) overall. Almost one quarter of employed Chinese-born men work in occupations related to information technology, sciences, or engineering.[19]

These elite and professional immigrants are part of the "uptown, high-tech Chinese," who include English-speaking scientists, real estate moguls, capitalist entrepreneurs, and professional elites. Many of these professional immigrants have formed new ethnic enclaves in the suburbs, complete with Chinese-owned banks, restaurants, malls, and Chinese-language newspapers. Chinese make up more than one third of Monterey Park's population in southern California, for example, giving the city the nickname of "the first suburban Chinatown," while in New York City there are now numerous Chinatowns spread across the five boroughs.[20]

While these well-educated and high-earning Chinese Americans represent a portrait of stunning economic success, the Chinese American population is in fact overrepresented at both extremes of the socioeconomic ladder. There are also "downtown, low-tech" Chinese who are low-skilled workers, waiters, domestic workers, garment workers, cooks, and laundrymen.[21] For example, Chinese immigrant women made up 80 percent of the sewing machine operators in San Francisco in the early 1990s. Similarly, in New York City, Chinese immigrant women comprised 85 percent of the garment industry workforce. They juggled their multiple roles as wives, mothers, and wage earners. As workers, their wages made important financial contributions to their family economies. But at home, they were expected to conform to traditional caretaking roles of cooking, cleaning, laundry, grocery shopping, and caring for children, husbands, and sometimes parents.[22] Slowly, some things have changed at home. "My husband dares not look down on me," one Chinese garment worker told sociologist Min Zhou in 1992. "He knows he can't provide for the family by himself."[23]

51. Chinese garment workers (mother and child), New York City, 1976.

Still, with limited English abilities and job skills, many Chinese immigrant women not only felt trapped by the jobs available to them but also by the exploitative and low-paid work of the garment industry. Some women found ways to juggle their responsibilities and achieve some job security and improved working conditions. Garment workers in New York's Chinatown, for example, organized around the need for affordable child care. In 1977, a group of workers expressed their needs to their union, the International Ladies' Garment Workers' Union, the ILGWU. When their demands went unheeded, day care activists began to organize, sometimes bringing their babies with them to meet with union officials. When the ILGWU began negotiations for a new union contract in 1982, these activists played an important role in mobilizing 20,000 Chinatown workers to take to the streets in support of a strike. Negotiations resumed between the union and contractors, and in recognition of the work of day care activists, the ILGWU opened its first day care in 1984.[24]

52. Chinese waiters, Lunar New Year, New York City, 2012.

Other "downtown" Chinese include those who have entered the country without proper documentation. With neither professional skills nor relatives already in the United States who could sponsor them, an estimated

150,000 Chinese chose to enter without documentation beginning in the 1990s.[25] Many come from Fujian, a rural and impoverished coastal province in Southern China. They hope to strike it rich, taking great risks and paying huge sums to fulfill long-standing American dreams. As in the early twentieth century, countries in Latin America have become back doors into the United States and Canada, sometimes with the help of smugglers, or "snakeheads," who force the Chinese to take long, circuitous, and dangerous journeys into the north. In 1989, Lily Wang paid $30,000 to be guided from Fuzhou to Hong Kong, Thailand, Bolivia, Mexico, and across the border into the United States. By 2010, Chinese immigrants were being charged $80,000.[26]

Countless Chinese die en route. In 1995, eighteen Chinese suffocated to death inside a sealed trailer on its way to Hungary. Five years later, fifty-eight Chinese were found dead inside a refrigerator full of rotting tomatoes in Dover, England. In 1993, a ship called the *Golden Venture* ran aground on Rockaway Peninsula near New York City with 260 Chinese immigrants. Urged by the crew to swim ashore, the Chinese jumped overboard. Ten drowned. Between 2005 and 2008, the U.S. Border Patrol apprehended 6,000 Chinese nationals attempting to cross the U.S.-Mexico border without documentation. As of 2009, an estimated 120,000 unauthorized immigrants in the United States were from China.[27]

Even if they survive the journey to the United States, undocumented Chinese immigrants often face years of exploitation. Hidden in urban centers, they work menial jobs in an effort to pay back the exorbitant smuggler's fees and send money back home to waiting relatives. Some have been imprisoned, beaten, or forced to work for extremely low wages. A few repay their debts and even become financially successful. Others have found only hardship and even death in the United States.[28] Lily Wang, for example, began working in a garment factory but has ended up as a prostitute. "America is not a paradise; it's a hell," she concluded.[29]

Also coming to the United States beginning in the 1990s are adopted children from China. Strict enforcement of the communist government's one-child policy established in 1979 to curb explosive population growth led many families to put children up for adoption or to abandon them outright. Because of patriarchal values that led families to value sons over daughters, a large majority of these children have been girls. Orphanages became overcrowded and abuse was commonplace. In 1992, the government began to encourage large-scale international adoption, and the United States became a major receiving nation.

By 2000, China became the leading provider of children put up for international adoption, with over 5,000 Chinese adoptees arriving in the U.S. that year. Viewed as a both a humanitarian act and a symbol of progress for multicultural America, the Chinese adoption program has helped to create even more "global families" in the United States.[30]

Like Chinese immigrants, Filipinos have also come to the United States in increasing numbers since 1965. Almost 665,000 Filipinos entered the United States in the twenty years after the 1965 Immigration Act was passed. Between 1990 and 2000, the Filipino population grew by 66 percent. In 2010, there were 2.55 million Filipinos in the country, making up 18 percent of the adult Asian population. Sixty-nine percent were foreign-born; three quarters were U.S. citizens.[31]

Filipino immigration to the United States is only one part of a larger global movement out of the Philippines. As a result of global economic restructuring, export-based nations like the Philippines rely on the emigration of their citizens in order to bring foreign currency into their economies. Over 8 million Filipinos, or around 10 percent of the entire Philippine population, currently work overseas in 140 countries. Made up of nurses, doctors, schoolteachers, entertainers, domestic workers, and seafarers working aboard container ships and luxury cruise liners, the Filipino diaspora is perhaps the largest in the world. Reflecting patterns of gendered immigration, more than 60 percent of these overseas workers are women, and the remittances that they send home provide an economic lifeline to their families and to the country as a whole.[32]

Just as in earlier decades, the vast majority of Filipinos who have settled abroad permanently have come to the United States. The U.S. presence in the Philippines has sustained a culture of immigration. Just as in the early twentieth century, American education, abundance, and popular culture—not to mention relatives and friends already in the United States—have attracted the vast majority of Filipinos coming to the United States.

Filipino immigration continues to be shaped by the colonial and military relationships between the United States and the Philippines as well. Long after U.S. colonization of the Philippines ended in 1946, trade relations, foreign assistance, and the presence of U.S. military bases in the Philippines tied the two countries closely together and facilitated certain types of Filipino immigration into the United States, including and especially military service members and medical professionals. In 1970, the 14,000 Filipinos serving in the U.S. Navy outnumbered the number of Filipinos serving in the Philippine Navy, and today, Filipinos are the second largest group of foreign-born veterans in the United States armed forces after immigrants from Mexico.[33]

Likewise, since the 1960s, the Philippines has sent the largest number of professional immigrants to the United States. Filipino nurses, doctors, and other medical practitioners have been heavily recruited by American health institutions to help alleviate a shortage of medical personnel, especially in inner cities and rural areas. By the 1970s and 1980s, the Philippines became the largest supplier of health professionals to the United States. In 2010, over 15 percent of employed Filipino-born men worked in health care support occupations, and almost 23 percent of Filipino-born women worked as registered nurses. They have become the Philippines' "new national heroes."[34]

Political conditions in the Philippines, especially the repressive government of Ferdinand Marcos (1965–1985) and the civil unrest caused by communist rebels and Islamic separatists, also spurred immigration abroad. Marcos declared martial rule from 1972 to 1981 and exerted firm control over the media and the legislature. Many of his political opponents were arrested.

Continuing massive unemployment and underemployment as well as income inequality have sustained a culture of immigration. College graduates who had difficulty finding work at home took their skills to another country. Educated in the American-style educational system, fluent in English, and familiar with American culture, Filipinos have been well prepared to migrate to the United States, and their skills have been in demand. In 1972, the *Los Angeles Times* reported that over 2,000 Filipinos a day were asking for visas to come to the United States.[35]

Not all Filipino medical professionals are able to find commensurate professional opportunity in the United States, however. Additional examinations and state medical requirements as well as workplace racism often create employment barriers for new immigrants. While many successfully navigate what Dr. Edgar Gamboa calls the "subtle form of racism" directed toward foreign-born doctors, others undergo lengthy recertification processes and examinations or end up working in fields unrelated to their medical training.[36]

Filipina nurses have also faced obstacles in the United States and have responded with collective action. When a backlash against foreign-trained nurses and licensure requirements erupted in the 1970s and 1980s, Filipino nurses organized to provide a collective voice for their members, alleviate hardships that Filipino nurses faced abroad, and advocate for fair licensure procedures for foreign nurses. Filipina nurse Norma Ruspian Watson, executive secretary of the Foreign Nurse Defense Fund, for example, called attention to the discriminatory practices that permeated the profession in a letter to President Ronald Reagan. "Foreign nurses, particularly Fillippinas [sic] are the, "COOLIES OF THE MEDICAL WORLD. . . . We are sick and tired of being subservient and culturally non-aggressive. . . . I would like to see all foreign nurses walk out of the hospitals in this country, and see what happens." Watson's vision of a walkout never occurred, but by 1981 Filipino nurse organizations had successfully persuaded the California Board of Registered Nursing to establish nondiscriminatory licensure examinations.[37]

In the years directly following the passage of the U.S.'s 1965 Immigration Act, immigration from both India and Pakistan—independent nations created in 1947—has also increased. The U.S. Census recorded 371,630 South Asians in the country in 1980, including those from India, Pakistan, Bangladesh, and Sri Lanka. In 1990, the number had almost tripled to 919,626, and in 2010 there were 2.84 million Indians, 363,699 Pakistanis, 128,792 Bangladeshis, and 28,596 Sri Lankans in the United States.[38]

Immigrants from India make up the bulk of arrivals from South Asia. They are the third largest group among Asian Americans; 87 percent are foreign-born.[39] Unlike the small numbers of immigrants who arrived in the early twentieth century mostly from the Punjab region of what is now India and Pakistan, today's newcomers come from throughout India. In addition, people with Indian ancestry have also immigrated to the United

States from the Caribbean, East Africa, Canada, and the United Kingdom. While the early-twentieth-century immigration was almost exclusively male laborers, both men and women make up contemporary Indian immigrants. Compared to other immigrant groups, Indian immigrants are much better educated. The majority are fluent in English and are highly educated professionals, including physicians, engineers, and computer scientists. This is due to both economic conditions in India as well as favorable U.S. immigration policies. During the 1960s and 1970s, India's economy could not keep pace with the number of college graduates it was producing. In 1974, there were 100,000 engineers out of work in India. At the same time, the U.S. was recruiting these types of highly skilled individuals under the technical and professional preferences of the 1965 Immigration Act.[40]

Educated professionals sought opportunities abroad just as the United States' 1965 Immigration Act offered visas to those with technical skills. Ram Gada was one who arrived in the United States in the 1960s. He had received his engineering degree and was working at an auto company in Bombay, but he felt that his future lay outside India. Friends and relatives already in the United States encouraged him to come and helped him apply for scholarships in advanced mechanical engineering. His parents knew someone living in North Dakota, so he packed his bags, moved to North Dakota, earned his master's degree, and eventually settled in Minneapolis.[41]

Gada was hardly alone. Out of the 46,000 employed Indian immigrants in the United States in 1974, 16,000 were engineers, 4,000 were scientists, and 7,000 were physicians or surgeons. The next year, 93 percent of Indian immigrants admitted into the country were either "professional/technical workers" or their spouses. According to the 2010 census, 81 percent of recent Indian immigrants already hold a college degree, which makes them extremely competitive in the job market.[42] The arrival of so many highly educated and skilled workers has had a tremendous impact on American industry. Scholar A. L. Saxenian estimated that by 1998, Chinese and Indian immigrants had started over a quarter of the technology businesses (around 2,000) in California's Silicon Valley and generated 60,000 jobs. By 2012, 15.5 percent of all start-ups were founded by immigrant entrepreneurs born in India.[43] And almost half of all computer-related H-1B visas (given to highly trained workers with skills that meet current needs in the U.S.

economy) were given to workers from India at the turn of the twenty-first century. Over one quarter of employed Indian-born men worked in information technology, and one third of Indian-born women worked in business, management, and information technology fields.[44]

Since the 1990s, Indian immigration has diversified to include a growing number of arrivals coming as relatives of family members already in the country. In 1991, 35,000 out of 44,121 Indian immigrants had family members in the United States.[45] Unlike those with advanced degrees who find work in white-collar industries, these working-class immigrants often do not have college or university degrees and toil in small grocery stores, gas stations, or motels. In fact, Indian Americans own about half of all the motels in the United States. Typically from the Gujarat, a state in western India, motel owners have come from rural landowning families from the Bhakta and Patel lineages. Many are the siblings of professional immigrants already in the United States and have pooled their resources into their motels to provide economic security and a place of residence. Much of the success of these enterprises relies upon the unpaid labor of immigrant women in the family who clean rooms, do the laundry, and perform reception and office tasks on top of the household labor they perform for their own families. One motel owner's wife told an interviewer, "I get up at about 5:30 in the morning, make breakfast for the family, and get the two children ready for school. If there is a guest, I check him in. After the kids are gone I clean the rooms . . . and make beds, take out laundry . . . and clean house."[46] Arriving with few resources, some Indian motel owners have become economically successful. But they also remain highly marginalized from mainstream society.[47]

Just as there are class divisions among recent Indian immigrants, so are there differences of opportunity for male immigrants versus female immigrants. In July of 2012, the Indian newspaper *The Hindu* published an exposé on the "sea of broken dreams" that Indian women in the United States faced. Many were highly educated professionals in their own right but had come with H-4 visas as spouses of husbands working in the expanding IT industry with temporary H-1B visas. Caught in a net of visa restrictions that prevented them from working, these career women who had once been able to support themselves and nurture their own careers found themselves isolated, depressed, and without purpose. Rashi Bhatnagar, an H-4 visa-holder with a master's degree from India and years at a successful career, found only slammed doors when she relocated to the United States to join her IT-worker husband. She set up a Facebook group called "H-4 visa, a curse."[48]

Altogether, the 2010 census counted over 1.73 million Indian Americans. They were the fastest growing Asian American group in the 1990s and are highly diverse in terms of language, religion, and increasingly, class, as more working-class family members arrive to join those already here. They have settled throughout the country, but one of the first concentrations, or Little Indias, was in Jackson Heights, New York.[49]

Immigration from Pakistan, Bangladesh, and Sri Lanka to the United States has also increased since the 1990s, with most of the new arrivals coming through family-sponsored immigration. During the 1990s, the Pakistani American community grew by at least 88 percent. Over 134,000 came between 1990 and 2000. Over 70,000 Bangladeshis arrived during the same period. The 2010 U.S. Census reported over 409,000 Pakistanis in the U.S. and over 147,000 Bangladeshis.[50]

Many Pakistani immigrants come as part of a larger immigration of Pakistanis going to various places around the world. The dream of immigration, anthropologist Junaid Rana has found, is cultivated through word of mouth from relatives and friends already abroad, through Pakistani television serials, and through Bollywood films. The largest numbers head to Middle Eastern countries as laborers on construction projects. These *Dubai chalo* working-class immigrants differ from the *Amrikan* Pakistani, who are educated professionals working in the United States, Canada, or Europe.[51]

Newer groups like Bangladeshis and Sri Lankans are smaller in number but growing in their impact. Both have flocked to New York City, where the 74,000 Bangladeshis in the city are the eleventh-largest foreign-born population and the population of 5,000 Sri Lankans in Staten Island marks the area as having one of the highest concentrations of Sri Lankans outside Sri Lanka.[52]

Since 1965, Korean immigration (overwhelmingly from South Korea) to the United States has also skyrocketed. In 1970, the census reported 70,598 persons of Korean ancestry in the United States. Twenty years later, the census counted almost 800,000, and in 2010, the Korean population was estimated to be 1.26 million. Almost 80 percent were foreign-born, and 67 percent of the Korean population were U.S. citizens. This rapid immigration occurred within the context of political instability and economic dislocations in South Korea. During the Cold War, the United States invested heavily in the South Korean economy to help contain communism. The military dictatorship of Park Chung-hee initiated an accelerated industrialization program, and during the 1980s and early 1990s South Korea was known as an NIC—newly industrializing country—a "Little Tiger" of Asia (along with Taiwan, Hong Kong, and Singapore). This rapid industrialization expanded the pool of industrial laborers, but it also came with some costs: low wages, government suppression of labor strikes, and income inequality for large segments of the Korean working class, intense rural-to-urban immigration, and increased population density. Dramatic population growth also exacerbated conditions. From 1960 to 1975, the population increased from 25 to 35 million. As opportunities for socioeconomic mobility diminished, middle-class Koreans increasingly considered moving abroad. The South Korean government also actively promoted emigration as part of its population control program.[53]

Like the earlier wave of Korean immigrants to the United States, the newcomers are both men and women and tend to immigrate as families. A majority have quickly become naturalized citizens. Professionals and students made up the bulk of the initial wave of Korean immigrants, including physicians, nurses, pharmacists, and dentists. But like recent Filipino immigrants, they have not always been able to work within these same professions once in the United States. Professional certifications from Korea were not always accepted in the United States, and immigrants suffered from their lack of English fluency. Han Chol Hong, a Korean engineer who immigrated to the United States in 1983, for example, struggled to find employment. When he was turned away from engineering jobs, he enrolled at a plumbing and welding school but was unable to find work. He became licensed to paint houses, but again he had trouble finding a job. He finally became a janitor just to make ends meet.

As a result of their declining professional status, many Korean immigrants like Han pooled their resources with other Koreans in a credit-rotating system known as *kae* and opened up their own businesses. Koreans flocked to American inner cities and took over the ownership of grocery stores and other small businesses previously owned by older Jewish, Italian, and Greek immigrant and second-generation families. After a friend told Han about a grocery market that was for sale in South Central Los Angeles, he and his family bought it and became one of the many Korean immigrant entrepreneurs running small businesses in American cities by the 1990s. Rising at five every morning to pick up produce, the Hans then ran the store "from 8:00 a.m. to 8:00 p.m., seven days a week, three hundred sixty five days a year," he explained, and rarely took a day off. "Doing business like this takes hard work," Han admitted. "But I am my own boss. . . . Nobody tells me what to do." [54]

The peak years of Korean immigration were in the late 1970s and 1980s, when many family members of immigrants already in the country began to arrive. Since the 1990s, when South Korea's living standards and democratization have increased, immigration to the United States has declined, but the Korean American population remains vibrant. In 1997, there were almost 136,000 Korean-owned businesses in the United States.[55] In 2010, more than half of all Korean Americans had a bachelor's degree compared to the national rate of 28 percent. But like Chinese Americans, Koreans are overrepresented at both ends of the economic scale. In general, they have higher median annual personal earnings than the U.S. population. But they also have higher poverty rates as well.[56]

At the same time that new Asian immigrants began arriving in the United States, another equally dramatic change was taking place within Asian American communities. Diverse Asian American activists began working together and with others for recognition, political empowerment, and equality. They envisioned a new Asian America and a new America.

Some activists began fighting for equality and working across racial lines in the immediate post–World War II era. Japanese Americans and African Americans came together to challenge the whites-only rule in Los Angeles neighborhoods like Crenshaw, for example. Their interethnic alliances helped to move the city's civil rights agendas forward and laid important political foundations for interracial activism in later years.[57] During the 1960s and 1970s, a new generation of activists came of age and expanded the previous generations' struggles against racism and inequalities at home and abroad. They were simultaneously part of larger social justice movements that were transforming American society and politics as well as new campaigns organized around distinct Asian American–specific causes.

Yuri Kochiyama, Philip Vera Cruz, and Grace Lee Boggs were among those who got their start in the African American civil rights movement or the farmworkers' movement. Born to Japanese immigrants in California in 1921, Kochiyama was incarcerated along with other Japanese Americans at the Jerome, Arkansas, camp. At the end of the war, she moved back to California to persistent anti-Japanese sentiment. Every night, customers would call her "Jap" at her waitressing job, or worse, throw cups of hot coffee at her. She soon moved to New York City with her husband, Bill, and it was during these years that Yuri met Daisy Bates, the NAACP Little Rock chapter president who had guided the Little Rock Nine in their school desegregation movement. "It was after my meeting Daisy Bates," Kochiyama explains, "that I began to take a serious interest in the civil rights movement. I kept my eyes on the newspapers as civil unrest and demonstrations erupted all over the South." This new awareness set the stage for what would become a significant period for the Kochiyama family. "People were fighting for things that we had taken for granted," she recalled. "I started to realize that I needed to fight for my civil rights, too." Kochiyama would go on to become a community organizer, a close associate of Malcolm X, and an important force connecting the emerging Asian American movement on the East Coast to the ongoing African American civil rights movement. She gave her voice and energy to various causes, including protesting against U.S. imperialism in Asia and supporting ethnic studies in New York City schools. During the 1980s, she and Bill testified in the Commission on Wartime Relocation and Internment of Civilians. In her later years, she remained active in the movement to free political prisoners and to end racial profiling after September 11, 2001.[58]

Another early Asian American activist was Philip Vera Cruz. A member of the first wave of Filipinos who came to the United States in the early twentieth century, Cruz spent thirty years working on farms and in canneries and restaurants in Minnesota and Washington. When he moved to California in the 1950s, he became involved in the Filipino labor movement and helped organize the Agricultural Workers Organizing Committee in a series of effective strikes and boycotts that crippled the grape industry in Delano in 1965. These actions led to the formation of the United Farm Workers (UFW), which joined Filipino farm laborers with other ethnic groups, including Mexicans. Vera Cruz served as the UFW's vice president under Chicano Cesár Chávez until 1977. In his later years, he educated a new generation of activists with his messages of grassroots organizing, devotion to the rights of working people, commitment to democracy, and solidarity.[59]

Like Cruz and Kochiyama, Grace Lee Boggs became active in social justice movements in the 1960s. Born in 1915 to Chinese immigrant parents, Boggs grew up in Providence, Rhode Island. She attended Barnard College and then went on to Bryn Mawr, where she received her PhD in 1940. Unable to find a job in academia, she relocated to Chicago, where she became involved in African American civil rights activism through her work with West Indian Marxist C. L. R. James. She was inspired by African Americans' struggle for civil rights, especially labor leader A. Philip Randolph's successful campaign to establish fair hiring practices in American defense plants during the 1940s. "When I saw what a movement could do I said, 'Boy that's what I wanna do with my life,' " Boggs recalled. She married African American activist James Boggs and moved to Detroit in 1953. The pair worked together for decades playing a key role in the many social and what she calls "humanizing" movements of the

53. Yuri Kochiyama marching during a Chinese Restaurant Waiters' strike, New York City, 1980s.

late twentieth century, including civil rights, Black Power, labor issues, women's rights, antiwar campaigns, environmental concerns, and Asian American rights.[60] In her nineties when she published an autobiography and a collection of essays, Grace Lee Boggs still expressed her steadfast belief in the power of ideas and the need for organizing to build a twenty-first-century America in which people of all "races and ethnicities live together in harmony."[61]

54. Activist Grace Lee Boggs, 2012.

Like Boggs, Cruz, and Kochiyama, a growing number of Asian Americans began to push forward a new era in radical Asian American politics in the 1960s. Inspired by the civil rights, Black Power, and antiwar movements as well as the visions of prominent socialists and communists like Mao Zedong of the People's Republic of China, Ho Chi Minh in North Vietnam, Kim Il-sung in North Korea, Che Guevara in Argentina, Fidel Castro in Cuba, and

Frantz Fanon in Algeria, these new activists called for unity among Asian Americans and other peoples of color, economic justice, community services, and Asian American–centered education and arts. They rejected the label "Orientals," the prevailing term used in the United States, as well as the model minority stereotype and its emphasis on cooperation and assimilation. Instead, they proclaimed themselves Asian Americans, a pan-ethnic identity that emphasized commonalities across all Asian immigrant and ethnic groups. They "sought to achieve radical social change by building interracial coalitions and transnational solidarities," according to historian Daryl Maeda, and they worked to end oppression in the United States and beyond. Political, cultural, and community organizations were formed to finally give Asian Americans a place and voice in American politics.[62]

Most activists got their start in other social movements. Asian Americans participated in the civil rights movement in the South, the Free Speech movement on the UC Berkeley campus, and the anti–Vietnam War movement during the 1960s. But no Asian American organization existed to focus on issues unique to Asian American communities. As activist Yuji Ichioka remembered, there were "so many Asians out there in the political demonstrations, but we had no effectiveness. Everyone was lost in the larger rally." He and his partner, Emma Gee, thought that if Asian Americans could rally behind an "Asian American banner" they could have a larger impact.[63] Together with other activists, Ichioka and Gee formed the Asian American Political Alliance (AAPA) at UC Berkeley in May of 1968. It explicitly brought together a multigenerational group of Asian American women and men from different ethnic and class backgrounds and became the first organization to use "Asian American" to "stand for all of us Americans of Asian descent," as Ichioka put it.[64]

The Asian American Political Alliance focused on three goals that would help define the broader Asian American movements of the 1960s through the 1980s. First, AAPA sought to bring together all Asians as a political group regardless of ethnic or other differences. In one of its early documents describing the goals of the organization, the AAPA began each goal with the collective phrase "We Asian Americans." Second, AAPA explicitly critiqued the United States as a racist, imperialistic, and exploitative society. Rejecting the model minority premise that Asian Americans were not victims of American racism, the AAPA declared that "Asian Americans have been continuously exploited and oppressed by the racist majority." Third, AAPA affirmed its commitment to interracial solidarity with other "Third World people" in the United States and abroad and pledged its "support [of] all oppressed peoples and their struggles for Liberation." Identifying as part of the Third World in the United States, Asian Americans connected with other nonwhite people, including African Americans, Chicanos, Puerto Ricans, and Native Americans, who were similarly racially oppressed and economically exploited. In voicing a particular opposition to U.S. imperialism, the AAPA also specifically critiqued the Vietnam War.[65]

The AAPA in Berkeley had a short history and was disbanded in late 1969. It nevertheless helped to inspire similar organizations to form across the country in Los Angeles, New York, and Hawai'i, like New York's Asian Americans for Action (AAA) and I Wor Kuen, the largest revolutionary Asian American organization aligned with the Black Power movement. Together, these and other organizations helped forge a new Asian American consciousness and inspired the creation of new institutions that addressed the distinct needs of Asian Americans and gave voice to the growing community.[66]

Some of the first sites of activism occurred on college campuses. In 1968, the AAPA at San Francisco State University joined with Chicano, Native American, and African American students in the Third World Liberation Front (TWLF), which identified racism and colonialism as common sources of oppression of people of color in the United States and abroad. Demanding curricula and programs that reflected the histories, needs, and experiences of people of color, the Third World Liberation Front called a strike on the San Francisco State campus on November 6, 1968. The student organizers received support from Stokely Carmichael, the former chairman of the civil rights organization SNCC, the Student Nonviolent Coordinating Committee, who urged the students to seize power and to strive for "real control."[67] Protests, demonstrations, sit-ins, and building occupations followed, and more than 700 students were arrested over the next five months.

UC Berkeley's campus was similarly engulfed in activism. African American, Chicano, Asian American, and Native American student groups had similar grievances with the campus administration and the lack of what they viewed as relevant and accountable curricula and programs. The Berkeley Third World Liberation Front was formed as a way to express interracial solidarity, and a strike for what Daryl Maeda calls "self-determination in education" was called for January 22, 1969.[68] Over the next three months, student protesters and their allies went toe-to-toe with police as they blocked campus walkways and formed protest lines that wound throughout the campus. Police responded by using helicopters to dump tear gas onto demonstrators. Arrests multiplied and the police clashes with protesters became so violent that California governor Ronald Reagan threatened to establish martial law and send the National Guard to Berkeley's campus.

55. Third World Liberation Front strike supporters gather at UC Berkeley's Sather Gate, January 28, 1969.

Both the San Francisco State and UC Berkeley strikes ended within days of each other in March 1969. The San Francisco State strike culminated in the creation of the first School of Ethnic Studies in the nation. At Berkeley, an Ethnic Studies department was established. Over time, similar efforts spread on college and university campuses across the country and extended into communities and to mainstream culture and politics. What had begun on college campuses resulted in an entire generation consciously finding its voice and acting for change.[69]

Asian American activists' struggles on campus coincided with similar efforts by community-based activists to engage in "serve-the-people" programs to provide affordable housing, social services, health care, and labor rights for poor and working-class Asian Americans. Urban and rural campaigns sprang up around the country. One of the most important efforts involved the campaign to save the International Hotel, a single room occupancy building located on the edge of San Francisco's Chinatown and Manilatown that housed elderly working-class Filipino and Chinese men.

56. Establishing community-based health care services were an important aspect of the Asian American movement in the 1960s and 1970s. 1973 Chinatown Health Fair, New York City.

When the owners of the I-Hotel, as it was known, threatened the residents with eviction in 1969, community activists banded together to lease the building, renovate it, and bring in Asian American businesses and cultural and arts organizations as tenants. Three years later, the hotel was threatened again, and a coalition of Asian American groups, students, and tenants formed once more to fight eviction. Despite their efforts, eviction plans moved forward. On the night of the final eviction on August 3, 1977,

200 activists barricaded themselves inside the hotel while 2,000 supporters circled the hotel, created a human chain, chanted "Stop the Eviction! We Won't Move," and sang civil rights movement protest songs. In the early hours of the next day, 250 riot-equipped police officers began to break up the protesters with clubs. Sheriff's deputies used sledgehammers and axes to break down doors and led the tenants and protesters outside.

The campaign to save the I-Hotel had failed. The longtime tenants were forced out and the building was razed. However, the I-Hotel movement helped to inspire other campaigns for affordable housing in San Francisco's Chinatown and Japantown. Equally important, in bringing together a diverse group of supporters who crossed generational, ethnic, political, and class lines, it mobilized broad-based support and had a lasting legacy that created a new generation of political leaders who would continue to serve their communities and enter mainstream American politics in the following decades.[70]

As they struggled to meet the basic needs of community members in very specific local neighborhoods, Asian American activists also saw themselves as part of a larger global struggle against capitalism and imperialism. They expressed this internationalism by declaring their solidarity with the peoples of Asian nations affected by U.S. imperialism. And they fiercely opposed the Vietnam War. Many believed that the war was just the latest example of ongoing U.S. imperialism in Asia that had resulted in the bombings of Hiroshima and Nagasaki, the occupation of Okinawa, and the Korean War. Carrying banners that read "Stop the Bombing of Asian People" and "Stop Killing Our Asian Brothers and Sisters," Asian American antiwar protesters emphasized the similarities between the oppression of Asians within the United States and the violence against Asians in Asia.[71]

The Bay Area Asian Coalition Against the War (BAACAW) declared its goal to "build a solid, broad-based anti-imperialist movement of Asian people against the war in Vietnam" and connected the oppression of Asians in the United States to the war as part of its "One Struggle, Many Fronts" banner.[72] Some activists visited China, North Vietnam, and North Korea in an attempt to connect to Asians in Asia and to explore how socialism worked in these countries.[73] After the war ended, Asian American activists continued to act for change. They vowed to "bring the war back to the communities" to help provide health care and employment services to neglected poor and working-class Asian American neighborhoods.

Asian Americans' involvement in the civil rights and antiwar movements led to their engagement with other radical movements of the 1960s and 1970s, including the women's liberation and gay liberation movements. Reacting to the chauvinism that some of their fellow male activists displayed, Asian American women increasingly began to form their own organizations to address gender inequality inside and outside their communities. Like other women activists in the civil rights movements, Asian American women were often given secondary, background roles within Asian American organizations. While men made decisions, gave speeches, and were the public face of the organizations, women were called upon to type up leaflets and newsletters, take notes, make coffee, and even clean the toilets. Increasingly, Asian American women recognized their "triple oppression" of being people of color, women, and workers, and they organized to create change from within their communities.[74]

Groups like Asian Women United and the Organization of Asian Women flourished in the late 1960s and 1970s. Largely led by educated, middle-class women, these groups devoted themselves to promoting the status of women through educational and service projects. But there were countless other Asian American women activists, like Unsuk Perry, a Korean American hotel employee who as a union steward frequently translated for her Korean workers and made sure that they understood what rights they had. And there was also housing activist Chang Jok Lee, who worked tirelessly throughout the 1970s and 1980s to protect the rights of low-income tenants in San Francisco's Chinatown.[75]

Similar to the ways in which Asian American women's participation in women's liberation emerged from their marginalization in other social justice movements, Asian American LGBT activism also grew from other social justice movements. LGBT Asian Americans felt keenly their exclusion from mostly white mainstream LGBT organizations. In addition, other liberation movements were, at best, dismissive of LGBT issues or, at worst, homophobic. Activist, author, and journalist Helen Zia recalled being put on trial by other Asian American and black liberation activists in Boston in the 1970s. There was "no place for gays" in the liberation movement, Zia was told. "I had not yet come out, and they made it clear that if I did, I would also be out of the liberation community. That threatening message kept me in the closet for the next several years."[76]

57. Asian American women were active in the larger women's liberation movement. "A Day for Women's Rights to Ratify the ERA, 1977."

Working alongside other LGBT people of color and their allies, an Asian American LGBT movement began in October 1979 when more than 600 black, Latino, Native American, Asian, and white people attended the First National Third World Gay and Lesbian Conference in Washington, D.C. That same weekend, the First National March for Gay and Lesbian Rights began, including a newly formed Lesbian and Gay Asian Contingent. Activist Trinity Ordona marks this moment as the birth of "a seminal Asian gay and lesbian movement."[77] Another organization, the Asian/Pacific Lesbians and Gays (A/PLG), was established in Los Angeles 1980 as the first to represent the interests of gay and lesbian Asians in that city. These and other organizations highlighted the unique issues facing LGBT Asian Americans and enabled them to organize programs to fight homophobia inside and outside the Asian American community and to provide support for those living with HIV/AIDS.[78]

By the early twenty-first century, Asian American LGBTs were no longer at the margins of the Asian American community and were instead growing more active and visible. They worked to raise awareness and acceptance around issues that affected both the Asian American and LGBT communities, like equality. Asian American organizations were in fact central actors in the same sex marriage debates in some states. "With each individual who comes to realize there are Asian queers and queer Asians," explained Zia, who with her partner became one of the first same sex couples to marry in California, "that space where the gay zone meets the Asian zone opens a little more."[79]

Out of the civil rights and social justice movements of the 1960s also came a desire among Japanese Americans to revisit their experiences of forced removal and incarceration during World War II. It was Aiko Herzig-Yoshinaga's involvement in the antiwar and Asian American movements in New York City that triggered her own reappraisal of the treatment of Japanese Americans during the war years. Through her involvement with Asian Americans for Action, she started to think about "our own experience back in wartime, and why did it happen, and what we were suffering from as a result."[80]

During the 1970s, support for investigating and addressing the injustices during the war began to grow, and a number of different Japanese American organizations began a campaign to seek an official apology and restitution from the U.S. government for incarceration during the war. Deep divisions existed within the Japanese American community over political strategies and the meaning of incarceration, but the groups eventually found common ground in their efforts to obtain redress and reparations. After years of advocacy, the movement began to gain traction. In 1976, President Gerald Ford officially declared the wartime removal and relocation of Japanese Americans a "tragedy." The president acknowledged that "we now know what we should have known then—not only that evacuation was wrong but that Japanese Americans were and are loyal Americans."[81]

The U.S. Commission on Wartime Relocation and Internment of

Civilians was created in 1980. Over the next year, congressional hearings were held in twenty cities throughout the country. More than 500 Japanese Americans testified. It was the first time that many of them had ever spoken publicly about their wartime experiences. In 1982, the commission released its report, *Personal Justice Denied*, which included testimonies of camp inmates given at the hearings and highly important government documents discovered by Aiko Herzig-Yoshinaga and her research team that proved that Japanese Americans had not been disloyal. It also issued a scathing rebuke of the government's actions: "The promulgation of Executive Order 9066 was not justified by military necessity," the commission's report concluded. Instead, race prejudice, war hysteria, and a failure of political leadership led to an egregious policy. "A grave injustice was done to American citizens and resident nationals of Japanese ancestry who, without individual review or any probative evidence against them, were excluded, removed, and detained by the United States during World War II."[82]

58. Onlookers watch as President Ronald Reagan signs the Civil Liberties Act of 1988, which offered a national apology for the wartime removal and incarceration of Japanese Americans. August 10, 1988, Washington, D.C.

The commission recommended the passage of a joint congressional resolution officially apologizing for the removal and relocation, the establishment of an educational and humanitarian fund, and reparations paid to each survivor. In 1985, the Manzanar camp in southern California was designated a National Historic Landmark. At the same time, legal efforts proceeded to reconsider the three wartime Supreme Court cases (*Hirabayashi*, *Yasui*, and *Korematsu*) that had sanctioned the government's wartime actions. In 1988, the Civil Liberties Act was approved by Congress and signed into law by President Reagan. The act authorized a national apology for removal and incarceration, the payment of $20,000 to each surviving Japanese American affected by Executive Order 9066, and the establishment of educational and other programs.

In Canada, the government followed suit and offered an official apology and redress payments to Japanese Canadians. Efforts to obtain redress for Japanese Latin Americans have taken longer. In 1996, the United States officially apologized for its actions affecting Japanese Latin Americans and offered minimal reparations. The campaign to advocate for compensation equal to what was awarded to Japanese Americans, however, continues.[83]

The U.S. government's payments did not come close to repaying Japanese Americans for the financial disaster they experienced during the war. Nor could the payments make Japanese Americans spiritually whole again. Nevertheless, the Japanese American redress movement was instrumental in spearheading movements to right historical injustices, in creating enduring educational resources to help prevent a repeat of past mistakes, and as Senator Daniel Inouye explained, in helping make Americans' "concept of democracy get closer to perfection."[84] "We wrote a page in history—U.S. history," added activist Hitoshi H. Kajihara.[85]

14

In Search of Refuge: Southeast Asians in the United States

While immigration reform and community-based activism were creating a new Asian America in the decades of the late twentieth century, events halfway around the world in Southeast Asia were disrupting the lives of millions in ways that would force them to leave their homes and seek refuge in the United States. The U.S.'s aggressive anticommunist foreign policy led it to Southeast Asia at the end of World War II. By the 1950s, it had replaced France as the major Western power in the region and was engaged in a full-blown war with North Vietnamese communist forces and their allies in South Vietnam by the 1960s. The war transformed every aspect of life in Vietnam. Along with the contests for political power, war brought death, destruction, and displacement. As U.S. interventionism spread to neighboring Laos and Cambodia, these countries and peoples were also caught up in similar aftereffects of war. The United States came to rely on a "Secret Army" of soldiers (so named because the existence of the army and its actions were kept from the American public) made up of the Hmong, an ethnic minority in Laos, for example. When the war ended with a U.S. defeat, communist governments came to power in all three countries.

The story of how 1.2 million Vietnamese, Lao, Hmong, and Cambodian peoples have come to the United States from 1975 to 2010 reveals the multifaceted legacies of the war and the immense resilience of the refugees who have made the United States their home over the past forty years.[1] Unlike immigrants who choose to move, refugees are forced to flee their homelands because of persecution, extreme instability and trauma, or both. Their flight occurs on very short notice and under conditions of duress; their resettlement in another country can take months or years; they arrive with physical and psychological wounds of war and grief; and they often have to rebuild their communities from scratch.[2]

Like so many generations of Asian immigrants before them, many refugees have gone on to pursue the American Dream. But their history in the United States is also a story of contradictions and unfinished journeys. On the one hand, U.S. interventions in Southeast Asia helped produce the very conditions that forced people to flee. On the other hand, U.S. humanitarianism made it possible for so many to find refuge in the United States. Sponsors and communities across the country helped the newcomers begin new lives in the U.S., but there were often strings attached. And not all Americans welcomed the refugees with open arms. As a result, the refugee resettlement process has often been full of unforeseen struggles and setbacks.[3]

As part of the spread of European imperialism throughout Asia during the nineteenth century, France set its sights on acquiring an empire in Southeast Asia. French forces took Saigon in 1859, turned Cambodia into a French protectorate in 1863, and colonized Laos in 1893. Together, Vietnam, Laos, and Cambodia were known as Indochine Française, or French Indochina.

During World War II, Japanese troops were stationed in and eventually occupied French Indochina by March of 1945. At the end of the war, France tried desperately to recolonize Vietnam. Vietnamese nationalists led by Ho Chi Minh had different ideas. Ho had spent the previous twenty years trying to bring independence to his country. Rebuffed by Western powers in his attempts to gain rights for the French Indochinese colonies in the early twentieth century, Ho turned to communism, and French and Viet Minh forces fought each other for almost a decade in the First Indochina War. After a devastating two-month siege in 1954, France gave up its Indochinese empire, and the 1954 Geneva Accords divided Vietnam along the seventeenth parallel. The North was led by Ho Chi Minh's Viet Minh government. The

United States created a new government in South Vietnam led by anticommunist Roman Catholic Ngo Dinh Diem.

President Dwight Eisenhower was not ready to commit U.S. troops to Vietnam, but he was also not willing to let the country fall to communism. By incremental steps, the United States found itself enmeshed in the region in an escalating commitment that would last for twenty-one years. By the time Eisenhower left office, there were 1,000 U.S. military advisors in Vietnam. President Kennedy continued the campaign against communism and supported the Diem regime, which was proving to be corrupt and repressive.

In 1960, the National Liberation Front (NLF) was founded with the support of Ho Chi Minh's communist government and began to successfully challenge Diem in the South. President Kennedy began to increase the number of American military advisors and special forces in the country. The situation that President Johnson inherited after Kennedy's assassination was dire. With neither a formal congressional declaration of war nor a national debate, Johnson escalated U.S. involvement to prevent an NLF victory. When North Vietnamese ships fired on the U.S. destroyer *Maddox* in August of 1964, the president characterized the action as an act of unprovoked communist aggression. The U.S. Congress followed with the Gulf of Tonkin Resolution, which allowed Johnson to order U.S. planes to bomb North Vietnam and deploy U.S. combat troops into South Vietnam. The Second Indochina War had begun.

The first U.S. troops landed in Vietnam in 1965. By the end of 1966, there were 400,000 U.S. soldiers in the country. Two years later, that number had risen to 540,000. While the North Vietnamese communists and their southern counterparts (the Viet Cong) marshaled civilians to participate in the war against the United States, South Vietnamese troops were demoralized and deserting in droves. In the United States, protests against the war increased. The U.S. and North Vietnamese governments sat down for peace talks in 1968, but these efforts quickly stalled.

Meanwhile, the war took its toll on the Vietnamese people. More than a million tons of bombs were dropped on North Vietnam to destroy roads, bridges, power plants, moving vehicles, military installations, airfields, supply depots, dams, waterways, factories, and missile sites. Four million tons were also dropped on South Vietnam. The goal was to limit the North

Vietnamese government's ability to arm and supply its supporters in the south. The total tonnage dropped on Vietnam, Laos, and Cambodia was greater than what had been dropped on Nazi Germany and Nazi-occupied countries during World War II. The U.S. military also dropped napalm, a flammable gel, chemical defoliants, and herbicides that cleared trees and increased visibility for U.S. forces but caused massive destruction. Twelve million people in South Vietnam—about half the country's total population—were forced to leave their homes and became internally displaced people.[4] As one refugee later recalled, "I was born in Vietnam into a world at war. Our life was war. We lived and breathed war. We waited for peace, longing night after night . . . in the darkness only to see flares burst into bombs and hear the weeping of people who had lost their relatives."[5]

The North Vietnamese launched a major offensive during the Tet New Year celebrations in January 1968. Even though the Tet Offensive was ultimately a communist defeat, the two weeks of intensive fighting and the rising death toll of U.S. troops turned American public opinion even more against the war. Richard Nixon campaigned with a pledge of finding "peace with honor," and when he became president his Nixon Doctrine helped to shift the war to a new phase called "Vietnamization": the South Vietnamese forces would begin shouldering the bulk of the fighting while the United States began withdrawing its troops. A peace agreement between the United States and North Vietnam was signed on January 27, 1973, in Paris.

As U.S. troops were withdrawing from Vietnam, the war came increasingly to Cambodia and Laos, two countries that were officially neutral. Reflecting the domino theory of foreign relations that predicted that if one country fell to communism, then other countries in the surrounding region would also fall, U.S. foreign policy dictated American involvement on a wide scale. Beginning in the 1950s, the United States entangled both Laos and Cambodia in covert, clandestine operations and intervened in their domestic political affairs. Civilians in both countries suffered terribly as a consequence. U.S. bombings contributed to the political destabilization in Cambodia and Laos, and by 1975 both countries were under communist rule. The legacies of war—in the form of millions of land mines and unexploded ordnance—still plague the peoples of these two countries.[6]

In Laos, a civil war between the communist Pathet Lao and the anticommunist Royal Lao government was dividing the country. Fearing that a communist takeover of Laos was imminent, the United States tried to influence Lao politics through military and humanitarian aid programs beginning in 1955. The hope was to prevent a communist victory in the upcoming 1958 elections. When the Pathet Lao won a majority of the seats in the coalition government, the U.S. government began to take action against it.[7]

Over the next decade, the United States desired more active military intervention in Laos, but the 1962 Geneva Accords, which required that all foreign troops leave the country, hampered its ability. The Central Intelligence Agency thus set its sights on recruiting Hmong soldiers to take on covert actions on behalf of the United States. An ethnic group with roots in southwestern China, the Hmong had been living in the mountainous regions of Laos since the early nineteenth century. A man named Vang Pao became central to U.S. efforts. As a young military officer in the Royal Lao Army, Vang had sided with the French against Vietnamese nationalists and was a self-described anticommunist and Lao nationalist. Committed to protecting northwestern Laos, where most Hmong lived, from communist domination, Vang was receptive to U.S. overtures.

In 1961, CIA agent James William (Bill) Lair contacted Vang to recruit Hmong soldiers to the U.S. effort. He proposed a deal in which the United States would arm and train special Hmong guerrilla units to attack North Vietnamese communists coming through Laos. In exchange, the Hmong would receive military and humanitarian aid. Because there was no written documentation of the meeting between Lair and Vang, we may never know what deal the two men struck exactly, but many Hmong believe Vang Pao's explanation that the United States also promised a long-sought Hmong homeland or sanctuary in exchange for their service. Based out of the military base at Long Cheng and supplied by the CIA airline Air America, Hmong soldiers carried out espionage, sabotage, and propaganda missions. Because the United States paid the Hmong a fraction of what it paid its own military personnel, this was war on the cheap. And the Hmong did not disappoint. Vang Pao initially recruited 9,000 soldiers in 1961. By 1969, the secret army under his command numbered 40,000 and has been called "America's most lethal weapon."[8]

By the late 1960s, the United States increased its reliance on the Hmong. The war involved the entire Hmong population. Hmong men faced high casualties, with some records estimating that 25 percent of enlisted Hmong were killed. By 1970, more Hmong soldiers were boys only twelve or thirteen years old. An estimated 50,000 civilians were also killed or wounded, a devastating statistic, considering that the entire Hmong population before the war was only 300,000.[9]

In addition, Laos was engulfed in bombs. President Nixon ordered multiple bombings in Laos to support the Royal Lao government against the communist Pathet Lao and to disrupt the movement of North Vietnamese arms and personnel along the Laotian portion of the Ho Chi Minh Trail to the South. Beginning in 1964 and continuing until 1973, the United States dropped more than 2 million tons of ordnance on Laos during 580,000 bombing missions, rendering the Plain of Jars "the most intensely bombarded place on the face of the planet."[10] In 1970, an estimated one in four Laotians (more than 600,000) had been displaced due to the war. Many had been displaced more than once, making Laos the country with the most displaced population in the world.[11]

Although the war was directed by the U.S. embassy in Laos and the Central Intelligence Agency and was funded by congressional appropriations committees, the war remained out of America's public eye for years. The U.S. government maintained its position that the American presence in Laos was solely humanitarian. It was not until 1970 that the war was exposed to the general public.[12]

The Hmong army in Laos was not the United States's only secret in Southeast Asia. For fourteen months in 1969 and 1970, the United States launched bombing raids that dropped 108,823 tons of bombs on neutral Cambodia. Authorized by President Nixon but kept hidden from the American public, the bombings were targeted to destroy both the Ho Chi Minh Trail as well as the areas in Cambodia, where North Vietnamese troops retreated during firefights with U.S. forces. Although National Security Advisor Henry Kissinger claimed in 1973 that the bombings had taken place only in "unpopulated parts of Cambodia," U.S. officials were aware of casualties from the start. Over time, more civilian deaths occurred in these bombings than military deaths. Estimates range from 50,000, which is almost equal to the number of Americans who died in the Vietnam War, to 150,000.[13]

During this period of intense bombing, a protracted civil war raged within Cambodia between the U.S.-backed Lon Nol government and the communist Khmer Rouge led by Saloth Sar, who would later be known as Pol Pot. Scholars believe that the U.S. bombings—meant to thwart communist forces—were ironically an important factor in helping to increase support for the Khmer Rouge among rural Cambodians. The Khmer Rouge only had to point to the damage and devastation caused by U.S. bombs to recruit followers away from the U.S.-supported Nol government. The bombings also forced North Vietnamese troops to move deeper and deeper into Cambodia, where they provided military and political support to the Khmer Rouge.[14] On April 17, 1975, the Khmer Rouge entered Phnom Penh as victors. There they set up a new government called Democratic Kampuchea. Their reign over Cambodia was brief, only three years and eight months, from April 1975 to January 1979. But it would result in one of the greatest human tragedies in the modern age.

In Vietnam, the end of the war came quickly. By early 1975, it became clear to U.S. officials that the South Vietnamese government was about to fall. The removal of U.S. troops and funding as well as the weakness of the Nguyen Van Thieu regime led to a final collapse of the South Vietnamese government.[15] Plans to evacuate U.S. personnel and citizens as well as Vietnamese who would be vulnerable to persecution under the new regime began to form. By the end of April, U.S. officials described scenes of "absolute chaos" as people scrambled to find ways out of the country.[16] On April 21, Thieu announced his resignation as president of the Republic of Vietnam. More people began forming exit strategies.

One Vietnamese refugee recalled that in the days following Thieu's announcement, families in his neighborhood began to mysteriously disappear without a trace as they quietly left the country. His family began to make their own plans. "[We were] certain that we could not live under Communism," he explained. The man's mother, who had worked for a U.S. oil company, put all of her energy into getting exit permits and visas from the U.S. embassy in Saigon. On April 25, she finally received approval to be evacuated. She rushed home and announced that the family had just two hours to pack up their belongings. When they arrived at Saigon's Tan Son Nhut Airport, they joined thousands of other refugees clamoring to leave. After a night of anxious waiting, they boarded a bus and then a giant military transport plane. Four hours later, they landed at Clark Air Force Base in the Philippines. They stayed one day before flying to Wake Island. By the time they arrived in Honolulu, newspaper headlines blared that communist tanks had stormed into Saigon, and that the South Vietnamese government had surrendered. This man's family was safe, but the realization that he might never see his relatives or his homeland again made him extremely depressed. "I felt myself falling apart," he recalled. "I wanted to cry but did not. I told myself that I had to be strong and to remain calm. . . . My heart had shattered to pieces. I lost not only my country but also everything I had loved."[17]

When the U.S. evacuation process—officially known as "Operation New Life"—kicked into high gear, U.S. airplanes evacuated around 7,500 people a day. After the runways of Tan Son Nhut Airport were destroyed by North Vietnamese forces, giant helicopters took over the task and evacuated more than 7,000 before Saigon fell on April 30. Another 73,000 escaped by sea on South Vietnamese navy vessels or on anything seaworthy they could secure. They found their way to the waiting U.S. naval vessels that then took them to the naval base in the Philippines. From there, officials directed them to other processing camps on Guam and Wake Island before sending them to reception centers in the United States.[18]

Later referred to as the "first wave" of Vietnamese refugees, these evacuees usually spent just a short time in the camps before being relocated. Largely from elite or middle-class backgrounds, they came with education, some English or French fluency, job skills, and previous contact with Americans. All of these factors would greatly help their transition to their new lives in the United States.[19]

Around 4,600 Cambodians, mostly diplomats, high-level officials, and those who might face persecution in the new regime, were also admitted into the United States. Members of this first group of refugees were mostly educated, had professional backgrounds and work skills. They joined a small number of Cambodian students and professionals who were already in the

United States, and together would form the core group of Cambodian community leaders who could assist those arriving in later years.[20]

The fall of Saigon also had dire repercussions in Laos. The Pathet Lao slowly gained power in the country, and as they did so, they targeted the Hmong as former allies of the United States. Unlike what occurred in Saigon and Phnom Penh, there was no similar large-scale evacuation of Hmong. The CIA did airlift Vang Pao and his officers out of harm's way, and Vang eventually resettled in California, but the few planes that were sent to do this could not evacuate all who wanted to leave. Panic and chaos followed as huge crowds showed up every day at Long Cheng in the hope of being evacuated. Mao Vang Lee, who had worked at the CIA-sponsored radio station at Long Cheng, waited at the base for three days to board one of the few planes. The scene is seared in her memory. "As soon as the airplane lands, the crowd was already packed underneath it before it came to a halt. They would fight, step on each other to get into the plane." With a baby in tow, Mao explained that she and her husband decided that they just could not compete with the crowd. "Even though we feared for our lives . . . we decided to stay."[21]

Although 10,000 Hmong crowded onto the airbase at Long Cheng, only around 2,500 were evacuated by the United States in May 1975.[22] When the last U.S. planes took off from the airbase, the crews dumped duffel bags of Lao money onto the tarmac as a diversion. After the last plane took off, described Yia Lee, who witnessed the event, "Everyone cried. In those moments, there was sense of hopelessness. No dreams for the future. You become like thin air."[23]

With international media covering the dramatic events in Vietnam, the plight of Vietnamese refugees became front-page news. Newspapers captured in words and photographs refugees' desperate attempts to leave the country while Viet Cong rockets whistled overhead and exploded in what had recently been U.S. and South Vietnamese–controlled territory. "Large groups of Vietnamese clawed their way up the 10-foot wall of the [U.S.] embassy compound in desperate attempts to escape approaching Communist troops," the *New York Times* reported on April 30. U.S. Marines in battle gear pushed people off the wall in a desperate attempt at crowd control.

Some tried to jump the wall, but at least two missed and landed on top of the barbed wire strung along the top. One photographer captured a U.S. official punching a Vietnamese man in the face to try to break his hold on the doorway of an airplane already overloaded with refugees.[24]

59. An American official punches a man in the face to dislodge him from the doorway of an airplane already overloaded with refugees seeking to flee Nha Trang, South Vietnam, April 2, 1975.

Faced with a massive humanitarian crisis, President Ford, who succeeded Nixon after his resignation, established the Interagency Task Force (IATF) in April to coordinate federal funding and management of the evacuation and resettlement of refugees from Vietnam, Laos, and Cambodia. After the 1975 Indochina Migration and Refugee Assistance Act classified Vietnamese, Cambodian, and later, Lao and Hmong peoples as refugees to be resettled, U.S. officials began working with nongovernmental agencies, many of them religious charities, to sponsor refugees to be resettled in the United States.

60. Vietnamese refugees getting off a plane in Fort Chafee, Arkansas, 1978–1980.

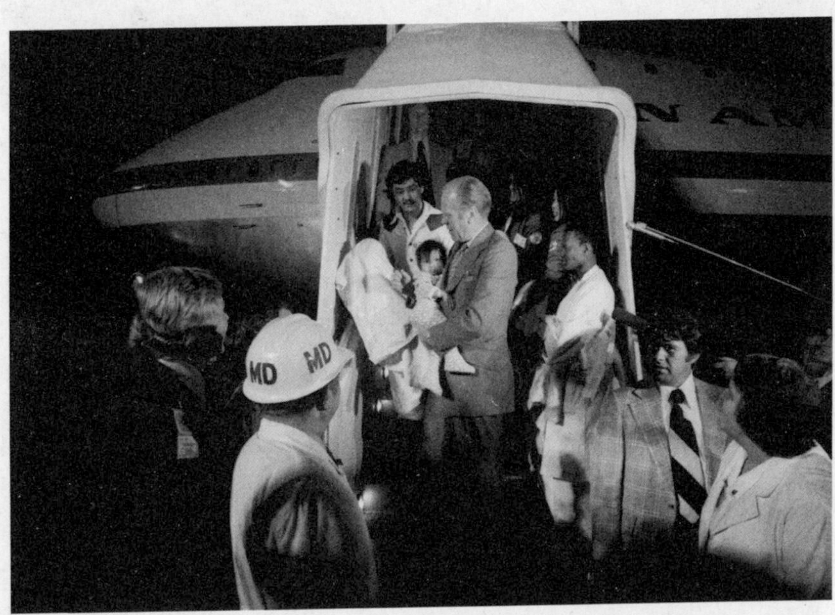

61. President Gerald R. Ford carries a Vietnamese baby from *Clipper 1742*, one of the planes that transported approximately 325 South Vietnamese orphans from Saigon to the United States, April 5, 1975.

From the very beginning, the resettlement of Southeast Asian refugees was cloaked in the heady rhetoric of U.S. humanitarianism. Ford described the U.S.'s admission of Vietnamese, for example, as a necessary "mission of mercy" involving the rescue of "helpless" refugees.[25] The first to be rescued were Vietnamese and Cambodian "orphans" (many fathered by U.S. military personnel). Between April 3 and April 15, over 1,700 were airlifted to the United States in what became known as "Operation Babylift." "This is the least we can do," Ford told reporters, "and we will do much more."[26] The president personally greeted one planeload of new arrivals at San Francisco International Airport on April 5.

Soon the president was committing the United States to "provide humanitarian aid to the helpless civilian victims of the war in Vietnam." "Let no ally or friend fear that our commitments will not be honored," he declared.[27] Over the next weeks, the president's public remarks on refugee resettlement emphasized the U.S.'s "moral obligation" to help refugees resettle and begin new lives in the United States. "By helping these refugees," the president told reporters, "we are living up to our heritage as a charitable and compassionate people."[28]

By December 31, 1975, the work of the Interagency Task Force was completed, and the processing and reception centers were closed. Eventually, around 130,000 Southeast Asian refugees were admitted during this first wave before the end of 1975. The vast majority—126,000—were Vietnamese, but there were also 4,600 Cambodians and 800 from Laos. In 1976, 10,200 more refugees from Laos who had escaped to Thai refugee camps were also allowed in.[29]

While many U.S. officials believed that the work of resettling Southeast Asian refugees would be completed in 1975, individuals and families from Vietnam, Cambodia, and Laos continued to seek refuge long after the evacuations ended. From 1975 to 1980, almost 433,000 refugees from Vietnam, Cambodia, and Laos arrived in the United States, peaking in 1980. By the early 1980s, an average of 50,000 refugees were admitted every year.[30]

In Vietnam, political persecution, economic restructuring, and ethnic discrimination all produced a mass exodus of new refugees. Within days of capturing Saigon, North Vietnamese forces targeted South Vietnamese elected officials, civil servants, military officers, policemen, members of noncommunist political parties, teachers, writers, artists, and religious leaders for "reeducation." A Vietnamese refugee in California vividly recalled the night "the Communists had stolen my father," a former government official who was incarcerated as a political prisoner. Some low-ranking officials were only kept for a few days. But the majority of political prisoners were incarcerated for years. In the reeducation camps, they were subjected to harsh labor, a near-starvation diet, and political indoctrination. The estimated number of South Vietnamese prisoners ranged from 40,000 by the North Vietnamese government to nearly 400,000 by a former South Vietnamese officer.[31] Once freed, many sought to escape their homeland to avoid further persecution.

These former political prisoners and their families were joined by more Vietnamese fleeing other types of persecution. As part of the new Vietnamese government's crackdown on "bourgeois trade," armed soldiers and cadres descended upon the many Chinese-owned businesses that had dominated the rice milling and wholesale and retail trade in both North and South Vietnam for centuries. In 1978, 30,000 small businesses were raided and closed, and Chinese began to leave Vietnam in droves. One refugee later explained that "fleeing the country was the only way out."[32]

An international crisis heated up when Vietnam invaded Cambodia in December 1978 and ousted the China-backed Khmer Rouge regime. China retaliated by invading Vietnam in February 1979. Afraid of more reprisals now that the two countries were at war, a growing number of the remaining ethnic Chinese in Vietnam fled by boat. In the first few months of 1978, 20,000 landed in neighboring countries.[33]

The flight had to be done under cover of darkness and with the utmost secrecy. Only a few items could be brought. One refugee recalled how her mother ingeniously sewed gold necklaces and jade jewelry inside the elastic waistbands of their pants, shirt collars, and luggage handles. Her cleverness allowed the family to retain their small savings.[34] Traveling with their most precious possessions, these "boat people," as they were known, took to the seas and often fell victim to pirates who preyed on them. In 1979, Le Tan Si and his family were fleeing on a boat with fifty-eight other people when the engine broke down. Groups of Thai pirates repeatedly robbed the refugees of their possessions, raped the girls and women, and killed all who resisted. Eventually, the survivors made their way to Malaysia with the help of a group of Thai fishermen. Le Tan Si's harrowing ordeal was not uncommon. Some estimate that 30 to 50 percent lost their lives in their escape to places of first asylum like Indonesia, Malaysia, the Philippines, Thailand, and Hong Kong.[35]

By June of 1979, there were 76,500 refugees in Malaysian refugee camps. With 17,000 refugees, Hong Kong housed the second-largest number of boat people fleeing Vietnam. Primarily from rural areas, these "second wave" Vietnamese refugees were generally less educated than those who had been evacuated in 1975. They came with fewer economic resources and marketable job skills. Some suffered from physical and mental wounds, and their flight from their country had been more perilous. Many had lost family members along the way or had been separated from their families for many years. They often faced anxiety-ridden weeks at sea followed by months in a refugee camp. When they arrived in the United States after 1982, there were fewer programs available to assist in their adjustment, and federal funds had been reduced.[36]

Over time, Vietnamese adjusted to their new lives in the United States. Although they were initially resettled all over the United States, many re-migrated to be closer together. By the 1990s, the city of Westminster in Orange County, California, became home to the Vietnamese neighborhood of Little Saigon, and by 2000, one quarter of all Vietnamese Americans lived in the Los Angeles–Orange County–San Diego area.[37]

Just as refugees were fleeing from Vietnam beginning in the late spring and summer of 1975, dramatic events were unfolding in Cambodia. On the day that the Khmer Rouge entered Phnom Penh, they began to put their revolutionary principles into action. Former military and government officials were executed. Markets, money, banks, and private property were abolished, as were Western medicine, schools, and Buddhism. Consequently, Buddhist monks were defrocked, while "class enemies" such as educated individuals, merchants, and landlords were killed. The 2 million residents of Phnom Penh were evacuated. Forced out of their homes and into the streets, tens of thousands died due to hunger, thirst, illness, and exposure to the elements.

Kassie Neou described this march of death: "We stepped over the dead bodies. We heard the loudspeakers: 'Move on. Move on.' "[38] Under this regime, resistance was futile.

The Khmer Rouge restructured society and transformed the entire country into a giant forced labor camp. Peasants were granted full rights in the regime, while urbanites were treated as enemies of the revolution and had no rights. Ethnic minorities, including Chinese and Vietnamese who had lived in Cambodia for generations, were expelled.[39] Fed only meals of thin rice gruel and forced to work long hours building dams and irrigation ditches and planting and harvesting crops with minimal or no tools, masses of Cambodians suffered from malnutrition, starvation, and illness. Loung Ung, a young child during the Khmer Rouge years, lived and worked in the labor camp for almost four years. An older sister died of food poisoning, and soon after, soldiers came for her mother and little sister. By the time the Khmer Rouge soldiers came to take her father away, she had become accustomed to unimaginable hardship at the tender age of seven. "I did not pray for the gods to spare his life, to help him escape, or even to return him to me. I prayed only that his death be quick and painless," she recalls.[40] Another survivor described the incalculable losses Cambodians suffered during these years in this way: "We not only lost our identities, but we lost our pride, our senses, our religion, our loved ones, our souls, ourselves."[41]

Eventually, the Khmer Rouge turned on its own. In 1978, Pol Pot and his commanders arrested and killed between 100,000 and 250,000 people who were suspected of disloyalty. The Khmer Rouge's control over Cambodia ended when a dissident Khmer Rouge group fled to Vietnam for assistance and returned with Vietnamese troops. Pol Pot was driven from Phnom Penh the first week of January of 1979. In total, some 1.7 million people, about 21 percent of the country's population, lost their lives during the three-and-a-half-year reign of the Khmer Rouge in Cambodia.[42]

Those who were able to leave sought refuge in other countries. By 1979, more than half a million Cambodians were trying to enter Thailand, but by this time this first country of asylum for Vietnamese, Lao, and Cambodian refugees was experiencing a growing refugee crisis. Because Western countries like the United States prioritized the resettlement of former U.S. allies like the Vietnamese, Hmong, and Lao, they were less willing to accept Cambodians. As a result, the camps in Thailand became overcrowded, the

Thai people grew weary of the number of refugees arriving in their country, and Cambodian refugees were sometimes treated with shocking violence.

Increased international attention about the crisis in Southeast Asia finally prompted the United States to admit Cambodians into the country. In 1979, *Time* magazine reported on survivors of Pol Pot's regime and described Cambodia's plight in dramatic terms: it was "a country soaked in blood, devastated by war, and its people are starving to death." The magazine profiled a young woman named Chan Khoun who had recently walked for three months through the woods and mountains to arrive at a Thai refugee camp with her dangerously malnourished infant sister.[43] Between 1980 and 1986, another 122,000 arrived in Thailand, where they applied for resettlement in a third country. The refugees tended to be rural farmers, fishermen, and artisans who had survived the Khmer Rouge years. With little education and a lack of familiarity with urban life, those who were eventually resettled in the United States struggled as they tried to heal from years of war and trauma and adapt to their new surroundings. Between 1987 and 1993, almost 28,000 more Cambodians were admitted into the United States, often as family members of those already in the country.[44]

The largest Cambodian community outside of Cambodia is in Long Beach, California, where a new Phnom Penh formed by the end of the twentieth century. A small number of students had already been living in and around Long Beach since the 1950s and 1960s and were well prepared to assist newcomers arriving after 1975. By the early 1990s, around 50,000 Cambodians lived in Long Beach. Seattle and Lowell, Massachusetts, are also home to sizable Cambodian communities.[45]

In Laos, another exodus began. From May to December of 1975, some 45,000 fled the country. An estimated 200,000 "lowland Lao"—the dominant group in Laos—made it to Thailand between 1975 and 1986. They left to avoid being punished for their anticommunist political beliefs and forced into reeducation "seminars," or because they were simply unable to support themselves in postwar Laos. Like the Hmong refugees, many Lao fled across the Mekong River to Thailand under fire from soldiers and at great risk to themselves. Over 10,000 Lao refugees arrived in Thailand in 1975. The next year, that number had almost doubled, and in 1978 almost 50,000 Lao fled to Thailand during the height of the exodus.[46]

Saengmany Ratsabout's family was part of this exodus. Forced to escape the aftermath of the civil war in Laos, the Ratsabouts made the long trek to the Mekong River in 1984. Leaving their homeland, possibly forever, was heart wrenching. "My parents once told me that the day we left Laos, my name was written on the sandy shores of the Mekong River," Saengmany recalls, "reminding me that Laos will always be a part of me."[47] The Ratsabouts made it to a refugee camp in Thailand, where they became family number NP002870. Camp life revolved around paperwork, medical examinations, and waiting. After two and a half years, the Ratsabouts received final clearance to resettle in the United States. Each member of the family was given a new identification number, photographed, and fingerprinted. Four-year-old Saengmany became refugee no. 129 337 5/6. They then boarded a plane to the Philippines, where they spent six months at the refugee processing center. Saengmany and his siblings attended day care and school while their parents attended classes in cultural orientation, English as a second language, and vocational training. On July 31, 1986, a series of Northwest Airlines flights took them from Manila to Seattle, Minneapolis, and finally, to Atlanta. They joined 120,000 ethnic Lao refugees who were admitted into the United States from 1972 to 1992. Today, the states with the largest Lao American populations are California, Texas, Minnesota, and Washington.[48]

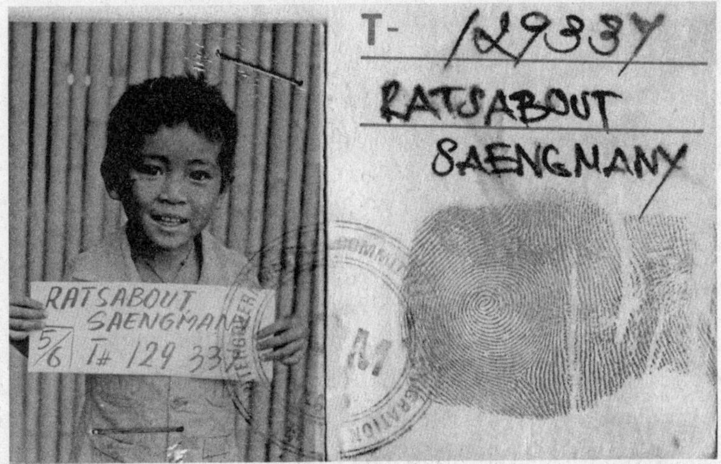

62. Saengmany Ratsabout, on the day that he left Na Pho refugee camp in Thailand for the United States, 1986. His father's fingerprint is attached to his photo and identification number.

Hmong who were not lucky enough to be evacuated from Laos in 1975 faced months and years of struggle. After the Pathet Lao declared the formation of the Lao People's Democratic Republic in December 1975, the new government made it clear that those who had fought against the communists, like the Hmong, would be punished. The official Pathet Lao newspaper announced that it was "necessary to extirpate, down to the root, the Hmong minority."[49]

At the former military base at Long Cheng and in other places, prisons were established to house all Hmong who were suspected of aiding General Vang Pao. Eventually, as many as 30,000 Hmong were either put in prison or placed under tight military security under the new government. They faced months and years of hard labor, starvation, and torture.[50] Hmong remaining in the country also came under attack from poisonous chemicals, including one called "yellow rain" to describe the colored liquid sprayed from helicopters and planes. According to Her Ge, who lived with his family in the area where these chemicals were released, helicopters came every other day in 1980 and spread poisons. As he recounted to a journalist, "the planes drop three different colors: yellow that is like dry power and people get very drunk and paralyzed; yellow that is sticky and people get fever with vomiting with blood; and the blue color which is sticky and . . . gives people the fever, dizziness and vomiting." The thirty-six-year-old, his wife, and their children were all struck by the toxins. His six-year-old son did not survive.[51]

Hmong families faced harrowing decisions about whether to leave, who should go, and how they would escape. As Mai Vang Thao explained, "We stayed as long as we could, but when we could no longer survive safely we followed General Vang Pao to Thailand." Trying to evade the communists, these escapees hid in the jungles for months and sometimes years before deciding to tackle the arduous trek to the Mekong and across to Thailand and the refugee camps. "We just kept running and hiding," Thao recalled.[52] Only half survived the journey. Ma Lee, her husband, and two young sons spent five years in the jungle hiding from Pathet Lao and Vietnamese forces. They survived by eating dirt and the pith from banana trees as they tried to stay one step ahead of their pursuers. One evening while Lee was sleeping, Vietnamese troops caught up with their group. "There were bullets flying everywhere. I mean, we could feel them going by our ears. There were so many bullets." One of them found her six-year-old son, and he died in her arms.[53]

Once families arrived at the banks of the Mekong, they faced more danger. Having lived most of their lives in the mountains, many had never learned how to swim. Yeng Xiong, her husband, and their three young children reached the river's banks in 1980. They made string out of bamboo reeds. Yeng was tied to her husband, and her oldest child was tied to her. She put her two youngest children, including her eleven-month-old baby boy, inside her baby carrier and strapped it on her back. Then they entered the river. The family struggled in the strong current, went under water, and the baby carrier became untied. The baby fell out and began to float away. "[My husband] tried to swim to catch him but couldn't," Yeng tearfully recalled. When the family finally made it to shore, Yeng looked everywhere for her son. "The people . . . who didn't make it, they all washed up on the bank. Only my baby wasn't there." Yeng and her husband were forced to abandon their search and went on to the refugee camp at Ban Vinai. They were eventually resettled in the United States after eight years and had three children in the refugee camp and five more in the United States. But more than thirty years after she crossed the Mekong River, the baby carrier that she used that fateful day remains a symbol of the great losses she suffered as part of her refugee journey. "We used this to carry our children to a better place in hopes of giving them a better life," she explained. "But things don't go the way you want them to. After my baby passed away, I never used that carrier again."[54]

Over 102,000 people fled Laos for Thailand by 1980. Ninety-five percent of them were Hmong.[55] The first camp established for Hmong refugees was at Ban Namphong, a military base in northeastern Thailand. Refugees who subsequently crossed the Mekong River to Thailand were settled in camps at Nong Khai, Wat Samakkhi, and Ban Vinai. As the exodus of Hmong from Laos continued, the camps ballooned. There were 22,000 Hmong crammed into Nong Khai by 1977. New arrivals were given only plastic sheeting to protect themselves from the rain, and they were forced to make their own shelter with little or no materials. When Dr. Mace Goldfarb volunteered at Ban Vinai camp in 1979, he found 42,000 people living in extremely crowded and unsanitary conditions, but he also found a "bustling marketplace" with tailors, restaurants, and barbershops, and weekend soccer games that helped to make life in camp a little bit more bearable.[56]

For the Hmong who were able to reach the refugee camps, there were three options available. The first was to return to Laos and face almost certain capture and death by the Pathet Lao and Vietnamese forces patrolling the border area. The second was to remain waiting in the camps despite growing tensions with the Thai government and rumors of cutbacks in essential aid. Or lastly, they could apply for permanent resettlement in another country.

Refugees faced difficult, heart-wrenching decisions. The Hmong contemplated long and hard before deciding to leave family members behind in the camp with no assurances that they would ever see each other again. Mao Heu Thao, who arrived in Minnesota from Ban Vinai in 1976, explained that her greatest fear was that she would be separated from her parents, aunts and uncles, and brothers and sisters forever. "What if they got sick or I got sick? What if one of us died? We wouldn't be able to be there for each other," she recalled years later. "The departure marked a sad and heartbreaking moment in my life, but I closed my eyes and tried to exist from day to day. I didn't want to be trapped in the refugee camp."[57] From the camps, Hmong refugees were resettled to the United States and to other Western countries.

15

Making a New Home: Hmong Refugees and Hmong Americans

The resettlement of Southeast Asian refugees in the United States begun in 1975 eventually brought 1.2 million Vietnamese, Cambodian, Lao, and Hmong refugees to the country and transformed America's involvement in refugee issues around the world. Their arrival in the United States, however, was just the beginning of their American journeys. "Compassion fatigue" soon set in, and as Americans expressed growing concern about immigration, Southeast Asian refugees struggled to feel at home in the United States.

More than a quarter of a million Hmong from Laos left for the United States. They fled with few resources and have faced considerable obstacles. In many cases, they have been set decidedly outside the model minority Asian American success narrative. In spite of these struggles, Hmong Americans have not only made new homes for themselves, they have also played important roles in the making of contemporary Asian America.

After years of war, escape, and waiting in refugee camps, coming to the United States was simultaneously joyful and terrifying for many Southeast Asian refugees. Pa Xiong Gonzalo, who resettled in the United States with her parents and five siblings from Laos in 1979, felt as if she had entered "a whole new world."[1] Understanding and learning basic survival skills in the United States was often difficult. Few Hmong had lived in cities before the war or had acquired enough formal education to learn how to read or write. Once proudly self-sufficient, many Hmong now felt helpless because they could not communicate with the people around them. Finding familiar foods, navigating through busy city streets, and surviving the bitterly cold weather in the northeastern and midwestern United States were all new challenges that often seemed insurmountable.

New appliances and technologies could also be a source of confusion. In 1983, a film crew followed two recently arrived Hmong refugee families in Seattle and captured their introduction to indoor plumbing, electricity, and various household appliances like the heater, kitchen fan, and thermostat in an urban public housing complex. Mang Vang, a widow with five children, expressed frustration. "How can I use all of these things?" she asked, overwhelmed. The apartment assistant manager, another Hmong refugee, patiently explained, "This is life in America. You have to learn."[2]

Over time, Hmong and other Southeast Asian refugees were able to manage their initial shock and settled into daily routines. Other challenges remained, however. The government's policy of dispersing refugees throughout the country meant that the first arrivals found themselves scattered across the states with few support networks to find employment and housing and to sustain and build communities in a new land. Ly Vang had taken comfort in the fact that there were a number of other Hmong families on her plane from Thailand to the United States in 1976. But when the plane landed in Chicago and the groups and families all started going their separate ways, Vang described feeling utterly alone and anxious. "You wonder where you're going, what you'll do, and what kind of life you will have. How will we survive? Will we be safe?" Vang and her husband arrived in Minnesota in 1976 and found that their sponsors had winter coats, an apartment, and food ready for them. Still, while they had everything they needed materially, Vang explains that "our hearts were empty." They were alone, and for some, these early years were overwhelming.[3]

Like other Southeast Asian refugees, Hmong were often placed in poor, urban neighborhoods and were mixed in with other low-income families in public housing complexes. In the Twin Cities, these included the Phillips and Near North neighborhoods in Minneapolis and Frogtown in St. Paul.

Liberty Plaza, managed by the Dayton Presbyterian Church in St. Paul, became home to some of the first groups of arrivals. As more Hmong arrived in the Twin Cities, word spread that Liberty Plaza, as well as St. Paul's Mount Airy, McDonough, and Roosevelt homes, were places where Hmong could live together and assist each other.[4]

The search for employment began almost immediately after securing housing. Many faced uphill battles with little English, nonagricultural skills or work experience, and inadequate job placement and training assistance. As a result, Hmong refugees had persistently high rates of unemployment, poverty, and dependency on federal and state assistance in the early years of resettlement. In 1982, only 20 percent of Hmong adults were employed in the Twin Cities area, and 85 percent of households were receiving some form of public assistance. Even those with jobs often had difficulty supporting their families on the low wages they earned.[5] The trend continued into the next decade. The 1990 U.S. Census found that 65 percent of Hmong Americans were unemployed and more than 60 percent lived below the poverty line.[6] The Hmong were among the most frustrated with their predicament. As one man interviewed in Minnesota explained in 1982: "Many Americans say that the Hmong are lazy and they do not want to work. Hmong do not like to hear that. If the Hmong get a chance to have a job and they turn out to be lazy, then the Americans can say that. But the Hmong do not have jobs, no chance to work, so how can people say they are lazy? Everybody wants to work."[7]

During and after the tumultuous years of war, flight, and resettlement, many Hmong families experienced tremendous change that contributed to the challenges they faced in the early resettlement years. Men's and women's roles changed, as did the relationships between children and parents, elders and youth, families and clans. Like many patriarchal cultures, authority and respect in Hmong families were granted to men, especially older men. Women played supporting and nurturing roles. After resettlement, however, some Hmong men, especially those whose skills did not match the jobs available to them, found their ability to support their families—and with it, their authority and sense of selves—changed and diminished. Some Hmong women were finding it easier to find work outside the home and to learn

English as compared to Hmong men. With more economic power, they were demanding equality in their homes and communities. Husbands like Soua Teng Vang, who had served in the Lao army as a physician's assistant and resettled in Fresno, California, for example, found his traditional role as a Hmong male provider turned upside down. "Is a Hmong man a man when he can't control his wife?" he asked an interviewer in 1998. "Here [in the United States] . . . Hmong women are really changing. I am confused. I don't know what to do. Women are supposed to serve their husband, but now they are arguing that sharing the duty is better. This makes many Hmong men feel stressful—to argue every day about equality around the house."[8]

Bilingual children also began to wield more power within families due to their English language capabilities and their skills as family translators. Lillian Faderman and Ghia Xiong explained a common predicament among the older refugee generation: "it's hard to present yourself as a wise man if your sons or daughters have to teach you how to cross the street or dial the phone." Struggling to adapt to so many changes at once, many Hmong refugees felt like they had been reduced to helpless children in their own homes.[9] Kia Vue told Faderman and Xiong that in the United States "everything I do, I just depend on my children. Whatever I need, I just have to wait and wait until they do it for me."[10] Others remarked on how this change in the generational power structure was causing Hmong youth to ignore their parents' authority. As Ka Pao Xiong explained to an interviewer, "Our children are assimilating into American society, so they no longer listen to us."[11]

During the 1980s and 1990s, Hmong parents and elders had reason to be anxious about how their children were faring. Researchers identified high dropout rates among women who married and had children while still in high school.[12] Poverty, feelings of powerlessness, and alienation among Hmong boys and young men all contributed to the rise in gang activity. Vicki Xiong, who escaped from Laos with her family as a young child, tried to explain to an interviewer how both of her brothers ended up in gangs during the 1990s. "My father did try to discipline them so they would be good boys, but they don't listen to him." Although their father was a policeman in Laos and led his entire extended family across the Mekong River to safety in Thailand, in America, her brothers only saw him as a helpless refugee. "He doesn't have any power here," Vicki explained. "He doesn't know what to do, how to get along in America. . . . So maybe my brothers just thought they had to find another family in gangs."[13]

Other young Hmong Americans struggled to go to school and take on the added responsibilities of caring for their younger siblings while their parents worked. Dawb and Kao Kalia Yang were just twelve and eleven years old when they started taking care of their two younger siblings after school and all night because their parents worked the nightshift in the factory. "We know it is illegal to leave children home at night in America, but we cannot do anything now. Help us make life possible in America," their parents told them. "We did our best to help," Kao Kalia remembers. "There was no time to learn how to take care of a baby; we learned by doing."[14]

As the numbers of Hmong refugees coming to the United States grew, media portrayals often presented them in stereotypical and demeaning ways. Instead of characterizing them as war veterans who had earned political asylum, the Hmong were portrayed as primitive and backward peoples who lacked the abilities to survive in the modern world and assimilate into the United States. "Laos Nomads Find U.S. Life Confusing," the *Minneapolis Star* explained in 1979. Hmong culture was "far removed from 20th century America" and "clashes with American ways." The reporter described his impressions of one St. Paul family who welcomed him into their home. They looked like they "just stepped out of a National Geographic magazine" with their "colorful" costumes and "darkened teeth," he explained.[15] Other press reports blamed the "vastly different customs" between Hmong and American cultures that made it difficult for Hmong to "cope with modern American ideas."[16]

Researchers and other journalists added to the idea that the "cultural differences" between Hmong and Americans were great, perhaps even insurmountable.[17] Anne Fadiman's bestselling book, *The Spirit Catches You and You Fall Down*, recounted the story of Lia Lee, an epileptic Hmong girl, and the clashes that occurred between her American doctors, who wanted to treat Lee with conventional drugs and procedures, and her parents, who believed that Lia's condition was related to her interaction with the Hmong spirit world, as a disastrous "collision of two cultures."[18] Unlike other Asian Americans, the Hmong—and other Southeast Asian refugees—were excluded from the model minority Asian American success story also circulating at the time.

Amid growing concerns about immigration in general and the number of refugee arrivals in particular, misunderstandings, conflicts, and outright discrimination and violence directed against Southeast Asians became common. Most Americans had little idea of who the Hmong were and why they were in the United States. It was easy for uninformed individuals to view the new arrivals as government freeloaders who were not assimilating into American society. Despite regulations that offered Southeast Asian refugees the same level of federal assistance as others in the same income bracket, many Americans complained that the newcomers received more financial assistance, priority for housing, and other benefits. "They're the aliens, living off my tax dollar, that's what fries me," a St. Paul resident complained to the *Saint Paul Dispatch* in 1980.[19] Hmong families in St. Paul public housing projects had Molotov cocktails thrown into their units or left in their mailboxes. Gunshots were fired into windows of refugee homes, injuring residents. Two Hmong brothers walking home in the middle of the night from their dishwashing jobs were beaten unconscious by two white attackers wielding clubs.[20] Not reported to the police or covered in the newspapers were the countless hate-filled interactions that many Hmong Americans experienced. Writer Kao Kalia Yang remembers that people often yelled at her and her family to "go home." "Next to waves of hello, we received the middle finger."[21]

Such news reports of violence, discrimination, and resentment directed toward refugees reflected the compassion fatigue that began to set in during the late 1970s and early 1980s. The initial resettlement of refugees from Vietnam in 1975 led to what seemed to be a never-ending international refugee crisis. A *Time* magazine article headline baldly stated that the United States had "no more room for refugees" in May of 1982.[22]

The U.S. government tried to keep pace with the growing exodus of peoples from Southeast Asia to address both "land" peoples who were mostly Hmong, Lao, and Cambodian, and Vietnamese "boat" peoples. A series of "parole" programs granted the U.S. attorney general ad hoc authority to allow into the United States any alien on an emergency basis with no real numerical limit or oversight from Congress. Eleven thousand were admitted in 1976. Another 15,000 were allowed into the country in 1977. From 1978 to 1980, around 268,000 refugees had been admitted into the United States.[23]

As more refugees continued to come from Southeast Asia, U.S. resettlement efforts began to highlight a late-twentieth-century phase of the debate over Asian immigration. Similar to past debates that focused on whether Asian immigration was good or bad for the country, there were vehement supporters and opponents. On the one hand, humanitarians pointed to the importance of keeping the doors open to those fleeing persecution in Southeast Asia, especially since they were being targeted because of their ties to the United States. Groups like the Citizens' Commission on Indochinese Refugees also emphasized the moral necessity of offering refuge to those fleeing the genocide in Cambodia. Highly publicized reports of refugees crowded into unseaworthy boats and cramped into makeshift refugee camps in Southeast Asia led to growing pressure on Washington to take action. Sympathetic lawmakers argued that traditional restrictionist and anti-immigrant sentiment had no place in the United States. Joseph Califano, secretary of the Department of Health, Education and Welfare, stated that the refugee issue required the United States to "reveal to the world—and more importantly to ourselves—whether we truly live by our ideals or simply carve them on our monuments."[24]

On the other hand, the initial welcome of refugees eventually led to debate, negative reaction, and a renewed anti-immigrant backlash as the numbers of new refugees (including those who were less educated and less skilled) as well as the cost of their resettlement grew. As early as April 1975, a Harris poll found that 54 percent of Americans surveyed believed that Southeast Asians should be excluded, while 36 percent believed they should be admitted. California congressman Burt Talcott echoed anti-Asian sentiment from the early twentieth century when he expressed American fears of another Asian invasion. "Damn it, we [already] have too many Orientals," he is quoted as saying.[25] The hatred was palpable to the Hmong. "It seems that Americans hate us," one refugee told a resettlement worker in 1983.[26]

By 1978, news and public opinion polls revealed that the majority of those questioned opposed the relaxation of immigration laws to admit additional refugees. In the wake of an economic recession, growing unemployment, high inflation, and the continuing divisions surrounding the Vietnam War, the specter of large numbers of Southeast Asian refugees needing economic assistance, jobs, and social welfare services prompted a strong backlash. In Minneapolis and St. Paul, rumors circulated that the government was granting higher welfare benefits, free apartments, and even tax-free income. Concerns that the new refugees would fail to assimilate and fears that they would take away jobs were also prevalent.[27]

An international refugee conference convened in Geneva in 1979 tried to put more order into the resettlement system. By November 1980 the United Nations High Commissioner for Refugees reported that forty nations had resettled 300,000 people from Southeast Asian and Hong Kong refugee camps. And while the number of people leaving Vietnam slowed, it did not stop altogether. Refugee camps continued to be overcrowded. One year after the conference, in May of 1979, there were still 97,000 people in the camps.[28]

In the United States, the Refugee Act of 1980 tried to solve some of these problems. It affirmed the U.S.'s commitment to humanitarianism, but it also restricted the number of refugees admitted into the country and imposed new regulations on where they would be resettled and how they would be integrated into the country. It became the first comprehensive refugee legislation in U.S. history. With its explicit welcome to refugees fleeing communist countries, the new law served the U.S.'s Cold War politics. But it also incorporated the broad language of the United Nations' definition of "refugee" as a person who had a "well-founded fear of persecution" owing to race, religion, nationality, or membership in a social group or political movement and thus allowed refugees from all over the world to come to the United States, not just those who were refugees from communist countries as was previously the case.

The act was characterized by remarkable political consensus from both the left and the right. Co-sponsored by Democratic senator Edward Kennedy and Republican senator Strom Thurmond, the bill was hailed by lawmakers as further evidence of the nation's egalitarian and humanitarian policy toward immigrants and refugees. Congressman Peter Rodino defined the Refugee Act as "one of the most important pieces of humanitarian legislation ever enacted by a U.S. Congress. . . . The United States once again [has] demonstrated its concern for the homeless, the defenseless, and the persecuted people who fall victim to tyrannical and oppressive government regimes."[29] The 1980 Refugee Act marked the United States' new involvement in refugee affairs globally and would transform the ways in which the country would administer refugee resettlement for decades after.

Obscured by this humanitarian rhetoric, however, was the act's new restrictions on the number of new refugees allowed into the country through a 50,000 annual quota that actually slowed the admission of Southeast Asian refugees. The act did, however, allow for the admission of asylees, refugees already in the United States who wanted to apply for entry and permanent residence. To minimize the growing public backlash against refugees, other aspects of the bill focused on geographic dispersal, economic self-sufficiency, and assimilation.[30]

Such resettlement policies backfired in many ways and actually slowed and thwarted refugee integration. Isolated from long-lost family members and others who were sometimes the only ones who could understand their experiences of war, dislocation, loss, and struggle, Southeast Asian refugees often felt lost and alone. Many host communities also lacked culturally and linguistically appropriate social services.[31] The strong Hmong patriarchal clan system, made up of approximately eighteen different clans, had traditionally been the core means of organizing and responding to community needs. Resettlement and dispersal, however, disrupted these ties and roles. Faced with these problems, many Hmong rejected U.S. policies and resettled themselves a second time to be among family members and other Hmong as a form of survival in a new land.[32] Many went to the Twin Cities of Minneapolis and St. Paul.

With its long, harsh winters, Minnesota was an unlikely place to resettle Hmong refugees. But with a number of social service providers, a history of refugee resettlement, the activism and organization of the Hmong community itself, and a strong economy, the state of Minnesota became a magnet for Hmong refugees. By the late twentieth century, enough families had either been resettled or voluntarily relocated there that St. Paul emerged as the "Hmong Capital of the World."[33]

In 1976, the first Hmong refugees began to arrive in Minnesota when the International Institute social service agency and members of the Dayton Presbyterian Church in St. Paul sponsored the first families to the state. Neither group had ever heard of the Hmong before, but when International Institute case worker Olga Zoltai, herself a Hungarian refugee, learned that her agency could help resettle Southeast Asian refugees as part of new assistance programs, she phoned her institute's director to lobby for the organization to get involved. Once she received the green light, Zoltai took charge of the resettlement program and soon welcomed the first Hmong family to the Twin Cities.[34]

63. Hmong students at the Lao Family Community Center, Young Men's Christian Association, St. Paul.

From this early trickle of refugees came a steady stream by the late 1970s. As the primary refugee group in the region, the Hmong benefited from a number of assistance programs designed especially for their needs, including employment, English language classes, farming, and vocational training programs. By the early 1980s, city and state governments as well as schools and private organizations had responded with programs of their own. Catholic Charities, Lutheran Immigration and Refugee Service, and Church World Service all began their own resettlement programs, and there were state government committees, offices, and advisory councils established to address refugee resettlement as well. Because of these programs, the Twin Cities were able to offer more bilingual language classes and job training programs than many other resettlement sites.[35]

As the number of new arrivals grew in the state, Hmong living elsewhere in the country began to relocate and move to Minnesota as well. News spread via audiocassette tapes and word of mouth that life was "nice" in Minnesota, and ethnic leaders began recruiting individuals with specific skills to join them. Family reunification was another key reason. Sixty-four percent of Hmong surveyed in a 1982 community study told researchers that they moved to the Twin Cities to be with family.[36] This secondary migration happened almost immediately after the initial resettlement phase. Gaoly Yang described how Minnesota seemed to provide a "friendlier environment for newcomers." There was housing, schools, and jobs. "I recruited my sister, who [had] resettled in Philadelphia. My husband encouraged many of his relatives to move here."[37] Mao Vang Lee's first stop had been Manchester, Connecticut, in 1978. She and her family had started to feel at home there. But when they traveled to Minnesota for a Hmong New Year celebration, they found themselves in a larger community, and the Lees began to imagine a new life in the upper Midwest. "Mom and dad: we belong here," Mao's children said. "People look like us. We don't belong in Connecticut." In 1995, the family moved to Minnesota.[38] By 1991, the Hmong population in the state had grown more than tenfold, making it the fastest growing minority group in the state according to the U.S. Census. By 2000, the Twin Cities had the largest concentration of Hmong people in the country.[39]

Secondary migration has allowed the Hmong in the Twin Cities to reunite families, rebuild communities, establish mutual assistance organizations, gain some economic stability, and become involved in local and national politics. For many, family and clan remain central sources of strength in their new lives in Minnesota. Kao Kalia Yang remembers huge extended-family gatherings where the adults would talk about how to survive in the United States and exchange strategies for advancement. Uncles, aunts, and older cousins gathered together to share information about daily survival tactics as well as larger philosophical questions: How can a family save money? Which job training programs are the best? Where is the best place to buy a 100-pound bag of Kokuho rice? How can the Hmong survive in America? Over the years, these big family meetings were used to instill certain values in the younger generation in order to spur them on toward socioeconomic success. Adults called meetings, Yang recalls, when "they were worried that their children were wasting opportunities to become educated people in America." The "bad older cousins," who spoke English at home, hung out with friends, and did not listen to their parents, were not to be looked up to. The role models were those who graduated from high school and went on to college. As Yang recalled, the message in her family was clear: "We almost died in the war. Many Hmong people died in the war. We are fortunate to have made it to America. . . . Your mothers and fathers are not educated people. We never had the chance. We do not speak English. You can."[40]

Hmong families in the Twin Cities also found ways of building organizations that served their new needs in the United States. In particular, a new generation of Hmong Americans, especially those who could speak English, became important leaders and advocates in the region. In 1977, the Association of Hmong in Minnesota was formed to assist Hmong refugees in finding jobs and getting access to programs and services. It also worked closely with government and sponsoring agencies, schools, social service providers, and others to advocate for the needs of Hmong refugees and to act as cultural brokers.[41] Another organization, Hmong American Partnership, was formed in 1990 to provide culturally appropriate social services like classes in English and technology, academic and career mentorship for at-risk teenagers, parental support, and job placement.[42] Hmong women also formed their own organizations, like the Association for the Advancement of Hmong Women in Minnesota, to address the specific issues and needs of women.[43]

By the 1990s, local newspapers were recognizing Hmong students graduating from college and "blazing new trails." In 1992, one newspaper article covered six college graduations in one extended family. The graduates included Mee Moua, who would later become the first Hmong American elected to a state legislature.[44] By the early twenty-first century, the English-language *Hmong Times*, the self-proclaimed "Newspaper of the Hmong Community," started running columns featuring "Hmong Firsts." In 2000, Yer Moua-Lor was heralded as the "first female Hmong chiropractor." In

2001, Mee Moua Vang was listed as the "first Hmong state certified court translator in the U.S.," and Lee Pao Xiong was congratulated as the first Asian president of the Minneapolis Urban Coalition, an organization known for addressing concerns of peoples of color.[45]

Other firsts were of a more personal nature. When Kao Kalia Yang's younger siblings were born in the United States, the family seemed to become more rooted than ever in their adopted country. Inspiration came from these "ready-made Americans in our arms, the little faces of boys and girls who spoke Hmong with American stiffness." With the newest family members growing up in the United States, Yang explains, "we could not remain just Hmong any longer. . . . We had no more lands to return to. . . . A new chapter of our lives unfolded as we strived to become Americans."[46]

By the 1990s, Hmong Americans were celebrating other firsts in local, state, and national politics. Choua Lee, a twenty-two-year-old expectant mother, made headlines when she became the first Hmong candidate for public office by running for a position on the St. Paul School Board. The mainstream press made a big issue about her candidacy being a "radical concept in male-dominated Hmong society." Lee's own message focused on the needs of students. Having tutored Hmong students in local high schools, she knew from firsthand experience that many were not learning how to read and write. But she also recognized that her victory signaled an important milestone for the entire Hmong American community.[47]

Hmong American politics has also emphasized the Hmong peoples' distinctive history as U.S. allies during the Vietnam War. Veterans tell and retell the story of how Hmong fought for the United States in its struggle against communism in order to portray themselves as "loyal Americans *before* they even set foot on American soil," according to historian Chia Vang. Elderly Hmong men often wear impressive military uniforms and medals at public events. This public display of Hmong military service and the advocacy of groups like the Lao Veterans of America have led to public recognition of the Hmong contribution in the nation's capital, in Arlington National Cemetery, and in many other locations around the country. Most notably, these efforts helped secure U.S. congressional support for the Hmong Veterans' Naturalization Act of 2000, which helped 45,000 people become citizens.[48]

Another political strategy involves mobilizing Hmong to exercise their voting rights and to elect Hmong American politicians to advocate on behalf of Hmong American issues. Some of this political activity first coalesced in the 1990s when welfare reform threatened to cut off aid to many elderly disabled veterans and their families. They and their advocates were quick to mobilize, and as a result Minnesota and thirteen other states developed a food assistance program for those—like the Hmong—who would no longer be covered under the federal government's program.[49]

Like other Asian Americans, Hmong Americans have also learned how to "put American politics to work for them."[50] In 2002, lawyer Mee Moua won election to the Minnesota Senate and helped to blaze a new trail in Hmong American politics. In the years since, Hmong Americans have held key staff positions in the offices of U.S. congressional representatives from the state as well as in the mayor's office in St. Paul.[51]

Homeland politics—or the political, financial, and cultural relations Hmong in the United States have maintained with Hmong in the Lao People's Democratic Republic and with Hmong around the world—make up another focus of political activism. Like other Asian Americans who retain ties to their native countries, Hmong Americans have been active in shaping events in their homelands. Over time, these ties have changed according to shifting priorities of Hmong Americans as well as changing international relations between the United States and Laos. Many of the former Hmong military leaders who arrived as refugees in the 1970s and 1980s worked with Vang Pao to raise awareness about continuing persecution of the Hmong in Laos and to support political and military resistance to communist rule in the country. The United Lao National Liberation Front (ULNLF), also known as Neo Hom, called on all Laotian people to support these efforts, and the organization played a large role in Hmong communities in the United States. By the 1990s, support for the organization had diminished. Many former supporters had become rooted in the United States and no longer desired to return home. Charges of corruption and questionable fundraising tactics also tarnished the group's image, and when Vang was arrested by U.S. authorities in California for allegedly purchasing illegal weapons and for plotting to overthrow the Lao government in 2007—charges that were later dropped—the organization suffered another damaging blow.[52]

Other Hmong American efforts have centered on advocating for the resettlement of remaining Hmong refugees in the United States. When news that the United Nations–sponsored refugee camps in Thailand were beginning to close in 1992, Hmong American activists took to the streets to voice their concern that relatives and friends would be persecuted by the Lao government. They pressured President Bill Clinton's administration to keep Thai refugee camps open or ease U.S. immigration rules. Between 1992 and 1994, more than 25,000 Hmong were resettled in the United States, and an additional 15,000 arrived in the country between 2004 and 2008.[53]

Like other Asian Americans today, Hmong Americans represent a diverse community in the midst of great growth and change. Statistics tell us certain things. The 2010 U.S. Census counted 260,073 persons of Hmong origin living in the United States. This represents a 40 percent increase from the last count in 2000. The states with the largest Hmong American populations are California, Minnesota, and Wisconsin. The Minneapolis–St. Paul metropolitan area continues to be home to the largest urban Hmong population in the country.[54] The percentage of Hmong Americans with jobs increased from 24 percent in 1990 to 56 percent in 2010 (compared to a 60 percent employment rate for the general U.S. population in 1990 and a 65 percent employment rate in 2010). The decline in overall poverty in the Hmong population from 64 percent in 1990 and 38 percent in 2000 to 25 percent in 2010 is also significant. The number of Hmong Americans graduating from colleges and universities is growing, from 3 percent in 1990 to over 11 percent in 2009. And the kinds of jobs they are getting have changed, too. More hold management or professional jobs than in previous years.[55]

Other markers include Hmong homeownership and entrepreneurship. In 1990, 40 percent of Hmong Americans owned their own homes. By 2006, Hmong homeownership had increased to 54 percent, though it declined slightly during the economic recession beginning in 2008. Beginning in the 1970s, Hmong farmers began using vacant lots to grow vegetables that they could not find in local markets. In the 1990s, Hmong farmers in the Twin Cities helped revitalize the struggling farmer's market in Minneapolis and were central to the emergence of a new market in St. Paul. Benefiting from the burgeoning interest in eating more local and organic produce, Hmong farmers have become important to this growing segment of the regional economy.[56]

Hmong-owned companies in Minnesota generated more than $100 million in 2004 and ethnic businesses like real estate companies, restaurants, markets, and the only Hmong bookstore in the country dot St. Paul streets. In 1999, the *St. Paul Pioneer Press* dubbed the city's University Avenue "the Asian Main Street." The Hmong Village Shopping Center in St. Paul houses professional offices, restaurants, an arcade, and a market full of booths selling everything from roasted chicken legs, bubble tea, DVDs, pizza, and eyebrow waxing services.[57]

Nevertheless, the same set of statistics also reveals remaining gaps and obstacles that persist among many Asian American groups. Ninety-one percent of Hmong American households had earnings in 2010, but their per capita income lags dramatically behind that of the general U.S. population. In 2010, per capita income for the general U.S. population was $26,279, whereas it was $11,766 for Hmong Americans. They are heavily concentrated in the declining manufacturing job sector. They have some of the lowest bachelor's degree attainment rates across racial and ethnic groups. Just 14.5 percent of Hmong Americans twenty-five years and older hold bachelor's degrees, compared to 31.4 percent of non-Hispanic whites, 18 percent of non-Hispanic blacks, 50.2 percent of non-Hispanic Asians, and 13.1 percent of Hispanics. Hmong women lag even further behind their male counterparts in obtaining post-secondary education. Few Hmong American households have any retirement income, and as the population ages, financial support for elders is a challenge. Most strikingly, the Hmong remain one of the poorest groups in the United States. In 2009, almost 27 percent of all Hmong American families remained in poverty. In general, Hmong men earn a median annual income almost $16,000 less than other men in the country. And Hmong American women earn less in median annual income than men. The Hmong poverty rate is twice as high as that of the general U.S. population.[58]

Media stereotyping, racism, and discrimination continue to be problems as well. Portrayals of Hmong as backward, primitive, resistant to change, patriarchal, and unable to assimilate persisted through the early twenty-first century in newspapers and popular culture. Such media portrayals contributed to the ways in which real-life tragedies and racial tensions have played out in recent years. In 2005, Hmong American Chai Soua Vang was found guilty of shooting six white hunters to death in the northern Wisconsin woods. He claimed that he acted in self-defense after being subjected to racial slurs and intimidation. Two years later in the same state, Hmong American hunter Cha Vang was killed by a white hunter who told police that the Hmong "are mean and kill everything." In the weeks following the Chai Soua Vang incident, media coverage focused on the alleged "culture clash" between Hmong and American peoples that portrayed the former as unassimilated lawbreakers and trespassers. Bumper stickers reading "Save a Deer. Shoot a Mung" appeared in Wisconsin, and Hmong Americans in Minnesota and Wisconsin reported being victims of hate crimes. Some had "Killers" spray-painted on their homes. Others received death threats.[59]

These stereotypes echoed those projected onto other Asian immigrants and Asian Americans: the unassimilable foreigner and immigrant invasion that endangers the United States. Hmong have also been uniquely stereotyped as "perpetual refugees" regardless of their immigration or citizenship status or how long they have been in the United States.[60] Victories like the 2000 Hmong Veterans' Naturalization Act represented the political inclusion of Hmong Americans into the country. At the same time, the Hmong have simultaneously been portrayed as rescued, yet unassimilated, refugees, "natural" soldiers who were effective in the mountains of Laos, but dangerous on American city streets, anticommunist friends of freedom during the Cold War who became dangerous terrorists during the War on Terror, and emerging Asian American model minorities and new citizens, but also violent gangbangers and criminals.[61]

Like other Asian Americans, Hmong Americans are engaging in lively debates about identity, asking themselves what it means to be Hmong, Hmong American, and American. In the forty years since the first Hmong refugees arrived, the population has grown and diversified. Many members of the refugee generation still long for Laos. Their children and grandchildren see themselves as American, but they also honor and preserve Hmong history and culture. If the war years were focused on fighting for freedom and the early years in the United States were characterized by the struggle to survive, the twenty-first century has brought a number of new questions and issues.

A new generation of Hmong American leaders has risen up to organize against racism and discrimination. "We're not going to stand for racism anymore!" protesters declared in 1998 when Twin Cities radio host Tom Barnard made racist statements about Hmong culture following an infanticide committed by a thirteen-year-old Hmong girl in Wisconsin. Using the tragic event to ridicule Hmong customs and peoples, Barnard vehemently declared that the Hmong should "Assimilate or hit the goddamn road!" in his KQRS broadcast. Objectionable comments, jokes, and the use of an offensive "Asian" character who spoke in broken English continued to be mainstays of Barnard's show over the next several days.

Hmong activists responded by forming Community Action Against Racism (CAAR), a multiracial coalition of whites, Latinos, and Asian and African Americans that staged protests and publicized the issues. After the radio station and its hosts refused to apologize, CAAR successfully organized an economic boycott of the station and urged corporations and businesses to pull their advertising contracts. By the fall of 1998, KQRS had issued an official apology and agreed to air public service announcements to raise awareness about Hmong history and pride. CAAR accepted that it had won a major victory, but signaled that it would be ready to mobilize community members and their allies around future incidents. "The battle is won," CAAR leaders told the *Hmong Times* in November 1998, "but the war is not over."[62]

Hmong Americans are also questioning gender and family roles within their community. Specific expectations of what Hmong men and women should do and how they should act continue to be central in shaping their identity and their educational, life, and career choices. But what it means to be Hmong men and women—and how these norms are lived on a daily basis—have changed in the process of war and resettlement in the United States.[63] It is common for Hmong American boys, for example, to take on greater homemaking responsibilities, including such traditionally feminine duties as cooking, cleaning, and care of younger siblings, because their parents are busy working multiple jobs.[64]

And Hmong women are continuing to question and push against gender norms that confer an unequal status on women. Writer Ka Vang describes how "good Hmong girls" are constantly reminded that they are to prepare meals for the family, maintain their virtue, and pursue only feminine activities. Women and girls in Vang's family are also supposed to feed the men first at big gatherings and are not allowed to eat until the men finish. "I am tired of sitting at the women's table, gnawing on the little meat on a chicken neck while an uncle chews a hearty piece of chicken breast," Vang writes with frustration. Hmong women "deserve to be at the table with the Hmong men," she declares. And if they are not invited to the men's table, "then we will just have to create our own women's table and the men will have to refill their own dishes."[65]

Lesbian, gay, transgender, and bisexual Hmong American youth are also pushing the boundaries of gender roles, sexual orientation, and what it means to be both LGBT and Hmong American. Like other LGBT Asian Americans, Hmong Americans have begun to create support networks that serve the specific needs of the Hmong American LGBT community. There are now LGBT Hmong New Year celebrations as well as organizations that advocate for LGBT Hmong youth.[66]

Like other Asian Americans in the twenty-first century, Hmong Americans are also creating new ways of understanding and expressing cultural identities. One example is the changing meaning and production of *paj ntaub*, or "story cloths," a textile art unique to Hmong culture. Traditionally, Hmong girls and women sewed intricate patterns into clothing, baby carriers, and other functional art objects. Hmong women began creating *paj ntaub Amerika* story cloths in Thai refugee camps during the 1970s as a means of recording wartime experiences and remembering life in Laos through depictions of Hmong New Year celebrations, daily rural life, and folktales. They were also produced for a growing consumer market in Thailand and the United States, and the proceeds of *paj ntaub Amerika* sales could account for up for 90 percent of a family's income while in the refugee camps. The commercialization and commodification of *paj ntaub* gave some women the potential to earn money for the first time and contributed to their economic independence. The sewing arts and the production of *paj ntaub* remain culturally significant in Hmong American communities as a way of expressing memory, survival, individual creativity, collective identity, and Hmong culture in the past and present. But the messages have changed. While older *paj ntaub* record the history of the Hmong escape from Laos into Thailand, new *paj ntaub* tell of Hmong American achievements in education, what many Hmong families believe is a necessary first step toward achieving the American Dream.[67]

64. *Paj ntaub* depicting the Hmong fleeing persecution in Laos, crossing the Mekong River, and arriving at a refugee camp in Thailand.

In addition, there are now two Hmong New Year celebrations in the Twin Cities every fall. Reflecting the older generation's desire to hold on to Hmong traditions, the Minnesota Hmong New Year in St. Paul tries to keep Laos as the Hmong homeland and Hmong and Lao culture and identities front and center. In contrast, the Hmong American New Year in Minneapolis emphasizes a changing and fluid Hmong American identity. In St. Paul, the Hmong beauty queen wears a traditional Hmong dress and is photographed next to former military leaders. In Minneapolis, she wears an evening gown and is photographed next to that year's "Prince Charming," a young Hmong American man.[68]

65. *Paj ntaub* telling the story of Hmong Americans achieving academic success in the United States.

The role of memory and history—including documenting past practices of U.S. imperialism in Southeast Asia and continuing inequalities and human rights abuses for Hmong people—also affects the multiple ways in which Hmong Americans express their identities in local and global contexts. For Hmong American hip-hop artist Tou Saiko Lee, honoring and preserving Hmong culture and history means connecting with others around the corner and around the world. Growing up in the inner cities of Syracuse and St. Paul after being born in a Thai refugee camp, Tou Saiko and his brother Vong started writing rap music as a way to document and share their experiences as Hmong Americans.

66. Tou Saiko Lee and his grandmother Zhoua Cha perform as "Fresh Traditions," February 2011.

Tou Saiko's desire to write songs that are "relevant to Hmong no matter where we are in the world" also reflects the global and multigenerational dimensions of contemporary Hmong American life. And his attention to history in understanding his community's place in the United States and the world reflects a common trait shared across Asian American communities. The Lee brothers' hit song "30-Year Secret" recalls the suffering of the Hmong people, who were "persecuted and scorned" after the end of the war and the struggle to survive "working overtime" and "slug[ging] it out against the winter and snow" in the United States. It ends with a declaration that while Hmong Americans are "survivors," it is imperative to "remind your elders and educate the young," for discrimination in the United States and human rights abuses in Laos continue to threaten the Hmong people. More recently, Lee has formed a new group with his grandmother to pass on elders' stories in a blend of Hmong poetry chanting and American hip-hop. Blending old and new, the duo calls themselves "Fresh Traditions."[69]

16

Transnational Immigrants and Global Americans

Dipa Patel and her husband, Pratik, find themselves simultaneously rooted in both the United States and India. Pratik came to the United States from a small Gujarati town where he had grown up, earned a computer science degree, and opened a computer school with his cousins. When he moved to the United States, he found a job working the assembly line of a large telecommunications firm in the Boston area. At night, he works on his master's degree at Boston University. Dipa is a quality insurance supervisor at a computer manufacturing firm. After being in the country for five years, Pratik and Dipa filed for U.S. citizenship. Their two young daughters are growing up learning American nursery rhymes, and recently the Patel family bought their own home in the southern New Hampshire suburbs. By all appearances, the Patels are living the American Dream.

But as sociologist Peggy Levitt has shown, families like the Patels are pursuing the Indian Dream as well. Pratik and Dipa regularly send money home to support their retired parents in Gujarat. Pratik donates to the computer school he helped found in his home village, and in addition to paying the mortgage of their new home in New Hampshire, they have also renovated their family home in Bodeli, which now includes a new second story with a Western-style bathroom. Another way that they remain connected to their home state of Gujarat is through religion. They worship every weekend at the Hindu temple in Lowell, Massachusetts, and belong to the ISSO, a Hindu denomination in Gujarat that maintains its connections with its members around the world.

Dipa's and Pratik's transnational lives are made possible through their socioeconomic success in the United States, their close relationships to family remaining in India, and their strong Gujarati identities. Neither the U.S. nor the Indian government tries to limit this transnational activity. Recognizing the important role that nonresident Indians play in the economic development in India, the Indian government has worked very hard to facilitate these linkages. Beginning in 2003, India approved dual citizenship for Indians in the United States and the United Kingdom.[1]

Dipa and Pratik highlight one of the most defining features of recent Asian immigration to the United States: its transnational nature. Just as transpacific steamship travel revolutionized immigration from Asia in the late nineteenth century, recent technological advances in transportation and communication like frequent and cheaper air travel, email, cell phones, and social media have similarly transformed the ways in which people move and how they live their lives across borders today.

Contemporary immigrants come as part of new global patterns in which people are moving around the world, sometimes to multiple places over the course of their lifetimes, in search of better lives for themselves and for their families. Sometimes the move is temporary; sometimes it is permanent. Other times, it is circular, with people returning to the land of their birth or to the land of their parents' or even grandparents' birth. In the late twentieth and early twenty-first centuries, Asian immigrants practice all of these types of patterns: ongoing transnational migration across the Pacific, remigrations within the Americas, and even "return" migration to Asia. They are paving new ways of "becoming American" and of becoming "global" by figuring out how to situate themselves in a changing world.[2]

Not all immigrants are transnational, and living transnationally is not without risks or unintended consequences. Class status, gender, education, and income are important mitigating factors. U.S. international relations and concerns about national security also allow for some types of immigrant transnationalism to be accepted, and even celebrated, while the transnational activities of other immigrants—notably those who are connected to homelands suspected of terrorist activities—are viewed as threats.[3] But despite persistent inequalities, some have found a balance between "here" and "there" without rejecting an ethnic or a single national identity. This affects all of us. Recent immigrants and their children are a growing proportion of the United States. (In 2011, they made up 18 percent of the total population.) And Americans are becoming increasingly interconnected to the larger world, with all the promises and challenges that globalization brings. Thus, to understand transnational immigrant experiences is to understand what it means to be American in a global age.[4]

At one end of the economic spectrum are Asians who are "flexible citizens," the term that anthropologist Aihwa Ong uses to describe very elite immigrants who seek out the best sites for investment, work, and family relocation. "New strategies of flexible accumulation," Ong writes, "have promoted a flexible attitude toward citizenship." But so have real fears about political uncertainty. In the 1990s, 10 percent of all Hong Kong residents (around 600,000) held foreign passports as insurance against the former British colony's impending return to mainland Chinese rule in 1997. Caught between the declining economic power of Britain and surging capitalism in Asia, but unsure of what communist China's control over Hong Kong would be like, many sought out safe havens abroad.[5]

Some governments have adapted quickly to facilitate the entry of such individuals. Immigrant investors who bring a significant amount of capital with them, for example, have special access to the United States and Canada. An estimated 700,000 Chinese business immigrants brought billions of dollars of investment funds with them to Canada between 1983 and 1996, for example.[6] Together with other Asian immigrants from India, the Philippines, Hong Kong, Sri Lanka, Pakistan, and Taiwan, they have helped reinvigorate a "globally connected Pacific Canada" whose trade flows as well as social, cultural, and political connections have increasingly reoriented Canada to the Pacific.[7] In the United States, the immigrant investor (EB-5) visa program grants lawful permanent residence to foreign nationals who invest $500,000 or $1 million in U.S. businesses and create or preserve at least ten American jobs. Created as part of the Immigration Act of 1990, the immigration investor program sparked little interest until recently; now Asian immigrant investors, particularly from China, have almost maxed out the annual cap of 10,000 visas given to investors and their immediate family members.[8]

Globalization and new immigration laws have also created new types of sojourners engaged in "the Pacific shuttle." The Chinese farmer who left his home village for a life of hard work in a restaurant or laundry in the United States during the late nineteenth century has been replaced. Now there is the "astronaut" father who shuttles across the Pacific by air while his wife and children relocate to the United States to earn residency rights.

These new flexible family relationships—intact families living apart—oftentimes bump up against everyday realities that challenge prior arrangements, expectations, and family and gender roles. Some marriages end. Some parent-child relations suffer. Family relationships change. Chinese wives sent to the United States to manage suburban homes and lifestyles while their husbands jet around the world sarcastically refer to themselves as "widows." Other women in California's Silicon Valley have become successful entrepreneurs in their own right and have turned their years of living and raising children in the region into lucrative real estate careers helping other newly arrived astronaut families settle into their new lives.[9]

Another group of new Asian immigrants are "parachute kids" who live in the United States alone or with caretakers and relatives to attend elementary, middle, and high school. Among a group of highly select young people ranging in age from eight to seventeen, these children come from families whose parents are either engaged in the Pacific shuttle themselves or who remain in Asia full-time. During the 1980s and 1990s, the majority of parachute kids were from Taiwan, with a large number living in southern California, but there are also parachute kids with roots in Hong Kong, China, India, Korea, and the Philippines.[10]

International students have always been an important group of Asian immigrants to the United States. But a new set of conditions in both Asia and the United States has set in motion a type of younger student whose family is attempting to live concurrently in two societies. Squeezed by the competitive educational environment at home in Taiwan and Hong Kong, for example, some parachute kids seek a pre-college American education in order to better their chances of getting into prestigious American colleges and universities and obtaining good jobs in either Asia or the United States. Either alternative is acceptable, and it is understood that any future decision will be based on what is strategically better for the children and their families. "Dropping parachute kids into the United States not only fulfills the family's educational goals," writes sociologist Min Zhou, "it is also a practical way of investing in the future."[11]

Globalization and new migration patterns have also created a new generation of "transnational mothers." At the other end of the economic spectrum from the Chinese astronaut fathers and Taiwanese parachute kids, these are women who migrate for work abroad and almost always work in gendered female positions of domestic service, teaching, or health care. Many Filipina workers fall into this category. Forced abroad in the face of economic inequalities at home, they leave families and young children in the Philippines for long stretches of time while they work to send money back. Their wages are oftentimes the main support for the family. Vicky Diaz, a thirty-four-year-old mother of five young children working in the United States, has spent only three months with her husband and children in the Philippines over a span of nine years. She tries to compensate for her physical absence with material goods—a washing machine, car, and TV—along with financial support. Nevertheless, the heartache is devastating. "What saddens me the most about my situation is that during the formative years of their childhood, I was not there for them," she laments. She is hardly alone. Scores of Filipinas (and other immigrant women) are now transnational mothers.[12]

Today's transnational immigrants not only live across borders through their immigration and family patterns. They also live transnationally through the things that they buy (and where they buy them), the films and TV shows that they watch, and the news that they consume. Living transnationally does not require actual crossing of national borders but can be achieved through culture and consumption. Indian immigrants in the Bay Area, for example, frequently visit Indian grocery stores to purchase lentils, spices, and other ingredients crucial to Indian cooking. They also buy a variety of other consumer goods imported from India like cosmetics, music, Bollywood films, religious icons, clothes, and jewelry. Purchasing these goods, anthropologist Purnima Mankekar explains, reminds immigrants of home and allows them to remain connected to India. "People don't just come here to buy groceries," one store owner told Mankekar. "They come for the whole package. They come for 'India shopping.' "[13] The stores also serve as crucial community meeting places where information about jobs, housing, and schools as well as the latest gossip can be exchanged. It is here, too, that traditional gender roles and community sanctions can also be played out. For some immigrant women, the grocery store is the one "safe" place that their controlling husbands allow them to go on their own.[14]

Media is another way in which transnational immigrants remain connected to each other and to their homelands. To serve the growing and diverse Chinese American population, Chinese-language media has experienced a dramatic increase in recent years, for example. Sociologist Min Zhou found at least 200 Chinese-language media outlets across the United States putting out newspapers, television and radio programs, and communicating online. Owned by either Chinese American or transnational Chinese entrepreneurs, and in a few cases by overseas Chinese media corporations, these media outlets cover events in local Chinese communities as well as economic, political, social, and cultural news in the homeland (China, Hong Kong, or Taiwan) and around the world. Chinese-language media serves as an excellent example of how immigrants can integrate into local societies while staying connected to their homeland. Newspapers in southern California, for example, provide crucial information on jobs, housing, schooling, child care, health care, taxes, and immigration through classified ads, business directories, and news stories. Radio programs give Chinese-language coverage of the Los Angeles Lakers playoff game, California's energy crisis, and Hollywood gossip, as well as the latest developments in U.S.-China relations. "Without speaking a single word of English," Zhou explains, "immigrants know what is going on in the world around them," whether it be down the street or halfway across the world.[15]

Just as previous generations of immigrants sent money back to families, hometowns, organizations, and governments in their homelands, today's immigrants continue the trend on an even larger scale. And they are aggressively courted by homeland governments who grant special access, privileges, and honors in order to keep immigrants tied to the land of their birth through tangible investments. The Vietnamese government, for example, adopted a policy called *dôi mói* in 1986 to invite foreign capital, including remittances from the Vietnamese diaspora, into the country. During the 1990s, Vietnamese abroad (known as *Viêt Kiêu*, or temporary sojourners) sent an estimated $600 to $700 million a year back to families in Vietnam.[16]

This is a global phenomenon. Indian immigrants in the United States also maintain strong transnational homeland ties, and both the Indian American community and the Indian government encourage financial contributions to homeland projects. Beginning in the 1970s, the English-language newspaper *India Abroad* routinely featured thinly veiled pleas for investment in India. The Indian government participated in some of these efforts by sponsoring investment planning sessions. It was a smart strategy. India has a larger number of people living abroad than any other nation, and by the 1990s, Indian Americans were growing in number and in wealth. In 1999, the Indian government began to issue special immigration documents known as "Persons of Indian Origin Cards" that allow "non-resident Indians" (NRIs) to visit India without a visa, own property, buy government bonds, and apply to universities in India. In 2000, the Indian government created the High Commission on the Indian Diaspora to strengthen and facilitate contributions from overseas Indians for development and philanthropic projects. Indians in North America have responded with enthusiasim. In 2005 alone, India received $27 billion in remittances. Nonresident Indians have become the "new VIPs."[17]

Like Indian immigrants in North America, Filipino *balikbayan*, permanent residents of the United States, have long been championed as national Filipino heroes for the remittances they send to their families and native villages. In 2009, the *Philippine Daily Inquirer* reported that Filipino Americans remitted $8 billion to the Philippines. As a result, *balikbayan* are treated to all kinds of perks during their "homecomings," like reduced airfare, extended visas, tax breaks, and priority immigration and customs service when they arrive in Manila.[18]

Filipino Americans are now linked to the Philippines by thousands of transnational hometown, regional, and national associations, as well as professonal and alumni organizations. Since the 1980s, Filipino Americans have developed new institutions explicitly focused on direct investment and partnership with communities in the Philippines. Led by Filipino immigrant professionals, these groups range widely in their purpose and focus on what scholar Joyce Mariano calls "homeland development" and "diasporic giving." There are medical missions led by Filipino American doctors and nurses as well as volunteer-abroad programs for Filipino American youth. Filipino Americans contribute to charity and social development efforts in the Philippines on a massive scale. Their philanthropy serves multiple purposes. It allows Filipino Americans to contribute to their homeland. It also reaffirms the status of diasporic Filipinos as heroic *balikbayan*, helps define themselves in the United States and in the diaspora, and maintains connections with the Philippines for the U.S.-born generation.[19]

Transnational Asians are not content to simply contribute financially to relatives, hometowns, or national governments. Just like previous generations, they are also active in affecting social and political change in their homelands. Again the Indian and Filipino communities provide helpful examples. In the United States, the first Indian women's organizations were founded to help immigrant women adapt to American society. By the 1980s and 1990s, groups like Manavi in New Jersey focused on issues like domestic violence in their own communities as well as women's issues in India. A new generation of South Asian feminists began to form organizations that had both local and international dimensions and that transcended national and religious identities.[20] Like earlier immigrants, some Indian Americans view their involvement in India's politics as a reflection of their lives and identities in both their native and adopted homelands. When Prime Minister Narendra Modi visited the United States in 2014, 30,000 people crowded into New York City's Madison Square Garden to attend a program that highlighted both the prime minister and the accomplishments of Indian Americans, like the first Indian American Miss America winner, Nina Davuluri. Modi's visit and the rockstar treatment he received in the United States, Indian American Manisha Verma explained, "brings hope of change in India which will help Indians have better self-esteem and image in the United States."[21]

Beginning in the early 1970s, several Filipino organizations in the United States like Kalayaan (Freedom Collective), the Support Committee for a Democratic Philippines in New York, and the Samahan ng Makabayang Pilipino (SAMAPI-Association of Nationalist Filipinos) in Chicago focused their political activities on the Philippines. These organizations were ready to respond when Philippine president Ferdinand Marcos declared martial law on September 21, 1972. He suspended democratic governance and his government carried out the mass arrests of civilians. Hundreds of dissenters were reportedly tortured, and many others fled abroad, primarily to the United States.

Marcos's actions inspired a new generation of activists who worked to create change in the Philippines and the United States. One of these was Carol Ojeda-Kimbrough. She was a medical student in the Philippines when martial law was imposed, and she joined a group of community activists engaged in organizing the urban poor in Manila. As the Marcos government's political repression continued, military officials began to visit Ojeda-Kimbrough's home and interrogate her about the whereabouts of other activists. Fearing arrest, she joined her parents in the United States. In Los Angeles, she began to participate in meetings of the Anti-Martial Law alliance and joined members of the KDP (Katipunan ng mga Demokratikong Pilipino, or the Union of Democratic Filipinos), which exercised a "two-sided" political program that spanned the Pacific. For Ojeda-Kimbrough, her residence in the United States did not dampen her commitment to effecting change in the Philippines. She continued her anti-Marcos activism and also began to work on issues affecting Filipino Americans.[22] In 1986, the United States government abandoned its support of the Marcos government, in large part as a result of the activism of Filipinos in the United States.

In addition to being highly transnational across the Pacific, contemporary Asian migration is also transnational within the Americas. Take the case of Beleza Li, a Chinese Brazilian immigrant in the United States. "My family history is a history of a never ending search for better opportunities, whether in China, Brazil or the United States," she told an interviewer. The family's immigration history began when Beleza's great-aunt immigrated to the United States in the 1950s and sent money back to the family remaining in China while she worked in a San Francisco sweatshop. Beleza's grandfather used these funds to immigrate to Brazil in 1961 and opened up a *pastelaria* (café). It took over twenty years for him to bring his wife and son over, but once they arrived in Brazil, the family quickly adapted. Even with her grandmother working sixteen-hour nonstop factory shifts, "Brazil was like heaven on Earth," for the Lis, Beleza recalled. But in 2002, the family picked up and moved to the United States. "They believed this was the ultimate dream, the 'American Dream,' " she explains.[23]

The Lis are hardly alone. Beginning in the 1970s, middle-class and elite Chinese Panamanians viewed studying abroad in the United States as an important way of gaining fluency in English, earning a prestigious American university degree, and possibly acquiring U.S. citizenship. Transnational families and circular migrations between Panama and the United States have since become commonplace.[24]

In Peru and Cuba, Chinese have also moved northward to escape political instability. A large number of Peruvian Chinese left the country for the United States and Canada when General Juan Velasco Alvarado seized power from President Fernando Belaúnde in 1968 and confiscated agricultural properties and industrial enterprises that many Chinese were engaged in. Similarly, Chinese Cubans fled to Miami, New York, Toronto, Madrid, and elsewhere when Fidel Castro's revolutionary government nationalized private commerce and threatened the livelihood of many Chinese Cubans who owned small shops and restaurants. By the 1960s and 1970s, thousands of Chinese Cubans had fled to the United States alongside other Cubans.[25]

South Asians and Koreans in Latin America also followed a path northward to the United States for economic reasons. Beginning in the 1970s, a growing number of South Asians from the Caribbean, Guyana, and Suriname migrated to the United States. In 2000, there were an estimated 150,000 to 250,000 Indo-Caribbeans, as they are known, in New York City alone. Blending their British colonial, Caribbean, and Indian identities, they are known for running small businesses that reflect their mixed heritage such as food trucks and restaurants serving jerk chicken alongside roti and dal.[26]

A sizable number of Korean immigrants from Latin America also arrived in the United States by the 1990s. In Argentina, guerrilla warfare and high inflation convinced some families to leave in the early 1970s. High inflation in Brazil and economic uncertainty similarly led to an exodus of Brazilians, including Korean Brazilians, to the United States in the early 1990s. A 1999 survey of the Korean community in Los Angeles estimated that 10 percent, or 20,000 to 30,000 people, were secondary migrants from South America. Most had migrated to Brazil or Argentina beginning in the 1970s and had lived there for fifteen to twenty years before coming to the United States.[27]

Asian immigrants from Latin America have helped create new communities and identities. In Los Angeles, these Asian Latinos can draw from a high concentration of multilingual services and express their *latinidad*, or "Latinness," as they try to honor and express both their Asian and Latino heritages in the United States. Japanese Peruvian restaurants, Korean Brazilian associations, and Chinese Brazilian churches draw community members together. In New York City, Chinese Latino or Chino Cubano restaurants have served Chinese immigrants from Cuba since the 1970s. Offering both Cuban and Chinese American cuisine to a diverse clientele, these restaurants bring Chinese, Latino, and American cultures together. Koreans who grew up in Argentina and then remigrated to the United States use both Spanish and Korean in their work with Asian and Latino immigrants in the United States. Reconstructing their identities as Korean, Latino, and American, these migrants "float" back and forth between nations and communities, creating new diasporic cultures and redefining racial and ethnic identities at the same time.[28]

In addition to new migrations of Asians from Latin America, increasing rates of intermarriage among Asians and Latinos in the United States have also created a growing community of mixed race Asian Latinos. According to the 2000 census, there are more than 400,000 individuals of Asian Latino ancestry living in the United States. These Chino Chicanos, as historian Robert Chao Romero has explained, are in the midst of forging their own unique identities, drawing from their Asian, Latin American, and U.S. American experiences.[29]

Just as recent Asian migrations to the Americas and within the Americas serve as important indicators of late-twentieth- and early-twenty-first-century global trends, so does the new increase in "return" migration to Asia. In the new global race for highly skilled workers and entrepreneurs, the United States is no longer the only preferred destination for many prospective immigrants. In particular, Asia and its strong economies are drawing people back to their homelands. Home country recruitment policies have drawn people to Taiwan, South Korea, India, and China. In some cases, the children and even grandchildren of Asian immigrants who had arrived in the United States in earlier decades are choosing to "return" to their ancestral homelands for economic and other opportunities. As many of these new immigrants are sometimes one to two generations removed from their ancestral homelands and often do not speak the native language, this return is not a traditional one to a native land, but rather a symbolic one.[30]

Japanese Latin Americans made up the first large wave of returnees to Asia. In the 1980s and 1990s, Japan's booming economy drew on Latin American Japanese to work as temporary laborers performing the "3K jobs" that most native-born Japanese rejected: *kitanai*/dirty, *kitsui*/demanding, and *kiken*/dangerous. In 1990, the Japanese government reformed its immigration laws to create a new "long-term resident" status (*teijusha*) for Japanese nationals and children and grandchildren of Japanese emigrants born abroad. The next year, 83,875 Brazilians of Japanese descent entered the country. By 1996 a culture of migration was firmly established among Japanese communities in many Latin American countries.[31]

The rapid growth of China and India in the early twenty-first century now offers increased economic opportunities for returning immigrants and their offspring. Chinese and Indian students who come to the United States or Canada are increasingly returning after receiving their degrees.[32] Indian Americans born and raised in the United States are also increasingly living and working in the country that their parents had left decades ago. As Anand Giridharadas, an Indian American who moved to India in 2003, explains, the second-generation children of immigrants are increasingly exploring motherland opportunities "as economies convulse in the West and jobs dry up." The idea of moving to India, he continues, "is spreading virally in émigré homes."[33]

Chinese immigrants, especially an increasing number of middle-class professionals, are also returning to China to take advantage of that country's robust economy. The Chinese government lures them back with promises of housing and a guaranteed spot in one of the new business parks that have cropped up in big and small cities. Like Chinese astronauts with their multiple passports, these returnees also seek to maximize future options. They secure naturalized U.S. citizenship as a means of putting down roots in the United States and also to take advantage of its other privileges. U.S. citizenship offers, among other things, more international mobility, protection from political uncertainties in mainland China, and an advantage in the global labor market, where higher salaries are often paid to U.S. citizens.[34]

While the search for economic opportunity has spurred the return of immigrants and their descendants to Asia, another group has traveled to the country of their birth in search of their roots, and in some cases to change the system that prompted their international movement in the first place. Scholar Kim Park Nelson estimates that around one in four Korean adoptees has returned to Korea for short visits, or less commonly, to settle permanently.[35] Special visas issued by the South Korean government and the option of dual citizenship allow Korean adoptees special access to and rights in their birth country. Korean adoptee author and activist Jane Jeong Trenka is one of these returnees and works with other internationally adopted Koreans to question the processes and consequences of international adoption and to advocate for Korean adoptees in Korea.[36]

During this time of increasing globalization and mass immigration, Asian Americans are also forging new diasporas. The number of Indian-born people living outside of India and the number of Chinese-born people living outside of China have both doubled since 1990 to 14 million and 9 million, respectively.[37] The Korean diaspora, formed out of necessity during and after Japanese colonialism and the Korean War, encompasses an estimated 5.7 million Koreans living in 160 different countries.[38] Vietnamese in the United States and Canada have family scattered across the border, and in France and Vietnam.[39] By the mid-1990s, there were 620,370 people of Japanese descent in Brazil; 760,370 in the United States; 55,472 in Peru; 55,111 in Canada; 29,262 in Argentina; 14,725 in Mexico; and 6,054 in Paraguay.[40]

And within these diasporas are new identities and organizations that connect these communities to their Asian homelands and to each other within the Americas. These are not new phenomena, but instead continue patterns established over the centuries. Globalization has intensified diasporic and transnational identities, communities, and activism of Asian-descended peoples around the world. They have formed connections with other peoples of Asian descent outside their own communities, states, and nations, and in doing so have helped document shared histories and create bonds across borders.

Just as Chinese Americans formed transnational commercial and cultural linkages in the early twentieth century, for example, today's Chinese communities continue to maintain connections across national borders in informal and formal ways, including annual conventions that bring the Chinese in Central America together. Beginning in the 1980s, Japanese in the Americas also began to form connections and organizations, including the Pan American Nikkei Association to link Japanese-descended peoples together within the Western Hemisphere.[41] Similar to the ways in which South Asians in the United States and Canada forged political and support networks across the border in the early twentieth century, today's South Asian immigrants also maintain active transnational family networks that span several countries on different continents. South Asians in Canada, Great Britain, and the United States, for example, have formed what scholar Jigna Desai calls "Brown Atlantic" identities that link them to each other and to South Asia.[42]

Today's Asian immigrant journeys are fluid, multidirectional, and global. Similarly, identities are not tied to one place, but to many places at once. Immigrants balance time, loyalties, money, and identities between the countries they move from, as well as the many other places that they have been or hope to go next. Whether the children and grandchildren of recent immigrants will keep or change these transnational practices is unclear, but how they figure this out will be important, because in a world increasingly connected through globalization, we're all learning to become global Americans.

PART FIVE

Twenty-first-Century Asian Americans

17

The "Rise of Asian Americans"? Myths and Realities

In recent years, U.S. news outlets have applauded the "rise of Asian Americans." They are not only the fastest growing group in the United States, they are supposedly also the most educated, wealthiest, and even happiest. *The Wall Street Journal* has heralded the "rise of the Tiger Nation," using economists' label for the competitive, fast-growing, and successful "Little Tiger" economies of South Korea, Taiwan, Hong Kong, and Singapore to apply to Asian Americans as well.[1] Business magazines have proclaimed that Indian immigrants have "conquered Silicon Valley" and serve as important examples for "women and other races" seeking similar success.[2] And researchers at the Pew Research Center have declared that Asian American achievement represents nothing less than major "milestones of economic success and social assimilation" in the United States as a whole. Even as they acknowledged differences among Asian Americans, the Pew researchers found that as a group they enjoyed shared economic mobility and high education rates and collectively valued "cultural" traits such as the importance of family, respect for elders, and a "pervasive belief in the rewards of hard work."[3]

Once cast as inassimilable and racially inferior foreigners who were threats to the United States, Asian Americans are now the poster children of American success and are sometimes even called "honorary whites."[4] But this portrait is misleading. It masks persistent inequalities and disparities among Asian Americans and relies on a new and divisive language of racism. Moreover, it obscures the unstable place of Asian Americans in contemporary America. Depending on domestic economic and global political conditions, some Asian Americans are accepted as full and equal citizens in the United States while others find themselves marginalized as dangerous outsiders. Since the 1980s, the growing strength of the Japanese and Chinese economies and the outsourcing of U.S. jobs to places like India, for example, have affected the ways in which Asian Americans are seen as economic competitors in the United States. U.S.-China tensions have particularly cast a shadow of suspicion on the loyalties of Chinese Americans. And the War on Terror's focus on Muslim, Arab, and Muslim-looking peoples after 9/11 has dramatically affected South Asian American and other immigrant communities. This simultaneous acceptance and rejection of Asian Americans reflects their complex place in contemporary American society as well as the myths and realities of the so-called rise of Asian Americans.

The model minority concept remains by far the most common way that Americans view Asian Americans today. With its roots in World War II and the Cold War, the Asian American model minority stereotype gained even more traction in American public discourse during the 1980s, when newspapers and magazines routinely praised Asian Americans for holding the formula for success. In 1984, *Newsweek* reported that Asian Americans "pack the honor rolls of some of the country's most highly regarded schools." They outscored other racial groups on the math portion of the Scholastic Aptitude Test (SAT) year after year.[5] The next year, *The New Republic* noted the group's "spectacular" presence in some of the country's most elite schools. Other superlatives were peppered throughout the article: "outstanding," "astonishing."[6] *Fortune* magazine's description of Asian Americans as "America's Super Minority" went even further. Asian Americans were "smarter and better educated and make more money than everyone else" because of upbringing, but also because of genetics. "Asian Americans," the magazine flatly declared, "are smarter than the rest of us."[7]

This late-twentieth-century praise of Asian Americans was both similar and different from previous decades. Like the 1960s version of the Asian

American model minority stereotype, the 1980s edition also explained Asian American success through so-called Asian values and culture that emphasized "a traditional reverence for learning" and strong family structures.[8] And like earlier versions of the model minority stereotype, the Asian explanation separates them from other Americans in negative ways.

The perceived educational and socioeconomic successes of Asian Americans are also still used to compare them to other racial minorities, especially African Americans. Rather than referencing a slowing U.S. economy, the growing disappearance of blue-collar jobs, deteriorating inner cities and public schools, and the continuing legacies of centuries of institutionalized discrimination, African American poverty has been increasingly explained as the by-product of a dysfunctional culture with delinquent family values.[9]

The media's Asian–African American comparison was brought to the forefront during the 1992 Los Angeles riots that followed the acquittal of four Los Angeles police officers of brutally beating African American motorist Rodney King. The April 29 riots, known by Koreans as Sa-I-Gu (Korean for 4-2-9), destroyed more than 2,300 Korean businesses and uprooted more than 10,000 Korean Americans from their homes and places of business. Almost half of the city's $1 billion loss in property damage was sustained by Korean American small business owners.[10] From the outset, media reporting characterized the event as a black-Korean conflict. Despite the fact that participants in the demonstrations, acts of civil disobedience, rioting, and looting were white, black, Latino, and Asian, mainstream media described the events as a clash of black-Korean cultures. African Americans living in South Central Los Angeles were portrayed as unproductive citizens and welfare recipients who resented the growing economic presence of Korean Americans in their neighborhoods. In contrast, Korean American shopkeepers were portrayed as hardworking immigrants trying to achieve the American Dream. But they were bigoted and kept to themselves. A clash between the two groups was almost inevitable, according to media accounts. Such media coverage pitted African Americans against Korean Americans while ignoring the larger structural inequalities that helped to create the conditions for the Los Angeles riots. Korean American reporter K. W. Lee went so far as to call the coverage a "media-fanned minority vs. minority bogus race war." He observed that "even before Koreans and African Americans had a chance to get to know each other with their common struggles and sorrows . . . both groups watched themselves pitted against each other . . . in the shouting sound bites and screaming headlines."[11]

African Americans are not the only points of comparison to the Asian American model minority in the media. The contemporary Asian American success story is also used as a cautionary tale aimed at white Americans. Underlying the praise is an undercurrent of anxiety that Asian Americans may be *too* successful for their own good, hurting deserving white Americans and competing with other more deserving minorities. During the 1980s, some made sardonic references to schools being allegedly overrun with Asians. MIT was nicknamed "Made in Taiwan," while UCLA was supposedly the "University of Caucasians Lost Among Asians."[12]

In both comparisons—with blacks and whites—Asian American success is viewed as coming at the expense of other groups.

Social scientists, demographers, and policymakers have consistently pointed out flaws in the characterization of all Asian Americans as model minorities. There are many examples of educational and economic success, but the community is far from homogeneous. And highlighting only the successful characteristics obscures the significant proportion of Asian Americans who still struggle to survive, live in poverty, are unemployed or underemployed, and have low rates of education. Asian Americans are in fact what some call a "community of contrasts," with significant diversity and disparities within and between different groups.[13]

U.S. Census data confirm that Asian Americans are overrepresented at both ends of the educational and socioeconomic spectrum of privilege and poverty. More Asian Americans (49 percent) have college degrees compared with all other U.S. adults (28 percent).[14] These figures include highly educated immigrants who arrive in the United States with advanced degrees in hand and individuals whose families have been in the United States for generations. At the same time, five times as many Asians as non-Hispanic whites had zero to four years of education in 2000.[15] By 2010, a greater proportion of the Asian American population (8 percent) still had less than a ninth-grade education than the total U.S. population (6 percent).[16] For many groups, including more recent arrivals from countries with uneven educational opportunities and refugees who have lacked access to formal education in the refugee camps, school can be a challenge and dropout rates are high.

The 2010 census revealed that Indian Americans, Chinese Americans, and Japanese Americans have higher median annual personal earnings than the general U.S. population. At the same time, Korean Americans, Vietnamese Americans, and Filipino Americans have lower median annual personal earnings than the U.S. general population, and these same groups plus Chinese and "other U.S. Asian" (as the census describes them) Americans also have a higher poverty rate than the general population. They work in low-wage service industries and live in crowded apartments. Many who already lived at the economic margins of society fell deeper into poverty during recent recessions, and like African Americans have had a much more difficult time regaining their economic stability. Some communities, like Chinese Americans, are represented at both ends of the economic spectrum. In 2010, Chinese Americans had higher median annual personal earnings than the general U.S. population, but at the same time 14 percent of all Chinese Americans lived in poverty, higher than the rate for both the overall Asian Americans and the general U.S. populations.[17]

Data for the state of California, home to the nation's largest Asian American population, confirm that Asian Americans are a community of contrasts. The state's Asian American population grew by 34 percent between 2000 and 2010. They owned over half a million businesses in 2007 and have experienced increased citizenship, voter registration, and political participation in recent years. Some are among the most educated in California, including Taiwanese and Indians, but statewide, Asian Americans twenty-five years and older are less likely than whites to have earned a high school diploma or a GED (86 percent versus 93 percent). This is a rate similar to African Americans (87 percent). Hmong, Cambodian, Laotian, and Vietnamese American adults have the lowest educational attainment of Asian American ethnic groups in the state. In addition, Asian Americans in California had the highest growth in unemployment (196 percent) among all racial groups statewide from 2006 to 2010. Compared to whites, more Asian Americans are low income (20 percent and 24 percent, respectively), and they have a lower per capita income ($42,052 and $29,841, respectively). Lastly, Asian Americans have a higher poverty rate than whites (10 percent and 8 percent, respectively). Between 2007 and 2011, the number of Asian Americans living in poverty statewide increased by roughly 50 percent, to over half a million. Hmong and Cambodian American children have higher rates of poverty (42 percent and 31 percent, respectively) than African American and Latino children (27 percent and 26 percent, respectively.)[18] And Asian American Californians are not alone. In recent years, Asian Americans in New York City plunged deeper into poverty and are now the poorest New Yorkers.[19]

A closer look at Cambodian Americans serves to illustrate the dangers of grouping diverse Asian Americans into one monolithic portrait of success. In 2009, there were over 275,000 Cambodian Americans (naturalized citizens, native-born citizens, and noncitizens) in the country. More than a third of the adult population (38.5 percent) twenty-five years and over had not graduated from high school, as compared with 14.7 percent of the overall U.S. population and 14.2 percent of the overall Asian American population. Over 15 percent of Cambodian families were living in poverty compared to 10.5 percent of the overall U.S. population and 8.7 percent of the overall Asian American population. In addition, they had lower median household incomes than both groups.

The lower levels of education and higher levels of poverty have been persistent aspects of Cambodian American life since the first refugees began to arrive in 1979, often with severe physical and psychological wounds inflicted during the Cambodian genocide. Many adults suffered from post-traumatic stress disorder, and families—many of them headed by widowed mothers—struggled to survive in the United States. They had to learn English, find jobs, attend school, and adapt to the crime-ridden neighborhoods where they were placed. Some Cambodian children became alienated from school, were bullied on the streets, and as a result sought protection with Cambodian gangs.[20]

The criminal behavior—ranging from petty crimes to murder—that some of these individuals engaged in often landed them in jail. Mao So, for example, was fourteen when he began to sell drugs at his high school in Santa Ana, California. The next year, he joined a gang and dropped out of school. He was making up to $500 a day. He soon had twenty armed men working for him and was a well-known and successful drug dealer in the area. He was routinely closing $100,000 drug deals. But eventually he was caught, arrested, and sentenced to five years in prison. He served two and a half years of his sentence and was released in 2001.[21]

Cambodian Americans like Mao So are the extreme opposite from the Asian American model minority. In fact, new immigration laws that have targeted noncitizens with criminal records have pushed So and hundreds of others so far to the margins of American society that they have been banished from the country altogether. In 1996, the U.S. Congress increased the list of crimes labeled "aggravated felonies" as part of the Illegal Immigration Reform and Immigrant Responsibility Act, and it expanded the categories of mandatory deportation with the Antiterrorism and Effective Death Penalty Act passed that same year. With these laws, legal permanent residents who are not U.S. citizens can be deported if they have been convicted of "aggravated felonies," even if they have served their time. After the terrorist attacks of September 11, 2001, the government stepped up efforts to remove undesirable foreigners and pressured countries like Cambodia to accept deportees.

As of 2010, over 200 Cambodian Americans have been deported to Cambodia under these mandatory regulations, including drug dealers like Mao So. The laws have also swept up people like Louen Lun, who as a teenager fired a gun in the air at a Tacoma shopping mall as he fled a group of young men he and a friend had been arguing with. Lun was arrested on assault charges and spent eleven months in the county jail. After his release, he became a model citizen. He got a job, started a family, and applied for naturalization. But when he showed up at the Seattle immigration office in 2002, he was arrested under the new laws for his prior conviction.[22]

Approximately 2,000 more await deportation with little or no chance of appeal and regardless of model behavior, length of residence in the United States, and family ties, including U.S. citizen children. Most of the returnees are male, fled Cambodia as small children with their refugee families in 1979 and 1980, and have no memory of Cambodia. Many do not speak the Khmer language, have no family in Cambodia, and know little of the country that their families struggled so hard to escape. They arrive in a country ill prepared to assist the new arrivals. They leave behind families, including mothers who kept them alive under horrific circumstances in Cambodia only to see them returned there, and U.S.-born children. These separations of "exiled Americans" are permanent, for U.S. law bars them from reentering the United States.[23]

In spite of real factual evidence that illustrates the broad diversity of Asian American populations, high levels of poverty, unemployment and underemployment, and low levels of education among some groups, the model minority label has persisted. Some social scientists point to the negative repercussions of this stereotype for Asian Americans and for American race relations. Historian Franklin Odo argues that the model minority label "encourages Asian Americans to endure contemporary forms of racism without complaint and to provide brave and loyal service above and beyond that required of other Americans." It also allows Americans in general to "turn a blind eye" to enduring inequalities in the United States, he explains.[24] And sociologist Lisa Sun-Hee Park finds that the model minority myth not only plays an ongoing role in perpetuating the marginal status of Asian Americans, but also hinders progressive social change among the second generation.[25] Musician Vijay Iyer goes further: privileged and unquestioning Asian Americans have become "complicit" in their acceptance of ongoing American inequality.[26]

Others point out that Americans' perpetuation and celebration of the Asian American model minority masks the growth in a new racism that affects us all. A new language of "culture" instead of "race" has become commonplace to explain different, and often, related notions of superiority and inferiority. Proponents of this perspective argue that it is not a person's race or skin color that explains their abilities, it is their culture. There are two things wrong with this line of thinking. First, these arguments often ignore institutional factors such as immigration laws that give preference to highly educated individuals and those with technical skills. Professional class status and family reunification are by far the two most common pathways into the United States for Asian immigrants today. This means that they already have high educational status (and likely a work visa that will lead to steady and high-paying income) before they even arrive. For others, relatives already in the United States can help provide economic capital as well as personal resources to help navigate and succeed in the new land.[27] Where Asian

Americans fit into America's existing racial hierarchy as model minorities also makes a difference in the types of neighborhoods, schools, and societal resources they have access to. As anthropologist Nancy Foner explains, Asians face less discrimination in housing, for example, which translates into being able to live in areas with good public schools and in turn helps prepare their children for academic success.[28]

Second, the cultural explanations for success and failure treat culture in the same way that we used to talk about race; that is, as unchanging, inheritable traits that determine things like intelligence, morality, and ability. Some cultures, like particular Asian ones, are held up as superior, while others are found to be lacking or clashing with American culture. Beginning in the 1960s, Asian Americans and their so-called traditional Asian cultures were pitted against African Americans who were said to have dysfunctional families and culture. In the 1990s, some pundits turned to the growing population of Latinos as an example of unfit cultures. Harvard professor Samuel Huntington, for example, claimed that "Hispanic traits" such as a "mistrust of people outside the family, lack of initiative, self-reliance, and ambition" were not only holding Latinos back, but were at great odds to American culture and presented a profound "Hispanic challenge" to the United States.[29] New racialists don't just denigrate certain cultures like Huntington. They also hold others (like Asian Americans) up as exemplary and invite invidious comparisons with others to explain serious problems like the achievement gap, poverty, and crime among some groups in America. Racism does not look the same as it did in decades past. Cloaked in praise and using culture instead of race, the new racism, however, is still destructive and divisive.[30]

While much of the media discourse about the rise of Asian Americans is rooted in changing social, economic, and political conditions in the United States, the international context shaping Asian Americans' status remains equally important. Just as in the past, Asian Americans continue to be linked to Asia and to the United States' shifting relationships with various Asian countries. These media-produced linkages are different from the transnational connections that immigrants themselves maintain. Instead, Asian Americans are seen as Asians, not Americans, and come to embody whatever threat the land of their ancestry allegedly poses to the United States.

During the 1980s, the stunning economic success of "Japan Inc.," which was turning out automobiles and electronics at a phenomenal rate, stood in stark contrast to the economic malaise of the U.S. economy with its high unemployment rate and inflation. In Detroit, proud home of the U.S.'s auto industry, autoworkers found themselves out of work. Japanese cars, Japanese autoworkers, and the Japanese auto industry were blamed for the woes of the entire U.S. auto industry and its workers. In this context, older strains of anti-Asian racism resurfaced, including the treatment of all Asians as indistinguishable from each other and viewing Asian Americans as representatives of a foreign Asian country. Beginning in the 1980s, a rash of hate crimes—including murder, intimidation, and other violent acts—increasingly targeted Asian Americans. The 1982 killing of Vincent Chin, a Chinese American engineer out on the town for his bachelor party, became emblematic of the trend.

The fight began in a Detroit bar, where Chin exchanged heated words with Ronald Ebens and his stepson, Michael Nitz. Things escalated and then the two white American autoworkers chased Chin down and beat him with a baseball bat. Ebens and Nitz claimed that Chin's death was accidental and pled guilty to manslaughter. But witnesses suggested a clear motive. Ebens, an automobile plant foreman, had called Chin a "Jap" and yelled, "It's because of you motherf—ers that we're out of work!" When Ebens and Nitz were sentenced to only three years' probation and $3,800 in fines and no jail time, a significant new phase of Asian American activism and political awakening was set in motion. To many, what happened to Chin represented a double tragedy: the murder of a young man with a promising future and a criminal justice system that failed to adequately punish the killers.[31]

Civil rights activist and journalist Helen Zia was among those who gathered at a local steak house to discuss possible actions. The huge public outpouring of anger and frustration was a first. "Suddenly people who had endured a lifetime of degrading treatment were wondering if their capacity to suffer in silence might no longer be a virtue," she recalled.[32]

The Chinese American community was the first to organize, but soon they were joined by Japanese Americans, Korean Americans, Filipino Americans, and African Americans in one of the first large-scale pan–Asian American and interracial campaigns to call attention to hate crimes targeting Asian Americans. Under the name "American Citizens for Justice," this multiracial coalition of activists worked to demonstrate how the killing had been racially motivated. They also had to convince a skeptical public and judicial system that Asian Americans—the so-called model minorities who had made it in America—could indeed be victims of terrible discrimination. In 1983, American Citizens for Justice filed a civil rights suit on behalf of Vincent Chin and a federal grand jury indicted Ebens and Nitz for violating Chin's civil rights. At the end of the trial in 1984, the federal jury found Ebens guilty and acquitted Nitz, but the conviction was overturned on appeal. In 1987, a retrial resulted in an acquittal.

The outcome was a severe disappointment, and filmmakers Christine Choy and Renee Tajima-Peña pointedly criticized the lack of justice in the case by asking "who killed Vincent Chin?" in their well-known documentary of the same name. Ebens and Nitz did, but so did U.S. racism and persistent stereotypes of Asian Americans as threatening outsiders.[33]

67. Vincent Chin protest, Detroit, 1983.

By the 1990s, another Asian country was on the rise. With the demise of the Soviet Union in 1989, China began to emerge as a military and economic power that might someday rival the United States. At the same time, a deindustrializing United States sank into a recession first in the 1980s and again in the early twenty-first century. China is now seen as both an important business partner and a dangerous rival. Sensationalist bestsellers with titles such as *When China Rules the World* and *Death by China* feed a fear that China will topple American hegemony, and some even go so far as to describe China's ascent as an all-out assault on the United States from both within and without.[34]

As in the past, Chinese Americans have found that their loyalty to the United States has been questioned. They have been treated as dangerous foreigners rather than full-fledged U.S. citizens. This has happened in countless everyday interactions as well as in high-profile investigations, acts of violence, and discriminatory racial profiling by government agencies. There have been, for example, a number of cases in which Chinese American scientists have been accused of spying for the People's Republic of China. Aerospace engineers, computer scientists, and others were targeted by FBI officers and unjustifiably accused of passing information to the Chinese. The most egregious case involved the wrongly accused Wen Ho Lee, a research scientist at Los Alamos National Laboratory in New Mexico. The Taiwanese-born American physicist came under investigation in 1999, when the *New York Times* raised suspicions that the Los Alamos lab had been involved in giving China nuclear warhead technology. U.S. intelligence officers quickly focused on Lee due to his ethnic heritage and his access to the weapons information. Lee was thrown in jail and placed in solitary confinement for more than 200 days. After an intensive investigation lasting five years, the U.S. government could find no evidence of espionage and the U.S. District Court judge in New Mexico in charge of Lee's case issued a formal apology.[35]

68. Wen Ho Lee, c. 2001.

The rise of Asian Americans and the rise of Asia were also forcefully linked in the media coverage around Yale law professor Amy Chua's bestselling family memoir, *Battle Hymn of the Tiger Mother*, published in 2011. Chua describes raising her successful and Ivy League university–attending children in the strict "Chinese" way that she learned from her Chinese immigrant parents, and the "Tiger Mom" image of the overbearing, strict, and success-driven Asian American mom became a powerful cultural symbol. An excerpt from the book published in *The Wall Street Journal* was provocatively titled "Why Chinese Mothers Are Superior." It went on to give expert advice on how "Chinese parents raise such stereotypically successful kids [who are] math whizzes and music prodigies" by refusing indulgent, American-style play dates and sleepovers and by instilling a strict regime of discipline and practice.[36]

Some commentators applauded Chua for instilling high expectations and hard work in her children and the "Asian drive to succeed," while others were dismayed that Chua's writing reinforced the stereotypes that Chinese and American cultures were distinctly different from each other. Frances Kai-Hwa Wang, a mother and journalist, told the *San Francisco Chronicle* that "It's one thing to say, 'This is my particular hardcore way of parenting, take it or leave it, do whatever you want.' But the article is saying, 'This is how *Chinese people* do it'—implying that we *all* treat our kids this way. You spend so much time trying to break down racial stereotypes and after something like this, it all goes out the window."[37] Many commentators also worried that Chua's book—set against U.S. anxiety about the "rise of China"—would further fuel anti-Chinese rhetoric already present in the media and in Congress. Chua's retelling of the model minority myth, explains scholar Mitchell Chang, "can be readily turned into a Yellow Peril one that supports . . . the dangerous claim that Asians are dominating the real world."[38]

The tragic attacks on the World Trade Center and the Pentagon on September 11, 2001, highlighted the ways in which the United States' global War on Terror resulted in another backlash against some Asian American populations. For South Asians in North America, the terrorist attacks and the War on Terror ushered in a new wave of anti-immigrant sentiment, racial profiling, heightened government scrutiny, deportations, and hate crimes.

In the search for the perpetrators, entire Middle Eastern, South Asian, and Muslim immigrant communities were vulnerable to blanket racially motivated charges that they were terrorists, potential terrorists, or terrorist sympathizers. The new "Islamic peril" discourse follows a pattern of immigrant scapegoating during wartime, and as was the case for Japanese Americans during World War II, Muslim and other immigrant groups have felt the repercussions.[39]

Within days of the attacks, law enforcement officials had arrested more than 1,200 people, only a handful of whom were proven to have any links to terrorism. Reflecting the United States' belief that Pakistan was a national security risk as a terrorist feeder state that exported terrorism abroad, almost 40 percent of the detainees were believed to be Pakistani nationals. Like Japanese immigrant male leaders taken into custody after the attack on Pearl Harbor, Muslim men began to disappear from their families and communities. Mass deportations also occurred, often with little or no public awareness.[40]

In the weeks and months after 9/11, hate crimes directed against Muslim, Middle Eastern, and South Asian Americans increased by 1,600 percent throughout the nation, according to the Federal Bureau of Investigation, resulting in murders, property damage, physical violence, and harassment.[41] Practicing Sikh men wearing the distinctive turbans of their faith were easy targets in more than half of the incidents involving South Asians. On September 15, 2001, Balbir Singh Sodhi, a Sikh gas station owner in Mesa, Arizona, was murdered by a self-proclaimed American "patriot" who blamed him for the terrorist attacks. A Pakistani-born grocer was killed in Texas, as was an Egyptian-born merchant in Los Angeles. Mosques were attacked and businesses vandalized. Racialized as the latest immigrant menace that conflated Muslim and Muslim-appearing peoples with terrorism, South Asians found themselves scrutinized and under siege. There were almost 650 bias incidents reported by media organizations from September 11 to September 17 alone. In the eight weeks that followed 9/11, more than a thousand incidents of racial violence were reported, including nineteen murders, attacks on places of worship, and personal intimidation and harassment.[42]

The global War on Terror abroad was directly linked to controlling immigration in the United States, and the U.S. government instituted drastic changes in immigration policy in a few short months immediately following the attack. No formal legislation was passed that restricted immigration from countries suspected of being breeding grounds for terrorists, but important new controls on immigration, and especially on immigrants already in the United States, were instituted as part of other laws. Immigration policies were amended to track, control, and detain immigrants suspected of terrorist activity or those deemed a potential threat to national security. Detainees reported violations of civil liberties and human rights as well as abuse.[43]

In June 2002, Attorney General John Ashcroft proposed new Justice Department regulations that required men from twenty-five countries, twenty-four of them Arab and Muslim, to be fingerprinted, photographed, and registered with the Immigration and Naturalization Service. The measure—similar to the Geary Act of 1892, which required Chinese laborers to register with the U.S. federal government—was to provide a "vital line of defense" against terrorists, in the words of the attorney general. Critics claimed that the program, known as the National Security Entry-Exit Registration System, institutionalized racial profiling and suspended immigrants' civil liberties. U.S. government officials themselves publicly questioned the merit of the program. Of the more than 83,000 immigrants suspected to have ties to terrorism, only six were further investigated by the newly created Department of Homeland Security. Nearly 13,000 were found to be in the country without proper immigration documentation.[44]

While South Asian American communities had flourished under the new professional class provisions of the 1965 Immigration Act and had achieved a type of "probationary status" of acceptance in the United States, as scholar Vijay Prashad explains, everything changed after 9/11. In the new heightened vilification of Islamic terrorism that was facilitated and spread through the media, a general atmosphere of suspicion, fear, and distrust resulted in racism and racial profiling on a daily basis. South Asian Americans became easily mistaken as terrorists and paid the price.[45] Even more than ten years after 9/11, Sikhs remained targets of extreme racial violence, as seen in the shooting rampage at Oak Creek, Wisconsin, in August of 2012 that left six Sikh Americans dead and a responding police officer severely wounded.[46]

South Asians in the United States have responded in various ways. Some have left the country voluntarily to avoid the immigrant backlash and real threats of detention and deportation. By March 2003, over 2,100 Pakistanis from the United States had applied for political asylum in Canada. In the ten years since, the number of Pakistani returnees is estimated to be over 100,000.[47] Others have organized to provide community assistance and legal aid, and to advocate for civil rights for those affected by the new policies. Legal organizations like the Asian American Legal Defense and Education Fund represented young victims of racial, ethnic, and religious profiling based on Muslim appearance by school administrators as well as peer harassment. Practicing what scholar Sunaina Maira calls "dissenting citizenship," many Muslim American youth have been particularly vocal critics of the anti-Muslim backlash that erupted in the weeks and months after 9/11 and connect the global War on Terror with a domestic war on immigrants.[48]

69. Sikh Americans at a candlelight vigil in Central Park, September 15, 2001.

The impact of post-9/11 policies on Asian Americans highlighted just how quickly the status of some Asian Americans could change from model minorities to suspected dangerous immigrant threats. It also reveals how fragile Asian Americans' inclusion in the United States has been. In the early twenty-first century, the place of Asian Americans in American society is a paradoxical one. While making great strides economically, academically, and politically, Asian Americans are still vulnerable to global economic shifts and political struggles. "The miasma of international relations interrupts our lives constantly," Vijay Prashad observes, as U.S. interventions in Asia and the Middle East in the global War on Terror translated into the mistreatment and marginalization of some Asian American and other communities in the United States.[49] In this context, they have become threatening foreigners rather than members of the American community. It is a pattern that Japanese Americans had experienced during World War II and that Chinese Americans had experienced during the Cold War. For some, the much-touted "rise of Asian Americans" seems more myth than reality.

Epilogue: Redefining America in the Twenty-first Century

In telling the story of the making of Asian America, we have traveled across the centuries, around the world, and back again. The complexity of this history runs from families like mine who are now seven generations in the United States to the most recent arrivals like the Chinese international students I see in my classrooms today and the Karen and Bhutanese refugee children I'll likely see in a few years. Asian Americans have experienced both the limits and the possibilities of America. There are highly successful and visible Asian American politicians, writers, artists, and professional athletes. But there are also many recent Asian immigrants and refugees and others who live in poverty, struggle to learn English, and are at the margins of society.

Despite attempts to lump them together or tell their story through a simplistic and monolithic "model minority" lens, Asian Americans and their histories are in fact exceedingly diverse and complicated. To be Asian American in the twenty-first century is an exercise in coming to terms with a contradiction: benefiting from new positions of power and privilege while still being victims of hate crimes and microaggressions that dismiss Asian American issues and treat Asian Americans as outsiders in their own country.[1]

But one thread that connects this history across time is how Asian

Americans have—over successive generations—continued to build communities and shape American life in ways that have been central to the making of the United States. Today, while the bulk of U.S. media attention focuses on Asian Americans' rise as economically successful overachievers, Asian Americans are rising and becoming more visible in other ways. They are redefining the country through their growing political participation, their leadership in campaigns for justice, and their efforts to make America and the very meaning of American more inclusive in the twenty-first century.

As the fastest growing group in the United States, Asian Americans are beginning to flex their political power. They have been especially successful running as Democrats and gaining statewide office in Hawai'i and California, where there are large Asian American populations. But the recent elections and reelections of Republicans Bobby Jindal as governor of Louisiana and Nikki Haley as governor of South Carolina—two states with much smaller Asian American populations—also demonstrate the broad appeal and geographic and political diversity of contemporary Asian American politicians.

Despite their long history in the United States, Asian immigrants were denied the right of naturalization until the decades during and after World War II. While European immigrants and their descendants quickly capitalized on their ability to deliver votes, Asians, like African Americans, remained disfranchised. With the ability to become naturalized U.S. citizens, Asian Americans slowly began to enter into politics. Chinese American Wing F. Ong was the first Asian American to be elected to state office when he became a state representative in Arizona in 1946. Californian Dalip Singh Saund, a native of India, was the first Asian American to be elected as a U.S. representative in 1956. Three years later, Hiram Fong of Hawai'i became the first Asian American elected to the U.S. Senate, and in 1964 Patsy Takemoto Mink from Hawai'i became the first Asian American woman elected to the U.S. House of Representatives. That growth has continued. During the last decades of the late twentieth century, the number of elected officials of Asian Pacific American descent almost tripled.[2] Asian American politicians have served in some of the highest positions of political leadership. Daniel Inouye represented Hawai'i as a U.S. senator from 1963 to 2012. As president pro tempore of the Senate, he was both the highest-ranking Asian

American elected official in the country and also the most senior member in the Senate and the second-longest serving senator in history. Gary Locke of Washington was the first Chinese American governor and went on to serve as both the secretary of commerce and the ambassador to China under President Barack Obama.

But it is up-and-coming politicians like Mee Moua who best capture both the recent gains of Asian Americans in American politics and the work that remains to be done. Moua was nine years old when her family fled the communist invasion in Laos and came to the United States as Hmong refugees. Her family resettled in Appleton, Wisconsin, where she struggled to learn English and adjust to her new surroundings. She eventually joined the Girl Scouts, the debate club, the basketball team, and the choir at the local Catholic church.

After graduating from high school, she intended to become a doctor. But as an undergraduate at Brown University, she found a different calling to serve her community after becoming more aware of racial and economic injustice in the United States. She went on to receive public policy and law degrees before being elected to the Minnesota State Senate in 2002 at the age of thirty-two. As chair of the powerful judiciary committee, Moua was known to call attention to racial profiling practices and civil rights issues. She also opened the door for other Asian American politicians who have followed in her footsteps. She has insisted that it is time for Asian Americans to play a more central role in American politics. "The issue is not whether the Asian American politicians are ready," she has said. "It's really whether America is ready."[3]

When she retired from the State Senate in 2010, Moua became the president and executive director of Asian Americans Advancing Justice (AAJC), a civil rights advocacy organization based in Washington, D.C. In her new position, Moua has called attention to the persistent poverty rate among Asian Americans, the importance of immigration reform and voting rights for Asian American families, and the need to "build a movement where those who have been dismissed, disadvantaged, disenfranchised and disengaged . . . could be visible, exert influence and wield political power."[4] On the fiftieth anniversary of the 1963 March on Washington, Moua expressed "renewed hope for the American Dream," but also recognized the need to challenge continuing inequalities. Asian Americans marched in 1963 in solidarity with African Americans and others, she noted. Fifty years later, Asian Americans marched again, she declared, "because not to would be fatal."[5]

70. Mee Moua campaigning for state senate in Minnesota, 2002.

If Mee Moua represents a new generation of Asian American politicians seeking to make visible the needs and concerns of contemporary Asian Americans, Fred Korematsu, the Japanese American who refused to comply with the U.S. government's exclusion order and challenged the constitutionality of Executive Order 9066 during World War II, spent his last years making sure that Americans would remember the lessons learned from the struggles of past generations. Forty years after his conviction, Korematsu, along with other Japanese American plaintiffs in separate cases, Minoru Yasui and Gordon Hirabayashi, was back in the courts again. But this time

Korematsu was there to file legal motions with a writ of *coram nobis* to vacate his wrongful conviction. Newly uncovered documents by legal scholar Peter Irons revealed that Justice Department lawyers handling the Supreme Court case had knowingly suppressed evidence that the army's claims of Japanese American espionage were false.[6]

After learning of the government's misconduct, Korematsu agreed to reopen his case. There was "no question in my mind," he explained. "I was prepared to do it and I wanted to do it."[7] A team of lawyers welcomed the chance to, as lawyer Dale Minami explained, take advantage of the "last opportunity to achieve justice denied forty years ago."[8] Their goal was to not only vindicate Japanese American families but to also contribute to the larger civil rights movement on behalf of all Americans.

On November 10, 1983, Korematsu had his day in court. He made his case before a packed courtroom in the U.S. District Court for the Northern District of California. Forty years before, he explained, he had entered the court in handcuffs and was sent to a camp that was unfit for human habitation. He entreated the court to vacate his conviction not just for him personally, but for the benefit of the entire country. "As long as my record stands in federal court," he declared, "any American citizen can be held in prison or concentration camps without a trial or a hearing."[9]

Judge Marilyn Hall Patel vacated Korematsu's criminal conviction on the grounds that the Supreme Court had made its decision based on false information. Although her opinion did not overturn the Supreme Court decision, which still stands as legal precedent, it underscored the importance of the case and the rationale for her decision. Korematsu's case, she explained, "stands as a caution that in times of distress the

71. Fred Korematsu with his Presidential Medal of Freedom, 1998.

shield of military necessity and national security must not be used to protect governmental actions from close scrutiny and accountability."[10] Patel's decision energized the parallel movement to seek reparations for Japanese Americans and influenced the passage of the Civil Liberties Act of 1988.

In the intervening decades, Fred Korematsu was recognized as one of the country's most important civil rights leaders. When President Bill Clinton awarded Korematsu the Presidential Medal of Freedom, he likened him to a select group of "ordinary citizens" who helped lead the struggle for justice: African American Homer Plessy, who challenged Louisiana's segregation law in 1892, and African American Rosa Parks, who refused to give up her seat in the "colored section" of a Montgomery, Alabama, bus to a white passenger in 1955. "To that distinguished list," the president proclaimed, "today we add the name of Fred Korematsu."[11]

Korematsu used his personal experiences and history to call attention to the need to protect the civil liberties of all people. He was an outspoken critic of the U.S. government's national security measures after 9/11 and warned that they were reminiscent of civil liberties violations in the past. He filed an amicus brief with the Supreme Court on behalf of U.S. citizen Yaser Hamdi, designated an "enemy combatant" by the U.S. government and held for two years without access to a lawyer or prospect of a trial. Korematsu also filed an amicus brief on behalf of two non-American citizens imprisoned at Guantánamo Bay without trial. Citing similarities between the wrongful imprisonment of Japanese Americans during World War II and Muslims following 9/11, Korematsu argued that "even in times of crisis, we must guard against prejudice and keep uppermost our commitment to law and justice." For Fred Korematsu, this transcended race, religion, and nationality. It was about civil rights for all Americans and human rights for all.[12]

With histories of both exclusion and inclusion, Asian Americans are uniquely positioned to raise questions about what it means to be American in the twenty-first century. One recent campaign has focused on changing the way in which racial identity is measured to better encompass the growing population of multiracial Americans. While many states had prohibited interracial marriages—including those between whites and Asians—since the nineteenth century, these laws were slowly dismantled after World

War II. California struck down its antimiscegenation laws in 1948. The U.S. Supreme Court prohibited all remaining laws banning interracial marriage in its 1967 decision *Loving* v. *Virginia*. From the 1960s to the 1990s, interracial marriages in the United States increased 800 percent.[13] Correspondingly, the number of children living in mixed race families grew as well. In 1970, there were 460,000 children in mixed race families recorded by the U.S. Census. By 1990, the number had increased to almost 2 million, or 4 percent of all children.[14] But the government's system of counting people through the census was not keeping up with these dramatic demographic changes. Until 2000, respondents could only identify as a member of one race.

Beginning in the 1990s, a movement to change the U.S. Census forms to allow individuals to choose multiple races gained momentum among a broad coalition of multiracial organizations. The Hapa Issues Forum, a group that uses the Hawaiian term "hapa" (meaning "part" or "mixed") to identify multiracial Asian Americans, declared the need to count mixed race Asian Americans in order to better represent and serve all of America's diverse peoples. By 2000, the campaign had succeeded, and beginning with the 2000 census individuals could check off multiple races and/or write in their own ethnicity. That year, multiracial individuals made up 2.4 percent of the total population (6.8 million). Ten years later in 2010, the numbers had increased by 32 percent to over 9 million or 2.9 percent of the population.[15] Among Asian Americans, 2.6 million reported being Asian and one or more races in the 2010 census. This multiracial population had grown by an astounding 60 percent since 2000. Today about 13 percent of Asian Americans in California are multiracial.[16]

Outside the political arena, multiracial Asian Americans have helped reframe discussions about race and identity in popular culture. Golfer Tiger Woods corrected reporters who consistently identified him as African American that he was "the product of two great cultures, one African-American and the other Asian. Truthfully, I feel very fortunate, and equally proud, to be both."[17] Photographer and filmmaker Kip Fulbeck's "Hapa Project" photographed 1,200 self-identified hapas as a way of promoting awareness and recognition of the growing communities of multiracial Asian Americans living in the United States. Volunteers were photographed and then allowed to identify their ethnicities in their own words rather than choose an identity from prescribed categories that obscured their rich backgrounds. Tired of answering the question "What are you?," participants gave a range of answers. One young woman wrote: "I am a person of color. I am not half-'white.' I am not half-'Asian.' I am a whole 'other.' "[18]

While Asian Americans' involvement in the multiracial movement reflects America's growing diversity, their role in the debates over comprehensive immigration reform has raised questions about other pressing issues facing the United States: What should America's relationship to immigration and immigrant communities be? And what does it mean to be American?

Debates over immigration, especially undocumented immigration, resurfaced in the 1980s after new caps on immigration from the Western Hemisphere increased undocumented immigration. By the end of the twentieth century, divisive border battles had erupted in many states along the U.S.-Mexico border, in small towns throughout the country, and in the halls of the U.S. Congress. Most of the discussion is concentrated on border security issues along the U.S.'s southern border and the status of undocumented immigrants in the United States. It is one of the most divisive political issues in contemporary America. On one side of the debate are those who characterize undocumented immigration as an "invasion" of lawbreaking "illegal aliens" who should be deported. On the other side are those who point out how global forces, including U.S. economic policies, as well as U.S. employer needs, fuel a demand for immigrants with or without papers. Despite the fact that many undocumented immigrants come from Asia, Europe, and Africa, the latest immigration debates are mostly seen as a Chicano/Latino issue, and organizations from these communities have taken the lead in demanding reform and in protesting the record number of deportations affecting them.

Yet Asian Americans and Asian American–serving organizations have also become significantly involved in the growing immigrant rights movement and in the movement to reform immigration laws. Advocates cite the enormous visa backlogs that affect immigration from Asia, the need for more H-1B visas, the deportation of Cambodian Americans, and the plight of an estimated 1.3 million undocumented Asian immigrants (around 10 percent of the total undocumented population). Among the last group are immigrants from China, India, the Philippines, Korea, and Vietnam, who come without authorization or overstay their student, work, or visitor's visa and end up in the same underground economy living in fear of detection like other undocumented immigrants.[19] "The time has come for us to mobilize and let other Americans know how the broken immigration system is separating and hurting Asian American and Pacific Islander families and communities," declared Betty Hung, policy director of the Asian Pacific American Legal Center in 2013. That same year, the Asian American Center for Advancing Justice launched the "18 Million Hearts" project to represent diverse Asian American communities in the national dialogue about immigration.[20]

Journalist Jose Antonio Vargas has also become a leading figure in the immigrant rights campaign. Born in the Philippines, Vargas arrived in the United States as a child and was raised by his grandparents in Mountain View, California. Growing up American, Vargas did not realize he had fraudulent identification papers until he applied for his driver's license. With the help of teachers, employers, allies, and other benefactors who became part of what he calls his "underground railroad," he kept a low profile and managed to graduate from high school and college before becoming a journalist. At the *Washington Post*, he won a Pulitzer Prize. In 2011, he "came out" as an undocumented immigrant in an essay in the *New York Times Magazine*. In the years since, he has become an effective spokesperson for the estimated 11 million undocumented immigrants in the United States. He travels the country discussing immigration issues and uses social media to profile the lives of undocumented immigrants and garner support for immigration reform.[21]

Vargas was among the first speakers invited to testify before a 2013 Senate Judiciary Committee hearing on immigration reform. "I come to you as one of our country's 11 million undocumented immigrants, many of us Americans at heart but without the right papers to show for it," he told the senators. "We dream of a path to citizenship so that we can actively participate in our American democracy. We dream of contributing to the country we call our home." Holding up President John F. Kennedy's book *A Nation of Immigrants*, Vargas ended his testimony with pointed questions: "What do you want to do with me? For all the undocumented immigrants . . . what do you want to do with us?"[22]

72. Pulitzer Prize–winning journalist, immigration rights activist, and self-declared undocumented immigrant Jose Antonio Vargas testifies on Capitol Hill in Washington, D.C., before the Senate Judiciary Committee hearing on comprehensive immigration reform, February 13, 2013.

Vargas's activism is one aspect of the growing immigrant rights movement that has evolved and grown in recent years in conjunction with the national debates over immigration reform, the growing power of the Latino and Asian American vote, and changing demographics in the country. Borrowing many of their strategies of direct political action, mass rallies, and acts of civil disobedience from the civil rights movement of the 1960s, the immigrant rights movement explicitly identifies itself as a "continuation" of earlier struggles as well as a product of the ongoing movements to protect civil and human rights. Partnerships with African American civil rights organizations like the Black Immigration Network and the NAACP highlight areas of common ground, including inclusion and racial equality, "full civic participation and citizenship for all," economic justice, and the recognition of historical injustice.[23]

Vargas identifies himself as a "student of the civil rights movement" and has likened the unequal status of undocumented immigrants to the history of slavery in the United States. On the fiftieth anniversary of Dr. Martin

Luther King Jr.'s speech at the March on Washington in 1963, Vargas published online an "Undocumented Immigrant Version" of King's "I Have a Dream" speech. "I have a dream . . . of citizenship, in a country I call my home, to a nation I want to keep contributing to," he wrote. "I have a dream . . . of not being judged by the pieces of papers I lack, but by the content of my character and the talent and skills I offer . . . I have a dream . . . of being a free human being."[24]

Linking the campaign for comprehensive immigration reform to a longer history of civil rights in the country has been an effective means of securing allies and building support for specific legislative action. But it has also served a larger role in helping to redefine the very essence of what it means to be American. Along those lines, Vargas has spearheaded the "Define American" campaign to start a "renewed conversation" about immigration and its place in the United States. The online project invites participants to "define American." "Why is America special to you? What values do we, as Americans, share? What is the role of immigrants and immigration in America?" the project asks. Marshaling the power of social media to engage people in participatory democracy, users upload photos, written texts, or short videos to join the conversation. "It starts with us," the "Define American" site declares.[25]

Vargas himself has set the tone of the conversation by proactively claiming his American identity. For him, it is one based on ideals and practice rather than on papers and legal status. Undocumented immigrants are "Americans at heart," Vargas claims, "for defining American runs deeper than documentation."[26] A *Time* magazine profile of Vargas featured a cover that helped to popularize this message with the bold title: "WE ARE AMERICANS (Just not legally)."[27] A year later, Vargas repeated his claim of being an American and added a call for action: "As far as I'm concerned, I'm an American. I'm just waiting for my country to recognize it."[28]

The "Define American" project is hugely popular. Notable politicians and media personalities like former Secretary of State Hillary Rodham Clinton, Senator Harry Reid, and TV personality Stephen Colbert have participated, but there are also hundreds of videos uploaded by everyday Americans, including an anonymous undocumented immigrant who, as a young child, crossed three borders to travel from El Salvador to Los Angeles. A college graduate, the author identifies as a DREAMer (a reference to those who support the DREAM Act, an acronym for Development, Relief, and Education for Alien Minors), that would allow individuals who arrived in the United States at a young age to gain legal status. Hiding his face on camera to avoid identification and possible arrest and deportation, the anonymous author writes on the "Define American" site, "to be an American is a matter of the values that define our lives . . . It's true, I did not come here with the 'right' papers. BUT I've been raised with the right values."[29] Representing an important and growing segment of the contemporary Asian American population, Jose Antonio Vargas and his personal stand to advocate for the rights of undocumented Americans has grown into a larger movement to create a more inclusive and equitable America for all.

There are a wide variety of Asian American voices now being heard from, from Tiger Mom Amy Chua to DREAMer Jose Antonio Vargas. Asian Americans include those who have just arrived today as well as those whose families have been in the United States for several generations. They are working-class families who struggle to make ends meet as well as professionals with multiple advanced degrees, passports, and homes. Some embrace the model minority label while others actively work to dispel it. Their multiethnic and multiracial families are headed by same sex parents, single parents, and grandparents. They are adoptees, refugees, immigrants, naturalized citizens, undocumented immigrants, and U.S.-born Americans. They symbolize stories of American success and privilege as well as struggle and poverty.

As diverse as they are, they are part of a larger Asian American community that—through its complexity—uniquely captures the story of America. Theirs is a history of immigrant dreams, American realities, and global connections that has helped to make the United States what it is today. And as the fastest growing group in the country, Asian Americans are also helping to create the nation that we'll be in the future.

Bibliographic Essay

This book draws from both community-based research and archives as well as academic scholarship from a wide range of disciplines. The following sources have been among the most helpful in the writing of this book and are included here as a general introduction to the study of Asian American history and communities. See the Notes section for a complete record of all sources.

Earlier syntheses of Asian American history include Ronald T. Takaki, *Strangers from a Different Shore: A History of Asian Americans* (Boston: Little, Brown, 1989); Sucheng Chan, *Asian Americans: An Interpretive History* (Boston: Twayne, 1991); and Shelley Sang-Hee Lee, *A New History of Asian America* (New York: Routledge, 2013). Useful publications covering multiple aspects of Asian American history and contemporary communities include Gary Y. Okihiro, *Margins and Mainstreams: Asians in American History and Culture* (Seattle: University of Washington Press, 1994) and *The Columbia Guide to Asian American History* (New York: Columbia University Press, 2001); Franklin Odo, *The Columbia Documentary History of the Asian American Experience* (New York: Columbia University Press, 2002); Min Zhou and James V. Gatewood, eds., *Contemporary Asian America: A Multidisciplinary Reader* (New York: New York University Press, 2000); Jean Yu-wen Shen Wu and Min Song, eds., *Asian American Studies: A Reader* (New Brunswick, NJ: Rutgers University Press, 2000); Shirley Hune and Gail M. Nomura, *Asian/Pacific Islander American Women: A Historical Anthology* (New York: New York University Press, 2003); Lon Kurashige and Alice Yang Murray, eds., *Major Problems in*

Asian American History (Boston: Houghton Mifflin, 2003); and Pawan Dhingra and Robyn Magalit Rodriguez, *Asian America: Sociological and Interdisciplinary Perspectives* (Malden, MA: Polity Press, 2014).

This book uses Asian Americans to retell U.S. history and follows others in the fields of African American and Native American Studies, such as: Mary Helen Washington, " 'Disturbing the Peace: What Happens to American Studies If You Put African American Studies at the Center?': Presidential Address to the American Studies Association, October 29, 1997," *American Quarterly* 50, no. 1 (March 1998): 1–12 and Susan Sleeper-Smith, Juliana Barr, Jean M. O'Brien, Nancy Shoemaker, and Scott Manning Stevens, eds., *Why You Can't Teach United States History without American Indians* (Chapel Hill: University of North Carolina Press, 2015).

An important part of understanding U.S. history today is through its transnational, international, and global contexts and connections. I have found broad definitions of global American history and transnational studies to be the most helpful. See for example: Thomas Bender, *Rethinking American History in a Global Age* (Berkeley: University of California Press, 2002); David Thelen, "The Nation and Beyond: Transnational Perspective on United States History," *Journal of American History* 86, no. 3 (1999): 965–75; Richard White, "The Nationalization of Nature," *The Journal of American History* 86, no. 3 (1999): 976–86; Shelley Fisher Fishkin, "Crossroads of Cultures: The Transnational Turn in American Studies—Presidential Address to the American Studies Association, November 12, 2004," *American Quarterly* 57, no. 1 (2005): 17–57; Sanjeev Khagram and Peggy Levitt, eds., *The Transnational Studies Reader: Intersections and Innovations* (New York: Taylor & Francis, 2008); and Sandhya Shukla and Heidi Tinsman, eds., *Imagining Our Americas: Toward a Transnational Frame* (Durham, NC: Duke University Press, 2007).

A growing number of works exploring the overlapping histories of Asians in the U.S., Canada, and Latin America have also been instrumental in placing this history of Asian Americans within a larger "globalized Americas" context. Evelyn Hu-DeHart's pioneering work, including "Coolies, Shopkeepers, Pioneers: The Chinese of Mexico and Peru, 1849–1930," *Amerasia* 15, no. 2 (1989): 91–116 and "From Area Studies to Ethnic Studies: The Study of the Chinese Diaspora in Latin America," in *Asian Americans: Comparative and Global Perspectives*, ed. Shirley Hune (Pullman: Washington State University Press, 1991), 5–16, has been instrumental in this regard, as are the works of W. Peter Ward, *White Canada Forever: Popular Attitudes and Public Policy Toward Orientals in British Columbia* (Montreal: McGill-Queens University Press, 1978); Joan M. Jensen, *Passage from India: Asian Indian Immigrants in North America* (New Haven: Yale University Press, 1988); Patricia Roy, *A White Man's Province: British Columbia Politicians and Chinese and Japanese Immigrants,*

1858–1914 (Vancouver: University of British Columbia Press, 1989); Walton Look Lai, *Indentured Labor, Caribbean Sugar: Chinese and Indian Migrants to the British West Indies, 1838–1918* (Baltimore: Johns Hopkins University Press, 1993); Lynn Pan, ed., *The Encyclopedia of the Chinese Overseas* (Cambridge: Harvard University Press, 1999); Seiichi Higashide, *Adios to Tears: The Memoirs of a Japanese-Peruvian Internee in U.S. Concentration Camps* (Seattle: University of Washington Press, 2000); Adam McKeown, *Chinese Migrant Networks and Cultural Change: Peru, Chicago, Hawaii, 1900–1936* (Chicago: University of Chicago Press, 2001); Akemi Kikumura-Yano, ed., *Encyclopedia of Japanese Descendants in the Americas: An Illustrated History of the Nikkei* (Walnut Creek, CA: AltaMira, 2002); Lane Ryo Hirabayashi, Akemi Kikumura-Yano, and James A. Hirabayashi, eds., *New Worlds, New Lives: Globalization and People of Japanese Descent in the Americas and from Latin America in Japan* (Stanford: Stanford University Press, 2002); Daniel M. Masterson and Sayaka Funada-Classen, *The Japanese in Latin America* (Urbana: University of Illinois Press, 2004); Lisa Yun, *The Coolie Speaks: Chinese Indentured Laborers and African Slaves in Cuba* (Philadelphia: Temple University Press, 2008); Moon-Ho Jung, *Coolies and Cane: Race, Labor, and Sugar in the Age of Emancipation* (Baltimore: Johns Hopkins University Press, 2008); Edward R. Slack, Jr., "Los Chinos in New Spain: A Corrective Lens for a Distorted Image," *Journal of World History* 20, no. 1 (2009): 35–67 and "Sinifying New Spain: Cathay's Influence on Colonial Mexico via the Nao de China," in *The Chinese in Latin America and the Caribbean*, eds. Walton Look Lai and Chee Beng Tan (Leiden, Netherlands: Brill, 2010): 7–34. Robert Chao Romero, *The Chinese in Mexico, 1882–1940* (Tucson: University of Arizona Press, 2011); Julia María Schiavone Camacho, *Chinese Mexicans: Transpacific Migration and the Search for a Homeland, 1910–1960* (Chapel Hill, NC: University of North Carolina Press, 2012); Grace Delgado, *Making the Chinese Mexican: Global Migration, Localism, and Exclusion in the U.S.-Mexico Borderlands* (Stanford, CA: Stanford University Press, 2012); Kathleen M. López, *Chinese Cubans: A Transnational History: A Transnational History* (Chapel Hill: University of North Carolina Press, 2013).

Some of the most important works published recently on Chinese immigration, the anti-Chinese movement, and the Chinese exclusion era include Sucheng Chan, *This Bittersweet Soil: The Chinese in California Agriculture, 1860–1910* (Berkeley: University of California Press, 1989); Sucheng Chan, ed., *Entry Denied: Exclusion and the Chinese Community in America, 1882–1943* (Philadelphia: Temple University Press, 1991); Lucy Salyer, *Laws Harsh as Tigers: Chinese Immigrants and the Shaping of Modern Immigration Law* (Chapel Hill: University of North Carolina Press, 1995); Judy Yung, *Unbound Feet: A Social History of Chinese Women in San*

Francisco (Berkeley: University of California Press, 1995); Andrew Gyory, *Closing the Gate: Race, Politics, and the Chinese Exclusion Act* (Chapel Hill: University of North Carolina Press, 1998); George Anthony Peffer, *If They Don't Bring Their Women Here: Chinese Female Immigration Before Exclusion* (Urbana: University of Illinois Press, 1999); Robert G. Lee, *Orientals: Asian Americans in Popular Culture* (Philadelphia: Temple University Press, 1999); Madeline Hsu, *Dreaming of Gold, Dreaming of Home: Transnationalism and Migration Between the United States and South China, 1882–1943* (Stanford: Stanford University Press, 2000); Nayan Shah, *Contagious Divides: Epidemics and Race in San Francisco's Chinatown* (Berkeley: University of California Press, 2001); Erika Lee, *At America's Gates: Chinese Immigration During the Exclusion Era, 1882–1943* (Chapel Hill: University of North Carolina Press, 2003); Kevin Scott Wong, *Americans First: Chinese Americans and the Second World War* (Cambridge: Harvard University Press, 2005); Karen J. Leong, *The China Mystique: Pearl S. Buck, Anna May Wong, Mayling Soong, and the Transformation of American Orientalism* (Berkeley: University of California Press, 2005); Jean Pfaelzer; *Driven Out: The Forgotten War Against Chinese Americans* (Berkeley: University of California Press, 2008); and Erika Lee and Judy Yung, *Angel Island: Immigrant Gateway to America* (New York: Oxford University Press, 2010). Oral histories and poetry of Chinese detainees on Angel Island are preserved by Him Mark Lai, Genny Lim, and Judy Yung in *Island: Poetry and History of Chinese Immigrants on Angel Island, 1910–1940* (San Francisco: HOC DOI, 1980) and 2nd ed. (Seattle: University of Washington Press, 2014) and through the Angel Island Immigration Station Foundation's "Immigrant Voices" project: http://www.aiisf.org/immigrant-voices.

Important recent works on Japanese immigration, the anti-Japanese movement, and Japanese American communities include Roger Daniels, *The Politics of Prejudice: The Anti-Japanese Movement in California and the Struggle for Japanese Exclusion* (Berkeley: University of California Press, 1962); Ronald T. Takaki, *Pau Hana: Plantation Life and Labor in Hawaii, 1835–1920* (Honolulu: University of Hawaii Press, 1984); Evelyn Nakano Glenn, *Issei, Nisei, War Bride: Three Generations of Japanese American Women in Domestic Service* (Philadelphia: Temple University Press, 1986); Eiichiro Azuma, *Between Two Empires: Race, History, and Transnationalism in Japanese America* (New York: Oxford University Press, 2005); and Valerie Matsumoto, *City Girls: The Nisei Social World in Los Angeles, 1920–1950* (New York: Oxford University Press, 2014). The Densho Digital Archive (www.densho.org) is one of the best repositories of historical material related to the Japanese American experience, with visual history interviews and transcripts, photos, documents, and newspapers spanning the early 1900s to the redress movement in the 1980s, with a particular focus on the World War II mass incarceration. John Kuo Wei Tchen and Dylan Yeats have collected an impressive archive of yellow peril material in *Yellow Peril!: An Archive of Anti-Asian Fear* (London: Verso, 2014).

The best first-person account of Korean immigration and Korean American communities before World War II is Mary Paik Lee, *Quiet Odyssey: A Pioneer Korean Woman in America*, ed. Sucheng Chan (Seattle: University of Washington Press, 1990). See also Richard S. Kim, *The Quest for Statehood: Korean Immigrant Nationalism and U.S. Sovereignty, 1905–1945* (New York: Oxford University Press, 2011). The Korean American Digital Archive has collected documents, photographs, and sound files in a searchable archive at: http://digitallibrary.usc.edu/cdm/landingpage/collection/p15799coll126.

On South Asian immigration and exclusion before World War II, see Joan M. Jensen, *Passage from India*; Nayan Shah, *Stranger Intimacy: Contesting Race, Sexuality and the Law in the North American West* (Berkeley: University of California Press, 2011); Vivek Bald, *Bengali Harlem and the Lost Histories of South Asian America* (Cambridge: Harvard University Press, 2013); and Seema Sohi, *Echoes of Mutiny: Race, Surveillance, and Indian Anticolonialism in North America* (New York: Oxford University Press, 2014). The South Asian American Digital Archive preserves and shares South Asian American history with documents, photographs, oral histories, and first person accounts at: https://www.saadigitalarchive.org/.

The rich and growing body of literature on the Filipino experience in the United States includes Yen Le Espiritu, *Home Bound: Filipino American Lives Across Cultures, Communities, and Countries* (Berkeley: University of California Press, 2003); Catherine Ceniza Choy, *Empire of Care: Nursing and Migration in Filipino American History* (Durham, NC: Duke University Press, 2003); Rick Baldoz, *The Third Asiatic Invasion: Migration and Empire in Filipino America, 1898–1946* (New York: New York University Press, 2011); and Dawn Bohulano Mabalon, *Little Manila Is in the Heart: The Making of the Filipina/o American Community in Stockton, California* (Durham, NC: Duke University Press, 2013).

New scholarship has illustrated how undocumented Asian immigration was an essential Asian immigration strategy during the exclusion era and that the U.S. response helped create the United States' modern border security system. See Erika Lee, *At America's Gates*; Chao Romero, *The Chinese in Mexico*; Delgado, *Making the Chinese Mexican*; and Elliott Young, *Alien Nation: Chinese Migration in the Americas from the Coolie Era Through World War II* (Chapel Hill: University of North Carolina Press, 2014). Mae Ngai's *Impossible Subjects: Illegal Immigration and the Making of Modern America* (Princeton: Princeton University Press, 2004) uses several examples of Asian immigration to examine the shaping of modern immigration law.

Among the most comprehensive studies of the mass removal and incarceration of Japanese Americans during World War II are Roger Daniels, *Prisoners Without Trial: Japanese Americans in World War II* (New York: Hill & Wang, 1993); Greg Robinson, *By Order of the President: FDR and the Internment of Japanese Americans* (Cambridge: Harvard University Press, 2001) and *A Tragedy of Democracy: Japanese Confinement in North America* (New York: Columbia University Press, 2009); and Roger Daniels, *The Japanese American Cases: The Rule of Law in Time of War* (Lawrence: University Press of Kansas, 2013). See also the U.S. Commission on Wartime Relocation and Internment of Civilians report titled *Personal Justice Denied* (Washington, DC; Seattle: Civil Liberties Public Education Fund; University of Washington Press, 1997). For Japanese Peruvians in the U.S., see: C. Harvey Gardiner's *Pawns in a Triangle of Hate: The Peruvian Japanese and the United States* (Seattle: University of Washington Press, 1981).

A number of new studies have explored the impact of Cold War international and domestic politics on Asian American communities, including Ji-yeon Yuh, *Beyond the Shadow of Camptown: Korean Military Brides in America* (New York: New York University Press, 2002); Xiaojian Zhao, *Remaking Chinese America: Immigration, Family, and Community, 1940–1965* (New Brunswick, NJ: Rutgers University Press, 2002); Christina Klein, *Cold War Orientalism: Asia in the Middlebrow Imagination* (Berkeley: University of California Press, 2004); Ellen Wu, *The Color of Success: Asian Americans and the Origins of the Model Minority* (Princeton: Princeton University Press, 2013); and Catherine Ceniza Choy, *Global Families: A History of Asian International Adoption in America*, 2013).

Studies on the causes of recent Asian immigration have focused on changes in U.S. immigration policy after 1965, global economic restructuring in both the United States and Asia, and increased U.S. political, economic, and military roles in Asia. Helpful overviews include Eric Yo Ping Lai and Dennis Arguelles, eds., *The New Face of Asian Pacific America: Numbers, Diversity and Change in the 21st Century* (Los Angeles: AsianWeek with UCLA's Asian American Studies Center Press, 2003); Philip Q. Yang, "A Theory of Asian Immigration to the United States," *Journal of Asian American Studies* 13, no. 1 (2010): 1–34; and Philip Q. Yang, *Asian Immigration to the United States* (Hoboken, NJ: Wiley, 2011). On the 1965 Act, see David M. Reimers, *Still the Golden Door: The Third World Comes to America* (New York: Columbia University Press, 1985). Studies of specific Asian immigrant groups include Eui-Young Yu and Elaine H. Kim, eds., *East to America: Korean American Life Stories* (New York: New Press, 1996); Min Zhou, *Contemporary Chinese America: Immigration, Ethnicity, and Community Transformation*, 2nd ed. (Philadelphia: Temple University Press, 2009); Junaid Rana, *Terrifying Muslims: Race and Labor in the South Asian Diaspora* (Durham, NC: Duke University Press, 2011); and Espiritu, *Home Bound*.

Important new perspectives on the Asian American movements of the 1960s and 1970s include works by Daryl J. Maeda, including *Chains of Babylon: The Rise of Asian America* (Minneapolis: University of Minnesota Press, 2009) and *Rethinking the Asian American Movement* (New York: Routledge, 2012); Sonia Shah, ed., *Dragon Ladies: Asian American Feminists Breathe Fire* (Boston: South End, 1997); and David L. Eng and Alice Y. Hom, eds., *Q+A: Queer in Asian America* (Philadelphia: Temple University Press, 1998).

Oral history collections of Southeast Asian refugees include Sucheng Chan, ed., *Hmong Means Free: Life in Laos and America* (Philadelphia: Temple University Press, 1994), *Survivors: Cambodian Refugees in the United States* (Champaign: University of Illinois Press, 2004); *Vietnamese American 1.5 Generation* (Philadelphia: Temple University Press, 2006); Sucheng Chan and Audrey U. Kim, *Not Just Victims: Conversations with Cambodian Community Leaders in the United States* (Champaign: University of Illinois Press, 2003); Lillian Faderman and Ghia Xiong, *I Begin My Life All Over: The Hmong and the American Immigrant Experience* (Boston, MA: Beacon Press, 2005). See also Yen Le Espiritu, *Body Counts: The Vietnam War and Militarized Refugees* (Berkeley: University of California Press, 2014), and Chia Youyee Vang, *Hmong America: Reconstructing Community in Diaspora* (Champaign, IL: University of Illinois Press, 2010). The digital collections of the Southeast Asian Archive at the University of California, Irvine, can be found at SEAAdoc: Documenting the Southeast Asian Experience, http://seaadoc.lib.uci.edu/.

For recent studies that have documented and analyzed the War on Terror's impact on immigrant, including Asian, communities, see Tram Nguyen, *We Are All Suspects Now: Untold Stories from Immigrant Communities After 9/11* (Boston: Beacon, 2005). The special issue of the *Asian American Literary Review* 2:1.5 (Fall 2011) on the tenth anniversary of 9/11 explores the impact of 9/11 on Asian Americans through a range of excellent first-person narratives, interviews, art, and commentary.

Image Credits

1. From Abraham Ortelius, *Theatrum orbis terrarum* (His Epitome of the Theater of the World) (London, Ieames Shawe, 1603). Courtesy of the James Ford Bell Library, University of Minnesota.
2. From Carl Nebel, *Viaje pintoresco y arqueológico sobre la parte más interesante de la República Mexicana, en los años transcurridos desde 1829 hasta 1834* (México: Librería de M. Porrúa, 1963).
3. New York Public Library Digital Gallery.
4. Courtesy MS AM 2211 (9), Houghton Library, Harvard University.
5. From the collections of the University of Minnesota Libraries.
6. National Archives at Philadelphia, PA.
7. Author's family photo.
8. Pajaro Valley Historical Association.
9. Beinecke Rare Book and Manuscript Library, Yale University.
10. Courtesy of the Bancroft Library, University of California, Berkeley.
11. Scan by Vincent Chin, National Archives at San Francisco.
12. San Francisco History Center, San Francisco Public Library.
13. Library of Congress.
14. Courtesy of California State Parks 2015.
15. National Archives at Washington, DC.
16. Library and Archives Canada/Department of Employment and Immigration fonds/e008222747. © Government of Canada. Reproduced with the permission of the Minister of Public Works and Government Services Canada (2014).

17. By Jose Angel Espinoza (1932).
18. Courtesy of California State Parks 2015.
19. Library of Congress.
20. Denshopd-p25-00002: Courtesy of Densho, the Yamada Family Collection.
21. Japanese American National Museum (Gift of the Takeya Family, 99.208.1).
22. From the collections of the University of Minnesota Libraries.
23. Courtesy of the Wong Ching Foo Collection, NYU A/P/A Institute.
24. Courtesy of USC Korean American Digital Archive.
25. Courtesy of Rani Bagai.
26. Courtesy of Rani Bagai.
27. *The Hindusthanee Student*, January 1916. Courtesy of the South Asian American Digital Archive.
28. *San Francisco Daily News*.
29. Courtesy Vancouver Public Library. Special Collections, VPL 6231.
30. Bhagat Singh Thind Collection, South Asian American Digital Archive. Courtesy of David Thind and the South Asian American Digital Archive.
31. Stockton Chapter, Filipino American National Historical Society.
32. Bancroft Library, University of California, Berkeley.
33. Stockton Chapter, Filipino American National Historical Society.
34. San Francisco History Center, San Francisco Public Library.
35. Dr. Seuss Collection, Special Collections & Archives, UC San Diego Library
36. World War Poster Collection (Mss 36), Literary Manuscripts Collection, University of Minnesota Libraries, Minneapolis, Minnesota.
37. Photographer: Dorothea Lange. Bancroft Library, University of California, Berkeley.
38. Photographer: Dorothea Lange. Bancroft Library, University of California, Berkeley.
39. Photographer: Dorothea Lange. Bancroft Library, University of California, Berkeley.
40. Photographer: Dorothea Lange. Bancroft Library, University of California, Berkeley.
41. Photo courtesy of Karen Korematsu and the Korematsu Institute.
42. Photographer: Dorothea Lange. Bancroft Library, University of California, Berkeley.
43. Denshopd-p7-00008: Courtesy of Densho, the Kaneko Family Collection.
44. Photograph No. 53. Records of the Office of Controls, Special War Problems Division. RG 59. General Records of the Department of State, National Archives at Washington, DC.

45. Photograph No. 75. Records of the Office of Controls, Special War Problems Division. RG 59. General Records of the Department of State, National Archives at Washington, DC.
46. © Bettmann/CORBIS.
47. Courtesy of Teresa Swartz.
48. Denshopd-p113-00039: Courtesy of Densho, the Uyeda Groves Family Collection.
49. Photo by Ed Clark/The LIFE Picture Collection/Getty Images.
50. LBJ Library photo by Yoichi Okamoto.
51. © Corky Lee. Courtesy of the artist.
52. © Corky Lee. Courtesy of the artist.
53. © Corky Lee. Courtesy of the artist.
54. © Corky Lee. Courtesy of the artist.
55. Photo by Douglas Wachter, copyright 2014.
56. © Corky Lee. Courtesy of the artist.
57. © Corky Lee. Courtesy of the artist.
58. Denshopd-p10-00006: Courtesy of Densho, the Kinoshita Family Collection.
59. © Bettmann/CORBIS.
60. MS-SEA 025, Special Collections and Archives, The UCI Libraries, Irvine, California.
61. Courtesy Gerald R. Ford Library.
62. Courtesy of Saengmany Ratsabout.
63. Minnesota Historical Society.
64. Unknown artist, c. 2000. Author's collection.
65. Unknown artist, c. 2000. Author's collection.
66. Courtesy of Justin Schell.
67. Copyright by the Estate of Vincent Chin, used with permission.
68. © Deborah Feingold/Corbis.
69. © Corky Lee. Courtesy of the artist.
70. *Star Tribune*/Minneapolis-St. Paul 2014.
71. Photo by Shirley Nakao, Courtesy of the Korematsu Institute.
72. © Susan Walsh/AP/Corbis.

Acknowledgments

This book began many years ago when I was in college and started learning about Asian American history for the first time. There had been no mention of Asian Americans in my high school history classes, and like many Chinese American families who had lived under the shadow of the Chinese exclusion laws, my own family did not talk about our past. I'll never forget my shock when I learned about the history of the violent and hate-filled anti-Chinese movement for the first time. "I never knew that this happened," I remember thinking.

By the time I finished college, Sucheng Chan and Ron Takaki had published their seminal histories of Asian Americans. I had the privilege of meeting both of them when they visited Tufts University where I was an undergraduate. They helped me imagine the possibility of becoming a historian and contributing to the ongoing work of preserving and writing Asian American history. Sucheng was especially encouraging and she became an important mentor.

A lot has changed since then. There are now award-winning books, documentary films, and historic sites that preserve many aspects of Asian American history. However, more often than not, my students still tell me that they "never knew this happened." I hear this nearly every semester at the University of Minnesota and whenever I give a public talk around the country and abroad. I could be talking to undergraduates at an elite Ivy League university, New York City museum docents, or high school teachers from the South. "I never knew that this happened" has become a constant refrain and points to the continuing invisibility of Asian Americans in American history and life.

Countless individuals, institutions, and community organizations have countered this invisibility by documenting and preserving Asian American history and saving historic sites. They have collectively insisted that Asian American history matters. This book has drawn generously from their efforts and from the amazing research that historians and others have done in the past twenty-five years. The work of Sucheng Chan, Ron Takaki, Evelyn Hu-DeHart, Roger Daniels, and Gary Okihiro has been especially important to me.

Many colleagues, students, and research assistants also helped shape this book with their ideas, feedback, and assistance over the past ten years. Judy Yung and K. Scott Wong have been supportive colleagues, friends, and mentors since my graduate school days, and their encouragement and feedback have continued to be important to me. I strive every day to follow Judy's example of community-engaged research. My close friend and former colleague Donna Gabaccia has shaped the way I think about history in more ways than one. I am much more of a world historian than I used to be due to her influence, and her globe-trotting, interdisciplinary work continues to amaze and inspire me. In this book, I have tried to emulate her practice of doing "premature synthesis," as she calls it. Her timely advice helped fight off bouts of anxiety when I felt overwhelmed. She also read the manuscript in its entirety and offered insightful suggestions on just how the book was (and was not) global history. Gary Okihiro's commitment to writing "anti-history" that challenges dominant paradigms has shaped this book in many ways, and his encouragement on this project has been especially appreciated. Roger Daniels also lent his keen and exacting eye to the manuscript more than once and I am grateful for both his suggestions and his support. Special thanks to other friends and colleagues who generously read drafts of this work in various forms and offered helpful feedback, including Eiichiro Azuma, Catherine Ceniza Choy, Sarah Chambers, Jigna Desai, Saje Mathieu, Mae Ngai, Lisa Sun-hee Park, Kong Pha, Edward Slack, Jr., Chia Youyee Vang, Barbara Welke, Scott Wong, and Judy Yung. I also thank the anonymous reviewers at Princeton University Press, University of California Press, and Yale University Press for their instructive and timely feedback early in the process of writing this book.

The University of Minnesota has generously supported this research in numerous ways, including the President's Multicultural Research Award, the McKnight Land Grant Professorship, the McKnight Presidential Fellowship, an Institute for Advanced Study Fellowship, and the Rudolph J. Vecoli Chair in Immigration History. The Center for Writing Studies' ”Hunkers" provided an encouraging writing community for many summers. Wonderful friends and colleagues in the Department of History, the Asian American Studies Program, and the Immigration History

Research Center at the University of Minnesota have provided valuable feedback, suggestions, and support, including David Chang, Ted Farmer, Karen Ho, Josephine Lee, MJ Maynes, Rich Lee, Elaine Tyler May, Pat McNamara, Lisa Norling, Jean O'Brien, Yuichiro Onishi, Lisa Sun-hee Park, Carla Rahn Philipps, Saengmany Ratsabout, J. B. Shank, Teresa Swartz, and Ann Waltner. Thanks especially to my Asian American Studies colleagues who helped to vet book titles and cover images. Good friends near and far have cheered me on over the years. Thank you especially to Daniel Slager who gave me helpful publishing advice at a crucial time.

A small army of research assistants provided crucial labor on this project over more than ten years, including Erika Busse, Lothar Busse, Grant Grays, Ben Hartmann, Lisong Liu, Joyce Mariano, Masako Nakamura, Yuichiro Onishi, Andrea Moerer, Kim Park Nelson, Juliana Hu Pegues, Kong Pha, Nicole Phelps, Kelly Condit-Shrestha, Mary Strasma, Jasmine Kar Tang, and Andrew Urban. Librarians and archivists at multiple institutions helped me track down sources far and wide, especially the interlibrary staff, Daniel Necas, Marguerite Ragnow, Justin Schell, and Rafael Tarrago, at the University of Minnesota. Nancy Sims shared her expertise on copyright use. Photographer Corky Lee shared more than 200 of his classic photographs documenting Asian American life with me, and it is an honor to include a few of them in this book. Helen Zia, Teresa Swartz, Justin Schell, Rani Cardona, and Saengmany Ratsabout also allowed me to use photos from their personal collections.

Invited lectures at several institutions helped me share research-in-progress and receive valuable feedback. I thank the faculty, staff, and students especially at Stanford University, UC Berkeley, Brown University, University of Toronto, Ohio State University, University of British Columbia, Smith College, Indiana University, the Huntington Library, Pennsylvania State University, Academia Sinica (Taiwan), University of Wisconsin, Milwaukee, Harvard University, Macalester College, the Japanese Association for Migration Studies, the Wing Luke Museum of the Asian Pacific American Experience, and the University of Colorado.

Portions of this book have been previously published in different form, and I thank the journal editors and readers for their helpful feedback shaping my ideas. Sections of Chapter 4 appeared in "Orientalisms in the Americas: A Hemispheric Approach to Asian American History," *Journal of Asian American Studies* (October 2005): 235–56; portions of Chapter 5 appeared in "Hemispheric Orientalism and the 1907 Race Riots on the Pacific Coast," *Amerasia Journal* 33:2 (September, 2007): 19–48 and in "The 'Yellow Peril' in the United States and Peru: A Transnational History of Japanese Exclusion, 1920s-World War Two," in Camilla Fojas and Rudy Guevera, eds., *Transnational Crossroads: Remapping the Americas and the Pacific* (Lincoln: University of Nebraska Press, 2012) 315–58.

My agent, Sandra Dijkstra, believed in this book and in my ability to tell this story. She expertly and enthusiastically ushered it forward with the passion and style that she is known for. She and Elise Capron cheered me on and provided wise counsel and timely support during some unexpected twists and turns. I feel so fortunate to be represented by an agency that believes in the power of books to make the world a better place.

The amazing team at Simon & Schuster provided the kind of insightful and hands-on editorial support that every author dreams about. Editor Thomas LeBien was an indispensable partner on this project from the very beginning. He understood this book's potential and guided me every step of the way, even if I might have thrown him for a loop by turning in a 220,000-word first draft. He asked smart questions, made thoughtful suggestions, and with amazing insight and skill, helped me see the big picture. Because of him, this is a better book, and I am now a better writer. Brit Hvide moved the manuscript into the first stage of production. I am deeply grateful to Jonathan Karp, Alice Mayhew, and especially Priscilla Painton, who lent their support to the project at a crucial time. Priscilla pushed me in all the right ways to bring more focus to the final manuscript. She and Sydney Tanigawa moved the book into the last stage of production, and with copyeditor Fred Chase, recommended important edits that shaped the book into its final form. The press's proofreaders suggested helpful corrections and clarifications. Production editor Mara Lurie deftly managed additional edits and saw the book all the way to the printer. Elisa Rivlin offered valuable feedback, and Erin Reback and Dana Trocker made sure to publicize and market the book far and wide. My deepest thanks go to editorial assistant Sophia Jimenez, who expertly managed the hectic final stages of production, provided timely and helpful support, offered design advice, and answered my many questions with cheer.

Thank you to my family, including my parents, Fay and Howard Lee, sisters Kristen Lee and Laurel Lee-Alexander, and in-laws Bill and Molly Buccella, who were always in the background cheering me on. My husband, Mark Buccella, and our two sons, Ben and Billy, have lived with this book every day and have felt all of the ups and downs that have come with it. Thank you, Ben and Billy, for being such great kids and for listening patiently to the many "history matters" stories at the dinner table. Your own convictions about justice and injustice make me proud. Thank you, Mark, for giving wise and supportive advice on everything from the text, images, and book design and for still being my best friend and love after all of these years.

This book is dedicated to the many undergraduate and graduate students I have taught. They continually push me to rethink what it means to be Asian American, and I am a better scholar and teacher because of them.

Notes

Repositories

Asian American Studies Center Library, University of California, Los Angeles
Bancroft Library, University of California, Berkeley
Centro de Estudios de Historia de México, Mexico City, Mexico
Densho Digital Archive
Ethnic Studies Library, University of California, Berkeley
Gerald R. Ford Presidential Digital Library
Hmong Resource Center Library, St. Paul, Minnesota
Hoover Institution Archives, Stanford University, Stanford, California
Immigration History Research Center Archives, University of Minnesota, Minneapolis, Minnesota
James Ford Bell Library, University of Minnesota, Minneapolis, Minnesota
Kauai Historical Society, Lihui, Kauai, Hawai'i
Labor Archives and Research Center, San Francisco State University, San Francisco, California
Library and Archives Canada, Ottawa
Minnesota Historical Society, St. Paul, Minnesota
San Francisco History Center, San Francisco Public Library, San Francisco, California
South Asian American Digital Archive
Special Collections, University of California, Los Angeles
U.S. National Archives at College Park, Maryland [NA CP]

U.S. National Archives at Philadelphia, Pennsylvania

U.S. National Archives at San Francisco, California

U.S. National Archives at Seattle, Washington

U.S. National Archives, Washington, D.C.

Government Records

Asiatics, Orientals (Japanese, Chinese, and East Indians), Records of the Immigration Branch, RG 76, Library and Archives Canada, Ottawa.

General Records of the Department of State. RG 59. Decimal File, 1940–1944. U.S. National Archives, College Park, Maryland.

Records of the Immigration and Naturalization Service. RG 85. Chinese General Correspondence, 1898–1908. U.S. National Archives, Washington, D.C.

Records of the Immigration and Naturalization Service. RG 85. Entry 9. Immigration and Naturalization Service Central Office Subject Correspondence and Case Files, ca. 1906–1957. U.S. National Archives, Washington, D.C.

Records of the Immigration and Naturalization Service. RG 85. Chinese Arrivals, 1900–1923. U.S. National Archives, Philadelphia, Pennsylvania.

Records of the Immigration and Naturalization Service. RG 85. Chinese Exclusion Case Files, 1894–1943. U.S. National Archives, Seattle, Washington.

Records of the Immigration and Naturalization Service. RG 85. Investigation Arrival Case Files, 1884–1944. U.S. National Archives, San Francisco, California.

Records of the Office of Strategic Services. RG 226. Research and Analysis Branch Divisions. Intelligence Series, 1941–1945. U.S. National Archives, College Park, Maryland.

Manuscript and Digital Collections

Angel Island Interviews, Bancroft Library, University of California, Berkeley

Angel Island Oral History Project, Ethnic Studies Library, University of California, Berkeley

Asiatic Exclusion League Records, 1906–1910, Labor Archives and Research Center, San Francisco State University, San Francisco, California

Becoming Minnesotan: Stories of Recent Immigrants and Refugees, Minnesota Historical Society, St. Paul, Minnesota

Densho Visual History Collection, Densho Digital Archive

The Diaries of William Lyon Mackenzie King, Library and Archives Canada, Ottawa

Edward Norton Barnhart Papers, 1942–1954, Japanese American Research Project, Special Collections, University of California, Los Angeles

Immigrant Stories Archive, Immigration History Research Center, University of Minnesota, Minneapolis, Minnesota

"Immigrant Voices," Angel Island Immigration Station Foundation, San Francisco, California

International Institute of San Francisco Records, Immigration History Research Center Archives, University of Minnesota, Minneapolis, Minnesota

"Operation Babylift," Gerald R. Ford Presidential Digital Library

Press Clippings, Hmong Resource Center Library, St. Paul, Minnesota

Refugee Studies Center Collections, Immigration History Research Center Archives, University of Minnesota, Minneapolis, Minnesota

Survey of Race Relations: A Canadian-American Study of the Oriental on the Pacific Coast, Hoover Institution on War, Revolution, and Peace, Stanford University, Stanford, California

Introduction

1 Emma Britz, Jeanne Batalova, and Migration Policy Institute, "Frequently Requested Statistics on Immigrants and Immigration in the United States," *The Migration Information Source*, January 2013, http://www.migrationinformation.org/USfocus/display.cfm?id=931 (accessed March 13, 2014); Audrey Singer, "The Rise of New Immigrant Gateways," *The Brookings Institution*, February 2004, http://www.brookings.edu/research/reports/2004/02/demographics-singer (accessed March 13, 2014); Karen Humes, Nicholas A. Jones, and Roberto R. Ramirez, *Overview of Race and Hispanic Origin, 2010* (Washington, DC: US Department of Commerce, Economics and Statistics Administration, US Census Bureau, 2011), 5, 19; U.S. Census Bureau News, "Asian/Pacific American Heritage Month: May 2014," April 23, 2014, http://www.census.gov/content/dam/Census/newsroom/facts-for-features/2014/cb14-ff13_asian.pdf (accessed February 7, 2015); "U.S. Hispanic and Asian Populations Growing, But for Different Reasons," Pew Research Center, June 26, 2014, http://www.pewresearch.org/fact-tank/2014/06/26/u-s-hispanic-and-asian-populations-growing-but-for-different-reasons/ (accessed February 7, 2015).

2 "South Asia" refers to the present-day countries of Bangladesh, Bhutan, India, Maldives, Nepal, Pakistan, and Sri Lanka. During the nineteenth and twentieth centuries, the U.S. government categorized all persons from South Asia as "Indian," "East Indian," or "Hindoo." These terms are confusing. South

Asian immigrants practiced a variety of faiths including Sikhism, Hinduism, and Islam. The Indian subcontinent, under the colonial rule of Great Britain from 1612 to 1947, included all of the present-day countries of South Asia (not just India). I thus use "South Asia" or "British India," unless a more specific label such as "Punjabi" or "Madrasi" was used in the original source. "India" and "Indian" are used in reference to nationalist activism related to that nation-state inside and outside the Indian subcontinent during the early twentieth century. On this terminology, see Sugata Bose and Ayesha Jalal, *Modern South Asia: History, Culture, Political Economy*, 3rd ed. (London: Routledge, 2011), 31; Joan M. Jensen, *Passage from India: Asian Indian Immigrants in North America* (New Haven: Yale University Press, 1988), 101; and Nazli Kibria, "Not Asian, Black, or White? Reflections on South Asian American Racial Identity," in *Asian American Studies: A Reader*, ed. Min Song and Jean Wu (New Brunswick, NJ: Rutgers University Press, 2000), 247–54.

3 Although Native Hawaiians and Pacific Islanders are also sometimes included in a larger Asian American and Pacific Islander umbrella label, as indigenous peoples, Native Hawaiians and Pacific Islanders have related, but also separate, histories from the peoples of Asia who arrived in the Americas as settlers. In this book, I have chosen to focus on those who have come from Asia and their descendants. On both the commonalities and the differences of Asian American and Native Hawaiian/Pacific Islander experiences and history, see: Keith L. Camacho, "Transoceanic Flows: Pacific Islander Interventions Across the American Empire," *Amerasia Journal* 37, no. 3 (2011): ix–xxxiv and Roderick N. Labrador and Erin Kahunawaika'ala Wright, "Engaging Indigeneity in Pacific Islander and Asian American Studies," *Amerasia Journal* 37, no. 3 (2011): 135–47.

4 Others have suggested similar starting points for Asian American history. See Gary Okihiro, *Margins and Mainstreams: Asians in American History and Culture* (Seattle: University of Washington Press, 1994), 28–29; Evelyn Hu-DeHart and Kathleen López, "Asian Diasporas in Latin America and the Caribbean: An Historical Overview," *Afro-Hispanic Review* 27, no. 1 (2008): 9.

5 "Uprooted" is from Oscar Handlin, *The Uprooted: The Epic Story of the Great Migrations That Made the American People* (Boston: Little, Brown, 1951). "Transplanted" is from John Bodnar, *The Transplanted: A History of Immigrants in Urban America* (Bloomington: Indiana University Press, 1985). For an analysis of this historiography, see Donna Gabaccia, "Do We Still Need Immigration History?" *Polish American Studies* 55 (1998): 45–68.

6 Donna Gabaccia, *Foreign Relations: American Immigration in Global Perspective* (Princeton: Princeton University Press, 2012).

7 Sometimes these processes are called "migration" and the people involved are called "migrants." I use "immigration" and "immigrants" to refer to processes and individuals that seem to involve voluntary and permanent or long-term residence in another country, and "migration" and "migrants" to better capture multidirectional movements and the peoples who made them. Together, both terms capture the complexity of human movement across time and space. On similarly broad definitions of migration, see Donna R. Gabaccia and Dirk Hoerder, eds., *Connecting Seas and Connected Ocean Rims: Indian, Atlantic, and Pacific Oceans and China Seas Migrations from the 1830s to the 1930s* (Leiden, Netherlands: Brill, 2011), 1–11; Gabaccia, "Do We Still Need Immigration History?"; Madeline Y. Hsu, "Transnationalism and Asian American Studies as a Migration-Centered Project," *Journal of Asian American Studies*, Transnational and Asian American Studies 11, no. 2 (2008): 185–97; and Philip Q. Yang, "A Theory of Asian Immigration to the United States," *Journal of Asian American Studies* 13, no. 1 (2010): 1–34.

8 Citizenship is both political and cultural. See, for example, Aihwa Ong, *Buddha Is Hiding: Refugees, Citizenship, the New America* (Berkeley: University of California Press, 2003), 2–7; and William V. Flores and Rina Benmayor, eds., *Latino Cultural Citizenship: Claiming Identity, Space, and Rights*, 1st ed. (Boston: Beacon, 1998).

9 Pew Research Center, *The Rise of Asian Americans* (Washington, DC, 2013), 1.

10 See, for example, Thomas A. Guglielmo, *White on Arrival: Italians, Race, Color, and Power in Chicago, 1890–1945* (New York: Oxford University Press, 2004).

11 Eduardo Bonilla-Silva, *Racism Without Racists: Color-Blind Racism and the Persistence of Racial Inequality in America* (New York: Rowman & Littlefield, 2013), 25–26, 76–77.

12 Derald Wing Sue et al., "Racial Microaggressions and the Asian American Experience," *Cultural Diversity and Ethnic Minority Psychology* 13, no. 1 (2007): 72.

13 Edward Said, *Orientalism* (New York: Vintage, 1979).

14 Okihiro, *Margins and Mainstreams*, 3–30; Robert G. Lee, *Orientals: Asian Americans in Popular Culture* (Philadelphia: Temple University Press, 1999); John Kuo Wei Tchen, *New York Before Chinatown: Orientalism and the Shaping of American Culture, 1776–1882* (Baltimore: Johns Hopkins University

Press, 1999); and Shelley Sang-Hee Lee, *A New History of Asian America* (New York: Routledge, 2013), 5–26.

15 Ellen Wu, *The Color of Success: Asian Americans and the Origins of the Model Minority* (Princeton: Princeton University Press, 2013), 2.

16 Erika Lee, *At America's Gates: Chinese Immigration During the Exclusion Era, 1882–1943* (Chapel Hill: University of North Carolina Press, 2003), 6–7.

17 Lisa Lowe, *Immigrant Acts: On Asian American Cultural Politics* (Durham, NC: Duke University Press, 1996), 5–6; Mia Tuan, *Forever Foreigners or Honorary Whites?: The Asian Ethnic Experience Today* (New Brunswick, NJ: Rutgers University Press, 1998); Edward J. W. Park and John S. W. Park, *Probationary Americans: Contemporary Immigration Policies and the Shaping of Asian American Communities* (New York: Routledge, 2005); and Vijay Prashad, *Uncle Swami: South Asians in America Today* (New York: New Press, 2012), ix–x, 11–12.

18 Evelyn Nakano Glenn, "Split Household, Small Producer and Dual Wage Earner: An Analysis of Chinese-American Family Strategies," *Journal of Marriage and the Family* 45, no. 1 (1983): 35–46.

19 Yen Le Espiritu, *Home Bound: Filipino American Lives Across Cultures, Communities, and Countries* (Berkeley: University of California Press, 2003), 4–5.

20 Peggy Levitt, *God Needs No Passport: Immigrants and the Changing American Religious Landscape* (New York: New Press, 2007), 2, 12, 26.

21 Ibid., 2, 12, 26.

Chapter 1: *Los Chinos* in New Spain and Asians in Early America

1 William D. Phillips and Carla Rahn Phillips, *The Worlds of Christopher Columbus* (New York: Cambridge University Press, 1992), 37–44, 84; Seana Locklin, "Orientalism and the Nation: Asian Women in Spanish American Literature" (PhD diss., Cornell University, 1998), 2–3.

2 Okihiro, *Margins and Mainstreams*, 8–9.

3 Mary B. Campbell, *The Witness and the Other World: Exotic European Travel Writing, 400–1600* (Ithaca: Cornell University Press, 1991), 3.

4 Phillips and Phillips, *The Worlds of Christopher Columbus*, 11, 16–21; Campbell, *The Witness*, 3.

5 Phillips and Phillips, *The Worlds of Christopher Columbus*, 11, 16–23.

6 Marco Polo, *The Travels of Marco Polo, Greatly Amended and Enlarged from Valuable Early Manuscripts Recently Published by the French Society of*

Geography, and in Italy by Count Baldelli Boni (New York: Harper & Brothers, 1845), 125; Phillips and Phillips, *The Worlds of Christopher Columbus*, 46.

7 John Mandeville, *The Travels of Sir John Mandeville* (London: Penguin, 1983), 141–45; Iain Macleod Higgins, *Writing East: The "Travels" of Sir John Mandeville* (Philadelphia: University of Pennsylvania Press, 1997), vii.

8 Sir Walter Raleigh, *The Works of Sir Walter Ralegh, Kt: Miscellaneous Works* (Oxford: The University Press, 1829), 325.

9 Phillips and Phillips, *The Worlds of Christopher Columbus*, 20, 47–49, 83.

10 Christopher Columbus, *The Log of Christopher Columbus*, trans. Robert H. Fuson (Camden, ME: International Marine Publishing Company, 1987); Phillips and Phillips, *The Worlds of Christopher Columbus*, 205, 12.

11 New Spain's territory included what is the Bay Islands (until 1643), the Cayman Islands (until 1670), Central America (as far as the southern border of Costa Rica), Cuba, Florida, Hispaniola (including Haiti until 1697), Jamaica (until 1655), the Mariana Islands, Mexico, the Philippines, Puerto Rico, Trinidad (until 1797), and nearly all of the Southwest United States (including all or parts of the modern-day U.S. states of California, Nevada, Utah, Colorado, Wyoming, Arizona, New Mexico, Texas, and Florida), but the northern boundary of New Spain remained undefined until the Adams-Onís Treaty of 1819. In 1821, Spain lost the continental territories when it recognized the independence of Mexico. However, Cuba, Puerto Rico, and the Spanish East Indies (including the Mariana Islands and the Philippines) remained under Spanish rule until the Spanish-American War (1898).

12 Locklin, "Orientalism," 1–5.

13 Carla Phillips, "Spain and the Pacific: Voyaging into Vastness," *Mains'l Haul* 41–42 (Fall 2005/Winter 2006), 7–12.

14 Teobaldo Filesi, *China and Africa in the Middle Ages*, trans. David Morison (London: F. Cass, 1972), 57–61. Gavin Menzies has argued that Zheng and his fleet came to the Americas in 1421, but his assertions have been roundly discounted by historians. See Gavin Menzies, *1421: The Year China Discovered the World* (New York: William Morrow, 2003); Robert Finlay, "How Not to (Re)Write World History: Gavin Menzies and the Chinese Discovery of America," *Journal of World History* 15, no. 2 (2004): 229–42; Edward L. Dreyer, "Review of Gavin Menzies, 1421: The Year China Discovered America," *Ming Studies*, no. 1 (2004): 131–38.

15 On Chinese emigration during the Ming and Qing Empires, see Ching-Hwang Yen, *Coolies and Mandarins: China's Protection of Overseas Chinese*

During the Late Ch'ing Period (1851–1911) (Singapore: Singapore University Press, 1985), 1–31. On migration of Chinese traders within Asia, see Philip A. Kuhn, *Chinese Among Others: Emigration in Modern Times* (Lanham, MD: Rowman & Littlefield, 2008), 7–106; and Sucheng Chan, *Asian Americans: An Interpretive History* (Boston: Twayne, 1991), 5.

16 William Lytle Schurz, "Acapulco and the Manila Galleon," *The Southwestern Historical Quarterly* 22, no. 1 (1918): 31, 50.

17 William Lytle Schurz, *The Manila Galleon* (New York: E. P. Dutton, 1939), 195; Paul S. Taylor, "Spanish Seamen in the New World During the Colonial Period," *Hispanic American Historical Review* 5, no. 4 (1922): 642; Rainer F. Buschmann et al., *Navigating the Spanish Lake: The Pacific in the Iberian World, 1521–1898* (Honolulu: University of Hawaii Press, 2014), 26.

18 Schurz, *The Manila Galleon*, 195–97.

19 Susan Bacon, *Manila Galleon Voyages*, Spotlight on PSD Research (U.S. Department of Commerce, National Oceanic & Atmospheric Administration, NOAA Research, Earth System Research Laboratory, Physical Sciences Division, Summer 2004), http://www.esrl.noaa.gov/psd/spotlight/2004/manila-galleon.html (accessed November 8, 2012); Taylor, "Spanish Seamen," 647, 649; Alexander Von Humboldt, *Political Essay on the Kingdom of New Spain: With Physical Sections and Maps Founded on Astronomical Observations and Trigonometrical and Barometrical Measurements* (London: Longman, Hurst, Rees, Orme, and Brown, 1822), vol. 4, 71–81.

20 On Asian goods, see Schurz, "Acapulco and the Manila Galleon," 31, 50. On the demand for silver in China, see Dennis O. Flynn and Arturo Giráldez, "Born with a 'Silver Spoon': The Origin of World Trade in 1571," *Journal of World History* 6, no. 2 (1995): 201 and Dennis O. Flynn and Arturo Giráldez, "Cycles of Silver: Global Economic Unity Through the Mid-Eighteenth Century," *Journal of World History* 13, no. 2 (2002): 398.

21 Because Asian sailors were crewmembers on both the official Manila galleons and the accompanying vessels that also made the transpacific voyage, Edward R. Slack, Jr., estimates that 100,000 Asian immigrants would "be within the realm of probability." See Edward R. Slack, Jr., "Los Chinos in New Spain: A Corrective Lens for a Distorted Image," *Journal of World History* 20, no. 1 (2009): 37 (fn 3). See also Jonathan Irvine Israel, *Race, Class and Politics in Colonial Mexico, 1610–1670* (London: Oxford University Press, 1975), 75–76.

22 Jose Maria S. Luengo, A *History of the Manila–Acapulco Slave Trade (1565–1815)* (Tubigon, Bohol, Philippines: Mater Dei Publications, 1996),

99–105; Floro L. Mercene, *Manila Men in the New World: Filipino Migration to Mexico and the Americas for the Sixteenth Century* (Diliman, Quezon City, Philippines: University of the Philippines Press, 2007), 40, 70–71; and Matt K. Matsuda, *Pacific Worlds* (West Nyack, NY: Cambridge University Press, 2012), 119.

23 On the diversity of Asians in New Spain, see Slack Jr., "Los Chinos," 38; Melba E. Falck Reyes and Héctor Palacios, *El Japonés Que Conquistó Guadalajara: La Historia de Juan de Páez En La Guadalajara Del Siglo XVII* (Guadalajara, Jalisco, México: Universidad de Guadalajara: Biblioteca Pública del Estado de Jalisco Juan José Arreola, 2009), 119–23.

24 Schurz, *The Manila Galleon*, 209–10; Edward R. Slack Jr., "Sinifying New Spain: Cathay's Influence on Colonial Mexico via the Nao de China," in *The Chinese in Latin America and the Caribbean*, ed. Walton Look Lai and Chee Beng Tan (Leiden, Netherlands: Brill, 2010), 9–11.

25 Francisco Leandro de Viana, "Demonstración del Misero Deplorable Estado de las Islas Philipinas, Manila, February 10, 1765," trans. in Blair and Robertson, *The Philippine Islands*, vol. 48 (1751–1765), 301.

26 Pedro Cubero Sebastián, *Peregrinación del Mundo de D. Pedro Cubero Sebastián* (Zaragoza, 1688), 268, cited in ibid., vol. 1, 105 (fn 66).

27 Giovanni Francesco Gemelli Careri, *A Voyage Round the World* (1693) in Awnsham Churchill and John Churchill, *A Collection of Voyages and Travels, Some Now First Printed from Original Manuscripts, Others Translated out of Foreign Languages, and Now First Published in English* (London: A. and J. Churchill, 1704), vol. 4, 486–91. Crew quarters described in ibid., vol. 1., 213.

28 Schurz, *The Manila Galleon*, 211–12 and Taylor, "Spanish Seamen," 649–50, 653.

29 Hernando de los Ríos Coronel, "Reforms Needed in the Filipinas" (Madrid, 1619–1620), trans. in Blair and Robertson, *The Philippine Islands*, vol. 18 (1617–1620), 287.

30 Careri, *A Voyage Round the World*, 491; Taylor, "Spanish Seamen," 650; and Slack Jr., "Los Chinos," 39. Details of 1618 ship from Sebastián de Pineda, "Philippine Ships and Shipbuilding" (1619), trans. in Blair and Robertson, *The Philippine Islands*, vol. 18 (1617–1620), 174–75; Taylor, "Spanish Seamen," 652.

31 Schurz, *The Manila Galleon*, 252; Slack Jr., "Sinifying New Spain," 13.

32 Tatiana Seijas, "The Portuguese Slave Trade to Spanish Manila: 1580–1640," *Itinerario* 32, no. 1 (2008): 21–23; Ward, "Slavery in Southeast Asia, 1420–1804,"

in *The Cambridge World History of Slavery: Volume 3, AD 1420–AD 1804*, eds., David Eltis et al. (Cambridge: Cambridge University Press, 2011), 180–81.

33 Gonzalo Aguirre Beltrán, "The Slave Trade in Mexico," *The Hispanic American Historical Review* 24, no. 3 (1944): 412–14, 420; Israel, *Race, Class, and Politics*, 12–13, 27; William D. Phillips Jr., "Slavery in the Atlantic Islands and the Early Modern Spanish Atlantic World," in Eltis et al., eds., *The Cambridge World History of Slavery*, 337.

34 Pedro Chirino, "Relación de las Islas Filipinas" (1604), trans. in Blair and Robertson, *The Philippine Islands*, vol. 12 (1601–1604), 192.

35 Israel, *Race, Class, and Politics*, 75–76.

36 Seijas, "The Portuguese Slave Trade," 24–25.

37 Beltrán, "Slave Trade," 421.

38 Seijas, "The Portuguese Slave Trade," 24–25; Schurz, *The Manila Galleon*, 272.

39 Schurz, *The Manila Galleon*, 33; Slack Jr., "Sinifying New Spain," 28; Slack Jr., "Los Chinos," 65.

40 The use of the misnomer *los chinos* to refer to all Asians reflects Europe's long history of describing all of the vast and diverse lands of Asia as either India or, more typically, China. On Europe's long history of treating the separate kingdoms, empires, peoples, and later, nations of Asia as one undifferentiated mass, see Donald F. Lach, *Asia in the Making of Europe, Volume I: The Century of Discovery* (Chicago: University of Chicago Press, 1994), 3–4. On the use of *chino* in New Spain to refer to all Asians, see Israel, *Race, Class, and Politics*, 751 (fn51); Slack Jr., "Los Chinos," 57–67; Slack Jr., "Sinifying New Spain," 7, 24–25; and Locklin, "Orientalism," 54–56.

41 Slack, Jr. "Los Chinos," 40, 37–38. See also Schurz, "Acapulco and the Manila Galleon," 21–22; and Dubs and Smith, "Chinese in Mexico City," 388.

42 Reyes and Palacios, *El Japonés*, 33–37; Daniel M. Masterson and Sayaka Funada-Classen, *The Japanese in Latin America* (Urbana: University of Illinois Press, 2004), 13–14.

43 Henry F. Dobyns and Paul L. Doughty, *Peru: A Cultural History* (New York: Oxford University Press, 1976), 117–18.

44 Ching Chieh Chang, "The Chinese in Latin America: A Preliminary Geographical Survey with Special Reference to Cuba and Jamaica" (PhD diss., University of Maryland, 1956), 9–10.

45 Thomas Gage, *A New Survey of the West-Indies, 1648: The English-American* (New York: RM McBride, 1929), 84. See also Slack Jr., "Los Chinos," 40–42 and "Sinifying New Spain," 12.

46 Dubs and Smith, "Chinese in Mexico City," 387.
47 Ríos Coronel, "Reforms Needed," 324.
48 Slack Jr., "Los Chinos," 48–52; Slack Jr., "Sinifying New Spain," 16–19.
49 Reyes and Palacios, *El Japonés*, 43–56.
50 Ibid., 59–67, 87, 95–98, 103–16, 119–23.
51 Seijas, "The Portuguese Slave Trade," 19; Gauvin Alexander Bailey, *A Mughal Princess in Baroque New Spain: Catarina de San Juan (1606–1688), the China Poblana*, Annales del Instituto de Investigaciones Estéticas (Universidad Nacional Autónoma de México, 1997), 47.
52 She told her biographers that she was hidden in a house in Manila where a "lewd and cruel man stole her honesty." Translated from Alonso Ramos, *Primera Parte de Los Prodigios de La Omnipotencia, y Milagros de la Gracia en la Vida de la Venerable Sierva de Dios Catharina de S. Joan, Natural del Gran Mogor, Difunta en Esta Imperial Ciudad de La Puebla de los Angeles en La Nueva España Núñez de Miranda, Antonio, 1618–1695* (En la Puebla : En la Imprenta Plantiniana de Diego Fernández de León, 1689), vol. I, 27.
53 Bailey, *A Mughal Princess*, 40–41, 67–70; Ronald J. Morgan, *Spanish American Saints: And the Rhetoric of Identity, 1600–1810* (Tucson: University of Arizona Press, 2002), 119, 122, 141–142; Kathleen Ann Myers, *Neither Saints nor Sinners: Writing the Lives of Women in Spanish America* (New York: Oxford University Press, 2003), 44, 48–50, 66–68; Roshni Rustomji-Kerns, "Mirrha-Catarina de San Juan: From India to New Spain," *Amerasia Journal* 28, no. 2 (2002): 33–34.
54 Locklin, "Orientalism," 42, 58–82; Hu-DeHart and López, "Asian Diasporas," 10; Rustomji-Kerns, "Mirrha-Catarina de San Juan," 29–37.
55 On "China-mania" and the importance of tea and porcelain in early America, see Caroline Frank, *Objectifying China, Imagining America: Chinese Commodities in Early America* (Chicago: University of Chicago Press, 2012), 3, 29, 99. Washington's taste for Chinese goods is from John Kuo Wei Tchen, *New York Before Chinatown: Orientalism and the Shaping of American Culture, 1776–1882* (Baltimore: Johns Hopkins University Press, 1999), xv, 4.
56 Frank, *Objectifying China*, 10, 24, 179–82, 188, 201; Kariann Akemi Yokota, *Unbecoming British: How Revolutionary America Became a Postcolonial Nation* (New York: Oxford University Press, 2011), 83–84.
57 Yokota, *Unbecoming British*, 115.
58 Frank, *Objectifying China*, 10, 204.
59 Yokota, *Unbecoming British*, 115, 119.
60 Frank, *Objectifying China*, 204; David Igler, *The Great Ocean: Pacific Worlds from Captain Cook to the Gold Rush* (New York: Oxford University Press,

2013), 20, 32–36; Yokota, *Unbecoming British*, 144–52; Tchen, *New York Before Chinatown*, xvi–xix, 3–24.

61 Filipinos as crew described in Mercene, *Manila Men*, 11, 70–71. The *Pallas* and John Huston described in Tchen, *New York Before Chinatown*, 31–40, 76–80.

62 *New York Times*, July 9, 1836, available at National Women's History Museum, "Chinese American Women: A History of Resilience and Resistance," http://www.nwhm.org/online-exhibits/chinese/4.html (accessed September 26, 2012). See also John Haddad, "The Chinese Lady and China for the Ladies: Race, Gender, and Public Exhibition in Jacksonian America," *Chinese America: History and Perspectives* (2011), 7–9.

63 Afong Moy may have proceeded to Europe for a tour. Krystyn R. Moon, *Yellowface: Creating the Chinese in American Popular Music and Performance, 1850s–1920s* (New Brunswick, NJ: Rutgers University Press, 2005), 60–63; Haddad, "The Chinese Lady," 16.

64 The early presence of Filipinos in Louisiana is a source of some debate. Marina E. Espina's claim that Filipinos arrived in Louisiana as early as 1765 as an extension of the settlement of Filipinos in Mexico has been cited in numerous Asian American histories. However, Malcolm H. Churchill has offered a corrective to this interpretation. See Marina Estrella Espina, *Filipinos in Louisiana* (New Orleans: AF Laborde, 1988); and Malcolm H. Churchill, "Louisiana History and Early Filipino Settlement: Searching for the Story," *Bulletin of the American Historical Collection Foundation* 27, no. 2 (1999): 26–49.

65 Lafcadio Hearn, "Saint Malo: A Lacustrine Village in Louisiana," *Harper's Weekly*, March 31, 1883, 198–99.

Chapter 2: Coolies

1 The term "coolie" has various origins. In Hindi, *koli* referred to a race in India; in Tamil, *kuli* meant wages or hire; in Turkic *kuli* related to slaves. Although "coolie" has also been connected to the Chinese term *k'u-li*, or "bitter labor" or "bitter strength," historians agree that the Hindi term was probably adopted by foreigners, especially the British, to refer to Chinese and South Asian menial laborers in European treaty ports. "Culi," the Spanish equivalent, was likely adopted from its English equivalent. "Coolie" has also been used as a pejorative term to castigate foreign indentured laborers and their lowly positions in colonial societies. In some places, it took on racial overtones. In the West Indies, for example, Indians—regardless of their profession or generation in the country—were called "coolies." Although some have sought to reclaim

the word as a way of identifying with their indentured laborer origins, today the word is still used in denigrating ways to describe cheap laborers in the U.S. and abroad. I use "coolie" here as the historical term used to refer to Asian indentured laborers and as a term that marks both their colonial origins and their unequal status in the Americas. On various definitions and usage of the term "coolie," see Robert L. Irick, *Ch'ing Policy Toward the Coolie Trade, 1847–1878* (Taipei: Chinese Materials Center, 1982), 2–7; Hugh Tinker, *A New System of Slavery: The Export of Indian Labour Overseas, 1830–1920* (London: Hansib, 1993), 41–43; Lisa Yun, *The Coolie Speaks: Chinese Indentured Laborers and African Slaves in Cuba* (Philadelphia: Temple University Press, 2008), xix; and Gaiutra Bahadur, *Coolie Woman: The Odyssey of Indenture* (Chicago: University of Chicago Press, 2014), xix–xxi.

2 Lynn Pan, *The Encyclopedia of the Chinese Overseas* (Cambridge: Harvard University Press, 1999), 249; Andrew R. Wilson, *The Chinese in the Caribbean* (Princeton: M. Wiener, 2004), 5; Lisa Yun and Ricardo Rene Laremont, "Chinese Coolies and African Slaves in Cuba, 1847–74," *Journal of Asian American Studies* 4, no. 2 (2001): 100; Watt Stewart, *Chinese Bondage in Peru: A History of the Chinese Coolie in Peru, 1849–1874* (Durham, NC: Duke University Press, 1951), 73.

3 Basdeo Mangru, *Indenture and Abolition: Sacrifice and Survival on the Guyanese Sugar Plantations* (Toronto: TSAR, 1993), 100; Walton Look Lai, *Indentured Labor, Caribbean Sugar: Chinese and Indian Migrants to the British West Indies, 1838–1918* (Baltimore: Johns Hopkins University Press, 1993), 51–52, 266–67.

4 Yun and Laremont, "Chinese Coolies and African Slaves," 101.

5 On distinctions between Asian immigration to the United States and Latin America, see, for example, Sucheng Chan, *This Bittersweet Soil: The Chinese in California Agriculture, 1860–1910* (Berkeley: University of California Press, 1989), 25–26; Hugh Tinker, *A New System of Slavery: The Export of Indian Labour Overseas, 1830–1920* (London: Hansib, 1993).

6 David Brion Davis, *Inhuman Bondage: The Rise and Fall of Slavery in the New World* (New York: Oxford University Press, 2006).

7 Yun and Laremont, "Chinese Coolies and African Slaves," 101; Look Lai, *Indentured Labor*, 5–11.

8 Tinker, *A New System of Slavery*, 1, 18.

9 Eugenio Chang-Rodríguez, "Chinese Labor Migration into Latin America in the Nineteenth Century," *Revista de Historia de America* 46 (December 1958): 377; Yen, *Coolies and Mandarins*, 59–60.

10 Okihiro, *Margins and Mainstreams*, 39.

11 Look Lai, *Indentured Labor*, 109, 19; David Northrup, *Indentured Labor in the Age of Imperialism, 1834–1922* (Cambridge: Cambridge University Press, 1995), 120–21, 4; Mangru, *Indenture and Abolition*, 63, 4.

12 Denis Judd, *The Lion and the Tiger: The Rise and Fall of the British Raj, 1600–1947* (New York: Oxford University Press, 2004), 2, 28, 47; Sucheng Chan, "European and Asian Immigration into the United States in Comparative Perspective, 1820s to 1920s," in *Immigration Reconsidered: History, Sociology, and Politics*, ed. Virginia Yans McLaughlin (New York: Oxford University Press, 1990), 53–54.

13 Lucie Cheng and Edna Bonacich, eds., *Labor Immigration Under Capitalism: Asian Immigrant Workers in the United States Before World War II* (Berkeley: University of California Press, 1984), 216; Sucheta Mazumdar, "Colonial Impact and Punjabi Emigration to the United States," in *Labor Immigration Under Capitalism*, Cheng and Bonacich, eds., 322–24, 326–28; Northrup, *Indentured Labor*, 65.

14 Look Lai, *Indentured Labor*, 24–25; Tinker, *A New System of Slavery*, 49; Northrup, *Indentured Labor*, 67; Sucheng Chan, *Asian Americans: An Interpretive History* (Boston: Twayne, 1991), 20.

15 Tinker, *A New System of Slavery*, 43–44, 121–23; Northrup, *Indentured Labor*, 60.

16 Tinker, *A New System of Slavery*, xiii; Look Lai, *Indentured Labor*, 19; Steven Vertovec, "Indian Indentured Migration to the Caribbean," in *The Cambridge Survey of World Migration*, ed. Robin Cohen (Cambridge: Cambridge University Press, 1995), 57.

17 Look Lai, *Indentured Labor*, 107; Northrup, *Indentured Labor*, 24–26.

18 Look Lai, *Indentured Labor*, 27–29, 51, 124; Northrup, *Indentured Labor*, 74–77; K. O. Laurence, *Immigration into the West Indies in the 19th Century* (St. Lawrence, Barbados: Caribbean Universities Press, 1971), 46.

19 Look Lai, *Indentured Labor*, 29.

20 Rosemarijn Hoefte, *In Place of Slavery: A Social History of British Indian and Javanese Laborers in Suriname* (Gainesville: University Press of Florida, 1998), 109.

21 James McNeill and Chimman Lal, *Report to the Government of India on the Conditions of Indian Immigrants in Four British Colonies and Surinam* (Simla, India: Government Central Press, 1915), 93.

22 Hoefte, *In Place of Slavery*, 106–10.

23 John Geoghegan, *Note on Emigration from India* (Calcutta, India: Office of Superintendent of Government Printing, 1873), 6.

24 Tinker, *A New System of Slavery*, 126–27.

25 Mangru, *Indenture and Abolition*, 6; Northrup, *Indentured Labor*, 97.

26 E. Swinton and Jane Swinton, *The Other Middle Passage: Journal of a Voyage from Calcutta to Trinidad, 1858* (London: Alfred Bennett, 1859), 3. Mortality rates between 1857 and 1862 from Mangru, *Indenture and Abolition*, 25. 1870s mortality rates from Tinker, *A New System of Slavery*, 165.

27 Look Lai, *Indentured Labor*, 57; Northrup, *Indentured Labor*, 4, 64; Vertovec, "Indian Indentured Migration to the Caribbean," 58–60.

28 Look Lai, *Indentured Labor*, 109, 114; John Scoble, *Hill Coolies: A Brief Exposure of the Deplorable Conditions of the Hill Coolies in British Guiana and Mauritius* (London: Harvey & Danton, 1840), 14.

29 Look Lai, *Indentured Labor*, 117–118.

30 Mangru, *Indenture and Abolition*, 88.

31 Hoefte, *In Place of Slavery*, 108–9.

32 Look Lai, *Indentured Labor*, 143–44; Mangru, *Indenture and Abolition*, 83.

33 Laurence, *Immigration into the West Indies*, 53.

34 Tinker, *A New System of Slavery*, 191–95; Look Lai, *Indentured Labor*, 127–36.

35 Tinker, *A New System of Slavery*, 19, 63.

36 McNeill and Lal, *Report to the Government of India*, 4.

37 Mangru, *Indenture and Abolition*, 81–83, 94; Tinker, *A New System of Slavery*, 226–29, 187; Look Lai, *Indentured Labor*, 144–45.

38 Look Lai, *Indentured Labor*, 219, 221; Laurence, *Immigration into the West Indies*, 53.

39 Northrup, *Indentured Labor*, 149; Aisha Khan, *Callaloo Nation: Metaphors of Race and Religious Identity Among South Asians in Trinidad* (Durham, NC: Duke University Press, 2004), 8; Look Lai, *Indentured Labor*, 122, 257; Tinker, *A New System of Slavery*, 221; Noor Kumar Mahabir, *The Still Cry: Personal Accounts of East Indians in Trinidad and Tobago During Indentureship, 1845–1917* (Tacarigua, Trinidad: Calaloux Publications, 1985), 15; Hoefte, *In Place of Slavery*, 158, 163.

40 Laurence, *Immigration into the West Indies*, 74–75. See also Tinker, *A New System of Slavery*, 283–84, 300, 308, 312–14, 334; Mangru, *Indenture and Abolition*, 98, 100–101.

41 Tinker, *A New System of Slavery*, 341; Mangru, *Indenture and Abolition*, 108–9, 113–15.

42 Laurence, *Immigration into the West Indies*, 75; Tinker, *A New System of Slavery*, 364; Mangru, *Indenture and Abolition*, 119–20.

43 Chinese Emperor Qianlong's 1793 message to British King George III in Sir Edmund Backhouse and John Otway Percy Bland, *Annals and Memoirs of the Court of Peking from the 16th to the 20th Century, Illustrated* (New York: Houghton Mifflin, 1914), 325–31.

44 Adam McKeown, "Conceptualizing Chinese Diasporas, 1842–1949," *Journal of Asian Studies* 58 (1999), 313–15; Grace Delgado, *Making the Chinese Mexican: Global Migration, Localism, and Exclusion in the U.S.-Mexico Borderlands* (Stanford: Stanford University Press, 2012), 15, 19.

45 Ta Chen, *Chinese Migrations, with Special Reference to Labor Conditions* (Washington, DC: U.S. Government Printing Office, 1923), 4, 51–56, 75.

46 Pan, *Encyclopedia*, 62; Chan, *This Bittersweet Soil*, 16.

47 Chan, "European and Asian Immigration," 44. Quote from Northrup, *Indentured Labor*, 95 (fn 30); Look Lai, *Indentured Labor*, 38, 44–45.

48 China Cuba Commission, *The Cuba Commission Report: A Hidden History of the Chinese in Cuba, The Original English-Language Text of 1876* (Baltimore: Johns Hopkins University Press, 1993), 20; Benjamin Nicolas Narvaez, "Chinese Coolies in Cuba and Peru: Race, Labor, and Immigration, 1839–1886" (PhD diss., University of Texas, 2010), 76–77; Northrup, *Indentured Labor*, 51; Stewart, *Chinese Bondage in Peru*, 61.

49 Yun and Laremont, "Chinese Coolies and African Slaves," 101.

50 Stewart, *Chinese Bondage*, 30–31; Yun and Laremont, "Chinese Coolies and African Slaves," 107, 111.

51 Yun and Laremont, "Chinese Coolies and African Slaves," 109.

52 China Cuba Commission, *The Cuba Commission Report*, 24. See also Stewart, *Chinese Bondage*, 32–34, 38–39.

53 Petition 41, *The Cuba Commission Report*, cited in Yun, *The Coolie Speaks*, 96.

54 China Cuba Commission, *The Cuba Commission Report*, 37.

55 Kathleen María López, "Migrants Between Empires and Nations: The Chinese in Cuba, 1874–1959" (PhD diss., University of Michigan, 2005), 36; Delgado, *Making the Chinese Mexican*, 23; Yun, *The Coolie Speaks*, 28.

56 Yen, *Coolies and Mandarins*, 59–60; Irick, *Ch'ing Policy*, 26–27.

57 Northrup, *Indentured Labor*, 57; Yun, *The Coolie Speaks*, 18.

58 Stewart, *Chinese Bondage in Peru*, 55.

59 Irick, *Ch'ing Policy*, 209–210.

60 China Cuba Commission, *The Cuba Commission Report*, 42–46.

61 Yun, *The Coolie Speaks*, 18; Yen, *Coolies and Mandarins*, 61–62; Yun and Laremont, "Chinese Coolies and African Slaves," 110, 112; Evelyn

Hu-Dehart, "Chinese Coolie Labour in Cuba in the Nineteenth Century: Free Labour or Neo-Slavery," *Slavery and Abolition* 14, no. 1 (1993): 45.

62 *New York Times*, June 22, 1871, cited in Narvaez, "Chinese Coolies in Cuba and Peru," 1–3.

63 Arnold J. Meagher, *The Coolie Trade: The Traffic in Chinese Laborers to Latin America 1847–1874* (Philadelphia: Xlibris, 2008), 171.

64 Yun, *The Coolie Speaks*, 243; China Cuba Commission, *The Cuba Commission Report*, 47–48.

65 Narvaez, "Chinese Coolies in Cuba and Peru," 77–79; López, "Migrants Between Empires and Nations," 51; Stewart, *Chinese Bondage*, 103.

66 Yun, *The Coolie Speaks*, 66–71.

67 Narvaez, "Chinese Coolies in Cuba and Peru," 83; Yun and Laremont, "Chinese Coolies and African Slaves," 116; Evelyn Hu-DeHart, "Coolies, Shopkeepers, Pioneers: The Chinese of Mexico and Peru, 1849–1930," *Amerasia* 15, no. 2 (1989): 92, 103; Humberto Rodríguez Pastor, *Los Herederos del Dragon: Historia de La Comunidad China en el Peru* (Lima: Fondo Editorial del Congreso del Peru, 2000), 54–56; Stewart, *Chinese Bondage*, 95–98.

68 Rights described in Northrup, *Indentured Labor*, 109; Hu-Dehart, "Chinese Coolie Labour in Cuba," 42, 44. Unique labor system explained in Narvaez, "Chinese Coolies in Cuba and Peru," 93, 155–67, 24–25, 168.

69 China Cuba Commission, *The Cuba Commission Report*, 56.

70 Yun, *The Coolie Speaks*, 11; China Cuba Commission, *The Cuba Commission Report*, 21; Hu-Dehart, "Chinese Coolie Labour in Cuba," 43.

71 Petition 40, *The Cuba Commission Report*, cited in Yun, *The Coolie Speaks*, 84.

72 Petition 41, *The Cuba Commission Report*, cited in Yun, *The Coolie Speaks*, 97.

73 China Cuba Commission, *The Cuba Commission Report*, 50.

74 Yun and Laremont, "Chinese Coolies and African Slaves," 114.

75 Philip S. Foner, *A History of Cuba and Its Relations with the United States* (New York: International Publishers, 1962), 224.

76 Yun, *The Coolie Speaks*, 150, 83, 176, 178; Hu-Dehart, "Chinese Coolie Labour in Cuba," 50.

77 China Cuba Commission, *The Cuba Commission Report*, 50.

78 Deposition 18, *The Cuba Commission Report*, cited in Yun, *The Coolie Speaks*, 148.

79 Kathleen López, *Chinese Cubans: A Transnational History* (Chapel Hill, NC: University of North Carolina Press, 2013), 117, 133.

80 Matthew Guterl and Christine Skwiot, "Atlantic and Pacific Crossings: Race, Empire, and the 'Labor Problem' in the Late Nineteenth Century," *Radical History Review* 91 (Winter 2005): 41–42; Stewart, *Chinese Bondage*, 138, 144; Hu-Dehart, "Chinese Coolie Labour in Cuba," 70.

81 The 1862 law (passed February 19, 1862) was officially known as the "Act to Prohibit the 'Coolie Trade' by American Citizens in American Vessels" (12 Stat. 340). Moon-Ho Jung, *Coolies and Cane: Race, Labor, and Sugar in the Age of Emancipation* (Baltimore: Johns Hopkins University Press, 2008), 5, 33–38.

82 Stewart, *Chinese Bondage*, 158–59, 204.

83 Yun, *The Coolie Speaks*, 36.

84 Stewart, *Chinese Bondage*, 204.

85 Hu-Dehart, "Chinese Coolie Labour in Cuba," 43; Yun, *The Coolie Speaks*, 118.

86 López, "Migrants Between Empires and Nations," 112; Narvaez, "Chinese Coolies in Cuba and Peru," 409–24; Pan, *Encyclopedia*, 249; Chang, "The Chinese in Latin America," 93–97, 63; Evelyn Hu-DeHart, "Coolies, Shopkeepers, Pioneers: The Chinese of Mexico and Peru, 1849–1930," *Amerasia* 15, no. 2 (1989): 107–108, 110.

87 Narvaez, "Chinese Coolies in Cuba and Peru," 436, 440–41.

88 On remigration in general, see López, "Migrants Between Empires and Nations," 11. On Chinese in New York, see Tchen, *New York Before Chinatown*, 227–28. On Chinese to Louisiana, see Jung, *Coolies and Cane*, 76–84, 91–92.

Chapter 3: Chinese Immigrants in Search of Gold Mountain

1 Kil Young Zo, *Chinese Emigration into the United States, 1850–1880* (San Francisco: Arno, 1978), 83.

2 Statistics from Ronald T. Takaki, *Strangers from a Different Shore: A History of Asian Americans* (Boston: Little, Brown, 1998), 79, 34. Advertisement from Xiao-huang Yin, *Chinese American Literature Since the 1850s* (Urbana: University of Illinois Press, 2000), 14.

3 The U.S. government agency charged with administering the country's immigration laws changed names multiple times over the years. Customs officials under the Office of Superintendent of Immigration in the Treasury Department were the first immigration officials. The Bureau of Immigration was established in 1895, the Bureau of Immigration and Naturalization in 1906, the Immigration and Naturalization Service in 1933, and the U.S. Citizenship and

Immigration Services in 2002. "Our History," Department of Homeland Security, http://www.uscis.gov/about-us/our-history (accessed November 23, 2014).

4 Inspector's Investigation, 1907, File 514-C (Moy Wah Chung) Investigation Arrival Case Files, Philadelphia, PA, National Archives, Philadelphia, PA; Interrogation of Moy Wah Chung, May 21, 1928, File 35100/177, Investigation Arrival Case Files, Seattle, National Archives, Seattle, WA; Interview with Gladys Huie (Moy Sau Bik) by author, Walnut Creek, California, September 9, 1993.

5 Molly O'Neill, *New York Cookbook* (New York: Workman, 1992), 254.

6 Kevin Scott Wong, *Americans First: Chinese Americans and the Second World War* (Cambridge: Harvard University Press, 2005).

7 Quote from Kin Huie, *Reminiscences* (Peiping: San Yu Press, 1932), in *Chinese American Voices: From the Gold Rush to the Present*, ed. Judy Yung, Gordon H. Chang, and H. Mark Lai (Berkeley: University of California Press, 2006), 58.

8 Pan, *The Encyclopedia of the Chinese Overseas*, 62.

9 Adam McKeown, *Chinese Migrant Networks and Cultural Change: Peru, Chicago, Hawaii, 1900–1936* (Chicago: University of Chicago Press, 2001), 76–78.

10 Robert Eric Barde, *Immigration at the Golden Gate: Passenger Ships, Exclusion, and Angel Island* (Westport, CT: Praeger, 2008), 54.

11 Victor Nee, *Longtime Californ': A Documentary Study of an American Chinatown* (Boston: Houghton Mifflin, 1974), 16.

12 Marlon Hom, "Some Cantonese Folksongs on the American Experience." *Western Folklore* 42, no. 2 (1983): 128.

13 Hamilton Holt, *The Life Stories of Undistinguished Americans as Told by Themselves* (New York, NY: James Pott & Company, 1906), 287–288.

14 Erika Lee and Judy Yung, *Angel Island: Immigrant Gateway to America* (New York: Oxford University Press, 2010), 71.

15 Interview with Lee Chi Yet (Wallace Lee) by author, Buffalo, New York, February 20, 1990.

16 "Petition of the Chinese Six Companies to Prince Tsai Tao on His Visit to the United States," printed in *Chung Sai Yat Po*, May 2, 1910, translated by the U.S. Bureau of Immigration, File 52961/24-B, INS Subject Correspondence, National Archives, Washington, D.C.

17 Gold Mountain firms described in Hsu, *Dreaming of Gold*, 34–40. "Grooves" from McKeown, *Chinese Migrant Networks*, 84–86.

18 Judy Yung, *Unbound Feet: A Social History of Chinese Women in San Francisco* (Berkeley: University of California Press, 1995), 99.

19 Lee, *At America's Gates*, 117–19; McKeown, *Chinese Migrant Networks*, 31, 36.

20 On "Gold Mountain widows" or "grass widows," see Judy Yung, *Unbound Feet: A Social History of Chinese Women in San Francisco* (Berkeley: University of California Press, 1995), 20; and Hsu, *Dreaming of Gold*, 104, 213 (fn 25).

21 Letters reprinted in Yung, Chang, and Lai, eds., *Chinese American Voices*, 97–102.

22 Yung, *Unbound Feet*, 27.

23 Ibid., 26–29.

24 Ruthanne Lum McCunn, *Thousand Pieces Of Gold* (San Francisco: Design Enterprises of San Francisco, 1981).

25 Tye Leung's life described in Lee and Yung, *Angel Island*, 36–37, 82. Rescue homes described in Yung, *Unbound Feet*, 36–37.

26 Lee, *At America's Gates*, 117–19.

27 File 26002/1-9, Investigation Arrival Case Files, San Francisco, National Archives, San Francisco, CA; Interview with Wong Lan Fong (Mary Lee), by author, Buffalo, New York, February 20, 1990.

28 Lee and Yung, *Angel Island*, 72–73.

29 Chan, *This Bittersweet Soil*, 56.

30 Cited in *The Economist*, July 24, 1869, 874.

31 Edwin Legrand Sabin, *Building the Pacific Railway: The Construction-Story of America's First Iron Thoroughfare Between the Missouri River and California, from the Inception of the Great Idea to the Day, May 10, 1869, When the Union Pacific and the Central Pacific Joined Tracks at Promontory Point, Utah, to Form the Nation's Transcontinental* (Philadelphia: J. B. Lippincott, 1919), 111.

32 Takaki, *Strangers from a Different Shore*, 84–85.

33 Yung, Chang, and Lai, eds., *Chinese American Voices*, 3.

34 Nee, *Longtime Californ'*, 41.

35 Edward Lydon, *The Anti-Chinese Movement in the Hawaiian Kingdom, 1852–1886* (San Francisco, CA: R and E Research Associates, 1975), 18.

36 Takaki, *Strangers from a Different Shore*, 24; Clarence Glick, *Sojourners and Settlers: Chinese Migrants in Hawaii* (Honolulu: University of Hawaii Press, 1980), 46, 102–3.

37 Paul M. Ong, "Chinese Labor in Early San Francisco: Racial Segmentation and Industrial Expansion," *Amerasia Journal* 8, no. 1 (1981): 70–75.

38 Takaki, *Strangers from a Different Shore*, 94–95; Jung, *Coolies and Cane*, 194–95, 197, 214; Leslie Bow, "Racial Interstitiality and the Anxieties of the 'Partly

Colored': Representations of Asians under Jim Crow," in *Asian Americans in Dixie: Race and Migration in the South*, ed. Khyati Y. Joshi and Jigna Desai (Urbana: University of Illinois Press, 2013), 54–76.

39 Chan, *This Bittersweet Soil*, 76, 120, 171, 191, 74–75.

40 Carey McWilliams, *Factories in the Field: The Story of Migratory Farm Labor in California* (Berkeley: University of California Press, 1939), 67, 71.

41 Chan, *This Bittersweet Soil*, 328.

42 Ruthanne Lum McCunn, *Chinese American Portraits* (Seattle: University of Washington Press, 1988), 32–39.

43 Sucheng Chan, "The Economic Life of the Chinese in California, 1850–1920," in *Early Chinese Immigrant Societies: Case Studies from North America and British Southeast Asia*, ed. Tai To Lee (Singapore: Heinemann Asia, 1988), 112.

44 Holt, *The Life Stories*, 289–90.

45 Chin Foo Wong, "The Chinese in New York," *The Cosmopolitan*, October 1888, 298.

46 Paul Chan Pang Siu, *The Chinese Laundryman: A Study of Social Isolation* (New York: New York University Press, 1987), 456, 46; Chan, *Asian Americans*, 33.

47 Holt, *The Life Stories*, 292–93.

48 Tung Pok Chin, *Paper Son: One Man's Story* (Philadelphia, PA: Temple University Press, 2000), 13.

49 Siu, *The Chinese Laundryman*, 85.

50 Takaki, *Strangers from a Different Shore*, 117–18, 79.

51 Ching Chao Wu, "Chinatowns: A Study of Symbiosis and Assimilation" (PhD diss., University of Chicago, 1928), 158.

52 Peter Kwong and Dusanka Miscevic, *Chinese America: The Untold Story of America's Oldest New Community* (New York: New Press, 2006), 111.

53 Jacob Riis, *How the Other Half Lives* (New York: Dover, 1971), 83.

54 Tchen, *New York Before Chinatown*, 90–92. Appo later spent several stints in prison after being accused of murder and assault. He died in a mental hospital in 1912. See Tyler Anbinder, *Five Points: The Nineteenth-Century New York City Neighborhood That Invented Tap Dance, Stole Elections and Became the World's Most Notorious Slum* (New York: Free Press, 2001), 389–95.

55 Anbinder, *Five Points*, 389, 420.

56 Yung, *Unbound Feet*, 7.

57 Ibid., 42.

58 Ibid., 55.

59 Judy Yung, *Unbound Voices: A Documentary History of Chinese Women in San Francisco* (Berkeley: University of California Press, 1999), 181–87.

60 Ibid., 224–41.

61 Yung, *Unbound Feet*, 86–92.

62 Ibid., 106.

63 Pardee Lowe, *Father and Glorious Descendant* (Boston: Little, Brown, 1943), 19–20.

64 Wendy Rouse Jorae, *Children of Chinatown: Growing Up Chinese American in San Francisco, 1850–1920* (Chapel Hill: University of North Carolina Press, 2009), 63–64.

65 Thomas Lathrop Stedman and Kuei-p'an Li, *A Chinese and English Phrase Book* (New York: William R. Jenkins, 1888), 61, 112.

66 Takaki, *Strangers from a Different Shore*, 128.

67 McCunn, *Chinese American Portraits*, 41–45; Mae M Ngai, *The Lucky Ones: One Family and the Extraordinary Invention of Chinese America* (Boston: Houghton Mifflin Harcourt, 2010), 43–57.

68 *United States v. Wong Kim Ark*, 169 U.S. 649 (1898); Erika Lee, "Wong Kim Ark v. United States: Immigration, Race, and Citizenship," in *Race Law Stories*, ed. Devon Carbado and Rachel Moran (New York: Foundation, 2008), 89–109.

69 Scott D. Seligman, *The First Chinese American: The Remarkable Life of Wong Chin Foo* (Hong Kong: Hong Kong University Press, 2013), 45, 195–208, 212–13.

70 Chinese Equal Rights League, *Appeal of the Chinese Equal Rights League to the People of the United States for Equality of Manhood* (New York: Chinese Equal Rights League, 1892), 2–3.

71 She-Hong Chen, "Republicanism, Confucianism, Christianity, and Capitalism in American Chinese Ideology," in *Chinese American Transnationalism: The Flow of People, Resources, and Ideas Between China and America During the Exclusion Era*, ed. Sucheng Chan (Philadelphia: Temple University Press, 2006), 178.

72 Renqui Yu, *To Save China, To Save Ourselves: The Chinese Hand Laundry Alliance of New York* (Philadelphia: Temple University Press, 1995).

73 Siu, *The Chinese Laundryman*, 199.

74 Ibid., 123.

75 Yung, *Unbound Feet*, 168–69.

76 Kit King Louis, "A Study of American-Born and American-Reared Chinese in Los Angeles" (MA thesis, University of Southern California, 1931), 127.

Chapter 4: "The Chinese Must Go!": The Anti-Chinese Movement

1 Congressional testimony, cited in Gyory, *Closing the Gate: Race, Politics and the Chinese Exclusion Act* (Chapel Hill, University of North Carolina Press, 1998), 223–38.

2 Ibid., 224–227.

3 Ibid., 238.

4 The Chinese Exclusion Act (May 6, 1882) was officially titled "An Act to Execute Certain Treaty Stipulations Relating to the Chinese" (22 Stat. 58).

5 Lee, *At America's Gates*, 25.

6 Stuart Creighton Miller, *The Unwelcome Immigrant: The American Image of the Chinese, 1785–1882* (Berkeley: University of California Press, 1969); Tchen, *New York Before Chinatown*, xx–xxiv; Lee, *Orientals*, 27–43.

7 Samuel Gompers, *Some Reasons for Chinese Exclusion—Meat vs. Rice—American Manhood Against Asiatic Coolieism—Which Shall Survive?* (Washington, D.C.: U.S. Government Printing Office, 1902).

8 Miller, *The Unwelcome Immigrant*, 163–64; R. Lee, *Orientals*, 90–91, 104–5; Karen J. Leong, " 'A Distant and Antagonistic Race': Constructions of Chinese Manhood in the Exclusionist Debates, 1869–1878," in *Across the Great Divide: Cultures of Manhood in the American West*, ed. Laura McCall and Matthew Basso (New York: Routledge, 2000), 131–48.

9 Charles J. McClain, "The Chinese Struggle for Civil Rights in Nineteenth-Century America: The First Phase, 1850–1870," *California Law Review* 72, no. 4 (1984): 544, 555.

10 Lucy Salyer, *Laws Harsh as Tigers: Chinese Immigrants and the Shaping of Modern Immigration Law* (Chapel Hill, NC: University of North Carolina Press, 1995), 8.

11 Charles J. McClain, *In Search of Equality: The Chinese Struggle Against Discrimination in Nineteenth-Century America* (Berkeley: University of California Press, 1996), 17–18.

12 Jean Pfaelzer, *Driven Out: The Forgotten War Against Chinese Americans* (Berkeley: University of California Press, 2008), 10–16.

13 John Johnson, "How Los Angeles Covered Up the Massacre of 17 Chinese," *LA Weekly*, March 10, 2011.

14 Pfaelzer, *Driven Out*, 121–33, 209–15.

15 1862 Coolie Trade Act (12 Stat. 340); The 1875 Page Law ("An Act Supplementary to the Acts in Relation to Immigration"), March 3, 1875 (18 Stat. 477); Chinese Exclusion Act, May 6, 1882 (22 Stat. 58); Act of October 1,

1888 (25 Stat. 504, section 2); Act of May 5, 1892 (27 Stat. 25); Act of April 29, 1902, "Chinese Immigration Prohibited" (32 Stat. 176).

16 Him Mark Lai, Genny Lim, and Judy Yung, eds., *Island: Poetry and History of Chinese Immigrants on Angel Island, 1910–1940*, 2nd ed. (Seattle, WA: University of Washington Press, 2014), 162.

17 *San Francisco Morning Call*, September 14, 1892, 8.

18 The constitutionality of the Chinese exclusion laws was upheld in 1888 by the U.S. Supreme Court in *Chae Chan Ping* v. *United States* and again in *Fong Yue Ting* v. *United States* (1893). On Chinese challenges to the laws, see McClain, *In Search of Equality*; Sucheng Chan, "The Exclusion of Chinese Women, 1875–1943," in *Entry Denied: Exclusion and the Chinese Community in America, 1882–1943*, ed., Sucheng Chan (Philadelphia: Temple University Press, 1994) 94–146; and Salyer, *Laws Harsh as Tigers*.

19 Interview with Ted Chan by Judy Yung and Him Mark Lai, April 17, 1977, San Francisco, Interview 23, Angel Island Oral History Project, Ethnic Studies Library, University of California, Berkeley.

20 Him Mark Lai, Genny Lim, and Judy Yung. *Island: Poetry and History of Chinese Immigrants on Angel Island 1910–1940* (Seattle, WA: University of Washington Press, 1991), 111; Lee, *At America's Gates*, 147; Hsu, *Dreaming of Gold*, 71–72.

21 Lai, Lim, and Yung, eds., *Island*, 2nd ed., 339–40.

22 "Lee Puey You: 'A Bowlful of Tears,'" in Lai, Lim, and Yung, eds., *Island*, 2nd ed., 330–331.

23 Wen-hsien Chen, "Chinese under Both Exclusion and Immigration Laws," (PhD diss., University of Chicago, 1940), 107.

24 Lee and Yung, *Angel Island*, 88–89.

25 Lai, Lim, and Yung, eds., *Island*, 2nd ed., 21.

26 Ibid., 22.

27 Ibid., 24–31, 36.

28 Ibid., 80.

29 Lee and Yung, *Angel Island*.

30 Edward Lydon, *The Anti-Chinese Movement in the Hawaiian Kingdom, 1852–1886* (San Francisco, CA: R &and E Research Associates, 1975), 43–44.

31 A. Marques, "The Chinese Question," *Hawai'i Gazette*, October 7, 1885.

32 *Planters' Monthly* 2, no. 3 (June 1883): 49.

33 Statistics include both Native Hawaiian and part Hawaiian, from Robert C. Schmitt, *Historical Statistics of Hawaii* (Honolulu: University of Hawaii Press, 1977), 25.

34 Lydon, *The Anti-Chinese Movement*, 37, 45, 47. On Gibson, see also Esther Leonore Sousa, "Walter Murray Gibson's Rise to Power in Hawaii" (MA thesis, University of Hawaii, 1942).

35 Ralph Kuykendall, *The Hawaiian Kingdom, 1874–1893: The Kalakaua Dynasty* (Honolulu: University of Hawaii Press, 1963), 135–36, 140, 151–52; Glick, *Sojourners and Settlers*, 17, 19–22.

36 Noel Kent, *Hawaii: Islands Under the Influence* (New York: Monthly Review Press, 1983), 60.

37 John L. Stevens, "A Plea for Annexation," *North American Review* 157 (1893): 743.

38 Annexation of the Hawaiian Islands, H. Rep. 1355, 55th Cong., 2nd Sess. (May 17, 1898), 50; Roger J. Bell, *Last Among Equals: Hawaiian Statehood and American Politics* (Honolulu: University of Hawaii Press, 1984), 34.

39 Hearings before the Committee on the Philippines of the United States Senate, Sen. Doc. No. 331, pt. 1, 57th Cong., 1st Sess. (Washington, DC: U.S. Government Printing Office, 1902), 151; Clark L. Alejandrino, *A History of the 1902 Chinese Exclusion Act: American Colonial Transmission and Deterioration of Filipino-Chinese Relations* (Manila: Kaisa Para Sa Kaunlaran, 2003), 31–34, 39; Delber McKee, *Chinese Exclusion versus the Open Door Policy, 1900–1906: Clashes over China Policy in the Roosevelt Era* (Detroit: Wayne State University Press, 1977), 35.

40 López, *Chinese Cubans*, 152.

41 Ibid., 195–98.

42 W. Peter Ward, *White Canada Forever: Popular Attitudes and Public Policy Toward Orientals in British Columbia* (Montreal: McGill-Queens University Press, 1978), 36, 53–54, 171. On the making of a "white man's province" and a "white Canada," see also Patricia Roy, *A White Man's Province: British Columbia Politicians and Chinese and Japanese Immigrants, 1858–1914* (Vancouver: University of British Columbia Press, 1989); and Patricia Roy, *The Oriental Question: Consolidating a White Man's Province, 1914–1941* (Vancouver: University of British Columbia Press, 2003).

43 Erika Lee, "Orientalisms in the Americas: A Hemispheric Approach to Asian American History," *Journal of Asian American Studies* 8, no. 3 (2005): 235–56.

44 An Act to Restrict and Regulate Chinese Immigration into Canada, July 20, 1885, ch. 71, 1885, S.C. 207–12 (Can); Roy, *A White Man's Province*, 59–63, 66–68, 92, 102; Harry Con and Edgar Wickberg, *From China to Canada: A History of the Chinese Communities in Canada* (Vancouver, Canada: McClelland & Stewart, 1982), 57.

45 Robert E. Wynne, *Reaction to the Chinese in the Pacific Northwest and British Columbia, 1850–1910* (New York: Arno, 1978), 399, 446, 460; Peter S. Li, *The Chinese in Canada* (New York: Oxford University Press, 1998), 38.

46 Evelyn Huang and Lawrence Jeffery, *Chinese Canadians: Voices from a Community* (Vancouver: Douglas & McIntyre, 1992), 5, 267.

47 Robert Chao Romero, *The Chinese in Mexico, 1882–1940* (Tucson: University of Arizona Press, 2011), 1, 26–27, 51; Kenneth Cott, "Mexican Diplomacy and the Chinese Issue," *Hispanic American Historical Review* 67 (1987): 66–73.

48 Evelyn Hu-DeHart, "Racism and Anti-Chinese Persecution in Sonora, Mexico, 1876–1932," *Amerasia* 9, no. 2 (1982): 1–27.

49 Hu-DeHart, "Coolies, Shopkeepers, Pioneers," 101–2; Chao Romero, *Chinese in Mexico*, 158–60.

50 José Angel Espinoza, *El Ejemplo de Sonora* (México, D.F., 1932), 22.

51 Espinoza, *El Ejemplo de Sonora*, 77, 36; Chao Romero, *Chinese in Mexico*, 83; Robert Chao Romero, " 'El Destierro de los Chinos': Popular Perspectives on Chinese-Mexican Intermarriage in the Early Twentieth Century," *Aztlán: A Journal of Chicano Studies* 32, no. 1 (2007): 113–44; Delgado, *Making the Chinese Mexican*, 112.

52 Alan Knight, "Racism, Revolution, and Indigenismo: Mexico, 1910–1940," in *The Idea of Race in Latin America, 1870–1940*, ed. Richard Graham (Austin, TX: University of Texas Press, 1990), 81; Evelyn Hu-DeHart, "Immigrants to a Developing Society: The Chinese in Northern Mexico, 1875–1932," *The Journal of Arizona History* 21, no. 3 (1980): 276, 283, 285, 289; Chao Romero, *Chinese in Mexico*, 90; Charles C. Cumberland, "The Sonora Chinese and the Mexican Revolution," *Hispanic American Historical Review* 40, no. 2 (1960): 208; Delgado, *Making the Chinese Mexican*, 164–68.

53 Gerardo Rénique, "Race, Region, and Nation. Sonora's Anti-Chinese Racism and Mexico's Post-Revolutionary Nationalism, 1920s–1930s," in *Race and Nation in Modern Latin America*, ed. Nancy P. Appelbaum, Anne S. Macpherson, and Karin Alejandra Rosemblatt (Chapel Hill, NC: University of North Carolina Press, 2003), 220–221; Gordon V. Krutz, "Chinese Labor, Economic Development and Social Reaction," *Ethnohistory* 18, no. 4 (Autumn 1971), 328.

54 Espinoza, *El Ejemplo de Sonora*, 62; Hu-DeHart, "Racism and Anti-Chinese Persecution," 19.

55 Wilfley and Bassett, *Memorandum on the Law and the Facts in the Matter of the Claim of China against Mexico for Losses of Life and Property Suffered by*

Chinese Subjects at Torreon on May 13, 14, and 15, 1911 (Mexico: American Book & Print Co., 1911), 3, 4–7; Chao Romero, *Chinese in Mexico*, 147–55.

56 Chao Romero, *Chinese in Mexico*, 93–94; Delgado, *Making the Chinese Mexican*, 118, 165–66; Leo M. D. Jacques, "The Anti-Chinese Campaign in Sonora, Mexico, 1900–1931" (PhD diss., University of Arizona, 1974), 174.

57 Jacques, "The Anti-Chinese Campaign in Sonora," 37–38; Chao Romero, *Chinese in Mexico*, 185–86.

58 Theresa Alfaro-Velcamp, *So Far from Allah, So Close to Mexico* (Austin: University of Texas Press, 2007), 102–3.

59 Chang, "The Chinese in Latin America," 32, 73.

60 Aristide Zolberg, "The Great Wall Against China: Responses to the First Immigration Crisis, 1885–1925," in *Migration, Migration History, History: Old Paradigms and New Perspectives*, ed. Jan Lucassen and Leo Lucassen (New York: Peter Lang, 1999), 292.

Chapter 5: Japanese Immigrants and the "Yellow Peril"

1 Kazuo Ito, *Issei: A History of Japanese Immigrants in North America* (Seattle: Japanese Community Service, 1973), 27.

2 Akemi Kikumura-Yano, ed., *Encyclopedia of Japanese Descendants in the Americas: An Illustrated History of the Nikkei* (Walnut Creek, CA: AltaMira, 2002), 275.

3 Ronald T. Takaki, *Pau Hana: Plantation Life and Labor in Hawaii, 1835–1920* (Honolulu: University of Hawaii Press, 1984), 42.

4 Eiichiro Azuma, *Between Two Empires: Race, History, and Transnationalism in Japanese America* (New York: Oxford University Press, 2005), 17–20.

5 Ayumi Takenaka, "The Japanese in Peru: History of Immigration, Settlement, and Racialization," *Latin American Perspectives* 31, no. 3 (2004): 78–80.

6 Azuma, *Between Two Empires*, 27–29; Alan Takeo Moriyama, *Imingaisha: Japanese Emigration Companies and Hawaii, 1894–1908* (Honolulu: University of Hawaii Press, 1985), 3, 18–20; Yuji Ichioka, *The Issei: The World of the First Generation Japanese Immigrants, 1885–1924* (New York: Free Press, 1988), 42–46; and Masterson and Funada-Classen, *The Japanese in Latin America*, 54; Takenaka, "The Japanese in Peru," 80–81.

7 Takaki, *Pau Hana*, 43, 45.

8 Azuma, *Between Two Empires*, 29.

9 Ichioka, *The Issei*, 46, 65.

10 Moriyama, *Imingaisha*, 26.

11 Ito, *Issei*, 29.

12 Ichioka, *The Issei*, 28–39, 42–46, 167–68.

13 Takaki, *Strangers from a Different Shore*, 47.

14 Ichioka, *The Issei*, 28–39.

15 Evelyn Nakano Glenn, *Issei, Nisei, War Bride: Three Generations of Japanese American Women in Domestic Service* (Philadelphia: Temple University Press, 1986), 43–44; Ichioka, *The Issei*, 168–69.

16 Lee and Yung, *Angel Island*, 113, 117–20.

17 Roger Daniels, *The Politics of Prejudice: The Anti-Japanese Movement in California and the Struggle for Japanese Exclusion* (Berkeley: University of California Press, 1962), 5.

18 Takaki, *Pau Hana*, 57.

19 Takaki, *Strangers from a Different Shore*, 135.

20 Ibid.

21 Takaki, *Pau Hana*, 59. See also Franklin Odo, *Voices from the Canefields: Folksongs from Japanese Immigrant Workers in Hawai'i* (New York: Oxford University Press, 2013).

22 Takaki, *Strangers from a Different Shore*, 135.

23 Takaki, *Pau Hana*, 153, 155, 160–163; Takaki, *Strangers from a Different Shore*, 142–55.

24 Ichioka, *The Issei*, 51, 69; U.S. Immigration Commission, *Japanese and Other Immigrant Races in the Pacific Coast and Rocky Mountain States* (Washington, D.C, 1911), vol. 1, 33–46.

25 Ito, *Issei*, 312, 343, 362, 435.

26 Ibid., 248; Nakano Glenn, *Issei, Nisei, War Bride*, 67–76.

27 Ichioka, *The Issei*, 150; Takaki, *Strangers from a Different Shore*, 188–89.

28 "Visit with Mr. George Shima, 'Potato King' of California," Interview, July 14, 1924, 1–3, Survey of Race Relations, Hoover Institution Archives, Stanford University; Takaki, *Strangers from a Different Shore*, 192.

29 Yamato Ichihashi, *Japanese in the United States: A Critical Study of the Problems of the Japanese Immigrants and Their Children* (Stanford: Stanford University Press, 1932), 110; Takaki, *Strangers from a Different Shore*, 186.

30 Ito, *Issei*, 703–5, 710, 722; "Rise and Fall of an Empire Furuya: Immigrant, 1890," *International Examiner*, August 29, 2005.

31 Ichioka, *The Issei*, 184–96, 202–4.

32 Monica Sone, *Nisei Daughter* (Boston: Little, Brown, 1953), 22.

33 Yoshiko Uchida, *Desert Exile: The Uprooting of a Japanese American Family* (Seattle: University of Washington Press, 1982), 40–45.

34 Valerie Matsumoto, *City Girls: The Nisei Social World in Los Angeles, 1920–1950* (New York: Oxford University Press, 2014), 1.

35 Yuji Ichioka, "The Early Japanese Quest for Citizenship: The Background of the 1922 *Ozawa* Case," *Amerasia Journal* 4:1 (1977): 11.

36 Both World War I and delicate U.S.-Japan relations caused several delays in the case from the time that it was passed on to the Supreme Court to the time that the Court ruled. See Ian F. Haney Lopez, *White by Law: The Legal Construction of Race* (New York: New York University Press, 1996), 56–61; Takaki, *Strangers from a Different Shore*, 208; Ichioka, *The Issei*, 211, 219–26; Mae M. Ngai, "The Architecture of Race in American Immigration Law: A Reexamination of the Immigration Act of 1924," *The Journal of American History* 86:1 (June 1999): 81.

37 Takaki, *Strangers from a Different Shore*, 211.

38 Ichioka, *The Issei*, 5, 156–58, 186–96, 202–4.

39 Azuma, *Between Two Empires*, 3–14, 163–86.

40 *The Review of Reviews* (London), December 1895, 474–75; Okihiro, *Margins and Mainstreams*, 118–20.

41 Takaki, *Strangers from a Different Shore*, 180.

42 Daniels, *The Politics of Prejudice*, 20–21, 25–26.

43 Takaki, *Strangers from a Different Shore*, 181.

44 Asiatic Exclusion League, *Proceedings of the First International Convention* (Seattle, WA: San Francisco, 1908), 68; Robert E. Wynne, "American Labor Leaders and the Vancouver Anti-Oriental Riot," *Pacific Northwest Quarterly* 57, no. 4 (1966): 174.

45 Asiatic Exclusion League, *Proceedings*, 68.

46 Executive Order 589, March 14, 1907; Daniels, *The Politics of Prejudice*, 43–44, 130 (fn 42).

47 *New York Times*, May 30, 1907.

48 U.S. Congress, *Japanese in the City of San Francisco, Cal.; Message from the President of the United States, Transmitting the Final Report of Secretary Metcalf on the Situation Affecting the Japanese in the City of San Francisco* (Washington, DC: U.S. Government Printing Office, 1907); Philip C. Jessup, *Elihu Root*, vol. 2: 1905–1937 (Hamden, CT: Archon, 1938), 16, 22; Thomas A. Bailey, *Theodore Roosevelt and the Japanese-American Crisis* (Gloucester, MA: Peter Smith, 1964), 194–96, 199–200.

49 Daniels, *The Politics of Prejudice*, 38–39.

50 William Lyon Mackenzie King, *Report of W. L. Mackenzie King: Commissioner Appointed to Enquire into the Methods by Which Oriental Labourers Have Been Induced to Come to Canada* (Ottawa: S. E. Dawson, 1908), 15, 21–22.

51 *New York Times*, September 8, 1907, and September 10, 1907.
52 Jensen, *Passage from India*, 62, 64.
53 *Vancouver Daily Province*, September 5, 1907.
54 Roy, *A White Man's Province*, 191.
55 Asiatic Exclusion League, *Proceedings*, 13.
56 *New York Times*, September 11, 1907; Jensen, *Passage from India*, 67; Erika Lee, "Hemispheric Orientalism and the 1907 Pacific Coast Race Riots," *Amerasia Journal* 33, no. 2 (2007): 19–47.
57 Howard H. Sugimoto, *The Vancouver Riots of 1907* (Santa Barbara, CA: American Bibliographical Center-Clio Press, 1972), 93–94.
58 Jensen, *Passage from India*, 67.
59 Will Irwin, "The Japanese and the Pacific Coast," *Collier's*, September 28, 1907, 13; *New York Times*, September 14, 1907.
60 *New York Times*, September 10, 1907; Sugimoto, *The Vancouver Riots of 1907*, 97.
61 Ito, *Issei*, 103–4.
62 Wynne, "American Labor Leaders," 172–79; Woan-Jen Wang, "Perspectives on the 1907 Riots in Selected Asian Languages and International Newspapers," *Discovering Pacific Canada, Pacific Migrations Research and Asian Canadian Studies at the University of British Columbia*, 2007, http://www.instrcc.ubc.ca/1907_riotwj (accessed July 25, 2012).
63 Daniels, *The Politics of Prejudice*, 44. On the Canadian agreement, see Ken Adachi, *The Enemy That Never Was: A History of the Japanese Canadians* (Toronto: McClelland & Stewart, 1991), 81; and Sugimoto, *The Vancouver Riots of 1907*, 166–68.
64 Charles H. Pearson, *National Life and Character: A Forecast* (London: Macmillan, 1894); Madison Grant, *The Passing of the Great Race* (New York: Charles Scribner's Sons, 1918); Homer Lea, *The Valor of Ignorance* (New York: Harper & Brothers, 1909).
65 Lothrop Stoddard, *The Rising Tide of Color Against White World-Supremacy* (New York: Scribner, 1920), 14; R. Lee, *Orientals*, 136.
66 Stoddard, *The Rising Tide*, 17–53, 229. See also Jesse Frederick Steiner, *The Japanese Invasion: A Study in the Psychology of Interracial Contacts* (Chicago: A. C. McClurg, 1917), 35–36.
67 Stoddard, *The Rising Tide*, 41, 48–49, 229, 241–49.
68 Ibid., 251.
69 Eiichiro Azuma, "Historical Overview of Japanese Emigration, 1868–2000," in *Encyclopedia of Japanese Descendants in the Americas: An Illustrated*

History of the Nikkei, ed. Akemi Kikumura-Yano (Walnut Creek, CA: AltaMira, 2002), 32–48; Charles J. Woodsworth, *Canada and the Orient* (Toronto: Macmillan, 1941), 289.

70 *San Francisco Examiner*, February 27, 1924, cited in Jules Becker, "The Course of Exclusion, 1882–1924: San Francisco Newspaper Coverage of the Chinese and Japanese in the United States" (PhD diss., University of California, Berkeley, 1986), 191.

71 *San Francisco Examiner*, January 21, 1924.

72 Ibid.

73 Daniels, *The Politics of Prejudice*, 63, 88.

74 Steiner, *The Japanese Invasion*, v–vi, 197, 209.

75 Lea, *The Valor of Ignorance*, 115, 157–59, 192, 249–51, 264–78, 343.

76 Daniels, *The Politics of Prejudice*, 70.

77 Jack London, "The Yellow Peril," in *Revolution and Other Essays* (New York: Macmillan, 1910), 82–85, 220–37; Peter B. Kyne, *The Pride of Palomar* (New York: Cosmopolitan, 1921); Montaville Flowers, *The Japanese Conquest of American Opinion* (New York: G. H. Doran, 1917); Wallace Irwin, *Seed of the Sun* (New York: G. H. Doran, 1921); Daniels, *The Politics of Prejudice*, 92; Carey McWilliams, *Prejudice: Japanese Americans: Symbol of Racial Intolerance* (Boston: Little, Brown, 1944), 60–61; Colleen Lye, *America's Asia: Racial Form and American Literature, 1882–1945* (Princeton: Princeton University Press, 2004), 119, 128–29.

78 R. Lee, *Orientals*, 114, 116–17, 121, 125, 127–28, 130.

79 James Francis Abbott, *Japanese Expansion and American Policies* (New York: Macmillan, 1916), 2, 143–82, 190.

80 Madison Grant, Introduction to Stoddard, *The Rising Tide*, xxix–xxxii.

81 Stoddard, *The Rising Tide*, 221, 255, 276, 282.

82 Zolberg, "The Great Wall Against China," 291–316. See also Mae M. Ngai, *Impossible Subjects: Illegal Aliens and the Making of Modern America* (Princeton: Princeton University Press, 2004), 17–20.

83 The Quota Act of 1921 (42 Stat. 5, section 2); Immigration Act of 1924 (43 Stat. 153); John Higham, *Strangers in the Land: Patterns of American Nativism, 1860–1925* (New Brunswick, NJ: Rutgers University Press, 1963), 308–24; Ngai, *Impossible Subjects*, 21–55.

84 Patricia Roy, *Mutual Hostages: Canadians and Japanese During the Second World War* (Toronto: University of Toronto Press, 1990), 16; Ward, *White Canada Forever*, 131–33.

85 Masterson and Funada-Classen, *The Japanese in Latin America*, 53, 73, 79.

86 Nobuya Tsuchida, "The Japanese in Brazil, 1908–1941," (PhD diss., University of California, Los Angeles, 1978), 244–45, 280–82, 287, 290, 293–95; Jeffrey Lesser, *Negotiating National Identity: Immigrants, Minorities, and the Struggle for Ethnicity in Brazil* (Durham, NC: Duke University Press, 1999), 120.

87 In 1936, the quota was raised to 3,480 and in fact the number of actual entrants (over 8,000) was much higher than that due to lax enforcement. Tsuchida, "The Japanese in Brazil," 246–47; Lesser, *Negotiating National Identity*, 127.

88 *El Comercio*, May 29, 1924, and *Accíon*, April 30, 1934, cited in Molinari Morales, *El Fascismo En El Peru: La Unión Revolucionaria 1931–36* (Lima, Peru: Fondo Editorial de la Facultad de Ciencias Sociales, 2006), 233–34.

89 *La Prensa*, November 30, 1934.

90 João Frederico Normano, *The Japanese in South America: An Introductory Survey with Special Reference to Peru* (New York, NY: The John Day Company, 1943), 8, 113–15; C. Harvey Gardiner, *The Japanese and Peru, 1873–1973* (Albuquerque: University of New Mexico Press, 1975), 77, 114–16; Takenaka, "The Japanese in Peru," 87.

91 Gardiner, *The Japanese and Peru*, 50; Amelia Morimoto, *Los Inmigrantes Japoneses en El Perú* (Lima: Taller de Estudios Andinos Universidad Nacional Agraria Departamento de Ciencias Humanas, 1979), 71–72; Normano et al., *The Japanese in South America*, 117; Takenaka, "The Japanese in Peru," 87; Kodani, "The Japanese Peruvians," 76.

92 Normano, *The Japanese in South America*, 113, 116; Morimoto, *Los Inmigrantes Japoneses*, 74; Masterson and Funada-Classen, *The Japanese in Latin America*, 152; Edward N. Barnhart, "Japanese Internees from Peru," *Pacific Historical Review* 31, no. 2 (1962): 170.

93 Seiichi Higashide, *Adios to Tears: The Memoirs of a Japanese-Peruvian Internee in U.S. Concentration Camps* (Seattle: University of Washington Press, 2000), 105–10; Normano, *The Japanese in South America*, 52–53.

94 Iichiro Tokutomi, *Japanese-American Relations* (New York: Macmillan, 1922), 109–10.

Chapter 6: "We Must Struggle in Exile": Korean Immigrants

1 Mary Paik Lee, *Quiet Odyssey: A Pioneer Korean Woman in America*, ed. Sucheng Chan (Seattle: University of Washington Press, 1990), xxxix, 6–7; Richard S. Kim, *The Quest for Statehood: Korean Immigrant Nationalism and U.S. Sovereignty, 1905–1945* (New York: Oxford University Press, 2011), 15.

2 Takaki, *Strangers from a Different Shore*, 282.

3 Wayne Patterson, *The Korean Frontier in America: Immigration to Hawaii, 1896–1910* (Honolulu: University of Hawaii Press, 1988), 103–13; Linda Pomerantz, "The Background of Korean Emigration," in *Labor Immigration Under Capitalism*, eds. Cheng and Bonacich, 277–93.

4 Pomerantz, "The Background of Korean Emigration," 289.

5 Patterson, *The Korean Frontier in America*, 54.

6 Ibid., 193.

7 Bong Youn Choy, *Koreans in America* (Chicago: Nelson-Hall, 1979), 74.

8 Takaki, *Strangers from a Different Shore*, 56; Patterson, *The Korean Frontier in America*, 191.

9 Patterson, *The Korean Frontier in America*, 190.

10 Ibid., 105–10; Choy, *Koreans in America*, 77–78; Takaki, *Strangers from a Different Shore*, 53–56, 272–73; Lee, *Quiet Odyssey*, xli.

11 Wayne Patterson, *The Ilse: First-Generation Korean Immigrants in Hawai'i, 1903–1973* (Honolulu: University of Hawaii Press, 2000), 25.

12 Takaki, *Strangers from a Different Shore*, 137.

13 Lee and Yung, *Angel Island*, 87–88.

14 Ibid., 181–82.

15 Sun Bin Yim, "The Social Structure of Korean Communities in California, 1903–1920," in *Labor Migration Under Capitalism*, eds. Cheng and Bonacich, 518.

16 Warren Y. Kim, *Koreans in America* (Seoul: Po Chin Chai, 1971), 22–23; Pomerantz, "The Background of Korean Emigration," 305–8.

17 Patterson, *The Ilse*, 84.

18 Ibid., 87–88.

19 Ibid., 88.

20 Ibid., 91.

21 Choy, *Koreans in America*, 88–89.

22 Patterson, *The Ilse*, 93.

23 Ibid., 97.

24 Sonia Shinn Sunoo, *Korean Picture Brides: 1903–1920: A Collection of Oral Histories* (Bloomington, IN: Xlibris Corporation, 2002), 21–41.

25 Choy, *Koreans in America*, 105, 123–26, 130; Hyung-chan Kim, "Ethnic Enterprises Among Korean Immigrants in America," in *The Korean Diaspora: Historical and Sociological Studies of Korean Immigration and Assimilation in North America*, ed. Hyung-chan Kim, (Santa Barbara, CA: Clio Books, 1977), 90; Kim, *The Quest for Statehood*, 23.

26 Lee, *Quiet Odyssey*, xlv, lvii, 14.

27 Choy, *Koreans in America*, 114; Kim, *Koreans in America*, 66–68.

28 Lee, *Quiet Odyssey*, xlviii.

29 Choy, *Koreans in America*, 99–101; Kim, *Koreans in America*, 29; Lee, *Quiet Odyssey*, xlix.

30 Lee, *Quiet Odyssey*, 58.

31 Kim, *The Quest for Statehood*, 26.

32 Ibid., 8–10.

33 Ibid., 26. See also Kim, *Koreans in America*, 49; and Takaki, *Strangers from a Different Shore*, 283.

34 Kim, *The Quest for Statehood*, 41.

35 Choy, *Koreans in America*, 141–49; Lee, *Quiet Odyssey*, xxix.

36 Choy, *Koreans in America*, 148–52.

37 Kim, *The Quest for Statehood*, 6.

38 Choy, *Koreans in America*, 149–52.

39 Patterson, *The Ilse*, 98; Lee, *Quiet Odyssey*, lviii; Lili M. Kim, "Redefining the Boundaries of Traditional Gender Roles: Korean Picture Brides, Pioneer Korean Immigrant Women, and Their Benevolent Nationalism in Hawai'i," in *Asian/Pacific Islander American Women: A Historical Anthology*, eds. Shirley Hune and Gail M. Nomura (New York: New York University Press, 2003), 106–22; Kim, *The Quest for Statehood*, 49.

40 Kim, *The Quest for Statehood*, 46; Lee, *Quiet Odyssey*, xxx–xxxi.

41 Kim, *The Quest for Statehood*, 6, 53–56. See also Choy, *Koreans in America*, 152–61; and Kim, *Koreans in America*, 91–99.

42 Kim, *The Quest for Statehood*, 160.

43 Howard Brett Melendy, *Asians in America: Filipinos, Koreans, and East Indians* (Boston: Twayne, 1977), 134.

44 Lee, *Quiet Odyssey*, 12, 54–57.

45 Sonia Shinn Sunoo, *Korea Kaleidoscope: Oral Histories, Early Korean Pioneers in USA: 1903–1905*, vol. 1 (Sacramento: Sierra Mission Area United Presbyterian Church, 1982), 69.

46 Melendy, *Asians in America*, 136.

47 Yim, "The Social Structure of Korean Communities in California, 1903–1920," 529.

48 Brenda Paik Sunoo, ed., *Korean American Writings: Selected Material from Insight, Korean American Bimonthly* (New York: Insight, 1975), 25.

49 Lee, *Quiet Odyssey*, 14, 103.

Chapter 7: South Asian Immigrants and the "Hindu Invasion"

1 *San Francisco Chronicle*, April 6, 1899.

2 "Hindu Cheap Labor a Menace to Prosperity of the Coast," *Chico Enterprise*, December 20, 1909; "Turn Back the Hindu Invasion," *San Francisco Call*, February 1, 1910.

3 Jensen, *Passage from India*, 24–25; Mazumdar, "Colonial Impact and Punjabi Emigration to the United States," 316–17, 325.

4 Mazumdar, "Colonial Impact and Punjabi Emigration," 323.

5 Ibid., 331; Norman Buchignani, Doreen Marie Indra, and Ram Srivastava, *Continuous Journey: A Social History of South Asians in Canada* (Toronto: McClelland and Stewart, 1985), 12–13.

6 William Lyon Mackenzie King, *Report of W. L. Mackenzie King: Commissioner Appointed to Enquire into the Methods by Which Oriental Labourers Have Been Induced to Come to Canada* (Ottawa: S. E. Dawson, 1908), 80.

7 Interview of Sucha Singh, August 18, 1924, Survey of Race Relations, Hoover Institution Archives, Stanford University.

8 Hugh J. M. Johnston, *The East Indians in Canada* (Ottawa: Canadian Historical Association, 1984), 6.

9 Profile of Tuly Singh Johl from Jensen, *Passage from India*, 29–34.

10 H. A. Millis, "East Indian Immigration to British Columbia and the Pacific Coast States," *American Economic Review* 1 (March 1911): 74.

11 Jensen, *Passage from India*, 34–36, 38–39.

12 Vivek Bald, *Bengali Harlem and the Lost Histories of South Asian America* (Cambridge: Harvard University Press, 2013), chapters 1 and 2.

13 Ibid.

14 Board of Special Inquiry in the Matter of the Application of Vasaka Singh, October 25, 1913, File 12993/2-1, Investigation Arrival Case Files, San Francisco, National Archives, San Francisco, CA.

15 Board of Special Inquiry in the Matter of the Application of Suchiat Singh, October 6, 1914, File 13831/4-1, ibid.

16 Lee and Yung, *Angel Island*, 145–46, 153–55, 173. Profile of Kala Bagai is also available from Rani Bagai, " 'Bridges Burnt Behind': The Story of Vaishno Das Bagai," *Immigrant Voices, Angel Island Immigration Station Foundation*, http://www.aiisf.org/stories-by-author/876-bridges-burnt-behind-the-story-of-vaishno-das-bagai (accessed December 1, 2013).

17 Interview with Inder Singh, El Centro, California, May 31, 1924, Survey of Race Relations, Hoover Institution Archives, Stanford University;

Punjabi-Mexican families from Karen Isaksen Leonard, *Making Ethnic Choices: California's Punjabi Mexican Americans* (Philadelphia: Temple University Press, 1992), 37–38, 40, 50.

18 Nayan Shah, *Stranger Intimacy: Contesting Race, Sexuality and the Law in the North American West* (Berkeley: University of California Press, 2011), 1.

19 Rajani Kanta Das, *Hindustani Workers on the Pacific Coast* (Berlin: Walter DeGruyter, 1923), 88–89; Jogesh C. Misrow, *East Indian Immigration on the Pacific Coast* (San Francisco: R & E Research Associates, 1971), 14–15, 26–27.

20 Lee and Yung, *Angel Island*, 160.

21 Das, *Hindustani Workers*, 88–89.

22 Arun Coomer Bose, "Indian Nationalist Agitations in the USA and Canada Till the Arrival of Har Dayal in 1911," *Journal of Indian History* 43, no. 1 (1965): 235; Tapan K. Mukherjee, *Taraknath Das: Life and Letters of a Revolutionary in Exile* (Calcutta: National Council of Education, Bengal, Jadavpur University, 1998), 10, 16, 25; Arun Bose, *Indian Revolutionaries Abroad, 1905–1922: In the Background of International Developments* (Patna: Bharati Bhawan, 1971), 55; Mark Juergensmeyer, "The Ghadar Syndrome: Nationalism in an Immigrant Community," *Punjab Journal of Politics* 1, no. 1 (October 1977): 7; Jensen, *Passage from India*, 121.

23 Buchignani, Indra, and Srivastava, *Continuous Journey*, 51–53; Jensen, *Passage from India*, 186–87, 190–91; Jane Singh, "The Gadar Party: Political Expression in an Immigrant Community," in *Asian American Studies: A Reader*, eds. Min Song and Jean Yu-wen Shen Wu (New Brunswick, NJ: Rutgers University Press, 2000), 38–39; Lee and Yung, *Angel Island*, 163–69.

24 Juergensmeyer, "The Ghadar Syndrome," 8.

25 Johnston, *The East Indians in Canada*, 9; Buchignani, Indra, and Srivastava, *Continuous Journey*, 52.

26 Bellingham *Reveille*, September 6, 1907, cited in Gerald L. Hallberg, "Bellingham, Washington's Anti-Hindu Riot," *Journal of the West* 12 (January 1973): 172.

27 Jensen, *Passage from India*, 51.

28 H. A. Millis, "East Indian Immigration to the Pacific Coast," *Survey* 28 (1912): 381; U.S. Senate, *Reports of the Immigration Commission: Immigrants in Industries, Part 25: Japanese and Other Immigrant Races in the Pacific Coast and Rocky Mountain States*, vol. 1: Japanese and East Indians (Washington, DC: U.S. Government Printing Office, 1911), 349. On the committee's definitions of "races," see "Dictionary of Races or Peoples," ibid., 8. The

recommendations on South Asian exclusion appear in "Brief Statement of the Investigations of the Immigration Commission, with Conclusions and Recommendations, and Views of Minority," ibid., 47.

29 Jensen, *Passage from India*, 43.

30 *Bellingham Herald*, September 5, 1907; Hallberg, "Bellingham, Washington's Anti-Hindu Riot," 164–68; Jensen, *Passage from India*, 43–48; Robert E. Wynne, "American Labor Leaders and the Vancouver Anti-Oriental Riot," *Pacific Northwest Quarterly* 57, no. 4 (1966): 172–79; *New York Times*, September 6, 1907.

31 On the relationship between the Bellingham and Vancouver riots, see Lee, "Hemispheric Orientalism and the 1907 Pacific Coast Race Riots."

32 William Lyon Mackenzie King, *Report by W. L. Mackenzie King . . . Deputy Minister of Labour, on Mission to England to Confer with the British Authorities on the Subject of Immigration to Canada from the Orient and Immigration from India in Particular* (Ottawa: S. E. Dawson, 1908), 5, 7–8, 10; Jensen, *Passage from India*, 82.

33 U.S. Department of Labor, "Memorandum Regarding Hindu Migration to the United States," n.d., ca. January 1914, File 52903/110C, U.S. INS Subject Correspondence, National Archives, DC.

34 "Hindus by Thousands Coming to Coast Because the Railroads Want Cheap Labor," *Oakland Mail*, June 4, 1910; "Hindu Immigration and Conspiracy," *San Francisco Call*, June 15, 1910; "San Francisco Now Sole Dumping Ground for the Undesirable, Unspeakable Hindu, Barred by His Master from Sister Colonies," *San Francisco Daily News*, June 3, 1910, in File 52600/48, INS Subject Correspondence, National Archives, Washington, DC.; Agnes Foster Buchanan, "The West and the Hindu Invasion," *Overland Monthly*, April 1908; Girindra Mukerji, "The Hindu in America," *Overland Monthly*, April 1908; "The Hindu Invasion," *Collier's*, March 26, 1910.

35 Julius Kahn to Daniel J. Keefe, May 3, 1910, File 52903/110, U.S. INS Subject Correspondence, National Archives, DC.

36 Daniel Keefe to Hart Hyatt North, April 27, 1910, File 52903/110, ibid.

37 Jensen, *Passage from India*, 108.

38 Daniel Keefe, Memorandum for the Secretary, April 7, 1913, File 52903/110-A, U.S. INS Subject Correspondence, National Archives, DC.

39 Daniel Keefe to Hart Hyatt North, Commissioner of Immigration, SF, April 27, 1910, File 52903/110, ibid.

40 U.S. Department of Labor Memorandum Regarding Hindu Migration to the United States, n.d., ca. January 1914, File 52903/110C, ibid.

41 U.S. Department of Labor Memorandum Regarding Hindu Migration to the United States, n.d., ca. January 1914, File 52903/110C, ibid; Millis, "East Indian Immigration to British Columbia and the Pacific Coast States," 74.

42 Board of Special Inquiry Hearing, July 16, 1910, File 10414/7-9, Investigation Arrival Case Files, San Francisco, National Archives, San Francisco, CA.

43 Das, *Hindustani Workers*, 114.

44 Statistics drawn from Table 3: Alien Applicants for Admission to U.S. and Percent Debarred by Nationality July 1, 1910–June 30, 1932, in Lee and Yung, *Angel Island*, 328.

45 "Congratulations! Congratulations!! Congratulations!!!" (translation), Enclosure 4, in Governor [of Hong Kong] to Secretary of State, March 28, 1914, in File 879545, pt. 1, "Hindoo Immigration, Sailing of 400 Hindoos by chartered vessel (*Komagata Maru*)," RG 76, Vol. 601, Records from the Immigration Branch, Canada, Library and Archives, Canada.

46 Buchignani, Indra, and Srivastava, *Continuous Journey*, 54–55.

47 See government correspondence and newspaper clippings in File 879545, pt. 1, "Hindoo Immigration, Sailing of 400 Hindoos by chartered vessel (*Komagata Maru*)."

48 Jensen, *Passage from India*, 131–32.

49 See newspaper clippings for May 1914 in File 879545, pt. 1, "Hindoo Immigration, Sailing of 400 Hindoos by chartered vessel (*Komagata Maru*)."

50 W. C. Hopkinson to W. W. Cory, Deputy Minister of the Interior, June 1, 1914, in File 879545, pt. 2, "Hindus sailing from Shanghai to Vancouver, B.C. on SS. *KOMAGATA MARU*," RG 76, Volume 480, Records from the Immigration Branch, Canada, Library and Archives, Canada.

51 Mukherjee, *Taraknath Das*, 57–59; Buchignani, Indra, and Srivastava, *Continuous Journey*, 57.

52 E. B. Robertson, Asst. Superintendent of Immigration to Sir Robert Borden, July 20, 1914, in File 879545, pt. 4, "Hindus sailing from Shanghai to Vancouver, B.C. on SS. *KOMAGATA MARU*," RG 76, Volume 601, Records from the Immigration Branch, Canada, Library and Archives, Canada.

53 Jensen, *Passage from India*, 121–38.

54 Anthony Caminetti to the Secretary, June 12, 1914; Caminetti to John L. Burnett, July 3, 1914, in "Hindu Immigration," File 52903/110-D, U.S. INS Subject Correspondence, National Archives, DC.

55 Canadian Superintendent of Immigration to U.S. Commissioner of Immigration, Montreal, September 15, 1913, in "Hindu Immigration, 1910," File 52903/110-A, ibid.

56 Jensen, *Passage from India*, 191–93, 217; Lee and Yung, *Angel Island*, 165.

57 Jensen, *Passage from India*, 142, 154.

58 Immigration Act of 1917 (39 Stat. 874).

59 Das, *Hindustani Workers*, 113–15.

60 Willard A. Schurr, "Hindus in Los Angeles," Document No. 273-A, Survey of Race Relations, Hoover Institution Archives, Stanford University.

61 "Hindus Too Brunette to Vote Here," *The Literary Digest*, March 10, 1923, South Asian American Digital Archive, http://www.saadigitalarchive.org/item/20101210-148 (accessed November 24, 2013); *United States v. Bhagat Singh Thind*, 261 U.S. 204 (1923); Lopez, *White by Law*, 61–77.

62 *San Francisco Examiner*, March 17, 1928; Lee and Yung, *Angel Island*, 145–46, 153–55, 173.

63 Interview of Kala Bagai Chandra, Nov. 26, 1982, courtesy of Rani Bagai.

Chapter 8: "We Have Heard Much of America": Filipinos in the U.S. Empire

1 Francisco Carino, "My Life History," August 1924, Survey of Race Relations, Major Document No. 85, Hoover Institution Archives, Stanford University.

2 Ibid. Anti-Filipino signs in Dawn Bohulano Mabalon, *Little Manila Is in the Heart: The Making of the Filipina/o American Community in Stockton, California* (Durham, NC: Duke University Press, 2013), 113.

3 Carlos Bulosan, *America Is in the Heart: A Personal History* (Seattle: University of Washington Press, 1943), 121.

4 Espiritu, *Home Bound*, 46–62.

5 Leon Wolff, *Little Brown Brother: How the United States Purchased and Pacified the Philippine Islands at the Century's Turn* (Garden City, NY: Doubleday, 1961), xi; Mabalon, *Little Manila*, 31.

6 Espiritu, *Home Bound*, 50–51; Stuart Creighton Miller, *Benevolent Assimilation: The American Conquest of the Philippines, 1899–1903* (New Haven: Yale University Press, 1982), 134.

7 Cheng and Bonacich, *Labor Immigration Under Capitalism*, 217; Miriam Sharma, "The Philippines: A Case of Migration to Hawaii, 1906–1946," in ibid., 340–49; Mabalon, *Little Manila*, 40–45.

8 "Benevolent Assimilation," Proclamation of President William McKinley, December 21, 1898, in *The Statutes at Large of the United States of America from March 1897 to March 1899 and Recent Treaties, Conventions, Executive Proclamations, and the Concurrent Resolutions of the Two Houses of Congress* (Washington, DC: U.S. Government Printing Office, 1899).

9 Espiritu, *Home Bound*, 28–30, 61, 100, 129–33.

10 Francisco Carino, "My Life History."

11 James D. Sobredo, "From American 'Nationals' to the Third 'Asiatic Invasion': Racial Transformation and Filipino Exclusion (1898–1934)" (PhD diss., University of California, Berkeley, 1998), 56.

12 Takaki, *Strangers from a Different Shore*, 60–61.

13 Dolores Quinto, "Life Story of a Filipino Immigrant," *Social Process in Hawaii* 4 (1938): 73.

14 Takaki, *Pau Hana*, 53–54.

15 Milton Murayama, *All I Asking for Is My Body* (Honolulu: University of Hawaii Press, 1988), 28, 96; see also Takaki, *Pau Hana*, 57, 91, 112–13.

16 Takaki, *Pau Hana*, 52.

17 Quoted in Bruno Lasker, *Filipino Immigration to Continental United States and to Hawaii* (Manchester, NH: Ayer, 1969), 212–17.

18 Linda España-Maram, *Creating Masculinity in Los Angeles's Little Manila: Working-Class Filipinos and Popular Culture in the United States* (New York: Columbia University Press, 2006), 4.

19 Lasker, *Filipino Immigration*, 1, 31, 347–48.

20 Cases of Filipinos who entered via Canada and were admitted through San Francisco can be found in Investigation Arrival Case Files, National Archives, San Francisco, CA. An example of Filipinos in Mexico can be found in España-Maram, *Creating Masculinity*, 15–16.

21 Mabalon, *Little Manila*, 163–73.

22 Espiritu, *Home Bound*, 64.

23 Manuel Buaken, *I Have Lived with the American People* (Caldwell, ID: Caxton, 1948), 188, 82.

24 Carey McWilliams, "Exit the Filipino," *The Nation*, September 4, 1935. 60 percent from Takaki, *Strangers from a Different Shore*, 318.

25 Melendy, *Asians in America*, 75; Buaken, *I Have Lived*, 195.

26 España-Maram, *Creating Masculinity*, 5.

27 Interview with Eliseo Felipe by Judy Yung, April 23, 2009, cited in Lee and Yung, *Angel Island*, 278–79.

28 Takaki, *Strangers from a Different Shore*, 319; Mabalon, *Little Manila*, 77.

29 España-Maram, *Creating Masculinity*, 21; McWilliams, "Exit the Filipino."

30 Melendy, *Asians in America*, 82–83; Mabalon, *Little Manila*, 71.

31 Melendy, *Asians in America*, 82–83.

32 Buaken, *I Have Lived*, 62; Mabalon, *Little Manila*, 90.

33 Howard A. DeWitt, "The Filipino Labor Union: The Salinas Lettuce Strike of 1934," *Amerasia* 5, no. 2 (1978): 1; Takaki, *Strangers from a Different Shore*, 322–23.

34 Mabalon, *Little Manila*, 220–23.

35 Dorothy B. Fujita-Rony, *American Workers, Colonial Power: Philippine Seattle and the Transpacific West, 1919–1941* (Berkeley: University of California Press, 2003); and España-Maram, *Creating Masculinity*.

36 Mabalon, *Little Manila*, 112–29, 133.

37 Ibid., 147.

38 *San Francisco Examiner*, September 9, 1930, and November 28, 1930.

39 Melendy, *Asians in America*, 66.

40 Ibid., 65; Takaki, *Strangers from a Different Shore*, 325.

41 Buaken, *I Have Lived*, 169–70.

42 "Ban Demanded on Philippine Influx to U.S.," *San Francisco Examiner*, Sept. 9, 1930.

43 "Welch Assails Invasions of Filipinos Here," *San Francisco Examiner*, Nov. 28, 1930. See also "Filipinos Declared Unfit by Citizenship Speaker," *San Francisco Chronicle*, Feb. 22, 1930.

44 Melendy, *Asians in America*, 67.

45 Ibid., 52–53.

46 Bulosan, *America Is in the Heart*, 121. See also Ngai, *Impossible Subjects*, 113, 116; Dawn Bohulano Mabalon, "Life in Little Manila: Filipinas/os in Stockton, California, 1917–1972" (PhD dissertation, Stanford University, 2003), 61, 63; Rick Baldoz, "Valorizing Racial Boundaries: Hegemony and Conflict in the Racialization of Filipino Migrant Labour in the United States," *Ethnic and Racial Studies* 27:6 (2004), 983.

47 Espiritu, *Home Bound*, 66.

48 Buaken, *I Have Lived*, 89–94.

49 Mabalon, "Life in Little Manila," 60–1; Mabalon, *Little Manila*, 92–95; Melendy, *Asians in America*, 53–54; Baldoz, "Valorizing Racial Boundaries," 977–79; Ngai, *Impossible Subjects*, 105, 114; Brett Melendy, "California's Discrimination against Filipinos, 1927–1935," in *Letters in Exile: An Introductory Reader on the History of Pilipinos in America*, ed. UCLA Asian American Studies Center (Los Angeles: UCLA Asian American Studies Center, 1976), 40; Takaki, *Strangers from a Different Shore*, 327–28.

50 Rick Baldoz, *The Third Asiatic Invasion: Migration and Empire in Filipino America, 1898–1946* (New York: New York University Press, 2011), 157, 160, 164–65, 174–76.

51 Philippine Independence Act (48 Stat. 456), March 24, 1934; España-Maram, *Creating Masculinity*, 172–73 (fn 9); Ngai, *Impossible Subjects*, 119; Baldoz, *The Third Asiatic Invasion*, 177.

52 Marcelo Domingo is a pseudonym. File 34028/14–20, Investigation Arrival Case Files, National Archives, San Francisco, CA; Lee and Yung, *Angel Island*, 281–85.

53 Edward Cahill to Col. D. W. MacCormack, August 26, 1935, in "Filipinos, Mistreatment of by Officers of the Service," File 55874/464B, INS Subject Correspondence, National Archives, DC; Lee and Yung, *Angel Island*, 290–91.

54 Pedro B. Buncan, New York City, to the Secretary of Labor, June 6, 1935, and other letters from writers across the country, in "Filipinos, Mistreatment of by Officers of the Service."

55 Lee and Yung, *Angel Island*, 290–93.

56 Buaken, *I Have Lived*, 79.

Chapter 9: Border Crossings and Border Enforcement: Undocumented Asian Immigration

1 Translated letter included in F. W. Berkshire, Supervising Inspector, Mexican Border District, to Commissioner-General of Immigration, August 27, 1918, File 54270/1, INS Subject Correspondence, National Archives, Washington, DC.

2 Because no full record exists for both the northern and southern borders, this estimate is compiled from a number of sources: U.S. Department of Commerce and Labor, *Annual Report of the Commissioner-General of Immigration* (Washington, DC: U.S. Government Printing Office) (hereafter cited as *AR-CGI*) (1903), 102; George E. Paulsen, "The Yellow Peril at Nogales: The Ordeal of Collector William M. Hoey," *Arizona and the West* 13, no. 2 (Summer 1971): 113–28; U.S. Department of Commerce and Labor, *Annual Report of the Commissioner-General of Immigration*, (hereafter cited as *AR-CGI*) (1910), 146; and C. Luther Fry, "Illegal Entry of Orientals into the United States Between 1910 and 1920," *Journal of American Statistical Association* 23, no. 162 (1928): 173–77.

3 Fry, "Illegal Entry of Orientals," 173.

4 David Lai, *Chinatowns: Towns Within Cities in Canada* (Vancouver: University of British Columbia Press, 1988), 52.

5 Hyung-chan Kim and Richard W. Markov, "The Chinese Exclusion Laws and Smuggling Chinese into Whatcom County," *Annals of the Chinese Historical Society of the Pacific Northwest* (1983): 16–30; U.S. Department of Commerce and Labor, *AR-CGI* (1903), 98–99.

6 U.S. Congress, 49th Cong., 1st sess., "Reports on Charge of Fraudulent Importation of Chinese," Senate Executive Doc. 103 (Washington, DC: Government Printing Office, 1886), 8.

7 James Reynolds, "Enforcement of the Chinese Exclusion Law," *Annals of the American Academy of Political and Social Sciences* 34 (September, 1909): 368; U.S. Department of Commerce and Labor, *AR-CGI* (1904), 137–141 and *AR-CGI* (1909), 128.

8 Stanford Lyman, *Chinese Americans* (New York: Random House, 1974), 106.

9 U. S. Bureau of Immigration, *Compilation from the Records of the Bureau of Immigration of Facts Concerning the Enforcement of the Chinese-Exclusion Laws: Letter from the Secretary of Commerce and Labor, Submitting, in Response to the Inquiry of the House, a Report as to the Enforcement of the Chinese-Exclusion Laws* (Washington, DC: Government Printing Office, 1906), 63.

10 U.S. Department of Commerce and Labor, *AR-CGI* (1909), 130.

11 Julian Ralph, "The Chinese Leak," *Harper's New Monthly Magazine*, March 1891, 520; Lee, *At America's Gates*, 154, 175–76.

12 Ralph, "The Chinese Leak," 524; U.S. Department of Commerce and Labor, *AR-CGI* (1907), 111; Raymond B. Craib, "Chinese Immigrants in Porfirian Mexico: A Preliminary Study of Settlement, Economic Activity and Anti-Chinese Sentiment," Research Paper Series No. 28 (Albuquerque: Latin American Institute, May 1996), 8; J. W. Berkshire to Commissioner-General of Immigration, Oct. 17, 1907, File 52212/2, part 1, p. 3, INS Subject Correspondence, National Archives, Washington, DC.

13 Clifford Perkins, *Border Patrol: With the U.S. Immigration Service on the Mexican Boundary, 1910–54* (El Paso, TX: University of Texas at El Paso, 1978), 17.

14 U.S. Department of Commerce and Labor, *AR-CGI* (1907), 111.

15 U.S. Department of Commerce and Labor, *AR-CGI* (1909), 127.

16 Charles Babcock to U.S. Commissioner-General of Immigration, September 28, 1907, and October 7, 1907, "Smuggling-Vancouver," File 51893/102, INS Subject Correspondence, National Archives, Washington, DC.

17 John H. Clark to F. P. Sargent, November 18, 1907, File 51931/14A, ibid.

18 Newspaper articles in "Japanese via Kumeric, Seattle, 1907," File 51630/44, ibid.

19 Marcus Braun to F. P. Sargent, June 10, 1907, in "Braun's Second Detail to Mexico, Braun's Report," File 52320/1A, ibid.

20 Chizuko Watanabe, "The Japanese Immigrant Community in Mexico: Its History and Present," (Los Angeles: California State University, 1983), 28.

21 Ito, *Issei*, 67–68.

22 Ibid., 70–72.

23 Ibid., 67–68.

24 U.S. Department of Commerce and Labor, *AR-CGI* (1907), 110; Report by Marcus Braun to Frank P. Sargent, Feb. 12, 1907, File 52320/1, INS Subject Correspondence; Telegram, April 12, 1907; and Marcus Braun to Commissioner-General of Immigration, April 13, 1907, in "Japanese Conditions—Mexican Border, 1907," File 51931/11, INS Subject Correspondence, National Archives, Washington, DC.

25 U.S. Department of Labor, *AR-CGI* (1914), 348–49.

26 Lee, *At America's Gates*, 164.

27 Frank R. Stone to Supervising Inspector, El Paso, TX, April 23, 1910, File 52801/4A, 7, INS Subject Correspondence, National Archives, Washington, DC.

28 Lee, *At America's Gates*, 161–62.

29 Ito, *Issei*, 68–70.

30 Eiichiro Azuma, "Community Formation Across the National Border: The Japanese of the U.S.-Mexican Californias," *Review: Literature and Arts of the Americas* 39, no. 1 (2006): 34–35.

31 Lee, *At America's Gates*, 164.

32 T. F. Schmucker to Commissioner-General of Immigration, April 8, 1907, File 51931/7, INS Subject Correspondence, National Archives, Washington, DC.

33 F. P Sargent to Marcus Braun, November 12, 1906, File 52320/1, ibid.

34 Marcus Braun to F. P. Sargent, June 10, 1907, in "Braun's Second Detail to Mexico, Braun's Report," File 52320/1A, ibid.

35 Lee, *At America's Gates*, 175.

36 Marcus Braun to Commissioner-General of Immigration, "Report," Feb. 12, 1907, File 52320/1, 11, INS Subject Correspondence, National Archives, Washington, DC.

37 Lee, *At America's Gates*, 186.

38 Ibid., 176–79. On Canadian-U.S. negotiations, see for example, John H. Clark, U.S. Commissioner of Immigration, Montreal, Canada, to U.S. Commissioner-General of Immigration, July 16, 1912, File 51931/21, INS Subject Correspondence, National Archives, Washington, DC.

39 Lee, *At America's Gates*, 179–87.

40 Perkins, *Border Patrol*, 9; John M. Myers, *The Border Wardens* (Englewood Cliffs, NJ: Prentice Hall, 1971), 23.

41 U.S. Department of Commerce and Labor, *AR-CGI* (1906), 95.

42 Lee, *At America's Gates*, 180–87.

43 U.S. Department of Labor, *AR-CGI* (1914), 21.

44 Ito, *Issei*, 77.

45 U.S. Department of Labor, *AR-CGI* (1917), xxiv.

46 Statement of Shinji Kawamoto, Taken at County Jail, El Paso, Texas, April 30, 1908, by George J. Harris, in "Investigation of Immigration Officials—El Paso, 1908," in File 51893/55B, INS Subject Correspondence, National Archives, Washington, DC.

47 See series of letters from C. O. Cowley to Frank P. Sargent, Commissioner General of Immigration, D.C., May 9, 1904, May 3, 1904, and June 5, 1904, 51841/164 and American Vice Consul, Kingston, Jamaica, to Secretary of State, June 25, 1912, in File 52090/4D, ibid. See also U.S. Department of Labor, *AR-CGI* (1914), 233.

48 Lee, *At America's Gates*, 155–57.

49 Marcus Braun to F. P. Sargent, June 10, 1907, in "Braun's Second Detail to Mexico, Braun's Report," File 52320/1A, INS Subject Correspondence, National Archives, Washington, DC.

50 "Four Smuggled Japanese Aliens—El Paso, 1908," File 51893/55 and "Investigation of Japanese Smuggler—El Paso, 1908," File 51893/55A, ibid. For a summary of the case, see Richard Taylor, Inspector in Charge, El Paso, TX, to Frank Sargent, Commissioner-General of Immigration, March 18, 1908, in File 51893/55A, ibid.

51 U.S. House, 63rd Cong., 2nd Sess., "Hindu Immigration," Hearings before the Committee on Immigration Relative to Restriction of Immigration of Hindu Laborers, February 26, 1914, pt. 3 (Washington, DC: U.S. Government Printing Office, 1914), 118–19.

52 U.S. Department of Labor, *AR-CGI* (1923), 20, 15–21.

53 Patrick Ettinger, " 'We Sometimes Wonder What They Will Spring on Us Next': Immigrants and Border Enforcement in the American West, 1882–1930," *Western Historical Quarterly* 37, no. 2 (Summer 2006): 180.

54 *New York Times*, June 19, 1927; Emily Ryo, "Through the Back Door: Applying Theories of Legal Compliance to Illegal Immigration During the Chinese Exclusion Era," *Law & Social Inquiry* 31 (2006): 127.

55 Secretaria de Gobernación, *El Servicio de Migración en Mexico por Landa y Pina Jefe del Departamento de Migración* (México, D.F.: Talleres Gráficos de la Nación, 1930), 5, 24, 6; Chao Romero, *The Chinese in Mexico*, 183–85.

56 Francisco E. Balderrama and Raymond Rodriguez, *Decade of Betrayal: Mexican Repatriation in the 1930s* (Albuquerque: University of New Mexico Press, 1995), 133–34, 121.

57 Espinoza, *El Ejemplo de Sonora*, 176, 185 (emphasis mine).

58 Jacques, "The Anti-Chinese Campaign in Sonora, Mexico, 1900–1931," 229–30, 232; Chao Romero, *Chinese in Mexico*, 186–87.

59 Chao Romero, *Chinese in Mexico*, 264.

60 Evelyn Hu-DeHart, "Immigrants to a Developing Society: The Chinese in Northern Mexico, 1875–1932," *The Journal of Arizona History* 21, no. 3 (1980): 305.

61 Humberto Monteón González and José Luis Trueba Lara, *Chinos y Antichinos en México: Documentos para Su Estudio* (Gobierno de Jalisco, Secretaría General, Unidad Editorial, 1988), 134–37; Espinoza, *El Ejemplo de Sonora*, 110–11.

62 *Arizona Daily Star*, September 1, 1931, and September 4, 1931.

63 Espinoza, *El Ejemplo de Sonora*, 140; Charles C. Cumberland, "The Sonora Chinese and the Mexican Revolution," *Hispanic American Historical Review* 40, no. 2 (1960): 191, 203.

64 U.S. Department of Justice, *AR-CGI* (1932), 5.

65 *Arizona Daily Star*, September 1, 1931; *New York Times*, September 4, 1931.

66 *San Francisco Chronicle*, January 13, 1932.

67 *New York Times*, March 20, 1932, and August 6, 1932.

68 U.S. Department of Labor, *Annual Report of the Secretary of Labor* (Washington, DC: U.S. Government Printing Office, 1933), 59.

69 U.S. Department of Justice, *AR-CGI* (1932), 5.

70 Ibid.

71 Hom, *Songs of Gold Mountain*, 89.

Chapter 10: "Military Necessity": The Uprooting of Japanese Americans During World War II

1 Uchida, *Desert Exile*.

2 Roger Daniels, "The Decisions to Relocate the North American Japanese: Another Look," *Pacific Historical Review* 51, no. 1 (1982): 71. Peruvian statistics from Akemi Kikumura-Yano, ed., *Encyclopedia of Japanese Descendants in the Americas: An Illustrated History of the Nikkei* (Walnut Creek, CA: AltaMira, 2002), 273.

3 A variety of terms have been used to describe the wartime removal and confinement of Japanese Americans, Japanese Canadians, and Japanese Latin Americans during World War II. The U.S. government itself created

positive-sounding euphemisms like "evacuation," "relocation," and "assembly center" to describe its wartime actions. The most common terms are "internment," "internee," and "internment camp." As scholars, activists, and community members have pointed out, these terms are not correct. "Internment" refers to a legal process applied to nationals of a country with which a country is at war. In the United States, a system of international laws regulated treatment of prisoners of war and civilian enemy nationals in World War II. These could include an individual hearing before a government board that could lead to some recourse. An estimated 11,000 Japanese, German, and Italian nationals were interned during the war by the United States. In contrast, the vast majority of the Japanese Americans who were forcibly removed from their communities were U.S. citizens and had no such recourse. As historian Roger Daniels points out, "they were incarcerated not for suspected subversion or membership, but because of their ethnicity." The terms "internment" and "internee" may be technically correct for noncitizens of Japanese descent, but in this book I follow the lead of the Civil Liberties Public Education Fund and use the terms "removal," "incarceration," "confinement," and "inmate" to best describe the experiences of Japanese American citizens who were forcibly relocated and incarcerated during the war. See Roger Daniels, "Words Do Matter: A Note on Inappropriate Terminology and the Incarceration of the Japanese Americans," in *Nikkei in the Pacific Northwest: Japanese Americans and Japanese Canadians in the Twentieth Century*, eds. Gail M. Nomura and Louis Fiset (Seattle: University of Washington Press, 2005): 190–214; Civil Liberties Public Education Fund, "CLPEF Resolution Regarding Terminology" http://www.momomedia.com/CLPEF/backgrnd.html#Link%20to%20terminology (accessed March 18, 2013).

4 United States and Commission on Wartime Relocation and Internment of Civilians, *Personal Justice Denied* (Washington, DC; Seattle: Civil Liberties Public Education Fund; University of Washington Press, 1997), 54 (hereafter cited as U.S. CWRIC, *Personal Justice Denied*); Greg Robinson, *A Tragedy of Democracy: Japanese Confinement in North America* (New York: Columbia University Press, 2009), 47–48.

5 Robinson, *A Tragedy of Democracy*, 46.

6 Ibid., 39, 36–37, 44–47.

7 Roger Daniels, *Prisoners Without Trial: Japanese Americans in World War II* (New York: Hill & Wang, 1993), 25–26.

8 "Memorandum on C. B. Munson's Report 'Japanese on the West Coast,' " November 7, 1941, Commission on Wartime Relocation and Internment of

Civilians," Densho ID: denshopd-i67-00011, Densho Digital Archive (accessed March 19, 2013).

9 Robinson, *A Tragedy of Democracy*, 32–33.

10 Roy, *Mutual Hostages*, 23, 31–32; Robinson, *A Tragedy of Democracy*, 40.

11 Robinson, *A Tragedy of Democracy*, 41–43.

12 H. L. Keenleyside, "The Canada-United States Permanent Joint Board of Defence, 1940–1945," *International Journal* 16, no. 1 (1960–1961): 50–77; Robinson, *A Tragedy of Democracy*, 43; Daniels, "The Decisions," 75; Roy, *Mutual Hostages*, 36, 38–39, 46; Roy, *The Oriental Question*, 228.

13 Daniels, "The Decisions," 75; Robinson, *A Tragedy of Democracy*, 43, 65; Ann Gomer Sunahara, *The Politics of Racism: The Uprooting of Japanese Canadians During the Second World War* (Toronto: Lorimer, 1981), 36.

14 Peter H. Smith, *Talons of the Eagle: Latin America, the United States, and the World* (New York: Oxford University Press, 2000), 29–30, 36, 63–64 68–69, 75, 80–81, 85.

15 Max Paul Friedman, *Nazis and Good Neighbors: The United States Campaign–Against the Germans of Latin America in World War II* (Cambridge: Cambridge University Press, 2003), 77–78.

16 Interview with Senator Daniel Inouye, Go for Broke National Education Center, http://www.goforbroke.org/oral_histories/oral_histories_video_display_public.asp?publicclip=13701 (accessed March 30, 2013).

17 U.S. CWRIC, *Personal Justice Denied*, 55.

18 Ibid., 61.

19 Roger Daniels, "Words do Matter," 195; Daniels, *Prisoners Without Trial*, 26–27.

20 Daniels, "Words do Matter," 209 (fn 22).

21 Robinson, *A Tragedy of Democracy*, 62.

22 U.S. CWRIC, *Personal Justice Denied*, 56.

23 Ibid., 65.

24 Ibid., 65–66.

25 Ibid., 66.

26 Federal Communications Commission (FCC) to Francis Biddle, April 4, 1944, Commission on Wartime Relocation and Internment of Civilians (UW Libraries microfilm A7378, Reel 2, Box 3, Frames 622–25, Items 1918–1921); Densho ID: denshopd-i67-00076, "War Hysteria," Densho Digital Archive (accessed March 19, 2013); Robinson, *A Tragedy of Democracy*, 68.

27 U.S. CWRIC, *Personal Justice Denied*, 64.

28 Ibid., 82 (italics added).

29 Akiko Kurose Interview I, Segment 13, July 17, 1997, Densho ID: denshovh-kakiko-01-0013, Densho Visual History Collection, Densho Digital Archive, http://archive.densho.org/main.aspx (accessed May 22, 2013).

30 Robinson, *A Tragedy of Democracy*, 86–87.

31 Daniels, *Prisoners Without Trial*, 37; Robinson, *A Tragedy of Democracy*, 79–81.

32 Daniels, *Prisoners Without Trial*, 29.

33 Leo Carillo to Congressman Leland Ford, January 6, 1942, 740.00115 PACIFIC WAR/61, U.S. Department of State Records, National Archives, College Park, MD.

34 *Seattle Times*, January 30, 1942.

35 *Los Angeles Times*, February 2, 1942, quoted in U.S. CWRIC, *Personal Justice Denied*, 71–72; Robinson, *A Tragedy of Democracy*, 82–84.

36 *Washington Post*, February 12, 1942.

37 Daniels, *Prisoners Without Trial*, 45; Robinson, *A Tragedy of Democracy*, 84.

38 Robinson, *A Tragedy of Democracy*, 87–93; Godfrey Hodgson, *The Colonel: The Life and Wars of Henry Stimson, 1867–1950* (New York: Alfred A. Knopf, 1990), 259; Brian Niiya, "Francis Biddle," *Densho Encyclopedia*, http://encyclopedia.densho.org/Francis%20Biddle/ (accessed March 19, 2013); Brian Niiya, "Henry Stimson," *Densho Encyclopedia*, http://encyclopedia.densho.org/Henry%20Stimson/ (accessed April 5, 2013).

39 Greg Robinson, *By Order of the President: FDR and the Internment of Japanese Americans* (Cambridge: Harvard University Press, 2001).

40 Robinson, *A Tragedy of Democracy*, 93, 113–19; Takaki, *Strangers from a Different Shore*, 382.

41 Robinson, *A Tragedy of Democracy*, 74, 102–3.

42 The Diaries of William Lyon Mackenzie King, February 19, 1942, Library and Archives of Canada, http://www.collectionscanada.gc.ca/king/index-e.html (accessed April 21, 2013).

43 Roy, *Mutual Hostages*, 95–96; Robinson, *A Tragedy of Democracy*, 99. "P.C." stands for "Privy Council" and is used in Canadian law.

44 Gardiner, *Pawns in a Triangle of Hate*, viii.

45 Jorge Larrañaga to L. S. Rowe, in L. S. Rose to Laurence Duggan, March 17, 1942, File 894.20223/119 and Jorge Larrañaga to L. S. Rowe, March 26, 1941, File 894.20223/123, U.S. Department of State Records, National Archives, College Park, MD.

46 John K. Emmerson, "Japanese in Peru," October 9, 1943, iv, 16, 23, 54, 58, 64, 65, 78, File 894.20223/196; Emmerson to Norweb, April 18, 1942, File 894.20223/124, Ibid.

47 Undersecretary of State to Francis Biddle, August 20, 1942, File 740.00115/PACIFIC WAR 1002 2/6, Ibid.

48 *New York Times*, February 1, 1942, January 29, 1942; Friedman, *Nazis and Good Neighbors*, 121, 76, 3.

49 "Japanese Activities in Peru: Summary of FBI Report," June 27, 1942, File 894.20223/154, U.S. Department of State Records, National Archives, College Park, MD.

50 Department of State Telegram, August 12, 1942, File 740.00115/PACIFIC WAR 1001 2/6, ibid.

51 Friedman, *Nazis and Good Neighbors*, 121–22; Gardiner, *Pawns in a Triangle of Hate*, 16–18.

52 Edward N. Barnhart, "Japanese Internees from Peru," *Pacific Historical Review* 31, no. 2 (1962): 171; Friedman, *Nazis and Good Neighbors*, 16–18.

53 Gardiner, *Pawns in a Triangle of Hate*, 41; U.S. CWRIC, *Personal Justice Denied*, 307.

54 Recent Developments in Peru," in J. Edgar Hoover to William Donovan, March 6, 1942, File 13280, Intelligence Series, 1941–1945, Records of the Office of Strategic Services, RG 226, National Archives, College Park, MD; Gardiner, *Pawns in a Triangle of Hate*, 14–16.

55 John K. Emmerson, "Japanese in Peru," October 9, 1943, 22, File 894.20223/196, U.S. Department of State Records, National Archives, College Park, MD.

56 Ibid.

57 "Memorandum on the Control of Japanese in Peru," in Norweb to Secretary of State, July 7, 1943; John K. Emmerson, "Japanese in Peru," October 9, 1943, 22, 40, 68–75, File 894.20223/196, ibid.

58 Seiichi Higashide, *Adios to Tears: The Memoirs of a Japanese-Peruvian Internee in U.S. Concentration Camps* (Seattle: University of Washington Press, 2000), 115–116, 119, 125; Gardiner, *Pawns in a Triangle of Hate*, 27.

59 Art Shibayama Interview, Segment 9, interview by Alice Ho, Oct. 26, 2003, Densho ID: denshovh-sart-01-0009, Densho Visual History Collection, Densho Digital Archive, http://archive.densho.org/main.aspx (accessed May 10, 2013).

60 Elsa Kudo Interview, Segment 6, interview by Kelli Nakamura, February 6, 2012, Densho ID: denshovh-kelsa-01-0006, Densho Visual History Collection, Densho Digital Archive, (accessed May 10, 2013).

61 Higashide, *Adios to Tears*, 140–42.

62 Gardiner, *Pawns in a Triangle of Hate*, 25.

63 Ibid., 106–8.

64 Barnhart, "Japanese Internees from Peru," 172; U.S. CWRIC, *Personal Justice Denied* 312. In September, 1,340 Japanese, 55 percent of them from Latin America, were repatriated to Japan in an exchange of nationals between the United States and Japan. See Gardiner, *Pawns in a Triangle of Hate*, 84–85.

65 Figures are for 1937 from Masterson and Funada-Classen, *The Japanese in Latin America*, 112, 140–47.

66 Ibid., 122, 130–46.

Chapter 11: "Grave Injustices": The Incarceration of Japanese Americans During World War II

1 Uchida, *Desert Exile*, 102, 111, 142. Statistics from Michi Nishiura Weglyn, *Years of Infamy: The Untold Story of America's Concentration Camps*, 2nd ed. (Seattle: University of Washington Press, 1996), 21.

2 Shigeko Sese Uno Segment 18, September 18, 1998, Densho ID: denshovh-ushigeko-01-0018, Densho Visual History Collection, Densho Digital Archive, http://archive.densho.org/main.aspx (accessed May 10, 2013).

3 U.S. CWRIC, *Personal Justice Denied*, 122–26, 118.

4 Tom Akashi Interview, Segment 15, Interview by Tom Ikeda and Chizu Omori, July 3, 2004, Densho ID: denshovh-atom-01-0015, Densho Visual History Collection, Densho Digital Archive, (accessed May 11, 2013).

5 Sone, *Nisei Daughter*, 166.

6 U.S. CWRIC, *Personal Justice Denied*, 141–42.

7 Bob Utsumi Interview, Segment 11, Interview by Megan Asaka, July 31, 2008, Densho ID: denshovh-ubob-01-0011, Topaz Museum Collection, Densho Digital Archive, http://archive.densho.org/main.aspx, (accessed May 11, 2013).

8 May K. Sasaki, Segment 14, Interview by Lori Hoshino and Alice Ito, October 28, 1997, Densho ID: denshovh-smay-01-0014, Densho Visual History Collection, Densho Digital Archive, http://archive.densho.org/main.aspx (accessed May 11, 2013).

9 Leland Ford to Secretary of State Cordell Hull, Jan. 16, 1942, File 740.00115/PACIFIC WAR/79, Decimal File, 1940–1944, U.S. Department of State Records, National Archives, College Park, MD.

10 Roger Daniels, *The Japanese American Cases: The Rule of Law in Time of War* (Lawrence: University Press of Kansas, 2013), 28–30.

11 Gordon Hirabayashi Interview II, Segment 16, Interview by Tom Ikeda and Alice Ito, May 25, 1999, denshovh-hgordon-02-0016; Gordon Hirabayashi Interview, Segment 10, October 25, 1983, Densho ID: denshovh-hgordon-06-0010,

Densho Visual History Collection, Densho Digital Archive, (accessed May 11, 2013); Daniels, *The Japanese American Cases*, 31–34; *Hirabayashi v. United States*, 320 US. 81 (1943).

12 *New York Times*, April 1, 2005.

13 Daniels, *The Japanese American Cases*, 34–36, 49, 51, 55–59, 62–63, 67–76, 78–79; *Toyosaburo Korematsu v. United States*, 323 U.S. 214 (1944).

14 U.S. CWRIC, *Personal Justice Denied*, 156–57, 161; Sone, *Nisei Daughter*, 192.

15 U.S. CWRIC, *Personal Justice Denied*, 162–67.

16 Ibid., 168.

17 Ibid., 172.

18 Delphine Hirasuna et al., *The Art of Gaman: Arts and Crafts from the Japanese American Internment Camps 1942–1946* (Berkeley: Ten Speed, 2005); Chiura Obata and Kimi Kodani Hill, *Topaz Moon: Chiura Obata's Art of the Internment* (Berkeley: Heyday, 2000); Bill T. Manbo, *Colors of Confinement: Rare Kodachrome Photographs of Japanese American Incarceration in World War II*, ed. Eric L. Muller (Chapel Hill: University of North Carolina Press, 2012).

19 U.S. CWRIC, *Personal Justice Denied*, 176–80.

20 Eric L. Muller, *American Inquisition: The Hunt for Japanese American Disloyalty in World War II* (Chapel Hill: University of North Carolina Press, 2007), 31–38.

21 Frank Miyamoto Interview III, Segment 21, Interview by Stephen Fujita, April 29, 1998, Densho ID: denshovh-mfrank-03-0021, Densho Visual History Collection, Densho Digital Archive (accessed May 11, 2013).

22 Taneyuki Dan Harada Interview Segment 15, Interview by Martha Nakagawa, November 30, 2010, Densho ID: denshovh-htaneyuki-01-0015, Densho Visual History Collection, Densho Digital Archive (accessed May 11, 2013).

23 U.S. CWRIC, *Personal Justice Denied*, 193–194.

24 Ibid., 195.

25 Ibid., 208; Robinson, A *Tragedy of Democracy*, 192.

26 Weglyn, *Years of Infamy*, 156–73; Ngai, *Impossible Subjects*, 184–86; Barbara Takei, "Tule Lake," *Densho Encyclopedia*, http://encyclopedia.densho.org/Tule%20Lake/ (accessed May 12, 2014).

27 Weglyn, *Years of Infamy*, 15.

28 Ex Parte Mitsuye Endo, 323 U.S. 283 (1944); Robinson, *Tragedy of Democracy*, 224–25.

29 Weglyn, *Years of Infamy*, 244.

30 U.S. CWRIC, *Personal Justice Denied*, 208; Robinson, A *Tragedy of Democracy*, 192. On the renunciation of citizenship, see Ngai, *Impossible Subjects*,

189–201; Daniels, *The Japanese American Cases*, 119–30; Weglyn, *Years of Infamy*, 243; Takei, "Tule Lake."

31 Fred Shiosaki Interview, Segment 8, Interview by Andrea Dilley, 2003–2004, Densho ID: denshovh-sfred-02-0008, Densho Visual History Collection, Densho Digital Archive (accessed December 16, 2014).

32 Fred Matsumura Interview, Segment 20, Interview by Tom Ikeda and Beverly Kashino, July 2, 1998, Densho ID: denshovh-mfred-01-0020, Densho ID: denshovh-mfred-01-0200, Densho Visual History Collection, Densho Digital Archive (accessed December 16, 2014).

33 Fred Shiosaki Interview, Segment 8, 2003–2004, Densho ID: denshovh-sfred-02-0008, Densho Visual History Collection, Densho Digital Archive (accessed December 16, 2014).

34 U.S. CWRIC, *Personal Justice Denied*, 253–59; "442nd Regimental Combat Team" and "100th Infantry Battalion" in Densho Encyclopedia, http://encyclopedia.densho.org/100th_Infantry_Battalion/ and http://encyclopedia.densho.org/442nd_Regimental_Combat_Team/ (accessed May 11, 2013).

35 Mits Koshiyama Interview, Segment 4, Interview by Frank Abe, August 15 and 16, 1993, Densho ID: denshovh-kmits-03-0004, Densho Visual History Collection, Densho Digital Archive (accessed May 21, 2013).

36 The punishment meted out to the draft resisters differed from camp to camp. See Stephen Fugita and Marilyn Fernandez, *Altered Lives, Enduring Community: Japanese Americans Remember Their World War II Incarceration* (Seattle: University of Washington Press, 2004), 93.

37 Roger Daniels Interview, Segment 8, Interview by Frank Abe and Frank Chin, May 20, 1995, Densho ID: denshovh-droger-01-0008, Frank Abe Collection, Densho Digital Archive (accessed May 21, 2013); Daniel Inouye, Preface, in Eric L. Muller, *Free to Die for Their Country: The Story of the Japanese American Draft Resisters in World War II* (Chicago: University of Chicago Press, 2003); "Heart Mountain Fair Play Committee," Densho Encyclopedia, http://encyclopedia.densho.org/Heart%20Mountain%20Fair%20Play%20Committee/ (accessed May 21, 2013).

38 Art Shibayama Interview, Segment 8, October 26, 2003, Densho ID: denshovh-sart-01-0008, Densho Visual History Collection, Densho Digital Archive (accessed May 10, 2013).

39 Gardiner, *Pawns in a Triangle of Hate*, 29.

40 Elsa Kudo Interview, Segment 14, February 6, 2012, Densho ID: denshovh-kelsa-01-0014, Densho Visual History Collection, Densho Digital Archive (accessed May 10, 2013).

41 "Report on Civilian Detention Station, Seagoville, Texas," May 23, 1942, File 740.00115 EUROPEAN WAR 1939/4004; "Report on Civilian Detention Station, Camp Kenedy," May 22, 1942, File 740.00115 EUROPEAN WAR 1939/4715, Decimal File, 1940–1944, U.S. Department of State Records, National Archives, College Park, MD; Gardiner, *Pawns in a Triangle of Hate*, 82–83.

42 Art Shibayama Interview, Segment 8, October 26, 2003, Densho ID: denshovh-sart-01-0008, Densho Visual History Collection, Densho Digital Archive (accessed May 10, 2013).

43 Gardiner, *Pawns in a Triangle of Hate*, 59–61.

44 "Report on Civilian Detention Station, Seagoville, Texas," May 23, 1942, File 740.00115 EUROPEAN WAR 1939/4004; "Report on Civilian Detention Station, Camp Kenedy," May 22, 1942, File 740.00115 EUROPEAN WAR 1939/4715, U.S. Department of State Records, National Archives College Park.

45 Higashide, *Adios to Tears*, 168, 170.

46 WRA Resettlement Image. Denshopd-p7-00008. Kaneko Family Connection. Densho Digital Archive (accessed May 23, 2013).

47 Greg Robinson, *After Camp: Portraits in Midcentury Japanese American Life and Politics* (Berkeley: University of California Press, 2012), 48.

48 Brian Komei Dempster, *Making Home from War: Stories of Japanese American Exile and Resettlement* (Berkeley: Heyday, 2011), xxi.

49 "Twin Cities JACL Oral History," Japanese American Citizens League, Twin Cities (MN) Chapter, https://www.youtube.com/watch?v=aEsTX_2hBV8 (accessed May 21, 2013).

50 Daniels, *Concentration Camps*, 156–57.

51 See, for example, "Jap Hunting License" badge in Dempster, *Making Home from War*, 28.

52 Frank Yamasaki, Segment 31, interview by Lori Hoshino and Stephen Fujita, August 18, 1997, Densho ID: denshovh-yfrank-01-0031, Densho Visual History Collection, Densho Digital Archive (accessed May 23, 2013); Greg Robinson, Foreword, in Dempster, *Making Home from War*, x; Kurashige, *The Shifting Grounds of Race*, 195–97.

53 Uchida, *Desert Exile*, 149.

54 Robinson, *After Camp*, 223–32.

55 "The Story and Diary of Mrs. Kami Kamisato," in Takeo Kaneshiro, ed., *Internees: War Relocation Center Memoirs and Diaries* (New York: Vantage, 1976), 35–36.

56 John K. Emmerson, "Japanese in Peru," October 9, 1943, 82–83, File 894.20223/196, U.S. Department of State Records, National Archives, College Park.

57 Masterson and Funada-Classen, *The Japanese in Latin America*, 171, 174–78; Gardiner, *Pawns in a Triangle of Hate*, 112.

58 Higashide, *Adios to Tears*, 173.

59 "The Story and Diary of Mrs. Kami Kamisato," in Kaneshiro, ed., *Internees*, 35–36.

60 Higashide, *Adios to Tears*, 178.

61 Wayne M. Collins to George C. Marshall, February 7, 1947, Folder 2, Edward Norton Barnhart Papers, 1942–1954, Japanese American Research Project, Special Collections, University of California, Los Angeles.

62 Higashide, *Adios to Tears*, 179.

63 Robinson, *After Camp*, 45.

64 Higashide, *Adios to Tears*, 223–24.

65 Art Shibayama Interview, Segments 25 and 28, Densho ID: denshovh-sart-01-0025 and denshovh-sart-01-0028, Densho Visual History Collection, Densho Archive, http://archive.densho.org/main.aspx (accessed May 10, 2013).

Chapter 12: Good War, Cold War

1 Yu, *To Save China, To Save Ourselves*.

2 Him Mark Lai, "The Kuomintang in Chinese American Communities Before World War II," in *Entry Denied*, ed. Sucheng Chan, 194–97; Yung, *Unbound Feet*, 227–28.

3 R. Lee, *Orientals*, 147–48; Yung, *Unbound Feet*, 239.

4 *Congressional Record*, 78th Cong., 1st Sess., 1943, vol. 89, part 6, 8594.

5 Wu, *The Color of Success*, 191.

6 "How to Tell Japs from the Chinese," *Life*, December 22, 1941.

7 "How to Tell Your Friends from the Japs," *Time*, December 22, 1941.

8 Wong, *Americans First*, 80–81.

9 Wu, *The Color of Success*, 4; Charlotte Brooks, *Alien Neighbors, Foreign Friends: Asian Americans, Housing, and the Transformation of Urban California* (Chicago: University of Chicago Press, 2009), 17.

10 Wong, *Americans First*, 61–64.

11 Yung, *Unbound Feet*, 252, 257.

12 Wong, *Americans First*, 50.

13 Ibid., 47–49.

14 Ibid., 50.

15 Ibid., 204.

16 "The First Lady of China," *Time*, March 1, 1943, cited in ibid., 97.

17 Karen J. Leong, *The China Mystique: Pearl S. Buck, Anna May Wong, Mayling Soong, and the Transformation of American Orientalism* (Berkeley: University of California Press, 2005), 1, 106–7, 131–141, 145–54; Wong, *Americans First*, 89–109.

18 *New York Times*, October 12, 1943.

19 The repeal of Chinese exclusion was officially titled "An Act to Repeal the Chinese Exclusion Acts, to Establish Quotas, and for Other Purposes," Act of Dec. 17, 1943 (57 Stat. 600; 8 U.S.C. 212(a).

20 David M. Reimers, *Still the Golden Door: The Third World Comes to America* (New York: Columbia University Press, 1985), 11–22.

21 Xiaojian Zhao, *Remaking Chinese America: Immigration, Family, and Community, 1940–1965* (New Brunswick, NJ: Rutgers University Press, 2002), 26–28.

22 Ibid., 80.

23 Pan, *The Encyclopedia of the Chinese Overseas*, 239.

24 Takaki, *Strangers from a Different Shore*, 358.

25 Mabalon, *Little Manila Is in the Heart*, 217–18.

26 Buaken, *I Have Lived with the American People*, 322–23.

27 The Tydings-McDuffie Act had changed Filipinos' status to "aliens" for immigration purposes, but they remained U.S. nationals in other contexts. Shelley Sang-Hee Lee, A *New History of Asian America* (New York, NY: Routledge, 2013) 226–27.

28 Mabalon, *Little Manila*, 233; Takaki, *Strangers from a Different Shore*, 359, 432.

29 Mabalon, *Little Manila*, 232–33, 241.

30 Philip Q. Yang, *Asian Immigration to the United States* (Cambridge, U.K.: Polity, 2011), 102–3; Mabalon, *Little Manila*, 247.

31 R. T. Feria, "War and the Status of Filipino Immigrants," *Sociology and Social Research* 31, no. 1 (1946): 52.

32 Lee, *Quiet Odyssey*, 95.

33 Melendy, *Asians in America*, 157.

34 Kim, *The Quest for Statehood*, 129–30.

35 Patterson, *The Ilse*, 198.

36 Lee, *Quiet Odyssey*, 95–96.

37 Won Soon Lee to U.S. Secretary of State Cordell Hull, DECEMBER 16, 1941, File 740.00115 PACIFIC WAR/20, Decimal File, 1940–1944, U.S. Department of State Records, National Archives, College Park, MD.

38 Takaki, *Strangers from a Different Shore*, 366.

39 Kim, *The Quest for Statehood*, 132–33; Patterson, *The Ilse*, 203.

40 Takaki, *Strangers from a Different Shore*, 366–67.

41 Kim, *The Quest for Statehood*, 153–54.

42 Ibid., 156–63.

43 Act of July 2, 1946 (60 Stat. 416).

44 Yang, *Asian Immigration to the United States*, 93.

45 Christina Klein, *Cold War Orientalism: Asia in the Middlebrow Imagination* (Berkeley: University of California Press, 2004), 5.

46 John Dower, *War Without Mercy: Race and Power in the Pacific War* (New York: Pantheon, 1987); Naoko Shibusawa, *America's Geisha Ally: Reimagining the Japanese Enemy* (Cambridge: Harvard University Press, 2010).

47 Masako Nakamura, "Families Precede Nation and Race?: Marriage, Migration, and Integration of Japanese War Brides After World War II" (PhD diss., University of Minnesota, 2010), 2, 15–16, 37.

48 Nakano Glenn, *Issei, Nisei, War Bride*, 59–60.

49 Nakamura, "Families Precede Nation and Race?," 237–41.

50 Ibid., 3–4, 242–43.

51 Ibid., 23–74.

52 Ibid., 2.

53 Ibid., 99–100.

54 Ibid., 18, 77, 92–93.

55 Benjamin Hartmann, "Chiyoko Toguchi Swartz: There's Not a Book on That," Immigrant Stories Digital Archive, Immigration History Research Center, https://www.youtube.com/watch?v=i78px7r048k (accessed September 1, 2014).

56 Ji-Yeon Yuh, "Moved by War: Migration, Diaspora, and the Korean War," *Journal of Asian American Studies* 8, no. 3 (2005): 277–91; Yang, *Asian Immigration to the United States*, 84.

57 Ji-Yeon Yuh, "Imagined Community: Sisterhood and Resistance Among Korean Military Brides in America, 1950–1996," in *Asian/Pacific Islander American Women*, eds. Hune and Nomura, 221–36.

58 Ji-Yeon Yuh, *Beyond the Shadow of Camptown: Korean Military Brides in America* (New York: New York University Press, 2002), 43–47.

59 Ibid., 42–43, 222. Percentage of post-1965 Korean immigration tied to military brides from Yuh, "Moved by War," 278.

60 Yuh, "Imagined Community," 223.

61 Catherine Ceniza Choy, *Global Families: A History of Asian International Adoption in America* (New York: New York University Press, 2013). See also

Kim Park Nelson, *Mapping Multiple Histories of Korean American Transnational Adoption*, U.S.-Korea Institute Working Paper Series (Johns Hopkins University: U.S.-Korea Institute, School of Advanced International Studies, January 2009), 4–5; Richard Lee and Matthew Miller, "History and Psychology of Adoptees in Asian America," in *Asian American Psychology* (Mahwah, NJ: Lawrence Erlbaum, 2008), 337–63; Eleana Jean Kim, *Adopted Territory: Transnational Korean Adoptees and the Politics of Belonging* (Durham, NC: Duke University Press, 2010), 45; SooJin Pate, *From Orphan to Adoptee: U.S. Empire and Genealogies of Korean Adoption* (Minneapolis: University of Minnesota Press, 2014).

62 *First Person Plural*, VHS, directed by Deann Borshay Liem (2000; San Francisco, CA: National Asian American Telecommunications Association [NAATA], 2000), and *In the Matter of Cha Jung Hee*, DVD, directed by Deann Borshay Liem (2010; Berkeley, CA: Mu Films, 2010).

63 Park Nelson, *Mapping Multiple Histories*, 4–5.

64 Peter Kwong and Dusanka Miscevic, *Chinese America: The Untold Story of America's Oldest New Community* (New York: New Press, 2006), 231–33; Madeline Y. Hsu, "The Disappearance of America's Cold War Chinese Refugees, 1948–1966," *Journal of American Ethnic History* 31, no. 4 (2012): 12–33.

65 Iris Chang, *The Chinese in America: A Narrative History* (New York: Penguin, 2004), 300–303.

66 Kwong and Miscevic, *Chinese America*, 231–33; Hsu, "The Disappearance of America's Cold War Chinese Refugees," 13; Choy, *Empire of Care*, 59–118.

67 Ngai, *Impossible Subjects*, 238.

68 Reimers, *Still the Golden Door*, 19–22.

69 Jere Takahashi, *Nisei Sansei: Shifting Japanese American Identities and Politics* (Philadelphia: Temple University Press, 1997), 127–31; Nakamura, "Families Precede Nation and Race?," 61.

70 Cindy I-fen Cheng, *Citizens of Asian America: Democracy and Race During the Cold War* (New York: New York University Press, 2013), 2; Brooks, *Alien Neighbors, Foreign Friends*, 2.

71 Wu, *The Color of Success*, 4–5, 51.

72 Ibid., 72–110; 126–38; Cheng, *Citizens of Asian America*, 85–116.

73 "Made in America," *Time*, January 9, 1956; "Jackie and the Judge," *Time*, February 27, 1956; "Living Proof," *Time*, November 19, 1956.

74 Dalip Singh Saund, *Congressman from India* (New York: Dutton, 1960), 153.

75 "The Salesman," *Time*, December 16, 1957.

76 Ibid.

77 Ibid.
78 Saund, *Congressman from India*, v, 3–6.
79 Wu, *The Color of Success*, 111–14; Klein, *Cold War Orientalism*, 240–41; Brooks, *Alien Neighbors, Foreign Friends*, 4.
80 Helen Zia, *Asian American Dreams: The Emergence of an American People* (New York: Farrar, Straus & Giroux), 45.
81 Lee, *At America's Gates*, 240–42.
82 Wu, *The Color of Success*, 190–98.
83 Ellen D. Wu, "Asian Americans and the 'Model Minority' Myth," *Los Angeles Times*, January 23, 2014.
84 R. Lee, *Orientals*, 11, 149–53.
85 William Petersen, "Success Story, Japanese-American Style." *The New York Times Magazine*, January 9, 1966.
86 Robert Chang, *Disoriented: Asian Americans, Law, and the Nation-State* (New York: New York University Press, 1999), 54; Wu, *The Color of Success*, 244.
87 "Success Story of One Minority Group in U.S.," *U.S. News & World Report*, December 26, 1966.
88 Wu, *The Color of Success*, 147.
89 Ibid., 1.
90 Ibid., 2, 6.

Chapter 13: Making a New Asian America Through Immigration and Activism

1 John F. Kennedy, A *Nation of Immigrants* (New York: Harper & Row, 1964).
2 "President Lyndon Baines Johnson's Statement at the Signing of the 1965 Immigration and Nationality Bill, Liberty Island, New York, October 3, 1965," Lyndon B. Johnson, *Public Papers of the Presidents of the United States: Lyndon B. Johnson, 1963–1964*, Bk. 1, Nov. 22, 1963, to June 30, 1964 (Washington, DC: U.S. Government Printing Office, 1965).
3 "Annual Message to the Congress on the State of the Union," January 8, 1964, in ibid., 116; Donna Gabaccia and Maddalena Marinari, "American Immigration Policy," in A *Companion to Lyndon B. Johnson*, ed. Mitchell B. Lerner (Hoboken, NJ: Wiley-Blackwell, 2012), 210–27.
4 Reimers, *Still the Golden Door*, 81.
5 Ibid., 84; Immigration and Nationality Act (79 Stat. 911).
6 U.S. Immigration and Naturalization Service, *Statistical Yearbook of the Immigration and Naturalization Service* (Washington, DC: U.S. Government

Printing Office, 1998); "Immigration Growth at Highest Rate in 150 Years," *Washington Times*, June 5, 2002.

7 Elizabeth M. Grieco et al., *The Foreign-Born Population in the United States: 2010* (Washington, DC: U.S. Census, U.S. Department of Commerce, 2012), http://www.census.gov/prod/2012pubs/acs-19.pdf (accessed February 22, 2013).

8 Roger Daniels and Otis L. Graham, "Two Cheers for Immigration," in *Debating American Immigration, 1882–Present* (Lanham, MD: Rowman & Littlefield, 2001), 6; Grieco et al., *The Foreign-Born Population in the United States*; Elizabeth M. Hoeffel et al., *The Asian Population: 2010* (Washington, DC: U.S. Department of Commerce, Economics and Statistics Administration, U.S. Census Bureau, 2012), 1, 4; Pew Research Center, *The Rise of Asian Americans*, 2–3; Humes, Jones, and Ramirez, *Overview of Race and Hispanic Origin, 2010*; Nathan P. Walters and Edward N. Trevelyan, "The Newly Arrived Foreign-Born Population of the United States: 2010" (Washington, DC: U.S. Department of Commerce, Economics and Statistics Administration, U.S. Census Bureau, 2011), 2.

9 Park and Park, *Probationary Americans*, 21–24; Pew Research Center, *The Rise of Asian Americans*, 27.

10 Hoeffel et al., *The Asian Population*, 8; Ajantha Subramanian, "Indians in North Carolina: Race, Class, and Culture in the Making of Immigrant Identity," in *Contemporary Asian America*, ed. Min Zhou and James V. Gatewood, 2nd ed. (New York: New York University Press, 2000), 158–75; Mark E. Pfeifer et al., "Hmong Population and Demographic Trends in the 2010 Census and 2010 American Community Survey," *Hmong Studies Journal* 13 (2012): 2.

11 Pew Research Center, *The Rise of Asian Americans*, 21.

12 Ibid., 23–24.

13 Ibid., 54.

14 Eric Yo Ping Lai and Dennis Arguelles, eds., *The New Face of Asian Pacific America: Numbers, Diversity and Change in the 21st Century* (Los Angeles: AsianWeek with UCLA's Asian American Studies Center Press, 2003), 13; Pew Research Center, *The Rise of Asian Americans*, 21.

15 Wei Li and Emily Skop, "Diaspora in the United States: Chinese and Indians Compared," *Journal of Chinese Overseas* 6, no. 2 (2010): 296; Kristen McCabe and Migration Policy Institute, *Chinese Immigrants in the United States*, January 18, 2012, http://www.migrationinformation.org/USfocus/print.cfm?ID=841 (accessed November 12, 2012); Hoeffel et al., *The Asian Population*, 14; Pew Research Center, *The Rise of Asian Americans*, 38; Min Zhou,

Contemporary Chinese America: Immigration, Ethnicity, and Community Transformation, 2nd ed. (Philadelphia: Temple University Press, 2009), 43.

16 Reimers, *Still the Golden Door*, 94.

17 Kenny and Siu Wing Lai, "Where To from Here? Kenny and Siu Wing Lai," in *Asian Americans: Oral Histories of First to Fourth Generation Americans from China, the Philippines, Japan, India, the Pacific Islands, Vietnam and Cambodia*, ed. Joann Faung Lee (New York: W.W. Norton, 1991), 70.

18 Chang, *The Chinese in America*, 336–38.

19 Li and Skop, "Diaspora in the United States," 299; Wei Li and Lucia Lo, "New Geographies of Migration? A Canada-US Comparison of Highly-Skilled Chinese and Indian Migration," *Journal of Asian American Studies* 15, no. 1 (2012), 10; Pew Research Center, *The Rise of Asian Americans*, 39; McCabe and Migration Policy Institute, *Chinese Immigrants in the United States*, 9.

20 "Uptown" Chinese from Peter Kwong, *The New Chinatown* (New York: Hill & Wang, 1996), 5. "First Suburban Chinatown" from Timothy Fong, *The First Suburban Chinatown: The Remarking of Monterey Park, California* (Philadelphia: Temple University Press, 1994). Numerous Chinatowns in New York City from Kirk Semple, "How Do You Get to Little Guyana? Take the A Train," *New York Times*, June 9, 2013. See also Zhou, *Contemporary Chinese America*, 47, 83.

21 Kwong, *The New Chinatown*, 5.

22 San Francisco figure from Rhacel Salazar Parrenas, "Asian Immigrant Women and Global Restructuring, 1970s–1990s," in *Asian/Pacific Islander American Women*, eds. Hune and Nomura, 277. New York figure from Zhou, *Contemporary Chinese America*, 73. Fu Lee, "Immigrant Women Speak Out on Garment Industry Abuse," in Yung, Chang, and Lai, eds., *Chinese American Voices*, 359–362.

23 Zhou, *Contemporary Chinese America*, 182–83.

24 Xiaolan Bao, "Politicizing Motherhood: Chinese Garment Workers' Campaign for Daycare Centers in New York City, 1977–1982," in *Asian/Pacific Islander American Women*, eds. Hune and Nomura, 286–300.

25 Chang, *The Chinese in America*, 376.

26 Lily Wang, "A Journey of Bitterness (1999)," in Yung, Chang, and Lai, eds., *Chinese American Voices*, 355–58; "Mexico Captures Suspected Chinese Migrant Smuggler," *CNN Justice*, October 23, 2010, http://www.cnn.com/2010/CRIME/10/23/mexico.smuggling.arrest/index.html?_s=PM:CRIME (accessed October 27, 2013).

27 Chang, *The Chinese in America*, 375–81; "Mexico Captures Suspected Chinese Migrant Smuggler."

28 Chang, *The Chinese in America*, 381–88.

29 Wang, "A Journey of Bitterness (1999)," 355–58.

30 Sara K. Dorow, *Transnational Adoption: A Cultural Economy of Race, Gender, and Kinship* (New York: New York University Press, 2006); "International Adoption Facts," Evan B. Donaldson Adoption Institute, http://www.adoptioninstitute.org/FactOverview/international.html (accessed October 17, 2011); Choy, *Global Families*.

31 Hoeffel et al., *The Asian Population*, 14; Pew Research Center, *The Rise of Asian Americans*, 42.

32 Steven C. McKay, "Filipino Sea Men: Identity and Masculinity in a Global Labor Niche," in *Asian Diasporas: New Formations, New Conceptions*, ed. Rhacel Salazar Parrenas and Lok C. D. Siu (Stanford: Stanford University Press, 2007), 63; Parrenas, "Asian Immigrant Women and Global Restructuring, 1970s–1990s," 272–73; Espiritu, *Home Bound*, 24, 71, 73–74.

33 Figure is from 2010. See Aaron Terrazas, Jeanne Batalova, and Migration Policy Institute, *Filipino Immigrants in the United States*, April 7, 2010, http://www.migrationinformation.org/USfocus/print.cfm?ID=777 (accessed November 12, 2012).

34 Espiritu, *Home Bound*, 259, 263; Catherine Ceniza Choy, "Relocating Struggle: Filipino Nurses Organize in the United States," in *Asian/Pacific Islander American Women*, eds. Hune and Nomura, 336. 2010 statistics from Terrazas, Batalova, and Migration Policy Institute, *Filipino Immigrants in the United States*, 6.

35 Takaki, *Strangers from a Different Shore*, 433; Carl L. Bankston III and Danielle Antionette Hidalgo, "The Waves of War: Immigrants, Refugees, and New Americans from Southeast Asia," in *Contemporary Asian America: A Multidisciplinary Reader*, ed. Min Zhou and James V. Gatewood, 1st ed. (New York: New York University Press, 2007), 140–43.

36 Edgar Gamboa, "International Medical Graduates Are Tested Every Step of the Way," in *Filipino American Lives*, ed. Yen Espiritu (Philadelphia: Temple University Press, 1995), 128, 133–34.

37 Choy, "Relocating Struggle: Filipino Nurses Organize in the United States," 345 (emphasis in original).

38 Harold Coward, John R. Hinnells, and Raymond Brady Williams, "South Asians in the United States," in *The South Asian Religious Diaspora in Britain, Canada, and the United States* (Albany: State University of New York Press, 2000), 215; Hoeffel et al., *The Asian Population*, 14.

39 Pew Research Center, *The Rise of Asian Americans*, 45.

40 Takaki, *Strangers from a Different Shore*, 446. Comparison with other immigrant groups from Aaron Terrazas, Christina Batog, and Migration Policy Institute, *Indian Immigrants in the United States*, June 9, 2010, http://www.migrationinformation.org/USfocus/print.cfm?ID=785 (accessed November 12, 2012); Prashad, *Uncle Swami*, 96.

41 Ram Gada, "I Thought I Could Go Abroad," December 7, 1994, in "Becoming Minnesotan: Stories of Recent Immigrants and Refugees," Minnesota Historical Society, http://education.mnhs.org/immigration/narrators/asian-indian/ram-gada/i-thought-if-i-could-go-abroad-i-could-expand-my-horizons (accessed February 10, 2012).

42 Coward, Hinnells, and Williams, "South Asians in the United States," 215; Pew Research Center, *The Rise of Asian Americans*, 25.

43 A. L. Saxenian, *Silicon Valley's New Immigrant Entrepreneurs* (San Francisco: Public Policy Institute of California, 1999), 23–24; Vivek Wadhwa, "The Face of Success, Part I: How the Indians Conquered Silicon Valley," *Inc.com*, January 13, 2012, http://www.inc.com/vivek-wadhwa/how-the-indians-succeeded-in-silicon-valley.html (accessed November 8, 2013).

44 Terrazas, Batog, and Migration Policy Institute, *Indian Immigrants in the United States*, 6.

45 Li and Skop, "Diaspora in the United States," 300–302; Yang, *Asian Immigration to the United States*, 114; Coward, Hinnells, and Williams, "South Asians in the United States," 215.

46 Suvarna Thaker, "The Quality of Life of Asian Indian Women in the Motel Industry," *Comparative Studies of South Asia, Africa and the Middle East* 2, no. 1 (1982): 70.

47 Ibid., 68–73; Pawan Dhingra, *Life Behind the Lobby: Indian American Motel Owners and the American Dream* (Stanford: Stanford University Press, 2012). Lack of college degrees from Terrazas, Batog, and Migration Policy Institute, *Indian Immigrants in the United States*, 6.

48 "For Indian Women in America, a Sea of Broken Dreams," *The Hindu*, July 29, 2012 http://www.thehindu.com/news/international/for-indian-women-in-america-a-sea-of-broken-dreams/article3697211.ece (accessed May 16, 2013).

49 Sandhya Shukla, "New Immigrants, New Forms of Transnational Community: Post-1965 Indian Migrations," *Amerasia Journal* 25, no. 3 (1999): 30–33; Hoeffel et al., *The Asian Population*, 14.

50 Yang, *Asian Immigration to the United States*, 117, 124; Lai and Arguelles, *The New Face of Asian Pacific America*, 107–9.

51 Junaid Rana, *Terrifying Muslims: Race and Labor in the South Asian Diaspora* (Durham, NC: Duke University Press, 2011), 12–13, 99, 109–13.

52 Semple, "How Do You Get to Little Guyana?"

53 Yang, *Asian Immigration to the United States*, 114; Takaki, *Strangers from a Different Shore*, 436–45; Pew Research Center, *The Rise of Asian Americans*, 51.

54 Han Chol Hong, "Strong Determination," in *East to America: Korean American Life Stories*, ed. Kim Elaine H. and Eui-Young Yu (New York: New Press, 1996), 180–86.

55 Yang, *Asian Immigration to the United States*, 114; Eui-Young Yu and Peter Choe, "Korean Population in the United States as Reflected in the Year 2000 US Census," *Amerasia Journal* 29, no. 3 (2003): 2, 5.

56 Pew Research Center, *The Rise of Asian Americans*, 52.

57 Scott Kurashige, *The Shifting Grounds of Race: Black and Japanese Americans in the Making of Multiethnic Los Angeles* (Princeton: Princeton University Press, 2008).

58 Yuri Kochiyama, "Then Came the War: Yuri Kochiyama," in *Asian Americans*, ed., Joann Faung Jean Lee, 16–17; Yuri Kochiyama, *Passing It On: A Memoir* (Los Angeles: UCLA Asian American Studies Center Press, 2004), 45; Diane C. Fujino and S. Shah, "Revolution's from the Heart: The Making of an Asian American Woman Activist, Yuri Kochiyama," in Sonia Shah, ed., *Dragon Ladies: Asian American Feminists Breathe Fire* (Boston: South End, 1997), 171.

59 Craig Scharlin and Lilia V. Villanueva, *Philip Vera Cruz: A Personal History of Filipino Immigrants and the Farmworkers Movement* (Seattle: University of Washington Press, 2000), 99; Glenn Omatsu, " 'The Four Prisons' and the Movement of Liberation: Asian American Activism from the 1960s to the 1990s," in *Contemporary Asian America: A Multidisciplinary Reader*, ed. Min Zhou and James V. Gatewood, 2nd ed. (New York: New York University Press, 2007), 81–83.

60 Bill Moyers, "Grace Lee Boggs," *Bill Moyers Journal* (Public Broadcasting Corporation, June 15, 2007), http://www.pbs.org/moyers/journal/06152007/profile2.html (accessed October 18, 2011); Grace Lee Boggs, *The Next American Revolution: Sustainable Activism for the Twenty-first Century* (Berkeley: University of California Press, 2011), 4, 29.

61 Boggs, *The Next American Revolution*, 30.

62 Daryl J. Maeda, *Rethinking the Asian American Movement* (New York: Routledge, 2012), 1, 148.

63 Ibid., 10.

64 Yen Le Espiritu, *Asian American Panethnicity: Bridging Institutions and Identities* (Philadelphia: Temple University Press, 1992), 32.

65 Maeda, *Rethinking the Asian American Movement*, 107–8, 10–11, 15–17.

66 Daryl J. Maeda, *Chains of Babylon: The Rise of Asian America* (Minneapolis: University of Minnesota Press, 2009), 92.

67 Maeda, *Rethinking the Asian American Movement*, 37.

68 Ibid., 38, 46.

69 Ibid., 49–50; Karen Umemoto, "On Strike!: San Francisco State College Strike, 1968–1969: The Role of Asian American Students," in *Contemporary Asian America*, eds. Zhou and Gatewood, 2nd ed., 25–55.

70 Maeda, *Rethinking the Asian American Movement*, 58–64; Estella Habal, *San Francisco's International Hotel: Mobilizing the Filipino American Community in the Anti-Eviction Movement* (Philadelphia: Temple University Press, 2007).

71 Maeda, *Chains of Babylon*, 110–11.

72 Maeda, *Rethinking the Asian American Movement*, 118–19; Maeda, *Chains of Babylon*, 97.

73 Maeda, *Rethinking the Asian American Movement*, 121–22; Judy Tzu-Chun Wu, *Radicals on the Road: Internationalism, Orientalism, and Feminism During the Vietnam Era* (Ithaca: Cornell University Press, 2013).

74 Merilynne Hamano Quon, "Individually We Contributed, Together We Made a Difference," in *Asian Americans: The Movement and the Moment*, eds. Steve Louie and Glenn K. Omatsu (Los Angeles: UCLA Asian American Studies Center Press, 2001), 210.

75 Sonia Shah, "Introduction: Slaying the Dragon Lady," in *Dragon Ladies*, ed. Shah, xvi. Unsuk Perry example from Yoichi Shimatsu and Patricia Lee, "Dust and Dishes: Organizing Workers," in *Making Waves: An Anthology of Writings by and About Asian American Women*, ed. Asian Women United of California (Boston: Beacon, 1989), 386–95. Chang Jok Lee example from Nancy Diao, "From Homemaker to Housing Advocate: An Interview with Mrs. Chang Jok Lee," in ibid., 377–86.

76 Helen Zia, "Where the Queer Zone Meets the Asian Zone: Marriage Equality and Other Intersections," *Amerasia Journal* 32, no. 1 (January 1, 2006): 3. See also Trinity A. Ordona, "Asian Lesbians in San Francisco: Struggles to Create a Safe Space, 1970s–1980s," in *Asian/Pacific Islander American Women*, eds. Hune and Nomura, 320; Daniel C. Tsang, "Slicing Silence: Asian Progressives Come Out," in *Asian Americans*, eds. Louie and Omatsu, 224.

77 Ordona, "Asian Lesbians in San Francisco," 319.

78 Eric C. Wat, *The Making of a Gay Asian Community: An Oral History of Pre-AIDS Los Angeles* (Lanham, MD: Rowman & Littlefield, 2002), 1–2.

79 Zia, "Where the Queer Zone Meets the Asian Zone," 12; Gary Gates, Holning Lau, and R. Bradley Sears, "Asians and Pacific Islanders in Same-Sex Couples in the United States: Data from Census 2000," *Amerasia Journal* 32, no. 1 (January 1, 2006): 15–32; Bryant Yang, "Seeing *Loving* in Gay Marriages: Parallels of Asian American History and the Same-Sex Marriage Debates," *Amerasia Journal* 32, no. 1 (January 1, 2006): 33–44.

80 Aiko Yoshinaga Herzig Interview, Segment 2, Interview by Larry Hashima and Glen Kitayama, September 11, 1997, Densho ID: denshovh-haiko-01-0002, Densho Visual History Collection, Densho Digital Archive (accessed November 8, 2013).

81 Robinson, *A Tragedy of Democracy*, 291–93.

82 U.S. CWRIC, *Personal Justice Denied*, 18.

83 Ayako Hagihara and Grace Shimizu, "The Japanese Latin American Wartime and Redress Experience," *Amerasia* 28, no. 2 (2002): 203–17.

84 Interview with Daniel Inouye, Segment 3, Interview by Tom Ikeda, July 5, 2008, Densho ID: denshovh-idaniel-02-0003, Japanese American National Museum Collection, Densho Digital Archive (accessed November 8, 2013).

85 Interview with Hitoshi H. Kajihara, Segment 13, Interview by Tom Ikeda, September 11, 1997, Densho ID: denshovh-khitoshi-01-0013, Densho Visual History Collection, Densho Digital Archive (accessed November 8, 2013).

Chapter 14: In Search of Refuge: Southeast Asians in the United States

1 These figures include 145,230 Cambodians (Khmer, Cham, Khmer Loeu), 257,587 Lao (Hmong, Iu Mien, Khmu, Tai Dam, Tai Leu, and Lao), and 771,834 Vietnamese (Vietnamese, Khmer Kampuchea Krom, Montagnards). Southeast Asia Resource Action Center, *Southeast Asian Americans at a Glance: Statistics on Southeast Asians Adapted from the American Community Survey* (Washington, DC, 2011), 7.

2 The legal definition of a "refugee" as established by the United Nations High Commissioner for Refugees in 1951 identifies a refugee as someone who has been forced to leave their homeland "owing to a well-founded fear of being persecuted for reasons of race, religion, nationality, membership of a particular social group or political opinion." This definition leaves out those who are forced to leave because of natural disasters, famine, civil unrest, and war. Many of the Southeast Asians seeking refuge abroad after 1975 fit the legal

definition of refugee. But there are many others who fled kinds of danger other than formal persecution. Some scholars have offered terms such as "refuge migration" or "refuge seekers" to better reflect the variety of conditions and peoples who have been displaced and who seek peace and safety outside their homelands. See Yuh, "Moved by War," 287; and Sucheng Chan, *Survivors: Cambodian Refugees in the United States* (Champaign: University of Illinois Press, 2004), xxiv.

3 Refugee resettlement reflects what scholar Mimi Nguyen calls the "gift of freedom"; the promise of helping refugees that is simultaneously humanitarian and imperialistic; refugees are constantly subjected to intervention, regulation, and rehabilitation. Mimi Thi Nguyen, *The Gift of Freedom: War, Debt, and Other Refugee Passages* (Durham, NC: Duke University Press, 2012), xi–xii.

4 Sucheng Chan, *Vietnamese American 1.5 Generation* (Philadelphia: Temple University Press, 2006), 50–51, 56.

5 Ibid., 97.

6 Kenton Clymer, "Cambodia and Laos in the Vietnam War," in *Columbia History of the Vietnam War*, ed. David L. Anderson (New York: Columbia University Press, 2011), 375; Legacies of War, "Leftover Unexploded Ordnance (UXO)," http://legaciesofwar.org/about-laos/leftover-unexploded-ordnances-uxo/ (accessed July 19, 2013).

7 Martin E. Goldstein, *American Policy Towards Laos* (Hackensack, NJ: Fairleigh Dickinson University Press, 1973), 195; Paul Hillmer, *A People's History of the Hmong* (St. Paul: Minnesota Historical Society Press, 2010), 70.

8 Chia Youyee Vang, *Hmong America: Reconstructing Community in Diaspora* (Champaign: University of Illinois Press, 2010), 27, 30; Keith Quincy, *Harvesting Pa Chay's Wheat: The Hmong and America's Secret War in Laos* (Spokane: Eastern Washington University Press, 2000), 177–80. "America's most lethal weapon" from Keith Quincy, "From War to Resettlement: How Hmong Have Become Americans," in *Hmong and American: From Refugees to Citizens*, ed. Vincent K. Her and Mary Louise Buley-Meissner (St. Paul: Minnesota Historical Society Press, 2012), 64.

9 Vang, *Hmong America*, 6; Nengher Vang, "Political Transmigrants: Rethinking Hmong Political Activism in America," *Hmong Studies Journal* 12 (2011): 10; Quincy, "From War to Resettlement," 65.

10 Alfred W. McCoy, "America's Secret War in Laos, 1955–75," in *A Companion to the Vietnam War*, ed. Marilyn B. Young and Robert Buzzanco (New York: Blackwell, 2002), 290–92.

11 "Laos: The Not So Secret War" (CBS, 1970), National Archives and Records Administration, http://archive.org/details/gov.archives.arc.657070 (accessed July 12, 2013).

12 Vang, *Hmong America*, 30.

13 Clymer, "Cambodia and Laos," 373; Ben Kiernan, "The American Bombardment of Kampuchea, 1969–1973," *Vietnam Generation* 1, no. 1 (Winter 1989): 6, 8.

14 Kiernan, "American Bombardment," 21; Clymer, "Cambodia and Laos," 369; Sucheng Chan and Audrey U. Kim, *Not Just Victims: Conversations with Cambodian Community Leaders in the United States* (Champaign: University of Illinois Press, 2003), 8.

15 Chan, *Vietnamese American*, 60.

16 David Schiaccitano, "The River," in *To Bear Any Burden: The Vietnam War and Its Aftermath in the Words of Americans and Southeast Asians*, ed. Al Santoli (Bloomington: Indiana University Press, 1999), 11–17.

17 Chan, *Vietnamese American*, 104–12.

18 Ibid., 62–63.

19 Bankston and Hidalgo, "The Waves of War," 147.

20 Chan and Kim, *Not Just Victims*, 48.

21 Vang, *Hmong America*, 36.

22 Anne Fadiman, *The Spirit Catches You and You Fall Down: A Hmong Child, Her American Doctors, and the Collision of Two Cultures* (New York: Farrar, Straus & Giroux, 1998), 138.

23 Vang, *Hmong America*, 36. Quincy, "From War to Resettlement," 69.

24 *New York Times*, April 30, 1975.

25 "Remarks of the President to the San Francisco Bay Area Council," April 4, 1975, Operation Babylift Press Releases, "Operation Babylift," Gerald R. Ford Presidential Digital Library, http://www.fordlibrarymuseum.gov/library/exhibits/babylift/babylift.asp (accessed July 12, 2013).

26 "Opening Statement at Press Conference in San Diego, April 3, 1975," in "Indochina Refugees—Orphan Airlift" from Theodore Marrs Files, "Operation Babylift," ibid.

27 Text of Remarks by the President to the National Association of Broadcasters, Las Vegas, Nevada, April 7, 1975, Operation Babylift Press Releases, "Operation Babylift," ibid.

28 Memorandum from Ron Nessen to the President, May 6, 1975, in "Indochina Refugees—Orphan Airlift" from Theodore Marrs Files, "Operation Babylift," ibid.

29 Bankston and Hidalgo, "Waves of War," 146; Chan, *Vietnamese American*, 63–64.

30 Linda Trinh Vo, "The Vietnamese American Experience: From Dispersion to the Development of Post-Refugee Communities," in *Asian American Studies*, eds. Wu and Song, 291; Rubén G. Rumbaut, "Vietnamese, Laotian, and Cambodian Americans," in *Contemporary Asian America*, eds. Zhou and Gatewood, 182.

31 Chan, *Vietnamese American*, 65–66, 171–78.

32 Ibid., 191.

33 Ibid., 77.

34 Ibid., 192.

35 Le Tan Si, "Le Tan Si Writes a College Essay About His Terrifying Escape by Boat from Vietnam," in Lon Kurashige and Alice Yang Murray, eds., *Major Problems in Asian American History* (Boston: Houghton Mifflin Company, 2003), 394–97.

36 Chan, *Vietnamese American*, 74–75, 77; Vo, "The Vietnamese American Experience," 292.

37 Bankston and Hidalgo, "Waves of War," 148.

38 Kassie Neou, "City of Phantoms," in *To Bear Any Burden*, ed. Al Santoli, 7–10.

39 Michael Vickery, *Cambodia, 1975–1982* (Boston: South End, 1984), 29–30, 64, 81–82; Ben Kiernan, *The Pol Pot Regime: Race, Power, and Genocide in Cambodia Under the Khmer Rouge, 1975–79* (New Haven: Yale University Press, 1996), 80–83, 252–96, 298–309; Chan, *Survivors*, 15–26.

40 Loung Ung, *Lucky Child: A Daughter of Cambodia Reunites with the Sister She Left Behind* (New York: Harper Perennial, 2006), xi–xii.

41 Teeda Butt Mam, "Worms from Our Skin," in *Children of Cambodia's Killing Fields: Memoirs by Survivors*, ed. Dith Pran and Kim DePaul (New Haven: Yale University Press, 1997), 11–12, 14–15.

42 Chan, *Survivors*, 22–23, 26–28; David P. Chandler, *Voices from S-21: Terror and History in Pol Pot's Secret Prison* (Berkeley: University of California Press, 2000), viii; Kiernan, *The Pol Pot Regime*, 323–25, 337–48, 369–76, 386–439, 400, 437. Cambodian Genocide Program, www.yale.edu/cgp (accessed July 16, 2013).

43 "Deathwatch in Cambodia," *Time*, November 12, 1979.

44 Carol A. Mortland, "Cambodian Resettlement in America," in *Cambodian American Experiences: Histories, Communities, Cultures and Identities*, ed. Jonathan H. X. Lee (Dubuque, IA: Kendall Hunt, 2010), 76–102.

45 Bankston and Hidalgo, "Waves of War," 148; Susan Needham and Karen Quintiliani, "Cambodians in Long Beach, California: The Making of a Community," *Journal of Immigrant & Refugee Studies* 5, no. 1 (2007): 29–53; Chan, *Survivors*, 85–91.

46 Vang, *Hmong America*, 41; Bindi V. Shah, *Laotian Daughters Working Toward Community, Belonging, and Environmental Justice* (Philadelphia: Temple University Press, 2012), 23; Wanni W. Anderson, "Between Necessity and Choice: Rhode Island Lao American Women," in *Displacements and Diasporas: Asians in the Americas*, ed. Robert G. Lee and Wanni W. Anderson (New Brunswick, NJ: Rutgers University Press, 2005), 196; Jeremy Hein, *From Vietnam, Laos, and Cambodia: A Refugee Experience in the United States* (New York: Twayne, 1995), 47; Bankston and Hidalgo, "Waves of War," 148.

47 Saengmany Ratsabout, "Saengmany Ratsabout," Immigrant Stories Digital Archive, Immigration History Research Center, https://www.youtube.com/watch?v=_S4A1K6gSgI (accessed December 6, 2014).

48 Ibid.; Southeast Asia Resource Action Center, *Southeast Asian Americans*, 5.

49 Quincy, *Harvesting Pa Chay's Wheat*, 394.

50 Ibid., 395–97, 399; Lillian Faderman and Ghia Xiong, *I Begin My Life All Over: The Hmong and the American Immigrant Experience* (Boston: Beacon, 2005), 8.

51 Jane Hamilton-Merritt, *Tragic Mountains: The Hmong, the Americans, and the Secret Wars for Laos, 1942–1992* (Bloomington: Indiana University Press, 1993), 440–41.

52 Interview with Mai Vang Thao, "Becoming Minnesotan: Stories of Recent Immigrants and Refugees," Minnesota Historical Society, http://education.mnhs.org/immigration/narrators/hmong/mai-vang-thao/when-we-could-no-longer-survive-safely-we-followed-general-vang-pao-to (accessed February 10, 2012).

53 "This Is Home: The Hmong in Minnesota," Minnesota Public Radio, March 12, 1999 http://news.minnesota.publicradio.org/features/199903/08_nymanl_home/portraits/lee.shtml (accessed June 29, 2013); Vang, *Hmong America*, 38.

54 Yeng Xiong (edited and translated by Mai Tong Yang), "Yeng Xiong," Immigrant Stories Digital Archive, Immigration History Research Center, https://www.youtube.com/watch?v=LI4ylxTzR2s (accessed January 16, 2015).

55 Vang, *Hmong America*, 41.

56 Ibid., 38; Quincy, "From War to Resettlement," 69–70; Mace Goldfarb, *Fighters, Refugees, Immigrants: A Story of the Hmong* (Minneapolis: Carolrhoda, 1982).

57 Vang, *Hmong America*, 77–80.

Chapter 15: Making a New Home: Hmong Refugees and Hmong Americans

1 Pa Xiong Gonzalo, "Growing Up Hmong in Laos and America: Two Generations of Women Through My Eyes," *Amerasia Journal* 36, no. 1 (2010): 72.

2 Ken Levine and Ivory Waterworth, *Becoming American* (New Day Films, 2005).

3 Vang, *Hmong America*, 12–13.

4 Ibid., 15.

5 United States Office of Refugee Resettlement, Simon M. Fass, and Diana D. Bui, *The Hmong Resettlement Study: Final Report*, vol. 1 (Washington, DC: Office of Refugee Resettlement, 1985), 67; Appendix, 3–4 (hereafter cited as U.S. Hmong Resettlement Study).

6 Ibid., 104; Kou Yang, "The American Experience of the Hmong: A Historical Review," in *Diversity in Diaspora: Hmong Americans in the Twenty-first Century*, ed. Mark Edward Pfeifer (Honolulu: University of Hawaii Press, 2013), 8.

7 U.S. Hmong Resettlement Study, 94.

8 Faderman and Xiong, *I Begin My Life All Over*, 146; Vang, *Hmong America*, 55–56; Kou Yang, "Hmong Men's Adaptation to Life in the United States," *Hmong Studies Journal* 1, no. 2 (1997): 1–22.

9 Faderman and Xiong, *I Begin My Life All Over*, 164.

10 Ibid., 174.

11 Sucheng Chan, *Hmong Means Free: Life in Laos and America* (Philadelphia: Temple University Press, 1994), 85.

12 U.S. Hmong Resettlement Study, 175, 208; Bic Ngo, "Contesting 'Culture': The Perspectives of Hmong American Female Students on Early Marriage," *Anthropology & Education Quarterly* 33, no. 2 (2002): 163–66.

13 Faderman and Xiong, *I Begin My Life All Over*, 193.

14 Kao Kalia Yang, *The Latehomecomer: A Hmong Family Memoir* (Minneapolis: Coffee House Press, 2008).

15 *Minneapolis Star*, January 3, 1979.

16 *St. Paul Dispatch*, October 20, 1980.

17 Ngo, "Contesting 'Culture,' " 163–68.

18 Monica Chiu, "Medical, Racist, and Colonial Constructions of Power: Creating the Asian American Patient and the Cultural Citizen in Anne Fadiman's The Spirit Catches You and You Fall Down," *Hmong Studies Journal* 5 (2004): 6.

19 *St. Paul Dispatch*, Oct. 20, 1980.

20 Ibid.

21 Yang, *The Latehomecomer*, 133.

22 "No More Room for Refugees," *Time*, May 10, 1982.

23 Chan, *Vietnamese American 1.5 Generation*, 71.

24 Bill Ong Hing, *Making and Remaking Asian America Through Immigration Policy, 1850–1990* (Stanford: Stanford University Press, 1993), 126.

25 Gail Paradise Kelly, *From Vietnam to America: A Chronicle of the Vietnamese Immigration to the United States* (Boulder: Westview, 1977), 18.

26 David Palumbo-Liu, *Asian/American: Historical Crossings of a Racial Frontier* (Stanford, CA: Stanford University Press, 1999), 245; U.S. Office of Refugee Resettlement, *The Hmong Resettlement Study Site Report: Fresno, California* (Washington, DC: Office of Refugee Resettlement, 1983), 15.

27 Reimers, *Still the Golden Door*, 178; Bruce T. Downing and United States Office of Refugee Resettlement, *The Hmong Resettlement Study Site Report: Minneapolis-St. Paul* (Washington, DC, 1984), 9; Gil Loescher, *Calculated Kindness* (New York: Free Press, 1986), 130.

28 Chan, *Vietnamese American*, 81–82.

29 Loescher, *Calculated Kindness*, 130–43.

30 Hing, *Making and Remaking Asian America*, 127–28; Reimers, *Still the Golden Door*, 197; Norman L. Zucker and Naomi Flink Zucker, *Desperate Crossings: Seeking Refuge in America* (Armonk, NY: Sharpe, 1996), 6–7; Kevin R. Johnson, "Race, the Immigration Laws, and Domestic Race Relations: A Magic Mirror into the Heart of Darkness," *Indiana Law Journal* 73, no. 4 (1998): 1134; Harvey Gee, "The Refugee Burden: A Closer Look at the Refugee Act of 1980," *North Carolina Journal of International Law and Commercial Regulation* 26, no. 2 (2000): 579.

31 Vo, "The Vietnamese American Experience," 294.

32 Vang, *Hmong America*, 18–19.

33 Ibid., 55, 58–60.

34 Ibid., 13; Kitty Gogins, *My Flag Grew Stars* (Charleston, SC: BookSurge, 2009), 231–32.

35 Vang, *Hmong America*, 10–11, 19; U.S. Hmong Resettlement Study, 165; Appendix, 3.

36 Vang, *Hmong America*, 51–52; U.S. Hmong Resettlement Study, 43–44.

37 Vang, *Hmong America*, 17.

38 Ibid.

39 *St. Paul Pioneer Press*, June 12, 1991; Vang, *Hmong America*, 47, 55; Yang Lor, "Hmong Political Involvement in St. Paul, Minnesota and Fresno, California," *Hmong Studies Journal* 10 (2010): 14–15.

40 Yang, *The Latehomecomer*, 136, 169–170.

41 Vang, *Hmong America*, 72–73.

42 "HAP Programs," Hmong American Partnership Website, www.hmong.org/programs.aspx (accessed July 14, 2013); Vang, *Hmong America*, 36.

43 Vang, *Hmong America*, 73–75.

44 "Hmong Clan Celebrates 6 College Graduations," *St. Paul Pioneer Press-Dispatch*, July 19, 1992.

45 *Hmong Times*, May 1, 2000, May 1, 2001, May 16, 2001.

46 Yang, *The Latehomecomer*, 179, 202–3.

47 *St. Paul Pioneer Press*, September 30, 1991; Vang, *Hmong America*, 56, 59–60; *St. Paul Pioneer Press*, August 14, 1995; Lor, "Hmong Political Involvement."

48 Vang, *Hmong America*, 123, 129; Ma Vang, "The Refugee Soldier: A Critique of Recognition and Citizenship in the Hmong Veterans' Naturalization Act of 1997," *Positions* 20, no. 3 (2012): 708 (fn 14).

49 Vang, *Hmong America*, 126.

50 "Hmong Putting American Politics to Work for Them," *Star Tribune*, August 18, 1997.

51 "New Senator Makes History," Minnesota Public Radio, January 30, 2002, http://news.minnesota.publicradio.org/features/200201/29_wilcoxenw_moua/ (accessed July 14, 2013); Vang, *Hmong America*, 57; Lor, "Hmong Political Involvement," 18–19.

52 N. Vang, "Political Transmigrants," 1–46; Vang, *Hmong America*, 136–42; Vang, "The Refugee Soldier," 712 (fn 81).

53 *St. Paul Pioneer Press*, March 8, 1993; Yang, "The American Experience," 34; Grit Grigoleit, "Coming Home? The Integration of Hmong Refugees from Wat Tham Krabok, Thailand into American Society," *Hmong Studies Journal* 7, no. 1 (2006): 4–10.

54 Pfeifer et al., "Hmong Population and Demographic Trends," 1–31.

55 Chia Youyee Vang, "Making Ends Meet: Hmong Socioeconomic Trends in the U.S.," *Hmong Studies Journal* 13, no. 2 (2012): 1–20; Yang Sao Xiong, "Hmong Americans' Educational Attainment: Recent Changes and Remaining Challenges," *Hmong Studies Journal* 13, no. 2 (2012): 1–18; Yang, "The American Experience," 23–24; Kou Yang, "Forging New Paths, Confronting New Challenges: Hmong Americans in the Twenty-first Century," in *Hmong and American: From Refugees to Citizens*, ed. Vincent K. Her and Mary Louise Buley-Meissner (St. Paul: Minnesota Historical Society Press, 2012), 168.

56 Yang, "The American Experience," 22–23; Daniel F. Detzner, *Elder Voices: Southeast Asian Families in the United States* (Walnut Creek, CA: AltaMira, 2004), 19.

57 Lor, "Hmong Political Involvement," 16–17; Minneapolis Foundation, *Immigration in Minnesota: Discovering Common Ground* (Minneapolis:

Minneapolis Foundation, 2004), 13; *St. Paul Pioneer Press*, May 30, 1999; Yang, "The American Experience," 28–29.

58 Vang, "Making Ends Meet"; Hmong National Development, "The State of the Hmong American Community: 2010 U.S. Census Report, 2013" (Washington, DC: 2013).

59 Louisa Schein and Va-Megn Thoj, "Violence, Hmong American Visibility, and the Precariousness of Asian Race," *PMLA* 123, no. 5 (2008): 1752; Louisa Schein and Va-Megn Thoj, "Gran Torino's Boys and Men with Guns: Hmong Perspectives," *Hmong Studies Journal* 10, no. 1 (2009): 2; Louisa Schein, Va-Megn Thoj, and with Bee Vang and Ly Chong Thong Jalao, "Beyond Gran Torino's Guns: Hmong Cultural Warriors Performing Genders," *Positions* 20, no. 3 (2012): 767; Vang, *Hmong America*, 146–47.

60 Vang, *Hmong America*, 9.

61 Vang, "The Refugee Soldier," 685, 688.

62 *Hmong Times*, November 16, 1998, February 1, 1999; Zia, *Asian American Dreams*, 157–60.

63 Dia Cha, "Women in the Hmong Diaspora," in *Hmong and American*, ed. Her and Buley-Messner, 165–87.

64 Bic Ngo and Pa Nhia Lor, "Great Expectations: The Struggles of Hmong American High School Boys," in *Hmong and American*, ed. Her and Buley-Messner, 156; Cha, "Women in the Hmong Diaspora," 172.

65 Ka Vang, "The Good Hmong Girl Eats Raw Laab," in *Hmong and American*, ed. Her and Buley-Messner, 101–12.

66 Bic Ngo, " 'There Are No GLBT Hmong People': Hmong American Young Adults Navigating Culture and Sexuality," in *Hmong and American*, ed. Her and Buley-Messner, 113–32.

67 Mary Louise Buley-Meissner, "Stitching the Fabric of Hmong Lives: The Value of Studying Paj Ntaub and Story Cloth in Multicultural Education," in *Hmong and American*, ed. Her and Buley-Messner, 233–60; Lynellyn Long, *Ban Vinai, the Refugee Camp* (New York: Columbia University Press, 1993), 85–86; Faderman and Xiong, *I Begin My Life All Over*, 70.

68 Vang, *Hmong America*, 101–17.

69 "What Generation Gap?," *Star Tribune*, March 28, 2012, http://www.startribune.com/entertainment/blogs/144649305.html (accessed April 17, 2013); "Tou SaiKo Lee Visits Thailand in *Travel in Spirals*," *City Pages*, March 29, 2013, http://blogs.citypages.com/dressingroom/2013/03/tou_saiko_lee_visits_thailand_in_travel_in_spirals.php (accessed April 17, 2013); "Hmong Hip Hop Heritage," *New York Times*, http://www.youtube.com/watch?v=XIrN9hV62D8 (accessed July 14, 2013); Nicholas Poss, " 'Reharmonizing' the Generations:

Rap, Poetry, and Hmong Oral Tradition," in *Diversity in Diaspora*, ed. Pfeifer, Chiu, and Yang, 233–246.

Chapter 16: Transnational Immigrants and Global Americans

1 Dipa and Pratik Patel are pseudonyms assigned by sociologist Peggy Levitt in her research, from which this example is drawn. Levitt, *God Needs No Passport*, 37–46.

2 Ibid., 37.

3 On what some see as the "extreme dangers of transnational migration" and Islamic militancy, see Rana, *Terrifying Muslims*, 4.

4 Levitt, *God Needs No Passport*, 29.

5 Aihwa Ong, *Flexible Citizenship: The Cultural Logics of Transnationality* (Durham, NC: Duke University Press, 1999), 1, 17, 123.

6 Valerie Knowles, *Strangers at Our Gates: Canadian Immigration and Immigration Policy, 1540–2006* (Toronto: Dundurn, 2007), 208–10; Lloyd L. Wong and Connie Ho, "Chinese Transnationalism: Class and Capital Flows," in *Transnational Identities and Practices in Canada*, ed. Lloyd L. Wong and Vic Satzewich (Vancouver: UBC Press, 2006), 252.

7 Knowles, *Strangers at Our Gates*, 276; Henry Yu, "Global Migrants and the New Pacific Canada," *International Journal* 64, no. 4 (2009): 1011–14.

8 Muzaffar Chishti and Claire Bergeron, "Recession Breathes New Life into U.S. Immigrant Investor Visa Program," Migration Policy Institute, December 15, 2009 http://www.migrationpolicy.org/article/recession-breathes-new-life-us-immigrant-investor-visa-program (accessed December 5, 2014); "Why a U.S. Immigrant Investor Program Is Being Maxed Out by Chinese Applicants," *Washington Post*, September 5, 2014.

9 Ong, *Flexible Citizenship*, 110–38.

10 Zhou, *Contemporary Chinese America*, 203.

11 Ibid., 202, 207.

12 Rhacel Salazar Parreñas, "New Household Forms, Old Family Values: The Formation and Reproduction of the Filipino Transnational Family in Los Angeles," in *Contemporary Asian America*, 2nd ed., eds. Zhou and Gatewood, 214–16. See also Charlene Tung, "Caring Across Borders: Motherhood, Marriage, and Filipina Domestic Workers in California," in *Asian/Pacific Islander American Women*, eds. Hune and Nomura, 301–18.

13 Purnima Mankekar, " 'India Shopping': Indian Grocery Stores and Transnational Configurations of Belonging," *Ethnos* 67, no. 1 (2002): 80, 86.

14 Ibid., 91.

15 Zhou, *Contemporary Chinese America*, 129, 138, 141.

16 Louis-Jacques Dorais, "From Refugees to Transmigrants: The Vietnamese in Canada," in *Displacements and Diasporas*, 176–77. See also Linda Trinh Vo, "Vietnamese American Trajectories: Dimensions of Diaspora," *Amerasia Journal* 29, no. 1 (2003): x.

17 Shukla, "New Immigrants, New Forms of Transnational Community," 19, 23–26; "Indian Leader Narendra Modi, Once Unwelcome in U.S., Gets Rock Star Reception," *New York Times*, September 27, 2014; Margaret Walton-Roberts, "Transnational Geographies: Indian Immigration to Canada," *The Canadian Geographer/Le Géographe Canadien* 47, no. 3 (2003): 235–50; Verne A. Dusenbery and Darshan S. Tatla, Introduction, in *Sikh Diaspora Philanthropy in Punjab: Global Giving for Local Good* (London: Oxford University Press, 2009), 3–4, 7–8.

18 L. Joyce Zapanta Mariano, "Homeland Developments: Filipino America and the Politics of Diaspora Giving" (PhD diss., University of Minnesota, 2011), 198, 102–3; Espiritu, *Home Bound*, 86.

19 Mariano, "Homeland Developments," 3–4, 52–56, 102–26. For examples of Indian diasporic identity and activity, see Shukla, "New Immigrants, New Forms of Transnational Community."

20 Madhulika S. Khandelwal, "Opening Spaces: South Asian American Women Leaders in the Late Twentieth Century," in *Asian/Pacific Islander American Women*, eds. Hune and Nomura, 355.

21 "Indian Leader Narendra Modi."

22 Carol Ojeda-Kimbrough, "The Chosen Road," in *Asian Americans*, eds. Louie and Omatsu, 71–72; Catherine Ceniza Choy, "Towards Trans-Pacific Social Justice: Women and Protest in Filipino American History," *Journal of Asian American Studies* 8, no. 3 (2005): 297–99.

23 Beleza Li, "On the Meaning of Being Chinese," Immigrant Voices, Angel Island Immigration Station Foundation, http://aiisf.org/stories-by-author/590-li-beleza (accessed March 8, 2012).

24 Lok C. D. Siu, *Memories of a Future Home: Diasporic Citizenship of Chinese in Panama* (Stanford: Stanford University Press, 2005), 132–33.

25 Kathleen López, "The Revitalization of Havana's Chinatown: Invoking Chinese Cuban History," in *The Chinese in Latin America and the Caribbean*, eds. Lai and Tan, 220; Lok C. D. Siu, "In Search of Chino Latinos in Diaspora," in *Cuba: Idea of a Nation Displaced*, ed. Andrea O'Reilly Hervera (Albany: State University of New York Press, 2007), 123–31.

26 Lai and Arguelles, eds., *The New Face of Asian Pacific America*, 55.

27 Kyeyoung Park, "I'm Floating in the Air: Creation of a Korean Transnational Space Among Korean-Latino American Remigrants," *Positions* 7, no. 3 (1999): 669, 680–83.

28 Steven Masami Ropp, "Secondary Migration and the Politics of Identity for Asian Latinos in Los Angeles," *Journal of Asian American Studies* 3, no. 2 (2000): 219–29; Siu, "In Search of Chino Latinos in Diaspora," 123–31; Park, "I'm Floating in the Air," 690–92.

29 Romero, *The Chinese in Mexico*, 196; Lai and Arguelles, *The New Face of Asian Pacific America*, 12.

30 Takeyuki Tsuda, *Strangers in the Ethnic Homeland: Japanese Brazilian Return Migration in Transnational Perspective* (New York: Columbia University Press, 2003), xii.

31 Ibid., 92–5, 99; Masato Ninomiya, "The Dekasegi Phenomenon and the Education of Japanese Brazilian Children in Japanese Schools," in *New Worlds, New Lives*, ed. L. Hirabayashi, Kikumura-Yano, and J. A. Hirabayashi, 250, 304; Edson Mori, "The Japanese-Brazilian Dekasegi Phenomenon—An Economic Perspective," in ibid., 94–97.

32 Associated Press, "Green Card Petitions Down Sharply," *Arizona Republic*, August 6, 2009.

33 Anand Giridharadas, "India Calling," *New York Times*, November 22, 2008.

34 Lisong Liu, "Return Migration and Selective Citizenship: A Study of Returning Chinese Professional Migrants from the United States," *Journal of Asian American Studies* 15, no. 1 (2012): 55–56.

35 Kim Ja Park Nelson, "Korean Looks, American Eyes: Korean American Adoptees, Race, Culture and Nation" (PhD diss., University of Minnesota, 2009), 43.

36 Jane Trenka, "About," *Jane's Blog*, http://jjtrenka.wordpress.com/about/ (accessed October 28, 2013); Maggie Jones, "Why a Generation of Adoptees is Returning to South Korea," *New York Times Magazine*, January 14, 2015.

37 Christopher Inkpen, "7 Facts about World Migration," Fact Tank, Pew Research Center, September 2, 2014, http://www.pewresearch.org/fact-tank/2014/09/02/7-facts-about-world-migration/ (accessed December 4, 2014).

38 Edward Taehan Chang, "What Does It Mean to Be Korean Today? One Hundred Years of Koreans in America and More," *Amerasia Journal* 29, no. 3 (2003): xxiii; Yuh, "Moved by War," 287.

39 Dorais, "From Refugees to Transmigrants: The Vietnamese in Canada," 176–77, 184.

40 L. Hirabayashi, Kikumura-Yano, and J. A. Hirabayashi, *New Worlds, New Lives*, xvii; Masterson and Funada-Classen, *The Japanese in Latin America*, 240–41, 276–77.

41 Siu, *Memories of a Future Home*, 164–70; "The XVI Panamerican Nikkei Convention 2011," Discover Nikkei, http://www.discovernikkei.org/en/events/2011/09/01/3236 (accessed December 19, 2011); Yuji Ichioka, "Nikkei in the Western Hemisphere," *Amerasia Journal* 15, no. 2 (1989): 175. L. Hirabayashi, Kikumura-Yano, and J. A. Hirabayashi, *New Worlds, New Lives*, xiv–xv.

42 Dhiru Patel, "The Maple-Neem Nexus: Transnational Links of South Asian Canadians," in *Transnational Identities and Practices in Canada*, ed. Vic Satzewich and Lloyd L. Wong (Vancouver: University of British Columbia Press, 2006), 155–56; Jigna Desai, *Beyond Bollywood: The Cultural Politics of South Asian Diasporic Film* (New York: Routledge, 2004).

Chapter 17: The "Rise of Asian Americans"? Myths and Realities

1 Lee Siegel, "Rise of the Tiger Nation," *Wall Street Journal*, October 27, 2012.

2 Wadhwa, "The Face of Success."

3 Pew Research Center, *The Rise of Asian Americans*, 1, 68. See also Karthick Ramakrishnan, "When Words Fail: Careful Framing Needed in Research on Asian Americans," *Hyphen: Asian America Unabridged*, June 27, 2012, http://www.hyphenmagazine.com/blog/archive/2012/06/when-words-fail-careful-framing-needed-research-asian-americans (accessed June 28, 2012).

4 Tuan, *Forever Foreigners or Honorary Whites?*

5 Dennis William et al., "A Formula for Success," *Newsweek*, April 23, 1984.

6 David A. Bell, "The Triumph of Asian-Americans," *The New Republic*, July 15, 1985.

7 Anthony Ramirez, "America's Super Minority," *Fortune*, November 24, 1986.

8 William et al., "A Formula for Success."

9 Bonilla-Silva, *Racism Without Racists*, 73–100; Wu, *The Color of Success*, 242–58.

10 K. W. Lee, "The Fire Next Time?: Ten Haunting Questions Cry Out for Answers and Redress," *Amerasia Journal* 38, no. 1 (2012): 86.

11 On media portrayals, see Wu, *The Color of Success*, 252; Elaine H. Kim, "Home Is Where the Han Is: A Korean American Perspective on the Los Angeles Upheavals," *Social Justice* 20 (1-2) (Spring-Summer, 1993): 1, 3, 8; and Kyung Won Lee, "Legacy of Sa-Ee-Gu: Goodbye Hahn, Good Morning, Community Conscience," *Amerasia Journal* 25, no. 2 (1999): 43–64. On riots

as multiracial/multiethnic, see Nancy Abelman and John Lie, *Blue Dreams: Korean Americans and the Los Angeles Riots* (Cambridge: Harvard University Press, 1995), 7–8, 148–80; and Kyeyoung Park, "An Analysis of Latino-Korean Relations in the Workplace: Latino Perspectives in the Aftermath of 1992 Los Angeles Civil Unrest," *Amerasia Journal* 38, no. 1 (2012): 143–69. Quote from Lee, "The Fire Next Time?," 87.

12 Chang, *The Chinese in America*, 329; Takaki, *Strangers from a Different Shore*, 479.

13 Congressional Asian Pacific American Caucus, "CAPAC Chair Judy Chu Comments on New Pew Report on Asian Americans," *Congressional Asian Pacific American Caucus*, June 19, 2012, https://capac-chu.house.gov/press-release/capac-chair-judy-chu-comments-new-pew-report-asian-americans.

14 Pew Research Center, *The Rise of Asian Americans*, 13.

15 Lai and Arguelles, *The New Face of Asian Pacific America*, 13.

16 Asian American data from the 2013 American Community Survey ("Sex by Educational Attainment for the Population 25 Years and Older, Asian Alone"), http://factfinder2.census.gov/faces/tableservices/jsf/pages/productview.xhtml?pid=ACS_13_1YR_B15002D&prodType=table (accessed December 5, 2014). General U.S. population data from the 2009–2013 American Community Survey ("Educational Attainment"), http://factfinder2.census.gov/faces/tableservices/jsf/pages/productview.xhtml?pid=ACS_13_5YR_S1501&prodType=table (accessed December 5, 2014).

17 Pew Research Center, *The Rise of Asian Americans*, 7, 43, 45, 49, 52, 55; Rachel L. Swarns, "In a Flourishing Queens, Prosperity Eludes Some Asian Families," *New York Times*, May 4, 2014.

18 Asian Americans Advancing Justice, *A Community of Contrasts: Asian Americans, Native Hawaiians and Pacific Islanders in California, 2013* (Asian Americans Advancing Justice, 2013), 3–5, 12, 18, 20, 22.

19 "Nearly Half of New Yorkers Are Struggling to Get By, Study Finds," *New York Times*, April 30, 2014.

20 Aihwa Ong, *Buddha Is Hiding: Refugees, Citizenship, the New America* (Berkeley, CA: University of California Press, 2003).

21 "Cambodia's Black Sheep Return to Fold," *Los Angeles Times*, March 28, 2003.

22 Deborah Sontag, "In a Homeland Far from Home," *New York Times Magazine*, November 16, 2003.

23 Leitner Center for International Law and Justice, *Removing Refugees: U.S. Deportation Policy and the Cambodian American Community* (New York:

Fordham Law School, 2010); Soo Ah Kwon, "Deporting Cambodian Refugees: Youth Activism, State Reform, and Imperial Statecraft," *Positions* 20, no. 3 (Summer 2012): 737–62. "Exiled Americans" from "My Asian Americana (2011)—Studio Revolt," http://studio-revolt.com/?p=305.

24 National Asian American Telecommunications Association, Inc., Franklin Odo, "Beyond the Model Minority Myth," *Searching for Asian America*, 2004, http://www.pbs.org/searching/popup/cc_fodo.html# (accessed November 7, 2013).

25 Lisa Sun-Hee Park, "Continuing Significance of the Model Minority Myth: The Second Generation," *Social Justice* 35, no. 2 (2008): 136.

26 Vijay Iyer, "Our Complicity with Excess," *Asian American Writers' Workshop*, May 7, 2014, http://aaww.org/complicity-with-excess-vijay-iyer/ (accessed May 9, 2014).

27 Suketu Mehta, "The Superiority Complex," *Time*, February 3, 2014.

28 Nancy Foner, "Questions of Success: Lessons from the Last Great Immigration," in *Helping Young Refugees and Immigrants Succeed: Public Policy, Aid, and Education*, ed. Gerhard Sonnert and Gerald Holton (New York: Palgrave Macmillan, 2010), 19.

29 Samuel P. Huntington, "The Hispanic Challenge," *Foreign Policy*, March 1, 2004, http://www.foreignpolicy.com/articles/2004/03/01/the_hispanic_challenge (accessed May 12, 2014).

30 Bonilla-Silva, *Racism Without Racists*, 73–100; Mehta, "The Superiority Complex."

31 Christine Choy and Renee Tajima-Peña, "Who Killed Vincent Chin?" (Film News Now Foundation, 1987).

32 Zia, *Asian American Dreams*, 61, 63.

33 Choy and Tajima-Peña, "Who Killed Vincent Chin?"; Espiritu, *Asian American Panethnicity*, 153, 160.

34 See, for example, Steven W. Mosher, *Hegemon: China's Plan to Dominate Asia and the World* (San Francisco: Encounter, 2000); Martin Jacques, *When China Rules the World* (New York: Penguin, 2009); James Kynge, *China Shakes the World: A Titan's Rise and Troubled Future—and the Challenge for America* (Boston: Houghton Mifflin, 2006); and Peter Navarro and Greg Autry, *Death by China: Confronting the Dragon—A Global Call to Action* (Upper Saddle River, NJ: Prentice Hall, 2011).

35 Kwong and Miscevic, *Chinese America*, 359–69; Wen Ho Lee and Helen Zia, *My Country Versus Me: The First-Hand Account by the Los Alamos Scientist Who Was Falsely Accused of Being a Spy* (New York: Hyperion, 2001).

36 Amy Chua, "Why Chinese Mothers Are Superior," *Wall Street Journal*, January 8, 2011, http://online.wsj.com/news/articles/SB10001424052748704111504576059713528698754 (accessed January 9, 2011).

37 Jeff Yang, "Mother, Superior?," *SFGate*, January 13, 2001, http://www.sfgate.com/entertainment/article/Mother-superior-2383957.php#src=fb (accessed November 8, 2013).

38 Mitchell James Chang, "Battle Hymn of the Model Minority Myth," *Amerasia Journal* 37, no. 2 (2011): 141–42.

39 Scholars have explained how a new "Muslim" racial category has emerged after 9/11 that consolidates Arab, Muslim, Middle Eastern, and Muslim-looking peoples together and conflates them with being terrorists and non-citizens. See, for example, Rana, *Terrifying Muslims*, 7, 159.

40 Ibid., 7; Tram Nguyen, *We Are All Suspects Now: Untold Stories from Immigrant Communities After 9/11* (Boston: Beacon, 2005).

41 Richard A. Serrano, "Hate Crimes Against Muslims Soar, Report Says," *Los Angeles Times*, November 26, 2002, http://articles.latimes.com/2002/nov/26/nation/na-hate26, (accessed May 9, 2014).

42 South Asian American Leaders of Tomorrow, *American Backlash: Terrorists Bring War Home in More Ways than One* (Washington, DC: South Asian American Leaders of Tomorrow, 2001). See also the documentary by Valarie Kauer, *Divided We Fall: Americans in the Aftermath* (2006).

43 Rana, *Terrifying Muslims*, 161–66.

44 Erika Lee, "A Nation of Immigrants/A Gatekeeping Nation: American Immigration Law and Policy, 1875–Present," in *A Companion to American Immigration History*, ed. Reed Ueda (Hoboken, NJ: Blackwell, 2006), 26–28.

45 Prashad, *Uncle Swami*, ix–x, 11–12.

46 "Wisconsin Sikh Temple Shooting," CNN, http://www.cnn.com/SPECIALS/us/sikh-temple-shooting (accessed May 10, 2014).

47 Sunaina Maira, "Youth Culture, Citizenship and Globalization: South Asian Muslim Youth in the United States After September 11th," *Comparative Studies of South Asia, Africa and the Middle East* 24, no. 1 (2004): 220; Rana, *Terrifying Muslims*, 160.

48 Maira, "Youth Culture, Citizenship and Globalization," 226.

49 Prashad, *Uncle Swami*, 45–47.

Epilogue: Redefining America in the Twenty-first Century

1 Iyer, "Our Complicity with Excess."

2 Lai and Arguelles, eds., *The New Face of Asian Pacific America*, 210.

3 National Asian American Telecommunications Association, Inc., "Asian American Politicians: Mee Moua," *Searching for Asian America*, 2004, http://www.pbs.org/searching/aap_mmoua.html (accessed November 7, 2013).

4 Mee Moua, "Asian Americans: The Up-for-Grabs Electorate," *Huffington Post*, November 6, 2012, http://www.huffingtonpost.com/mee-moua/asian-american-voters_b_2082193.html (accessed May 10, 2014).

5 Mee Moua, "50th Anniversary of the March on Washington: A Renewed Hope for the American Dream," *Huffington Post*, August 23, 2013, http://www.huffingtonpost.com/mee-moua/50th-anniversary-of-the-march_b_3805885.html (accessed May 10, 2014).

6 Peter Irons Interview II, Segment 12, Interview by Lorraine Bannai and Alice Ito, October 27, 2000, Densho ID: denshovh-ipeter-02-0012, Densho Visual Archive (accessed May 15, 2014).

7 Eric Paul Fournier, "Of Civil Wrongs and Rights: The Fred Korematsu Story," Public Broadcasting Service, 2000.

8 Daniels, *The Japanese American Cases*, 171–72.

9 Shiho Imai, "Korematsu v. United States," in Densho Encyclopedia, http://encyclopedia.densho.org/Korematsu%20v.%20United%20States/ (accessed March 19, 2013); Fournier, "Of Civil Wrongs and Rights."

10 Fournier, "Of Civil Wrongs and Rights." Gordon Hirabayashi's conviction was also vacated. Minoru Yasui died before a final appeal of his case could be heard.

11 Ibid.

12 Korematsu Institute for Civil Rights and Education, "Fred Korematsu Bio," About Fred Korematsu, http://korematsuinstitute.org/institute/aboutfred/ (accessed November 9, 2013); Nat Hentoff, "Fred Korematsu v. George W. Bush," *Village Voice*, February 17, 2004, http://www.villagevoice.com/2004-02-17/news/fred-korematsu-v-george-w-bush/ (accessed May 15, 2014).

13 Lai and Arguelles, *The New Face of Asian Pacific America*, 17.

14 U.S. Census Bureau, U.S. Department of Commerce, *Questions and Answers for Census 2000 Data on Race*, March 14, 2001, http://www.census.gov/census2000/raceqandas.html (accessed February 21, 2013).

15 Humes, Jones, and Ramirez, *Overview of Race and Hispanic Origin, 2010*, 4.

16 Hoeffel et al., *The Asian Population*, 4; Asian American Center for Advancing Justice, *A Community of Contrasts*, 11.

17 Takaki, *Strangers from a Different Shore*, 506.

18 Kip Fulbeck, *Part Asian, 100% Hapa* (San Francisco: Chronicle, 2006), 254.

19 Michael Hoefer, Nancy Rytina, and Bryan Baker, "Estimates of the Unauthorized Immigrant Population Residing in the United States: January 2011," March 2012, p. 5, Office of Immigration Statistics, Department of Homeland Security, http://www.dhs.gov/xlibrary/assets/statistics/publications/ois_ill_pe_2011.pdf (accessed December 16, 2014); "U.S. Is Home to 1.5 Million Undocumented Asian Immigrants," NPR, November 28, 2014, http://www.npr.org/2014/11/28/367154343/u-s-is-home-to-1-5-million-undocumented-asian-immigrants (accessed December 16, 2014); Zi Heng Lim, "For Asian Undocumented Immigrants, a Life of Secrecy," *The Atlantic*, May 14, 2013, http://www.theatlantic.com/national/archive/2013/05/for-asian-undocumented-immigrants-a-life-of-secrecy/275829/ (accessed December 16, 2014).

20 "18 Million Hearts: Asian Americans and Pacific Islanders for Immigration Reform Launches Today," *AsianWeek*, February 28, 2013, http://www.asianweek.com/2013/02/28/18-million-hearts-asian-americans-and-pacific-islanders-for-immigration-reform-launches-today/ (accessed March 1, 2013).

21 Jose Antonio Vargas, "My Life as an Undocumented Immigrant," *New York Times*, June 22, 2011; Jose Antonio Vargas, "Not Legal Not Leaving," *Time*, June 25, 2012.

22 Michael Scherer, "Jose Antonio Vargas' Emotional Senate Testimony," *Time*, February 14, 2013, http://swampland.time.com/2013/02/14/jose-antonio-vargas-emotional-senate-testimony/ (accessed February 15, 2013).

23 Mónica Novoa, "Telling a Different Story," *Define American*, March 22, 2013, http://www.defineamerican.com/blog/post/black-immigrants-and-african-american-allies-make-history-and-tell-a-different-story (accessed November 15, 2013).

24 Jose Antonio Vargas, " 'I Have a Dream': An Undocumented Immigrant Version," *Define American*, August 28, 2013, http://www.defineamerican.com/blog/post/i-have-a-dream-an-undocumented-immigrant-version (accessed November 15, 2013).

25 Mónica Novoa, "Defining American Runs Deeper than Documentation," *Define American*, January 29, 2013, http://www.defineamerican.com/blog/post/defining-american-runs-deeper-than-documentation/; *Define American*, June 2011, http://www.defineamerican.com/ (accessed November 15, 2013).

26 Jose Antonio Vargas, "The America in Me," *Define American*, July 4, 2011, http://www.defineamerican.com/blog/post/the-america-in-me/ (accessed November 15, 2013); Novoa, "Defining American Runs Deeper than Documentation."

27 Vargas, "Not Legal Not Leaving."

28 Define American and *FWD.us "Documented" Screening*, 2013, http://www.youtube.com/watch?v=iaJGlbU_80k&feature=youtube (accessed August 16, 2013).

29 Anonymous, "Define American: A Matter of Faith," November 15, 2011, http://www.defineamerican.com/story/post/425/a-matter-of-faith-/ (accessed November 15, 2013).

Index

Page numbers in *italics* refer to illustrations and maps.

3 0053 01339 2504